Vauxhall Frontera
Service and Repair Manual

John S Mead and Mark Coombs

(3454-400-5AC1)

Models covered
Vauxhall Frontera 3- and 5-door models, including special/limited editions
1998 cc, 2198 cc & 2410 cc petrol engines
2260 cc, 2499 cc & 2771 cc diesel engines

© Haynes Publishing 1999

A book in the **Haynes Service and Repair Manual Series**

ABCDE
FGHIJ
KLMN

Printed in USA

All rights reserved. No part of this book may be reproduced or transmitted in any form or by any means, electronic or mechanical, including photocopying, recording or by any information storage or retrieval system, without permission in writing from the copyright holder.

ISBN **1 85960 454 4**

British Library Cataloguing in Publication Data
A catalogue record for this book is available from the British Library.

Haynes Publishing
Sparkford, Nr Yeovil, Somerset BA22 7JJ, England

Haynes North America, Inc
861 Lawrence Drive, Newbury Park, California 91320, USA

Editions Haynes S.A.
4, Rue de l'Abreuvoir
92415 COURBEVOIE CEDEX, France

Haynes Publishing Nordiska AB
Box 1504, 751 45 UPPSALA, Sweden

Contents

LIVING WITH YOUR VAUXHALL FRONTERA

Introduction	Page	0•4
Safety First!	Page	0•5

Roadside Repairs

Introduction	Page	0•6
If your car won't start	Page	0•6
Jump starting	Page	0•7
Wheel changing	Page	0•8
Identifying leaks	Page	0•9
Towing	Page	0•9

Weekly Checks

Introduction	Page	0•10
Underbonnet check points	Page	0•10
Engine oil level	Page	0•12
Brake and clutch fluid level	Page	0•13
Power steering fluid level	Page	0•13
Coolant level	Page	0•14
Battery	Page	0•14
Tyre condition and pressure	Page	0•15
Wiper blades	Page	0•16
Washer fluid level	Page	0•16
Bulbs and fuses	Page	0•16

Lubricants and fluids

	Page	0•17

Tyre pressures

	Page	0•18

MAINTENANCE

Routine Maintenance and Servicing

Vauxhall Frontera petrol models	Page	1A•1
Maintenance schedule	Page	1A•3
Maintenance procedures	Page	1A•6
Vauxhall Frontera diesel models	Page	1B•1
Maintenance schedule	Page	1B•3
Maintenance procedures	Page	1B•7

Contents

REPAIRS AND OVERHAUL

Engine and Associated Systems

2.0 litre petrol engine in-car repair procedures   Page 2A•1

2.2 litre petrol engine in-car repair procedures   Page 2B•1

2.4 litre petrol engine in-car repair procedures   Page 2C•1

2.3 litre diesel engine in-car repair procedures   Page 2D•1

2.5 litre diesel engine in-car repair procedures   Page 2E•1

2.8 litre diesel engine in-car repair procedures   Page 2F•1

Petrol engine removal and general overhaul procedures   Page 2G•1

Diesel engine removal and general overhaul procedures   Page 2H•1

Cooling, heating and ventilation systems   Page 3•1

Fuel and exhaust system - petrol engine models   Page 4A•1

Fuel and exhaust system - diesel engine models   Page 4B•1

Emission control systems   Page 4C•1

Starting and charging systems   Page 5A•1

Ignition system - petrol engine models   Page 5B•1

Preheating system - diesel engine models   Page 5C•1

Transmission

Clutch   Page 6•1

Transmission   Page 7•1

Propeller shafts and driveshafts   Page 8•1

Front and rear axles   Page 9•1

Brakes and Suspension

Braking system   Page 10•1

Suspension and steering   Page 11•1

Body equipment

Bodywork and fittings   Page 12•1

Body electrical system   Page 13•1

Wiring Diagrams   Page 13•20

REFERENCE

Dimensions and Weights   Page REF•1

Conversion Factors   Page REF•2

Buying Spare Parts and Vehicle Identification   Page REF•3

General Repair Procedures   Page REF•4

Jacking and Vehicle Support   Page REF•5

Radio/cassette unit Anti-theft System - precaution   Page REF•5

Tools and Working Facilities   Page REF•6

MOT Test Checks   Page REF•8

Fault Finding   Page REF•12

Glossary of Technical Terms   Page REF•20

Index   Page REF•25

The Vauxhall Frontera was introduced into the UK at the end of 1991. At its launch, the Frontera range consisted of a 2.0 litre (1998 cc) petrol engine 3-door model, and a 2.4 litre (2410 cc) petrol engine or 2.3 litre (2260 cc) diesel engine 5-door model. The engines are all well-proven units which have appeared in many Vauxhall vehicles. All engines are of four-cylinder overhead camshaft design, mounted at the front of vehicle with the transmission mounted on its rear.

All models have fully-independent front suspension incorporating upper and lower arms, shock absorbers and torsion bars and were originally fitted with a leaf spring rear axle.

A wide range of standard and optional equipment is available within the range to suit most tastes, including central locking, electric windows and an electric sunroof. An air conditioning system was available as an option on certain models.

In early 1994 a soft-top 3-door model was introduced and in early 1995 the model range was completely revised. A new 2.2 litre (2198 cc) 16-valve petrol engine was bought in to replace the 2.4 litre engine and the 2.3 litre Diesel engine was replaced with a new 2.8 litre (2771 cc) engine. At the same time, the body underwent a major overhaul and the leaf spring rear axle was replaced with a new coil spring rear axle arrangement to improve road-holding and handling. The only other change to the Frontera models range was the introduction of a new 2.5 litre (2499 cc) diesel engine in the middle of 1996.

Provided that regular servicing is carried out in accordance with the manufacturer's recommendations, the vehicle should prove reliable and very economical. The engine compartment is well-designed, and most of the items requiring frequent attention are easily accessible.

Vauxhall Frontera 5-door

Vauxhall Frontera Sport

Your Vauxhall Frontera manual

The aim of this manual is to help you get the best value from your vehicle. It can do so in several ways. It can help you decide what work must be done (even should you choose to get it done by a garage). It will also provide information on routine maintenance and servicing, and give a logical course of action and diagnosis when random faults occur. However, it is hoped that you will use the manual by tackling the work yourself. On simpler jobs it may even be quicker than booking the vehicle into a garage and going there twice, to leave and collect it. Perhaps most important, a lot of money can be saved by avoiding the costs a garage must charge to cover its labour and overheads.

The manual has drawings and descriptions to show the function of the various components so that their layout can be understood. Tasks are described and photographed in a clear step-by-step sequence.

References to 'left' and 'right' of the vehicle are in the sense of a person in the driver's seat facing forwards.

Acknowledgements

Thanks are due to Champion Spark Plug, who supplied the illustrations showing spark plug conditions. Certain illustrations are the copyright of Vauxhall Motors Limited, and are used with their permission. Thanks are also due to Draper Tools Limited, who provided some of the workshop tools, and to all those people at Sparkford who helped in the production of this manual.

We take great pride in the accuracy of information given in this manual, but vehicle manufacturers make alterations and design changes during the production run of a particular vehicle of which they do not inform us. No liability can be accepted by the authors or publishers for loss, damage or injury caused by any errors in, or omissions from, the information given.

Working on your car can be dangerous. This page shows just some of the potential risks and hazards, with the aim of creating a safety-conscious attitude.

General hazards

Scalding

• Don't remove the radiator or expansion tank cap while the engine is hot.
• Engine oil, automatic transmission fluid or power steering fluid may also be dangerously hot if the engine has recently been running.

Burning

• Beware of burns from the exhaust system and from any part of the engine. Brake discs and drums can also be extremely hot immediately after use.

Crushing

• When working under or near a raised vehicle, always supplement the jack with axle stands, or use drive-on ramps. *Never venture under a car which is only supported by a jack.*
• Take care if loosening or tightening high-torque nuts when the vehicle is on stands. Initial loosening and final tightening should be done with the wheels on the ground.

Fire

• Fuel is highly flammable; fuel vapour is explosive.
• Don't let fuel spill onto a hot engine.
• Do not smoke or allow naked lights (including pilot lights) anywhere near a vehicle being worked on. Also beware of creating sparks (electrically or by use of tools).
• Fuel vapour is heavier than air, so don't work on the fuel system with the vehicle over an inspection pit.
• Another cause of fire is an electrical overload or short-circuit. Take care when repairing or modifying the vehicle wiring.
• Keep a fire extinguisher handy, of a type suitable for use on fuel and electrical fires.

Electric shock

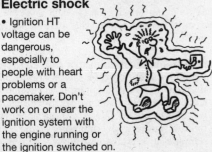

• Ignition HT voltage can be dangerous, especially to people with heart problems or a pacemaker. Don't work on or near the ignition system with the engine running or the ignition switched on.

• Mains voltage is also dangerous. Make sure that any mains-operated equipment is correctly earthed. Mains power points should be protected by a residual current device (RCD) circuit breaker.

Fume or gas intoxication

• Exhaust fumes are poisonous; they often contain carbon monoxide, which is rapidly fatal if inhaled. Never run the engine in a confined space such as a garage with the doors shut.
• Fuel vapour is also poisonous, as are the vapours from some cleaning solvents and paint thinners.

Poisonous or irritant substances

• Avoid skin contact with battery acid and with any fuel, fluid or lubricant, especially antifreeze, brake hydraulic fluid and Diesel fuel. Don't syphon them by mouth. If such a substance is swallowed or gets into the eyes, seek medical advice.
• Prolonged contact with used engine oil can cause skin cancer. Wear gloves or use a barrier cream if necessary. Change out of oil-soaked clothes and do not keep oily rags in your pocket.
• Air conditioning refrigerant forms a poisonous gas if exposed to a naked flame (including a cigarette). It can also cause skin burns on contact.

Asbestos

• Asbestos dust can cause cancer if inhaled or swallowed. Asbestos may be found in gaskets and in brake and clutch linings. When dealing with such components it is safest to assume that they contain asbestos.

Special hazards

Hydrofluoric acid

• This extremely corrosive acid is formed when certain types of synthetic rubber, found in some O-rings, oil seals, fuel hoses etc, are exposed to temperatures above 400°C. The rubber changes into a charred or sticky substance containing the acid. *Once formed, the acid remains dangerous for years. If it gets onto the skin, it may be necessary to amputate the limb concerned.*
• When dealing with a vehicle which has suffered a fire, or with components salvaged from such a vehicle, wear protective gloves and discard them after use.

The battery

• Batteries contain sulphuric acid, which attacks clothing, eyes and skin. Take care when topping-up or carrying the battery.
• The hydrogen gas given off by the battery is highly explosive. Never cause a spark or allow a naked light nearby. Be careful when connecting and disconnecting battery chargers or jump leads.

Air bags

• Air bags can cause injury if they go off accidentally. Take care when removing the steering wheel and/or facia. Special storage instructions may apply.

Diesel injection equipment

• Diesel injection pumps supply fuel at very high pressure. Take care when working on the fuel injectors and fuel pipes.

⚠️ *Warning: Never expose the hands, face or any other part of the body to injector spray; the fuel can penetrate the skin with potentially fatal results.*

Remember...

DO

• Do use eye protection when using power tools, and when working under the vehicle.

• Do wear gloves or use barrier cream to protect your hands when necessary.

• Do get someone to check periodically that all is well when working alone on the vehicle.

• Do keep loose clothing and long hair well out of the way of moving mechanical parts.

• Do remove rings, wristwatch etc, before working on the vehicle – especially the electrical system.

• Do ensure that any lifting or jacking equipment has a safe working load rating adequate for the job.

DON'T

• Don't attempt to lift a heavy component which may be beyond your capability – get assistance.

• Don't rush to finish a job, or take unverified short cuts.

• Don't use ill-fitting tools which may slip and cause injury.

• Don't leave tools or parts lying around where someone can trip over them. Mop up oil and fuel spills at once.

• Don't allow children or pets to play in or near a vehicle being worked on.

The following pages are intended to help in dealing with common roadside emergencies and breakdowns. You will find more detailed fault finding information at the back of the manual, and repair information in the main chapters.

If your car won't start and the starter motor doesn't turn

☐ Open the bonnet and make sure that the battery terminals are clean and tight.

☐ Switch on the headlights and try to start the engine. If the headlights go very dim when you're trying to start, the battery is probably flat. Get out of trouble by jump starting (see next page) using a friend's vehicle.

If your car won't start even though the starter motor turns as normal

☐ Is there fuel in the tank?

☐ Is there moisture on electrical components under the bonnet? Switch off the ignition, then wipe off any obvious dampness with a dry cloth. Spray a water-repellent aerosol product (WD-40 or equivalent) on ignition and fuel system electrical connectors like those shown in the photos. Pay special attention to the ignition coil wiring connector and HT leads. **Note**: *Diesel engines don't normally suffer from damp.*

A Check the condition and security of the battery connections.

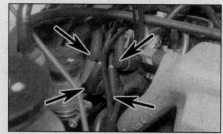

B On petrol engines, check that the spark plug HT leads are securely connected by pushing them onto the plugs and DIS module or coil and distributor (as applicable).

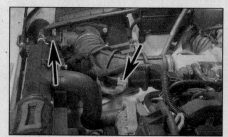

C Check that the fuel injection system wiring connectors are securely connected (where necessary).

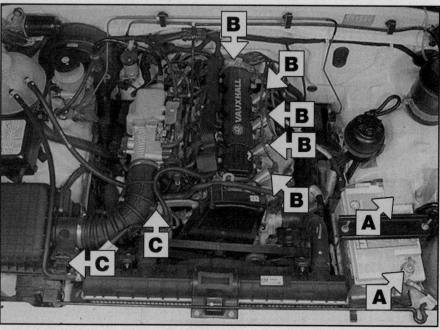

Check that electrical connections are secure (with the ignition switched off) and spray them with a water dispersant spray like WD-40 if you suspect a problem due to damp (fuel-injected model shown).

Jump starting

HAYNES HiNT *Jump starting will get you out of trouble, but you must correct whatever made the battery go flat in the first place. There are three possibilities:*

1) *The battery has been drained by repeated attempts to start, or by leaving the lights on.*
2) *The charging system is not working properly (alternator drivebelt slack or broken, alternator wiring fault or alternator itself faulty).*
3) *The battery itself is at fault (electrolyte low, or battery worn out).*

When jump-starting a car using a booster battery, observe the following precautions:

✔ Before connecting the booster battery, make sure that the ignition is switched off.

✔ Ensure that all electrical equipment (lights, heater, wipers, etc) is switched off.

✔ Take note of any special precautions printed on the battery case.

✔ Make sure that the booster battery is the same voltage as the discharged one in the vehicle.

✔ If the battery is being jump-started from the battery in another vehicle, the two vehicles MUST NOT TOUCH each other.

✔ Make sure that the transmission is in neutral (or PARK, in the case of automatic transmission).

1 Connect one end of the red jump lead to the positive (+) terminal of the flat battery

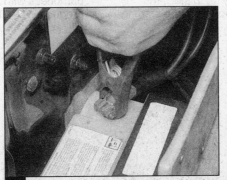

2 Connect the other end of the red lead to the positive (+) terminal of the booster battery

3 Connect one end of the black jump lead to the negative (-) terminal of the booster battery

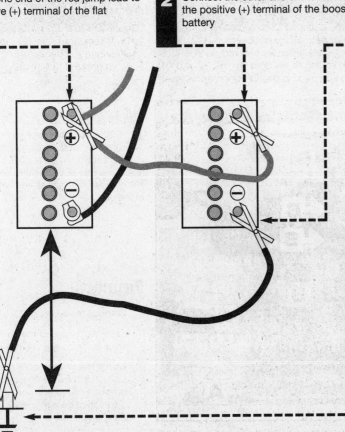

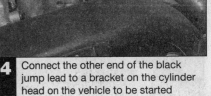

4 Connect the other end of the black jump lead to a bracket on the cylinder head on the vehicle to be started

5 Make sure that the jump leads will not come into contact with the fan, drivebelts or other moving parts of the engine

6 Start the engine using the booster battery and run it at idle speed. Switch on the lights, rear window demister and heater blower motor, then disconnect the jump leads in the reverse order of connection. Turn off the lights etc.

Wheel changing

- [ ] When a puncture occurs, stop as soon as it is safe to do so.
- [ ] Park on firm level ground, if possible, and well out of the way of other traffic.
- [ ] Use hazard warning lights if necessary.
- [ ] If you have one, use a warning triangle to alert other drivers of your presence.
- [ ] Apply the handbrake and engage first or reverse gear.
- [ ] Chock the wheel diagonally opposite the one being removed – a couple of large stones will do for this.
- [ ] If the ground is soft, use a flat piece of wood to spread the load under the jack.

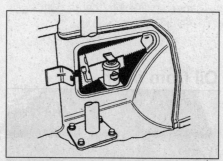

1 On 3-door models the jack and tools are stored behind the trim panel on the left-hand side of the luggage compartment. Remove the panel and lift out the tool kit and jack.

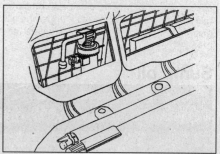

2 On 5-door models the jack and tools are stored in the base of the left-hand rear seat cushion. Lift up the seat cushion and remove the tool kit and jack.

3 Remove the cover then unscrew the retaining nuts and lift off the spare wheel from the tailgate.

4 Remove the wheel nut covers then slacken each wheel nut by half a turn. Remove the hub cap.

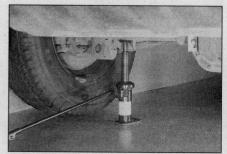

5 Make sure the jack is located on firm ground and engage the jack head correctly with the lifting point (see *Jacking and Vehicle Support* in the Reference section at the end of the this manual).

6 Raise the jack until the wheel is raised clear of the ground. Unscrew the wheel nuts and remove the wheel. Fit the spare wheel and screw on the nuts. Lightly tighten the nuts with the wheelbrace then lower the vehicle to the ground.

7 Securely tighten the wheel nuts in a diagonal sequence then refit the hub cap and wheel nut covers. Refit the punctured wheel to the carrier and securely tighten its retaining nuts.

Finally...

- [ ] Remove the wheel chocks.
- [ ] Stow the damaged tyre or wheel, jack and tools in the correct locations in the car.
- [ ] Check the tyre pressure on the wheel just fitted. If it is low, or if you don't have a pressure gauge with you, drive slowly to the nearest garage and inflate the tyre to the right pressure.
- [ ] Have the damaged tyre or wheel repaired as soon as possible.

Identifying leaks

Puddles on the garage floor or drive, or obvious wetness under the bonnet or underneath the car, suggest a leak that needs investigating. It can sometimes be difficult to decide where the leak is coming from, especially if the engine bay is very dirty already. Leaking oil or fluid can also be blown rearwards by the passage of air under the car, giving a false impression of where the problem lies.

⚠ **Warning: Most automotive oils and fluids are poisonous. Wash them off skin, and change out of contaminated clothing, without delay.**

 HAYNES HiNT *The smell of a fluid leaking from the car may provide a clue to what's leaking. Some fluids are distinctively coloured. It may help to clean the car and to park it over some clean paper as an aid to locating the source of the leak. Remember that some leaks may only occur while the engine is running.*

Sump oil

Engine oil may leak from the drain plug...

Oil from filter

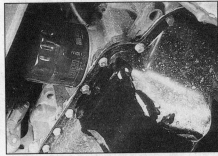

...or from the base of the oil filter.

Gearbox oil

Gearbox oil can leak from the seals at the inboard ends of the driveshafts.

Antifreeze

Leaking antifreeze often leaves a crystalline deposit like this.

Brake fluid

A leak occurring at a wheel is almost certainly brake fluid.

Power steering fluid

Power steering fluid may leak from the pipe connectors on the steering rack.

Towing

When all else fails, you may find yourself having to get a tow home – or of course you may be helping somebody else. Long-distance recovery should only be done by a garage or breakdown service. For shorter distances, DIY towing using another car is easy enough, but observe the following points:
☐ Both front and rear towing eyes are provided and are located on the right-hand side of the front and rear of the vehicle.
☐ Use a proper tow-rope – they are not

expensive. The vehicle being towed must display an ON TOW sign in its rear window.
☐ Always turn the ignition key to the 'on' position when the vehicle is being towed, so that the steering lock is released, and that the direction indicator and brake lights will work.
☐ Before being towed, release the handbrake and select neutral on the transmission.
☐ Note that greater-than-usual pedal pressure will be required to operate the brakes, since the vacuum servo unit is only operational with the engine running.

☐ On models with power steering, greater-than-usual steering effort will also be required.
☐ The driver of the car being towed must keep the tow-rope taut at all times to avoid snatching.
☐ Make sure that both drivers know the route before setting off.
☐ Only drive at moderate speeds and keep the distance towed to a minimum. Drive smoothly and allow plenty of time for slowing down at junctions.

Introduction

There are some very simple checks which need only take a few minutes to carry out, but which could save you a lot of inconvenience and expense.

These *Weekly checks* require no great skill or special tools, and the small amount of time they take to perform could prove to be very well spent, for example;

☐ Keeping an eye on tyre condition and pressures, will not only help to stop them wearing out prematurely, but could also save your life.

☐ Many breakdowns are caused by electrical problems. Battery-related faults are particularly common, and a quick check on a regular basis will often prevent the majority of these.

☐ If your vehicle develops a brake fluid leak, the first time you might know about it is when your brakes don't work properly. Checking the level regularly will give advance warning of this kind of problem.

☐ If the oil or coolant levels run low, the cost of repairing any engine damage will be far greater than fixing the leak, for example.

Underbonnet check points

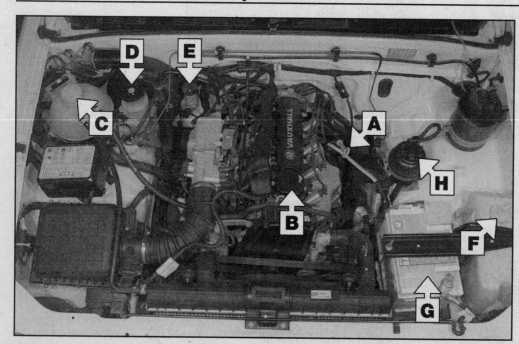

◀ **2.0 litre petrol engine (1995-on model shown)**

A *Engine oil dipstick*
B *Engine oil filler cap*
C *Coolant expansion tank*
D *Brake fluid reservoir*
E *Clutch fluid reservoir*
F *Screen washer fluid reservoir*
G *Battery*
H *Power steering fluid reservoir*

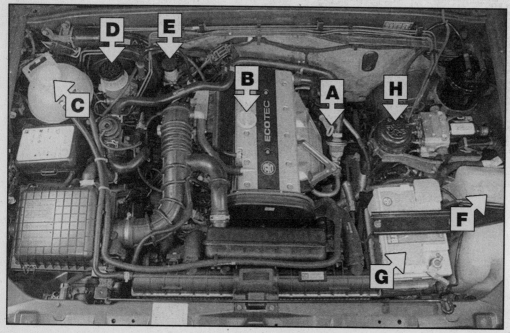

◀ **2.2 litre petrol engine**

A *Engine oil dipstick*
B *Engine oil filler cap*
C *Coolant expansion tank*
D *Brake fluid reservoir*
E *Clutch fluid reservoir*
F *Screen washer fluid reservoir*
G *Battery*
H *Power steering fluid reservoir*

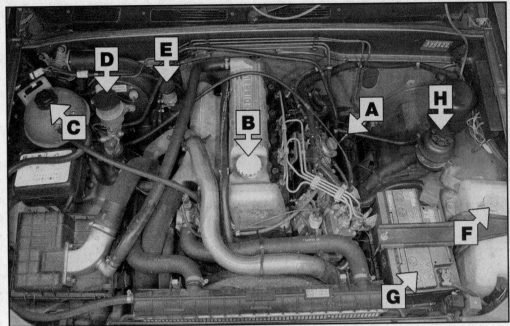

◄ **2.3 litre diesel engine**

A *Engine oil dipstick*
B *Engine oil filler cap*
C *Coolant expansion tank*
D *Brake fluid reservoir*
E *Clutch fluid reservoir*
F *Screen washer fluid reservoir*
G *Battery*
H *Power steering fluid reservoir*

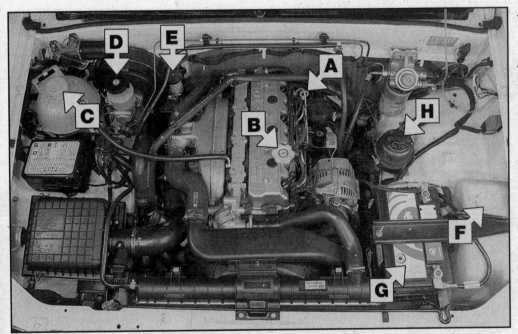

◄ **2.5 litre diesel engine**

A *Engine oil dipstick*
B *Engine oil filler cap*
C *Coolant expansion tank*
D *Brake fluid reservoir*
E *Clutch fluid reservoir*
F *Screen washer fluid reservoir*
G *Battery*
H *Power steering fluid reservoir*

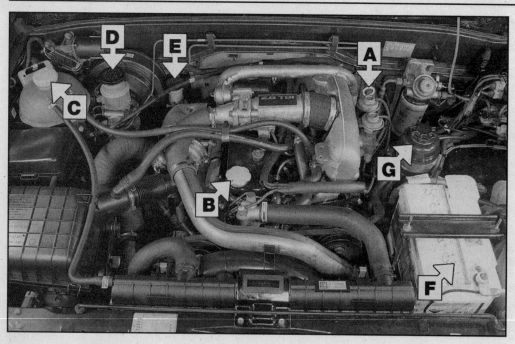

A *Engine oil dipstick*
B *Engine oil filler cap*
C *Coolant expansion tank*
D *Brake fluid reservoir*
E *Clutch fluid reservoir*
F *Battery*
G *Power steering fluid reservoir*

Engine oil level

Before you start

✔ Make sure that your car is on level ground.
✔ Check the oil level before the car is driven, or at least 5 minutes after the engine has been switched off.

 If the oil is checked immediately after driving the vehicle, some of the oil will remain in the upper engine components, resulting in an inaccurate reading on the dipstick

The correct oil

Modern engines place great demands on their oil. It is very important that the correct oil for your vehicle is used (See Lubricants and fluids).

Vehicle care

● If you have to add oil frequently, you should check whether you have any oil leaks. Place some clean paper under the vehicle overnight, and check for stains in the morning. If there are no leaks, the engine may be burning oil (see Fault finding).

1 The dipstick is located on the left-hand side of the engine (see *Underbonnet check points* for exact location). Withdraw the dipstick.

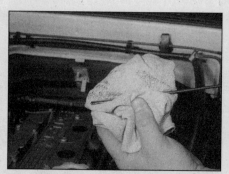

2 Using a clean rag or paper towel remove all oil from the dipstick. Insert the clean dipstick into the tube as far as it will go, then withdraw it again.

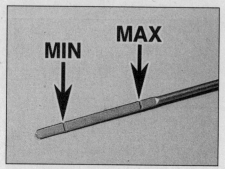

3 Note the oil level on the end of the dipstick, which should be between the upper (MAX) mark and lower (MIN) mark. Approximately 1.0 litre of oil will raise the level from the lower mark to the upper mark.

4 Oil is added through the filler cap. Rotate the cap through a quarter-turn anti-clockwise and withdraw it. Top-up the level. A funnel may help to reduce spillage. Add the oil slowly, checking the level on the dipstick often. Do not overfill.

Brake and clutch fluid level

Warning:

● **Brake fluid can harm your eyes and damage painted surfaces, so use extreme caution when handling and pouring it.**

● **Do not use fluid that has been standing open for some time, as it absorbs moisture from the air, which can cause a dangerous loss of braking effectiveness.**

Safety first!

● If the reservoir requires repeated topping-up this is an indication of a fluid leak somewhere in the system, which should be investigated immediately.

● If a leak is suspected, the vehicle should not be driven until the braking system has been checked. Never take any risks where brakes are concerned.

• **Make sure that your vehicle is on level ground.**
• **The fluid level in the reservoir will drop slightly as the brake pads wear down, but the fluid level must never be allowed to drop below the MIN mark.**

1 The upper (MAX) and lower (MIN or ADD) fluid level markings are on the side of the reservoir, which is located in the right-hand rear corner of the engine compartment. The fluid level must always be kept in between these two marks.

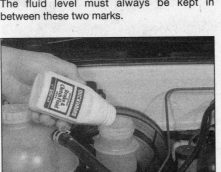

3 Carefully add fluid, avoiding spilling it on the surrounding paintwork. Use only the specified hydraulic fluid. After filling to the correct level, refit the cap and diaphragm and tighten it securely. Wipe off any spilt fluid.

2 If topping-up is necessary, first wipe clean the area around the filler cap with a clean cloth then unscrew the cap and remove it along with the rubber diaphragm.

4 Repeat the check with the clutch reservoir (level markings arrowed) and, if necessary, top up.

Power steering fluid level

Before you start:

✔ Park the vehicle on level ground.
✔ With the engine idling, turn the steering wheel slowly from lock to lock 2 or 3 times and set the front wheels at the straight-ahead position, then stop the engine.

Safety first!

● The need for frequent topping-up indicates a leak, which should be investigated immediately.

For the check to be accurate, the steering must not be turned once the engine has been stopped.

1 The power steering fluid reservoir is located on the left-hand side of the engine compartment. Wipe clean the reservoir before unscrewing and removing the cap.

2 Wipe clean the filler cap dipstick then refit the filler cap and remove it again. Note the fluid level on the dipstick.

3 When the engine is cold the fluid level should be up to the lower mark up the dipstick and when the engine is at operating temperature it should be at the upper mark. Top up the fluid level using the specified type of fluid (do not overfill) then securely refit the filler cap.

Coolant level

⚠️ **Warning:**
● **Do not attempt to remove the expansion tank pressure cap when the engine is hot, as there is a very great risk of scalding.**
● **Do not leave open containers of coolant about, as it is poisonous.**

● With a sealed-type cooling system, adding coolant should not be necessary on a regular basis. If frequent topping-up is required, it is likely there is a leak. Check the radiator, all hoses and joint faces for signs of staining or wetness, and rectify as necessary.

● It is important that antifreeze is used in the cooling system all year round, not just during the winter months. Don't top-up with water alone, as the antifreeze will become too diluted.

1 The coolant level varies with the temperature of the engine. When the engine is cold, the coolant level should be slightly above the KALT/COLD mark on the side of the tank. When the engine is hot, the level will rise.

2 If topping up is necessary, **wait until the engine is cold**. Slowly unscrew the expansion tank cap, to release any pressure present in the cooling system, and remove it.

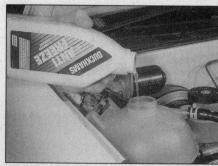

3 Add a mixture of water and antifreeze to the expansion tank until the coolant level is slightly above the KALT/COLD mark then securely refit the expansion cap tank.

Battery

Caution: Before carrying out any work on the vehicle battery, read the precautions given in Safety first! at the start of this manual.
✔ Make sure that the battery tray is in good condition, and that the clamp is tight. Corrosion on the tray, retaining clamp and the battery itself can be removed with a solution of water and baking soda. Thoroughly rinse all cleaned areas with water. Any metal parts damaged by corrosion should be covered with a zinc-based primer, then painted.
✔ Periodically (approximately every three months), check the charge condition of the battery as described in Chapter 5A.
✔ If the battery is flat, and you need to jump start your vehicle, see *Roadside Repairs*.

1 The battery is located at the front left-hand corner of the engine compartment. The exterior of the battery should be inspected periodically for damage such as a cracked case or cover.

2 Check the battery lead clamps for tightness to ensure good electrical connections and check the leads for signs of damage.

HAYNES HiNT

Battery corrosion can be kept to a minimum by applying a layer of petroleum jelly to the clamps and terminals after they are reconnected.

3 If corrosion (white, fluffy deposits) is evident, remove the cables from the battery terminals, clean them with a small wire brush, then refit them. Automotive stores sell a tool for cleaning the battery post . . .

4 . . . as well as the battery cable clamps.

Tyre condition and pressure

It is very important that tyres are in good condition, and at the correct pressure - having a tyre failure at any speed is highly dangerous. Tyre wear is influenced by driving style - harsh braking and acceleration, or fast cornering, will all produce more rapid tyre wear. As a general rule, the front tyres wear out faster than the rears. Interchanging the tyres from front to rear ("rotating" the tyres) may result in more even wear. However, if this is completely effective, you may have the expense of replacing all four tyres at once! Remove any nails or stones embedded in the tread before they penetrate the tyre to cause deflation. If removal of a nail does reveal that the tyre has been punctured, refit the nail so that its point of penetration is marked. Then immediately change the wheel, and have the tyre repaired by a tyre dealer.

Regularly check the tyres for damage in the form of cuts or bulges, especially in the sidewalls. Periodically remove the wheels, and clean any dirt or mud from the inside and outside surfaces. Examine the wheel rims for signs of rusting, corrosion or other damage. Light alloy wheels are easily damaged by "kerbing" whilst parking; steel wheels may also become dented or buckled. A new wheel is very often the only way to overcome severe damage.

New tyres should be balanced when they are fitted, but it may become necessary to re-balance them as they wear, or if the balance weights fitted to the wheel rim should fall off. Unbalanced tyres will wear more quickly, as will the steering and suspension components. Wheel imbalance is normally signified by vibration, particularly at a certain speed (typically around 50 mph). If this vibration is felt only through the steering, then it is likely that just the front wheels need balancing. If, however, the vibration is felt through the whole car, the rear wheels could be out of balance. Wheel balancing should be carried out by a tyre dealer or garage.

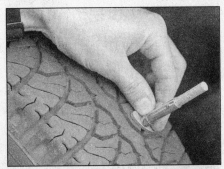

1 Tread Depth - visual check
The original tyres have tread wear safety bands (B), which will appear when the tread depth reaches approximately 1.6 mm. The band positions are indicated by a triangular mark on the tyre sidewall (A).

2 Tread Depth - manual check
Alternatively, tread wear can be monitored with a simple, inexpensive device known as a tread depth indicator gauge.

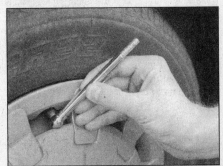

3 Tyre Pressure Check
Check the tyre pressures regularly with the tyres cold. Do not adjust the tyre pressures immediately after the vehicle has been used, or an inaccurate setting will result.

Tyre tread wear patterns

Shoulder Wear

Underinflation (wear on both sides)
Under-inflation will cause overheating of the tyre, because the tyre will flex too much, and the tread will not sit correctly on the road surface. This will cause a loss of grip and excessive wear, not to mention the danger of sudden tyre failure due to heat build-up.
Check and adjust pressures
Incorrect wheel camber (wear on one side)
Repair or renew suspension parts
Hard cornering
Reduce speed!

Centre Wear

Overinflation
Over-inflation will cause rapid wear of the centre part of the tyre tread, coupled with reduced grip, harsher ride, and the danger of shock damage occurring in the tyre casing.
Check and adjust pressures

If you sometimes have to inflate your car's tyres to the higher pressures specified for maximum load or sustained high speed, don't forget to reduce the pressures to normal afterwards.

Uneven Wear

Front tyres may wear unevenly as a result of wheel misalignment. Most tyre dealers and garages can check and adjust the wheel alignment (or "tracking") for a modest charge.
Incorrect camber or castor
Repair or renew suspension parts
Malfunctioning suspension
Repair or renew suspension parts
Unbalanced wheel
Balance tyres
Incorrect toe setting
Adjust front wheel alignment
Note: *The feathered edge of the tread which typifies toe wear is best checked by feel.*

Wiper blades

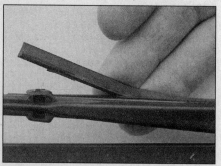

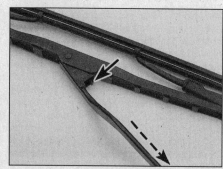

2 To remove a wiper blade, pull the arm fully away from the glass until it locks. Swivel the blade through 90°, then squeeze the locking clip, and detach the blade from the arm. When fitting the new blade, make sure that the blade locks securely into the arm, and that the blade is orientated correctly.

1 Check the condition of the wiper blades; if they are cracked or show any signs of deterioration, or if the glass swept area is smeared, renew them. Wiper blades should be renewed annually.

Washer fluid level

Screenwash additives not only keep the winscreen clean during foul weather, they also prevent the washer system freezing in cold weather - which is when you are likely to need it most. Don't top up using plain water as the screenwash will become too diluted, and will freeze during cold weather.
Caution: On no account use coolant antifreeze in the washer system - this could discolour or damage paintwork.

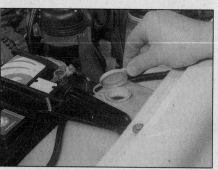

1 The reservoir for the windscreen washer systems is located on the front left-hand side of the engine compartment. If topping-up is necessary, open the cap.

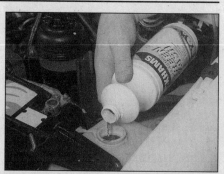

2 When topping-up the reservoir a screenwash additive should be added in the quantities recommended on the bottle.

Bulbs and fuses

✔ Check all external lights and the horn. Refer to the appropriate Sections of Chapter 13 for details if any of the circuits are found to be inoperative.

✔ Visually check all accessible wiring connectors, harnesses and retaining clips for security, and for signs of chafing or damage.

HAYNES HiNT *If you need to check your brake lights and indicators unaided, back up to a wall or garage door and operate the lights. The reflected light should show if they are working properly.*

1 If a single indicator light, stop light, sidelight or headlight has failed, it is likely that a bulb has blown and will need to be replaced. Refer to Chapter 13 for details. If both stop lights have failed, it is possible that the switch has failed (see Chapter 10).

2 If more than one indicator light or tail light has failed it is likely that either a fuse has blown or that there is a fault in the circuit (see Chapter 13). The fuses are located in the driver's compartment fusebox, behind the cover on the driver's end of the facia, and also in the engine compartment fusebox.

3 To replace a blown fuse, simply pull it out and fit a new fuse of the correct rating (see Chapter 13). If the fuse blows again, it is important that you find out why - a complete checking procedure is given in Chapter 13.

Lubricants and fluids

Engine:

Petrol . . . . Multigrade engine oil, viscosity SAE 10W/40 to 20W/50 to API SG/CD or SH/CD
(Duckhams QXR Premium Petrol Engine Oil, or Duckhams Hypergrade Petrol Engine Oil)

Diesel . . . . Multigrade engine oil, viscosity SAE 10W/40 to 20W/50 to API SG/CD or SH/CD
(Duckhams QXR Premium Diesel Engine Oil, or Duckhams Hypergrade Diesel Engine Oil)

Cooling system . . . . Ethylene glycol based antifreeze
(Duckhams Antifreeze and Summer Coolant)

Transmission . . . . Multigrade engine oil, viscosity SAE 10W/30 or 10W/40 to API SG or SH
(Duckhams QXR Premium Petrol or Diesel Engine Oil, or Duckhams Hypergrade Petrol or Diesel Engine Oil)

Brake fluid . . . . Hydraulic fluid DOT 3 or DOT 4 - refer to recommendations on fluid reservoir filler cap
(Duckhams Universal Brake and Clutch Fluid)

Clutch fluid . . . . Hydraulic fluid DOT 3 or DOT 4 - refer to recommendations on fluid reservoir filler cap
(Duckhams Universal Brake and Clutch Fluid)

Front and rear axles:

Standard differential . . . . Hypoid SAE 90 gear oil to API GL5
(Duckhams Hypoid 80W/90S Gear Oil)

Limited slip differential . . . . Hypoid SAE 90 gear oil to API GL5
(Duckhams Hypoid 90DL Gear Oil)

Power steering . . . . Special oil 19 40 763
(Duckhams Unimatic)

Propeller shaft joints/bearings . . . . GM 4750-M lithium-based grease - available from your Vauxhall dealer

Choosing your engine oil

Engines need oil, not only to lubricate moving parts and minimise wear, but also to maximise power output and to improve fuel economy. By introducing a simplified and improved range of engine oils, Duckhams has taken away the confusion and made it easier for you to choose the right oil for your engine.

HOW ENGINE OIL WORKS

• Beating friction

Without oil, the moving surfaces inside your engine will rub together, heat up and melt, quickly causing the engine to seize. Engine oil creates a film which separates these moving parts, preventing wear and heat build-up.

• Cooling hot-spots

Temperatures inside the engine can exceed 1000° C. The engine oil circulates and acts as a coolant, transferring heat from the hot-spots to the sump.

• Cleaning the engine internally

Good quality engine oils clean the inside of your engine, collecting and dispersing combustion deposits and controlling them until they are trapped by the oil filter or flushed out at oil change.

OIL CARE - FOLLOW THE CODE

To handle and dispose of used engine oil safely, always:

OIL CARE
OIL BANK LINE
0800 66 33 66

- **Avoid skin contact with used engine oil. Repeated or prolonged contact can be harmful.**
- **Dispose of used oil and empty packs in a responsible manner in an authorised disposal site. Call 0800 663366 to find the one nearest to you. Never tip oil down drains or onto the ground.**

DUCKHAMS ENGINE OILS

For the driver who demands a premium quality oil for complete reassurance, we recommend synthetic formula **Duckhams QXR Premium Engine Oils**.

For the driver who requires a straightforward quality engine oil, we recommend **Duckhams Hypergrade Engine Oils**.

For further information and advice, call the Duckhams UK Helpline on 0800 212988.

Note: *Pressures apply to original-equipment tyres only and may vary if any other make or type of tyre is fitted; check with the tyre manufacturer or supplier for correct pressures if necessary.*

Note: *Tyre pressures must always be checked with the tyres cold to ensure accuracy.*

Tyre size

3-door models:

225/75 R15:

Upto 2 passengers:

Front .... 25 psi (1.7 bar)
Rear .... 25 psi (1.7 bar)

Fully loaded:

Front .... 25 psi (1.7 bar)
Rear .... 35 psi (2.4 bar)

235/70 R16 and 255/65 R 16:

Upto 2 passengers:

Front .... 29 psi (2.0 bar)
Rear .... 32 psi (2.2 bar)

Fully loaded:

Front .... 29 psi (2.0 bar)
Rear .... 36 psi (2.5 bar)

5-door models:

225/75 R15:

Upto 3 passengers:

Front .... 25 psi (1.7 bar)
Rear .... 25 psi (1.7 bar)

Fully loaded:

Front .... 25 psi (1.7 bar)
Rear .... 35 psi (2.4 bar)

235/70 R16 and 255/65 R 16:

Upto 2 passengers:

Front .... 29 psi (2.0 bar)
Rear .... 32 psi (2.2 bar)

Fully loaded:

Front .... 29 psi (2.0 bar)
Rear .... 36 psi (2.5 bar)

Chapter 1 Part A
Routine maintenance and servicing - petrol engine models

Contents

Air cleaner element renewal	23	Handbrake check	25
Auxiliary drivebelt check and renewal	4	Headlight beam alignment check	19
Axle oil level check	14	Hinge and lock lubrication	18
Axle oil renewal	30	Hose and fluid leak check	8
Brake fluid renewal	20	Propeller shaft check and lubrication	12
Braking system load proportioning valve check	17	Rear brake pad and disc check	7
Coolant renewal	28	Rear brake shoe and drum check	26
Corrosion check	9	Regular maintenance	2
Driveshaft gaiter check	10	Road test	21
Engine oil and filter renewal	3	Spark plug renewal - 1995 onwards models	31
Exhaust emission check	5	Spark plug renewal - pre 1995 models	22
Front brake pad and disc check	6	Suspension and steering check	11
Front hub bearing check and adjustment	13	Timing belt renewal - 2.0 and 2.2 litre engine	32
Front hub bearing lubrication	27	Transmission unit oil level check	15
Fuel filter renewal	24	Transmission unit oil renewal	29
General information	1	Wheel nut tightness check	16

Degrees of difficulty

Easy, suitable for novice with little experience 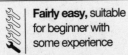	**Fairly easy,** suitable for beginner with some experience 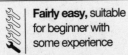	**Fairly difficult,** suitable for competent DIY mechanic 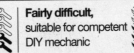	**Difficult,** suitable for experienced DIY mechanic	**Very difficult,** suitable for expert DIY or professional 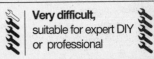

Servicing specifications

Capacities

Engine oil

At oil and filter change:	
2.0 and 2.2 litre engine	5.0 litres
2.4 litre engine	5.5 litres
Difference between MIN and MAX on dipstick	Approximately 1.0 litre

Cooling system

2.0 litre engine:	
Pre 1995 models (C20NE engine)	7.2 litres
1995 onwards models (X20SE engine)	8.3 litres
2.2 litre engine	8.3 litres
2.4 litre engine	7.8 litres

Transmission

2.0 litre engine	4.4 litres
2.2 and 2.4 litre engines:	
Transmission housing	2.95 litres
Transfer case	1.45 litres

Axles

Front axle:	
3-door models (9HU axle)	0.9 litres
5-door models (12HU axle)	1.7 litres
Rear axle:	
Standard	2.3 litres
Models with limited slip differential	1.9 litres

Fuel tank

All models	80 litres

Lubricants and fluids

Refer to *Weekly checks*

Engine

Oil filter:
2.0 and 2.2 litre engines	Champion G102
2.4 litre engine	Champion C103

Cooling system

Antifreeze mixture:
33% antifreeze	Protection down to -20°C (-4°F)
50% antifreeze	Protection down to -37°C (-35°F)

Note: *Refer to antifreeze manufacturer for latest recommendations.*

Fuel system

Air filter element	Champion U570
Fuel filter	Champion L201

Ignition system

Spark plugs:

	Type	Electrode gap*
2.0 litre engine:		
Models up to July 1995 (C20NE engine)	Champion RN9YCC	0.8 mm
Models from August 1995 onwards (X20SE engine)	Champion RC10DMC	Not adjustable
2.2 litre engine	Champion RC10DMC	Not adjustable
2.4 litre engine	Champion RL82YCC	0.8 mm

The spark plug gap quoted is that recommended by Champion for their specified plug listed above. If spark plugs of any other type are to be fitted, refer to their manufacturer's recommendations.

Brakes

Friction material minimum thickness:
Front and rear brake pads	1.0 mm
Rear brake shoes	1.0 mm

Torque wrench settings

	Nm	lbf ft
Air conditioning compressor fixings - 2.4 litre engine:		
Adjuster nut:		
Clamp bolt	45	33
Locknut	40	30
Mounting bolts	50	37
Alternator fixings:		
2.0 litre (C20NE engine) pre 1995 model	25	18
2.4 litre engine:		
Adjuster nut locknut	25	18
Lower mounting bolt	25	18
Oil filter - 1995 onwards models	15	11
Power steering pump fixings:		
2.0 litre (C20NE engine) pre 1995 model:		
Adjuster clamp bolt	25	18
Adjuster locknut	39	29
Lower mouning bolt	25	18
2.4 litre engine:		
Adjuster nut:		
Clamp bolt:		
Models with air conditioning	40	30
Models without air conditioning	25	18
Locknut	40	30
Mounting bolts	25	18
Spark plugs:		
2.0 and 2.2 litre engine	25	18
2.4 litre engine	40	30
Wheel nuts:		
Alloy wheels	120	89
Steel wheels	110	81

1 The maintenance intervals in this manual are provided with the assumption that you, not the dealer, will be carrying out the work. These are the minimum maintenance intervals recommended by us for vehicles driven daily. If you wish to keep your vehicle in peak condition at all times, you may wish to perform some of these procedures more often. **Note:** *For models after 1995, the manufacturers extended the service mileages from 4500 to 5000, 9000 to 10 000, etc. The time intervals remained the same. We encourage frequent maintenance, because it enhances the efficiency, performance and resale value of your vehicle.*

2 If the vehicle is driven in dusty areas, used to tow a trailer, or driven frequently at slow speeds (idling in traffic) or on short journeys, more frequent maintenance intervals are recommended.

3 When the vehicle is new, it should be serviced by a factory-authorised dealer service department, in order to preserve the factory warranty.

Every 4500 miles or 6 months, whichever comes first

☐ Renew the engine oil and filter (Section 3)

Note: *Vauxhall recommend that the engine oil and filter are changed at the annual specified mileage or every 12 months, whichever comes first. However, oil and filter changes are good for the engine and it is recommend that the oil and filter are renewed more frequently, especially if the vehicle is used on a lot of short journeys.*

Every 9000 miles or 12 months, whichever comes first

Note: *On vehicles covering more than 18 000 miles annually, carry out the items marked with an asterisk every 18 000 miles, regardless of time, then carry out the items not marked with an asterisk at the 12 month interval.*

☐ Check the condition and tension of the auxiliary drivebelt(s) (Section 4)*
☐ Check the exhaust emission level (Section 5)*
☐ Check the front brake pads and discs for wear (Section 6)*
☐ Check the rear brake pads and discs for wear (Section 7)*
☐ Check all components, pipes and hoses for fluid leaks (Section 8)
☐ Check the body and underbody for corrosion protection (Section 9)
☐ Check the condition of the driveshaft gaiters (Section 10)*
☐ Check the steering and suspension components for condition and security (Section 11)*
☐ Check the condition of the propeller shaft and lubricate the shaft bearings (Section 12)*. **Note:** *If the vehicle is used off-road frequently, the propeller shaft check should be performed every 6000 miles, or every 3000 miles if the vehicle is regularly driven through deep water.*
☐ Check and adjust the front hub bearings (Section 13)*
☐ Check the front and rear axle oil level (Section 14)*
☐ Check the transmission unit oil level (Section 15)*
☐ Check the roadwheel nuts are tightened to the specified torque (Section 16)*
☐ Check the operation of the braking system load proportioning valve (Section 17)*

Every 9000 miles or 12 months, whichever comes first (continued)

☐ Lubricate all door locks and hinges, door stops, bonnet lock and release, and tailgate lock and hinges (Section 18)
☐ Check and if necessary adjust the headlight beam alignment (Section 19)
☐ Renew the brake fluid (Section 20)
☐ Carry out a road test (Section 21)*

Every 18 000 miles or 2 years, whichever comes first

☐ Renew the spark plugs - pre 1995 models (Section 22)
☐ Renew the air cleaner element (Section 23)
☐ Renew the fuel filter (Section 24)
☐ Check and, if necessary, adjust the handbrake (Section 25)
☐ Check the rear brake shoes and drums for wear (Section 26)
☐ Lubricate the front hub bearings (Section 27)

Every 2 years, regardless of mileage

☐ Renew the coolant (Section 28)

Every 27 000 miles or 3 years, whichever comes first

☐ Renew the transmission unit oil (Section 29)
☐ Renew the front and rear axle oil (Section 30)

Every 36 000 miles or 4 years, whichever comes first

☐ Renew the spark plugs - 1995 onwards models (Section 31)
☐ Renew the timing belt - 2.0 and 2.2 litre engine (Section 32)

Note: *From 1997 model year, Vauxhall increased the specified interval for timing belt renewal. However, if the vehicle is used mainly for short journeys or a lot of stop-start driving it is recommended that this, earlier, recommendation is adhered to. The actual belt renewal interval is very much upto the individual owner but, bearing in mind that severe engine damage will result if the belt breaks in use, we recommend you err on the side of caution.*

1A

Underbonnet view of a 1995 onwards 2.0 litre model (X20SE engine)

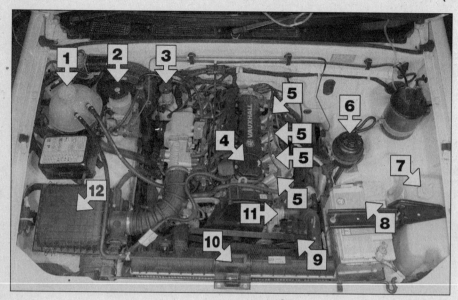

1 Coolant expansion tank
2 Brake fluid reservoir
3 Clutch fluid reservoir
4 Engine oil filler cap
5 Spark plugs
6 Power steering fluid reservoir
7 Washer fluid reservoir
8 Battery
9 Auxiliary drivebelt
10 Radiator
11 Thermostat housing
12 Air cleaner housing

Underbonnet view of a 2.2 litre engine model

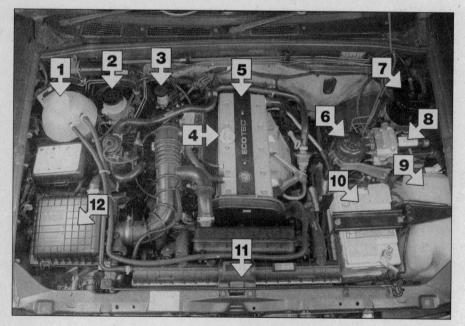

1 Coolant expansion tank
2 Brake fluid reservoir
3 Clutch fluid reservoir
4 Engine oil filler cap
5 Spark plug cover
6 Power steering fluid reservoir
7 Evaporative emission system canister
8 ABS unit
9 Washer fluid reservoir
10 Battery
11 Radiator
12 Air cleaner housing

Front underbody view - undercover removed
(1995 onwards 2.0 litre engine shown, others similar)

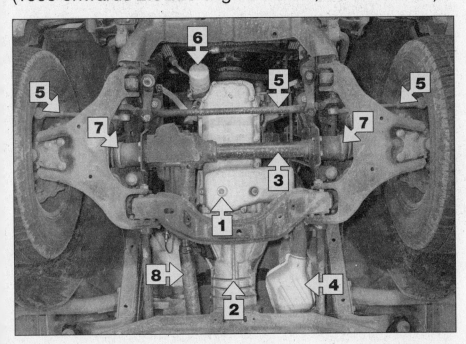

1 Engine sump drain plug
2 Transmission unit
3 Front axle
4 Exhaust pipe
5 Steering linkage
6 Oil filter
7 Driveshaft inner joint
8 Propeller shaft

1A

Rear underbody view (coil spring suspension shown)

1 Exhaust system
2 Propeller shaft
3 Fuel tank
4 Rear axle differential housing
5 Shock absorber
6 Anti-roll bar
7 Lateral rod
8 Trailing link
9 Handbrake cable
10 Fuel filter

1 General information

1 This Chapter is designed to help the home mechanic maintain his/her vehicle for safety, economy, long life and peak performance.

2 The Chapter contains a master maintenance schedule, followed by Sections dealing specifically with each task in the schedule. Visual checks, adjustments, component renewal and other helpful items are included. Refer to the accompanying illustrations of the engine compartment and the underside of the vehicle for the locations of the various components.

3 Servicing your vehicle in accordance with the mileage/time maintenance schedule and the following Sections will provide a planned maintenance programme, which should result in a long and reliable service life. This is a comprehensive plan, so maintaining some items but not others at the specified service intervals will not produce the same results.

4 As you service your vehicle, you will discover that many of the procedures can - and should - be grouped together, because of the particular procedure being performed, or because of the proximity of two otherwise-unrelated components to one another. For example, if the vehicle is raised for any reason, the exhaust can be inspected at the same time as the suspension and steering components.

5 The first step in this maintenance programme is to prepare yourself before the actual work begins. Read through all the Sections relevant to the work to be carried out, then make a list and gather all the parts and tools required. If a problem is encountered, seek advice from a parts specialist, or a dealer service department.

2 Regular maintenance

1 If, from the time the vehicle is new, the routine maintenance schedule is followed closely, and frequent checks are made of fluid levels and high-wear items, as suggested throughout this manual, the engine will be kept in relatively good running condition, and the need for additional work will be minimised.

2 It is possible that there will be times when the engine is running poorly due to the lack of regular maintenance. This is even more likely if a used vehicle, which has not received regular and frequent maintenance checks, is purchased. In such cases, additional work may need to be carried out, outside of the regular maintenance intervals.

3 If engine wear is suspected, a compression test (refer to relevant Part of Chapter 2) will provide valuable information regarding the overall performance of the main internal components. Such a test can be used as a basis to decide on the extent of the work to be carried out. If, for example, a compression test indicates serious internal engine wear, conventional maintenance as described in this Chapter will not greatly improve the performance of the engine, and may prove a waste of time and money, unless extensive overhaul work is carried out first.

4 The following series of operations are those most often required to improve the performance of a generally poor-running engine:

Primary operations

a) Clean, inspect and test the battery (refer to Weekly checks).
b) Check all the engine-related fluids (refer to Weekly checks).
c) Check the condition of the spark plugs (Section 22).
d) Check the condition and tension of the auxiliary drivebelt (Section 4).
e) Check the condition of the air cleaner element, and renew if necessary (Section 23).
f) Renew the fuel filter (Section 24).
g) Check the condition of all hoses, and check for fluid leaks (Section 8).

5 If the above operations do not prove fully effective, carry out the following secondary operations:

Secondary operations

All items listed under Primary operations, plus the following:
a) Check the charging system (refer to Chapter 5A).
b) Check the ignition system (refer to Chapter 5B).
c) Check the fuel system (refer to Chapter 4A).

Every 4500 miles or 6 months, whichever comes first

3 Engine oil and filter renewal

1 Frequent oil and filter changes are the most important preventative maintenance procedures which can be undertaken by the DIY owner. As engine oil ages, it becomes diluted and contaminated, which leads to premature engine wear.

2 Before starting this procedure, gather together all the necessary tools and materials. Also make sure that you have plenty of clean rags and newspapers handy, to mop up any spills. Ideally, the engine oil should be warm, as it will drain more easily, and more built-up sludge will be removed with it. Take care not to touch the exhaust or any other hot parts of the engine when working under the vehicle. To avoid any possibility of scalding, and to protect yourself from possible skin irritants and other harmful contaminants in used engine oils, it is advisable to wear gloves when carrying out this work.

3 If necessary, to improve access to the oil filter and sump drain plug, undo the retaining bolts and remove the undercover from beneath the engine.

4 Remove the oil filler cap from the cylinder head cover.

5 Using a spanner, or preferably a suitable socket and bar, slacken the drain plug about half a turn (see illustration). Position the draining container under the drain plug, then remove the plug completely (see Haynes Hint).

6 Allow some time for the oil to drain, noting that it may be necessary to reposition the container as the oil flow slows to a trickle.

7 After all the oil has drained, wipe the drain plug and the sealing washer with a clean rag. Examine the condition of the sealing washer, and renew it if it shows signs of scoring or other damage which may prevent an oil-tight seal. Clean the area around the drain plug

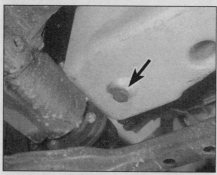

3.5 Sump drain plug - 1995 onwards 2.0 litre engine

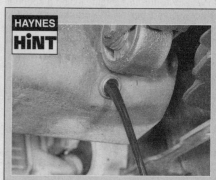

Hint: As the drain plug threads release, move it sharply away so the stream of oil issuing from the sump runs into the container, not up your sleeve

3.9 Using an oil filter removal tool to unscrew the oil filter

opening, and refit the plug complete with the washer and tighten it securely.

8 Move the container into position under the oil filter which is located at the front end of the engine, on the right-hand side.

9 Use an oil filter removal tool to slacken the filter initially, then unscrew it by hand the rest of the way **(see illustration)**. Empty the oil from the old filter into the container.

10 Use a clean rag to remove all oil, dirt and sludge from the filter sealing/housing area on the engine.

11 Apply a light coating of clean engine oil to the sealing ring on the new filter, then screw the filter into position on the engine. Tighten the filter firmly by hand only - **do not** use any tools. On 1995 onwards models, if a genuine filter is being fitted and the special oil filter tool (a socket which fits over the end of the filter) is available, tighten the filter to the specified torque setting.

12 Remove the old oil and all tools from under the vehicle then, where necessary, refit the undercover and securely tighten its retaining bolts.

13 Fill the engine through the filler hole, using the correct grade and type of oil (refer to *Weekly Checks* for details of topping-up).

Pour in half the specified quantity of oil first, then wait a few minutes for the oil to drain into the sump. Continue to add oil, a small quantity at a time, until the level is up to the lower mark on the dipstick. Adding approximately a further 1.0 litre will bring the level up to the upper mark on the dipstick.

14 Start the engine and run it for a few minutes, while checking for leaks around the oil filter seal and the sump drain plug. Note that there may be a delay of a few seconds before the low oil pressure warning light goes out when the engine is first started, as the oil circulates through the new oil filter and the engine oil galleries before the pressure builds up.

15 Stop the engine, and wait a few minutes for the oil to settle in the sump once more. With the new oil circulated and the filter now completely full, recheck the level on the dipstick, and add more oil as necessary.

16 Dispose of the used engine oil safely with reference to *General repair procedures*.

Every 9000 miles or 12 months, whichever comes first

4 Auxiliary drivebelt check and renewal

Checking

Note: *On pre 1995 2.0 litre engines (C20NE) and all 2.4 litre engines the alternator, power steering pump and (where fitted) air conditioning compressor are all driven by separate belts. On 1995 on 2.0 litre engines (X20SE) and all 2.2 litre engines a single belt is used to drive all auxiliary components.*

1 Due to their function and material makeup, drivebelts are prone to failure after a long period of time and should therefore be inspected regularly.

2 With the engine stopped, inspect the full length of the drivebelt(s) for cracks and separation of the belt plies. It will be necessary to turn the engine (using a spanner or socket and bar on the crankshaft pulley bolt - remove the undercover to gain access) in order to move the belt from the pulleys so that the belt can be inspected thoroughly. Twist the belt between the pulleys so that both sides can be viewed. Also check for fraying, and glazing which gives the belt a shiny appearance. Check the pulleys for nicks, cracks, distortion and corrosion.

3 If the belt shows signs of wear or damage, it must be renewed.

4 On pre 1995 2.0 litre engines (C20NE) and all 2.4 litre engines check the tension of each drivebelt and, if necessary, adjust as described under the relevant sub-heading in the renewal section.

5 On 1995 on 2.0 litre engines (X20SE) and all 2.2 litre engines, check the position of the drivebelt tensioner assembly arm, the arm should be inbetween the stops on the backplate and should be free to move **(see illustration)**. If the tensioner arm is against the stop, the belt must be renewed.

Renewal

6 Undo the retaining bolts and remove the undercover from beneath the engine. Proceed as described under the relevant sub-heading.

Alternator drivebelt - pre 1995 2.0 litre engines (C20NE)

7 Remove the cooling fan as described in Chapter 3.

8 Remove the power steering pump drivebelt as described in this Section.

9 Slacken the alternator upper and lower mounting bolts then pivot the alternator in towards the cylinder block and slip the belt off the pulleys. On some engines, the upper mounting is fitted with a threaded adjuster; on these engines slacken the locknut and back off the adjuster nut to release the drivebelt tension.

10 Manoeuvre the new belt into position and seat it on the pulleys. Using the adjuster nut (where fitted) or a piece of wood carefully inserted between the alternator body and cylinder block, position the alternator so that under firm thumb pressure there is about 10 mm of movement at the mid-point on the longest run of the belt. Once the belt is correctly tensioned, hold the alternator in position and tighten its mounting bolts to the

1A

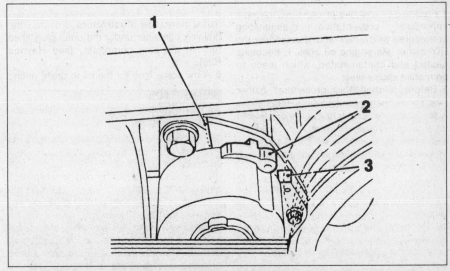

4.5 On 1995 on 2.0 litre engines (X20SE) and all 2.2 litre engines ensure the auxiliary drivebelt tensioner arm indicator (2) is between the stops (1 and 3) on the backplate

specified torque and retighten the adjuster locknut (where fitted) securely. Recheck the drivebelt tension and, if necessary, readjust.

11 Refit the power steering pump drivebelt as described in this Section.

12 Refit the cooling fan as described in Chapter 3.

Power steering pump drivebelt - pre 1995 2.0 litre engines (C20NE)

13 Slacken the power steering pump lower mounting bolt and loosen the bolt securing the adjuster clamp to the pump bracket.

14 Slacken the adjuster clamp locknut then back off the adjuster nut to release the drivebelt tension. Slip the belt off the pulleys and remove it from the engine.

15 Manoeuvre the new belt into position and seat it on the pulleys.

16 Tension the power steering pump belt using the adjuster nut so that under firm thumb pressure there is about 10 mm of movement at the mid-point on the longest run of the belt. Once the adjuster nut is correctly positioned, tighten the adjuster clamp bolt and the power steering pump lower mounting bolt to their specified torque settings then tighten the adjuster locknut. Refit the undercover and securely tighten its retaining bolts.

Auxiliary drivebelt - 1995 on 2.0 litre engines (X20SE) and all 2.2 litre engines

17 Prior to removal make a note of the correct routing of the belt around the various pulleys. If the belt is to be re-used, also mark the direction of rotation on the belt to ensure the belt is refitted the same way around.

18 Using a suitable spanner or socket fitted to the tensioner pulley centre bolt, lever the tensioner away from the belt until there is sufficient slack to enable the belt to be slipped off the pulleys. Carefully release the tensioner pulley until it is against its stop then remove the belt from the vehicle.

19 Manoeuvre the belt into position, routing it correctly around the pulleys; if the original belt is being fitted use the marks made prior to removal to ensure it is fitted the correct way around.

20 Lever the tensioner roller back against is spring, and seat the belt on the pulleys. Ensure the belt is centrally located on all pulleys then slowly release the tensioner pulley until the belt is correctly tensioned. **Do not** allow the tensioner to spring back and stress the belt. Refit the undercover and securely tighten its retaining bolts

Alternator drivebelt - 2.4 litre engine

21 Remove the cooling fan as described in Chapter 3.

22 Remove the power steering pump drivebelt or the air conditioning compressor drivebelt (as applicable) as described in this Section.

23 Slacken the alternator upper and lower mounting bolts then pivot the alternator in

towards the cylinder block and slip the belt off the pulleys. On some engines, the upper mounting is fitted with a threaded adjuster; on these engines slacken the locknut and back off the adjuster nut to release the drivebelt tension.

24 Manoeuvre the new belt into position and seat it on the pulleys. Using the adjuster nut (where fitted) or a piece of wood carefully inserted between the alternator body and cylinder block, position the alternator so that under firm thumb pressure there is about 10 mm of movement at the mid-point on the longest run of the belt. Once the belt is correctly tensioned, hold the alternator in position and tighten its mounting bolts to the specified torque and retighten the adjuster locknut (where fitted) securely. Recheck the drivebelt tension and, if necessary, readjust.

25 Refit the air conditioning compressor drivebelt or power steering pump drivebelt (as applicable) as described in this Section.

26 Refit the cooling fan as described in Chapter 3.

Power steering pump drivebelt - 2.4 litre engine

27 Where necessary, remove the air conditioning compressor drivebelt as described in this Section.

28 Slacken the power steering pump mounting bolts and loosen the nut and bolt securing the adjuster nut clamp to the pump bracket.

29 Slacken the adjuster nut locknut then back off the adjuster nut to release the drivebelt tension. Slip the belt off the pulleys and remove it from the engine.

30 Manoeuvre the new belt into position and seat it on the pulleys.

31 Refit the air conditioning compressor drivebelt (where fitted) and tension it as described in this Section.

32 Tension the power steering pump belt using the adjuster nut so that under firm thumb pressure there is about 10 mm of movement at the mid-point on the longest run of the belt. Once the adjuster nut is correctly positioned, tighten the adjuster nut clamp bolt, the power steering pump mounting bolts and the adjuster nut locknut to their specified torque settings. Refit the undercover and securely tighten its retaining bolts.

Air conditioning compressor drivebelt - 2.4 litre engine

33 Slacken the compressor mounting bolts and loosen the bolt securing the adjuster nut clamp to the compressor.

34 Slacken the adjuster bolt locknut then back off the adjuster nut to release the drivebelt tension. Slip the belt off the pulleys and remove it from the engine.

35 Manoeuvre the new belt into position and seat it on the pulleys. Tension the belt using the adjuster nut so that under firm thumb pressure there is about 10 mm of movement at the mid-point on the longest run of the belt. Once the adjuster nut is correctly positioned,

tighten the adjuster nut clamp bolt, the compressor mounting bolts and the adjuster nut locknut to their specified torque settings.

36 Check and, if necessary, adjust the power steering pump drivebelt then refit the undercover and securely tighten its retaining bolts.

5 Exhaust emission check

1 Vauxhall specify that this check should be carried out annually. The check involves checking the engine management system operation by plugging an electronic tester into the system diagnostic socket to check the electronic control unit (ECU) memory for faults (see Chapter 4A).

2 In reality, if the vehicle is running correctly and the engine management warning light in the instrument panel is functioning normally, then this check need not be carried out.

6 Front brake pad and disc check

1 Firmly apply the handbrake, then jack up the front of the vehicle and support it securely on axle stands. Remove the front roadwheels.

2 For a quick check, the pad thickness can be carried out via the inspection hole on the front of the caliper **(see Haynes Hint)**. Using a steel rule, measure the thickness of the friction material on each pad. This must not be less than that indicated in the Specifications.

3 The view through the caliper inspection hole gives a rough indication of the state of the brake pads. For a comprehensive check, the brake pads should be removed and cleaned. The operation of the caliper can then also be checked, and the condition of the brake disc itself can be fully examined on both sides. Chapter 10 contains a detailed

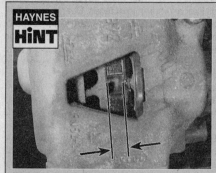

For a quick check, the thickness of friction material remaining on the brake pad can be measured through the aperture in the caliper body

description of how the brake disc should be checked for wear and/or damage.

4 If any pad's friction material is worn to the specified thickness or less, *all four pads must be renewed as a set.* Refer to Chapter 10 for details.

5 On completion, refit the roadwheels and lower the vehicle to the ground.

7 Rear brake pad and disc check

1 Firmly apply the handbrake, chock the front wheels, then jack up the rear of the vehicle and support it securely on axle stands. Remove the rear roadwheels.

2 For a quick check, the pad thickness can be carried out via the inspection hole on the rear of the caliper. Using a steel rule, measure the thickness of the friction material of each pad. This must not be less than that indicated in the Specifications.

3 The view through the caliper inspection hole gives a rough indication of the state of the brake pads. For a comprehensive check, the brake pads should be removed and cleaned. The operation of the caliper can then also be checked, and the condition of the brake disc itself can be fully examined on both sides. Chapter 10 contains a detailed description of how the brake disc should be checked for wear and/or damage.

4 If any pad's friction material is worn to the specified thickness or less, *all four pads must be renewed as a set.* Refer to Chapter 10 for details.

5 On completion, refit the roadwheels and lower the vehicle to the ground.

8 Hose and fluid leak check

1 Visually inspect the engine joint faces, gaskets and seals for any signs of water or oil leaks. Pay particular attention to the areas around the cylinder head cover, cylinder head, oil filter and sump joint faces. Bear in mind that, over a period of time, some very slight seepage from these areas is to be expected - what you are really looking for is any indication of a serious leak. Should a leak be found, renew the offending gasket or oil seal by referring to the appropriate Chapters in this manual.

2 Also check the security and condition of all the engine-related pipes and hoses, and all braking system pipes and hoses and fuel lines. Ensure that all cable ties or securing clips are in place, and in good condition. Clips which are broken or missing can lead to chafing of the hoses, pipes or wiring, which could cause more serious problems in the future.

3 Carefully check the radiator hoses and heater hoses along their entire length. Renew any hose which is cracked, swollen or

A leak in the cooling system will usually show up as white- or rust-coloured deposits on the area adjoining the leak

deteriorated. Cracks will show up better if the hose is squeezed. Pay close attention to the hose clips that secure the hoses to the cooling system components. Hose clips can pinch and puncture hoses, resulting in cooling system leaks. If the crimped-type hose clips are used, it may be a good idea to replace them with standard worm-drive clips.

4 Inspect all the cooling system components (hoses, joint faces, etc) for leaks **(see Haynes Hint)**.

5 Where any problems are found on system components, renew the component or gasket with reference to Chapter 3.

6 With the vehicle raised, inspect the fuel tank and filler neck for punctures, cracks and other damage. The connection between the filler neck and tank is especially critical. Sometimes a rubber filler neck or connecting hose will leak due to loose retaining clamps or deteriorated rubber.

7 Carefully check all rubber hoses and metal fuel lines leading away from the fuel tank. Check for loose connections, deteriorated hoses, crimped lines, and other damage. Pay particular attention to the vent pipes and hoses, which often loop up around the filler neck and can become blocked or crimped. Follow the lines to the front of the vehicle, carefully inspecting them all the way. Renew damaged sections as necessary. Similarly, whilst the vehicle is raised, take the opportunity to inspect all underbody brake fluid pipes and hoses.

8 From within the engine compartment, check the security of all fuel, vacuum and brake hose attachments and pipe unions, and inspect all hoses for kinks, chafing and deterioration.

9 Corrosion check

1 This work should be carried out by a Vauxhall/Opel dealer in order to validate the vehicle warranty. The work includes a thorough inspection of the vehicle paintwork and underbody for damage and corrosion.

10 Driveshaft gaiter check

1 With the vehicle raised and securely supported on stands, turn the steering onto full lock then slowly rotate the roadwheel. Inspect the condition of the outer constant velocity (CV) joint rubber gaiters while squeezing the gaiters to open out the folds. Check for signs of cracking, splits or deterioration of the rubber which may allow the grease to escape and lead to water and grit entry into the joint. Also check the security and condition of the retaining clips. Repeat these checks on the inner CV joints. If any damage or deterioration is found, the gaiters should be renewed as described in Chapter 8.

2 At the same time check the general condition of the CV joints themselves by first holding the driveshaft and attempting to rotate the wheel. Repeat this check by holding the inner joint and attempting to rotate the driveshaft. Any appreciable movement indicates wear in the joints, wear in the driveshaft splines or loose driveshaft retaining nut.

11 Suspension and steering check

Front suspension and steering check

1 Raise the front of the vehicle, and securely support it on axle stands.

2 Visually inspect the balljoint dust covers for splits, chafing or deterioration. Any wear of these components will cause loss of lubricant, together with dirt and water entry, resulting in rapid deterioration of the balljoints.

3 Check the power steering fluid hoses for chafing or deterioration, and the pipe and hose unions for fluid leaks.

4 Grasp the roadwheel at the 12 o'clock and 6 o'clock positions, and try to rock it. Very slight free play may be felt, but if the movement is appreciable, further investigation is necessary to determine the source. Continue rocking the wheel while an assistant depresses the footbrake. If the movement is now eliminated or significantly reduced, it is likely that the hub bearings are at fault. If the free play is still evident with the footbrake depressed, then there is wear in the suspension joints or mountings.

5 Now grasp the wheel at the 9 o'clock and 3 o'clock positions, and try to rock it as before. Any movement felt now may again be caused by wear in the hub bearings or the steering tie rod balljoints.

6 Using a large screwdriver or flat bar, check for wear in the suspension mounting bushes by levering between the relevant suspension component and its attachment point. Some

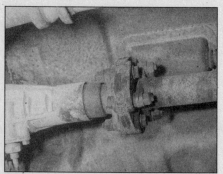

12.1 Check the propeller shaft joints and couplings for signs of wear or damage . . .

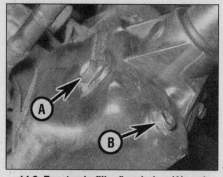

12.2 . . . and lubricate with the specified grease

movement is to be expected, as the mountings are made of rubber, but excessive wear should be obvious. Also check the condition of any visible rubber bushes, looking for splits, cracks or contamination of the rubber.

7 With the vehicle standing on its wheels, have an assistant turn the steering wheel back-and-forth, about an eighth of a turn each way. There should be very little lost movement between the steering wheel and roadwheels. If this is not the case, closely observe the joints and mountings previously described. If these appear satisfactory, check the steering adjustment, as described in Chapter 11.

Rear suspension check

8 Chock the front wheels, then jack up the rear of the vehicle and support securely on axle stands.

9 Working as described previously for the front suspension, check the rear hub bearings, the suspension bushes, springs and mountings for wear.

Shock absorber check

10 Check for any signs of fluid leakage around the shock absorber body, or from the area around the piston rod. Should any fluid be noticed, the shock absorber is defective internally, and should be renewed. **Note:** *Shock absorbers should always be renewed in pairs on the same axle.*

11 The efficiency of the shock absorber may be checked by bouncing the vehicle at each corner. Generally speaking, the body will return to its normal position and stop after being depressed. If it rises and returns on a rebound, the shock absorber is probably suspect. Also examine the shock absorber upper and lower mountings for any signs of wear.

12 Propeller shaft check and lubrication

Note: *If the vehicle is used off-road frequently, the propeller shaft check should be performed every 6000 miles, or every 3000 miles if the*

vehicle is regularly driven through deep water.

1 Check the propeller shaft joints for signs of wear or damage, paying particular attention to the rubber coupling (where fitted) **(see illustration)**. Check that all the propeller shaft bolts are tightened to the specified torque (see Chapter 8). If any damage is found, renew the affected item as described in Chapter 8.

2 Using a grease gun, work along the propeller shaft and lubricate each of the universal and sliding joint nipples with a good quality lithium-based grease (Vauxhall recommend the use of GM4750-M) **(see illustration)**. Wipe off excess grease.

13 Front hub bearing check and adjustment

Refer to the procedures contained in Chapter 11, Section 4.

14 Axle oil level check

Front axle

1 Park the vehicle on level ground. To further improve access, either position the vehicle

over an inspection pit, or jack up the front and rear of the vehicle and support it on axle stands. The vehicle **must** be level for the check to be accurate.

2 Clean the area around the filler/level plug which is located on the front of the differential housing, then slacken and remove the plug from the housing **(see illustration)**.

3 The oil level should be up to the lower edge of the filler/level plug aperture.

4 If necessary, top-up using the specified type of lubricant until the oil level is correct. Fill the axle until oil starts to flow out and allow excess oil to drain out.

5 Once the axle oil level is correct, refit the filler/level plug and tighten it securely. Lower the vehicle to the ground.

6 Note that frequent need for topping-up indicates a leakage, possibly through an oil seal. The cause should be investigated and rectified.

Rear axle

7 Check the oil level as described in paragraphs 1 to 6 noting that the filler/level plug is on the differential housing rear cover **(see illustration)**.

15 Transmission unit oil level check

1 Park the vehicle on level ground. To further improve access, either position the vehicle over an inspection pit, or jack up the front and rear of the vehicle and support it on axle stands. The vehicle **must** be level for the check to be accurate. The oil level must be checked before the vehicle is driven, or at least 5 minutes after the engine has been switched off. If the oil is checked immediately after driving the car, some of the oil will remain distributed around the transmission components, resulting in an inaccurate level reading.

2.0 litre engines

2 Wipe clean the area around the transmission housing filler/level plug which is

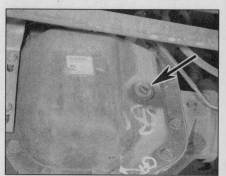

14.2 Front axle filler/level plug (A) and drain plug (B)

14.7 Rear axle filler/level plug

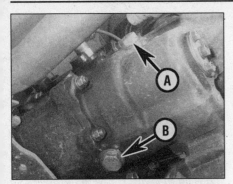

15.2 Transmission unit filler/level plug (A) and drain plug (B) - 2.0 litre engine

located on the left-hand side of the transmission unit, directly below the gearchange lever **(see illustration)**. Unscrew the plug and recover the sealing washers; if either washer shows signs of damage a new one must be used on refitting.

3 The oil level should reach the lower edge of the filler/level plug hole.

4 If topping-up is necessary, add the specified type of oil through the filler/level plug hole until oil begins to trickle out. Allow the excess oil to drain out.

5 Once the transmission oil level is correct, refit the filler/level plug complete with sealing washers and tighten securely. Wipe off any spilt oil.

2.2 and 2.4 litre engines

Note: *The transmission unit has separate oil supplies for the transmission housing and transfer case. Both oil levels must be checked at this interval.*

6 Wipe clean the area around the transmission housing and the transfer case filler/level plugs, both of which are located on the right-hand side of the transmission unit **(see illustration)**. Unscrew the plugs and recover the sealing washers; if either washer shows signs of damage a new one must be used on refitting.

7 The oil level should reach the lower edge of the each filler/level plug hole.

8 If topping-up is necessary, add the specified type of oil through the relevant filler/level plug hole until oil begins to trickle out. Allow the excess oil to drain out.

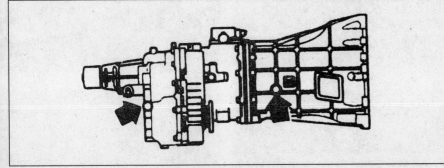

15.6 Transmission unit housing and transfer case filler/level plug locations (arrowed) - 2.2 and 2.4 litre engines

9 Once both the transmission and transfer case oil levels are correct, refit the level plugs complete with sealing washers and tighten them securely. Wipe off any spilt oil.

16 Wheel nut tightness check

1 Remove the wheel trims and check the tightness of all the wheel nuts, using a torque wrench.

2 Refit the wheel trims on completion.

17 Braking system load proportioning valve check

1 At this interval Vauxhall specify that the braking system load proportioning valve should be checked and adjusted. Adjustment of the valve is a complex procedure which involves loading the vehicle accurately so that the rear axle weight is at the specified weight for the check. The task should therefore be entrusted to a Vauxhall dealer. In reality, if the braking system is functioning correctly and there having been no problems noted with the rear wheels locking under heavy braking then this check need not be carried out (if the vehicle is over 3 years old, the braking system operation will be checked as part of the MOT test anyway).

18 Hinge and lock lubrication

1 Work around the vehicle and lubricate the hinges of the bonnet, doors and tailgate with a light machine oil.

2 Lightly lubricate the bonnet release mechanism and exposed section of inner cable with a smear of grease.

3 Check carefully the security and operation of all hinges, latches and locks, adjusting them where required. Check the operation of the central locking system.

19 Headlight beam alignment check

1 Refer to Chapter 13 for details

20 Brake fluid renewal

 Warning: *Brake hydraulic fluid can harm your eyes and damage painted surfaces, so use extreme caution when handling and pouring it. Do not use fluid that has been standing open for some time, as it absorbs moisture from the air. Excess moisture can cause a dangerous loss of braking effectiveness.*
Caution: *The engine should be running at idling speed. Depressing the brake pedal fully without the engine running can cause damage to the vacuum servo unit.*

1 The procedure is similar to that for the bleeding of the hydraulic system as described in Chapter 10.

2 Working as described in Chapter 10, open the first bleed screw in the sequence, and pump the brake pedal gently until nearly all the old fluid has been emptied from the master cylinder reservoir. Top-up to the MAX level with new fluid, and continue pumping until only the new fluid remains in the reservoir, and new fluid can be seen emerging from the bleed screw. Be careful to keep the master cylinder reservoir topped-up to above the MIN level at all times, or air may enter the system and greatly increase the length of the task. Tighten the screw, and top the reservoir level up to the MAX level line.

3 Work through all the remaining bleed screws in the sequence until new fluid can be seen at all of them.

4 When the operation is complete, check that all bleed screws are securely tightened, and that their dust caps are refitted. Wash off all traces of spilt fluid, and recheck the master cylinder reservoir fluid level.

5 Check the operation of the brakes before taking the vehicle on the road.

21 Road test

Instruments and electrical equipment

1 Check the operation of all instruments and electrical equipment.

2 Make sure that all instruments read correctly, and switch on all electrical equipment in turn, to check that it functions properly.

1A

Steering and suspension

3 Check for any abnormalities in the steering, suspension, handling or road feel.

4 Drive the vehicle, and check that there are no unusual vibrations or noises.

5 Check that the steering feels positive, with no excessive sloppiness, or roughness, and check for any suspension noises when cornering and driving over bumps.

Drivetrain

6 Check the performance of the engine, clutch, transmission and driveshafts.

7 Listen for any unusual noises from the engine, clutch and transmission.

8 Make sure that the engine runs smoothly when idling, and that there is no hesitation when accelerating.

9 Check that the clutch action is smooth and progressive, that the drive is taken up

smoothly, and that the pedal travel is not excessive. Also listen for any noises when the clutch pedal is depressed.

10 Check that all gears can be engaged smoothly without noise, and that the gear lever action is not abnormally vague or notchy.

11 Listen for a metallic clicking sound from the front of the vehicle, as the vehicle is driven slowly in a circle with the steering on full-lock. Carry out this check in both directions. If a clicking noise is heard, this indicates wear in a driveshaft joint (see Chapter 8).

Check the operation and performance of the braking system

12 Make sure that the vehicle does not pull to one side when braking, and that the wheels do not lock prematurely when braking hard.

13 Check that there is no vibration through the steering when braking. **Note:** *The ABS system will cause the pedal to pulse when operating - this is not a fault.*

14 Check that the handbrake operates correctly, without excessive movement of the lever, and that it holds the vehicle stationary on a slope.

15 Test the operation of the brake servo unit as follows. Depress the footbrake four or five times to exhaust the vacuum, then start the engine. As the engine starts, there should be a noticeable give in the brake pedal as vacuum builds up. Allow the engine to run for at least two minutes, and then switch it off. If the brake pedal is now depressed again, it should be possible to detect a hiss from the servo as the pedal is depressed. After about four or five applications, no further hissing should be heard, and the pedal should feel considerably harder.

Every 18 000 miles or 2 years, whichever comes first

> **22 Spark plug renewal -** pre 1995 models

Spark plug renewal

1 The correct functioning of the spark plugs is vital for the correct running and efficiency of the engine. It is essential that the plugs fitted are appropriate for the engine; suitable types are specified at the beginning of this Chapter, or in the vehicle's Owner's Handbook. If the correct type is used and the engine is in good condition, the spark plugs should not need attention between scheduled replacement intervals. Spark plug cleaning is rarely necessary, and should not be attempted unless specialised equipment is available, as damage can easily be caused to the firing ends.

2 If the marks on the original-equipment spark plug (HT) leads cannot be seen, mark the leads to correspond to the cylinder the lead serves. Pull the leads from the plugs by gripping the end fitting, not the lead,

otherwise the lead connection may be fractured.

3 It is advisable to remove the dirt from the spark plug recesses using a clean brush, vacuum cleaner or compressed air before removing the plugs, to prevent dirt dropping into the cylinders.

4 Unscrew the plugs from the cylinder head using a spark plug spanner, suitable box spanner or a deep socket and extension bar. Keep the socket aligned with the spark plug - if it is forcibly moved to one side, the ceramic insulator may be broken off.

5 Examination of the spark plugs will give a good indication of the condition of the engine. If the insulator nose of the spark plug is clean and white, with no deposits, this is indicative of a weak mixture or too hot a plug (a hot plug transfers heat away from the electrode slowly, a cold plug transfers heat away quickly).

6 If the tip and insulator nose are covered with hard black-looking deposits, then this is indicative that the mixture is too rich. Should the plug be black and oily, then it is likely that the engine is fairly worn, as well as the mixture being too rich.

7 If the insulator nose is covered with light tan to greyish-brown deposits, then the mixture is correct and it is likely that the engine is in good condition.

8 Most engines are fitted with multi-electrode plugs as standard by Vauxhall **(see illustration)**. On these plugs, the electrode gaps are all preset and no attempt should be made to bend the electrodes.

9 If single electrode plugs are to be installed, the spark plug electrode gap is of considerable importance. If the gap is too large or too small, the size of the spark and its efficiency will be seriously impaired and it will not perform correctly under all engine speed and load conditions. The gap should be set to the value specified by the spark plug manufacturer.

10 To set the gap, measure it with a feeler blade or spark plug gap gauge and then carefully bend the outer plug electrode until the correct gap is achieved. The centre electrode should never be bent, as this may crack the insulator and cause plug failure, if nothing worse. If using feeler blades, the gap is correct when the appropriate-size blade is a firm sliding fit **(see illustrations)**.

22.8 Multi-electrode spark plugs are preset and should not be adjusted

22.10a If single electrode plugs are being fitted, check the electrode gap using a feeler gauge . . .

22.10b . . . or wire gauge . . .

22.11 . . . and if necessary adjust the gap by bending the electrode

11 Special spark plug electrode gap adjusting tools are available from most motor accessory shops, or from some spark plug manufacturers **(see illustration)**.

12 Before fitting the spark plugs, check that the threaded connector sleeves are tight, and that the plug exterior surfaces and threads are clean **(see Haynes Hint)**.

13 Tighten the plug to the specified torque using the spark plug socket and a torque wrench. Refit the remaining spark plugs in the same manner. Check the HT leads as follows before reconnecting them in the correct order.

Ignition system check

Warning: Voltages produced by an electronic ignition system are considerably higher than those produced by conventional ignition systems. Extreme care must be taken when working on the system with the ignition switched on. Persons with surgically-implanted cardiac pacemaker devices should keep well clear of the ignition circuits, components and test equipment.

14 The spark plug (HT) leads should be checked whenever new spark plugs are fitted.

15 Ensure that the leads are numbered before removing them, to avoid confusion when refitting. Pull the leads from the plugs by gripping the end fitting, not the lead, otherwise the lead connection may be fractured.

16 Check inside the end fitting for signs of corrosion, which will look like a white crusty powder. Push the end fitting back onto the spark plug, ensuring that it is a tight fit on the plug. If not, remove the lead again and use pliers to carefully crimp the metal connector inside the end fitting until it fits securely on the end of the spark plug.

17 Using a clean rag, wipe the entire length of the lead to remove any built-up dirt and grease. Once the lead is clean, check for burns, cracks and other damage. Do not bend the lead excessively, nor pull the lead lengthwise - the conductor inside might break.

18 Disconnect the other end of the lead from the distributor and check for corrosion and a tight fit in the same manner as the spark plug end. Refit the lead securely on completion.

HAYNES HiNT

It is very often difficult to insert spark plugs into their holes without cross-threading them. To avoid this possibility, fit a short length of rubber hose over the end of the spark plug. The flexible hose acts as a universal joint to help align the plug with the plug hole. Should the plug begin to cross-thread, the hose will slip on the spark plug, preventing thread damage to the cylinder head

19 Check the remaining leads one at a time, including the lead connecting the distributor to the ignition coil, in the same way.

20 If new spark plug (HT) leads are required, purchase a set for your specific vehicle and engine.

21 On 2.0 litre engines undo the retaining screws and lift off the distributor cap, complete with sealing ring, from the end of the cylinder head to gain access to the rotor arm. On 2.4 litre engines release the retaining clips and lift the cap off from the distributor body.

22 On all engines, wipe the cap clean, and carefully inspect it inside and out for signs of cracks, black carbon tracks (tracking) and worn, burned or loose contacts. Check that the cap centre carbon brush is in good condition and is free to move against spring pressure, allowing it to make good contact with the top of the rotor arm.

23 Inspect the metal terminals on the inside the cap. Surface corrosion and light deposits can be removed with fine-grade emery paper, but more serious wear will mean the renewal of the distributor cap.

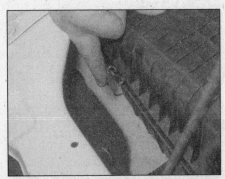

23.2 Release the retaining clips . . .

24 Inspect the rotor arm closely. Light deposits can be removed with fine-grade emery paper, but if the contacts are badly pitted, the rotor arm should be renewed; the arm is retained by screws on 2.0 litre engines and is a push-fit on 2.4 litre engines.

HAYNES HiNT *When fitting a new distributor cap, transfer the HT leads from the old cap to the new one in sequence, one at a time, so that the firing order is preserved.*

25 Even with the ignition system in first-class condition, some engines may still occasionally experience poor starting attributable to damp ignition components. To disperse moisture, a water-dispersant aerosol can be very effective.

26 If all is well, securely refit the distributor cap and reconnect the HT leads to the spark plugs.

23 Air cleaner element renewal

1 The air cleaner is located in the front right-hand corner of the engine compartment.

2 Release the securing clips, and lift the air cleaner cover sufficiently to enable removal of the filter element **(see illustration)**. On 1995 on 2.0 litre engines (X20SE) and 2.2 litre engines, take care not to strain the wiring for the airflow meter as the cover is lifted.

3 Lift out the filter element **(see illustration)**.

4 Wipe out the casing and the cover. Fit the new filter, noting that the rubber locating flange should be uppermost, and secure the cover with the clips.

24 Fuel filter renewal

1 The fuel filter is located under the rear of the vehicle where it is mounted onto the right-hand side of the chassis, in front of the rear axle.

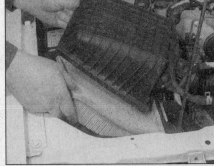

23.3 . . . then lift the lid slightly and remove the air cleaner filter element

1A

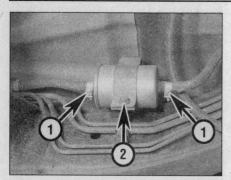

24.4 Fuel filter hose retaining clips (1) and clamp bolt (2)

2 Depressurise the fuel system as described in Chapter 4A.

3 Position a suitable container below the fuel filter, to catch spilt fuel.

4 Slacken the retaining clips securing the fuel hoses to the filter and carefully disconnect both hoses **(see illustration)**. Be prepared for fuel spillage, and take adequate fire precautions.

5 Slacken the clamp bolt and slide the filter out of position, noting which way around it is fitted. Discard the filter safely.

6 Slide the new filter into position making sure that the arrow on the filter body is pointing in the direction of fuel flow (towards the engine). Ensure the filter is correctly positioned then securely tighten the clamp bolt.

7 Reconnect the fuel hoses to the filter and securely tighten their retaining clips.

8 On completion, start the engine and check for leaks. If leakage is evident, stop the engine immediately and rectify the problem without delay.

25 Handbrake check

1 Check and, if necessary, adjust the handbrake as described in Chapter 10. Check that the handbrake cables are free to move easily and lubricate all exposed linkages/cable pivots.

26 Rear brake shoe and drum check

1 Referring to Chapter 10, remove the brake drums and check the brake shoes and drums for signs of wear and the wheel cylinders for signs of leakage.

27 Front hub bearing lubrication

1 Referring to Chapter 11, Section 4, remove the front hub assemblies from the vehicle and clean the bearings and races. Check all components for wear or damage then pack the bearings with fresh grease and refit the hubs to the vehicle.

Every 2 years, regardless of mileage

28 Coolant renewal

Cooling system draining

Warning: Wait until the engine is cold before starting this procedure. Do not allow antifreeze to come in contact with your skin, or with the painted surfaces of the vehicle. Rinse off spills immediately with plenty of water. Never leave antifreeze lying around in an open container, or in a puddle in the driveway or on the garage floor. Children and pets are attracted by its sweet smell, but antifreeze can be fatal if ingested.

1 With the engine completely cold, remove the expansion tank filler cap. Turn the cap anti-clockwise, wait until any pressure remaining in the system is released, then unscrew it and lift it off.

2 Where necessary, unbolt and remove the engine undercover to improve access to the radiator drain plug.

3 Position a suitable container beneath the radiator then unscrew the drain plug and allow the coolant to drain into the container. Where no drain plug is fitted, slacken the retaining clip and disconnect the bottom hose from the radiator.

4 When the flow of coolant stops, securely tighten the drain plug or reconnect the hose and securely tighten its retaining clip (as applicable).

5 If the coolant has been drained for a reason other than renewal, then provided it is clean and less than two years old, it can be re-used, though this is not recommended.

Cooling system flushing

6 If coolant renewal has been neglected, or if the antifreeze mixture has become diluted, then in time, the cooling system may gradually lose efficiency, as the coolant passages become restricted due to rust, scale deposits, and other sediment. The cooling system efficiency can be restored by flushing the system clean.

7 The radiator should be flushed independently of the engine, to avoid unnecessary contamination.

Radiator flushing

8 Disconnect the top and bottom hoses and any other relevant hoses from the radiator, with reference to Chapter 3.

9 Insert a garden hose into the radiator top inlet. Direct a flow of clean water through the radiator, and continue flushing until clean water emerges from the radiator bottom outlet.

10 If after a reasonable period, the water still does not run clear, the radiator can be flushed with a good proprietary cleaning agent. It is important that the manufacturer's instructions are followed carefully. If the contamination is particularly bad, insert the hose in the radiator bottom outlet, and reverse-flush the radiator.

Engine flushing

11 Remove the thermostat as described in Chapter 3 then, if the radiator top hose has been disconnected from the engine, temporarily reconnect the hose.

12 With the top and bottom hoses disconnected from the radiator, insert a garden hose into the top hose. Direct a clean flow of water through the engine, and continue flushing until clean water emerges from the radiator bottom hose.

13 On completion of flushing, refit the thermostat and reconnect the hoses with reference to Chapter 3.

Cooling system filling

14 Before attempting to fill the cooling system, make sure that all hoses and clips are in good condition, and that the clips are tight. Note that an antifreeze mixture must be used all year round, to prevent corrosion of the engine components.

15 Remove the expansion tank filler cap and slowly fill the system until the coolant level reaches the KALT/COLD mark on the side of the expansion tank.

16 Once the coolant level is correct, refit the expansion tank cap and tighten securely.

17 Start the engine, and allow it to run until it reaches normal operating temperature (until the cooling fan cuts in and out).

18 Stop the engine, and allow it to cool, then re-check the coolant level with reference to *Weekly checks*. Top-up the level if necessary and refit the expansion tank filler cap.

Antifreeze mixture

19 The antifreeze should always be renewed at the specified intervals. This is necessary not only to maintain the antifreeze properties, but also to prevent corrosion which would otherwise occur as the corrosion inhibitors become progressively less effective.

20 Always use an ethylene-glycol based antifreeze which is suitable for use in mixed-metal cooling systems. The quantity of

antifreeze and levels of protection are given in the Specifications.

21 Before adding antifreeze, the cooling system should be completely drained, preferably flushed, and all hoses checked for condition and security.

22 After filling with antifreeze, a label should be attached to the expansion tank, stating the type and concentration of antifreeze used, and the date installed. Any subsequent topping-up should be made with the same type and concentration of antifreeze.

23 Do not use engine antifreeze in the windscreen/tailgate washer system, as it will cause damage to the vehicle paintwork. A screenwash additive should be added to the washer system in the quantities stated on the bottle.

Every 27 000 miles or 3 years, whichever comes first

29 Transmission unit oil renewal

1 This operation is much more efficient if the vehicle is first taken on a journey of sufficient length to warm the engine/transmission up to normal operating temperature. *Caution: If the procedure is to be carried out on a hot transmission unit, take care not to burn yourself on the hot exhaust or the transmission/engine unit.*

2 Park the vehicle on level ground. To further improve access, either position the vehicle over an inspection pit, or jack up the front and rear of the vehicle and support it on axle stands ensuring the vehicle remains level. Where necessary, undo the retaining screws and remove the undercover from beneath the transmission unit.

2.0 litre engine

Note: *The transmission unit has separate oil baths for the transmission housing and transfer case components. Both must be renewed at this interval.*

3 Wipe clean the area around the transmission housing filler/level plug on the left-hand side of the transmission unit (see Section 15). Unscrew the plug and recover the sealing washer; if the washer shows signs of damage a new one must be used on refitting.

4 Wipe clean the area around the drain plug on the base of the transmission unit **(see illustration 15.2).**

5 Position a suitable container underneath the transmission unit then unscrew the drain plug and allow the transmission oil to drain in

to the container. Recover the sealing washer and discard it; a new one should be used on refitting.

6 Allow the oil to drain completely into the container. If the oil is hot, take precautions against scalding.

7 When the oil has finished draining, clean the drain plug threads and those of the transmission casing. Fit a new sealing washer then refit the drain plug, tightening it securely.

8 Refilling the transmission is an extremely awkward operation. Above all, allow plenty of time for the oil level to settle properly before checking it. Note that the vehicle **must** be parked on flat level ground when checking the oil level.

9 Refill the transmission with the exact amount of the specified type of oil then check the oil level as described in Section 15. When the level is correct, refit the filler/level plug and sealing washer and tighten securely. Refit the undercover (where removed). **Note:** *If the correct amount was poured in and a large amount flows out on checking the level, refit the filler/level plug and take the vehicle on a short journey so that the new oil is distributed fully around the transmission components, then check the level again on your return.*

2.2 and 2.4 litre engine

Note: *The transmission unit has separate oil baths for the transmission housing and transfer case components. Both must be renewed at this interval.*

10 Wipe clean the area around the transmission housing and the transfer case filler/level plugs, both of which are located on the right-hand side of the transmission

unit (see Section 15). Unscrew the plugs and recover the sealing washers; if either washer shows signs of damage a new one must be used on refitting.

11 Wipe clean the area around the transmission and transfer case drain plugs, both of which are located on the left-hand side of the transmission unit **(see illustration).**

12 Position a suitable container underneath the transmission unit then unscrew both drain plugs and allow the transmission oil to drain in to the container. Recover the sealing washer from each drain plug and discard them; new ones should be used on refitting.

13 Allow the oil to drain completely into the container. If the oil is hot, take precautions against scalding.

14 When the oil has finished draining, clean the drain plug threads and those of the transmission/transfer housing casing. Fit a new sealing washer to each drain plug, and refit both plugs, tightening them securely.

15 Refilling the transmission/transfer case is an extremely awkward operation. Above all, allow plenty of time for the oil level to settle properly before checking it. Note that the vehicle **must** be parked on flat level ground when checking the oil level.

16 Refill the transmission and transfer case with the exact amount of the specified type of oil then check the oil level as described in Section 15. When the level is correct, refit the filler/level plugs complete with sealing washers and tighten securely. Refit the undercover (where removed). **Note:** *If the correct amount was poured into either the transmission or transfer case and a large amount flows out on checking the level, refit the filler/level plug and take the vehicle on a short journey so that the new oil is distributed fully around the transmission components, then check the level again on your return.*

1A

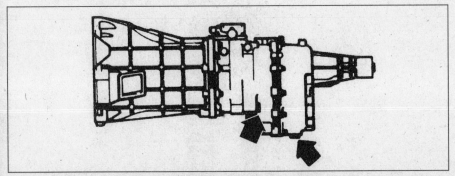

29.11 Transmission unit housing and transfer case drain plug locations (arrowed) - 2.2 and 2.4 litre engines

30 Axle oil renewal

Front axle

1 This operation is much more efficient if the vehicle is first taken on a journey of sufficient length to warm the engine/transmission up to normal operating temperature.

Caution: If the procedure is to be carried out on a hot axle, take care not to burn yourself on the hot exhaust or the axle.

2 Park the vehicle on level ground. To further improve access, either position the vehicle over an inspection pit, or jack up the front and rear of the vehicle and support it on axle stands ensuring the vehicle remains level. If necessary, slacken and remove the retaining screws and remove the undercover from beneath the engine unit.

3 Wipe clean the area around the axle filler/level plug (see Section 14) then unscrew the plug from the differential housing.

4 Wipe clean the area around the axle drain plug and position a suitable container underneath the differential housing. Unscrew the drain plug and allow the oil to drain in to the container.

5 Allow the oil to drain completely into the container. If the oil is hot, take precautions against scalding.

6 When the oil has finished draining, clean the drain plug threads and those of the housing then refit the drain plug and tighten securely.

7 Refilling the axle is an extremely awkward operation. Above all, allow plenty of time for the oil level to settle properly before checking it. Note that the vehicle **must** be parked on flat level ground when checking the oil level.

8 Refill the axle with the exact amount of the specified type of oil then check the oil level as described in Section 14. When the level is correct, refit the filler/level plug and tighten securely. Refit the undercover (where removed). **Note:** *If the correct amount was poured in and a large amount flows out on checking the level, refit the filler/level plug and take the vehicle on a short journey so that the new oil is distributed fully around the axle, then check the level again on your return.*

Rear axle

9 Renew the oil as described in paragraphs 1 to 8.

Every 36 000 miles or 4 years, whichever comes first

31 Spark plug renewal - 1995 onwards models

Spark plug renewal

1 Refer to Section 22. On 2.2 litre models note that it will be necessary to undo the retaining screws and remove the spark plug cover from the centre of the camshaft cover to gain access to the spark plugs; a HT lead removal tool should be clipped to one of the caps to ease the task of disconnecting the plug caps from the plugs.

Ignition system check

⚠️ **Warning: Voltages produced by an electronic ignition system are considerably higher than those produced by conventional ignition systems. Extreme care must be taken when working on the system with the ignition switched on. Persons with surgically-implanted cardiac pacemaker devices should keep well clear of the**

ignition circuits, components and test equipment.

2 The spark plug (HT) leads should be checked whenever new spark plugs are fitted.

3 Ensure that the leads are numbered before removing them, to avoid confusion when refitting. Pull the leads from the plugs by gripping the end fitting, not the lead, otherwise the lead connection may be fractured (see paragraph 1).

4 Check inside the end fitting for signs of corrosion, which will look like a white crusty powder. Push the end fitting back onto the spark plug, ensuring that it is a tight fit on the plug. If not, remove the lead again and use pliers to carefully crimp the metal connector inside the end fitting until it fits securely on the end of the spark plug.

5 Using a clean rag, wipe the entire length of the lead to remove any built-up dirt and grease. Once the lead is clean, check for burns, cracks and other damage. Do not bend the lead excessively, nor pull the lead lengthwise - the conductor inside might break.

6 Disconnect the other end of the lead from the DIS module and check for corrosion and a

tight fit in the same manner as the spark plug end. Refit the lead securely on completion.

7 Check the remaining leads one at a time in the same way.

8 If new spark plug (HT) leads are required, purchase a set for your specific vehicle and engine.

HAYNES HiNT

When fitting a new set of HT leads, renew the leads one at a time to ensure the firing order is preserved.

9 Even with the ignition system in first-class condition, some engines may still occasionally experience poor starting attributable to damp ignition components. To disperse moisture, a water-dispersant aerosol can be very effective.

32 Timing belt renewal - 2.0 and 2.2 litre engine

1 Refer to Chapter 2A (2.0 litre engine) or Chapter 2B (2.2 litre engine).

Chapter 1 Part B
Routine maintenance and servicing - diesel engine models

Contents

Air cleaner element renewal 23
Auxiliary drivebelt check and renewal 5
Axle oil level check 15
Axle oil renewal 31
Brake fluid renewal 21
Braking system load proportioning valve check 18
Coolant renewal 29
Corrosion check 10
Driveshaft gaiter check 11
Engine oil and filter renewal 3
Front brake pad and disc check 7
Front hub bearing check and adjustment 14
Front hub bearing lubrication 28
Fuel filter renewal 24
Fuel filter water draining 4
General information 1
Handbrake check 25
Headlight beam alignment check 20
Hinge and lock lubrication 19
Hose and fluid leak check 9
Idle speed and exhaust emission check 6
Propeller shaft check and lubrication 13
Rear brake pad and disc check 8
Rear brake shoe and drum check 27
Regular maintenance 2
Road test 22
Suspension and steering check 12
Timing belt renewal - 2.8 litre engine 32
Transmission unit oil level check 16
Transmission unit oil renewal 30
Valve clearance check and adjustment - 2.3 and 2.8 litre engines . . 26
Wheel nut tightness check 17

Degrees of difficulty

Easy, suitable for novice with little experience	**Fairly easy,** suitable for beginner with some experience	**Fairly difficult,** suitable for competent DIY mechanic 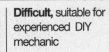	**Difficult,** suitable for experienced DIY mechanic	**Very difficult,** suitable for expert DIY or professional

Servicing specifications

Capacities

Engine oil

At oil and filter change:
2.3 litre engine	5.70 litres
2.5 litre engine	6.25 litres
2.8 litre engine	5.50 litres
Difference between MIN and MAX on dipstick	Approximately 1.0 litre

Cooling system
2.3 litre engine	10.9 litres
2.5 and 2.8 litre engine	8.8 litres

Transmission
Transmission housing	2.95 litres
Transfer case	1.45 litres

Axles
Front axle	1.7 litres
Rear axle:	
Standard	2.3 litres
Models with limited-slip differential	1.9 litres

Fuel tank
All models	80 litres

Lubricants and fluids

Refer to *Weekly checks*

Cooling system

Antifreeze mixture:
33% antifreeze	Protection down to -20ºC (-4ºF)
50% antifreeze	Protection down to -37ºC (-35ºF)

Note: *Refer to antifreeze manufacturer for latest recommendations.*

Fuel system

Idle speed:
  2.3 litre engine:
Models with air conditioning	770 to 800 rpm (air conditioning turned on)
Models without air conditioning	720 to 740 rpm
2.5 litre engine	Controlled by EDC system
2.8 litre engine	700 to 800 rpm

Brakes

Friction material minimum thickness:
Front and rear brake pads	1.0 mm
Rear brake shoes	1.0 mm

Torque wrench settings

	Nm	lbf ft
2.3 litre engine		
Air conditioning compressor fixings:		
Adjuster nut:		
Clamp bolt	45	33
Locknut	40	30
Mounting bolts	50	37
Alternator fixings:		
Adjuster nut locknut	25	18
Lower mounting bolt	25	18
Power steering pump fixings:		
Adjuster nut:		
Clamp bolt:		
Models with air conditioning	40	30
Models without air conditioning	25	18
Locknut	40	30
Mounting bolts	25	18
Wheel nuts:		
Alloy wheels	120	89
Steel wheels	110	81
2.5 litre engine		
Auxiliary drivebelt tensioner pulley bolt - early models	47	35
Wheel nuts:		
Alloy wheels	120	89
Steel wheels	110	81
2.8 litre engine		
Alternator fixings:		
Lower mounting bolt	40	30
Upper mounting bolt	19	14
Power steering pump mounting bolts	37	27
Wheel nuts:		
Alloy wheels	120	89
Steel wheels	110	81

1 The maintenance intervals in this manual are provided with the assumption that you, not the dealer, will be carrying out the work. These are the minimum maintenance intervals recommended by us for vehicles driven daily. If you wish to keep your vehicle in peak condition at all times, you may wish to perform some of these procedures more often. **Note:** *For models after 1995, the manufacturers extended the service mileages from 4500 to 5000, 9000 to 10 000, etc. The time intervals remained the same. We encourage frequent maintenance, because it enhances the efficiency, performance and resale value of your vehicle.*

2 If the vehicle is driven in dusty areas, used to tow a trailer, or driven frequently at slow speeds (idling in traffic) or on short journeys, more frequent maintenance intervals are recommended.

3 When the vehicle is new, it should be serviced by a factory-authorised dealer service department, in order to preserve the factory warranty.

Every 4500 miles or 6 months, whichever comes first

- ☐ Renew the engine oil and filter (Section 3)*
- ☐ Drain water from fuel filter (Section 4)

* Note: *Vauxhall recommend that the engine oil and filter are changed at the annual specified mileage or every 12 months, whichever comes first. However, oil and filter changes are good for the engine and it is recommend that the oil and filter are renewed more frequently, especially if the vehicle is used on a lot of short journeys.*

Every 9000 miles or 12 months, whichever comes first

Note: *On vehicles covering more than 18 000 miles annually, carry out the items marked with an asterisk every 18 000 miles, regardless of time, then carry out the items not marked with an asterisk at the 12 month interval.*

- ☐ Check the condition and tension of the auxiliary drivebelt(s) (Section 5)*
- ☐ Check the engine idle speed and exhaust emission level (Section 6)*
- ☐ Check the front brake pads and discs for wear (Section 7)*
- ☐ Check the rear brake pads and discs for wear (Section 8)*
- ☐ Check all components, pipes and hoses for fluid leaks (Section 9)
- ☐ Check the body and underbody for corrosion protection (Section 10)
- ☐ Check the condition of the driveshaft gaiters (Section 11)*
- ☐ Check the steering and suspension components for condition and security (Section 12)*
- ☐ Check the condition of the propeller shaft and lubricate the shaft bearings (Section 13)*. **Note:** *If the vehicle is used off-road frequently, the propeller shaft check should be performed every 4500 mile,s or every 3000 miles if the vehicle is regularly driven through deep water.*
- ☐ Check and adjust the front hub bearings (Section 14)*
- ☐ Check the front and rear axle oil level (Section 15)*
- ☐ Check the transmission unit oil level (Section 16)*
- ☐ Check the roadwheel nuts are tightened to the specified torque (Section 17)*
- ☐ Check the operation of the braking system load proportioning valve (Section 18)*

Every 9000 miles or 12 months, whichever comes first (continued)

- ☐ Lubricate all door locks and hinges, door stops, bonnet lock and release, and tailgate lock and hinges (Section 19)
- ☐ Check and if necessary adjust the headlight beam alignment (Section 20)
- ☐ Renew the brake fluid (Section 21)
- ☐ Carry out a road test (Section 22)*

Every 18 000 miles or 2 years, whichever comes first

- ☐ Renew the air cleaner element (Section 23)
- ☐ Renew the fuel filter (Section 24)
- ☐ Check and, if necessary, adjust the handbrake (Section 25)
- ☐ Check and, if necessary, adjust the valve clearances - 2.3 and 2.8 litre engines (Section 26)
- ☐ Check the rear brake shoes and drums for wear (Section 27)
- ☐ Lubricate the front hub bearings (Section 28)

Every 2 years, regardless of mileage

- ☐ Renew the coolant (Section 29)

Every 27 000 miles or 3 years, whichever comes first

- ☐ Renew the transmission unit oil (Section 30)
- ☐ Renew the front and rear axle oil (Section 31)

Every 40 000 miles or 4 years, whichever comes first

- ☐ Renew the timing belt - 2.8 litre engine (Section 32)

Note: *Although the normal interval for timing belt renewal is 60 000 miles or 6 years, it is strongly recommended that the interval is reduced to 40 000 miles or 4 years on vehicles which are subjected to intensive use, ie, mainly short journeys or a lot of stop-start driving. The actual belt renewal interval is therefore up to the individual owner but, bearing in mind that severe engine damage will result should the belt break in use, we recommend you err on the side of caution.*

1B

Underbonnet view of a 2.3 litre diesel engine model

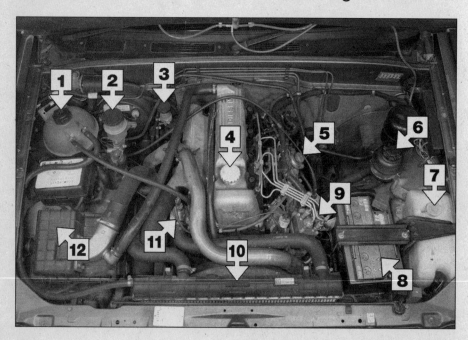

1 Coolant expansion tank
2 Brake fluid reservoir
3 Clutch fluid reservoir
4 Engine oil filler cap
5 Fuel filter
6 Power steering fluid reservoir
7 Washer fluid reservoir
8 Battery
9 Fuel injection pump
10 Radiator
11 Thermostat housing
12 Air cleaner housing

Underbonnet view of a 2.5 litre diesel engine model

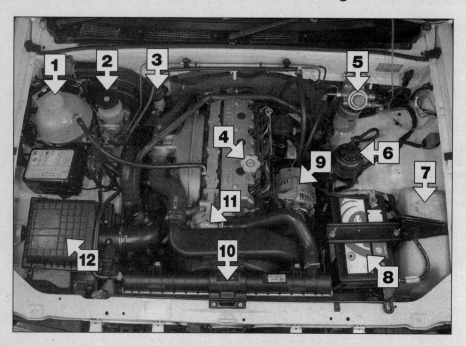

1 Coolant expansion tank
2 Brake fluid reservoir
3 Clutch fluid reservoir
4 Engine oil filler cap
5 Fuel filter
6 Power steering fluid reservoir
7 Washer fluid reservoir
8 Battery
9 Alternator
10 Radiator
11 Thermostat housing
12 Air cleaner housing

Underbonnet view of a 2.8 litre diesel engine model

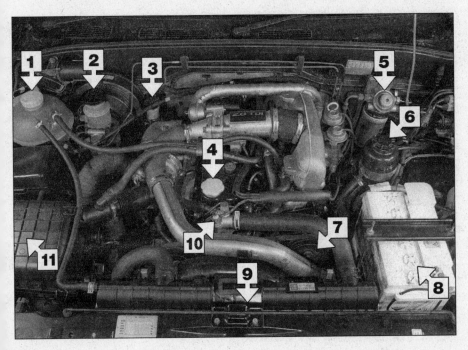

1 Coolant expansion tank
2 Brake fluid reservoir
3 Clutch fluid reservoir
4 Engine oil filler cap
5 Fuel filter
6 Power steering fluid reservoir
7 Power steering pump
8 Battery
9 Radiator
10 Thermostat housing
11 Air cleaner housing

Front underbody view - undercover removed
(2.5 litre engine shown, others similar)

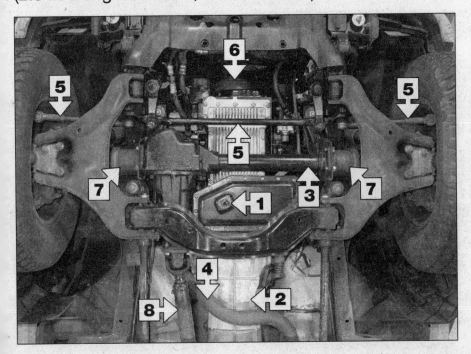

1 Engine sump drain plug
2 Transmission unit
3 Front axle
4 Exhaust pipe
5 Steering linkage
6 Crankshaft pulley
7 Driveshaft inner joint
8 Propeller shaft

Rear underbody view
(coil spring suspension shown)

1 Exhaust system
2 Propeller shaft
3 Fuel tank
4 Rear axle differential housing
5 Shock absorber
6 Anti-roll bar
7 Lateral rod
8 Trailing link
9 Handbrake cable

Maintenance procedures

1 General information

1 This Chapter is designed to help the home mechanic maintain his/her vehicle for safety, economy, long life and peak performance.
2 The Chapter contains a master maintenance schedule, followed by Sections dealing specifically with each task in the schedule. Visual checks, adjustments, component renewal and other helpful items are included. Refer to the accompanying illustrations of the engine compartment and the underside of the vehicle for the locations of the various components.
3 Servicing your vehicle in accordance with the mileage/time maintenance schedule and the following Sections will provide a planned maintenance programme, which should result in a long and reliable service life. This is a comprehensive plan, so maintaining some items but not others at the specified service intervals will not produce the same results.
4 As you service your vehicle, you will discover that many of the procedures can - and should - be grouped together, because of the particular procedure being performed, or because of the proximity of two otherwise-unrelated components to one another. For example, if the vehicle is raised for any reason, the exhaust can be inspected at the same time as the suspension and steering components.
5 The first step in this maintenance programme is to prepare yourself before the actual work begins. Read through all the Sections relevant to the work to be carried out, then make a list and gather all the parts and tools required. If a problem is encountered, seek advice from a parts specialist, or a dealer service department.

2 Regular maintenance

1 If, from the time the vehicle is new, the routine maintenance schedule is followed closely, and frequent checks are made of fluid levels and high-wear items, as suggested throughout this manual, the engine will be kept in relatively good running condition, and the need for additional work will be minimised.
2 It is possible that there will be times when the engine is running poorly due to the lack of regular maintenance. This is even more likely if a used vehicle, which has not received regular and frequent maintenance checks, is purchased. In such cases, additional work may need to be carried out, outside of the regular maintenance intervals.
3 If engine wear is suspected, a compression test or leakdown test (refer to relevant Part of Chapter 2) will provide valuable information regarding the overall performance of the main internal components. Such a test can be used as a basis to decide on the extent of the work to be carried out. If, for example, a compression or leakdown test indicates serious internal engine wear, conventional maintenance as described in this Chapter will not greatly improve the performance of the engine, and may prove a waste of time and money, unless extensive overhaul work is carried out first.
4 The following series of operations are those most often required to improve the performance of a generally poor-running engine:

Primary operations

a) Clean, inspect and test the battery (refer to Weekly checks).
b) Check all the engine-related fluids (refer to Weekly checks).
c) Check the condition and tension of the auxiliary drivebelt (Section 5).
d) Check the condition of the air cleaner element, and renew if necessary (Section 23).
e) Renew the fuel filter (Section 24).
f) Check the condition of all hoses, and check for fluid leaks (Section 9).
5 If the above operations do not prove fully effective, carry out the following secondary operations:

Secondary operations

All items listed under Primary operations, plus the following:
a) Check the charging system (refer to Chapter 5A).
b) Check the pre-heating system (refer to Chapter 5C).
c) Check the fuel system (refer to Chapter 4B).

Every 4500 miles or 6 months, whichever comes first

3 Engine oil and filter renewal

1 Frequent oil and filter changes are the most important preventative maintenance procedures which can be undertaken by the DIY owner. As engine oil ages, it becomes diluted and contaminated, which leads to premature engine wear.

2 Before starting this procedure, gather together all the necessary tools and materials. Also make sure that you have plenty of clean rags and newspapers handy, to mop up any spills. Ideally, the engine oil should be warm, as it will drain more easily, and more built-up sludge will be removed with it. Take care not to touch the exhaust or any other hot parts of the engine when working under the vehicle. To avoid any possibility of scalding, and to protect yourself from possible skin irritants and other harmful contaminants in used engine oils, it is advisable to wear gloves when carrying out this work.

3 If necessary, to improve access to the oil filter and sump drain plug, undo the retaining bolts and remove the under cover from beneath the engine.

4 Remove the oil filler cap from the cylinder head cover.

5 Using a spanner, or preferably a suitable socket and bar, slacken the drain plug about half a turn **(see illustration)**. Position the draining container under the drain plug, then remove the plug completely **(see Haynes Hint)**.

6 Allow some time for the oil to drain, noting that it may be necessary to reposition the container as the oil flow slows to a trickle.

7 After all the oil has drained, wipe the drain plug and the sealing washer with a clean rag. Examine the condition of the sealing washer,

and renew it if it shows signs of scoring or other damage which may prevent an oil-tight seal. Clean the area around the drain plug opening, and refit the plug complete with the washer and tighten it securely.

8 Move the container into position under the oil filter which is located at the front end of the engine, either on the left- or right-hand side **(see illustration)**.

9 On 2.5 litre engines where the oil filter is housed inside an alloy housing, unscrew the cover from the end of the housing and recover the sealing ring. Remove the filter element from the housing and allow the oil to drain into the container.

10 On all other engines, use an oil filter removal tool to slacken the filter initially, then unscrew it by hand the rest of the way. Empty the oil from the old filter into the container.

11 Use a clean rag to remove all oil, dirt and sludge from the filter sealing/housing area on the engine.

12 On 2.5 litre engines with a filter housing, insert the new filter element into the housing. Fit a new sealing ring to the cover then refit the cover to the housing and tighten it securely.

13 On all other engines, apply a light coating of clean engine oil to the sealing ring on the new filter, then screw the filter into position on the engine. Tighten the filter firmly by hand only - **do not** use any tools. On 2.5 and 2.8 litre engines, if a genuine filter is being fitted and the special oil filter tool (a socket which fits over the end of the filter) is available, screw on the filter until its sealing ring contacts the housing then tighten it through a further one and a quarter turns.

14 Remove the old oil and all tools from under the vehicle then, where necessary, refit the undercover and securely tighten its retaining bolts.

15 Fill the engine through the filler hole, using the correct grade and type of oil (refer to

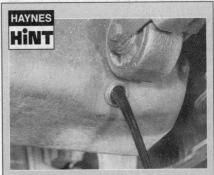

As the drain plug threads release, move it sharply away so the stream of oil issuing from the sump runs into the container, not up your sleeve

Weekly Checks for details of topping-up). Pour in half the specified quantity of oil first, then wait a few minutes for the oil to drain into the sump. Continue to add oil, a small quantity at a time, until the level is up to the lower mark on the dipstick. Adding approximately a further 1.0 litre will bring the level up to the upper mark on the dipstick.

16 Start the engine and run it for a few minutes, while checking for leaks around the oil filter seal and the sump drain plug. Note that there may be a delay of a few seconds before the low oil pressure warning light goes out when the engine is first started, as the oil circulates through the new oil filter and the engine oil galleries before the pressure builds up.

17 Stop the engine, and wait a few minutes for the oil to settle in the sump once more. With the new oil circulated and the filter now completely full, recheck the level on the dipstick, and add more oil as necessary.

18 Dispose of the used engine oil safely with reference to *General repair procedures*.

1B

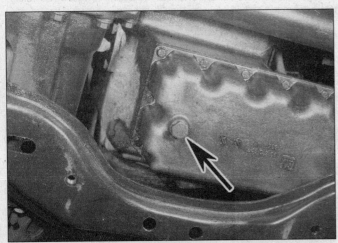

3.5 Sump drain plug - 2.3 litre engine

3.8 Oil filter location - 2.3 litre engine

4 Fuel filter water draining

Caution: Before starting any work on the fuel filter, wipe clean the filter assembly and the area around it; it is essential that no dirt or other foreign matter is allowed into the system. Obtain a suitable container into which the filter can be drained and place rags or similar material under the filter assembly to catch any spillages. Do not allow diesel fuel to contaminate components such as the alternator and starter motor, the coolant hoses and engine mountings, and any wiring.

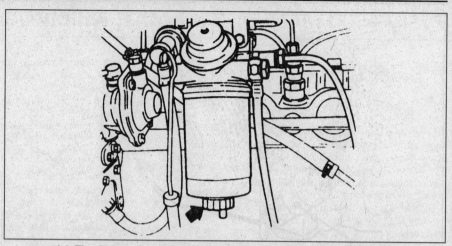

4.1 The drain screw (arrowed) is located on the base of the fuel filter

1 In addition to taking the precautions noted above to catch any fuel spillages, connect a tube to the drain screw on the base of the fuel filter; the filter is located on the left-hand side of the engine unit on 2.3 litre engines and in the left-hand rear corner of the engine compartment on 2.5 and 2.8 litre engines **(see illustration)**. Place the other end of the tube in a clean jar or can.

2 Unscrew the drain screw and allow the filter to drain until clean fuel, free of dirt or water, emerges from the tube (approximately 100 cc is usually sufficient). Note that it maybe necessary to pump the priming pump to drain the fuel from the filter.

3 Securely close the drain screw and remove the tube, containers and rag, mopping up any spilt fuel.

4 On completion, dispose safely of the drained fuel. Check carefully all disturbed components to ensure that there are no leaks (of air or fuel) when the engine is restarted. If necessary, bleed the fuel system as described in Chapter 4B.

Every 9000 miles or 12 months, whichever comes first

5 Auxiliary drivebelt check and renewal

Checking

Note: *On 2.3 litre engines, the alternator, power steering pump and (where fitted) air conditioning compressor are all driven by separate belts. On 2.5 litre engines, a single belt is used to drive all auxiliary components. On 2.8 litre engines, one belt drives the alternator and another the power steering pump and (where fitted) air conditioning compressor.*

1 Due to their function and material makeup, drivebelts are prone to failure after a long period of time and should therefore be inspected regularly.

2 With the engine stopped, inspect the full length of the drivebelt(s) for cracks and separation of the belt plies. It will be necessary to turn the engine (using a spanner or socket and bar on the crankshaft pulley bolt - remove the undercover to gain access) in order to move the belt from the pulleys so that the belt can be inspected thoroughly. Twist the belt between the pulleys so that both sides can be viewed. Also check for fraying, and glazing which gives the belt a shiny appearance. Check the pulleys for nicks, cracks, distortion and corrosion.

3 If the belt shows signs of wear or damage, it must be renewed.

4 On 2.3 and 2.8 litre engines, check the tension of each drivebelt and, if necessary, adjust as described under the relevant sub-heading.

Renewal

5 Undo the retaining bolts and remove the undercover from beneath the engine. Proceed as described under the relevant sub-heading.

Alternator drivebelt - 2.3 litre engine

6 Remove the cooling fan as described in Chapter 3.

7 Remove the power steering pump drivebelt or the air conditioning compressor drivebelt as described in this Section.

8 Slacken the alternator lower mounting bolt and the adjuster bolt locknut then back off the adjuster nut to release the drivebelt tension. Slip the belt off the pulleys and remove it from the engine.

9 Manoeuvre the new belt into position and seat it on the pulleys. Tension the belt using the adjuster nut so that under firm thumb pressure there is about 10 mm of movement at the mid-point on the longest run of the belt. Once the adjuster nut is correctly positioned, tighten the alternator lower mounting bolt to the specified torque then tighten the adjuster bolt locknut to the specified torque.

10 Refit the air conditioning compressor drivebelt or power steering pump drivebelt as described in this Section.

11 Refit the cooling fan as described in Chapter 3.

Power steering pump drivebelt - 2.3 litre engine

12 Where necessary, remove the air conditioning compressor drivebelt as described in this Section.

13 Slacken the power steering pump mounting bolts and loosen the nut and bolt securing the adjuster nut clamp to the pump bracket **(see illustration)**.

14 Slacken the adjuster nut locknut then back off the adjuster nut to release the drivebelt tension. Slip the belt off the pulleys and remove it from the engine.

15 Manoeuvre the new belt into position and seat it on the pulleys.

16 Refit the air conditioning compressor drivebelt (where fitted) and tension it as described in this Section.

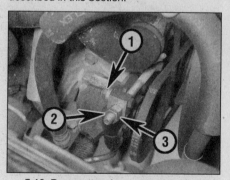

5.13 Power steering pump drivebelt adjuster nut clamp bolt (1), adjuster nut locknut (2) and adjuster nut (3)

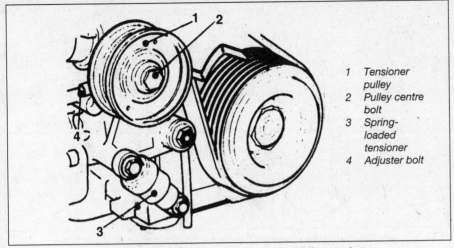

1 Tensioner pulley
2 Pulley centre bolt
3 Spring-loaded tensioner
4 Adjuster bolt

5.20 Auxiliary drivebelt adjuster - early 2.5 litre engine

17 Tension the power steering pump belt using the adjuster nut so that under firm thumb pressure there is about 10 mm of movement at the mid-point on the longest run of the belt. Once the adjuster nut is correctly positioned, tighten the adjuster nut clamp bolt, the power steering pump mounting bolts and the adjuster nut locknut to their specified torque settings. Refit the undercover and securely tighten its retaining bolts.

Air conditioning compressor - 2.3 litre engine

18 Slacken the compressor mounting bolts and loosen the bolt securing the adjuster nut clamp to the compressor. Slacken the adjuster bolt locknut then back off the adjuster nut to release the drivebelt tension. Slip the belt off the pulleys and remove it from the engine.

19 Manoeuvre the new belt into position and seat it on the pulleys. Tension the belt using the adjuster nut so that under firm thumb pressure there is about 10 mm of movement at the mid-point on the longest run of the belt. Once the adjuster nut is correctly positioned, tighten the adjuster nut clamp bolt, the compressor mounting bolts and the adjuster nut locknut to their specified torque settings. Check and, if necessary, adjust the power steering pump drivebelt tension. Refit the undercover and securely tighten its retaining bolts.

Drivebelt - 2.5 litre engine

20 There are two possible types of drivebelt tensioner on this engine. On some early models, an adjustable tensioner assembly incorporating an spring-loaded tensioner is fitted whereas on later models, a fully-automatic spring loaded tensioner is used **(see illustration)**. On early models, some means of compressing the tensioner will be required in order to allow the drivebelt to be removed (Vauxhall use service tool KM-8078).

21 Remove the cooling fan as described in Chapter 3 and make a note of the correct routing of the drivebelt. If the belt is to be re-used, mark the direction of rotation on the belt prior to removal.

22 On early models compress the spring-loaded tensioner to relieve the drivebelt tension. In the absence of the special service tool (KM-8078), the tensioner can be compressed with a large pair of water pump pliers. Slip the drivebelt off the from the pulleys and remove it from the engine. Slowly release the water pump pliers to relieve the tensioner.

23 On later models, using a 1/2 inch drive ratchet or bar fitted to the square-section hole in the top of the tensioner pulley assembly, lever the tensioner away from the belt until there is sufficient slack to enable the belt to be slipped off the pulleys. Carefully release the tensioner pulley until it is against its stop then remove the belt from the vehicle. If necessary, the tensioner can be locked in the released position by aligning the holes in the tensioner arm and backplate and inserting a bolt or punch **(see illustrations)**.

24 Manoeuvre the belt into position, routing it correctly around the pulleys; if the original belt is being fitted, use the marks made prior to removal to ensure it is fitted the correct way around.

25 Move the tensioner pulley away from the belt and seat the belt on the pulleys. Ensure the belt is centrally located on all pulleys then slowly release the tensioner pulley until it is in contact with the belt again.

26 On early models check the belt is correctly tensioned by measuring the distance between the centres of the tensioner retaining bolts. This should be between 81 and 83 mm. If adjustment is necessary, slacken the tensioner pulley centre bolt (note that this bolt has a left-hand thread - rotate clockwise to loosen, anti-clockwise to tighten) and the pulley adjuster bolt locknut. Rotate the adjuster bolt until the distance is as specified then tighten the pulley centre bolt to the specified torque and securely tighten the adjuster bolt locknut.

1B

5.23a On later 2.5 litre engines, move the tensioner pulley away from the drivebelt . . .

5.23b . . . and hold it in position by inserting a bolt or pin through the holes in the tensioner arm and backplate (shown with engine removed for clarity)

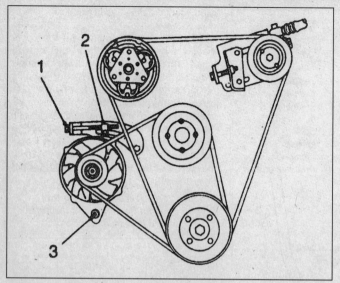

5.30 On 2.8 litre engines, slacken the alternator upper and lower mounting bolts (2 and 3) and adjust the belt tension with the adjuster bolt (1)

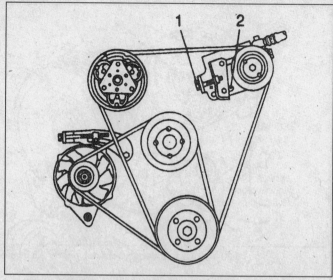

5.33 On 2.8 litre engines, slacken the power steering pump mounting bolts (2) and adjust the belt tension with the adjuster bolt (1)

27 On later models the belt tension is automatically set by the tensioner spring and requires no checking or adjustment.

28 On all models, refit the cooling fan as described in Chapter 3 then refit the undercover, tightening its retaining bolts securely.

Alternator drivebelt - 2.8 litre engine

29 Remove the power steering pump/air conditioning compressor drivebelt as described in this Section.

30 Slacken the alternator upper and lower mounting bolts then back off the adjuster bolt until the drivebelt can be slipped off the pulleys and removed from the engine **(see illustration)**.

31 Manoeuvre the new belt into position, seating it on the pulleys, and tension it using the adjuster bolt. Adjust the belt tension, so that there is 10 mm of movement in the belt when a force of 98 N (equivalent to 10 kg) is applied to the mid-point on the upper run of the belt the belt. When the belt tension is correctly set, tighten the alternator mounting bolts to the specified torque.

32 Refit the power steering pump/air conditioning compressor drivebelt as described in this Section.

Power steering pump/air conditioning compressor drivebelt - 2.8 litre engine

33 Slacken the power steering pump mounting bolts then back off the adjuster bolt until the drivebelt can be slipped off the pulleys and removed from the engine **(see illustration)**.

34 Manoeuvre the new belt into position, seating it on the pulleys, and tension it using the adjuster bolt.

35 On models with just power steering, adjust the belt tension so there is 14 to 17 mm of movement in the belt when a force of 98 N (equivalent to 10 kg) is applied to the mid-point on the upper run of the belt the belt.

36 On models with power steering and air conditioning, adjust the belt tension so that there is 12 to 15 mm of movement in the belt when a force of 98 N (equivalent to 10 kg) is applied to the mid-point on the upper run of the belt the belt.

37 When the belt tension is correctly set, tighten the power steering pump mounting bolts to the specified torque then refit the undercover.

---

6 Idle speed and exhaust emission check

Idle speed check

2.3 litre engine

1 The usual type of tachometer (rev counter), which works from ignition system pulses, cannot be used on diesel engines. If it is not felt that adjusting the idle speed by ear is satisfactory, it will be necessary to purchase or hire an appropriate tachometer, or else leave the task to a Vauxhall dealer or other suitably-equipped specialist.

2 Make sure that the accelerator cable is correctly adjusted (see Chapter 4B).

3 Warm the engine up to normal operating temperature and check that it idles at the specified speed.

4 If adjustment is necessary, slacken the locknut and rotate the idle speed adjustment screw which is located on the top of the injection pump **(see illustration)**. Once the engine is idling at the specified speed, securely tighten the locknut.

5 Switch off the engine and (where applicable) disconnect the tachometer on completion.

2.5 litre engine

6 On these engines, the engine idle speed is automatically controlled by the EDC (Electronic Diesel Control) system and therefore requires no adjustment (see Chapter 4B for further information). If a problem has been noted, the vehicle should be taken to a Vauxhall dealer for testing using special diagnostic equipment.

2.8 litre engine

7 Warm the engine up to normal operating temperature and connect the tachometer to the engine (see paragraph 1).

8 Unclip the accelerator outer cable from its mounting bracket to ensure the injection pump accelerator lever remains in contact with the idle speed adjusting screw.

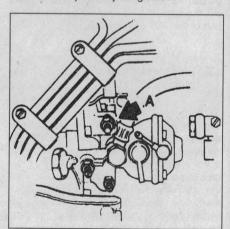

6.4 Idle speed adjustment screw (A) - 2.3 litre engine

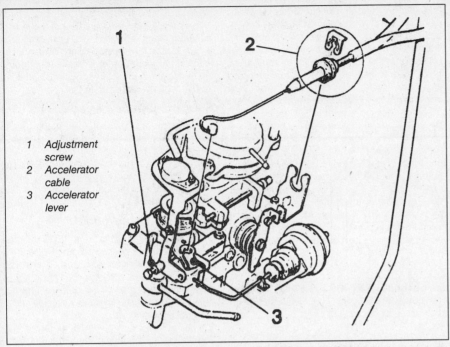

1 Adjustment
screw
2 Accelerator
cable
3 Accelerator
lever

6.9 Idle speed adjustment details - 2.8 litre engine

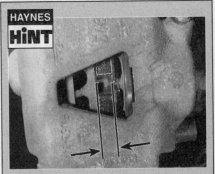

For a quick check, the thickness of friction material remaining on the brake pad can be measured through the aperture in the caliper body

sides. Chapter 10 contains a detailed description of how the brake disc should be checked for wear and/or damage.

4 If any pad's friction material is worn to the specified thickness or less, *all four pads must be renewed as a set*. Refer to Chapter 10 for details.

5 On completion, refit the roadwheels and lower the vehicle to the ground.

9 Hose and fluid leak check

1 Visually inspect the engine joint faces, gaskets and seals for any signs of water or oil leaks. Pay particular attention to the areas around the cylinder head cover, cylinder head, oil filter and sump joint faces. Bear in mind that, over a period of time, some very slight seepage from these areas is to be expected - what you are really looking for is any indication of a serious leak. Should a leak be found, renew the offending gasket or oil seal by referring to the appropriate Chapters in this manual.

2 Also check the security and condition of all the engine-related pipes and hoses, and all braking system pipes and hoses and fuel lines. Ensure that all cable ties or securing clips are in place, and in good condition. Clips which are broken or missing can lead to chafing of the hoses, pipes or wiring, which could cause more serious problems in the future.

3 Carefully check the radiator hoses and heater hoses along their entire length. Renew any hose which is cracked, swollen or deteriorated. Cracks will show up better if the hose is squeezed. Pay close attention to the hose clips that secure the hoses to the cooling system components. Hose clips can pinch and puncture hoses, resulting in cooling system leaks. If the crimped-type hose clips are used, it may be a good idea to replace them with standard worm-drive clips.

9 Start the engine and check that the idle speed is within the specified range. If adjustment is necessary, slacken the locknut and rotate the adjustment screw as necessary **(see illustration)**. Once the idle speed is correctly set, hold the screw stationary and securely tighten the locknut.

10 Disconnect the tachometer from the engine then reconnect and adjust the accelerator cable as described in Chapter 4B.

Exhaust emission check

11 Specialised equipment is needed to check the exhaust gas emission levels so this check must be entrusted to a Vauxhall dealer or a suitably-equipped garage. In reality, if the vehicle is running correctly and no problems have been noticed then this check need not be carried out (if the vehicle is over 3 years old, the exhaust emissions will be checked as part of the MOT test anyway).

7 Front brake pad and disc check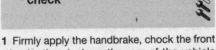

1 Firmly apply the handbrake, then jack up the front of the vehicle and support it securely on axle stands. Remove the front roadwheels.

2 For a quick check, the pad thickness can be carried out via the inspection hole on the front of the caliper **(see Haynes Hint)**. Using a steel rule, measure the thickness of the friction material on each pad. This must not be less than that indicated in the Specifications.

3 The view through the caliper inspection hole gives a rough indication of the state of the brake pads. For a comprehensive check, the brake pads should be removed and cleaned. The operation of the caliper can then also be checked, and the condition of the brake disc itself can be fully examined on both sides. Chapter 10 contains a detailed description of how the brake disc should be checked for wear and/or damage.

4 If any pad's friction material is worn to the specified thickness or less, *all four pads must be renewed as a set*. Refer to Chapter 10 for details.

5 On completion, refit the roadwheels and lower the vehicle to the ground.

8 Rear brake pad and disc check

1 Firmly apply the handbrake, chock the front wheels, then jack up the rear of the vehicle and support it securely on axle stands. Remove the rear roadwheels.

2 For a quick check, the pad thickness can be carried out via the inspection hole on the rear of the caliper. Using a steel rule, measure the thickness of the friction material of each pad. This must not be less than that indicated in the Specifications.

3 The view through the caliper inspection hole gives a rough indication of the state of the brake pads. For a comprehensive check, the brake pads should be removed and cleaned. The operation of the caliper can then also be checked, and the condition of the brake disc itself can be fully examined on both

A leak in the cooling system will usually show up as white- or rust-coloured deposits on the area adjoining the leak

4 Inspect all the cooling system components (hoses, joint faces, etc) for leaks **(see Haynes Hint)**.

5 Where any problems are found on system components, renew the component or gasket with reference to Chapter 3.

6 With the vehicle raised, inspect the fuel tank and filler neck for punctures, cracks and other damage. The connection between the filler neck and tank is especially critical. Sometimes a rubber filler neck or connecting hose will leak due to loose retaining clamps or deteriorated rubber.

7 Carefully check all rubber hoses and metal fuel lines leading away from the fuel tank. Check for loose connections, deteriorated hoses, crimped lines, and other damage. Pay particular attention to the vent pipes and hoses, which often loop up around the filler neck and can become blocked or crimped. Follow the lines to the front of the vehicle, carefully inspecting them all the way. Renew damaged sections as necessary. Similarly, whilst the vehicle is raised, take the opportunity to inspect all underbody brake fluid pipes and hoses.

8 From within the engine compartment, check the security of all fuel, vacuum and brake hose attachments and pipe unions, and inspect all hoses for kinks, chafing and deterioration.

10 Corrosion check

1 This work should be carried out by a Vauxhall/Opel dealer in order to validate the vehicle warranty. The work includes a thorough inspection of the vehicle paintwork and underbody for damage and corrosion.

11 Driveshaft gaiter check

1 With the vehicle raised and securely supported on stands, turn the steering onto full lock then slowly rotate the roadwheel.

Inspect the condition of the outer constant velocity (CV) joint rubber gaiters while squeezing the gaiters to open out the folds. Check for signs of cracking, splits or deterioration of the rubber which may allow the grease to escape and lead to water and grit entry into the joint. Also check the security and condition of the retaining clips. Repeat these checks on the inner CV joints. If any damage or deterioration is found, the gaiters should be renewed as described in Chapter 8.

2 At the same time check the general condition of the CV joints themselves by first holding the driveshaft and attempting to rotate the wheel. Repeat this check by holding the inner joint and attempting to rotate the driveshaft. Any appreciable movement indicates wear in the joints, wear in the driveshaft splines or loose driveshaft retaining nut.

12 Suspension and steering check

Front suspension and steering check

1 Raise the front of the vehicle, and securely support it on axle stands.

2 Visually inspect the balljoint dust covers for splits, chafing or deterioration. Any wear of these components will cause loss of lubricant, together with dirt and water entry, resulting in rapid deterioration of the balljoints.

3 Check the power steering fluid hoses for chafing or deterioration, and the pipe and hose unions for fluid leaks.

4 Grasp the roadwheel at the 12 o'clock and 6 o'clock positions, and try to rock it. Very slight free play may be felt, but if the movement is appreciable, further investigation is necessary to determine the source. Continue rocking the wheel while an assistant depresses the footbrake. If the movement is now eliminated or significantly reduced, it is likely that the hub bearings are at fault. If the free play is still evident with the footbrake depressed, then there is wear in the suspension joints or mountings.

5 Now grasp the wheel at the 9 o'clock and 3 o'clock positions, and try to rock it as before. Any movement felt now may again be caused by wear in the hub bearings or the steering tie rod balljoints.

6 Using a large screwdriver or flat bar, check for wear in the suspension mounting bushes by levering between the relevant suspension component and its attachment point. Some movement is to be expected, as the mountings are made of rubber, but excessive wear should be obvious. Also check the condition of any visible rubber bushes, looking for splits, cracks or contamination of the rubber.

7 With the vehicle standing on its wheels, have an assistant turn the steering wheel

back-and-forth, about an eighth of a turn each way. There should be very little lost movement between the steering wheel and roadwheels. If this is not the case, closely observe the joints and mountings previously described. If these appear satisfactory, check the steering adjustment, as described in Chapter 11.

Rear suspension check

8 Chock the front wheels, then jack up the rear of the vehicle and support securely on axle stands.

9 Working as described previously for the front suspension, check the rear hub bearings, the suspension bushes, springs and mountings for wear.

Shock absorber check

10 Check for any signs of fluid leakage around the shock absorber body, or from the area around the piston rod. Should any fluid be noticed, the shock absorber is defective internally, and should be renewed. **Note:** *Shock absorbers should always be renewed in pairs on the same axle.*

11 The efficiency of the shock absorber may be checked by bouncing the vehicle at each corner. Generally speaking, the body will return to its normal position and stop after being depressed. If it rises and returns on a rebound, the shock absorber is probably suspect. Also examine the shock absorber upper and lower mountings for any signs of wear.

13 Propeller shaft check and lubrication

Note: *If the vehicle is used off-road frequently, the propeller shaft check should be performed every 6000 miles, or every 3000 miles if the vehicle is regularly driven through deep water.*

1 Check the propeller shaft joints for signs of wear or damage **(see illustration)**, paying particular attention to the rubber coupling (where fitted). Check that all the propeller shaft bolts are tightened to the specified torque (see Chapter 8). If any damage is found, renew the affected item as described in Chapter 8.

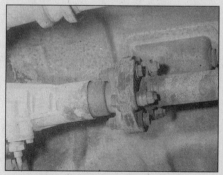

13.1 Check the propeller shaft joints and couplings for signs of wear or damage . . .

13.2 . . . and lubricate with the specified grease

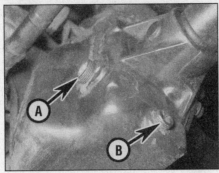

15.2 Front axle filler/level plug (A) and drain plug (B)

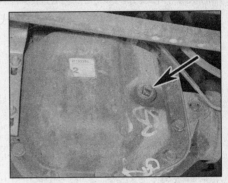

15.7 Rear axle filler/level plug

2 Using a grease gun, work along the propeller shaft and lubricate each of the universal and sliding joint nipples with a good quality lithium-based grease (Vauxhall recommend the use of GM4750-M) **(see illustration)**. Wipe off excess grease.

14 Front hub bearing check and adjustment

Refer to the procedures contained in Chapter 11, Section 4.

15 Axle oil level check

Front axle

1 Park the vehicle on level ground. To further improve access, either position the vehicle over an inspection pit, or jack up the front and rear of the vehicle and support it on axle stands. The vehicle **must** be level for the check to be accurate.
2 Clean the area around the filler/level plug which is located on the front of the differential housing, then slacken and remove the plug from the housing **(see illustration)**.
3 The oil level should be up to the lower edge of the filler/level plug aperture.
4 If necessary, top-up using the specified type of lubricant until the oil level is correct.

Fill the axle until oil starts to flow out and allow excess oil to drain out.
5 Once the axle oil level is correct, refit the filler/level plug and tighten it securely. Lower the vehicle to the ground.
6 Note that frequent need for topping-up indicates a leakage, possibly through an oil seal. The cause should be investigated and rectified.

Rear axle

7 Check the oil level as described in paragraphs 1 to 6 noting that the filler/level plug is on the differential housing rear cover **(see illustration)**.

16 Transmission unit oil level check

Note: *The transmission unit has separate oil supplies for the transmission housing and transfer case. Both oil levels must be checked.*
1 Park the vehicle on level ground. To further improve access, either position the vehicle over an inspection pit, or jack up the front and rear of the vehicle and support it on axle stands. The vehicle **must** be level for the check to be accurate. The oil level must be checked before the vehicle is driven, or at least 5 minutes after the engine has been switched off. If the oil is checked immediately after driving the car, some of the oil will remain distributed around the transmission

components, resulting in an inaccurate level reading.
2 Wipe clean the area around the transmission housing level plug and the transfer case level plug, both of which are located on the right-hand side of the transmission unit **(see illustration)**. Unscrew the plugs and recover the sealing washers; if either washer shows signs of damage a new one must be used on refitting.
3 The oil level should reach the lower edge of the each level plug hole.
4 If topping-up is necessary, add the specified type of oil through the relevant filler/level plug hole until oil begins to trickle out. Allow the excess oil to drain out.
5 Once both the transmission and transfer case oil levels are correct, refit the level plugs complete with sealing washers and tighten them securely. Wipe off any spilt oil.

17 Wheel nut tightness check

1 Remove the wheel trims and check the tightness of all the wheel nuts, using a torque wrench
2 Refit the wheel trims on completion.

18 Braking system load proportioning valve check

1 At this interval Vauxhall specify that the braking system load proportioning valve should be checked and adjusted. Adjustment of the valve is a complex procedure which involves loading the vehicle accurately so that the rear axle weight is at the specified weight for the check. The task should therefore be entrusted to a Vauxhall dealer. In reality, if the braking system is functioning correctly and there having been no problems noted with the rear wheels locking under heavy braking then this check need not be carried out (if the vehicle is over 3 years old, the braking system operation will be checked as part of the MOT test anyway).

1B

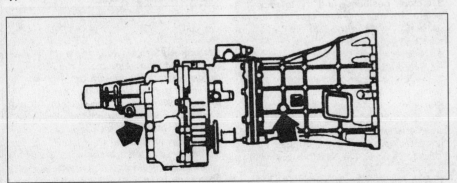

16.2 Transmission unit housing and transfer case filler/level plug locations (arrowed)

19 Hinge and lock lubrication
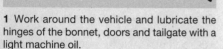

1 Work around the vehicle and lubricate the hinges of the bonnet, doors and tailgate with a light machine oil.
2 Lightly lubricate the bonnet release mechanism and exposed section of inner cable with a smear of grease.
3 Check carefully the security and operation of all hinges, latches and locks, adjusting them where required. Check the operation of the central locking system.

20 Headlight beam alignment check

1 Refer to Chapter 13 for details

21 Brake fluid renewal
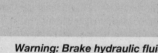

 Warning: Brake hydraulic fluid can harm your eyes and damage painted surfaces, so use extreme caution when handling and pouring it. Do not use fluid that has been standing open for some time, as it absorbs moisture from the air. Excess moisture can cause a dangerous loss of braking effectiveness.
Caution: The engine should be running at idling speed. Depressing the brake pedal fully without the engine running can cause damage to the vacuum servo unit.
1 The procedure is similar to that for the bleeding of the hydraulic system as described in Chapter 10.
2 Working as described in Chapter 10, open the first bleed screw in the sequence, and pump the brake pedal gently until nearly all the old fluid has been emptied from the master cylinder reservoir. Top-up to the MAX level with new fluid, and continue pumping until new fluid can be seen emerging from the bleed screw. Be careful to keep the master cylinder reservoir topped-up to above the MIN level at all times, or air may enter the system and greatly increase the length of the task.Tighten the screw, and top the reservoir level up to the MAX level line.
3 Work through all the remaining bleed screws in the sequence until new fluid can be seen at all of them.
4 When the operation is complete, check that all bleed screws are securely tightened, and that their dust caps are refitted. Wash off all traces of spilt fluid, and recheck the master cylinder reservoir fluid level.
5 Check the operation of the brakes before taking the vehicle on the road.

22 Road test

Instruments and electrical equipment

1 Check the operation of all instruments and electrical equipment.
2 Make sure that all instruments read correctly, and switch on all electrical equipment in turn, to check that it functions properly.

Steering and suspension

3 Check for any abnormalities in the steering, suspension, handling or road feel.
4 Drive the vehicle, and check that there are no unusual vibrations or noises.
5 Check that the steering feels positive, with no excessive sloppiness, or roughness, and check for any suspension noises when cornering and driving over bumps.

Drivetrain

6 Check the performance of the engine, clutch, transmission and driveshafts.

7 Listen for any unusual noises from the engine, clutch and transmission.
8 Make sure that the engine runs smoothly when idling, and that there is no hesitation when accelerating.
9 Check that the clutch action is smooth and progressive, that the drive is taken up smoothly, and that the pedal travel is not excessive. Also listen for any noises when the clutch pedal is depressed.
10 Check that all gears can be engaged smoothly without noise, and that the gear lever action is not abnormally vague or notchy.
11 Listen for a metallic clicking sound from the front of the vehicle, as the vehicle is driven slowly in a circle with the steering on full-lock. Carry out this check in both directions. If a clicking noise is heard, this indicates wear in a driveshaft joint (see Chapter 8).

Check the operation and performance of the braking system

12 Make sure that the vehicle does not pull to one side when braking, and that the wheels do not lock prematurely when braking hard.
13 Check that there is no vibration through the steering when braking. **Note:** *The ABS system will cause the pedal to pulse when operating - this is not a fault.*
14 Check the handbrake operates correctly, without excessive movement of the lever, and that it holds the vehicle stationary on a slope.
15 Test the operation of the brake servo unit as follows. Depress the footbrake four or five times to exhaust the vacuum, then start the engine. As the engine starts, there should be a noticeable give in the brake pedal as vacuum builds up. Allow the engine to run for at least two minutes, and then switch it off. If the brake pedal is now depressed again, it should be possible to detect a hiss from the servo as the pedal is depressed. After about four or five applications, no further hissing should be heard, and the pedal should feel considerably harder.

Every 18 000 miles or 2 years, whichever comes first

23 Air cleaner element renewal

1 The air cleaner is located in the front right-hand corner of the engine compartment.
2 Release the securing clips, and lift the air cleaner cover sufficiently to enable removal of the filter element. On 2.5 litre engines take care not to strain the wiring for the air mass meter as the cover is lifted.
3 Lift out the filter element **(see illustration)**.
4 Wipe out the casing and the cover. Fit the new filter, noting that the rubber locating flange should be uppermost, and secure the cover with the clips.

23.3 Removing the air cleaner filter element

24 Fuel filter renewal
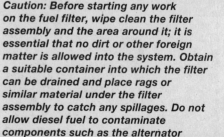

Caution: Before starting any work on the fuel filter, wipe clean the filter assembly and the area around it; it is essential that no dirt or other foreign matter is allowed into the system. Obtain a suitable container into which the filter can be drained and place rags or similar material under the filter assembly to catch any spillages. Do not allow diesel fuel to contaminate components such as the alternator and starter motor, the coolant hoses

and engine mountings, and any wiring.

1 Drain the fuel filter as described in Section 4.

2 Place absorbent rags around the base of the fuel filter then unscrew the filter and remove it from its housing. If the filter is tight it can be unscrewed using an oil filter removal tool.

3 Mop up any spilt fuel and recover the sealing rings from the old filter/filter housing (as applicable).

4 Ensure the filter housing surface is clean then fit the new sealing rings to top of the new filter element.

5 Smear a little fuel on the new sealing rings and screw the new filter onto the housing, tightening securely by hand only.

6 Bleed the fuel system as described in Chapter 4B then start the engine and check for leaks.

25 Handbrake check

1 Check and, if necessary, adjust the handbrake as described in Chapter 10. Check that the handbrake cables are free to move easily and lubricate all exposed linkages/cable pivots.

26 Valve clearance check and adjustment - 2.3 and 2.8 litre engines

1 Check and, if necessary, adjust the valve clearances as described in Chapter 2D (2.3 litre engine) or 2F (2.8 litre engine) (as applicable).

27 Rear brake shoe and drum check

1 Referring to Chapter 10, remove the brake drums and check the brake shoes and drums for signs of wear and the wheel cylinders for signs of leakage.

28 Front hub bearing lubrication

1 Referring to Chapter 11, Section 4, remove the front hub assemblies from the vehicle and clean the bearings and races. Check all components for wear or damage then pack the bearings with fresh grease and refit the hubs to the vehicle.

Every 2 years, regardless of mileage

29 Coolant renewal

Cooling system draining

 Warning: Wait until the engine is cold before starting this procedure. Do not allow antifreeze to come in contact with your skin, or with the painted surfaces of the vehicle. Rinse off spills immediately with plenty of water. Never leave antifreeze lying around in an open container, or in a puddle in the driveway or on the garage floor. Children and pets are attracted by its sweet smell, but antifreeze can be fatal if ingested.

1 With the engine completely cold, remove the expansion tank filler cap. Turn the cap anti-clockwise, wait until any pressure remaining in the system is released, then unscrew it and lift it off.

2 Where necessary, unbolt and remove the engine undercover to improve access to the radiator drain plug.

3 Position a suitable container beneath the radiator then unscrew the drain plug and allow the coolant to drain into the container. Where no drain plug is fitted, slacken the retaining clip and disconnect the bottom hose from the radiator.

4 When the flow of coolant stops, securely tighten the drain plug or reconnect the hose and securely tighten its retaining clip (as applicable).

5 If the coolant has been drained for a reason other than renewal, then provided it is clean and less than two years old, it can be re-used, though this is not recommended.

Cooling system flushing

6 If coolant renewal has been neglected, or if the antifreeze mixture has become diluted, then in time, the cooling system may gradually lose efficiency, as the coolant passages become restricted due to rust, scale deposits, and other sediment. The cooling system efficiency can be restored by flushing the system clean.

7 The radiator should be flushed independently of the engine, to avoid unnecessary contamination.

Radiator flushing

8 Disconnect the top and bottom hoses and any other relevant hoses from the radiator, with reference to Chapter 3.

9 Insert a garden hose into the radiator top inlet. Direct a flow of clean water through the radiator, and continue flushing until clean water emerges from the radiator bottom outlet.

10 If after a reasonable period, the water still does not run clear, the radiator can be flushed with a good proprietary cleaning agent. It is important that the manufacturer's instructions are followed carefully. If the contamination is particularly bad, insert the hose in the radiator bottom outlet, and reverse-flush the radiator.

Engine flushing

11 Remove the thermostat as described in Chapter 3 then, if the radiator top hose has been disconnected from the engine, temporarily reconnect the hose.

12 With the top and bottom hoses disconnected from the radiator, insert a garden hose into the top hose. Direct a clean flow of water through the engine, and continue flushing until clean water emerges from the radiator bottom hose.

13 On completion of flushing, refit the thermostat and reconnect the hoses with reference to Chapter 3.

Cooling system filling

14 Before attempting to fill the cooling system, make sure that all hoses and clips are in good condition, and that the clips are tight. Note that an antifreeze mixture must be used all year round, to prevent corrosion of the engine components.

15 Remove the expansion tank filler cap.

16 On 2.3 litre engines slacken and remove the bleed screw from the top of the thermostat housing cover.

17 On all engines, slowly fill the system until the coolant level reaches the MAX or KALT/COLD mark on the side of the expansion tank (as applicable).

18 On 2.3 litre engines keep an eye on the bleed screw hole whilst the system is being filled; when coolant which is free from air bubbles starts to flow from the hole, refit the bleed screw and tighten it securely.

19 Once the coolant level is correct, refit the expansion tank cap and tighten securely.

20 Start the engine, and allow it to run until it reaches normal operating temperature (until the cooling fan cuts in and out).

21 Stop the engine, and allow it to cool, then re-check the coolant level with reference to *Weekly checks*. Top-up the level if necessary and refit the expansion tank filler cap.

Antifreeze mixture

22 The antifreeze should always be renewed at the specified intervals. This is necessary not only to maintain the antifreeze properties, but also to prevent corrosion which would otherwise occur as the corrosion inhibitors become progressively less effective.

23 Always use an ethylene-glycol based antifreeze which is suitable for use in mixed-metal cooling systems. The quantity of antifreeze and levels of protection are given in the Specifications.

24 Before adding antifreeze, the cooling system should be completely drained, preferably flushed, and all hoses checked for condition and security.

1B

25 After filling with antifreeze, a label should be attached to the expansion tank, stating the type and concentration of antifreeze used, and the date installed. Any subsequent topping-up should be made with the same type and concentration of antifreeze.
26 Do not use engine antifreeze in the windscreen/tailgate washer system, as it will cause damage to the vehicle paintwork. A screenwash additive should be added to the washer system in the quantities stated on the bottle.

Every 27 000 miles or 3 years, whichever comes first

30 Transmission unit oil renewal

Note: *The transmission unit has separate oil baths for the transmission housing and transfer case components. Both must be renewed.*

1 This operation is much more efficient if the vehicle is first taken on a journey of sufficient length to warm the engine/transmission up to normal operating temperature.
Caution: If the procedure is to be carried out on a hot transmission unit, take care not to burn yourself on the hot exhaust or the transmission/engine unit.
2 Park the vehicle on level ground. To further improve access, either position the vehicle over an inspection pit, or jack up the front and rear of the vehicle and support it on axle stands ensuring the vehicle remains level. Where necessary, undo the retaining screws and remove the undercover from beneath the transmission unit.
3 Wipe clean the area around the transmission housing and the transfer case filler/level plugs, both of which are located on the right-hand side of the transmission unit (see Section 16). Unscrew the plugs and recover the sealing washers; if either washer shows signs of damage a new one must be used on refitting.
4 Wipe clean the area around the transmission and transfer case drain plugs, both of which are located on the left-hand side of the transmission unit **(see illustration)**.
5 Position a suitable container underneath the transmission unit then unscrew both drain plugs and allow the transmission oil to drain in to the container. Recover the sealing washer from each drain plug and discard them; new ones should be used on refitting.

6 Allow the oil to drain completely into the container. If the oil is hot, take precautions against scalding.
7 When the oil has finished draining, clean the drain plug threads and those of the transmission/transfer housing casing. Fit a new sealing washer to each drain plug, and refit both plugs, tightening them securely.
8 Refilling the transmission/transfer case is an extremely awkward operation. Above all, allow plenty of time for the oil level to settle properly before checking it. Note that the vehicle **must** be parked on flat level ground when checking the oil level.
9 Refill the transmission and transfer case with the exact amount of the specified type of oil then check the oil level as described in Section 16. When the level is correct, refit the filler/level plugs complete with sealing washers and tighten securely. Refit the undercover (where removed). **Note:** *If the correct amount was poured into either the transmission or transfer case and a large amount flows out on checking the level, refit the filler/level plug and take the vehicle on a short journey so that the new oil is distributed fully around the transmission components, then check the level again on your return.*

31 Axle oil renewal

Front axle

1 This operation is much more efficient if the vehicle is first taken on a journey of sufficient length to warm the engine/transmission up to normal operating temperature.
Caution: If the procedure is to be carried out on a hot axle, take care not to burn yourself on the hot exhaust or the axle.

2 Park the vehicle on level ground. To further improve access, either position the vehicle over an inspection pit, or jack up the front and rear of the vehicle and support it on axle stands ensuring the vehicle remains level. If necessary, slacken and remove the retaining screws and remove the undercover from beneath the engine unit.
3 Wipe clean the area around the axle filler/level plug (see Section 15) then unscrew the plug from the differential housing.
4 Wipe clean the area around the axle drain plug and position a suitable container underneath the differential housing. Unscrew the drain plug and allow the oil to drain into the container.
5 Allow the oil to drain completely into the container. If the oil is hot, take precautions against scalding.
6 When the oil has finished draining, clean the drain plug threads and those of the housing then refit the drain plug and tighten securely.
7 Refilling the axle is an extremely awkward operation. Above all, allow plenty of time for the oil level to settle properly before checking it. Note that the vehicle **must** be parked on flat level ground when checking the oil level.
8 Refill the axle with the exact amount of the specified type of oil then check the oil level as described in Section 15. When the level is correct, refit the filler/level plug and tighten securely. Refit the undercover (where removed). **Note:** *If the correct amount was poured in and a large amount flows out on checking the level, refit the filler/level plug and take the vehicle on a short journey so that the new oil is distributed fully around the axle, then check the level again on your return.*

Rear axle

9 Renew the oil as described in paragraphs 1 to 8.

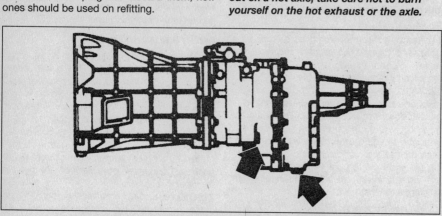

30.4 Transmission unit housing and transfer case drain plug locations (arrowed)

Every 40 000 miles or 4 years, whichever comes first

32 Timing belt renewal - 2.8 litre engine

Refer to Chapter 2F.

Chapter 2 Part A
2.0 litre petrol engine in-car repair procedures

Contents

Camshaft cover - removal and refitting 4
Camshaft followers and hydraulic tappets - removal,
  inspection and refitting 11
Camshaft housing and camshaft - removal, inspection and refitting 10
Camshaft oil seals - renewal 9
Compression test - description and interpretation 2
Crankshaft oil seals - renewal 17
Crankshaft pulley - removal and refitting 5
Cylinder head - removal and refitting 12
Engine oil and filter - renewal . . . . See Chapter 1A
Engine oil level check . . . . See Weekly checks

Engine/transmission mountings - inspection and renewal 18
Flywheel - removal, inspection and refitting 16
General engine checks . . . . See Chapter 1A
General information 1
Oil cooler (1995 onwards models) - removal and refitting 15
Oil pump - removal, overhaul and refitting 14
Sump - removal and refitting 13
Timing belt - removal and refitting 7
Timing belt covers - removal and refitting 6
Timing belt tensioner and sprockets - removal and refitting 8
Top dead centre (TDC) for No 1 piston - locating 3

Degrees of difficulty

Easy, suitable for novice with little experience	Fairly easy, suitable for beginner with some experience	Fairly difficult, suitable for competent DIY mechanic	Difficult, suitable for experienced DIY mechanic	Very difficult, suitable for expert DIY or professional

Specifications

General

Engine type . . . . Four-cylinder, in-line, water-cooled. Single overhead camshaft, belt-driven, acting on hydraulic tappets

Manufacturer's engine code*:
  Pre 1995 models C20NE
  1995 onwards models X20SE
Bore . . . . 86 mm
Stroke . . . . 86 mm
Capacity . . . . 1998 cc
Firing order . . . . 1-3-4-2 (No 1 cylinder at timing belt end)
Direction of crankshaft rotation . . . . Clockwise (viewed from timing belt end of engine)
Compression ratio:
  C20NE engine 9.2:1
  X20SE engine 10:1
* The engine code forms the first five digits of the engine number (see Vehicle identification section of this manual)

Timing belt

Belt tension settings using special (KM-510-A) tool - pre 1993 models (see text):
  New belt:
    Cold engine 0.5
    Hot engine 7.5
  Used belt:
    Cold engine 2.5
    Hot engine 7.0

Camshaft

Endfloat . . . . 0.09 to 0.21 mm
Maximum permissible radial run-out . . . . 0.03 mm
Cam lift . . . . 6.67 mm

Lubrication system

Oil pump type . . . . Gear type, driven directly from crankshaft
Minimum permissible oil pressure at idle speed, with engine
  at operating temperature (oil temperature of at least 70°C) . . . . 1.5 bar (22 psi)
Oil pump clearances:
  Gear teeth clearance . . . . 0.03 to 0.10 mm
  Gear endfloat . . . . 0.10 to 0.20 mm

2A

Torque wrench settings

	Nm	lbf ft
Camshaft cover bolts	8	6
Camshaft housing end cover bolts - X20SE engine	8	6
Camshaft sprocket bolt	45	34
Camshaft thrustplate bolts	8	6
Connecting rod big-end bearing cap bolt*:		
C20NE engine:		
Stage 1	35	26
Stage 2	Angle-tighten a further 45°	
X20SE engine:		
Stage 1	35	26
Stage 2	Angle-tighten a further 45°	
Stage 3	Angle-tighten a further 15°	
Coolant pump bolts	25	18
Crankshaft pulley bolts	20	15
Crankshaft sprocket bolt*:		
Stage 1	130	96
Stage 2	Angle-tighten a further 40 to 50°	
Cylinder head bolts*:		
Stage 1	25	18
Stage 2	Angle-tighten a further 90°	
Stage 3	Angle-tighten a further 90°	
Stage 4	Angle-tighten a further 90°	
Engine/transmission mounting bolts:		
Left- and right-hand mounting:		
Mounting-to-engine bracket nut	85	63
Mounting-to-body bolts	50	37
Rear mounting:		
Mounting-to-transmission bolts	80	59
Mounting-to-crossmember bolts	50	37
Engine-to-transmission unit bolts:		
C20NE engine	70	52
X20SE engine:		
M10 bolts	41	30
M12 bolts	68	50
Flywheel bolts*:		
Stage 1	65	47
Stage 2	Angle-tighten a further 30°	
Stage 3	Angle-tighten a further 15°	
Main bearing cap bolts*:		
C20NE engine:		
Stage 1	60	44
Stage 2	Angle-tighten a further 40 to 50°	
X20SE engine:		
Stage 1	50	37
Stage 2	Angle-tighten a further 40 to 50°	
Stage 3	Angle-tighten a further 15°	
Oil cooler hose union nuts - X20SE engine	25	18
Oil cooler mounting bolts	22	16
Oil pump:		
Retaining bolts	6	4
Pump cover screws	6	4
Oil pressure relief valve bolt	30	22
Oil pump pick-up/strainer bolts	8	6
Roadwheel nuts:		
Steel wheels	110	81
Alloy wheels	120	89
Sump bolts:		
Pre 1997 models:		
Engines with baffle plate and gaskets	8	6
Engines with gaskets bonded to baffle plate	15	11
1997 onwards models	20	15
Drain plug:		
C20NE engine	45	33
X20SE engine	55	41
Timing belt cover bolts	6	4
Timing belt tensioner pulley bolt - 1993 onwards models	25	18

New bolts should be used

1 General information

How to use this Chapter

Note: *Throughout this Chapter it is often necessary to identify engines either by their engine code or number (see paragraph 3). See Vehicle identification section for information on the engine number location; the engine code forms the first five digits of the number.*

1 This Part of Chapter 2 is devoted to in-car repair procedures for the 2.0 litre petrol engine. All procedures concerning engine removal and refitting, and engine block/cylinder head overhaul can be found in Chapter 2G.

2 Most of the operations included in this Part are based on the assumption that the engine is still installed in the car. Therefore, if this information is being used during a complete engine overhaul, with the engine already removed, many of the steps included here will not apply.

3 The engine underwent changes to the timing belt arrangement during late 1992 and was also modified in early 1995 and, throughout this Chapter, it is sometimes necessary to differentiate between engine types. All pre 1995 engines have the engine identification code C20NE whereas 1995 onwards engines are coded X20SE. Very early (pre 1993 - up to engine number 14608700) engines can be identified from the timing belt cover arrangement; the outer cover is clipped onto the inner cover as opposed to being bolted in position. In early 1995, most modifications involved detail changes to the fuel/ignition system with the engine internals being largely unchanged; pre 1995 (C20NE) engines can be identified by the distributor on the rear of the cylinder head as 1995 onwards (X20SE) engines are equipped with distributorless ignition systems (see Chapter 5B).

Engine description

4 The 2.0 litre petrol engine is a single overhead camshaft, four-cylinder, in-line unit, mounted at the front of the car, with the clutch and transmission at the rear.

5 The cylinder block is of the dry-liner type. The crankshaft is supported within the cylinder block on five shell-type main bearings. Thrustwashers are fitted to number 3 main bearing, to control crankshaft endfloat.

6 The connecting rods are attached to the crankshaft by horizontally split shell-type big-end bearings, and to the pistons by interference-fit gudgeon pins. The aluminium alloy pistons are of the slipper type, and are fitted with three piston rings, comprising two compression rings and a scraper-type oil control ring.

7 The camshaft runs directly in the camshaft housing, which is mounted on top of the cylinder head, and driven by the crankshaft via a toothed rubber timing belt (which also drives the coolant pump). The camshaft operates each valve via a follower. Each follower pivots on a hydraulic self-adjusting valve lifter (tappet) which automatically adjust the valve clearances.

8 Lubrication is by pressure-feed from a gear-type oil pump, which is mounted on the front end of the crankshaft. It draws oil through a strainer located in the sump, and then forces it through an externally mounted full-flow cartridge-type filter. The oil flows into galleries in the main bearing cap bridge arrangement and cylinder block/crankcase, from where it is distributed to the crankshaft (main bearings) and camshaft(s). The big-end bearings are supplied with oil via internal drillings in the crankshaft, while the camshaft bearings also receive a pressurised supply. The camshaft lobes and valves are lubricated by splash, as are all other engine components. On later engines an oil cooler is fitted to help keep the oil temperature stable under arduous operating conditions.

9 A semi-closed crankcase ventilation system is employed; crankcase fumes are drawn from cylinder head cover, and passed via a hose to the inlet manifold.

Repair operations possible with the engine in the car

10 The following operations can be carried out without having to remove the engine from the vehicle:

a) *Removal and refitting of the cylinder head.*
b) *Removal and refitting of the timing belt and sprockets.*
c) *Renewal of the camshaft oil seal(s).*
d) *Removal and refitting of the camshaft housing and camshaft.*
e) *Removal and refitting of the sump.*
f) *Removal and refitting of the connecting rods and pistons*.*
g) *Removal and refitting of the oil pump.*
h) *Removal and refitting of the oil cooler.*
i) *Renewal of the crankshaft oil seals.*
j) *Renewal of the engine mountings.*
k) *Removal and refitting of the flywheel.*

* Although the operation marked with an asterisk can be carried out with the engine in the car after removal of the sump, it is better for the engine to be removed, in the interests of cleanliness and improved access. For this reason, the procedure is described in Chapter 2G.

2 Compression test - description and interpretation

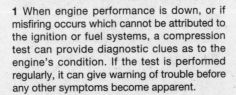

1 When engine performance is down, or if misfiring occurs which cannot be attributed to the ignition or fuel systems, a compression test can provide diagnostic clues as to the engine's condition. If the test is performed regularly, it can give warning of trouble before any other symptoms become apparent.

2 The engine must be fully warmed-up to normal operating temperature, the battery must be fully charged, and the spark plugs must be removed (see Chapter 1A). The aid of an assistant will also be required.

3 Disable the ignition system by disconnecting the wiring connector(s) from the ignition coil/DIS module (as applicable - see Chapter 5B) and the fuel system by removing the fuel pump fuse (see Chapter 13).

4 Fit a compression tester to the number 1 cylinder spark plug hole; the type of tester which screws into the plug thread is to be preferred.

5 Have the assistant hold the throttle wide open and crank the engine on the starter motor; after one or two revolutions, the compression pressure should build up to a maximum figure, and then stabilise. Record the highest reading obtained.

6 Repeat the test on the remaining cylinders, recording the pressure in each.

7 All cylinders should produce very similar pressures; a difference of more than 2 bar between any two cylinders indicates a fault. Note that the compression should build up quickly in a healthy engine; low compression on the first stroke, followed by gradually-increasing pressure on successive strokes, indicates worn piston rings. A low compression reading on the first stroke, which does not build up during successive strokes, indicates leaking valves or a blown head gasket (a cracked head could also be the cause). Deposits on the undersides of the valve heads can also cause low compression.

8 Although Vauxhall do not specify exact compression pressures, as a guide, any cylinder pressure of below 10 bar can be considered as less than healthy. Refer to a Vauxhall dealer or other specialist if in doubt as to whether a particular pressure reading is acceptable.

9 If the addition of a little oil temporarily improves the compression pressure, this indicates that bore or piston wear is responsible for the pressure loss. No improvement suggests that leaking or burnt valves, or a blown head gasket, may be to blame.

10 A low reading from two adjacent cylinders is almost certainly due to the head gasket having blown between them; the presence of coolant in the engine oil will confirm this.

11 If one cylinder is about 20 per cent lower than the others, and the engine has a slightly rough idle, a worn camshaft lobe could be the cause.

12 If the compression reading is unusually high, the combustion chambers are probably coated with carbon deposits. If this is the case, the cylinder head should be removed and decarbonised.

13 On completion of the test, refit the spark plugs (see Chapter 1A), refit the fuel pump fuse and reconnect the wiring to the ignition coil/DIS module (as applicable).

2A

3.5 On pre 1993 engines, align the camshaft sprocket mark with the mark on the top of the inner cover, and the crankshaft pulley notch with the pointer on the inner cover

3 Top dead centre (TDC) for No 1 piston - locating

1 In its travel up and down its cylinder bore, Top Dead Centre (TDC) is the highest point that each piston reaches as the crankshaft rotates. While each piston reaches TDC both at the top of the compression stroke and again at the top of the exhaust stroke, for the purpose of timing the engine, TDC refers to the piston position (usually number 1) at the top of its compression stroke.

2 Number 1 piston (and cylinder) is at the front (timing belt) end of the engine, and its TDC position is located as follows. Note that the crankshaft rotates clockwise when viewed from the front of the vehicle.

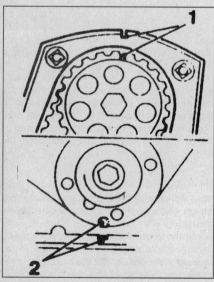

3.8 On 1993 onwards engines, align the camshaft sprocket mark with the mark on the top of the inner cover (1), and the crankshaft sprocket mark with the mark on the inner cover (2)

3 Disconnect the battery negative terminal. If necessary, remove all the spark plugs as described in Chapter 1A to enable the engine to be easily turned over. Continue as described under the relevant sub-heading.

Pre 1993 engines (up to engine number C20NE 14608700)

4 Unclip the timing belt upper outer cover and remove it from the engine (see Section 6).

5 Using a socket and extension bar on the crankshaft sprocket bolt, turn the crankshaft whilst keeping an eye on the camshaft sprocket. Rotate the crankshaft until the timing mark on the camshaft sprocket rim is correctly aligned with the mark on the top of the timing belt inner cover and the notch on the crankshaft pulley rim is aligned with the pointer on the timing belt inner cover **(see illustration)**.

6 With the crankshaft pulley and camshaft sprocket timing marks positioned as described, the engine is positioned with No1 piston at TDC on its compression stroke.

1993 on engines (engine number C20NE 14608701 onwards and all X20SE)

7 Remove the timing belt outer cover as described in Section 6.

8 Using a socket and extension bar on the crankshaft sprocket bolt, turn the crankshaft whilst keeping an eye on the camshaft sprocket. Rotate the crankshaft until the timing mark on the camshaft sprocket rim is correctly aligned with the mark on the top of the timing belt inner cover and the timing mark on the crankshaft sprocket rim is aligned with the cutout on the base of the timing belt inner cover **(see illustration)**.

9 With the crankshaft sprocket and camshaft sprocket timing marks positioned as described, the engine is positioned with No1 piston at TDC on its compression stroke.

4 Camshaft cover - removal and refitting

Removal

1 Release the retaining clip(s) and disconnect the breather hose(s) from the camshaft cover.

2 Slacken and remove the retaining bolts, noting the correct fitted location of any clips or brackets retained by the bolts (as applicable) then lift the camshaft cover from the camshaft housing. If the cover is stuck, do not lever between the cover and camshaft housing mating surfaces - if necessary, gently tap the cover sideways to free it. Recover the gasket; if it shows signs of damage or deterioration it must be renewed.

Refitting

3 Prior to refitting, examine the inside of the cover for a build-up of oil sludge or any other

contamination, and if necessary clean the cover with paraffin, or a water-soluble solvent. Examine the condition of the crankcase ventilation filter inside the camshaft cover, and clean as described for the inside of the cover if clogging is evident (if desired, the filter can be removed from the cover, after removing the securing bolts). Dry the cover thoroughly before refitting.

4 Ensure the cover is clean and dry and seat the gasket in the cover recess then refit the cover to the camshaft housing, ensuring the gasket remains correctly seated.

5 Refit the retaining bolts, ensuring all relevant clips/brackets are correctly positioned, and tighten them to the specified torque working in a diagonal sequence.

6 Reconnect the breather hose(s) securely to the cover.

5 Crankshaft pulley - removal and refitting

Removal

1 Remove the auxiliary drivebelt(s) as described in Chapter 1A.

2 On pre 1993 engines (up to engine number C20NE 14608700), position No 1 piston at TDC on its compression stroke as described in Section 3.

3 On all engines, slacken and remove the small retaining bolts securing the pulley to the crankshaft sprocket and remove the pulley from the engine. If necessary, prevent crankshaft rotation by holding the sprocket retaining bolt with a suitable socket.

Refitting

4 Refit the crankshaft pulley and refit its retaining bolts. On pre 1993 engines ensure the camshaft sprocket timing mark is still correctly aligned and align the crankshaft pulley notch with the pointer (see Section 3).

5 Lock the crankshaft by the method used on removal, and tighten the pulley retaining bolt to the specified torque setting.

6 Refit the auxiliary drivebelt(s) as described in Chapter 1A. On early engines, refit the timing belt outer cover ensuring it is clipped securely in position.

6 Timing belt covers - removal and refitting

Pre 1993 models (up to engine number C20NE 14608700)

Upper outer cover

1 Unclip the retaining clips situated around the cover and manoeuvre the cover away from the engine unit.

2 On refitting ensure the cover is correctly engaged with the other covers and secure it in position with the retaining clips.

Lower outer cover

3 Remove the upper outer cover as described in paragraph 1 then unclip and remove the lower cover.

4 On refitting fit the lower cover to the rear cover, securing it in position with the retaining clips, then refit the upper cover (see paragraph 2).

Inner cover

5 Remove the timing belt as described in Section 7.

6 Remove the camshaft and crankshaft sprockets as described in Section 8.

7 Slacken and remove the bolts securing the cover to the camshaft and oil pump housing then manoeuvre the cover out of position and remove it from the vehicle. With the main inner cover removed, if necessary, the small section can also be removed from the coolant pump.

8 Refitting is the reverse of removal, tightening the cover retaining bolts to the specified torque.

1993 to 1995 models (engine number C20NE 14608701 onwards)

Outer cover

9 Remove the cooling fan and coupling as described in Chapter 3.

10 Remove the crankshaft pulley as described in Section 5.

11 Unscrew the retaining bolts and remove the cooling fan drive pulley from its spindle

12 Slacken and remove the retaining bolts then remove the timing belt outer cover from the engine.

13 Refitting is the reverse of removal, tightening the cover retaining bolts to the specified torque.

Inner cover

14 Remove the outer cover as described in paragraphs 9 to 12

15 Remove the timing belt as described in Section 7.

16 Remove the camshaft sprocket, crankshaft sprocket and tensioner pulley as described in Section 8.

17 Slacken and remove the bolts securing the inner cover to the camshaft and oil pump housings. Remove the cover from the engine, taking care not to lose the spacer and rubber grommets from each of the retaining bolt holes.

18 Refitting is the reverse of removal. Ensure the rubber grommets and spacers are correctly fitted to the retaining bolt holes and tighten the bolts to the specified torque.

1995 onwards models (X20SE engine)

Outer cover

19 Remove the auxiliary drive belt as described in Chapter 1A. Where necessary, unscrew the retaining bolt and remove the belt idler pulley (where fitted) from the front of the engine.

20 Remove the crankshaft pulley as described in Section 5.

21 Slacken and remove the retaining bolts and remove the outer cover from the engine.

22 Refitting is the reverse of removal tightening the cover retaining bolts to the specified torque.

Inner cover

23 Remove the outer cover as described in paragraphs 9 to 12

24 Remove the timing belt as described in Section 7.

25 Remove the camshaft sprocket, crankshaft sprocket and tensioner pulley as described in Section 8.

26 Unclip the crankshaft sensor wiring from the rear of the timing belt inner cover and position, noting its correct routing.

27 Slacken and remove the bolts securing the inner cover to the camshaft and oil pump housings, and remove the cover from the engine.

28 Refitting is the reverse of removal, tightening the bolts to the specified torque. Ensure the crankshaft sensor wiring is correctly routed and clipped securely in position.

7 Timing belt - removal and refitting

Note: *The timing belt must be removed and refitted with the engine cold.*

Pre 1993 models (up to engine number C20SE 14608700) - engines without a timing belt tensioner pulley

Note: *On these engines Vauxhall specify the use of a special belt tension measuring tool (KM-510-A) to correctly set the timing belt tension. If access to this equipment cannot be obtained, an approximate setting can be achieved using the method described below. If the method described is used, the tension must be checked using the special electronic tool at the earliest possible opportunity. Do not drive the vehicle over large distances, or*

7.6 On engine without a timing belt tensioner pulley fit the adapter to the coolant pump

use high engine speeds, until the belt tension is known to be correct. Refer to a Vauxhall dealer for advice.

Note: *The timing belt tension is altered by rotating the coolant pump in the cylinder block, and a wrench which fits the hexagonal section of the pump housing will be required for the following procedure. In the absence of the special Vauxhall tool (KM-637), a suitable alternative should be purchased before starting work. The tool is in the form of an adaptor which is fitted to the end of a ratchet and should be readily available from most automotive tool and accessory shops.*

Removal

1 Remove the cooling fan and coupling as described in Chapter 3.

2 Remove the timing belt upper outer cover (see Section 6) then position No 1 cylinder at TDC on its compression stroke as described in Section 3.

3 Remove the crankshaft pulley as described in Section 5.

4 Unscrew the retaining bolts and remove the cooling fan drive pulley from its spindle.

5 Release the retaining clips and remove the timing belt lower outer cover (see Section 6).

6 Ensure the camshaft sprocket timing mark is still correctly aligned with the mark on the belt rear cover then fit the adaptor to the coolant pump **(see illustration)**.

7 Loosen the coolant pump retaining bolts then, using a ratchet or extension bar fitted to the adaptor, carefully rotate the pump to relieve the tension in the timing belt.

8 Slide the timing belt off from its sprockets and remove it from the engine. If the belt is to be re-used, use white paint or similar to mark the direction of rotation on the belt. **Do not** rotate the crankshaft until the timing belt has been refitted.

9 Check the timing belt carefully for any signs of uneven wear, splitting or oil contamination, and renew it if there is the slightest doubt about its condition. If the engine is undergoing an overhaul and has covered over 36 000 miles, or it was more than 4 years since the original belt was fitted, renew the belt as a matter of course, regardless of its apparent condition. If signs of oil contamination are found, trace the source of the oil leak and rectify it, then wash down the engine timing belt area and all related components to remove all traces of oil.

Refitting

10 On reassembly, thoroughly clean the timing belt sprockets then check that the camshaft sprocket timing mark is still correctly aligned with the cover cutout. Temporarily refit the crankshaft pulley to the sprocket and check that the pulley notch is still aligned with the pointer (see Section 3).

11 Fit the timing belt over the crankshaft and camshaft sprockets, ensuring that the belt front run is taut (ie, all slack is on the coolant pump side of the belt), then fit the belt over the coolant pump sprocket. Do not twist the

2A

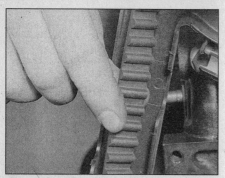

7.17 If the special tool is not available check the timing belt tension as described in text

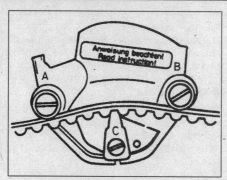

7.23 Fit the special measuring tool to the timing belt making sure that the outside of the belt is correctly positioned against the supports (A and B), and the tool arm (C) Is correctly located between the belt teeth

belt sharply while refitting it. Ensure that the belt teeth are correctly seated centrally in the sprockets, and that the timing marks remain in alignment. If a used belt is being refitted, ensure that the arrow mark made on removal points in the normal direction of rotation, as before.

12 Lightly tension the timing belt by rotating the coolant pump and securely tighten the pump retaining bolts.

13 Refit the crankshaft pulley and tighten its retaining bolts to the specified torque.

14 Check the camshaft sprocket and crankshaft pulley timing marks are still correctly aligned. If adjustment is necessary, release the belt tension again then disengage the belt from the sprockets and make any necessary adjustments before retensioning the belt.

15 If the marks are still correctly positioned, rotate the crankshaft smoothly through two complete turns (720°) in the normal direction of rotation to settle the timing belt in position.

16 Check that both the camshaft and crankshaft sprocket timing marks are realigned then tension the timing belt as described under the relevant sub-heading.

Tensioning without the special measuring tool

17 Ensuring that the front run of the belt, between the camshaft and crankshaft sprockets, is taut, working at the mid-point of the belt between the coolant pump and crankshaft sprockets, grip the belt between your thumb and forefinger and lightly twist the belt. Using only moderate pressure, it should just be possible to twist the belt through 90° **(see illustration)**. If adjustment is necessary, loosen the coolant pump retaining bolts and adjust the belt tension by rotating the pump as necessary. Once the belt tension is correctly set, tighten the pump retaining bolts to the specified torque.

18 Rotate the crankshaft smoothly through another two complete turns (720°) in the normal direction of rotation until the timing marks are correctly realigned then recheck the belt tension. If necessary, repeat the adjustment procedure the tension. Note that this procedure gives only an approximate

setting for the timing belt tension. To ensure the belt is correctly adjusted it is essential that the tension is checked using the special measuring tool at the earliest possible opportunity.

19 Refit the lower outer timing belt cover then install the upper outer cover. Ensure both covers are correctly seated and securely held by all the retaining clips.

20 Refit the cooling fan pulley, tightening its retaining bolts to the specified torque.

21 Refit the auxiliary drivebelts as described in Chapter 1A.

22 Refit the cooling fan assembly as described in Chapter 3.

Tensioning with the special measuring tool

23 Ensuring that the front run of the belt, between the camshaft and crankshaft sprockets, is taut, fit the measuring tool to the mid-point of the belt run between the coolant pump and camshaft sprockets. Ensure the belt is correctly engaged with the tool and lightly tap the tool to settle it in position **(see illustration)**. Read the value on the measuring tool scale and compare it to the values given in the specifications at the start of this Chapter.

24 If adjustment is necessary, slacken the coolant pump retaining bolts and rotate the pump as necessary. Once the tension is correctly set, tighten the coolant pump retaining bolts to the specified torque.

25 Remove the measuring tool from the timing belt then rotate the crankshaft smoothly through another two complete turns (720°) in the normal direction of rotation until the timing marks are correctly realigned.

26 Recheck the belt tension as described in paragraph 23.

27 If adjustment is necessary, repeat the operations described in paragraphs 24 to 26.

28 Once the belt tension is correctly adjusted, ensure the coolant pump retaining bolts are tightened to the specified torque then refit the lower outer timing belt cover and the upper outer cover. Ensure both covers are correctly seated and securely held by all the retaining clips.

29 Refit the cooling fan pulley, tightening its retaining bolts securely.

30 Refit the auxiliary drivebelts as described in Chapter 1A.

31 Refit the cooling fan assembly as described in Chapter 3.

1993 onwards models (engine number C20NE 14608701 onwards) - engines with a timing belt tensioner pulley

Removal

32 Remove the timing belt outer cover as described in Section 6.

33 Position No 1 cylinder at TDC on its compression stroke as described in Section 3.

34 Slacken the timing belt tensioner pulley bolt. Using an Allen key, rotate the tensioner arm clockwise to its stop, to relieve the tension in the timing belt, and hold it in position by securely tightening the retaining bolt.

35 Slide the timing belt off from its sprockets and remove it from the engine. If the belt is to be re-used, use white paint or similar to mark the direction of rotation on the belt. **Do not** rotate the crankshaft or camshafts until the timing belt has been refitted.

36 Check the timing belt carefully for any signs of uneven wear, splitting or oil contamination, and renew it if there is the slightest doubt about its condition. If the engine is undergoing an overhaul and has covered over 36 000 miles, or it was more than 4 years since the original belt was fitted, renew the belt as a matter of course, regardless of its apparent condition. If signs of oil contamination are found, trace the source of the oil leak and rectify it, then wash down the engine timing belt area and all related components to remove all traces of oil.

Refitting

37 On reassembly, thoroughly clean the timing belt sprockets and tensioner pulley.

38 Check that the camshaft and crankshaft sprocket timing marks are still correctly aligned with the marks on the rear cover (see Section 3).

39 Fit the timing belt over the crankshaft and camshaft sprockets, ensuring that the belt front run is taut (ie, all slack is on the tensioner side of the belt), then fit the belt over the coolant pump sprocket and tensioner pulley. Do not twist the belt sharply while refitting it. Ensure that the belt teeth are correctly seated centrally in the sprockets, and that the timing marks remain in alignment. If a used belt is being refitted, ensure that the arrow mark made on removal points in the normal direction of rotation, as before.

40 Slacken the timing belt tensioner bolt to release the tensioner spring. Rotate the tensioner arm anti-clockwise until the tensioner pointer is fully over against its stop, without exerting any excess strain on the belt.

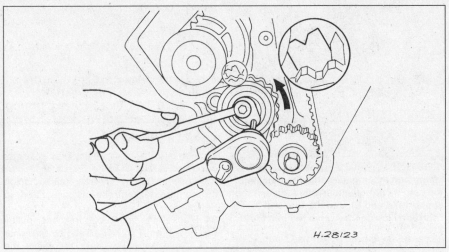

7.40 Tension the timing belt by rotating the tensioner arm fully anti-clockwise until the pointer is positioned as shown

Hold the tensioner in position and securely tighten its retaining bolt **(see illustration)**.

41 Check the sprocket timing marks are still correctly aligned. If adjustment is necessary, release the tensioner again then disengage the belt from the sprockets and make any necessary adjustments.

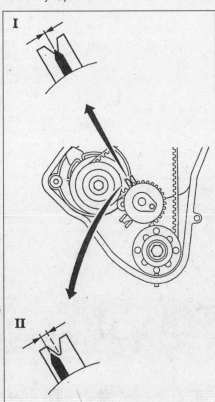

7.45 Timing belt tensioner pointer positions

I Location if a new belt is being fitted
II Location if the original belt is being re-used (pointer should be 4 mm to the left of the backplate cutout)

42 Using a socket on the crankshaft sprocket bolt, rotate the crankshaft smoothly through two complete turns (720º) in the normal direction of rotation to settle the timing belt in position.

43 Check that both the camshaft and crankshaft sprocket timing marks are correctly realigned then slacken the tensioner bolt again.

44 If a new timing belt is being fitted, adjust the tensioner so that the pointer is aligned with the cutout on the backplate **(see illustration)**. Hold the tensioner in the correct position and tighten its retaining bolt to the specified torque. Rotate the crankshaft smoothly through another two complete turns in the normal direction of rotation, to bring the sprocket timing marks back into alignment. Check that the tensioner pointer is still aligned with the backplate cutout.

45 If the original belt is being refitted, adjust the tensioner so that the pointer is positioned 4 mm to the left of the cutout on the backplate **(see illustration)**. Hold the tensioner in the correct position and tighten its retaining bolt to the specified torque. Rotate the crankshaft smoothly through another two complete turns in the normal direction of rotation, to bring the sprocket timing marks back into alignment. Check that the tensioner pointer is still correctly positioned in relation to the backplate cutout.

46 If the tensioner pointer is not correctly positioned in relation to the backplate, repeat the procedure in paragraph 44 (new belt) or 45 (original belt) (as applicable).

47 Once the tensioner pointer and backplate remain correctly aligned, refit the timing belt outer cover and tighten its retaining bolts to the specified torque.

48 On pre-1995 (C20NE engine) models, refit the cooling fan drive pulley and refit the cooling fan and coupling as described in Chapter 3.

49 On all models, refit the crankshaft pulley as described in Section 5.

7.44 If a new belt is being fitted, position the tensioner so that the pointer is aligned with the backplate cutout

8 Timing belt tensioner and sprockets - removal and refitting

Camshaft sprocket

Removal

1 Remove the timing belt as described in Section 7.

2 The camshaft must be prevented from turning as the sprocket bolt is unscrewed, and this can be achieved in one of two ways as follows.

a) *Make up a sprocket-holding tool using two lengths of steel strip (one long, the other short), and three nuts and bolts; one nut and bolt forms the pivot of a forked tool, with the remaining two nuts and bolts at the tips of the 'forks' to engage with the sprocket spokes.*

b) *Remove the camshaft cover as described in Section 4 and hold the camshaft with an open-ended spanner on the flats provided.*

3 Unscrew the retaining bolt and washer and remove the sprocket from the end of the camshaft. If the sprocket locating pin is a loose fit, remove it and store it with the sprocket for safe-keeping.

Refitting

4 Prior to refitting check the oil seal for signs of damage or leakage, if necessary, renewing it as described in Section 9.

5 Ensure the locating pin is in position then refit the sprocket, aligning its cutout with the pin. Refit the sprocket retaining bolt and washer.

6 Tighten the sprocket retaining bolt to the specified torque whilst prevent rotation using the method employed on removal.

7 Refit the timing belt as described in Section 7 then (where necessary) refit the camshaft cover as described in Section 4.

Crankshaft sprocket

Note: *A new sprocket retaining bolt must be used on refitting.*

Removal

8 Remove the timing belt as described in Section 7.

2A

9 Slacken the crankshaft sprocket retaining bolt. To prevent crankshaft rotation if the engine is in the vehicle, have an assistant select top gear and apply the brakes firmly. Alternatively retain the sprocket with a length of steel bar; drill two holes in the bar and bolt it to the crankshaft pulley retaining bolt threads on the sprocket. If the transmission has been removed, crankshaft rotation can be prevented by locking the flywheel (see Section 16).

10 Unscrew the retaining bolt and washer then slide the crankshaft sprocket off from the end of the crankshaft **(see illustrations)**. Discard the retaining bolt, a new one must be used on refitting.

11 If necessary, remove the Woodruff key from the crankshaft slot then slide off the spacer **(see illustrations)**.

Refitting

12 Prior to refitting, check the crankshaft oil seal for signs of damage or leakage, if necessary, renewing it as described in Section 17.

13 Slide the spacer onto the crankshaft and refit the Woodruff key to the crankshaft slot.

14 Refit the sprocket to the crankshaft, aligning its slot with the Woodruff key.

15 Fit the washer to the new retaining bolt and screw the bolt into position.

16 Lock the crankshaft by the method used on removal, and tighten the sprocket retaining bolt to the specified stage 1 torque setting then angle-tighten the bolt through the

8.10a Slacken and remove the retaining bolt and washer . . .

specified stage 2 angle, using a socket and extension bar. It is recommended that an angle-measuring gauge is used during the final stages of the tightening, to ensure accuracy **(see illustrations)**. If a gauge is not available, use white paint to make alignment marks between the bolt head and sprocket prior to tightening; the marks can then be used to check that the bolt has been rotated through the correct angle.

17 Refit the timing belt as described in Section 7.

Timing belt tensioner pulley - 1993 onwards models

Removal

18 Remove the timing belt as described in Section 7.

8.10b . . . and remove the crankshaft sprocket

19 Slacken and remove the retaining bolt and remove the tensioner assembly from the engine.

Refitting

20 Fit the tensioner to the engine, making sure that the lug on the backplate is correctly located in the oil pump housing hole. Ensure the tensioner is correctly seated then refit the retaining bolt. Using an Allen key, rotate the tensioner arm clockwise to its stop then securely tighten the retaining bolt.

21 Refit the timing belt as described in Section 7.

9 Camshaft oil seals - renewal

Front oil seal

1 Remove the camshaft sprocket as described in Section 8.

2 Carefully punch or drill small holes opposite each other in the oil seal. Screw a self-tapping screw into each, and pull on the screws to extract the seal **(see illustration)**.

3 Clean the seal housing, and polish off any burrs or raised edges which may have caused the seal to fail in the first place.

4 Lubricate the lips of the new seal with clean engine oil, and press it into position using a suitable tubular drift (such as a socket) which bears only on the hard outer edge of the seal

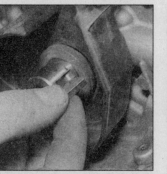

8.11a Remove the Woodruff key from the crankshaft . . .

8.11b . . . and slide off the spacer

8.16a Tighten the sprocket retaining bolt to the specified stage 1 torque . . .

8.16b . . . and then through the specified stage 2 angle

9.2 Removing a camshaft oil seal using a self-tapping screw and pliers

9.4 Using a socket to tap the new camshaft oil seal into position

(see illustration). Take care not to damage the seal lips during fitting; note that the seal lips should face inwards.

5 Refit the camshaft sprocket as described in Section 8.

Rear oil seal - pre 1995 models (C20NE engine)

6 Remove the distributor as described in Chapter 5B.

7 Using a large flat-bladed screwdriver, carefully lever the oil seal out of position taking great care not to damage the housing.

8 Fit the new seal as described in paragraphs 3 and 4.

9 Refit the distributor as described in Chapter 5B.

Rear gasket - 1995 onwards models (X20SE engine)

10 Disconnect the wiring connector from the DIS module which is mounted onto the rear of the cylinder head (see Chapter 5B). Slacken and remove the bolts secure the DIS module mounting bracket to the cylinder head, noting the correct fitted location of the engine lifting bracket.

11 Unclip the HT leads from the rear clip and position the module clear of the end cover.

12 Unbolt the camshaft housing end cover from the rear of the cylinder head, noting the correct fitted location of the HT lead clip and remove the gasket.

13 Ensure the mating surfaces are clean and dry then refit the cover using a new gasket.

Refitting the cover retaining bolts, complete with HT lead clip, and tighten them to the specified torque.

14 Refit the DIS module to the cylinder head, not forgetting the lifting bracket, and securely tighten the mounting bracket bolts. Clip the HT leads into the clip and reconnect the module wiring connector.

---

10 Camshaft housing and camshaft - removal, inspection and refitting

Removal

1 The camshaft can only be removed once the camshaft housing has been removed from the engine. Since the camshaft housing is secured in position by the cylinder head bolts, it is not possible to remove the camshaft without removing the cylinder head (see Section 12). **Note:** *In theory it is possible to remove the camshaft housing once the cylinder head bolts have been removed, and leave the head in position. However, this procedure carries a high risk of disturbing the head gasket, resulting in the head gasket 'blowing' once the camshaft and housing are refitted. If you wish to attempt this, proceed as described in Section 12, noting that it will not be necessary to remove the manifolds, etc. Be warned though that, after refitting, you may find the head gasket will need renewing, meaning that the cylinder head will have to be removed after all. The decision is yours as to whether this is a chance worth taking.*

2 On pre 1995 models (C20NE engine), with the camshaft housing removed, remove the distributor from the rear of the cylinder head (see Chapter 5B) then carefully lever out the camshaft rear oil seal.

3 On 1995 onwards models (X20SE engine), unbolt the end cover from the rear of the cylinder head, noting the correct fitted location of the HT lead clip and remove the gasket

4 On all models, measure the camshaft endfloat by inserting feeler gauges between the thrustplate and the camshaft; if the endfloat is not within the limits given in the Specifications then the thrustplate will need to be renewed. Unscrew the two retaining bolts

then slide out the camshaft thrustplate, noting which way round it is fitted (see illustration).

5 Carefully withdraw the camshaft from the rear of the housing, taking care not to damage the bearing journals (see illustration).

Inspection

6 With the camshaft removed, examine the bearings in the camshaft housing for signs of obvious wear or pitting. If evident, a new camshaft housing will probably be required. Also check that the oil supply holes in the camshaft housing are free from obstructions.

7 The camshaft itself should show no marks or scoring on the journal or cam lobe surfaces. If evident, renew the camshaft. If the camshaft lobes show signs of wear also examine the followers (see Section 11).

8 Check the camshaft thrustplate for signs of wear or grooves, and renew if necessary.

Refitting

9 Carefully prise the front oil seal out of from the camshaft housing, using a suitable screwdriver (see illustration). Ensure the housing is clean then press in the new seal, ensuring its sealing lip is facing inwards, until it is flush with the housing.

10 Liberally lubricate the camshaft and housing bearings and the oil seal lip with fresh engine oil.

11 Carefully insert the camshaft into the housing, taking care not to mark the bearing surfaces or damage the oil seal lip.

12 Slide the thrustplate into position, engaging it with the camshaft slot, and tighten its retaining bolts to the specified torque. Check the camshaft endfloat (see paragraph 4).

13 On pre 1995 models (C20NE engine), fit a new rear oil seal to the camshaft housing (see Section 9) then refit the distributor (see Chapter 5B).

14 On 1995 onwards models (X20SE engine), ensure the housing and rear cover mating surfaces are clean and dry then fit a new gasket to the housing. Refit the cover, ensuring the HT lead clip is correctly positioned, and tighten the retaining bolts to the specified torque.

15 Refit the camshaft housing as described in Section 12.

2A

10.4 Camshaft thrustplate is retained by two bolts

10.5 Removing the camshaft from the housing

10.9 Prise out the camshaft front oil seal and renew it before installing the camshaft

11.9a Remove the followers . . .

11.9b . . . and thrust pads . . .

11.9c . . . and withdraw the hydraulic tappets from the cylinder head

11 Camshaft followers and hydraulic tappets - removal, inspection and refitting

Using Vauxhall service tool (tool no. KM-565)

1 If access to the special tool or a suitable equivalent can be gained, the cam followers and tappets can be removed as follows, without disturbing the camshaft.

2 Remove the camshaft cover as described in Section 4.

3 Using a socket and extension bar, rotate the crankshaft in the normal direction of rotation until the camshaft lobe of the first follower/tappet to be remove is pointing straight upwards.

4 Fit the service tool to the top of the camshaft housing, making sure the tool end is correctly engaged with the top of the valve. Screw the tool stud into one of the housing bolt holes until the valve is sufficiently depressed to allow the follower to be slid out from underneath the camshaft. The hydraulic tappet can then also be removed from the top of the valve, as can the thrust pad. Inspect the components (see paragraphs 10 and 11) and renew if worn or damaged.

5 Lubricate the tappet and follower with fresh engine oil then slide the tappet into its bore in the cylinder head. Manoeuvre the follower into position, ensuring it is correctly engaged with the tappet and valve stem, then carefully remove the service tool.

6 Repeat the operation on the remaining followers and tappets.

Without the special tool

Removal

7 Without the use of the special tool, it will be necessary to remove the camshaft housing to allow the followers and tappets to be removed (see Section 10, paragraph 1).

8 With the housing removed, obtain eight small, clean plastic containers, and number them 1 to 8; alternatively, divide a larger container into eight compartments.

9 Lift out each follower, thrust pad and hydraulic tappet in turn, and place them in their respective container (see illustrations). Do not interchange the cam followers or tappets, or the rate of wear will be much increased.

Inspection

10 Examine the cam follower bearing surfaces which contact the camshaft lobes for wear ridges and scoring. Renew any follower on which these conditions are apparent. If a follower bearing surface is badly scored, also examine the corresponding lobe on the camshaft for wear, as it is likely that both will be worn. Also check the thrust pad for signs of wear or damage. Renew worn components as necessary.

11 If the hydraulic tappets are thought to be faulty they should be renewed; testing of the tappets is not possible.

Refitting

12 Lubricate the hydraulic tappets and their cylinder head bores with clean engine oil. Refit the tappets to the cylinder head, making sure they are fitted in their original locations.

13 Fit each thrust pad to the top of its respective valve.

14 Lubricate the followers with clean engine oil. Fit each follower, ensuring it is correctly engaged with both the tappet and thrust pad, then refit the camshaft housing (see Section 12).

12 Cylinder head - removal and refitting

Removal

Note: *The engine must be cold when removing the cylinder head. New cylinder head bolts must be used on refitting.*

1 Disconnect the battery negative lead.

2 Drain the cooling system and remove the spark plugs as described in Chapter 1A.

3 Remove the timing belt as described in Section 7.

4 Remove the inlet and exhaust manifolds as described in Chapter 4A. If no work is to be carried out on the cylinder head, the head can be removed complete with manifolds once the following operations have been carried out (see Chapter 4A).

a) Disconnect the various wiring connectors from the throttle housing and manifold and free the wiring harness from the inlet manifold.

b) Disconnect the fuel hoses from the fuel rail and the various vacuum and coolant hoses from the inlet manifold.

c) Disconnect the accelerator cable.

d) Unbolt the exhaust front pipe from manifold.

e) On 1995 onwards models (X20SE engine) unbolt the inlet manifold support bracket and the alternator support bracket from the manifold.

5 Remove the camshaft cover as described in Section 4.

6 Remove the camshaft sprocket as described in Section 8.

7 Undo the retaining bolts securing the timing belt inner cover to the camshaft housing.

8 Disconnect the wiring connector from the distributor/DIS module (as applicable) and the coolant temperature and gauge sender units. Free the wiring from its retaining clips, noting its correct routing, and position it clear of the cylinder head.

9 Slacken the retaining clips and disconnect the coolant hoses from the front and rear of the thermostat housing.

10 Referring to Chapter 5A, unbolt the alternator upper mounting bracket from the cylinder head.

11 On 1995 onwards models (X20SE engine) unbolt and remove the engine lifting bracket from the rear of the cylinder head.

12 On all models, make a final check to ensure that all relevant hoses, pipes and wires, etc, have been disconnected.

13 Working in the **reverse** of the tightening sequence **(see illustration 12.31a)**, progressively slacken the cylinder head bolts by a third of a turn at a time until all bolts can be unscrewed by hand. Remove each bolt in turn, along with its washer.

14 Lift the camshaft housing from the cylinder head. If necessary, tap the housing gently with a soft-faced mallet to free it from the cylinder head, but **do not** lever at the

12.23 Ensure the locating dowels are in position . . .

12.24 . . . then fit the new gasket making sure the OBEN/TOP marking is uppermost

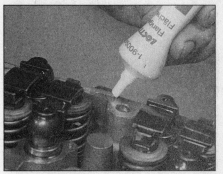

12.27 Apply sealant to the cylinder head upper mating surface then refit the camshaft housing

mating faces. Note the fitted positions of the two locating dowels, and remove them for safe keeping if they are loose.

15 Lift the cylinder head from the cylinder block, taking care not to dislodge the cam followers or thrust pads. If necessary, tap the cylinder head gently with a soft-faced mallet to free it from the block, but **do not** lever at the mating faces. Note the fitted positions of the two locating dowels, and remove them for safe keeping if they are loose.

16 Recover the cylinder head gasket, and discard it.

Preparation for refitting

17 The mating faces of the cylinder head and block must be perfectly clean before refitting the head. Use a scraper to remove all traces of gasket and carbon, and also clean the tops of the pistons. Take particular care with the aluminium surfaces, as the soft metal is damaged easily. Also, make sure that debris is not allowed to enter the oil and water channels - this is particularly important for the oil circuit, as carbon could block the oil supply to the camshaft or crankshaft bearings. Using adhesive tape and paper, seal the water, oil and bolt holes in the cylinder block. To prevent carbon entering the gap between the pistons and bores, smear a little grease in the gap. After cleaning the piston, rotate the crankshaft so that the piston moves down the bore, then wipe out the grease and carbon

with a cloth rag. Clean the piston crowns in the same way.

18 Check the block and head for nicks, deep scratches and other damage. If slight, they may be removed carefully with a file. More serious damage may be repaired by machining, but this is a specialist job.

19 If warpage of the cylinder head is suspected, use a straight-edge to check it for distortion. Refer to Chapter 2G if necessary.

20 Ensure that the cylinder head bolt holes in the crankcase are clean and free of oil. Syringe or soak up any oil left in the bolt holes. This is most important in order that the correct bolt tightening torque can be applied and to prevent the possibility of the block being cracked by hydraulic pressure when the bolts are tightened.

21 Renew the cylinder head bolts regardless of their apparent condition.

Refitting

22 Position number 1 piston at TDC, and wipe clean the mating faces of the head and block.

23 Ensure that the two locating dowels are in position at each end of the cylinder block/crankcase surface (**see illustration**).

24 Fit the new cylinder head gasket to the

block, making sure it is fitted with the correct way up with its OBEN or TOP mark uppermost (**see illustration**).

25 Carefully refit the cylinder head, locating it on the dowels.

26 Ensure the mating surfaces of the cylinder head and camshaft housing are clean and dry. Check the camshaft is still correctly positioned by temporarily fitting the camshaft sprocket and checking that the sprocket timing mark is still uppermost.

27 Apply a bead of suitable sealant to the cylinder head mating surface (**see illustration**).

28 Ensure the two locating dowels are in position then lubricate the camshaft followers with clean engine oil.

29 Carefully lower the camshaft housing assembly into position, locating it on the dowels.

30 Fit the washers to the new cylinder head bolts then carefully insert them into position (**do not drop**), tightening them finger-tight only at this stage (**see illustration**).

31 Working progressively and in the sequence shown, first tighten all the cylinder head bolts to the stage 1 torque setting (**see illustrations**).

32 Once all bolts have been tightened to the stage 1 torque, again working in the sequence shown, tighten each bolt through its specified stage 2 angle, using a socket and extension bar. It is recommended that an angle-

2A

12.30 Fit the washers to the new head bolts and screw all bolts into position

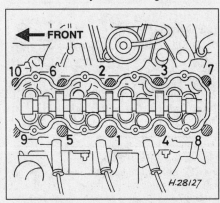

12.31a Cylinder head bolt tightening sequence

12.31b Working in the specified sequence, tighten the cylinder head bolts to the specified stage 1 torque setting . . .

12.32 . . . and then through the various specified angles (see text)

measuring gauge is used during this stage of the tightening, to ensure accuracy **(see illustration)**.

33 Working in the specified sequence, go around again and tighten all bolts through the specified stage 3 angle.

34 Finally go around in the specified sequence again and tighten all bolts through the specified stage 4 angle.

35 Refit the bolts securing the timing belt inner cover to the camshaft housing and tighten them to the specified torque.

36 Refit the camshaft sprocket as described in Section 8 then fit the timing belt as described in Section 7.

37 Reconnect the wiring connectors to the cylinder head components, ensuring all wiring is correctly routed, and secure it in position with the necessary clips.

38 Reconnect the coolant hoses to the thermostat housing and securely tighten their retaining clips.

39 Refit/reconnect the manifolds as described in Chapter 4A (as applicable).

40 Refit the roadwheel then lower the vehicle to the floor and tighten the wheel nuts to the specified torque.

41 Ensure all pipes and hoses are securely reconnected then refill the cooling system and refit the spark plugs as described in Chapter 1A.

42 Reconnect the battery then start the engine and check for signs of leaks.

13 Sump - removal and refitting

Removal

1 Disconnect the battery negative terminal.
2 Firmly apply the handbrake then jack up the front of the car and support it on axle stands.
3 Undo the retaining bolts and remove the engine undercover.
4 Drain the engine oil as described in Chapter 1A, then fit a new sealing washer and refit the drain plug, tightening it to the specified torque. If the engine is nearing its service interval when the oil and filter are due for

renewal, it is recommended that the filter is also removed and a new one fitted. After reassembly, the engine can then be refilled with fresh engine oil.

5 Remove the clutch slave cylinder as described in Chapter 6.

6 Position a jack underneath the transmission unit and raise the jack until it is supporting the weight of the transmission. Unscrew the nuts securing the rear engine mounting to the crossmember then slacken and remove the mounting bolts and remove the front suspension crossmember from underneath the engine/transmission unit.

7 Referring to Chapter 9, unbolt the front axle assembly from the chassis and lower it slightly to gain the necessary clearance required to remove the sump.

8 Progressively slacken and remove the bolts securing the sump to the base of the cylinder block/oil pump. Break the sump joint by striking the sump with the palm of the hand, then lower the sump away from the engine and withdraw it.

9 Undo the retaining bolts securing the oil pump pick-up/strainer in position and remove it from the base of the cylinder block, along with its gasket/sealing ring (as applicable).

10 Remove the baffle plate from the base of the cylinder block and discard the gaskets. **Note:** *On some engines the gaskets are bonded to the baffle plate, necessitating renewal of the baffle plate.*

Refitting

11 Remove all traces of dirt and oil from the mating surfaces of the sump and cylinder block and (where removed) the pick-up/strainer and oil pump housing. Also remove all traces of locking compound from the retaining bolts and threaded holes.

12 Apply a smear of suitable sealing compound (Vauxhall recommend the use of sealant 1503294 - Part No 90001851 - available from your Vauxhall dealer) to the cylinder block mating surface joints with the oil pump housing and rear main bearing cap **(see illustration)**.

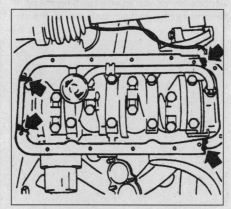

13.12 Apply sealant to the oil pump housing and rear main bearing cap joints (arrowed)

13 Fit a new gasket/sealing ring (as applicable) to the oil pump pick-up/strainer and apply a drop of locking compound (Vauxhall recommend the use of compound 1510177 - Part No 90167347 - available from your Vauxhall dealer) to the threads of the strainer retaining bolts.

14 Fit a new gasket to the top of the baffle plate (where necessary) then offer up the baffle plate and pick-up/strainer to the cylinder block. Ensure the baffle plate is correctly located then refit the pick-up/strainer retaining bolts and tighten them to the specified torque.

15 On pre 1997 models, apply locking compound (Vauxhall recommend the use of compound 1510177 - Part No 90167347 - available from your Vauxhall dealer) to the threads of the sump retaining bolts.

16 Fit a new gasket (where necessary) to the sump flange then offer up the sump to the cylinder block. Refit the retaining bolts and, working out from the centre in a diagonal sequence, progressively tighten them to the specified torque setting.

17 Refit the crossmember to the vehicle, engaging it with the rear mounting, and refit the mounting bolts. Tighten the mounting bolts to the specified torque setting then refit the engine mounting nuts and tighten them to the specified torque.

18 Refit the front axle as described in Chapter 9.

19 Refit the clutch slave cylinder as described in Chapter 6.

20 Refit the undercover then lower the vehicle to the ground.

21 Fill the engine with fresh oil, with reference to Chapter 1A and reconnect the battery.

14 Oil pump - removal, overhaul and refitting

Removal

1 Referring to Chapter 1A, drain the engine oil and remove the oil filter. If the filter is damaged on removal, which is likely, a new filter must be used on refitting and the engine filled with fresh oil.

2 Remove the timing belt inner cover as described in Section 6.

3 Remove the sump as described in Section 13.

4 Disconnect the wiring connector from the oil pressure switch.

5 Unbolt the crankshaft sensor mounting bracket and position it clear of the oil pump.

6 Slacken and remove the retaining bolts then slide the oil pump housing assembly off of the end of the crankshaft, taking great care not to lose the locating dowels. Remove the housing gasket and discard it.

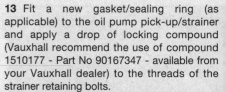

14.7 Undo the retaining screws and remove the pump cover

14.10 Oil pressure relief valve components

14.12a Using a feeler blade to check oil pump gear teeth clearance

Overhaul

7 Undo the retaining screws and lift off the pump cover from the rear of the housing (see illustration).

8 Using a suitable marker pen, mark the surface of both the pump inner and outer gears; the marks can then be used to ensure the rotors are refitted the correct way around.

9 Lift out the inner and outer gears from the pump housing.

10 Unscrew the oil pressure relief valve bolt from the front of the housing and withdraw the spring and plunger from the housing, noting which way around the plunger is fitted (see illustration). Remove the sealing washer from the valve bolt. **Note:** *The pressure relief valve can be removed with the pump in position on the engine unit. On models not fitted with air conditioning it will be necessary to remove the alternator (see Chapter 5A) to gain access to the valve and, on models with air conditioning, remove the power steering pump (see Chapter 1A).*

11 Clean the components, and carefully examine the gears, pump body and relief valve plunger for any signs of scoring or wear. Renew any component which shows signs of wear or damage; if the gears or pump housing are marked then the complete pump assembly should be renewed.

12 If the components appear serviceable, measure the inner gear-to-outer gear clearance using feeler blades. Also measure the gear endfloat, and check the flatness of the end cover (see illustrations). If the clearances exceed the specified tolerances, the pump must be renewed.

13 If the pump is satisfactory, reassemble the components in the reverse order of removal, noting the following.

a) *Ensure both gears are fitted the correct way around.*

b) *Fit a new sealing washer to the pressure relief valve bolt and tighten the bolt to the specified torque.*

c) *Remove all traces of locking compound from the cover screws. Apply a drop of fresh locking compound to each screw and tighten the screws to the specified torque.*

d) *On completion prime the oil pump by filling it with clean engine oil whilst rotating the inner gear.*

Refitting

14 Prior to refitting, carefully lever out the crankshaft oil seal using a flat-bladed screwdriver (see illustration). Fit the new oil seal, ensuring its sealing lip is facing inwards, and press it squarely into the housing using a tubular drift which bears only on the hard outer edge of the seal. Press the seal into position so that it is flush with the housing and lubricate the oil seal lip with clean engine oil.

15 Ensure the mating surfaces of the oil pump and cylinder block are clean and dry and the locating dowels are in position.

16 Fit a new gasket to the cylinder block (see illustration).

17 Carefully manoeuvre the oil pump into position and engage the inner gear with the crankshaft end. Locate the pump on the dowels, taking great care not damage the oil seal lip.

18 Refit the pump housing retaining bolts in their original locations and tighten them to the specified torque.

19 Reconnect the oil pressure sensor wiring connector.

20 Refit the sump as described in Section 13.

21 Refit the timing belt inner cover, timing belt sprockets and tensioner (where fitted) then refit the belt as described in Sections 6, 7 and 8.

22 On completion fit the oil filter and fill the engine with clean oil as described in Chapter 1A.

15 Oil cooler (1995 onwards models) - removal and refitting

Removal

1 Undo the retaining bolts and remove the undercover from the beneath the engine unit.

2 Drain the engine oil as described in Chapter

14.12b Using a straight edge and feeler blade to measure oil pump gear endfloat

14.14 Prise out the oil pump seal and renew it before refitting the pump

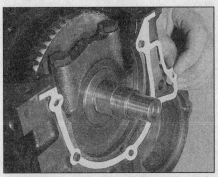

14.16 Ensure the locating dowels are in position and fit a new oil pump gasket to the cylinder block

2A

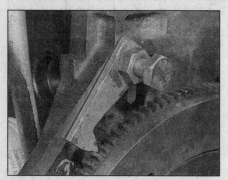

16.2 Lock the flywheel ring gear with a tool similar to that shown

1A. Refit the drain plug to the sump and tighten it to the specified torque.

3 Remove the radiator grille (see Chapter 12).

4 Wipe clean the area around the hose unions on the top of the oil cooler and position a container beneath to catch any spilt oil.

5 Unscrew the union nuts and disconnect the oil hoses from the cooler. Plug/cover the oil cooler and hose unions to prevent the entry of dirt into the system.

6 Slacken and remove the mounting bolts and spacers and manoeuvre the oil cooler out from underneath the vehicle. Recover the mounting rubbers from the oil cooler.

7 Inspect the oil cooler for signs of damage and renew if necessary. If the mounting rubbers show signs of wear or deterioration, they should be renewed.

Refitting

8 Ensure the mounting rubbers are correctly positioned then manoeuvre the oil cooler into position. Refit the spacers to the mounting rubbers then refit the mounting bolts, tightening them to the specified torque.

9 Reconnect the oil hoses to the cooler and tighten the union nuts to the specified torque.

10 Refit the radiator grille and refit the undercover to the vehicle.

11 Refill the engine with oil as described in Chapter 1A.

16 Flywheel - removal, inspection and refitting

Removal

Note: *New flywheel retaining bolts will be required on refitting.*

1 Remove the transmission as described in Chapter 7 then remove the clutch assembly as described in Chapter 6.

2 Make alignment marks between the flywheel and crankshaft using paint or a suitable marker pen. Prevent the flywheel from turning by locking the ring gear teeth with a similar arrangement to that shown **(see illustration)**. Alternatively, bolt a strap between the flywheel and the cylinder block/crankcase.

3 Slacken and remove the retaining bolts and remove the flywheel. Do not drop it, as it is very heavy.

Inspection

4 Examine the flywheel for scoring of the clutch face. If the clutch face is scored, the flywheel may be surface-ground, but renewal is preferable. Check for wear or chipping of the ring gear teeth. Renewal of the ring gear is also possible is not a task for the home mechanic; renewal requires the new ring gear to be heated (to 180° to 230ºC) to allow it to be fitted.

5 If there is any doubt about the condition of the flywheel, seek the advice of a Vauxhall dealer or engine reconditioning specialist. They will be able to advise if it is possible to recondition it or whether renewal is necessary.

Refitting

6 Clean the mating surfaces of the flywheel and crankshaft.

7 Offer up the flywheel and fit the new retaining bolts. If the original is being refitted align the marks made prior to removal.

8 Lock the flywheel by the method used on removal, and tighten the retaining bolts to the specified stage 1 torque setting then angle tighten the bolts through the specified stage 2 angle, using a socket and extension bar, and finally through the specified stage 3 angle. It is recommended that an angle-measuring gauge is used during the final stages of the tightening, to ensure accuracy **(see illustrations)**. If a gauge is not available, use white paint to make alignment marks between the bolt head and flywheel prior to tightening; the marks can then be used to check that the bolt has been rotated through the correct angle.

9 Refit the clutch as described in Chapter 6 then remove the locking tool, and refit the transmission as described in Chapter 7.

17 Crankshaft oil seals - renewal

Front (timing belt end) oil seal

1 Remove the crankshaft sprocket as described in Section 8. Note: On some engines it may also be necessary to remove the timing belt inner cover to gain access to the seal (see Section 6).

2 Carefully punch or drill two small holes opposite each other in the oil seal. Screw a self-tapping screw into each and pull on the screws with pliers to extract the seal. *Caution: Great care must be taken to avoid damage to the oil pump*

3 Clean the seal housing and polish off any burrs or raised edges which may have caused the seal to fail in the first place.

4 Lubricate the lips of the new seal with clean engine oil and ease it into position on the end of the shaft. Press the seal squarely into position until it is flush with the housing. If necessary, a suitable tubular drift, such as a socket, which bears only on the hard outer edge of the seal can be used to tap the seal

16.8a Tighten the flywheel retaining bolts to the specified stage 1 torque . . .

16.8b . . . and then through the specified angles

into position. Take great care not to damage the seal lips during fitting and ensure that the seal lips face inwards.

5 Wash off any traces of oil, then refit the timing belt inner cover (where removed), then refit the crankshaft sprocket as described in Section 8.

Rear (flywheel end) oil seal

6 Remove the flywheel as described in Section 16.

7 Renew the seal as described in paragraphs 2 to 4.

8 Refit the flywheel/driveplate as described in Section 16.

---

18 Engine/transmission mountings - inspection and renewal

Inspection

1 If improved access is required, raise the front of the car and support it securely on axle stands. Where necessary, undo the retaining bolts and remove the undercover from beneath the engine/transmission unit.

2 Check the mounting rubber to see if it is cracked, hardened or separated from the metal at any point; renew the mounting if any such damage or deterioration is evident.

3 Check that all the mountings' fasteners are securely tightened; use a torque wrench to check if possible.

4 Using a large screwdriver or a pry bar, check for wear in the mounting by carefully levering against it to check for free play; where this is not possible, enlist the aid of an assistant to move the engine/transmission unit back and forth, or from side-to-side, while you watch the mounting. While some free play is to be expected even from new components, excessive wear should be obvious. If excessive free play is found, check first that the fasteners are correctly secured, then renew any worn components as described below.

Renewal

Left- and right-hand side mountings

5 Slacken and remove the bolts securing both the left- and right-hand mountings to the chassis and unscrew the nut securing each mounting to its engine bracket.

6 Attach an engine hoist to the lifting brackets on the cylinder head and raise the engine slightly until there is sufficient clearance to manoeuvre the mountings out of position. On the left-hand side, note the correct fitted position of the mounting rubber heatshield on removal.

7 Refitting is the reverse of removal tightening the mounting nuts and bolts to the specified torque.

Rear mounting

8 Position a jack underneath the transmission unit and raise the jack until it is supporting the weight of the transmission.

9 Slacken and remove the bolts securing the mounting to the underside of the transmission housing.

10 Unscrew the nuts securing the mounting to crossmember then raise the transmission unit slightly and manoeuvre the mounting out of position.

11 Refitting is the reverse of removal, tightening the mounting nuts and bolts to their specified torque settings.

Notes

Chapter 2 Part B
2.2 litre petrol engine in-car repair procedures

Contents

Camshaft and followers - removal, inspection and refitting 10
Camshaft cover - removal and refitting 4
Camshaft oil seals - renewal 9
Compression test - description and interpretation 2
Crankshaft oil seals - renewal 16
Crankshaft pulley - removal and refitting 5
Cylinder head - removal and refitting 11
Engine oil and filter - renewal . . . . .See Chapter 1A
Engine oil level check .See Weekly checks
Engine/transmission mountings - inspection and renewal 17
Flywheel - removal, inspection and refitting 15
General engine checks . . . . .See Chapter 1A
General information 1
Oil cooler - removal and refitting 14
Oil pump - removal, overhaul and refitting 13
Sump - removal and refitting 12
Timing belt - removal and refitting 7
Timing belt covers - removal and refitting 6
Timing belt sprockets, tensioner and idler pulleys - removal and
  refitting 8
Top dead centre (TDC) for No 1 piston - locating 3

2B

Degrees of difficulty

Easy, suitable for novice with little experience		Fairly easy, suitable for beginner with some experience		Fairly difficult, suitable for competent DIY mechanic		Difficult, suitable for experienced DIY mechanic		Very difficult, suitable for expert DIY or professional	

Specifications

General

Engine type	Four-cylinder, in-line, water-cooled. Double overhead camshaft, belt-driven
Manufacturer's engine code*	X22XE
Bore	86.0 mm
Stroke	94.6 mm
Capacity	2198 cc
Firing order	1-3-4-2 (No 1 cylinder at timing belt end)
Direction of crankshaft rotation	Clockwise (viewed from timing belt end of engine)
Compression ratio	10.5:1

* The engine code forms the first five digits of the engine number (see Vehicle identification section of this manual)

Camshaft

Endfloat	0.04 to 0.15 mm
Maximum permissible radial run-out	0.06 mm
Cam lift (inlet and exhaust)	10.0 mm
Camshaft bearing journal diameter	27.960 to 27.939 mm
Camshaft bearing bore internal diameter	28.000 to 28.021 mm

Lubrication system

Oil pump type . . . .   Gear-type, driven directly from crankshaft
Minimum permissible oil pressure at idle speed, with engine
  at operating temperature (oil temperature of at least 70°C) . . . .   1.5 bar (22 psi)
Oil pump clearances:
  Inner-to-outer gear teeth clearance . . . .   0.10 to 0.20 mm
  Gear endfloat . . . .   0.03 to 0.10 mm

Torque wrench settings

	Nm	lbf ft
Camshaft bearing cap bolts	8	6
Camshaft cover bolts	8	6
Camshaft sprocket bolt*:		
Stage 1	50	37
Stage 2	Angle-tighten a further 60°	
Stage 3	Angle-tighten a further 15°	
Connecting rod big-end bearing cap bolt*:		
Stage 1	35	26
Stage 2	Angle-tighten a further 45°	
Stage 3	Angle-tighten a further 15°	
Crankshaft pulley bolts	20	15
Crankshaft sprocket bolt*:		
Stage 1	130	96
Stage 2	Angle-tighten a further 40 to 50°	
Cylinder head bolts*:		
Stage 1	25	18
Stage 2	Angle-tighten a further 90°	
Stage 3	Angle-tighten a further 90°	
Stage 4	Angle-tighten a further 90°	
Engine/transmission mounting bolts:		
Left- and right-hand mounting:		
Mounting-to-chassis bolts	50	37
Mounting-to-engine bracket nuts	85	63
Rear mounting:		
Mounting-to-transmission bolts	50	37
Mounting-to-subframe nuts	50	37
Engine-to-transmission unit bolts	68	50
Flywheel bolts:		
Stage 1	65	48
Stage 2	Angle-tighten a further 30°	
Stage 3	Angle-tighten a further 15°	
Main bearing cap bolts*:		
Stage 1	50	37
Stage 2	Angle-tighten a further 45°	
Stage 3	Angle-tighten a further 15°	
Oil cooler hose union nuts	25	18
Oil pump:		
Oil pressure relief valve bolt	30	22
Retaining bolts	6	4
Pump cover screws	6	4
Oil pump pick-up/strainer bolts	8	6
Sump bolts:		
Pre 1997 models	15	11
1997 onwards models	20	15
Drain plug	45	33
Timing belt cover bolts	6	4
Timing belt idler pulley:		
Mounting bracket bolts	25	18
Pulley bolt	25	18
Timing belt tensioner bolt	25	18
Transmission crossmember bolts	80	59

New bolts should be used

1 General information

How to use this Chapter

1 This Part of Chapter 2 is devoted to in-car repair procedures for the 2.2 litre petrol engine. All procedures concerning engine removal and refitting, and engine block/cylinder head overhaul can be found in Chapter 2G.

2 Most of the operations included in this Part are based on the assumption that the engine is still installed in the car. Therefore, if this information is being used during a complete engine overhaul, with the engine already removed, many of the steps included here will not apply.

Engine description

3 The engine is a double overhead camshaft (DOHC), four-cylinder, in-line unit, mounted at the front of the car, with the clutch and transmission on its rear.

4 The cylinder block is of the dry-liner type. The crankshaft is supported within the cylinder block on five shell-type main bearings. Thrustwashers are fitted to number 3 main bearing, to control crankshaft endfloat.

5 The connecting rods are attached to the crankshaft by horizontally split shell-type big-end bearings, and to the pistons by interference-fit gudgeon pins. The aluminium alloy pistons are of the slipper type, and are fitted with three piston rings, comprising two compression rings and a scraper-type oil control ring.

6 The camshafts run directly in the cylinder head, and driven by the crankshaft via a toothed rubber timing belt (which also drives the coolant pump). The camshafts operate each valve via a follower. Each follower incorporates a hydraulic self-adjusting valve which automatically adjusts the valve clearance.

7 Lubrication is by pressure-feed from a gear-type oil pump, which is mounted on the front end of the crankshaft. It draws oil through a strainer located in the sump, and then forces it through an externally-mounted full-flow cartridge-type filter. The oil flows into galleries in the main bearing cap bridge arrangement and cylinder block/crankcase, from where it is distributed to the crankshaft (main bearings) and camshaft(s). The big-end bearings are supplied with oil via internal drillings in the crankshaft, while the camshaft bearings also receive a pressurised supply. The camshaft lobes and valves are lubricated by splash, as are all other engine components. An oil cooler is fitted to keep the oil temperature stable under arduous operating conditions.

8 A semi-closed crankcase ventilation system is employed; crankcase fumes are drawn from the cylinder head cover, and passed via a hose to the inlet manifold.

Repair operations possible with the engine in the car

9 The following operations can be carried out without having to remove the engine from the vehicle.
a) Removal and refitting of the cylinder head.
b) Removal and refitting of the timing belt and sprockets.
c) Renewal of the camshaft oil seals.
d) Removal and refitting of the camshafts and followers.
e) Removal and refitting of the sump.
f) Removal and refitting of the connecting rods and pistons*.
g) Removal and refitting of the oil pump.
h) Renewal of the crankshaft oil seals.
i) Renewal of the engine mountings.
j) Removal and refitting of the flywheel.
* Although the operation marked with an asterisk can be carried out with the engine in the car after removal of the sump, it is better for the engine to be removed, in the interests of cleanliness and improved access. For this reason, the procedure is described in Chapter 2G.

2 Compression test - description and interpretation

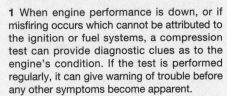

1 When engine performance is down, or if misfiring occurs which cannot be attributed to the ignition or fuel systems, a compression test can provide diagnostic clues as to the engine's condition. If the test is performed regularly, it can give warning of trouble before any other symptoms become apparent.

2 The engine must be fully warmed-up to normal operating temperature, the battery must be fully charged, and the spark plugs must be removed (see Chapter 1A). The aid of an assistant will also be required.

3 Disable the ignition system by disconnecting the wiring connector from the ignition system DIS module (see Chapter 5B) and the fuel system by removing the fuel pump relay (see Chapter 13).

4 Fit a compression tester to the number 1 cylinder spark plug hole; the type of tester which screws into the plug thread is to be preferred.

5 Have the assistant hold the throttle wide open and crank the engine on the starter motor; after one or two revolutions, the compression pressure should build up to a maximum figure, and then stabilise. Record the highest reading obtained.

6 Repeat the test on the remaining cylinders, recording the pressure in each.

7 All cylinders should produce very similar pressures; a difference of more than 2 bar between any two cylinders indicates a fault. Note that the compression should build up quickly in a healthy engine; low compression on the first stroke, followed by gradually-increasing pressure on successive strokes, indicates worn piston rings. A low compression reading on the first stroke, which does not build up during successive strokes, indicates leaking valves or a blown head gasket (a cracked head could also be the cause). Deposits on the undersides of the valve heads can also cause low compression.

8 Although Vauxhall do not specify exact compression pressures, as a guide, any cylinder pressure of below 10 bar can be considered as less than healthy. Refer to a Vauxhall dealer or other specialist if in doubt as to whether a particular pressure reading is acceptable.

9 If the addition of a little oil temporarily improves the compression pressure, this indicates that bore or piston wear is responsible for the pressure loss. No improvement suggests that leaking or burnt valves, or a blown head gasket, may be to blame.

10 A low reading from two adjacent cylinders is almost certainly due to the head gasket having blown between them; the presence of coolant in the engine oil will confirm this.

11 If one cylinder is about 20 per cent lower than the others, and the engine has a slightly rough idle, a worn camshaft lobe could be the cause.

12 If the compression reading is unusually high, the combustion chambers are probably coated with carbon deposits. If this is the case, the cylinder head should be removed and decarbonised.

13 On completion of the test, refit the spark plugs (see Chapter 1A), refit the fuel pump relay and reconnect the wiring connector to the DIS module.

3 Top dead centre (TDC) for No 1 piston - locating

1 In its travel up and down its cylinder bore, Top Dead Centre (TDC) is the highest point that each piston reaches as the crankshaft rotates. While each piston reaches TDC both at the top of the compression stroke and again at the top of the exhaust stroke, for the purpose of timing the engine, TDC refers to the piston position (usually number 1) at the top of its compression stroke.

2 Number 1 piston (and cylinder) is at the front (timing belt) end of the engine, and its TDC position is located as follows. Note that the crankshaft rotates clockwise when viewed from the front of the vehicle.

3 Disconnect the battery negative terminal. If necessary, remove all the spark plugs as described in Chapter 1A to enable the engine to be easily turned over.

4 To gain access to the camshaft sprocket timing marks, remove the timing belt outer cover as described in Section 6.

5 Remove the crankshaft pulley as described in Section 5.

2B

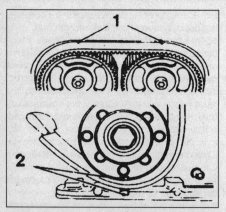

3.6 Align the camshaft sprocket marks with the marks on the top of the camshaft cover (1), and the crankshaft sprocket mark with the mark on the inner cover (2)

6 Using a socket and extension bar on the crankshaft sprocket bolt, rotate the crankshaft until the timing marks on the camshaft sprockets are both at the top and are correctly aligned with the marks on the camshaft cover. With the camshaft sprocket marks correctly positioned, align the mark on the crankshaft sprocket rim with the mark on the timing belt inner cover **(see illustration)**. The engine is now positioned with No 1 piston at TDC on its compression stroke.

4 Camshaft cover -
removal and refitting

Removal

1 Slacken the retaining clips and disconnect the breather hoses from the right-hand side of the cover.
2 Undo the retaining screws and remove the spark plug cover. Disconnect the plug caps from the plugs then unclip the HT leads and position them clear of the cover.
3 Disconnect the camshaft sensor wiring connector and unclip the wiring from the camshaft cover.
4 Evenly and progressively slacken and remove the camshaft cover retaining bolts.
5 Lift the camshaft cover away from the cylinder head and recover the cover seal and the sealing rings which are fitted to each of the retaining bolt holes. Examine the seal and sealing rings for signs of wear or damage and renew if necessary.

Refitting

6 Ensure the cover and cylinder head surfaces are clean and dry then fit the camshaft seal securely to the cover groove. Fit the sealing rings to the recesses around each retaining bolt hole, holding them in position with a smear of grease.
7 Carefully manoeuvre the camshaft cover into position, taking great care to ensure all the sealing rings remain correctly seated. Refit the cover retaining bolts and tighten the retaining bolts to the specified torque, working in a spiral pattern from the centre outwards.
8 Reconnect the breather hoses, securing them in position with the retaining clips, and securely reconnect the plug caps to the spark plugs.
9 Reconnect the wiring connector to the camshaft sensor, ensure it is correctly routed and retained by the cover clips. Refit the spark plug cover, tightening its retaining screws securely.

5 Crankshaft pulley -
removal and refitting

Removal

1 Remove the auxiliary drivebelt as described in Chapter 1A. Prior to removal, mark the direction of rotation on the belt to ensure the belt is refitted the same way around.
2 Slacken and remove the small retaining bolts securing the pulley to the crankshaft sprocket and remove the pulley from the engine. If necessary, prevent crankshaft rotation by holding the sprocket retaining bolt with a suitable socket.

Refitting

3 Ensure the crankshaft sprocket and pulley mating surfaces are clean and dry then refit the pulley, tightening its retaining bolts to the specified torque.
4 Refit the auxiliary drivebelt as described in Chapter 1A, using the mark made prior to removal to ensure the belt is fitted the correct way around.

6 Timing belt covers -
removal and refitting

Removal
Outer cover

1 Slacken the retaining clip and disconnect the intake hose from the resonator chamber which is located between the front of the engine and the radiator. Slacken and remove the retaining bolts and spacers and remove the resonator from the rear of the radiator, taking care not to lose the mounting rubbers or washer.
2 Remove the auxiliary drivebelt as described in Chapter 1A. Prior to removal, mark the direction of rotation on the belt to ensure the belt is refitted the same way around. Where necessary, unscrew the retaining bolt and remove the belt idler pulley (where fitted) from the front of the engine.
3 Slacken and remove the retaining bolts and remove the cover from the engine unit along with its seal **(see illustrations)**.

Rear cover

4 Remove the timing belt as described in Section 7.
5 Remove the camshaft sprockets, crankshaft sprocket, the timing belt tensioner and the idler pulley assembly as described in Section 8.
6 Undo the retaining bolts and remove the rear cover from the engine unit.

Refitting

7 Refitting is the reverse of removal, tightening all bolts to the specified torque.

7 Timing belt -
removal and refitting

Note: *The timing belt must be removed and refitted with the engine cold.*

Removal

1 Remove the crankshaft pulley as described in Section 5.
2 Remove the timing belt outer cover as described in Section 6.
3 Position No 1 cylinder at TDC on its compression stroke as described in Section 3.
4 With the timing marks correctly aligned, slacken the timing belt tensioner bolt. Using an Allen key, rotate the tensioner arm clockwise to its stop, to relieve the tension in

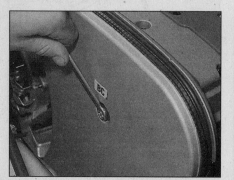

6.3a Unscrew the retaining bolts . . .

6.3b . . . then remove the timing belt outer cover from the engine, complete with seal

7.4 Slacken the tensioner pulley bolt (1) and rotate the tensioner arm clockwise using an Allen key in the arm cutout (2)

the timing belt, and hold it in position by and securely tighten the retaining bolt **(see illustration)**.

5 Slide the timing belt off from its sprockets and remove it from the engine. If the belt is to be re-used, use white paint or similar to mark the direction of rotation on the belt. **Do not** rotate the crankshaft or camshafts until the timing belt has been refitted.

6 Check the timing belt carefully for any signs of uneven wear, splitting or oil contamination, and renew it if there is the slightest doubt about its condition. If the engine is undergoing an overhaul and has covered over 36 000 miles, or it was more than 4 years since the original belt was fitted, renew the belt as a matter of course, regardless of its apparent condition. If signs of oil contamination are found, trace the source of the oil leak and rectify it, then wash down the engine timing belt area and all related components to remove all traces of oil.

Refitting

7 On reassembly, thoroughly clean the timing belt sprockets and tensioner/idler pulleys. Carefully check the tensioner/idler pulleys for any signs of damage, and particularly for any signs of cracking. It may be prudent to replace these components as a matter of course, regardless of their apparent condition, to avoid any future problems.

8 Check that the camshaft sprocket timing marks are still correctly aligned with the

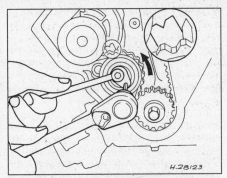

7.10 Tension the timing belt by rotating the tensioner arm fully anti-clockwise until the pointer is positioned as shown

camshaft cover marks and the crankshaft sprocket mark is still aligned with the mark on the cover.

9 Fit the timing belt over the crankshaft and camshaft sprockets and around the idler pulleys, ensuring that the belt run between the exhaust camshaft and crankshaft sprockets is taut (ie, all slack is on the tensioner side of the belt), then fit the belt over the coolant pump sprocket and tensioner pulley. Do not twist the belt sharply while refitting it. Ensure that the belt teeth are correctly seated centrally in the sprockets, and that the timing marks remain in alignment. If a used belt is being refitted, ensure that the arrow mark made on removal points in the normal direction of rotation, as before.

10 Slacken the timing belt tensioner bolt to release the tensioner spring. Rotate tensioner arm anti-clockwise until the tensioner pointer is fully over against its stop, without exerting any excess strain on the belt. Hold the tensioner in position and securely tighten its retaining bolt **(see illustration)**.

11 Check the sprocket timing marks are still correctly aligned **(see illustration)**. If adjustment is necessary, release the tensioner again then disengage the belt from the sprockets and make any necessary adjustments.

12 Using a socket on the crankshaft sprocket bolt, rotate the crankshaft smoothly through two complete turns (720°) in the normal direction of rotation to settle the timing belt in position.

13 Check that both the camshaft and

crankshaft sprocket timing marks are correctly realigned then slacken the tensioner bolt.

14 If a new timing belt is being fitted, adjust the tensioner so that the pointer is aligned with the cutout on the backplate **(see illustration)**. Hold the tensioner in the correct position and tighten its retaining bolt to the specified torque. Rotate the crankshaft smoothly through another two complete turns in the normal direction of rotation, to bring the sprocket timing marks back into alignment. Check that the tensioner pointer is still aligned with the backplate cutout.

15 If the original belt is being refitted, adjust the tensioner so that the pointer is positioned 4 mm to the left of the cutout on the backplate **(see illustration)**. Hold the tensioner in the correct position and tighten its retaining bolt to the specified torque. Rotate the crankshaft smoothly through another two complete turns in the normal direction of rotation, to bring the sprocket timing marks back into alignment. Check that the tensioner pointer is still correctly positioned in relation to the backplate cutout.

16 If the tensioner pointer is not correctly positioned in relation to the backplate, repeat the procedure in paragraph 14 (new belt) or 15 (original belt), as applicable.

17 Once the tensioner pointer and backplate remain correctly aligned, refit the timing belt cover and crankshaft pulley as described in Sections 5 and 6.

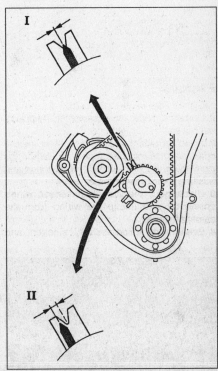

7.15 Timing belt tensioner pointer positions

I   *Location if a new belt is being fitted*
II *Location if the original belt is being re-used (pointer should be 4 mm to the left of the backplate cutout)*

7.11 Check that the sprocket timing marks are still correctly aligned

7.14 If a new belt is being fitted, position the tensioner so that the pointer is aligned with the backplate cutout

2B

8 Timing belt sprockets, tensioner and idler pulleys - removal and refitting

Camshaft sprockets

Note: *New sprocket retaining bolt(s) will be required on refitting.*

Removal

1 Remove the timing belt as described in Section 7.

2 The camshaft must be prevented from turning as the sprocket bolt is unscrewed, and this can be achieved in one of two ways as follows.

a) *Make up a sprocket-holding tool using two lengths of steel strip (one long, the other short), and three nuts and bolts; one nut and bolt forms the pivot of a forked tool, with the remaining two nuts and bolts at the tips of the 'forks' to engage with the sprocket spokes.*

b) *Remove the camshaft cover as described in Section 4 and hold the camshaft with an open-ended spanner on the flats provided* (see illustration).

3 Unscrew the retaining bolt and washer and remove the sprocket from the end of the camshaft. If the sprocket locating pin is a loose fit in the camshaft end, remove it and store it with the sprocket for safe-keeping.

4 If necessary, remove the remaining sprocket using the same method (both sprockets are the same).

Refitting

5 Prior to refitting check the oil seal(s) for signs of damage or leakage. If necessary, renew as described in Section 9.

6 Ensure the locating pin is in position in the camshaft end.

7 Both inlet and exhaust camshaft sprockets are the same, but each one is equipped with two locating pin cutouts. If the sprocket is being fitted to the inlet camshaft, engage the locating pin in the IN cutout, and if the sprocket is being fitted to the exhaust camshaft engage the locating pin in the EX (see illustration). Ensure the camshaft locating pin is engaged in the correct sprocket cutout then fit the washer and new retaining bolt.

8 Prevent rotation by the method used on removal, and tighten the sprocket retaining bolt to the specified stage 1 torque setting then angle-tighten the bolt through the specified stage 2 angle, using a socket and extension bar, and finally through the specified stage 3 angle. It is recommended that an angle-measuring gauge is used during the final stages of the tightening, to ensure accuracy. If a gauge is not available, use white paint to make alignment marks between the bolt head and sprocket prior to tightening; the marks can then be used to check that the bolt has been rotated through the correct angle.

9 Refit the timing belt as described in Section 7 then (where necessary) refit the camshaft cover as described in Section 4.

Crankshaft sprocket

Note: *A new crankshaft sprocket retaining bolt will be required on refitting.*

Removal

10 Remove the timing belt as described in Section 7.

11 Slacken the crankshaft sprocket retaining bolt. To prevent crankshaft rotation, have an assistant select top gear and apply the brakes firmly. If the engine is removed from the vehicle it will be necessary to lock the flywheel (see Section 15).

12 Unscrew the retaining bolt and washer then remove the crankshaft sprocket from the end of the crankshaft. If necessary, remove the Woodruff key from the crankshaft end then slide the spacer off of the crankshaft.

Refitting

13 Where necessary, slide the spacer onto the crankshaft then refit the Woodruff key to the crankshaft slot.

14 Align the sprocket groove with the Woodruff key and slide the sprocket into position. Fit the washer and new retaining bolt.

15 Lock the crankshaft by the method used on removal, and tighten the sprocket retaining bolt to the specified stage 1 torque setting then angle-tighten the bolt through the specified stage 2 angle, using a socket and extension bar. It is recommended that an angle-measuring gauge is used during the

final stages of the tightening, to ensure accuracy. If a gauge is not available, use white paint to make alignment marks between the bolt head and sprocket prior to tightening; the marks can then be used to check that the bolt has been rotated through the correct angle.

16 Refit the timing belt as described in Section 7.

Tensioner assembly

Removal

17 Remove the timing belt as described in Section 7.

18 Slacken and remove the retaining bolt and remove the tensioner assembly from the engine.

Refitting

19 Fit the tensioner to the engine, making sure that the lug on the backplate is correctly located in the oil pump housing hole. Ensure the tensioner is correctly seated then refit the retaining bolt. Using an Allen key, rotate the tensioner arm clockwise to its stop then securely tighten the retaining bolt.

20 Refit the timing belt as described in Section 7.

Idler pulleys

Removal

21 Remove the timing belt as described in Section 7.

22 Slacken and remove the retaining bolt(s) and remove the idler pulley(s) from the engine. If necessary, unbolt the pulley mounting bracket and remove it from the cylinder block.

Refitting

23 Refit the pulley mounting bracket (where removed) to the cylinder block and tighten its retaining bolts to the specified torque.

24 Refit the idler pulley(s) and tighten the retaining bolt(s) to the specified torque.

25 Refit the timing belt as described in Section 7.

9 Camshaft oil seals - renewal

1 Remove the relevant camshaft sprocket as described in Section 8.

2 Carefully punch or drill two small holes opposite each other in the oil seal. Screw a self-tapping screw into each, and pull on the screws with pliers to extract the seal.

3 Clean the seal housing, and polish off any burrs or raised edges which may have caused the seal to fail in the first place.

4 Lubricate the lips of the new seal with clean engine oil, and press it into position using a suitable tubular drift (such as a socket) which bears only on the hard outer edge of the seal. Take care not to damage the seal lips during fitting; note that the seal lips should face inwards.

5 Refit the camshaft sprocket as described in Section 8.

8.2 Using an open-ended spanner to retain the camshaft whilst the sprocket retaining bolt is slackened

8.7 Ensure the locating pin is engaged in the correct sprocket hole on refitting (see text)

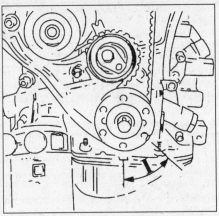

10.1 Prior to removing the timing belt, rotate the crankshaft 60° backwards to ensure the camshafts are correctly positioned

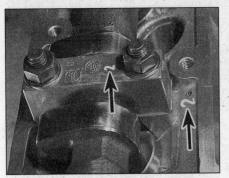

10.3 The identification numbers should be marked on both the bearing caps and cylinder head (arrowed)

10.6 Using a rubber sucker to remove a camshaft follower

10 Camshaft and followers - removal, inspection and refitting

Removal

1 Remove the timing belt as described in Section 7. Prior to releasing the timing belt tension and removing the belt, rotate the crankshaft **backwards** by approximately 60° (4 teeth of movement); this will position the camshafts so that the valve spring pressure is evenly exerted along the complete length of the shaft, reducing the risk of the bearing caps being damaged on removal/refitting **(see illustration)**.

2 Remove the camshaft sprockets as described in Section 8.

3 Starting on the inlet camshaft, working in a spiral pattern from the outside inwards, slacken the camshaft bearing cap retaining bolts by one turn at a time, to relieve the pressure of the valve springs on the bearing caps gradually and evenly. Once the valve spring pressure has been relieved, the bolts can be fully unscrewed and removed along with the caps; the bearing caps and the

cylinder head locations are numbered to ensure the caps are correctly positioned on refitting **(see illustration)**. Take care not to loose the locating dowels (where fitted).
Caution: If the bearing cap bolts are carelessly slackened, the bearing caps might break. If any bearing cap breaks then the complete cylinder head assembly must be renewed; the bearing caps are matched to the head and are not available separately.

4 Lift the camshaft out of the cylinder head and slide off the oil seal.

5 Repeat the operations described in paragraphs 3 and 4 and remove the exhaust camshaft.

6 Obtain sixteen small, clean plastic containers, and label them for identification. Alternatively, divide a larger container into compartments. Lift the followers out from the top of the cylinder head and store each one in its respective fitted position **(see illustration)**.
Note: *Store all the followers the correct way up to prevent the oil draining from the hydraulic valve adjustment mechanisms.*

Inspection

7 Examine the camshaft bearing surfaces and cam lobes for signs of wear ridges and scoring. Renew the camshaft if any of these conditions are apparent. Examine the condition of the bearing surfaces both on the camshaft journals and in the cylinder head. If

the head bearing surfaces are worn excessively, the cylinder head will need to be renewed.

8 Support the camshaft end journals on V-blocks, and measure the run-out at the centre journal using a dial gauge. If the run-out exceeds the specified limit, the camshaft should be renewed.

9 Examine the follower bearing surfaces which contact the camshaft lobes for wear ridges and scoring. Check the followers and their bores in the cylinder head for signs of wear or damage. If any follower is thought to be faulty or is visibly worn it should be renewed.

Refitting

10 Where removed, lubricate the followers with clean engine oil and carefully insert each one into its original location in the cylinder head.

11 Lubricate the camshaft followers with clean engine oil then lay the camshafts in position. Ensure the crankshaft is still positioned approximately 60° BTDC and position each camshaft so that the lobes of No 1 cylinder are pointing upwards. Temporarily refit the sprockets to the camshafts and position each one so that its sprocket timing mark is approximately 4 teeth before its TDC alignment position.

12 Ensure the mating surfaces of the bearing caps and cylinder head are clean and dry and lubricate the camshaft journals and lobes with clean engine oil.

13 Apply a smear of sealant to the mating surfaces of both the inlet and exhaust camshaft front bearing caps **(see illustration)**.

14 Ensure the locating dowels (where fitted) are in position then refit the camshaft bearing caps and the retaining bolts in their original locations on the cylinder head **(see illustration)**. The caps are numbered from front to rear and the corresponding numbers are marked on the cylinder head upper surface.

15 Working on the inlet camshaft, tighten the bearing cap bolts by hand only then, working in a spiral pattern from the centre outwards,

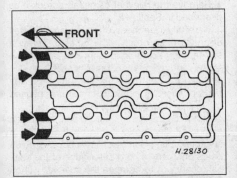

10.13 Apply a smear of sealant to the cylinder head mating surface of the front bearing caps

10.14 Refit the bearing caps using the identification markings to ensure each one is correctly fitted

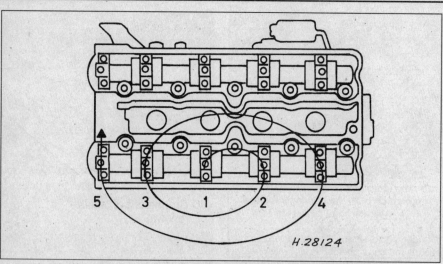

10.15 Camshaft bearing cap bolt tightening sequence (see text)

tighten the bolts by one turn at a time to gradually impose the pressure of the valve springs on the bearing caps **(see illustration)**. Repeat this sequence until all bearing caps are in contact with the cylinder head then go around and tighten the camshaft retaining bolts to the specified torque.
Caution: If the bearing cap bolts are carelessly tightened, the bearing caps might break. If any bearing cap breaks then the complete cylinder head assembly must be renewed; the bearing caps are matched to the head and are not available separately.
16 Tighten the exhaust camshaft bearing cap bolts as described in paragraph 15 **(see illustration)**.
17 Fit new camshaft oil seals as described in Section 9.
18 Refit the camshaft sprockets as described in Section 8.
19 Align all the sprocket timing marks to bring the camshafts and crankshaft back to TDC then refit the timing belt as described in Section 7.

20 Refit the camshaft cover and timing belt cover as described in Sections 4 and 6.

---

11 Cylinder head - removal and refitting

Removal

Note: *The engine must be cold when removing the cylinder head. New cylinder head bolts must be used on refitting.*
1 Disconnect the battery negative lead.
2 Drain the cooling system and remove the spark plugs as described in Chapter 1A.
3 Remove the camshafts as described in Section 10.
4 Remove the inlet and exhaust manifolds as described in Chapter 4A. If no work is to be carried out on the cylinder head, the head can be removed complete with manifolds once all the hoses/wiring, etc have been disconnected and the alternator and front pipe have been unbolted (see Chapter 4A).

5 Undo the retaining bolts securing the timing belt rear cover to the cylinder head.
6 Disconnect the wiring connectors from the DIS module, coolant temperature sensors, EGR valve and evaporative emission system purge valve, all which are mounted on the rear of the cylinder head. Free the wiring harness from its retaining clips and position it clear of the cylinder head.
7 Release the retaining clips and disconnect the all the coolant hoses from the cylinder head.
8 Make a final check to ensure that all relevant hoses, pipes and wires, etc, have been disconnected.
9 Working in the **reverse** of the tightening sequence **(see illustration 11.22a)**, progressively slacken the cylinder head bolts by a third of a turn at a time until all bolts can be unscrewed by hand. Remove each bolt in turn, along with its washer.
10 Lift the cylinder head from the cylinder block. If necessary, tap the cylinder head gently with a soft-faced mallet to free it from the block, but **do not** lever at the mating faces. Note the fitted positions of the two locating dowels, and remove them for safe keeping if they are loose.
11 Recover the cylinder head gasket, and discard it.

Preparation for refitting

12 The mating faces of the cylinder head and block must be perfectly clean before refitting the head. Use a scraper to remove all traces of gasket and carbon, and also clean the tops of the pistons. Take particular care with the aluminium surfaces, as the soft metal is damaged easily. Also, make sure that debris is not allowed to enter the oil and water channels - this is particularly important for the oil circuit, as carbon could block the oil supply to the camshaft or crankshaft bearings. Using adhesive tape and paper, seal the water, oil and bolt holes in the cylinder block. To prevent carbon entering the gap between the pistons and bores, smear a little grease in the gap.

10.16 Working as described in the text, carefully tighten the bearing cap bolts to the specified torque

11.19 Ensure the head gasket is fitted with the OBEN/TOP marking uppermost

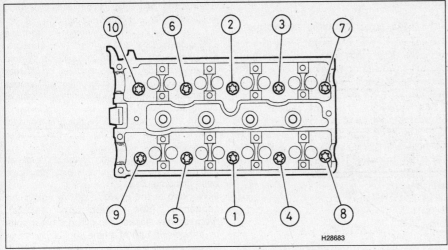

11.22 Cylinder head bolt tightening sequence

After cleaning the piston, rotate the crankshaft so that the piston moves down the bore, then wipe out the grease and carbon with a cloth rag. Clean the piston crowns in the same way.

13 Check the block and head for nicks, deep scratches and other damage. If slight, they may be removed carefully with a file. More serious damage may be repaired by machining, but this is a specialist job.

14 If warpage of the cylinder head is suspected, use a straight-edge to check it for distortion. Refer to Chapter 2G if necessary.

15 Ensure that the cylinder head bolt holes in the crankcase are clean and free of oil. Syringe or soak up any oil left in the bolt holes. This is most important in order that the correct bolt tightening torque can be applied and to prevent the possibility of the block being cracked by hydraulic pressure when the bolts are tightened.

16 Renew the cylinder head bolts regardless of their apparent condition.

Refitting

17 Ensure the crankshaft is till positioned approximately 60° BTDC and wipe clean the mating faces of the head and block.

18 Ensure that the two locating dowels are in position at each end of the cylinder block/crankcase surface.

19 Fit the new cylinder head gasket to the block, making sure it is fitted with the correct way up with its OBEN or TOP mark uppermost **(see illustration)**.

20 Carefully refit the cylinder head, locating it on the dowels.

21 Fit the washers to the new cylinder head bolts then carefully insert them into position **(do not drop)**, tightening them finger-tight only at this stage.

22 Working progressively and in the sequence shown, first tighten all the cylinder head bolts to the stage 1 torque setting **(see illustration)**.

23 Once all bolts have been tightened to the stage 1 torque, again working in the sequence shown, tighten each bolt through its specified stage 2 angle, using a socket and extension bar. It is recommended that an angle-measuring gauge is used during this stage of the tightening, to ensure accuracy.

24 Working in the specified sequence, go around again and tighten all bolts through the specified stage 3 angle.

25 Finally go around in the specified sequence again and tighten all bolts through the specified stage 4 angle.

26 Reconnect the coolant hoses, securing them in position with the retaining clips.

27 Refit the timing belt rear cover retaining bolts and tighten them to the specified torque.

28 Reconnect the wiring connectors to the components on the rear of the cylinder head (see paragraph 6), ensuring the harness is correctly routed and retained by all the necessary clips.

29 Refit the timing belt rear cover retaining bolts and tighten them to the specified torque.

30 Refit the camshafts as described in Section 10.

31 Refit/reconnect the inlet and exhaust manifolds (see Chapter 4A).

32 Ensure all pipes and hoses are securely reconnected then refill the cooling system and refit the spark plugs as described in Chapter 1A.

33 Reconnect the battery then start the engine and check for signs of leaks.

12 Sump - removal and refitting

1 Refer to Chapter 2A, Section 13.

13 Oil pump - removal, overhaul and refitting

1 Refer to Chapter 2A, Section 14.

14 Oil cooler - removal and refitting

1 Refer to Chapter 2A, Section 15.

15 Flywheel - removal, inspection and refitting

1 Refer to Chapter 2A, Section 16.

16 Crankshaft oil seals - renewal

Front (timing belt end) oil seal

1 Remove the crankshaft sprocket as described in Section 8.

2 Carefully punch or drill two small holes opposite each other in the oil seal. Screw a self-tapping screw into each and pull on the screws with pliers to extract the seal.

Caution: Great care must be taken to avoid damage to the oil pump

3 Clean the seal housing and polish off any burrs or raised edges which may have caused the seal to fail in the first place.

4 Lubricate the lips of the new seal with clean engine oil and ease it into position on the end of the shaft. Press the seal squarely into position until it is flush with the housing. If necessary, a suitable tubular drift, such as a socket, which bears only on the hard outer edge of the seal can be used to tap the seal into position. Take great care not to damage the seal lips during fitting and ensure that the seal lips face inwards.

5 Wash off any traces of oil, then refit the crankshaft sprocket as described in Section 8.

Rear (flywheel end) oil seal

6 Remove the flywheel as described in Section 15.

7 Renew the seal as described in paragraphs 2 to 4.

8 Refit the flywheel as described in Section 15.

17 Engine/transmission mountings - inspection and renewal

Inspection

1 If improved access is required, raise the front of the car and support it securely on axle stands. Where necessary, undo the retaining bolts and remove the undercover from beneath the engine/transmission unit.

2 Check the mounting rubber to see if it is cracked, hardened or separated from the

2B

metal at any point; renew the mounting if any such damage or deterioration is evident.

3 Check that all the mountings' fasteners are securely tightened; use a torque wrench to check if possible.

4 Using a large screwdriver or a pry bar, check for wear in the mounting by carefully levering against it to check for free play; where this is not possible, enlist the aid of an assistant to move the engine/transmission unit back and forth, or from side-to-side, while you watch the mounting. While some free play is to be expected even from new components, excessive wear should be obvious. If excessive free play is found, check first that the fasteners are correctly secured, then renew any worn components as described below.

Renewal

Left- and right-hand side mountings

5 Slacken and remove the bolts securing both the left- and right-hand mountings to the chassis and unscrew the nut securing each mounting to its engine bracket.

6 Attach an engine hoist to the lifting brackets on the cylinder head and raise the engine slightly until there is sufficient clearance to manoeuvre the mountings out of position. On the left-hand side, note the correct fitted position of the mounting rubber heatshield on removal.

7 Refitting is the reverse of removal tightening the mounting nuts and bolts to the specified torque.

Rear mounting

8 Position a jack underneath the transmission unit and raise the jack until it is supporting the weight of the transmission.

9 Slacken and remove the nuts securing the mounting to the crossmember then unbolt the crossmember from the chassis and remove it from underneath the vehicle.

10 Slacken and remove the nuts and bolts securing the exhaust pipe mounting bracket to the mounting.

11 Unbolt the rear mounting from the underside of the transmission unit, noting the correct fitted location of the heatshield, and remove it from underneath the vehicle.

12 Refitting is the reverse of removal; tightening all bolts to their specified torque settings.

Chapter 2 Part C
2.4 litre petrol engine in-car repair procedures

Contents

Camshaft - removal, inspection and refitting 11
Compression test - description and interpretation 2
Crankshaft oil seals - renewal 15
Crankshaft pulley - removal and refitting 6
Cylinder head - removal and refitting 12
Cylinder head cover - removal and refitting 5
Engine oil and filter renewal ....See Chapter 1A
Engine oil level check ....See Chapter 1A
Engine/transmission mountings - inspection and renewal 17
Flywheel - removal, inspection and refitting 16
General engine checks ....See Chapter 1A

General information 1
Hydraulic valve lifters - adjustment 4
Oil pump - removal, inspection and refitting 14
Rocker arms and hydraulic valve lifters - removal, inspection
   and refitting 10
Sump - removal and refitting 13
Timing chain and sprockets - removal, inspection and refitting 9
Timing chain cover - removal and refitting 7
Timing chain tensioner and guides - removal and refitting 8
Top dead centre (TDC) for No 1 piston - locating 3

Degrees of difficulty

| Easy, suitable for novice with little experience 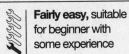 | Fairly easy, suitable for beginner with some experience 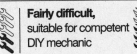 | Fairly difficult, suitable for competent DIY mechanic | Difficult, suitable for experienced DIY mechanic | Very difficult, suitable for expert DIY or professional |

Specifications

General

Engine type	Four-cylinder, in-line, water-cooled. Cam-in-head (CIH)
Manufacturer's engine code*	C24NE
Bore	95.0 mm
Stroke	69.8 mm
Capacity	2410 cc
Firing order	1-3-4-2 (No 1 cylinder at timing chain end of engine)
Direction of crankshaft rotation	Clockwise (viewed from timing chain end of engine)
Compression ratio	9.0:1

* The engine code forms the first five digits of the engine number (see Vehicle identification section of this manual)

Camshaft

Endfloat	0.1 to 0.2 mm
Maximum permissible radial run-out	0.025 mm
Cam lift (inlet and exhaust)	6.86 mm

Lubrication system

Oil pump type	Gear-type, driven by crankshaft via the distributor shaft
Minimum permissible oil pressure at idle speed, with engine at operating temperature (oil temperature of at least 80°C)	1.0 bar (15 psi)
Oil pump clearances:	
Gear teeth clearance	0.10 to 0.20 mm
Gear endfloat	0.10 to 0.20 mm

Torque wrench settings

	Nm	lbf ft
Camshaft sprocket bolts	25	18
Connecting rod big-end bearing cap bolt	43	32
Crankshaft pulley bolt	120	89
Cylinder head (main) bolts*:		
Stage 1	60	44
Stage 2	Angle-tighten a further 90°	
Warm engine up to normal operating temperature then:		
Stage 3	Angle-tighten a further 35°	
Cylinder head-to-timing chain cover bolts	25	18
Engine/transmission mounting bolts:		
Left- and right-hand mounting:		
Mounting-to-engine bracket nut	85	62
Mounting-to-body bolts	50	37
Rear mounting:		
Mounting-to-transmission bolts	80	58
Mounting-to-crossmember bolts	50	37
Engine-to-transmission unit bolts	45	33
Flywheel bolts	60	44
Main bearing cap bolts	110	81
Rocker arm stud	40	30
Sump retaining bolts:		
M8 bolts	20	15
M6 bolts	8	6
Timing chain cover bolts	15	11

New bolts should be used

1 General information

How to use this Chapter

1 This Part of Chapter 2 describes those repair procedures that can reasonably be carried out on the 2.4 litre petrol engine while it remains in the car. If the engine has been removed from the car and is being dismantled as described in Part G, any preliminary dismantling procedures can be ignored.

2 Note that, while it may be possible physically to overhaul items such as the piston/connecting rod assemblies while the engine is in the car, such tasks are not normally carried out as separate operations. Usually, several additional procedures (not to mention the cleaning of components and of oilways) have to be carried out. For this reason, all such tasks are classed as major overhaul procedures, and are described in Part G of this Chapter.

3 Part G also describes the removal of the engine/transmission unit from the vehicle, and the full overhaul procedures that can then be carried out.

Engine description

4 The 2.4 litre (2410 cc) petrol engine is a single overhead camshaft, four-cylinder, in-line unit, mounted at the front of the car, with the clutch and transmission at the rear. The engine design is known by Vauxhall as a cam-in-head (CIH) engine.

5 The crankshaft runs in five main bearings. Thrustwashers are fitted to the rear main bearing to control crankshaft endfloat.

6 The connecting rods rotate on horizontally-split bearing shells at their big-ends. The pistons are attached to the connecting rods by gudgeon pins, which are a sliding fit in the connecting rod small-end eyes and are retained by circlips. The aluminium-alloy pistons are fitted with three piston rings - two compression rings and an oil control ring.

7 The cylinder block is made of cast iron and the cylinder bores are an integral part of the block. On this type of engine the cylinder bores are sometimes referred to as having dry liners.

8 The inlet and exhaust valves are each closed by coil springs, and operate in guides pressed into the cylinder head.

9 The camshaft is driven by the crankshaft via a timing chain. The camshaft rotates directly in the head and operates the eight valves via rocker arms and hydraulic valve lifters. Valve clearances are automatically adjusted.

10 Lubrication is by means of an oil pump, which is driven off the front end of the crankshaft. It draws oil through a strainer located in the sump, and then forces it through an externally-mounted filter into galleries in the cylinder block/crankcase. From there, the oil is distributed to the crankshaft (main bearings) and camshaft. The big-end bearings are supplied with oil via internal drillings in the crankshaft, while the camshaft bearings also receive a pressurised supply. The camshaft lobes and valves are lubricated by splash, as are all other engine components.

Repair operations possible with the engine in the car

11 The following work can be carried out with the engine in the car:

a) Compression pressure - testing.
b) Hydraulic valve lifter - adjustment.
c) Cylinder head cover - removal and refitting.
d) Timing chain cover - removal and refitting.
e) Timing chain tensioner - removal and refitting.
f) Timing chain and sprockets - removal and refitting.
g) Rocker arms and hydraulic valve lifters - removal and refitting
h) Camshaft - removal, inspection and refitting.
i) Cylinder head - removal and refitting.
j) Connecting rods and pistons - removal and refitting*.
k) Sump - removal and refitting.
l) Oil pump - removal, overhaul and refitting.
m) Crankshaft oil seals - renewal.
n) Engine/transmission mountings - inspection and renewal.
o) Flywheel - removal, inspection and refitting.

* Although the operation marked with an asterisk can be carried out with the engine in the car after removal of the sump, it is better for the engine to be removed, in the interests of cleanliness and improved access. For this reason, the procedure is described in Chapter 2G.

2 Compression test - description and interpretation

1 When engine performance is down, or if misfiring occurs which cannot be attributed to the ignition or fuel systems, a compression test can provide diagnostic clues as to the engine's condition. If the test is performed regularly, it can give warning of trouble before any other symptoms become apparent.

2 The engine must be fully warmed-up to normal operating temperature, the battery must be fully charged, and the spark plugs must be removed (see Chapter 1A). The aid of an assistant will also be required.

3 Disable the ignition system by disconnecting the wiring connector(s) from the ignition coil (see Chapter 5B), and the fuel system by removing the fuel pump fuse (see Chapter 13).

4 Fit a compression tester to the number 1 cylinder spark plug hole; the type of tester which screws into the plug thread is to be preferred.

5 Have the assistant hold the throttle wide open and crank the engine on the starter motor; after one or two revolutions, the compression pressure should build up to a maximum figure, and then stabilise. Record the highest reading obtained.

6 Repeat the test on the remaining cylinders, recording the pressure in each.

7 All cylinders should produce very similar pressures; a difference of more than 2 bar between any two cylinders indicates a fault. Note that the compression should build up quickly in a healthy engine; low compression on the first stroke, followed by gradually-increasing pressure on successive strokes, indicates worn piston rings. A low compression reading on the first stroke, which does not build up during successive strokes, indicates leaking valves or a blown head gasket (a cracked head could also be the cause). Deposits on the undersides of the valve heads can also cause low compression.

8 Although Vauxhall do not specify exact compression pressures, as a guide, any cylinder pressure of below 10 bar can be considered as less than healthy. Refer to a Vauxhall dealer or other specialist if in doubt as to whether a particular pressure reading is acceptable.

9 If the addition of a little oil temporarily improves the compression pressure, this indicates that bore or piston wear is responsible for the pressure loss. No improvement suggests that leaking or burnt valves, or a blown head gasket, may be to blame.

10 A low reading from two adjacent cylinders is almost certainly due to the head gasket having blown between them; the presence of coolant in the engine oil will confirm this.

11 If one cylinder is about 20 per cent lower than the others, and the engine has a slightly rough idle, a worn camshaft lobe could be the cause.

12 If the compression reading is unusually high, the combustion chambers are probably coated with carbon deposits. If this is the case, the cylinder head should be removed and decarbonised.

13 On completion of the test, refit the spark plugs (see Chapter 1A), refit the fuel pump fuse and reconnect the wiring to the ignition coil.

3 Top dead centre (TDC) for No 1 piston - locating

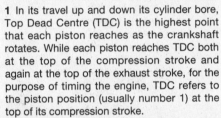

1 In its travel up and down its cylinder bore, Top Dead Centre (TDC) is the highest point that each piston reaches as the crankshaft rotates. While each piston reaches TDC both at the top of the compression stroke and again at the top of the exhaust stroke, for the purpose of timing the engine, TDC refers to the piston position (usually number 1) at the top of its compression stroke.

2 Number 1 piston (and cylinder) is at the front (timing chain) end of the engine, and its TDC position is located as follows. Note that the crankshaft rotates clockwise when viewed from the front of the vehicle.

3 Disconnect the battery negative terminal. To improve access to the crankshaft pulley, unbolt the undercover and remove it from underneath the engine.

4 Using a socket and extension bar on the crankshaft pulley bolt, rotate the crankshaft whilst observing the rear of the flywheel through the inspection aperture on the right-hand side of the cylinder block. Rotate the crankshaft until the pointer in the aperture is aligned with the raised mark on the rear of the flywheel. Once the mark is correctly aligned, No 1 and 4 pistons are at TDC.

5 To determine which piston is at TDC on its compression stroke, check the position of distributor rotor arm. Identify the location of No 1 HT lead on the cap then unclip the cap and remove it from the distributor (see illustration). When No 1 piston is at TDC on its compression stroke, the rotor arm tip will

3.5 Remove the distributor cap and check the rotor arm position as described in text

be in alignment with No 1 HT lead terminal of the cap; there is also an index mark on the distributor body (see Chapter 5B). If the rotor arm is in alignment with No 4 HT lead terminal of the distributor cap then No 4 cylinder is at TDC on its compression stroke; rotate the crankshaft through a further complete turn (360°) to bring No 1 cylinder to TDC on its compression stroke.

4 Hydraulic valve lifters - adjustment

1 The hydraulic valve lifters are designed to eliminate the need for adjustment during normal operation. However, they must be adjusted as follows if the rocker arms are disturbed during engine overhaul. The basic adjustment must be carried out before the engine is started for the first time and the final adjustment should be carried out once the engine has been warmed up to to normal operating temperature.

Basic adjustment

2 Remove the cylinder head cover as described in Section 5.

3 Position No 1 cylinder at TDC on its compression stroke as described in Section 3.

4 With No 1 cylinder at TDC on its compression stroke, slacken the front rocker arm retaining nut until freeplay is evident between the rocker arm and valve lifter. From this point, slowly tighten the nut until all freeplay has been removed, then tighten the nut through one more complete turn (360°). Repeat the operation on the remaining valve of No 1 cylinder.

5 Rotate the crankshaft through a half of a turn to bring No 3 cylinder to TDC on its compression stroke (rotor arm pointing towards No 3 HT lead terminal of the cap). Adjust the valve lifters of No 3 cylinder as described in paragraph 4.

6 Rotate the crankshaft through a half of a turn to realign the flywheel mark with the cylinder block pointer and bring No 4 cylinder to TDC on its compression stroke (rotor arm pointing towards No 4 HT lead terminal of the cap). Adjust the valve lifters of No 4 cylinder as described in paragraph 4.

7 Rotate the crankshaft through a half of a turn to bring No 2 cylinder to TDC on its compression stroke (rotor arm pointing towards No 2 HT lead terminal of the cap). Adjust the valve lifters of No 2 cylinder as described in paragraph 4.

8 Once all valve lifters have been adjusted, refit the cylinder head cover as described in Section 5 then warm the engine up and before carry out the final adjustment procedure as follows.

Final adjustment

9 Warm the engine up to normal operating temperature then switch it off.

2C

10 Remove the cylinder head cover as described in Section 5.

11 To prevent oil being sprayed around the engine compartment when the engine is running, make up a splash guard to fit over the top of the camshaft sprocket. Ensure the splash guard is fixed securely to the cylinder head and is in no danger of contacting the camshaft sprocket or timing chain once the engine is running.

12 Start up the engine and allow it to idle at the specified speed.

Caution: Take great care not to contact the moving parts of the engine during the following procedure.

13 Starting with the front valve lifter and working backwards adjust all the valve lifters as follows.

14 Slacken the rocker arm retaining nut until the arm beings to rattle then slowly tighten it until the rattling stops. From this point, tighten the nut through a further complete turn (360º), tightening it a quarter of a turn (90º) at a time with at least a ten second wait in between each quarter turn to allow the valve lifter hydraulic mechanism to settle (the engine will run roughly when the nut is first tightened but will idle smoothly again after a few seconds when the lifter has settled). This procedure preloads the valve lifter and ensures the hydraulic valve mechanism functions correctly.

15 Once all eight valve lifters have been correctly adjusted, switch off the engine, remove the splash guard and wipe up any spilt oil. Refit the cylinder head cover as described in Section 5.

5 Cylinder head cover - removal and refitting

Removal

1 Slacken the retaining clip and disconnect the breather hose from the cylinder head cover.

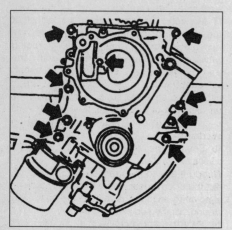

7.7 Timing chain cover retaining bolt locations (arrowed)

2 Slacken and remove the retaining bolts, noting the correct fitted location of any clips or brackets retained by the bolts (as applicable) then lift off the cylinder head cover. Recover the gasket; if it shows signs of damage or deterioration it must be renewed.

Refitting

3 Prior to refitting, examine the inside of the cover for a build-up of oil sludge or any other contamination, and if necessary clean the cover with paraffin, or a water-soluble solvent. Dry the cover thoroughly before refitting.

4 Ensure the cover is clean and dry and fit the gasket to the cover. Refit the cover to the cylinder head, ensuring the gasket remains correctly seated.

5 Refit the retaining bolts, ensuring all relevant clips/brackets are correctly positioned, and securely tighten them in a diagonal sequence.

6 Reconnect the breather hose securely to the cover.

6 Crankshaft pulley - removal and refitting

Removal

1 Remove the cooling fan and coupling as described in Chapter 3.

2 Remove the auxiliary drivebelts as described in Chapter 1A.

3 Slacken the crankshaft pulley retaining bolt. To prevent crankshaft rotation whilst the retaining bolt is slackened, have an assistant select top gear and apply the brakes firmly; if the engine is removed from the vehicle it will be necessary to lock the flywheel (see Section 16).

4 Unscrew the retaining bolt and washer and remove the crankshaft pulley from the end of the crankshaft. Whilst the pulley is removed check the oil seal for signs of wear or damage and, if necessary, renew as described in Section 15.

Refitting

5 Carefully locate the crankshaft pulley on the crankshaft end, aligning the pulley slot with

7.9 Check the timing chain tensioner blade and guide for wear or damage

the crankshaft key. Slide the pulley fully into position, taking great care not to damage the oil seal, then refit the washer and retaining bolt.

6 Lock the crankshaft by the method used on removal, and tighten the pulley retaining bolt to the specified torque setting.

7 Refit the auxiliary drivebelts as described in Chapter 1A.

8 Refit the cooling fan as described in Chapter 3.

7 Timing chain cover - removal and refitting

Removal

1 Remove the cylinder head as described in Section 12.

2 Remove the crankshaft pulley as described in Section 6.

3 Remove the coolant pump as described in Chapter 3. To further improve access also remove the radiator.

4 Remove the distributor as described in Chapter 5B.

5 Remove the sump as described in Section 13.

6 Remove the oil filter as described in Chapter 1A and discard it. Fit a new filter on refitting, and fill the engine with fresh oil.

7 Noting each bolts correct fitted location (the bolts are not all the same length), slacken and remove all the bolts securing the timing chain cover to the cylinder block **(see illustration)**. Do not forget the retaining bolt located in the coolant pump aperture.

8 Carefully ease the timing cover squarely away from the cylinder block and manoeuvre it out of position, noting the correct fitted positions of guide and tensioner blade fitted to the inside of the cover. Remove the cover gaskets and discard them, if the locating dowels are a loose fit, remove them and store with the cover for safe-keeping.

9 Inspect the timing chain guides and tensioner blade for signs of wear or damage and renew as necessary **(see illustration)**.

Refitting

10 Ensure the mating surfaces of the cover and cylinder block are clean and dry and the cover locating dowels are correctly positioned.

11 Fit the new gaskets to the cylinder block, using a smear of grease to hold them in position.

12 Ensure the timing chain guide and tensioner blade are correctly fitted to the inside of the cover.

13 Manoeuvre the cover into position, ensuring the gaskets remain correctly positioned, and locate it on the dowels.

14 Refit the cover retaining bolts, ensuring each bolt is refitted in its original location. Tighten all bolts by hand then go around and tighten them to the specified torque.

15 Carefully trim off the top of each timing chain cover gasket which protrudes above the cylinder head mating surface then refit the cylinder head as described in Section 12.

16 Refit the sump as described in Section 13.

17 Refit the distributor as described in Chapter 5B.

18 Renew the crankshaft front oil seal (see Section 15), then refit the crankshaft pulley as described in Section 5.

19 Refit the coolant pump as described in Chapter 3.

20 On completion, referring to Chapter 1A, fit a new oil filter and fill the engine with clean oil and refill the cooling system. Start the engine and check for signs of leaks.

8 Timing chain tensioner and guides - removal and refitting

Timing chain tensioner

Removal

1 To improve access to the tensioner, unbolt the undercover and remove it from underneath the engine unit.

2 The timing chain tensioner is located on the right-hand side of the timing chain cover, just above the oil filter.

3 If necessary, on models equipped with air conditioning, access to the tensioner can be improved by unbolting the compressor and positioning it clear of the mounting bracket once the drivebelt has been removed (see Chapter 3).

4 Unscrew the tensioner from the cover and remove it along with its sealing washer. Discard the sealing washer, a new one should be used on refitting.

Caution: Do not rotate the engine whilst the tensioner is removed.

5 Inspect the tensioner for signs of wear or damage and renew if necessary.

Refitting

6 Fit a new sealing washer to the tensioner then refit the tensioner to the timing chain cover, tightening it securely.

7 Refit the air conditioning compressor and drivebelt (where removed) then refit the undercover to the vehicle.

Timing chain guides

Removal

8 Remove the timing chain cover as described in Section 7.

9 The tensioner blade and smaller guide are fitted to the inside of the cover. Check the contact surface of each for signs of wear or damage and renew as necessary. If the pivot pins show signs of wear they should also be renewed.

10 Check the longer guide, which is bolted to the front of the cylinder block, for signs of wear or damage to its contact face. If renewal is necessary, unbolt the guide and remove it from the block. Remove all traces of locking compound from the retaining bolt threads and apply a drop of fresh locking compound (Vauxhall recommend the use of 1510177 - Part No 90167347 - available from your Vauxhall dealer) to the threads of each bolt. Fit the new guide to the cylinder block then refit the retaining bolts, tightening them securely.

11 Refit the timing chain cover as described in Section 7.

9 Timing chain and sprockets - removal, inspection and refitting

Removal

1 Remove the cylinder head as described in Section 12.

2 Remove the timing chain cover as described in Section 7.

3 Mark the outer face of the distributor drive gear then remove the gear from the end of the crankshaft **(see illustration)**. Remove the Woodruff key from the crankshaft and store it with the drivegear.

4 If the timing chain and sprockets are to be re-used, mark the outer surface of the chain using a suitable marker pen or a dab of paint. The mark can then be used to ensure the chain is fitted the same way around on refitting.

5 Lift the camshaft sprocket off of its support plate and remove the sprocket and timing chain from the engine. Separate the sprocket and chain.

6 Slide the sprocket off from the end of the crankshaft, noting which way around it is fitted, and remove the Woodruff key from the crankshaft slot. If the sprocket is a tight fit, carefully lever the gear off using a large flat-bladed screwdriver.

Inspection

7 Examine the teeth on the sprockets for any sign of wear or damage such as chipped, hooked or missing teeth. If there is any sign of

9.3 Removing the distributor drive gear from the crankshaft

wear or damage on either sprocket, both sprockets and the chain should be renewed as a set.

8 Inspect the links of the timing chain for signs of wear or damage on the rollers. The extent of wear can be judged by checking the amount by which the chain can be bent sideways; a new chain will have very little sideways movement. If there is an excessive amount of side play in a timing chain, it must be renewed.

9 Note that it is a sensible precaution to renew the timing chain, regardless of its apparent condition, if the engine has covered a high mileage, or if it has been noted that the chain has sounded noisy when the engine is running. Although not strictly necessary, it is always worth renewing the chain and sprockets as a matched set, since it is false economy to run a new chain on worn sprockets and *vice-versa*. If there is any doubt about the condition of the timing chain and sprockets, seek the advice of a Vauxhall dealer service department, who will be able to advise you as to the best course of action, based on their previous knowledge of the engine.

10 Examine the chain guides and tensioner blade for signs of wear or damage to their chain contact faces, renewing any which are badly marked (see Section 8).

Refitting

11 Ensure that the flywheel mark is correctly aligned with the pointer on the right-hand side of the cylinder block (No 1 and 4 pistons at TDC).

12 Fit the Woodruff key to the crankshaft and slide on the crankshaft sprocket, ensuring the sprocket is fitted the correct way around (teeth innermost). Align the sprocket groove with the key and slide it fully onto the crankshaft. If necessary, tap the sprocket fully up to its shoulder using a piece of tubing the same diameter as the sprocket flange.

13 Fit the camshaft sprocket to the timing chain. If the original chain is being re-used, ensure the mark made on the chain is on the same side as the timing mark on the sprocket.

14 Manoeuvre the timing chain and camshaft sprocket into position making sure the camshaft sprocket timing mark is facing outwards. Engage the chain with the crankshaft sprocket so that the camshaft sprocket timing mark is correctly aligned with the notch in the support plate when the left-hand run of the chain is taut and all slack is on the tensioner side **(see illustration overleaf)**.

15 Ensure the chain and sprockets are correctly mated then refit the second Woodruff key to the crankshaft. Slide on the distributor drivegear, using the mark made on removal to ensure it is refitted the same way around, aligning its slot with the key.

16 Refit the timing chain cover as described in Section 7, then refit the cylinder head as described in Section 12.

2C

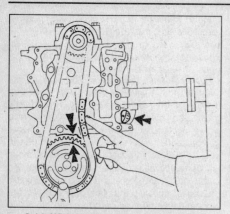

9.14 With No 1 and 4 pistons at TDC (flywheel mark aligned with pointer - arrowed), fit the timing chain and camshaft sprocket making sure the sprocket mark is correctly aligned with the support plate notch (arrowed) - shown with engine removed from vehicle and mounted upside-down

10.3a Slacken and remove the retaining nut . . .

10.3b . . . then lift off the pivot ball . . .

10 Rocker arms and hydraulic valve lifters - removal, inspection and refitting

Removal

1 Remove the cylinder head cover as described in Section 5.
2 Obtain eight small, clean plastic containers, and label them for identification. Alternatively, divide a larger container into compartments. All components can then be stored in groups which will help ensure all are refitted in their original locations.
3 Starting on the first rocker arm, unscrew the retaining nut then lift off the pivot ball and rocker arm. Slide the hydraulic valve lifter out from the cylinder head and store all associated components together **(see illustrations)**.
4 Repeat the operation in paragraph 3 and remove the remaining rocker arm and lifter assemblies.

Inspection

5 Check the rocker arms for signs of wear or damage on their contact surfaces and renew as necessary.

6 Inspect each valve lifter for signs of damage and renew as necessary. If the contact face of a lifter is badly marked, be sure to check the corresponding cam lobe for signs of damage (see Section 11). If the hydraulic adjustment mechanism of any lifter is thought to be faulty the lifter should be renewed; there is no satisfactory method of testing.
7 Check the rocker arm studs for signs of damage and replace as necessary. Each stud can be removed by locking two (M10 x 1) nuts together and then using the lower nut to unscrew the stud from the head. Remove all traces of locking compound from the cylinder head threads and transfer the nuts to the new stud. Apply a drop of locking compound (Vauxhall recommend the use of 1510177 - Part No 90167347 - available from your Vauxhall dealer) to the stud threads then fit the stud to the head and tighten it to the specified torque. Unlock the nuts and remove them from the stud.

Refitting

8 Lubricate the hydraulic valve lifters with clean engine oil and carefully insert each one into its original location in the cylinder head.
9 Fit each rocker arm to its respective stud, ensuring that they are all fitted the correct way around so that their peg are correctly located in the valve lifter ends. Fit the ball pivots and screw on the retaining nuts.
10 Referring to Section 4, carry out the hydraulic valve lifter basic adjustment on all rocker arms. Refit the cylinder head cover then warm the engine up to normal operating before removing the cover again to perform

the valve lifter final adjustment procedure on each rocker arm.
11 Refit the cylinder head cover as described in Section 5.

11 Camshaft - removal, inspection and refitting

Removal

1 Remove the cylinder head as described in Section 12.
2 Remove all the rocker arms and valve lifters as described in Section 10.
3 Unscrew the three retaining bolts and remove the access cover from the left-hand side of the cylinder head. Remove the cover gasket and discard it.
4 Carefully slide the camshaft out of the front of the cylinder **(see illustration)**. As the camshaft is removed, support it through the access cover aperture to ensure the bearings are not damaged.

Inspection

5 Examine the camshaft bearing surfaces and cam lobes for signs of wear ridges and scoring. Renew the camshaft if any of these conditions are apparent.
6 Support the camshaft end journals on V-blocks, and measure the run-out at the centre journal using a dial gauge. If the run-out exceeds the specified limit, the camshaft should be renewed.

10.3c . . . and rocker arm . . .

10.3d . . . and withdraw the hydraulic valve lifter from the cylinder head

11.4 Withdraw the camshaft from the front of the cylinder head

7 Examine the condition of the camshaft bearings and the bearings in the cylinder head. If the camshaft is worn it must be renewed, and if the cylinder head bearings are worn they should be renewed. Renewal of the bearings is a tricky operation requiring the use of several special tools and should therefore be entrusted to a Vauxhall dealer or suitably-equipped engineering firm.

Refitting

8 Lubricate the cylinder head and camshaft bearings with clean engine oil.
9 Carefully slide the camshaft into position, supporting it via the access cover aperture to help ensure the bearings are not damaged.
10 Ensure the mating surfaces of the cylinder head and access cover are clean and dry. Refit the cover, using a new gasket, and securely tighten the retaining bolts.
11 Refit the valve lifters and rocker arms as described in Section 10.
12 Refit the cylinder head as described in Section 12. Referring to Section 4, prior to refitting the head cover, carry out the hydraulic valve lifter basic adjustment on all rocker arms. Refit the cylinder head cover then warm the engine up to normal operating before removing the cover again to perform the valve lifter final adjustment procedure on each rocker arm.
13 Refit the cylinder head cover as described in Section 5.

12 Cylinder head - removal and refitting

Note: *The engine must be cold when removing the cylinder head. A splined socket bit will be required to remove the camshaft sprocket retaining bolts (Vauxhall service tool MKM320 or equivalent) and new cylinder head bolts will be needed for refitting. A new camshaft endfloat bolt will also be required.*

Removal

1 Disconnect the battery negative lead.
2 Drain the cooling system and remove the spark plugs as described in Chapter 1A. Unclip the HT leads and position them clear of the cylinder head.
3 Remove the inlet and exhaust manifolds as described in Chapter 4A. If no work is to be carried out on the cylinder head, the head can be removed complete with manifolds once the following operations have been carried out (see Chapter 4A).
a) *Disconnect the various wiring connectors from the throttle housing and manifold and free the wiring harness from the inlet manifold.*
b) *Disconnect the fuel hoses from the fuel rail and the intake duct and various vacuum and coolant hoses from the inlet manifold.*
c) *Disconnect the accelerator cable.*

d) *Unbolt the exhaust front pipe from manifold.*
e) *Unbolt the inlet manifold support bracket.*
4 Position No 1 cylinder at TDC on its compression stoke as described in Section 3.
5 Remove the cylinder head cover as described in Section 5.
6 Unscrew the retaining bolts and remove the end cover from the front of the cylinder head **(see illustration)**. Discard the cover gasket.
7 Unscrew the plastic endfloat bolt from the end of the camshaft, then slacken and remove the camshaft sprocket retaining bolts using a splined bit. Disengage the sprocket from camshaft, taking care not to dislodge the locating pin from the camshaft; a support plate is fitted to prevent the sprocket from falling down into the timing chain cover. **Do not** rotate the crankshaft until the sprocket is refitted to the camshaft.

> **HAYNES HINT** *To ensure the sprocket and timing chain remain correctly engaged secure them together with a cable tie.*

8 Slacken the retaining clips and disconnect the coolant hoses from the thermostat housing.
9 Disconnect the wiring connector from the coolant temperature sender unit.
10 Make a final check to ensure that all relevant hoses, pipes and wires, etc, have been disconnected.
11 Slacken and remove the two bolts securing the front of the cylinder head to the top of the timing chain cover.
12 Working in the **reverse** of the tightening sequence **(see illustration 12.28a)**, progressively slacken the cylinder head bolts by a third of a turn at a time until all bolts can be unscrewed by hand. Remove each bolt in turn, noting its correct fitted location; the bolts are of different lengths.
13 Lift the cylinder head from the cylinder block. If necessary, tap the cylinder head gently with a soft-faced mallet to free it from the block, but **do not** lever at the mating faces. Note the fitted positions of the two locating dowels, and remove them for safe keeping if they are loose.
14 Recover the cylinder head gasket and the

sealing ring from the top of the timing chain cover and discard them.
15 If the cylinder head is to be dismantled for overhaul, then refer to Part G of this Chapter.

Preparation for refitting

16 The mating faces of the cylinder head and cylinder block/crankcase must be perfectly clean before refitting the head. Use a hard plastic or wood scraper to remove all traces of gasket and carbon; also clean the piston crowns. Take particular care, as the surfaces are damaged easily. Also, make sure that the carbon is not allowed to enter the oil and water passages - this is particularly important for the lubrication system, as carbon could block the oil supply to any of the engine's components. Using adhesive tape and paper, seal the water, oil and bolt holes in the cylinder block/crankcase. To prevent carbon entering the gap between the pistons and bores, smear a little grease in the gap. After cleaning each piston, use a small brush to remove all traces of grease and carbon from the gap, then wipe away the remainder with a clean rag. Clean all the pistons in the same way.
17 Check the mating surfaces of the cylinder block/crankcase and the cylinder head for nicks, deep scratches and other damage. If slight, they may be removed carefully with a file, but if excessive, machining may be the only alternative to renewal.
18 Ensure that the cylinder head bolt holes in the crankcase are clean and free of oil. Syringe or soak up any oil left in the bolt holes. This is most important in order that the correct bolt tightening torque can be applied and to prevent the possibility of the block being cracked by hydraulic pressure when the bolts are tightened.
19 The cylinder head bolts must be discarded and renewed, regardless of their apparent condition.
20 If warpage of the cylinder head gasket surface is suspected, use a straight-edge to check it for distortion. Refer to Part G of this Chapter if necessary.

Refitting

21 Wipe clean the mating surfaces of the cylinder head and cylinder block/crankcase.
22 Fit a new sealing ring to the recess in the top of the timing chain cover **(see illustration)**.

12.6 Remove the end cover from the front of the cylinder head to gain access to the camshaft sprocket bolts

12.22 Fit a new sealing ring to the timing chain cover recess

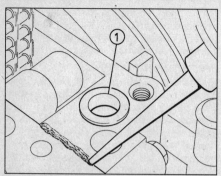

12.23 Apply sealant to the joints between the timing chain cover and cylinder block (see text) - sealing ring (1) arrowed

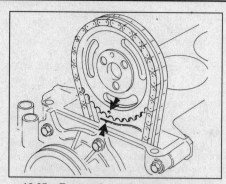

12.25a Ensure the camshaft sprocket timing mark is correctly aligned with the support plate notch (arrowed) . . .

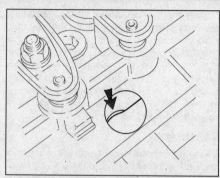

12.25b . . . and the camshaft is correctly positioned in the cylinder head so the notches allow access to the cylinder head bolts

23 Apply a bead of sealant (Vauxhall recommend the use of sealant 1503294 - Part No 90001851), approximately 3 mm thick to the joints between the timing chain cover and the front of the cylinder block **(see illustration)**.

24 Check that the two locating dowels are in position then fit a new gasket to the cylinder block.

25 Ensure the crankshaft is correctly positioned at TDC and check that the timing mark on the camshaft sprocket is still correctly aligned with the notch on the sprocket support plate. Make sure that the camshaft is still correctly positioned in the cylinder head with its sprocket locating pin uppermost; the camshaft recesses will be positioned to allow access to the cylinder head bolts **(see illustrations)**.

26 With the aid of an assistant, carefully refit the cylinder head assembly to the block. Take care not to dislodge the sealing ring from the top of the timing chain cover and locate the head on the dowels.

27 Apply a smear of oil to the threads and the underside of the heads of the new cylinder head bolts and carefully enter each bolt into its relevant hole (*do not drop them in*). Screw all bolts in, by hand only, until finger-tight.

28 Working progressively and in the sequence shown, tighten the cylinder head bolts to their stage 1 torque setting, using a torque wrench and suitable socket **(see illustrations)**.

29 Once all bolts have been tightened to the stage 1 torque, working again in the specified sequence, go around and tighten all bolts through the specified stage 2 angle. It is recommended that an angle-measuring gauge is used to ensure accuracy. If a gauge is not available, use white paint to make alignment marks prior to tightening; the marks can then be used to check that the bolt has been rotated through the correct angle.

30 Refit the two bolts securing the cylinder head to the timing chain cover and tighten them to the specified torque.

31 Align the camshaft sprocket with the locating pin and locate the sprocket on the camshaft. Refit the sprocket retaining bolts, tightening them to the specified torque, then remove the cable tie (where fitted) securing the chain to the sprocket **(see illustration)**.

32 Screw the new endfloat bolt securely into the end of the camshaft **(see illustration)**.

33 Ensure the mating surfaces are clean and dry then refit the end cover to front of the cylinder head, using a new gasket. Securely tighten the cover bolts then check the camshaft endfloat by measuring the clearance between the endfloat bolt and the inside of

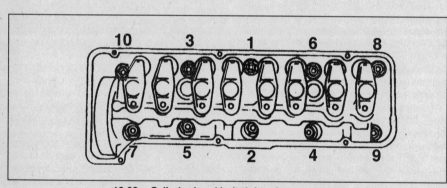

12.28a Cylinder head bolt tightening sequence

12.28b Tighten the cylinder head bolts as described in text

12.31 Refit the sprocket to the end of the camshaft and tighten its retaining bolts to the specified torque

12.32 Screw the new endfloat bolt securely into the camshaft end

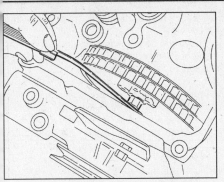

12.33 Checking camshaft endfloat

13.13a Apply sealant to the joints of the rear main bearing cap and cylinder block . . .

13.13b . . . and the timing chain cover and cylinder block before refitting the sump

the cover using feeler blades **(see illustration)**. If the endfloat is not within the limits given in the Specifications at the start of this Chapter, adjust it by deforming the end cover using a hammer and blunt-ended punch. If the clearance is excessive, adjust it by carefully tapping the centre of the cover inwards and if the clearance is insufficient adjust it by removing the cover again and gently tapping the centre of the cover back outwards.

34 Once the camshaft endfloat is correctly adjusted, reconnect the wiring connector to the coolant temperature sender unit.

35 Reconnect the coolant hoses to the thermostat housing and securely tighten their retaining clips.

36 Refit the cylinder head cover as described in Section 5.

37 Refit/reconnect the inlet and exhaust manifolds and associated components as described in Chapter 4A.

38 Refit the spark plugs and refill the cooling system as described in Chapter 1A.

39 Start the engine, warm it up to normal operating temperature then switch it off again.

40 Taking care not to burn your hands, remove the cylinder head cover again (see Section 5) and slacken the bolts securing the front of the cylinder head to the timing chain cover. Working in the specified sequence **(see illustration 12.28a)**, go around and tighten the ten main cylinder head bolts through the specified stage 3 angle (see paragraph 29). Tighten the cylinder head-to-timing chain cover bolts to the specified torque, then refit the cylinder head cover as described in Section 5.

13 Sump - removal and refitting

Note: *An engine hoist or support bar will be required for this procedure.*

Removal

1 Disconnect the battery negative terminal.

2 Firmly apply the handbrake then jack up the front of the car and support it on axle stands.

3 Undo the retaining bolts and remove the engine undercover.

4 Drain the engine oil as described in Chapter 1A, then fit a new sealing washer and refit the drain plug, tightening it securely. If the engine is nearing its service interval when the oil and filter are due for renewal, it is recommended that the filter is also removed and a new one fitted. After reassembly, the engine can then be refilled with fresh engine oil.

5 Position a jack underneath the transmission unit and raise the jack until it is supporting the weight of the transmission. Unscrew the nuts securing the rear engine mounting to the crossmember then slacken and remove the mounting bolts and remove the front suspension crossmember from underneath the engine/transmission unit.

6 Referring to Chapter 9, unbolt the front axle assembly from the chassis and lower it slightly to gain the necessary clearance required to remove the sump castings.

7 Attach the engine hoist or support bar (as applicable) to the engine and raise it until it is supporting the weight of the engine. Slacken and remove the bolts securing the left- and right-hand mountings to the chassis so the engine is free to be lifted. Raise the engine slightly to gain the clearance required to remove the sump castings, ensure the cooling fan does not damage the shroud.

8 Progressively slacken and remove the bolts securing the lower section of the sump to main casting. Break the joint by striking the lower section with the palm of the hand, then lower it away from the engine. Remove the gasket and discard it.

9 Progressively slacken and remove the bolts securing the main section of the sump to the cylinder block. Break the joint by striking the lower section with the palm of the hand, then lower the main sump casting away from the engine, disengaging it from the oil pump pick-up/strainer. Remove the gasket and discard it. **Note:** *On some engines the gasket may consist of four separate pieces.*

10 If necessary, undo the retaining bolts securing the oil pump pick-up/strainer in position and remove it from the base of the cylinder block. Discard the gasket.

Refitting

11 Remove all traces of dirt and oil from the mating surfaces of the sump castings, cylinder block and timing chain cover and (where removed) the pick-up/strainer.

12 Fit a new gasket to the oil pump pick-up/strainer (where removed) then refit it to the engine, tightening its retaining bolts securely.

13 Apply a smear of suitable sealing compound (Vauxhall recommend the use of sealant 1503294 - Part No 90001851 - available from your Vauxhall dealer) to the cylinder block mating surface joints with the timing chain cover and rear main bearing cap **(see illustrations)**.

14 Fit a new gasket to the top of the sump main casting then offer up the casting to the cylinder block. Refit the retaining bolts and tighten them all by hand. Working in a diagonal sequence, from the centre outwards, go around and tighten all the retaining bolts to the specified torque setting.

15 Fit a new gasket to the top of the sump lower section and refit the lower section to the main casting. Refit the casting retaining bolts and tighten them to the specified torque setting.

16 Lower the engine into position then refit the left- and right-hand mounting retaining bolts and tighten them to the specified torque. Detach the engine hoist/support bar (as applicable) and remove it.

17 Refit the crossmember to the vehicle, engaging it with the rear mounting, and refit the mounting bolts. Tighten the mounting bolts to the specified torque setting then refit the engine mounting nuts and tighten them to the specified torque.

18 Refit the front axle as described in Chapter 9.

19 Refit the undercover then lower the vehicle to the ground.

20 Fill the engine with fresh oil, with reference to Chapter 1A and reconnect the battery.

2C

14.4 Oil pump pressure relief valve components (shown with pump cover)

14 Oil pump - removal, inspection and refitting

Removal

1 Disconnect the battery negative terminal then undo the retaining bolts and remove the engine undercover. The oil pump is located on the base of the timing chain cover.

2 Unbolt the crankshaft sensor and position it clear of the oil pump cover.

3 Wipe clean the area around the pump cover and position a container beneath the cover, ready to catch any spilt oil.

4 Unscrew the oil pressure relief valve bolt and sealing washer from the pump cover and remove the spring and valve piston, noting which way around the piston is fitted **(see illustration)**.

5 Slacken and remove the pump cover retaining bolts then carefully remove the cover and collect the pump gears as they are released from the timing chain cover.

Inspection

6 Clean the components, and carefully examine the gears, pump body and valve piston for any signs of scoring or wear. Renew any component which shows signs of wear or damage; if the pump housing is marked then the timing chain cover assembly will have to be renewed. **Note:** *If the pump gears are to be renewed ensure the new gears are of the correct size. Vauxhall produced some timing*

chain covers with (0.2 mm) oversize gears. If oversize gears are fitted, '0.2' will be stamped on the left-hand side of the oil pump housing.

7 If the pump components appear to be satisfactory, insert the gears back into the housing and, using feeler blades, check the gear teeth backlash (clearance). Place a straight edge across the base of the timing chain cover and measure the endfloat of each gear **(see illustrations)**. Compare the results to those given in the Specifications, if the gears are worn beyond the specified limits they must be renewed.

Refitting

8 Ensure the pump cover and timing chain cover mating surfaces are clean and dry. Apply a smear of sealant (Vauxhall recommend the use of sealant 1503166 - Part No 90094714 - available from your Vauxhall dealer) to the pump cover mating surface. **Note:** *Do not apply excess sealant as this will only find its way into the oil pump.*

9 Refit the gears to the timing chain cover, making sure the drive gear is correctly engaged with the distributor shaft, and refit the cover. Refit the cover retaining bolts and tighten securely.

10 Engage the spring with the pressure relief valve piston and insert them into the oil pump cover. Fit a new sealing washer to the valve bolt then refit it to the cover, tightening it securely.

11 Refit the crankshaft sensor tightening its retaining bolt securely.

12 Using an Allen key, unscrew the small plug from the top of the oil pump housing. Prime the pump by filling it with clean engine oil, using an oil can, then securely refit the plug to the housing.

15 Crankshaft oil seals - renewal

Front (timing chain end) oil seal

1 Remove the crankshaft pulley as described in Section 6.

2 Using a large flat-bladed screwdriver,

carefully lever the seal out from the timing chain cover.

3 Clean the seal housing and polish off any burrs or raised edges which may have caused the seal to fail in the first place.

4 Lubricate the lips of the new seal with clean engine oil and press/tap it squarely into position until it is flush with the cover. If necessary, a suitable tubular drift, such as a socket, which bears only on the hard outer edge of the seal can be used to tap the seal into position.

5 Wash off any traces of oil, then refit the crankshaft pulley as described in Section 6.

Rear (flywheel end) oil seal

6 Remove the flywheel as described in Section 16.

7 Carefully punch or drill two small holes opposite each other in the oil seal. Screw a self-tapping screw into each and pull on the screws with pliers to extract the seal.

8 Clean the seal housing and polish off any burrs or raised edges which may have caused the seal to fail in the first place.

9 Lubricate the lips of the new seal with clean engine oil and ease it into position on the end of the crankshaft. Press the seal squarely into position until it is flush with the bearing cap. If necessary, a suitable tubular drift, such as a socket, which bears only on the hard outer edge of the seal can be used to tap the seal into position. Take great care not to damage the seal lips during fitting and ensure that the seal lips face inwards.

10 Refit the flywheel as described in Section 16.

16 Flywheel - removal, inspection and refitting

Removal

1 Remove the transmission as described in Chapter 7 then remove the clutch assembly as described in Chapter 6.

2 Before proceeding any further closely examine the flywheel retaining bolts. Find the bolt stamped with a P and mark its fitted location on the flywheel **(see illustration)**.

14.7a Using feeler blades, measure the oil pump gear clearance . . .

14.7b . . . and the gear endfloat and compare the results to those given in the Specifications

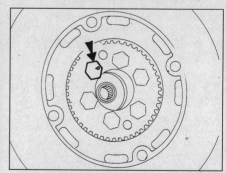

16.2 Mark the position of the bolt marked P on the flywheel prior to removal

16.3 Lock the flywheel ring gear with a tool similar to that shown

16.9 Ensure the flywheel locating bolt, which is marked with the letter P, is fitted in the correct location on refitting

3 Prevent the flywheel from turning by locking the ring gear teeth with a similar arrangement to that shown **(see illustration)**. Alternatively, bolt a strap between the flywheel and the cylinder block/crankcase. Make alignment marks between the flywheel and crankshaft.

4 Slacken and remove the retaining bolts and remove the flywheel. Do not drop it, as it is very heavy.

Inspection

5 Examine the flywheel for wear or chipping of the ring gear teeth. Renewal of the ring gear is possible but is not a task for the home mechanic; renewal requires the new ring gear to be heated (to 180° to 230°C) to allow it to be fitted.

6 Examine the flywheel for scoring of the clutch face. If the clutch face is scored, the flywheel may be surface-ground, but renewal is preferable.

7 If there is any doubt about the condition of the flywheel, seek the advice of a Vauxhall dealer or engine reconditioning specialist. They will be able to advise if it is possible to recondition it or whether renewal is necessary.

Refitting

8 Clean the mating surfaces of the flywheel and crankshaft and remove all traces of locking compound from the retaining bolt and crankshaft threads.

9 Apply a drop of locking compound (Vauxhall recommend the use of 1510177-Part No 90167347 - available from your Vauxhall dealer) to the threads of each retaining bolt then offer up the flywheel. Insert the bolts, making sure the bolt marked P is fitted in the correct position, and tighten all bolts by hand **(see illustration)**.

10 Lock the flywheel using the method employed on dismantling then, working in a diagonal sequence, evenly and progressively tighten the retaining bolts to the specified torque setting.

11 Refit the clutch as described in Chapter 6 then remove the locking tool and refit the transmission as described in Chapter 7.

17 Engine/transmission mountings - inspection and renewal

1 Refer to Chapter 2B, Section 17, noting that the heatshield is fitted to the right-hand engine mounting rather than the left-hand.

2C

Notes

Chapter 2 Part D
2.3 litre diesel engine in-car repair procedures

Contents

Camshaft - removal, inspection and refitting 10
Compression test - description and interpretation 2
Crankshaft oil seals - renewal 16
Crankshaft pulley - removal and refitting 6
Cylinder head - removal and refitting 12
Cylinder head cover - removal and refitting 5
Engine oil and filter renewal .See Chapter 1B
Engine oil level check . . . . .See Chapter 1B
Engine/transmission mountings - inspection and renewal 18
Flywheel - removal, inspection and refitting 17
General engine checks . . . . .See Chapter 1B

General information 1
Oil cooler and temperature control valve - removal and refitting . . . 15
Oil pump - removal, inspection and refitting 14
Rocker arms - removal, inspection and refitting 11
Sump - removal and refitting 13
Timing chain and sprockets - removal, inspection and refitting 9
Timing chain cover - removal and refitting 7
Timing chain tensioner and guides - removal and refitting 8
Top dead centre (TDC) for No 1 piston - locating 3
Valve clearance - adjustment 4

Degrees of difficulty

Easy, suitable for novice with little experience		Fairly easy, suitable for beginner with some experience		Fairly difficult, suitable for competent DIY mechanic		Difficult, suitable for experienced DIY mechanic		Very difficult, suitable for expert DIY or professional	

Specifications

General

Engine type	Four-cylinder, overhead camshaft (OHC) in-line, water-cooled.
Manufacturer's engine code*	23DTR
Bore	92 mm
Stroke	85 mm
Capacity	2260 cc
Direction of crankshaft rotation	Clockwise (viewed from timing chain end of engine)
Compression ratio	23.0:1

Note: *The engine code forms the first five digits of the engine number (see Vehicle identification section of this manual)*

Camshaft

Camshaft bearing outer diameter*:

No 1	33.950 to 33.975 mm
No 2	44.685 to 44.700 mm
No 3	44.935 to 44.950 mm
No 4	45.185 to 45.200 mm
No5	45.435 to 45.450 mm

Camshaft pedestal bearing inner diameter*:

No 1	34.000 to 34.025 mm
No 2	44.750 to 44.775 mm
No 3	45.000 to 45.025 mm
No 4	45.250 to 45.275 mm
No5	45.500 to 45.525 mm

These are standard measurements. Note that 0.1 mm undersize components are also available.

Valve clearance

Inlet	0.2 mm
Exhaust	0.3 mm

Lubrication system

Oil pump type	Gear-type, driven by crankshaft via the distributor shaft
Minimum permissible oil pressure at idle speed, with engine at operating temperature (oil temperature of at least 80°C)	1.8 bar (25 psi)

Oil pump clearances:

Gear teeth clearance	0.10 to 0.20 mm

Gear endfloat:

With gasket in position	0.10 to 0.25 mm
Without gasket	0.00 to 0.06 mm

2D

Torque wrench settings

	Nm	lbf ft
Camshaft pedestal retaining bolts	30	22
Camshaft sprocket bolt	150	111
Connecting rod big-end bearing cap bolt:		
Standard bolts	60	44
Bolts supplied pre-coated with locking compound (encapsulated)*:		
Stage 1	45	33
Stage 2	Angle-tighten a further 45°	
Crankshaft pulley bolt	220	162
Crossmember-to-chassis bolts	80	59
Cylinder head (main) bolts*:		
Stage 1	100	74
Stage 2	Angle-tighten a further 135°	
Warm engine up to normal operating temperature then:		
Stage 3	Angle-tighten a further 30°	
Stage 4	Angle-tighten a further 30°	
Cylinder head-to-timing chain cover bolts	22	16
Engine/transmission mounting bolts:		
Left- and right-hand mounting	85	63
Mounting-to-body bolts	50	37
Rear mounting:		
Mounting-to-transmission bolts	80	59
Mounting-to-crossmember nuts	50	37
Engine-to-transmission unit bolts	45	33
Flywheel bolts:		
Stage 1	80	59
Stage 2	Angle-tighten a further 30°	
Main bearing cap bolts*:		
M10 bolts:		
Stage 1	50	37
Stage 2	Angle-tighten a further 45 to 60°	
M12 bolts:		
Stage 1	70	52
Stage 2	Angle-tighten a further 60°	
Oil cooler mounting nuts	9	7
Oil cooler pipe union nuts	33	24
Oil filter adaptor bolt	15	11
Sump retaining bolts*:		
Main section-to-cylinder block bolts	8	6
Lower section-to-upper section bolts	5	4
Timing chain cover bolts	15	11

* New bolts should be used

1 General information

How to use this Chapter

1 This Part of Chapter 2 describes those repair procedures that can reasonably be carried out on the 2.3 litre diesel engine while it remains in the car. If the engine has been removed from the car and is being dismantled as described in Part H, any preliminary dismantling procedures can be ignored.

2 Note that, while it may be possible physically to overhaul items such as the piston/connecting rod assemblies while the engine is in the car, such tasks are not normally carried out as separate operations. Usually, several additional procedures (not to mention the cleaning of components and of oilways) have to be carried out. For this reason, all such tasks are classed as major overhaul procedures, and are described in Part H of this Chapter.

3 Part H describes the removal of the engine/ transmission unit from the vehicle, and the full overhaul procedures that can then be carried out.

Engine description

4 The 2.3 litre (2260 cc) petrol engine is a single overhead camshaft, four-cylinder, in-line unit, mounted at the front of the car, with the clutch and transmission at the rear.

5 The crankshaft runs in five main bearings. Thrustwashers are fitted to the rear main bearing to control crankshaft endfloat.

6 The connecting rods rotate on horizontally-split bearing shells at their big-ends. The pistons are attached to the connecting rods by gudgeon pins, which are a sliding fit in the connecting rod small-end eyes being retained by circlips. The aluminium-alloy pistons are fitted with three piston rings - two compression rings and an oil control ring.

7 The cylinder block houses the 'dry' cylinder liners which can be replaced if worn.

8 The inlet and exhaust valves are each closed by coil springs, and operate in guides pressed into the cylinder head.

9 The camshaft is driven by the crankshaft via a timing chain. The camshaft rotates in five pedestals, which are mounted onto the top of the cylinder head, and operates the eight valves via rocker arms. The valve clearances are manually adjusted using the rocker arm pivot screws which are screwed into the cylinder head.

10 Lubrication is by means of an oil pump, which is driven off the right-hand end of the crankshaft. It draws oil through a strainer located in the sump, and then forces it through an externally-mounted filter into galleries in the cylinder block/crankcase. From there, the oil is distributed to the crankshaft (main bearings) and camshaft. The big-end bearings are supplied with oil via internal drillings in the crankshaft, while the camshaft bearings also receive a pressurised supply. The camshaft lobes and valves are lubricated by splash, as are all other engine components. An oil cooler and temperature control valve arrangement is fitted to keep the oil temperature stable under all operating conditions.

Repair operations possible with the engine in the car

11 The following work can be carried out with the engine in the car:

a) Compression pressure - testing.
b) Valve clearance - adjustment.
c) Cylinder head cover - removal and refitting.
d) Timing chain cover - removal and refitting.
e) Timing chain tensioner - removal and refitting.
f) Timing chain and sprockets - removal and refitting.
g) Camshaft and rocker arms - removal, inspection and refitting.
h) Cylinder head - removal and refitting.
i) Connecting rods and pistons - removal and refitting*.
j) Sump - removal and refitting.
k) Oil pump - removal, overhaul and refitting.
l) Crankshaft oil seals - renewal.
m) Engine/transmission mountings - inspection and renewal.
n) Flywheel - removal, inspection and refitting.

* Although the operation marked with an asterisk can be carried out with the engine in the car after removal of the sump, it is better for the engine to be removed, in the interests of cleanliness and improved access. For this reason, the procedure is described in Chapter 2H.

2 Compression test - description and interpretation

Compression test

Note: *A compression tester specifically designed for diesel engines must be used for this test.*

1 When engine performance is down, or if misfiring occurs which cannot be attributed to the fuel system, a compression test can provide diagnostic clues as to the engine's condition. If the test is performed regularly, it can give warning of trouble before any other symptoms become apparent.

2 A compression tester specifically intended for diesel engines must be used, because of the higher pressures involved. The tester is connected to an adaptor which screws into the glow plug or injector hole. It is unlikely to be worthwhile buying such a tester for occasional use, but it may be possible to borrow or hire one - if not, have the test performed by a garage.

3 Unless specific instructions to the contrary are supplied with the tester, observe the following points:

a) *The battery must be in a good state of charge, the air filter must be clean, and the engine should be at normal operating temperature.*
b) *All the injectors (Chapter 4B) or glow plugs (Chapter 5C) should be removed before starting the test (as applicable).*

c) *Unscrew the retaining nut and disconnect the wiring connector from the fuel injection pump fuel cut-off solenoid (see Chapter 4B) to prevent fuel from being discharged.*

4 There is no need to hold the accelerator pedal down during the test, because the diesel engine air inlet is not throttled.

5 Crank the engine on the starter motor; after one or two revolutions, the compression pressure should build up to a maximum figure, and then stabilise. Record the highest reading obtained.

6 Repeat the test on the remaining cylinders, recording the pressure in each.

7 All cylinders should produce very similar pressures; a difference of more than 2 bar between any two cylinders indicates a fault. Note that the compression should build up quickly in a healthy engine; low compression on the first stroke, followed by gradually-increasing pressure on successive strokes, indicates worn piston rings. A low compression reading on the first stroke, which does not build up during successive strokes, indicates leaking valves or a blown head gasket (a cracked head could also be the cause). Deposits on the undersides of the valve heads can also cause low compression.

Note: *The cause of poor compression is less easy to establish on a diesel engine than on a petrol one. The effect of introducing oil into the cylinders (wet testing) is not conclusive, because there is a risk that the oil will sit in the swirl chamber or in the recess on the piston crown instead of passing to the rings.*

8 Although Vauxhall do not specify exact compression pressures, as a guide, any cylinder pressure of below 20 bar can be considered as less than healthy. Refer to a Vauxhall dealer or other specialist if in doubt as to whether a particular pressure reading is acceptable.

9 On completion of the test, reconnect the injection pump fuel cut-off solenoid wiring connector then refit the injectors or glow plugs as described in Chapter 4B or 5C (as applicable).

Leakdown test

10 A leakdown test measures the rate at which compressed air fed into the cylinder is lost. It is an alternative to a compression test, and in many ways it is better, since the escaping air provides easy identification of where pressure loss is occurring (piston rings, valves or head gasket).

11 The equipment needed for leakdown testing is unlikely to be available to the home mechanic. If poor compression is suspected, have the test performed by a suitably-equipped garage.

3 Top dead centre (TDC) for No 1 piston - locating

1 In its travel up and down its cylinder bore, Top Dead Centre (TDC) is the highest point that each piston reaches as the crankshaft rotates. While each piston reaches TDC both at the top of the compression stroke and again at the top of the exhaust stroke, for the purpose of timing the engine, TDC refers to the piston position (usually number 1) at the top of its compression stroke.

2 Number 1 piston (and cylinder) is at the front (timing chain) end of the engine, and its TDC position is located as follows. Note that the crankshaft rotates clockwise when viewed from the front of the vehicle.

3 Disconnect the battery negative terminal. To improve access to the crankshaft pulley, unbolt the undercover and remove it from underneath the engine.

4 Remove the cylinder head cover as described in Section 5 to gain access to the camshaft sprocket timing mark.

5 Working underneath the vehicle, remove the plug from the aperture on the base of the transmission bellhousing to reveal the bellhousing pointer **(see illustration)**.

6 Using a socket and extension bar on the crankshaft pulley bolt, rotate the crankshaft whilst observing the flywheel through the inspection aperture on the base of the bellhousing. Rotate the crankshaft until the OT (TDC) mark on the flywheel is aligned with the pointer in the bellhousing **(see illustration)**. Once the mark is correctly aligned, No 1 and 4 pistons are at TDC.

3.5 Remove the plug (arrowed) from the base of the transmission bellhousing to reveal the flywheel timing mark and pointer

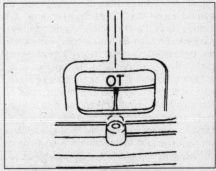

3.6 Align the OT (TDC) mark on the flywheel with the pointer on the bellhousing to position No 1 and 4 pistons at TDC

2D

3.7a With the flywheel mark aligned and the camshaft sprocket timing mark at the top (arrowed), No 1 cylinder is at TDC on its compression stroke

7 To determine which piston is at TDC on its compression stroke, check the position of camshaft sprocket timing mark. When No 1 piston is at TDC on its compression stroke, the mark should be at the top of the sprocket. If the mark is at the bottom and is aligned with the timing mark on the sprocket support then No 4 cylinder is at TDC on its compression stroke; rotate the crankshaft through a further complete turn (360°) to bring No 1 cylinder to TDC on its compression stroke **(see illustrations)**.

4 Valve clearance - adjustment

1 The importance of having the valve clearances correctly adjusted cannot be overstressed, as they vitally affect the performance of the engine. If the clearances are too big, the engine will be noisy (characteristic rattling or tapping noises) and engine efficiency will be reduced, as the valves open too late and close too early. A more serious problem arises if the clearances are too small, however. If this is the case, the valves may not close fully when the engine is

3.7b With the flywheel mark aligned and the camshaft sprocket timing mark is at the bottom (arrowed) and in alignment with the mark on the sprocket support, No 4 cylinder is at TDC on its compression stroke

hot, resulting in serious damage to the engine (eg. burnt valve seats and/or cylinder head warping/cracking). The clearances are checked and adjusted as follows, either with the engine hot or cold.

2 Remove the cylinder head cover as described in Section 5 then undo the retaining bolts and remove the oil splash guard from the top of the camshaft pedestals.

3 Position No 1 cylinder at TDC on its compression stroke as described in Section 3.

4 With the engine in this position, check that the clearances of No 1 cylinder inlet and exhaust valves, No 2 cylinder inlet and No 3 cylinder exhaust valve. The valve locations are as follows from front to rear; EX, IN, IN, EX, EX, IN, IN, EX **(see illustration)**.

5 Clearances are checked by inserting a feeler gauge of the correct thickness between the rocker arm and camshaft lobe. The feeler gauge should be a light, sliding fit. If adjustment is necessary, rotate the rocker arm pivot screw using an Allen key until the correct clearance is obtained.

6 Once all four valves are correctly adjusted, rotate the crankshaft a complete turn (360°) to bring No 4 cylinder to TDC. Note that the

timing mark on the camshaft will move through 180°, and will now be aligned with the mark on the sprocket support.

7 With the engine in this position, the clearances of No 2 cylinder exhaust valve, No 3 cylinder inlet valve and No 4 cylinder inlet and exhaust valves should be checked and adjusted as described in paragraph 5.

8 Once all the valve clearances have been checked, refit the splash guard to the top of the camshaft pedestals and securely tighten its retaining bolts.

9 Refit the cylinder head cover as described in Section 5 and refit the plug to the bellhousing timing aperture.

5 Cylinder head cover - removal and refitting

Removal

1 Slacken the retaining clip and disconnect the breather hose from the cylinder head cover.

2 Slacken and remove the retaining bolts, noting the correct fitted location of any clips or brackets retained by the bolts (as applicable) then lift off the cylinder head cover. Recover the gasket; if it shows signs of damage or deterioration it must be renewed.

Refitting

3 Prior to refitting, examine the inside of the cover for a build-up of oil sludge or any other contamination, and if necessary clean the cover with paraffin, or a water-soluble solvent. Dry the cover thoroughly before refitting.

4 Ensure the cover is clean and dry and fit the gasket to the cover. Refit the cover to the cylinder head, ensuring the gasket remains correctly seated.

5 Refit the retaining bolts, ensuring all relevant clips/brackets are correctly positioned, and securely tighten them in a diagonal sequence.

6 Reconnect the breather hose securely to the cover.

6 Crankshaft pulley - removal and refitting

Removal

1 Remove the cooling fan and coupling as described in Chapter 3.

2 Remove the auxiliary drivebelts as described in Chapter 1B.

3 Slacken the crankshaft pulley retaining bolt. To prevent crankshaft rotation whilst the retaining bolt is slackened, have an assistant select top gear and apply the brakes firmly; if the engine is removed from the vehicle it will be necessary to lock the flywheel (see Section 17).

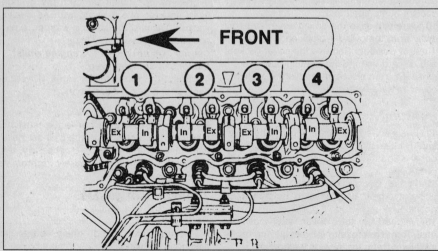

4.4 Inlet and exhaust valve locations

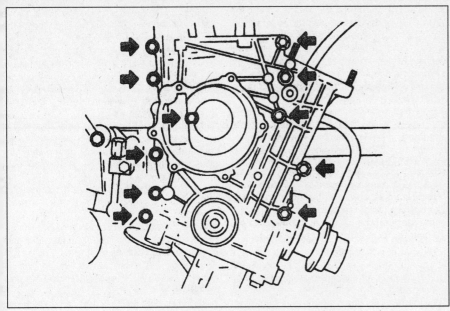

7.9 Timing chain cover bolt locations (arrowed)

4 Unscrew the retaining bolt and washer and remove the crankshaft pulley from the end of the crankshaft. Whilst the pulley is removed check the oil seal for signs of wear or damage and, if necessary, renew as described in Section 16.

Refitting

5 Carefully locate the crankshaft pulley on the crankshaft end, aligning the pulley slot with the crankshaft key. Slide the pulley fully into position, taking great care not to damage the oil seal then refit the washer and retaining bolt.
6 Lock the crankshaft by the method used on removal, and tighten the pulley retaining bolt to the specified torque setting.
7 Refit the auxiliary drivebelts as described in Chapter 1B.
8 Refit the cooling fan as described in Chapter 3.

7 Timing chain cover - removal and refitting

Removal

1 Remove the cylinder head as described in Section 12.
2 Remove the crankshaft pulley as described in Section 6.
3 Remove the coolant pump as described in Chapter 3. To further improve access also remove the radiator.
4 Remove the fuel injection pump and the lift pump as described in Chapter 4B.
5 Remove the sump as described in Section 13.
6 Remove the alternator as described in

Chapter 5A then unbolt and remove the alternator mounting bracket.
7 Unscrew the union bolt securing the turbocharger feed pipe to the side of the timing chain cover. Recover the sealing washer from each side of the union and discard; new sealing washers must be used on refitting.
8 Remove the oil filter as described in Chapter 1B and discard it. Fit a new filter on refitting and fill the engine with fresh oil. Unscrew the oil filter adaptor bolt and position the oil cooler temperature control valve assembly clear of the timing chain cover. Recover the sealing ring and discard it; a new one should be used on refitting.
9 Noting each bolts correct fitted location (the bolts are not all the same length), slacken and remove all the bolts securing the timing chain cover to the cylinder block **(see illustration)**. Do not forget the retaining bolt located in the coolant pump aperture.
10 Carefully ease the timing cover squarely away from the cylinder block and manoeuvre it out of position. Remove the cover gaskets and discard them, if the locating dowels are a loose fit, remove them and store with the cover for safe-keeping.

Refitting

11 Ensure the mating surfaces of the cover and cylinder block are clean and dry and the cover locating dowels are correctly positioned.
12 Fit the new gaskets to the cylinder block, using a smear of grease to hold them in position.
13 Manoeuvre the cover into position, ensuring the gaskets remain correctly positioned, and locate it on the dowels.
14 Refit the cover retaining bolts, ensuring

each bolt is refitted in its original location. Tighten all bolts by hand then go around and tighten them to the specified torque.
15 Carefully trim off the top of each timing chain cover gasket which protrudes above the cylinder head mating surface then refit the cylinder head as described in Section 12.
16 Fit a new sealing ring to the recess on the top of the oil cooler temperature control valve assembly. Offer the assembly up to the timing chain cover and refit the adaptor bolt. Ensure the valve assembly is correctly positioned then tighten the adaptor bolt to the specified torque.
17 Position a new sealing washer on each side of the turbocharger oil pipe union and refit the union bolt, tightening it securely.
18 Refit the sump as described in Section 13.
19 Refit the alternator as described in Chapter 5A.
20 Refit the fuel injection pump and lift pump as described in Chapter 4B.
21 Renew the crankshaft front oil seal (see Section 16) then refit the crankshaft pulley as described in Section 6.
22 Refit the coolant pump as described in Chapter 3.
23 On completion, referring to Chapter 1B, fit a new oil filter and fill the engine with clean oil and refill the cooling system. Start the engine and check for signs of leaks.

8 Timing chain tensioner and guides - removal and refitting

Timing chain tensioner

Removal

1 The timing chain tensioner is located on the right-hand side of the cylinder head.
2 If necessary, to improve access to the tensioner remove the metal intake duct linking the turbocharger to the intercooler (see Chapter 4B).
3 Unscrew the tensioner from the cylinder head and remove it along with its sealing washer. Discard the sealing washer, a new one should be used on refitting.
Caution: Do not rotate the engine whilst the tensioner is removed.
4 Inspect the tensioner for signs of wear or damage and renew if necessary.

Refitting

5 Fit a new sealing washer to the tensioner then refit the tensioner to the cylinder head, tightening it securely. Where necessary, refit the intake duct and securely tighten its retaining bolt and clips.

Timing chain guides

Removal

6 Remove the timing chain cover as described in Section 7.
7 The tensioner blade, guide and camshaft

9.3 Removing the injection pump drive gear from the crankshaft

sprocket support are fitted to the cylinder block. Check the contact surface of each for signs of wear or damage and renew as necessary; each one is retained by a circlip and washer. If the retaining pins show signs of wear they should also be renewed.

8 Refit the timing chain cover as described in Section 7.

9 Timing chain and sprockets - removal, inspection and refitting

Removal

1 Remove the cylinder head as described in Section 12.

2 Remove the timing chain cover as described in Section 7.

3 Mark the outer face of the injection pump drive gear then remove the gear from the end of the crankshaft **(see illustration)**. Remove the Woodruff key from the crankshaft and store it with the drivegear. If the drive gear is a tight fit, carefully lever the gear off or use a suitable puller to draw it off the end of the crankshaft.

4 If the timing chain and sprockets are to be reused, mark the outer surface of the chain using a suitable marker pen or a dab of paint. The mark can then be used to ensure the chain is fitted the same way around on refitting.

5 Lift the camshaft sprocket off of its support plate and remove the sprocket and timing chain from the engine. Separate the sprocket and chain.

6 Slide the sprocket off from the end of the crankshaft, noting which way around it is fitted, and remove the Woodruff key from the crankshaft slot. If the sprocket is a tight-fit, carefully lever the gear off using a large flat-bladed screwdriver or use the puller.

Inspection

7 Examine the teeth on the sprockets for any sign of wear or damage such as chipped, hooked or missing teeth. If there is any sign of wear or damage on either sprocket, both sprockets and the chain should be renewed as a set.

8 Inspect the links of the timing chain for signs of wear or damage on the rollers. The extent of wear can be judged by checking the amount by which the chain can be bent sideways; a new chain will have very little sideways movement. If there is an excessive amount of side play in a timing chain, it must be renewed.

9 Note that it is a sensible precaution to renew the timing chain, regardless of its apparent condition, if the engine has covered a high mileage, or if it has been noted that the chain has sounded noisy when the engine is running. Although not strictly necessary, it is always worth renewing the chain and sprockets as a matched set, since it is false economy to run a new chain on worn sprockets and *vice-versa*. If there is any doubt about the condition of the timing chain and sprockets, seek the advice of a Vauxhall dealer service department, who will be able to advise you as to the best course of action, based on their previous knowledge of the engine.

10 Examine the chain guide and tensioner blade for signs of wear or damage to their chain contact faces, renewing any which are badly marked (see Section 8).

Refitting

11 Ensure that the flywheel mark is correctly aligned with the pointer on the base of the transmission bellhousing (No 1 and 4 pistons at TDC).

12 Fit the Woodruff key to the crankshaft and slide on the crankshaft sprocket, ensuring the sprocket is fitted the correct way around (teeth innermost). Align the sprocket groove with the key and slide it fully onto the crankshaft. If necessary, tap the sprocket fully upto its shoulder using a piece of tubing the same diameter as the sprocket flange.

13 Fit the camshaft sprocket to the timing chain. If the original chain is being reused, ensure the mark made on the chain is on the same side as the timing mark on the sprocket.

14 Manoeuvre the timing chain and camshaft sprocket into position making sure the camshaft sprocket timing mark is facing outwards. Engage the chain with the crankshaft sprocket so that the camshaft sprocket timing mark is correctly aligned with the notch in the support plate when the left-hand run of the chain is taut and all slack is on the tensioner side (piston No 4 at TDC on its compression stroke).

15 Ensure the chain and sprockets are correctly mated and secure them in position by wrapping a stout elastic band around the top of the chain/sprocket support.

16 Refit the second Woodruff key to the crankshaft. Slide on the distributor drivegear, using the mark made on removal to ensure it is refitted the same way around, aligning its slot with the key.

17 Ensure the drive gear is correctly seated on the crankshaft then refit the timing chain cover as described in Section 7, and the cylinder head as described in Section 12.

10 Camshaft - removal, inspection and refitting

Removal

1 Remove the cylinder head cover as described in Section 5.

2 Referring to Section 3, position No 4 cylinder at TDC on its compression stoke so that the camshaft sprocket timing mark is correctly aligned with the mark on the sprocket support.

3 Undo the retaining bolts and remove the splash guard from the top of the camshaft pedestals.

4 Unscrew the timing chain tensioner from the right-hand side of the cylinder head and remove it along with its sealing washer.

5 Back off the rocker arm pivot screws to minimise the valve spring tension on the camshaft.

6 Fit the holding tool (KM 143 - a peg spanner which locates in the holes in the rear of the camshaft) to the rear of the camshaft then slacken the camshaft sprocket retaining bolt whilst using the tool to prevent rotation. In the absence of the special Vauxhall tool, the camshaft can be retained using a stout bar and two bolts the same size as the holes in the camshaft end; insert the bolts into the holes in the camshaft end then locate the bar in between the bolts and use it as a lever to prevent camshaft rotation.

7 Unscrew the retaining bolt and washer and free the sprocket from the camshaft end. If the sprocket locating pin is a loose fit, remove it and store it with the retaining bolt for safe-keeping.

 HAYNES HiNT *To ensure the sprocket and timing chain remain correctly engaged secure them together with a cable tie.*

8 Working in the **reverse** of the tightening sequence **(see illustration 10.17)**, slacken the camshaft pedestal retaining bolts by half-a-turn at a time, to gradually relieve the pressure of the valve springs. Once the valve spring pressure has been relieved, the bolts can be fully unscrewed and removed.

Caution: If the pedestal bolts are carelessly slackened, the pedestals might break.

9 Carefully lift the camshaft and pedestal assembly away from the top of the cylinder head and remove it from the engine. Recover the sealing ring which is fitted to the oil way on the centre pedestal and discard it; a new one must be used on refitting.

10 If the camshaft and pedestals assembly is to be dismantled, first check that the pedestal identification numbers are visible. The pedestals should be numbered 1 to 5 from front to rear. If the identifications marks are

not visible, number each cap before removing it. Starting at the front and working backwards, carefully slide the pedestals off the camshaft.

Inspection

11 Examine the camshaft bearing surfaces and cam lobes for signs of wear ridges and scoring. Renew the camshaft if any of these conditions are apparent. Examine the condition of the bearing surfaces both on the camshaft journals and the pedestals. If any of pedestal bearing surfaces are worn excessively, the pedestals must be renewed as a complete set. If the necessary measuring equipment is available, bearing wear can be checked by direct measurement (see values given in Specifications).

12 Examine the rocker arm bearing surfaces which contact the camshaft lobes for wear ridges and scoring and renew as necessary (see Section 11).

Refitting

13 Ensure the pedestals are clean and dry and that their oilways are unblocked.

14 Lubricate the camshaft and pedestal bearings with clean engine oil and slide the pedestals back onto the camshaft, using the identification numbers to ensure each one is correctly positioned.

15 Fit a new sealing ring to the centre pedestal oilway recess on the top of the cylinder head.

16 Position the camshaft so the lobes of No 4 cylinder are pointing upwards then lubricate the lobes and rocker arms with clean engine oil. Manoeuvre the camshaft and pedestal assembly into position and refit the retaining bolts.

17 Tighten the pedestal bolts by hand only then, working in the specified sequence, tighten the bolts by half-a-turn at a time to gradually impose the pressure of the valve springs on the pedestals and draw the pedestals squarely down onto the cylinder head **(see illustration)**. Once all pedestals are in contact with the cylinder head, go around in the specified sequence and tighten the retaining bolts to the specified torque.

Caution: If the pedestal bolts are carelessly tightened, the pedestals might break.

18 Ensure the locating pin is in position then locate the sprocket on the camshaft end, aligning its hole with the pin, and refit the retaining bolt and washer. Check that the flywheel timing mark is correctly aligned with its pointer and camshaft sprocket timing mark is correctly aligned with the mark on its support (see Section 3) then tighten the retaining bolt to the specified torque whilst preventing rotation using the method employed on removal. Where necessary, remove the cable-tie.

19 Fit a new sealing washer then refit the timing chain tensioner to the cylinder head and tighten it securely.

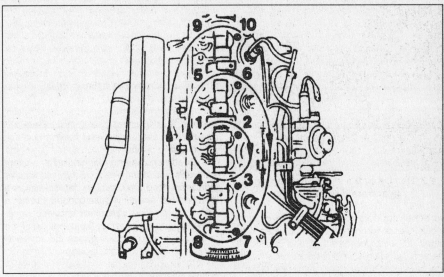

10.17 Camshaft pedestal retaining bolt tightening sequence

20 Adjust the valve clearances as described in Section 4 then refit the splash guard to the top of the pedestals, tightening its retaining bolts securely.

21 Refit the cylinder head cover as described in Section 5.

11 Rocker arms - removal, inspection and refitting

Removal

Note: *If the special Vauxhall service tool (KM 147) is available, the rocker arms can be removed without disturbing the camshaft. The tool is in the form of a lever which locates underneath the camshaft; with the cam lobe facing away from the rocker arm, the tool depresses the valve spring sufficiently to allow the rocker arm to be slid out of position. See your Vauxhall dealer for details. The following procedure assumes that the service tool is not available.*

1 Remove the camshaft as described in Section 10.

2 Obtain eight small, clean plastic containers, and number them 1 to 8; alternatively, divide a larger container into eight compartments.

3 Remove the retaining clips and lift off the rocker arms and thrust pads in turn. Place them in their respective container; do not interchange the rocker arms or the rate of wear will be much-increased. If necessary, unscrew the pivot bolts from the cylinder head and store them with their respective rocker arms.

Inspection

4 Examine the rocker arm bearing surfaces which contact the camshaft lobes for wear ridges and scoring. Renew any follower on which these conditions are apparent. If a

follower bearing surface is badly scored, also examine the corresponding lobe on the camshaft for wear, as it is likely that both will be worn. Also check the thrust pad, pivot screws and retaining clips for signs of wear or damage. Renew worn components as necessary.

Refitting

5 Screw the pivot screws fully into the cylinder head then fit each thrust pad to the top of its respective valve.

6 Lubricate the pivot screws with clean engine oil and fit each rocker arm. Ensure the rocker arms are correctly engaged with both the screws and thrust pads and secure then in position with the retaining clips.

7 Ensure the retaining clips are all securely fitted then refit the camshaft as described in Section 10.

12 Cylinder head - removal and refitting

Note: *The engine must be cold when removing the cylinder head. New cylinder head bolts must be used on refitting.*

Removal

1 Disconnect the battery negative lead.

2 Drain the cooling system as described in Chapter 1B.

3 Working as described in Chapter 4B, carry out the following procedures.

a) *Remove the inlet and exhaust manifolds.*

b) *Slacken the union nuts and remove the metal injector pipes connecting the injection pump to the injectors.*

c) *Disconnect the fuel return pipe from No 4 injector.*

d) *Unbolt the fuel filter and position it clear of the cylinder head.*

2D

4 Carry out the operations described in paragraphs 1 to 7 of Section 10 and unbolt the timing chain sprocket from the camshaft.

5 Unscrew the retaining nut and disconnect the main supply lead from the glow plug.

6 Slacken the retaining clips and disconnect the coolant hoses from the thermostat housing.

7 Disconnect the wiring connector from the coolant temperature which is screwed into the thermostat housing.

8 Make a final check to ensure that all relevant hoses, pipes and wires, etc, have been disconnected.

9 Slacken and remove the two bolts securing the front of the cylinder head to the top of the timing chain cover.

10 Working in a spiral sequence from the outside inwards, progressively slacken the cylinder head bolts by a third of a turn at a time until all bolts can be unscrewed by hand. Remove each bolt and washer in turn; discard the bolts as new ones must be used on refitting.

11 Lift the cylinder head from the cylinder block. If necessary, tap the cylinder head gently with a soft-faced mallet to free it from the block, but **do not** lever at the mating faces. Note the fitted positions of the two locating dowels, and remove them for safe keeping if they are loose.

12 Recover the cylinder head gasket and the sealing ring from the top of the timing chain cover. Keep the head gasket for identification purposes (see paragraph 19).

13 If the cylinder head is to be dismantled for overhaul, then refer to Part H of this Chapter.

Preparation for refitting

14 The mating faces of the cylinder head and cylinder block/crankcase must be perfectly clean before refitting the head. Use a hard plastic or wood scraper to remove all traces of gasket and carbon; also clean the piston crowns. Take particular care, as the surfaces are damaged easily. Also, make sure that the carbon is not allowed to enter the oil and water passages - this is particularly important for the lubrication system, as carbon could block the oil supply to any of the engine's components. Using adhesive tape and paper, seal the water, oil and bolt holes in the cylinder block/crankcase. To prevent carbon entering the gap between the pistons and bores, smear a little grease in the gap. After cleaning each piston, use a small brush to remove all traces of grease and carbon from the gap, then wipe away the remainder with a clean rag. Clean all the pistons in the same way.

15 Check the mating surfaces of the cylinder block/crankcase and the cylinder head for nicks, deep scratches and other damage. If slight, they may be removed carefully with a file, but if excessive, machining may be the only alternative to renewal.

16 Ensure that the cylinder head bolt holes in the crankcase are clean and free of oil. Syringe or soak up any oil left in the bolt holes. This is most important in order that the correct bolt tightening torque can be applied and to prevent the possibility of the block being cracked by hydraulic pressure when the bolts are tightened.

17 The cylinder head bolts must be discarded and renewed, regardless of their apparent condition.

18 If warpage of the cylinder head gasket surface is suspected, use a straight-edge to check it for distortion. Refer to Part H of this Chapter if necessary.

19 On this engine, the cylinder head-to-piston clearance is controlled by fitting different thickness head gaskets. The gasket thickness can be determined by looking at the number of holes punched in its identification tab.

Holes in gasket	Gasket thickness
One hole	1.3mm
Two holes	1.4 mm
Three holes	1.5 mm

The correct thickness of gasket required is selected by measuring the piston protrusions as follows.

20 Ensure that the crankshaft is positioned correctly at the TDC position. Mount a dial test indicator securely on the block so that its pointer can be easily pivoted between the piston crown and block mating surface. Zero the dial test indicator on the gasket surface of the cylinder block then carefully move the indicator over No 1 piston and measure its protrusion. Repeat this procedure on No 4 piston.

21 Remove the camshaft sprocket from the timing chain and rotate the crankshaft half-a-turn (180°) to bring No 2 and 3 pistons to TDC. Ensure the crankshaft is accurately positioned then measure the protrusions of No 2 and 3 pistons. Once both pistons have been measured, rotate the crankshaft through a further half a turn (180°) to bring No 1 and 4 pistons back to TDC. Realign the flywheel timing mark with the bellhousing pointer then engage the camshaft sprocket with the timing chain so that its timing mark is correctly aligned with the notch in the support plate

when the left-hand run of the chain is taut and all slack is on the tensioner side.

Caution: When rotating the crankshaft, keep the timing chain taut to prevent the chain jamming around the crankshaft sprocket.

22 Using the largest protrusion measurement of the four pistons, select the correct thickness of head gasket required using the following table.

Piston protrusion measurement	Gasket thickness required
Up to 0.60 mm	1.3 mm
0.61 to 0.70 mm	1.4 mm
0.71 to 0.85 mm	1.5 mm

Refitting

23 Wipe clean the mating surfaces of the cylinder head and cylinder block/crankcase.

24 Fit a new sealing ring to the recess in the top of the timing chain cover **(see illustration)**.

25 Apply a bead of sealant (Vauxhall recommend the use of sealant 1503294 - Part No 90001851), to the joints between the timing chain cover and the front of the cylinder block.

26 Check that the two locating dowels are in position then fit a new gasket to the cylinder block.

27 Referring to Section 3, ensure the flywheel timing mark is still correctly aligned with pointer on bellhousing and the timing mark on the camshaft sprocket is still correctly aligned with the notch on the sprocket support. Make sure that the camshaft is still correctly positioned with the lobes of No 4 cylinder pointing upwards.

28 With the aid of an assistant, carefully refit the cylinder head assembly to the block. Take care not to dislodge the sealing ring from the top of the timing chain cover and locate the head on the dowels.

29 Apply a smear of oil to the threads and the underside of the heads of the new cylinder head bolts and fit the washers to the bolts. Carefully enter each bolt into its relevant hole

12.24 Ensure the sealing ring (arrowed) is correctly fitted to the top of the timing chain cover

(*do not drop them in*) and screw all bolts in, by hand only, until finger-tight.

30 Working progressively, in a spiral sequence from the centre outwards, tighten the cylinder head bolts to their stage 1 torque setting, using a torque wrench and suitable socket.

31 Once all bolts have been tightened to the stage 1 torque, working again in spiral sequence from the centre outwards, go around and tighten all bolts through the specified stage 2 angle. It is recommended that an angle-measuring gauge is used to ensure accuracy. If a gauge is not available, use white paint to make alignment marks prior to tightening; the marks can then be used to check that the bolt has been rotated through the correct angle.

32 Refit the two bolts securing the cylinder head to the timing chain cover and tighten them to the specified torque.

33 Ensure the locating pin is in position then locate the sprocket on the camshaft end, aligning its hole with the pin, and refit the retaining bolt and washer. Check that the flywheel timing mark and camshaft sprocket timing marks are still correctly aligned with their marks (see Section 3) then tighten the retaining bolt to the specified torque whilst preventing rotation using the method employed on removal. Where necessary, remove the cable-tie.

34 Fit a new sealing washer then refit the timing chain tensioner to the cylinder head and tighten it securely.

35 Adjust the valve clearances as described in Section 4 then refit the splash guard to the top of the pedestals, tightening its retaining bolts securely.

36 Refit the cylinder head cover as described in Section 5.

37 Reconnect the wiring connector to the coolant temperature sender unit.

38 Reconnect the coolant hoses to the thermostat housing and securely tighten their retaining clips.

39 Reconnect the wiring to the glow plug and securely tighten the retaining nut.

40 Working as described in Chapter 4B, refit the inlet and exhaust manifolds and the injector pipes. Reconnect the return pipe to the injector and bolt the fuel filter back in position.

41 Refill the cooling system as described in Chapter 1B.

42 Start the engine, warm it up to normal operating temperature then switch it off again.

43 Taking care not to burn your hands, remove the cylinder head cover again (see Section 5) and slacken the bolts securing the front of the cylinder head to the timing chain cover. Working in a spiral sequence from the centre outwards, go around and tighten the ten main cylinder head bolts through the specified stage 3 angle (see paragraph 31). Finally go around in the same sequence and tighten them through the specified stage 4 angle. Tighten the cylinder head to timing

chain cover bolts to the specified torque then refit the cylinder head cover as described in Section 5.

13 Sump - removal and refitting

Note: *New sump lower and main section retaining bolts will be required on refitting.*

Removal

1 Disconnect the battery negative terminal.
2 Firmly apply the handbrake then jack up the front of the car and support it on axle stands.
3 Undo the retaining bolts and remove the engine undercover.
4 Referring to Chapter 1B, drain the engine oil and remove the oil filter. If the filter is damaged on removal, which is likely, a new filter must be used on refitting and the engine filled with fresh oil.
5 Position a jack underneath the transmission unit and raise the jack until it is supporting the weight of the transmission. Unscrew the nuts securing the rear engine mounting to the crossmember then slacken and remove the mounting bolts and remove the front suspension crossmember from underneath the engine/transmission unit.
6 Referring to Chapters 8 and 9, disconnect the propeller shaft then unbolt the front axle assembly from the chassis. Lower the axle slightly and rotate the differential drive flange downwards to gain the necessary clearance required to remove the sump casings.
7 Progressively slacken and remove the bolts securing the lower section of the sump to main casing. Break the joint by striking the lower section with the palm of the hand, then lower it away from the engine. Remove the gasket and retaining bolts and discard them.
8 Referring to Chapter 6, remove the clutch slave cylinder then unbolt the clutch housing support plate.
9 Unscrew the oil filter adaptor bolt and position the oil cooler temperature control valve assembly clear of the engine. Recover the sealing ring and discard it; a new one should be used on refitting.

10 Unscrew the retaining bolts and disconnect the turbocharger oil return hose end fitting from the main section of the sump. Release the retaining clips and disconnect the other oil and breather hoses from the sump, noting each ones correct fitted location.
11 Unbolt the fuel filter assembly and position it clear of the engine.
12 Progressively slacken and remove the bolts securing the main section of the sump to the cylinder block. Break the joint by striking the lower section with the palm of the hand, then lower the main sump casing away from the engine, taking care not to damage the oil pump pick-up/strainer. Remove the gasket pieces and retaining bolts and discard them.
13 If necessary, undo the retaining bolts securing the oil pump pick-up/strainer in position and remove it from the base of the cylinder block. Discard the gasket.

Refitting

14 Remove all traces of dirt and oil from the mating surfaces of the sump casings, cylinder block and timing chain cover and (where removed) the pick-up/strainer. Also thoroughly clean the retaining bolt hole threads.
15 Fit a new gasket to the oil pump pick-up/strainer (where removed) then refit it to the engine, tightening its retaining bolts securely.
16 Apply a smear of suitable sealing compound (Vauxhall recommend the use of sealant 1503295, Part No 90485251 - available from your Vauxhall dealer) to the cylinder block mating surface joints with the timing chain cover and rear main bearing cap (see illustrations). Fit the semi-circular end pieces of the gasket to the timing chain cover and rear main bearing cap, using the sealant to hold them in position.
17 Fit the new side sections of the gasket to the top of the sump main casting, sticking them in position with a smear of sealant.
18 Offer up the main casting to the cylinder block and fit the new retaining bolts. Tighten all bolts by hand then, working in a diagonal sequence from the centre outwards, go around and tighten all the retaining bolts to the specified torque setting.

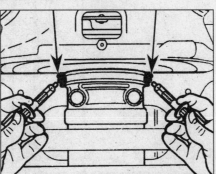

13.16a Apply sealant to the areas around the joints to the rear main bearing cap . . .

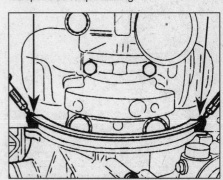

13.16b . . . and the timing chain cover joints

2D

19 Refit the fuel filter, tightening its retaining bolts securely.

20 Ensure the mating surfaces of the turbocharger hose end fitting and sump are clean and dry. Apply a smear of suitable sealing compound (Vauxhall recommend the use of sealant 1503166, Part No 90094714 - available from your Vauxhall dealer) to the end fitting then reconnect the hose to the sump, tightening its retaining bolts securely. Do not apply too much sealant to the end fitting as the excess sealant could find its way into the lubrication system. Apply a smear of the sealant to the other oil/breather hose unions then reconnect them to the sump and secure in position with the retaining clips.

21 Fit a new sealing ring to the recess on the top of the oil cooler temperature control valve assembly. Offer the assembly up to the timing chain cover and refit the adaptor bolt. Ensure the valve assembly is correctly positioned then tighten the adaptor bolt to the specified torque.

22 Referring to Chapter 6, refit the clutch housing support plate then refit the slave cylinder.

23 Apply a smear of suitable sealing compound (Vauxhall recommend the use of sealant 1503166, Part No 90094714 - available from your Vauxhall dealer) to the inner edge of the sump lower section mating surface then fit the new gasket. Refit the lower section to the main casting then fit the new retaining bolts and tighten them to the specified torque setting.

24 Refit the crossmember to the vehicle, engaging it with the rear mounting, and refit the mounting bolts. Tighten the mounting bolts to the specified torque setting then refit the engine mounting nuts and tighten them to the specified torque.

25 Refit the front axle as described in Chapter 9.

26 Fit a new oil filter and fill the engine with fresh oil as described in Chapter 1B. **Note:** *If the recommended Vauxhall sealants are being used, wait at least 12 hours before refilling the engine with oil. This will allow sufficient time for the sealing compounds to cure and prevent the risk of leakage.*

27 Refit the undercover then lower the vehicle to the ground and reconnect the battery.

14 Oil pump - removal, inspection and refitting

Removal

1 Disconnect the battery negative terminal then undo the retaining bolts and remove the engine undercover. The oil pump is located on the base of the timing chain cover.

2 Wipe clean the area around the pump cover and position a container beneath the cover, ready to catch any spilt oil.

3 Unscrew the oil pressure relief valve bolt and sealing washer from the pump cover and remove the spring and valve piston, noting which way around the piston is fitted **(see illustration)**.

4 Slacken and remove the pump cover retaining bolts then carefully remove the cover and collect the pump gears and gasket as they are released from the timing chain cover. A new gasket should be used on refitting.

Inspection

5 Clean the components, and carefully examine the gears, pump body, pump cover and valve piston for any signs of scoring or wear. Renew any component which shows signs of wear or damage; if the pump housing is marked then the timing chain cover assembly will have to be renewed.

6 If the pump components appear to be satisfactory, insert the gears back into the housing and, using feeler blades, check the gear teeth backlash (clearance) then place a straight edge across the base of the timing chain cover and measure the endfloat of each gear (either with or without the gasket in position) **(see illustrations)**. Compare the results to those given in the Specifications, if the gears are worn beyond the specified limits they must be renewed.

Refitting

7 Ensure the pump cover and timing chain cover mating surfaces are clean and dry then fit the gasket to the base of the cover, using a little grease to hold it in position.

8 Refit the gears to the timing chain cover, making sure the drive gear is correctly engaged with the injection pump drive shaft, then refit the pump cover. Refit the cover retaining bolts and tighten securely.

9 Engage the spring with the pressure relief valve piston and insert them into the oil pump cover. Fit a new sealing washer to the valve bolt then refit it to the cover, tightening it securely.

10 Unscrew the small plug from the top of the oil pump housing. Prime the pump by filling it with clean engine oil, using an oil can, then securely refit the plug to the housing.

11 Check the engine oil level (see *Weekly checks*) then reconnect the battery and start up the engine. Check for signs of leaks then refit the engine undercover.

15 Oil cooler and temperature control valve - removal and refitting

Oil cooler

Removal

1 Referring to Chapter 12, remove the radiator grille and the bonnet lock.

2 Wipe clean the area around the pipe unions on the side of the oil cooler and position a container beneath to catch any spilt oil. Make identification marks between one of the pipes and the cooler to ensure they are correctly reconnected on refitting.

3 Unscrew the union nuts and disconnect the oil pipes from the cooler. Plug/cover the oil cooler and pipe unions to minimise oil loss and prevent the entry of dirt into the system.

4 Slacken and remove the mounting nuts and washers then manoeuvre the oil cooler out of position. Recover the mounting rubber from the oil cooler lower mounting.

5 Inspect the oil cooler for signs of damage and renew if necessary. If the mounting rubber shows signs of wear or deterioration it should be renewed.

14.3 Oil pump pressure relief valve components (shown with pump cover)

14.6a Using feeler blades, measure the oil pump gear backlash . . .

14.6b . . . and the gear endfloat, and compare the results to those given in the Specifications

Refitting

6 Ensure the mounting rubber is correctly positioned then manoeuvre the oil cooler into position. Refit the washer and mounting nuts, tightening them to the specified torque.

7 Reconnect the oil pipes to the cooler and tighten the union nuts to the specified torque.

8 Refit the bonnet lock and radiator grille (see Chapter 12).

9 Check the engine oil level and, if necessary, top-up (see *Weekly checks*).

Temperature control valve

Removal

10 Disconnect the battery negative terminal then undo the retaining bolts and remove the engine undercover.

11 Referring to Chapter 1B, drain the engine oil and remove the oil filter. If the filter is damaged on removal, which is likely, a new filter must be used on refitting and the engine filled with fresh oil.

12 Wipe clean the area around the pipe unions on the side of the temperature control valve. Make identification marks between one of the pipes and the valve assembly to ensure they are correctly reconnected on refitting.

13 Unscrew the union nuts and disconnect the oil pipes from the valve. Plug/cover the valve and pipe unions to minimise oil loss and prevent the entry of dirt into the system.

14 Unscrew the oil filter adaptor bolt and position the oil cooler temperature control valve assembly clear of the engine. Recover the sealing ring and discard it; a new one should be used on refitting.

15 If necessary, remove the circlip then withdraw the end cap, spring and oil temperature thermostat from the valve body. Remove the sealing ring from the end cap and discard; a new one should be used on refitting. Inspect all components for signs of wear or damage and renew as necessary.

Refitting

16 If necessary, carefully fit the thermostat to the valve body and install the spring. Fit a new sealing ring to the end cap recess and

lubricate it with a smear of engine oil. Ease the end cap into the body and secure it in position with the circlip, making sure the circlip is correctly located.

17 Fit a new sealing ring to the recess on the top of the control valve and refit the valve assembly to the engine. Screw in the oil filter adaptor bolt and, making sure the valve unions are correctly positioned, tighten it to the specified torque.

18 Reconnect the oil pipes to the valve, tightening their union nuts to the specified torque.

19 Fit a new oil filter and fill the engine with fresh oil as described in Chapter 1B.

20 Refit the undercover and reconnect the battery.

16 Crankshaft oil seals - renewal

Front (timing chain end) oil seal

1 Remove the crankshaft pulley as described in Section 6.

2 Using a large flat-bladed screwdriver, carefully lever the seal out from the timing chain cover.

3 Clean the seal housing and polish off any burrs or raised edges which may have caused the seal to fail in the first place.

4 Lubricate the lips of the new seal with clean engine oil and press/tap it squarely into position until it is flush with the cover. If necessary, a suitable tubular drift, such as a socket, which bears only on the hard outer edge of the seal can be used to tap the seal into position.

5 Wash off any traces of oil, then refit the crankshaft pulley as described in Section 6.

Rear (flywheel end) oil seal

6 Remove the flywheel as described in Section 17.

7 Carefully punch or drill two small holes opposite each other in the oil seal. Screw a self-tapping screw into each and pull on the screws with pliers to extract the seal.

8 Clean the seal housing and polish off any burrs or raised edges which may have caused the seal to fail in the first place.

9 Lubricate the lips of the new seal with clean engine oil and ease it into position on the end of the crankshaft. Press the seal squarely into position until it is flush with the bearing cap. If necessary, a suitable tubular drift, such as a socket, which bears only on the hard outer edge of the seal can be used to tap the seal into position. Take great care not to damage the seal lips during fitting and ensure that the seal lips face inwards.

10 Refit the flywheel as described in Section 17.

17 Flywheel - removal, inspection and refitting

Note: *New flywheel retaining bolts must be used on refitting.*

Removal

1 Remove the transmission as described in Chapter 7 then remove the clutch assembly as described in Chapter 6.

2 Before proceeding any further, closely examine the flywheel retaining bolts. Find the bolt stamped with a P and mark its fitted location on the flywheel **(see illustration)**.

3 Prevent the flywheel from turning by locking the ring gear teeth with a similar arrangement to that shown **(see illustration)**. Alternatively, bolt a strap between the flywheel and the cylinder block/crankcase. Make alignment marks between the flywheel and crankshaft.

4 Slacken and remove the retaining bolts and remove the flywheel. Do not drop it, as it is very heavy. Discard the retaining bolts; new ones must be used on refitting.

Inspection

5 Examine the flywheel for wear or chipping of the ring gear teeth. Renewal of the ring gear is possible but is not a task for the home mechanic; renewal requires the new ring gear to be heated (to 180° to 230°C) to allow it to be fitted.

6 Examine the flywheel for scoring of the clutch face. If the clutch face is scored, the flywheel may be surface-ground, but renewal is preferable.

7 If there is any doubt about the condition of the flywheel, seek the advice of a Vauxhall dealer or engine reconditioning specialist. They will be able to advise if it is possible to recondition it or whether renewal is necessary.

Refitting

8 Clean the mating surfaces of the flywheel and crankshaft and remove all traces of locking compound from the crankshaft threads.

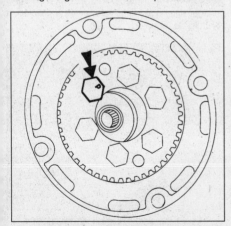

17.2 Mark the position of the bolt marked P on the flywheel prior to removal

17.3 Lock the flywheel ring gear with a tool similar to that shown

2D

17.9 Ensure the flywheel locating bolt, which is marked with the letter P is fitted in the correct location on refitting

9 Offer up the flywheel and insert the new retaining bolts, making sure the bolt marked P is fitted in the correct position **(see illustration)**. Tighten all bolts by hand.

10 Lock the flywheel using the method employed on removal then, working in a diagonal sequence, evenly and progressively tighten the retaining bolts to the specified stage 1 torque setting. Go around again in a diagonal sequence and angle-tighten the bolts through the specified stage 2 angle. It is recommended that an angle-measuring gauge is used during the final stages of the tightening, to ensure accuracy. If a gauge is not available, use white paint to make alignment marks between the bolt head and flywheel prior to tightening; the marks can then be used to check that the bolt has been rotated through the correct angle.

11 Refit the clutch as described in Chapter 6 then remove the locking tool and refit the transmission as described in Chapter 7.

---

18 Engine/transmission mountings -
inspection and renewal

Inspection

1 If improved access is required, raise the front of the car and support it securely on axle stands. Where necessary, undo the retaining bolts and remove the undercover from beneath the engine/transmission unit.

2 Check the mounting rubber to see if it is cracked, hardened or separated from the metal at any point; renew the mounting if any such damage or deterioration is evident.

3 Check that all the mounting s fasteners are securely tightened; use a torque wrench to check if possible.

4 Using a large screwdriver or a pry bar, check for wear in the mounting by carefully levering against it to check for free play; where this is not possible, enlist the aid of an assistant to move the engine/transmission unit back and forth, or from side to side, while you watch the mounting. While some free play is to be expected even from new components, excessive wear should be obvious. If excessive free play is found, check first that the fasteners are correctly secured, then renew any worn components as described below.

Renewal

Left- and right-hand side mountings

5 Slacken and remove the bolts securing both the left- and right-hand mountings to the chassis and unscrew the nut securing each mounting to its engine bracket.

6 Attach an engine hoist to the lifting brackets on the cylinder head and raise the engine slightly until there is sufficient clearance to manoeuvre the mountings out of position.

7 Refitting is the reverse of removal tightening the mounting nuts and bolts to the specified torque.

Rear mounting

8 Position a jack underneath the transmission unit and raise the jack until it is supporting the weight of the transmission.

9 Slacken and remove the nuts securing the mounting to the crossmember then unbolt the crossmember from the chassis and remove it from underneath the vehicle.

10 Slacken and remove the nuts and bolts securing the exhaust pipe mounting bracket to the mounting.

11 Unbolt the rear mounting from the underside of the transmission unit, noting the correct fitted location of the heatshield, and remove it from underneath the vehicle.

12 Refitting is the reverse of removal tightening all bolts to their specified torque settings.

Chapter 2 Part E
2.5 litre diesel engine in-car repair procedures

Contents

Compression and leakdown tests - description and interpretation . . 2
Crankshaft oil seals - renewal 17
Crankshaft pulley - removal and refitting 5
Cylinder head - dismantling and overhaul . . . . See Chapter 2H
Cylinder heads - removal and refitting 7
Cylinder head cover - removal and refitting 4
Engine mountings - inspection and renewal 18
Engine oil and filter renewal . . . . See Chapter 1B
Engine oil cooler - removal and refitting 13
Engine oil level check . . . . See Weekly checks
Flywheel - removal, inspection and refitting 19

General information 1
Oil filter adaptor - removal, and refitting 11
Oil filter thermostatic and by-pass valves - removal and refitting . . . 12
Oil pressure switch - removal and refitting 14
Oil pump - removal, inspection and refitting 9
Oil pump pressure relief valve - removal and refitting 10
Rocker arm assemblies - removal, inspection and refitting 6
Sump - removal and refitting 16
Timing cover - removal and refitting 8
Top dead centre (TDC) for No 1 piston - locating 3
Vacuum pump - removal and refitting 15

Degrees of difficulty

Easy, suitable for novice with little experience 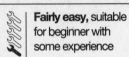	**Fairly easy,** suitable for beginner with some experience 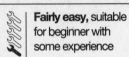	**Fairly difficult,** suitable for competent DIY mechanic 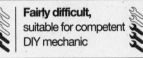	**Difficult,** suitable for experienced DIY mechanic 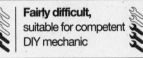	**Very difficult,** suitable for expert DIY or professional 

Specifications

General

Type	Four-cylinder, in-line, overhead valve
Designation	VM41B
Capacity	2499 cc
Bore	92.0 mm
Stroke	94.0 mm
Firing order	1-3-4-2 (No 1 cylinder at crankshaft pulley end)
Direction of crankshaft rotation	Clockwise viewed from front of engine
Compression ratio	22.5:1

Compression pressures

Maximum difference between cylinders (engine warm - approximately 80°C)	1 bar

Rocker arm assemblies

Rocker pedestal shaft diameter	21.979 to 22.000 mm
Rocker arm bush internal diameter	22.020 to 22.041 mm
Rocker arm running clearance	0.020 to 0.062 mm

Lubrication system

Oil pump clearances:	
Inner rotor tip to outer rotor	0.130 to 0.230 mm
Oil pump shaft endfloat	0.02 to 0.08 mm
Oil pressure relief valve spring free length	57.5 mm

Torque wrench settings

	Nm	lbf ft
Alternator support bracket bolts	83	61
Camshaft thrust plate bolts	24	18
Connecting rod big-end bearing cap bolts:		
Stage 1	29	21
Stage 2	Angle-tighten a further 60°	
Crankshaft bearing carrier retainers	54	40
Crankshaft two-piece bearing carrier retaining bolts	44	32
Crankshaft pulley nut	196	145
Cylinder head centre bolts:		
Stage 1	30	22
Stage 2	30	22
Stage 3	Angle-tighten a further 70°	
Stage 4	Angle-tighten a further 70°	
Run the engine for 20 minutes then allow it to cool completely. Slacken each bolt in turn and tighten to:		
Stage 5	30	22
Stage 6	Angle-tighten a further 65°	
Stage 7	Angle-tighten a further 65°	
12 000 miles (20 000 km) after overhaul:		
Stage 8	Angle tighten a further 15°	
Cylinder head outer bolts:		
Stage 1	30	22
Stage 2	Angle-tighten a further 80 to 90°	
Run the engine for 20 minutes then allow it to cool completely. Slacken each bolt in turn and tighten to:		
Stage 3	90	66
12 000 miles (20 000 km) after overhaul:		
Stage 4	Angle tighten a further 15°	
Cylinder head cover screws	16	12
Engine adaptor plate bolts	47	35
Engine adaptor plate nuts	27	20
Engine mounting bolts	50	37
Engine mounting nuts	85	63
Flywheel bolts:		
Stage 1	20	15
Stage 2	Angle tighten a further 60°	
Oil cooler hose banjo union bolts	33	24
Oil cooler mounting bolts	22	16
Oil cooler pipe and hose union nuts	33	24
Oil feed pipe-to-cylinder block adaptor banjo union bolt	23	17
Oil feed pipe-to-cylinder head banjo union bolts	13	10
Oil pump to cylinder block	27	20
Radiator visco-clutch fan pulley bolts	27	20
Rocker arm pedestals to cylinder head	29	21
Sump lower pan bolts	11	8
Sump-to-cylinder block bolts	11	8
Timing cover to cylinder block	11	8
Vacuum pump to cylinder block	27	20
Water manifold bolts	12	9

1 General information

How to use this Chapter

This Part of Chapter 2 is devoted to in-car repair procedures for the 2.5 litre diesel engine. Details on engine removal and refitting, and engine block/cylinder head overhaul, can be found in Chapter 2H.

Refer to *Buying spare parts and vehicle identification numbers* in the Reference Section of this manual for details of engine code locations.

Most of the operations in this Chapter assume that the engine is still installed in the car. Therefore, if this information is being used during a complete engine overhaul, with the engine already removed, many of the steps included here will not apply.

Engine description

The engine is of four-cylinder, in-line, overhead valve type, mounted longitudinally at the front of the vehicle with the transmission mounted on the rear end of the engine.

A cast iron cylinder block is used with replaceable wet liners, and an individual cylinder head is fitted for each cylinder.

The crankshaft is supported by a one-piece bush type main bearing at each end, and by three conventional shell-type intermediate main bearings. The rear and intermediate main bearings are located in aluminium alloy carriers, whereas the front main bearing is located directly in the cylinder block. Thrustwashers are fitted to the rear main bearing carrier to control crankshaft endfloat.

The connecting rods are attached to the crankshaft by horizontally-split shell-type big-end bearings and to the pistons by gudgeon pins. The gudgeon pins are fully-floating and are retained by circlips. The aluminium alloy pistons are fitted with three piston rings; two compression rings and a scraper-type oil control ring.

The camshaft is mounted in the cylinder block, and is driven by the crankshaft via a train of gears. Drive for the oil pump, vacuum pump and injection pump is included in this gear train.

The camshaft operates the valves by means of hydraulic tappets, push rods and rocker arms. Each pair of rocker arms is mounted on an individual shaft which is in turn mounted on one of the individual cylinder heads. The inlet and exhaust valves are mounted vertically in the cylinder heads and are each closed by a single valve spring.

Engine lubrication is by pressure feed from the oil pump located beneath the crankshaft. Engine oil is fed through an externally-mounted oil filter to the main oil gallery which feeds the crankshaft and camshaft internally, and the cylinder heads via an external oil supply pipe. A further external oil supply pipe is used to feed the turbocharger. An oil cooler is mounted in front of the radiator and is supplied via feed and return hoses connected to an adaptor located between the oil filter and cylinder block.

Repair operations possible with the engine in the vehicle

The following work can be carried out with the engine in the vehicle:

a) Compression pressure testing.
b) Removal and refitting of the cylinder head cover.
c) Removal and refitting of the rocker arm assemblies and push rods.
d) Removal and refitting of the cylinder heads.
e) Removal and refitting of the timing cover.
f) Removal and refitting of the oil pump and lubrication system components.
g) Removal and refitting of the vacuum pump.
h) Removal and refitting of the sump.
i) Removal and refitting of the connecting rods and pistons.*
j) Removal and refitting of the flywheel.
k) Renewal of the crankshaft oil seals.
l) Renewal of the engine mountings.

*Although the operation marked with an asterisk can be carried out with the engine in the vehicle after removal of the sump, it is better for the engine to be removed in the interests of cleanliness and improved access. For this reason, the procedure is described in Chapter 2H.

2 Compression and leakdown tests - description and interpretation

Compression test

Note: A compression tester specifically designed for diesel engines must be used for this test.

1 When engine performance is down, or if misfiring occurs which cannot be attributed to a fault in the fuel system, a compression test can provide diagnostic clues as to the engine's condition. If the test is performed regularly it can give warning of trouble before any other symptoms become apparent.

2 A compression tester specifically intended for diesel engines must be used, because of the higher pressures involved. The tester is connected to an adapter which screws into the fuel injector hole. It is unlikely to be worthwhile buying such a tester for occasional use, but it may be possible to borrow or hire one - if not, have the test performed by a garage.

3 Unless specific instructions to the contrary are supplied with the tester, observe the following points:

a) *The battery must be in a good state of charge, the air filter must be clean and the engine should be at normal operating temperature.*

b) *All the injectors should be removed before starting the test. When removing the injectors, also remove the fire seal washers (which must be renewed when the injectors are refitted - see Chapter 4B), otherwise they may be blown out.*

4 There is no need to hold the accelerator pedal down during the test because the diesel engine air inlet is not throttled.

5 Crank the engine on the starter motor for approximately four seconds. After one or two revolutions, the compression pressure should build up to a maximum figure and then stabilise. Record the highest reading obtained.

6 Repeat the test on the remaining cylinders, recording the pressure in each.

7 All cylinders should produce very similar pressures; any difference indicates the existence of a fault. Note that the compression should build up quickly in a healthy engine; low compression on the first stroke, followed by gradually increasing pressure on successive strokes, indicates worn piston rings. A low compression reading on the first stroke, which does not build up during successive strokes, indicates leaking valves or a blown head gasket (a cracked head could also be the cause). Deposits on the underside of the valve heads can also cause low compression.

8 On completion of the test, refit the fuel injectors as described in Chapter 4B.

Leakdown test

9 A leakdown test measures the rate at which compressed air fed into the cylinder is lost. It is an alternative to a compression test and in many ways it is better, since the escaping air provides easy identification of where pressure loss is occurring (piston rings, valves or head gasket).

10 The equipment needed for leakdown testing is unlikely to be available to the home mechanic. If poor compression is suspected, have the test performed by a suitably-equipped garage.

3 Top dead centre (TDC) for No 1 piston - locating

Note: *On later engines, a tool will need to be made from a length of dowel rod to lock the crankshaft in the TDC position. Details are given in the text.*

1 Top dead centre (TDC) is the highest point in the cylinder that each piston reaches as the crankshaft turns. Each piston reaches TDC at the end of the compression stroke and again at the end of the exhaust stroke; however, for the purpose of timing the engine, TDC refers to the position of No 1 piston at the end of its compression stroke. No 1 piston is at the crankshaft pulley end of the engine.

2 On early engines, when No 1 piston is at TDC, the timing mark on the crankshaft pulley should be aligned with the pointer on the timing cover. On later engines, a pointer is not fitted to the timing cover but instead a timing hole is provided in the engine rear adaptor plate into which a dowel rod can be inserted to engage with a corresponding hole in the flywheel. To determine which arrangement is fitted, check for the presence of a metal pointer on the timing cover just above the crankshaft pulley, then proceed as described under the following sub-headings.

Early engines with a timing cover pointer

3 To set the engine at TDC, the crankshaft must be turned. This should be done by using a spanner on the crankshaft pulley nut. If necessary, improved access to the pulley nut can be obtained from below after removing the engine undershield.

4 Remove the cylinder head cover as described in Section 4.

5 Turn the crankshaft pulley in a clockwise direction (as viewed from the front of the vehicle) to the point where the timing mark on the pulley aligns with the pointer on the timing cover (see illustration). As the pulley mark nears the pointer, No 1 piston is simultaneously approaching the top of its cylinder. To ensure that it is on its compression stroke and not its exhaust stroke, turn the crankshaft back and forth a few

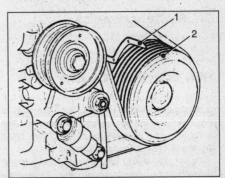

3.5 Timing pointer (1) and TDC timing mark (2) on early engines

2E

degrees from the TDC position and observe the action of the rocker arms and valves for No 1 and No 4 cylinders. When No 1 piston is at TDC on the compression stroke, the inlet and exhaust valve of No 1 cylinder will be closed, but the corresponding valves of No 4 cylinder will be seen to rock open and closed.

6 If the inlet and exhaust valves of No 1 cylinder are seen to rock whilst those of No 4 cylinder are shut, the crankshaft will need to be turned one full revolution clockwise to bring No 1 piston up to the top of its cylinder on the compression stroke.

7 Having determined that No 1 piston is on its compression stroke, re-align the timing mark and timing pointer ensuring that the pulley is always turned in a clockwise direction to finally align the marks.

8 On completion, refit the cylinder head cover unless other work in this vicinity is to be carried out.

Later engines without a timing cover pointer

9 On engines without a timing cover pointer, the only way to determine when No 1 cylinder is at TDC is by making a tool to insert into the timing holes in the engine adaptor plate and flywheel. The tool can be made from two dowel rods of diameters and lengths as shown **(see illustration)**. Drill a suitable hole in the centre of the larger dowel and insert the smaller dowel, using suitable adhesive. Alternatively, have the tool made up for you by a suitably-equipped garage. Once the tool is made, proceed as follows.

10 To set the engine at TDC, the crankshaft must be turned. This should be done by using a spanner on the crankshaft pulley nut. If necessary, improved access to the pulley nut can be obtained from below after removing the engine undershield.

11 Remove the cylinder head cover as described in Section 4.

12 Turn the crankshaft pulley in a clockwise direction (as viewed from the front of the vehicle) and observe the action of the rocker arms and valves for No 1 and No 4 cylinders. When No 1 piston is approaching TDC on the compression stroke, the inlet and exhaust valve of No 1 cylinder will be closed, but the exhaust valve of No 4 cylinder will be seen to still be closing.

13 If the exhaust valve of No 1 cylinder moving whilst those of No 4 cylinder are shut, the crankshaft will need to be turned one full revolution clockwise to bring No 1 piston up to the top of its cylinder on the compression stroke.

14 Having determined that No 1 piston is on compression, insert the tool into the timing hole located on the left-hand side of the engine rear adaptor plate, just above the crankshaft sensor. Push it in until it contacts the flywheel. While keeping slight pressure on the tool, continue turning the crankshaft slowly clockwise until the flywheel timing hole aligns and the tool is felt to engage further and

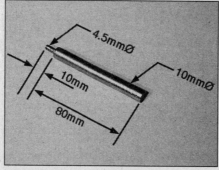

3.9 TDC setting tool dimensions for use on later engines

lock. No 1 piston is now at TDC on compression and will remain locked there by the tool. It is a good idea to put a notice on the engine warning that the crankshaft is locked and the tool is in position.

15 On completion, remove the tool and refit the cylinder head cover.

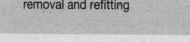

4 Cylinder head cover - removal and refitting

Removal

1 Release the clip and disconnect the crankcase breather hose from the rear of the cylinder head cover.

2 Progressively slacken, then unscrew the four cylinder head cover retaining screws. Withdraw the screws and collect the washers **(see illustration)**.

3 Lift off the cover and recover the gasket **(see illustrations)**. Obtain a new gasket for refitting.

Refitting

4 Thoroughly clean the cylinder head and cover mating faces and remove all traces of old gasket.

5 Position the new gasket on the cylinder head, then locate the cylinder head cover squarely over the gasket.

6 Refit the four screws and washers and tighten them progressively and evenly to the specified torque.

7 Reconnect the breather hose.

4.3a Remove the cylinder head cover . . .

4.2 Remove the cylinder head cover screws and washers

5 Crankshaft pulley - removal and refitting

Removal

Note: *Vauxhall special tool KM-8075 or a suitable heavy duty alternative puller is required to remove the pulley.*

1 Remove the auxiliary drive belt as described in Chapter 1B.

2 Slacken the crankshaft pulley retaining nut. To prevent crankshaft rotation whilst the retaining nut is slackened, have an assistant select top gear and apply the brakes firmly; if the engine is removed from the vehicle it will be necessary to lock the flywheel (see Section 19). Unscrew and remove the nut.

3 Attach Vauxhall puller KM-8075 or a suitable alternative to the pulley by means of the threaded holes in the centre of the pulley. Place a thrust piece over the end of the crankshaft to protect the crankshaft as the puller centre bolt is tightened.

4 Using the puller, draw the pulley off the crankshaft.

 Warning: The crankshaft pulley is a taper fit on the crankshaft and is likely to suddenly fly off when the taper releases. Stand to one side during this operation and protect yourself and surrounding areas of the vehicle.

5 With the pulley removed, check the oil seal in the timing cover for signs of leakage and, if

4.3b . . . and lift off the gasket

5.7a Apply Loctite 510 to the threads of the crankshaft . . .

5.7b . . . then screw on the pulley retaining nut

6.4 Lift the rocker assembly off the cylinder head studs

necessary renew it as described in Section 17.

Refitting

6 Lubricate the pulley boss with engine oil, then locate the pulley on the crankshaft aligning the slot in the pulley with the crankshaft Woodruff key.

7 Apply Loctite 510 to the crankshaft threads and screw on the retaining nut **(see illustrations)**.

8 Lock the crankshaft using the same procedure as for removal and tighten the nut to the specified torque.

9 Refit the auxiliary drivebelt as described in Chapter 1B.

6.6 Remove the pushrods from the hydraulic tappets

---

6 Rocker arm assemblies - removal, inspection and refitting

Removal

Note: *Each cylinder head has its own rocker assembly which can be individually removed.*

1 Remove the cylinder head cover as described in Section 4.

2 Remove the glow plugs as described in Chapter 5C.

3 Set the engine to the TDC position for No 1 cylinder as described in Section 3. From the TDC position turn the crankshaft anti-clockwise (as viewed from the front of the vehicle) one quarter of a turn. Do not turn the crankshaft until the rocker arm assemblies have been refitted.

4 Undo the two nuts securing the rocker assembly to the cylinder head, then lift the unit up and off the two studs **(see illustration)**.

5 Repeat this procedure for the remaining rocker assemblies as necessary. As each is removed, place them on a marked card or tie a label to them to identify the cylinder to which they were fitted.

6 With the rocker arm assemblies removed, the relevant push rods can be withdrawn from

their hydraulic tappets if required **(see illustration)**. Identify the push rod locations after removal.

Inspection

7 Lift off the spring plate then withdraw the inlet and exhaust rocker arm from each side of the pedestal. As each component is removed, wipe it clean then lay the parts out ready for inspection **(see illustrations)**.

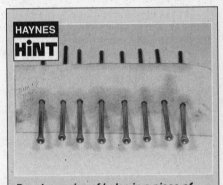

Punch a series of holes in a piece of card and label the holes 1 to 8, or as necessary depending on the number of pushrods being removed. Insert the push rods into their respective holes in the card to keep them in the correct order of fitting.

6.7a Lift off the rocker pedestal spring plate . . .

6.7b . . . remove the two rocker arms . . .

6.7c . . . and lay the parts out for inspection

2E

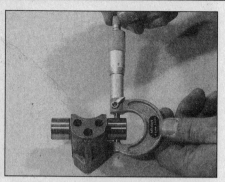

6.8 Measure the rocker pedestal shafts using a micrometer

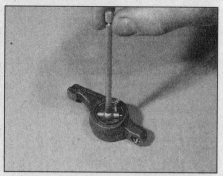

6.10a Measure the rocker bush internal diameter with an internal bore gauge . . .

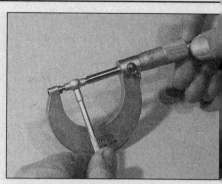

6.10b . . . then measure the gauge using a micrometer

8 Inspect the rocker pedestal shafts for signs of scoring or wear ridges. If the shafts appear satisfactory, measure their diameter at various points around the shaft using a micrometer **(see illustration)**. Record the dimensions obtained.

9 Examine the rocker arm pad and push rod location for signs of scoring or wear ridges. If any are apparent, the rocker arm should be renewed.

10 Examine the bush in each rocker arm for signs of excessive wear or lack of lubrication. If the bush appears satisfactory, measure its diameter at several points using an internal bore gauge. Measure the bore gauge using a micrometer to determine the bush internal diameter **(see illustrations)**.

11 Subtract the recorded rocker arm shaft diameter from the rocker arm bush diameter to

determine the running clearance and compare the figures obtained with those given in the specifications. If the components are excessively worn it will be necessary to obtain a new rocker pedestal and two new rocker arms.

12 The push rods should also be checked for straightness by rolling them along a level surface. If any signs of distortion are noticed, the push rod should be renewed.

Refitting

13 Make sure that the engine is still positioned as described in paragraph 3.

14 Lubricate both ends of the pushrods and fit them back into their respective hydraulic tappets.

15 Lubricate the rocker pedestal shafts with clean engine oil and fit the two rocker arms to the pedestal.

16 Slide the spring plate into position then locate the assembly over the studs on the cylinder head. Guide the assembly into place and engage the push rods with the rocker arms.

17 Refit the nuts and tighten to the specified torque.

18 Repeat this procedure on the remaining assemblies, as applicable.

19 Refit the cylinder head cover as described in Section 4.

20 Carefully turn the crankshaft clockwise (as viewed from the front of the vehicle) one complete revolution to check for any signs of piston to valve contact. If the valves are felt to contact the pistons, wait for 30 minutes to

allow the tappets to settle. When the crankshaft can be turned through a complete revolution without piston-to-valve contact, refit the glow plugs as described in Chapter 5C.

7 Cylinder heads - removal and refitting

Note: *A new cylinder head gasket must be fitted, and new cylinder head bolts may be required on refitting - see text.*

Removal

1 Remove the inlet and exhaust manifolds as described in Chapter 4B.

2 Release the clip and disconnect the heater hose from the rear of the cylinder head water manifold.

3 Progressively slacken the eight bolts securing the water manifold to the cylinder heads **(see illustration)**. Remove the bolts and washers and collect the hose bracket from the rear of the manifold.

4 Lift off the water manifold and recover the four gaskets **(see illustration)**.

5 Disconnect the engine wiring harness connectors at the rear of the engine **(see illustration)**.

6 Unscrew the locking collar and disconnect the injection pump main wiring plug from the harness socket.

7 Unscrew the pump wiring harness socket retaining ring and withdraw the socket from the harness bracket **(see illustration)**.

7.3 Undo the water manifold retaining bolts

7.4 Remove the water manifold and recover the gaskets

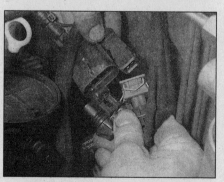

7.5 Disconnect the wiring harness connectors at the rear of the engine

7.7 Unscrew the injection pump wiring harness socket retaining ring and remove the socket

7.9 Disconnect the hose and remove the oil separator

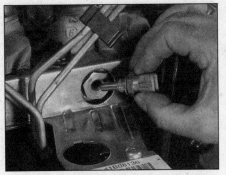

7.10 Unscrew the coolant temperature sensor from the cylinder head

7.11 Remove the wiring harness bracket

8 Disconnect the remaining wiring connectors at the harness bracket and detach the wiring sockets from the bracket.

9 Slacken the clips and detach the crankcase ventilation hoses from the oil separator. Release the oil separator and remove it from the wiring harness bracket **(see illustration)**.

10 Disconnect the wiring at the coolant temperature sensor located in the centre of the wiring harness bracket and unscrew the sensor from the cylinder head **(see illustration)**. Disconnect the wiring at the remaining sensor below No 1 cylinder fuel injector.

11 Undo the bolts and remove the wiring harness bracket **(see illustration)**.

12 Disconnect the wiring connector from the top of each glow plug and move the wiring harness to one side, clear of the cylinder heads **(see illustration)**.

13 Remove the fuel injectors as described in Chapter 4B.

14 Remove the cylinder head cover as described in Section 4.

15 Remove the rocker arm assemblies and push rods as described in Section 6.

16 Undo the four banjo union bolts securing the oil feed pipe to the cylinder head, and the remaining banjo union bolt securing the rear of the pipe to the cylinder block adaptor. Collect the two copper washers at each banjo union and remove the pipe from the engine **(see illustration)**. Note that new copper washers will be required for refitting.

17 Working progressively and in a spiral sequence, slacken the eighteen cylinder head retaining bolts. Remove the bolts, clamps and end plates and identify their locations to ensure correct refitting in their original positions **(see illustrations)**.

18 Lift the four cylinder heads off the engine and mark them one to four to ensure correct refitting **(see illustration)**. Remove the cylinder head gasket from the block.

19 If the cylinder heads are to be dismantled for overhaul, refer to Part H of this Chapter.

Preparation for refitting

20 The mating faces of the cylinder heads and block must be perfectly clean before refitting the heads. Use a scraper to remove all traces of gasket and carbon, and also clean the tops of the pistons. Take particular care as the surfaces are damaged easily.

Also, make sure that debris is not allowed to enter the oil and water channels - this is particularly important for the lubrication system, as carbon could block the oil supply to any of the engine's components. Using adhesive tape and paper, seal the water, oil and bolt holes in the cylinder block. Clean the piston crowns in the same way.

> **HAYNES HINT** *To prevent carbon entering the gap between the pistons and bores, smear a little grease in the gap. After cleaning the piston, rotate the crankshaft so that the piston moves down the bore, then wipe out the grease and carbon with a cloth rag.*

2E

7.12 Disconnect the glow plug wiring harness

7.16 Remove the oil feed pipe

7.17a Remove the cylinder head bolts and clamps . . .

7.17b . . . and lift off the end plates

7.18 Remove the four cylinder heads from the cylinder block

7.30 Locate a new gasket of the correct thickness on the cylinder block

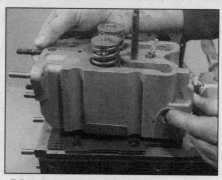

7.31a Lower No 1 cylinder head onto the gasket . . .

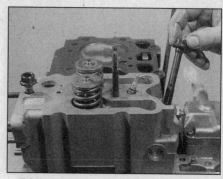

7.31b . . . and screw in the outer bolts

21 Check the block and heads for nicks, deep scratches and other damage. If slight, they may be removed carefully with a file. More serious damage may be repaired by machining, but this is a specialist job.

22 If warpage of the cylinder head is suspected, use a straight-edge to check it for distortion. Refer to Part H of this Chapter.

23 Clean out the bolt holes in the block using a pipe cleaner, or a rag and screwdriver. Make sure that all oil is removed, otherwise there is a possibility of the block being cracked by hydraulic pressure when the bolts are tightened.

24 Examine the bolt threads and the threads in the cylinder block for damage. If necessary, use the correct-size tap to chase out the threads in the block, and use a die to clean the threads on the bolts.

25 Although the manufacturers do not specify that the cylinder head bolts should be renewed after removing the heads, it is strongly recommended that new bolts are obtained. The bolts are tightened to a very high torque setting to the point where the bolts just start to stretch. The re-use of old bolts could lead to inaccurate torque settings when tightening, or breakage of the bolt(s).

26 Turn the crankshaft to bring piston Nos 1 and 4 to just below the TDC position (just below the top face of

the cylinder block). Position a dial gauge on the cylinder block, and zero it on the block face. Transfer the probe to a point near the edge of No 1 piston crown, then slowly turn the crankshaft back and forth past TDC, noting the highest reading produced on the indicator. Record this reading. Move the probe to a diametrically opposite point on No 1 piston and take another reading in the same way. Record this reading also.

27 Repeat this measurement procedure on No 4 piston, then turn the crankshaft half a turn (180º) and repeat the procedure on Nos 2 and 3 pistons.

28 Ascertain the greatest piston protrusion measurement, and use this to determine the correct cylinder head gasket from the following table.

Piston protrusion	Gasket grade and thickness
0.53 mm or more, but less than 0.63 mm	A (1.42 mm)
0.63 mm or more, but less than 0.73 mm	C (1.52 mm)
0.73 mm or more, but less than 0.83 mm	B (1.62 mm)

Refitting

29 Turn the crankshaft clockwise (viewed from the front of the engine) until Nos 1 and 4 pistons pass bottom dead centre (BDC) and begin to rise, then position them halfway up

their bores. Nos 2 and 3 pistons will also be at their mid-way positions, but descending their bores.

30 Ensure that the cylinder head locating dowels are fitted to the cylinder block, then fit the correct gasket the right way round on the cylinder block (see illustration).

31 Lower No 1 cylinder head onto the block. Lubricate the cylinder head bolt threads, and the undersides of the bolt heads with a little engine oil, then insert the two outer bolts into their locations (see illustrations). Screw the bolts into their threads as far as possible by hand.

32 Place the end plate in position then insert the two front retaining bolts together with their clamps. Screw the bolts in by hand (see illustrations).

33 Refit the remaining three cylinder heads in the same way making sure that the clamps are all positioned correctly (see illustration).

34 With all four cylinder heads in position, lightly tighten the cylinder head bolts until the bolt heads just contact the clamps. Do not tighten the bolts any further at this stage.

35 Using a new copper washer on each side of the banjo unions, refit the oil feed pipe to the cylinder head, and cylinder block adaptor. Screw in the banjo union bolts and tighten them finger

7.32a Place the end plate in position . . .

7.32b . . . and screw in the front retaining bolts and clamps

7.33 Check that all the head bolt clamps are positioned correctly

7.35 Refit the oil feed pipe using new copper washers

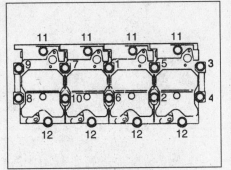

7.37a Cylinder head bolt tightening sequence

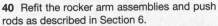

1 to 10 - centre bolts
11 and 12 - outer bolts

7.37b Tighten the cylinder head bolts to the specified torque using a torque wrench . . .

tight only at this stage **(see illustration)**.

36 Refit the inlet and exhaust manifolds to the cylinder heads as described in Chapter 4B, but do not tighten the manifold-to-cylinder head nuts to any more than 5 Nm (4 lbf ft). The manifolds must be in position to align the cylinder heads before any torque tightening can be carried out.

37 With the manifolds in place, tighten the ten centre cylinder head retaining bolts in the order shown, and in the stages given in the Specifications - ie, tighten the centre bolts in sequence to the Stage 1 torque, then in sequence to the Stage 2 torque using a torque wrench, then in sequence to the Stage 3 and Stage 4 angle using an angle tightening gauge **(see illustrations)**.

⚠️ *Warning: The final cylinder head bolt tightening stages involve very high forces. Ensure that the tools used are in good condition. If the engine is not in the car, engage the help of an assistant to steady and support the engine.*

38 With the ten centre bolts tightened fully, tighten the eight outer bolts in any order to the Stage 1 torque setting given in the Specifications, then to the Stage 2 angle.

39 The inlet and exhaust manifold nuts can now be tightened to the specified torque (see Chapter 4B), followed by the oil feed pipe banjo union bolts.

40 Refit the rocker arm assemblies and push rods as described in Section 6.

41 Refit the cylinder head cover as described in Section 4.

42 Refit the fuel injectors as described in Chapter 4B.

43 Feed the wiring harness back into position and reconnect the glow plug wiring.

44 Refit the wiring harness bracket, coolant temperature sensor and oil separator. Reconnect the ventilation hoses to the oil separator.

45 Refit the injection pump wiring socket to the wiring harness bracket and secure with the retaining ring. Reconnect the pump wiring plug to the socket and secure with the locking collar.

46 Reconnect the remaining wiring connectors and secure the sockets to the bracket. Reconnect the wires to the coolant temperature sensors.

47 Using new gaskets, locate the water manifold in position on the cylinder heads and refit the bolts and washers. Ensure that the hose bracket is in position under the two rear bolts. Progressively tighten the water manifold retaining bolts to the specified torque. Reconnect the heater hose and expansion tank hose to the water manifold.

48 Check that all hoses, wiring and components have been reconnected then fill and bleed the cooling system as described in Chapter 1B.

49 Prime and bleed the fuel system as described in Chapter 4B.

50 Start the engine and allow it to reach normal operating temperature.

51 Run the engine for a further twenty minutes then switch off and allow it to cool completely. Re-torque the cylinder head bolts as follows.

52 Using a small screwdriver, prise out the plastic inserts in the top of the cylinder head cover **(see illustration)**.

53 Re-torque the ten centre cylinder head retaining bolts in the order shown **(see illustration 7.37a)** by slackening, then immediately re-tightening each bolt, one at a time, to the Stage 5 torque setting then tighten it further through the Stage 6 and Stage 7 angles. The four bolts located inside the cylinder head cover can be reached through the access holes in the cover **(see illustration)**.

54 Now tighten the eight cylinder head outer bolts (without first slackening) in any order to the Stage 3 torque setting given in the Specifications.

55 Refit the cylinder head cover plastic inserts on completion.

56 A final tightening stage will be necessary once the vehicle has covered a further 12 000 miles (20 000 km). For the final stage, all the bolts must be tightened further, without slackening them initially. Tighten the ten centre bolts in the correct tightening sequence, and the eight outer bolts in any sequence.

2E

7.37c . . . then through the specified angle using an angle tightening gauge

7.52 Prise out the cylinder head cover plastic inserts . . .

7.53 . . . then re-torque the cylinder head bolts through the access holes

8.3 Cooling fan pulley retaining bolts (arrowed)

8.8 Note the location of the clip (arrowed) when removing the timing cover bolts

8.9 Withdraw the timing cover from the cylinder block

8 Timing cover - removal and refitting

Removal

1 Remove the auxiliary drivebelt as described in Chapter 1B.
2 Remove the radiator visco-clutch cooling fan as described in Chapter 3.
3 Undo the three bolts and remove the fan pulley (see illustration).
4 Remove the crankshaft pulley as described in Section 5.
5 Undo the nut securing the power steering pump pulley to the steering pump shaft. Prevent the pump shaft from turning as the

8.12 Apply a bead of sealant to the timing cover mating face

nut is undone using an Allen key or similar tool inserted into the end of the pump shaft.
6 Withdraw the pulley from the pump shaft, using a puller if the pulley is tight.
7 Slacken the clip and disconnect the vacuum pump oil drain hose from the adaptor on the front of the timing cover.
8 Undo the screws securing the timing cover to the cylinder block, noting the location of the hose clip and on early models, the timing pointer (see illustration).
9 Withdraw the timing cover from the cylinder block (see illustration). If the cover is tight, very carefully prise it away to break the bond formed by the sealant.
10 With the timing cover removed it is advisable to renew the oil seal as a matter of course as described in Section 17.
11 Thoroughly clean the cover and cylinder block ensuring all traces of sealer are removed.

Refitting

12 Apply a 3.0 mm bead of RTV sealant to the timing cover mating face, ensuring that the sealant bead passes around the inside of the bolt holes (see illustration).
13 Place the timing cover on the cylinder block and refit the retaining screws, bracket and clip as applicable. Progressively tighten the screws in a diagonal sequence to the specified torque.
14 Refit the vacuum pump oil drain hose and secure with the clip.

15 Refit the power steering pump pulley and tighten the retaining nut to the specified torque.
16 Refit the crankshaft pulley as described in Section 5.
17 Refit the fan pulley and secure with the three bolts tightened to the specified torque.
18 Refit the radiator visco-clutch cooling fan as described in Chapter 3.
19 Refit the auxiliary drivebelt as described in Chapter 1B.

9 Oil pump - removal, inspection and refitting

Removal

1 Remove the timing cover as described in Section 8.
2 Undo the three bolts securing the oil pump to the cylinder block (see illustration).
3 Withdraw the oil pump from the engine and remove the O-ring seal from the pump (see illustrations). Note that a new O-ring will be required for refitting.

Inspection

4 Carefully examine the pump body and inner and outer rotors for any signs of scoring or wear. Renew the complete pump assembly if excessive wear is evident (no spare parts are available separately).
5 If the components appear serviceable,

9.2 Undo the oil pump retaining bolts (arrowed)

9.3a Withdraw the oil pump . . .

9.3b . . . and remove the O-ring

9.6 Prime the oil pump by filling it with engine oil

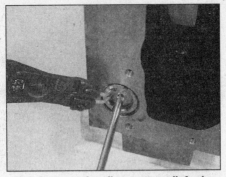

10.2 Depress the oil pressure relief valve cap and extract the circlip

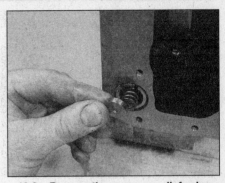

10.3a Remove the pressure relief valve cap . . .

measure the clearance between the inner rotor tip and outer rotor using feeler blades. Also check for signs of excessive endfloat of the shaft. If the clearances exceed the specified tolerances, the pump must be renewed.

6 If the pump is satisfactory, fit a new O-ring and fill the pump with engine oil **(see illustration)**.

Refitting

7 Lubricate the O-ring with clean engine oil, place the pump on the cylinder block and insert and fully tighten the retaining bolts.
8 Refit the timing cover as described in Section 8.

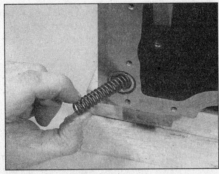

10.3b . . . spring . . .

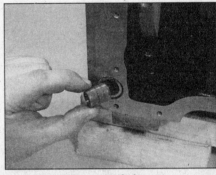

10.3c . . . and plunger

10 Oil pump pressure relief valve - removal and refitting

Removal

1 Remove the sump as described in Section 16.
2 Depress the centre of the relief valve cap using a screwdriver, to remove the tension on the circlip, then extract the retaining circlip using circlip pliers **(see illustration)**.
3 Slowly release the tension on the relief valve cap, and withdraw the cap, spring and plunger from the cylinder block **(see illustrations)**. Take care when doing this as it is likely that a carbon ridge may have formed in the orifice, initially preventing the cap from

releasing. The cap may then suddenly break free and the spring and plunger will fly out.
4 With all the components removed, clean them thoroughly and check for signs of scoring or wear ridges on the relief valve plunger.
5 Using vernier calipers, check the free length of the spring and compare the dimension obtained with that given in the Specifications **(see illustration)**. Renew the plunger if scoring or wear ridges are apparent, and renew the spring if the free length is less than specified, or if any distortion is noticed.

Refitting

6 Lubricate the plunger and the plunger bore with clean engine oil, then fit the plunger, spring and cap.
7 Depress the cap slightly with a screwdriver, and refit the retaining circlip, ensuring that the

circlip is fully located in the groove in the orifice.
8 Refit the sump as described in Section 16.

11 Oil filter adaptor - removal and refitting

Removal

1 Remove the oil filter cartridge as described in Chapter 1B.
2 Unscrew the oil cooler hose unions from the oil filter adaptor.
3 Using an Allen key, unscrew the adaptor centre retaining bolt **(see illustration)**.
4 Withdraw the oil filter adaptor from the cylinder block and remove the sealing O-ring **(see illustration)**. Note that a new O-ring will be required for refitting.

2E

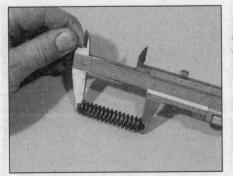

10.5 Measure the relief valve spring free length

11.3 Unscrew the oil filter adaptor retaining bolt (arrowed)

11.4 Withdraw the adaptor and remove the O-ring

12.2 Unscrew the by-pass valve end cap

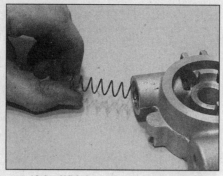

12.3a Withdraw the by-pass valve spring . . .

12.3b . . . and valve plunger

Refitting

5 Locate a new O-ring on the adaptor rear face and lubricate the ring with clean engine oil.

6 Fit the adaptor to the cylinder block, screw in the retaining bolt and tighten securely.

7 Connect the oil cooler hose unions, then fit a new oil filter, and refill the engine with oil as described in Chapter 1B.

12 Oil filter thermostatic and by-pass valves - removal and refitting

Removal

1 Remove the oil filter adaptor as described in Section 11.

By-pass valve

2 Unscrew the end cap from the oil filter adaptor and recover the copper washer (see illustration). Note that a new copper washer will be required for refitting.

3 Withdraw the spring and by-pass valve plunger from the adaptor (see illustrations).

4 Examine the components for any signs of scoring or wear ridges and renew as necessary.

Thermostatic valve

5 Unscrew the oil cooler banjo union from the bypass valve and recover the two copper washers (see illustration). Note that new copper washers will be required for refitting.

6 Unscrew the thermostatic valve and remove it from the adaptor, collecting the copper washer (see illustration).

Refitting

7 Refitting is a reversal of removal, but use new copper washers on all fittings.

13 Engine oil cooler - removal and refitting

Removal

Note: *On vehicles equipped with air conditioning, it will be necessary to discharge the system and remove various components for access to the oil cooler. On these vehicles, it is recommended that removal and refitting of the oil cooler is entrusted to a Vauxhall dealer.*

1 Drain the cooling system as described in Chapter 1B.

2 Remove the radiator grille as described in Chapter 12.

3 Remove the oil filter (refer to Chapter 1B).

4 Unscrew the union nuts and disconnect the oil cooler pipe assembly from the oil cooler, and from the oil filter adaptor supply and return hoses, being prepared for oil spillage. Remove the pipe assembly from under the oil cooler.

5 Undo the two oil cooler mounting bolts and collect the washers, bushes and spacers noting their arrangement for refitting.

6 Carefully lift the oil cooler out of the lower centre mounting bush and remove it from the front of the vehicle. Collect the mounting bush from the body mounting or oil cooler.

Refitting

7 Refitting is a reversal of removal, ensuring that the mounting components are fitted as noted during removal. On completion, refill the cooling system as described in Chapter 1B, and check and if necessary top up the engine oil as described in *Weekly checks*.

14 Oil pressure switch - removal and refitting

Removal

1 Disconnect the wiring connector from the oil pressure switch located on the right-hand side of the engine above the starter motor.

2 Unscrew the switch from its location and collect the copper washer (see illustration). Note that a new copper washer will be required for refitting.

Refitting

3 Refitting is a reversal of removal using a new copper washer.

12.5 Unscrew the oil cooler hose banjo union from the thermostatic valve . . .

12.6 . . . and unscrew the thermostatic valve from the oil filter adaptor

14.2 Unscrew the oil pressure switch and collect the copper washer

15.4 Unscrew the vacuum pump retaining bolts (arrowed)

15.5a Withdraw the vacuum pump . . .

15.5b . . . and remove the O-ring

15 Vacuum pump - removal, inspection and refitting

Removal

1 Remove the cylinder head cover as described in Section 4.
2 Set the engine to the TDC position for No 1 cylinder as described in Section 3.
3 Remove the timing cover as described in Section 8.
4 Undo the four bolts securing the vacuum pump to the cylinder block and collect the washers (see illustration).
5 Withdraw the vacuum pump from the engine and remove the O-ring seal (see illustrations). Note that a new O-ring will be required for refitting.

Inspection

6 Lift out the three vanes and carefully examine the vanes and pump body inner surfaces for any signs of scoring or wear. The vanes can be obtained separately, but if any are worn, all three should be renewed. If there is any signs of wear on the pump body, a complete new pump must be obtained.
7 If the pump is satisfactory, refit the vanes and fit a new O-ring to the pump body.

Refitting

8 Check that the engine is still positioned at

TDC for No 1 cylinder on compression as described in Section 3.
9 Check that the timing marks on the camshaft and injection pump gears are aligned (see illustration). The marks consist of a punch mark on two adjacent teeth on the camshaft gear and a letter B on one tooth of the injection pump gear which must be between the two camshaft marks. If necessary turn the camshaft gear until the marks line up.
10 Lubricate the vacuum pump O-ring and position the pump on the engine so that when fully in position the timing marks will be aligned with those on the adjacent gears. The marks consist of two punch marks on the vacuum pump which aligns with a single punch mark on the camshaft gear, and a single punch mark on the pump gear which aligns with two punch marks on the crankshaft gear (see illustration).
11 Slide the pump gear into engagement with the camshaft and crankshaft gear and, at the same time, move the pump outer anti-backlash ring into alignment using a screwdriver (see illustration). Push the pump fully into position.
12 Check that all the timing marks are aligned then secure the pump with the four bolts and washers tightened to the specified torque.
13 Refit the timing cover as described in Section 8.
14 Refit the cylinder head cover as described in Section 4.

15.9 Timing marks on the camshaft and injection pump gears in alignment

16 Sump - removal and refitting

Removal

1 Disconnect the battery negative lead.
2 Remove the engine undershield then drain the engine oil as described in Chapter 1B. Refit and tighten the drain plug using a new washer.
3 Remove the engine oil dipstick and disconnect the hose at the union on the sump top face (see illustration).
4 Jack up the front of the vehicle and support on axle stands (see Jacking and vehicle support).

2E

15.10 Timing marks on the vacuum pump, camshaft and crankshaft gears in alignment

15.11 Align the teeth on the vacuum pump anti-backlash gear as the pump is fitted

16.3 Disconnect the hose at the union on the sump

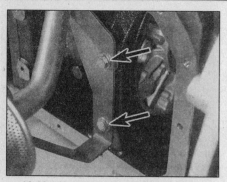
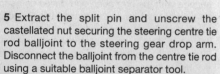

16.13a Undo the two oil pick-up pipe support bracket bolts and remove the pipe and strainer

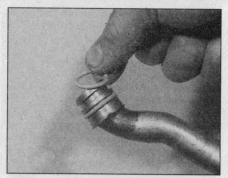
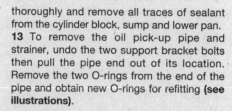

16.13b Remove the two O-rings from the end of the pipe

16.15 Apply a bead of RTV sealant to the sump mating face . . .

5 Extract the split pin and unscrew the castellated nut securing the steering centre tie rod balljoint to the steering gear drop arm. Disconnect the balljoint from the centre tie rod using a suitable balljoint separator tool.

6 Similarly extract the split pin and unscrew the castellated nut securing the steering centre tie rod to the idler pivot assembly drop arm. Disconnect the balljoint from the centre tie rod using a suitable balljoint separator tool. Move the centre tie rod clear of the axle front mounting bolts.

7 Position a trolley jack below and in contact with the front axle differential housing.

8 Undo the rear bolt and washer, and front bolt, nut and washer each side securing the axle mounting brackets to the chassis. Support the axle and driveshafts and lower the unit so that it rests on the suspension lower control arms.

9 Unscrew the bolts securing the sump to the cylinder block, but leave two diagonally opposite bolts entered on a few threads until the sump joint has been released.

10 Using a palette knife or similar tool, release the sump from the bottom of the cylinder block. Do not use a screwdriver as this may damage the mating surfaces.

11 Unscrew the two remaining bolts and lower the sump from the engine.

12 If required, the lower pan may be removed from the sump after undoing the retaining bolts and separating the two components as previously described. Clean the components

thoroughly and remove all traces of sealant from the cylinder block, sump and lower pan.

13 To remove the oil pick-up pipe and strainer, undo the two support bracket bolts then pull the pipe end out of its location. Remove the two O-rings from the end of the pipe and obtain new O-rings for refitting (see illustrations).

Refitting

14 Lubricate the two new oil pick-up pipe O-rings and fit them to the end of the pipe. Insert the pipe into the cylinder block then secure the support bracket with the two retaining bolts.

15 Apply a 3.0 mm bead of RTV sealant to the sump mating face, ensuring that the sealant bead passes around the inside of the bolt holes (see illustration).

16 Lift the sump into position, then insert the bolts and tighten them progressively to the specified torque (see illustration).

17 If the lower pan has been removed, apply a 3.0 mm bead of RTV sealant to the lower pan mating face, ensuring that the sealant bead passes around the inside of the bolt holes (see illustration).

18 Fit the lower pan to the sump, then insert the bolts and tighten them progressively to the specified torque (see illustration).

19 Raise the jack, locate the front axle in position and fit the front and rear mounting bolts, washers and nuts. Fit all four mountings hand tight initially, then tighten them in a

diagonal sequence to the specified torque (see Chapter 9 for torque wrench settings applicable to the front axle components).

20 Reconnect the steering centre tie-rod to the idler pivot drop arm and steering gear drop arm, fit the castellated nuts and tighten them to the specified torque. Align the split pin holes by further tightening the nuts slightly, if necessary, then secure the nuts using new split pins.

21 Refit the engine undershield then lower the vehicle to the ground.

22 Refit the engine oil dipstick and reconnect the hose at the union on the sump top face.

23 Refill the engine with oil as described in Chapter 1B and reconnect the battery.

17 Crankshaft oil seals - renewal

Front (timing cover) oil seal

1 Remove the crankshaft pulley, as described in Section 5.

2 Prise out the old oil seal using a small screwdriver, taking care not to damage the surface of the crankshaft. Alternatively, the oil seal can be removed by drilling two small holes diagonally opposite each other and inserting self-tapping screws in them. A pair of grips can then be used to pull out the oil seal, by pulling on each side in turn.

16.16 . . . then fit the sump to the cylinder block

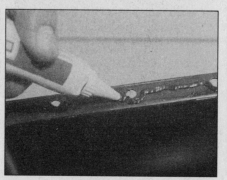

16.17 Apply RTV sealant to the lower pan mating face . . .

16.18 . . . and fit the lower pan to the sump

3 Wipe clean the oil seal seating, then dip the new seal in fresh engine oil, and locate it over the crankshaft with its closed side facing outwards. Make sure that the oil seal lip is not damaged as it is located on the crankshaft.

4 Using a tube of suitable diameter, drive the oil seal squarely into the housing until flush. A block of wood cut to pass over the end of the crankshaft may be used instead.

5 Refit the crankshaft pulley as described in Section 5.

Rear (flywheel end) oil seal

6 Remove the flywheel as described in Section 19.

7 Lift off the two crankshaft endfloat half thrustwashers noting their fitted direction for refitting **(see illustrations)**.

8 Remove the old seal and fit the new seal using the procedures described previously in paragraphs 2 to 4.

9 Locate the thrustwashers in their correct positions as noted during removal then refit the flywheel as described in Section 19.

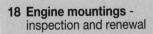

18 Engine mountings - inspection and renewal

Inspection

1 Visually inspect the rubber pads on the two engine mountings for signs of cracking and deterioration. Careful use of a lever will help to determine the condition of the rubber pads. If there is excessive movement in the mounting, or if the rubber has deteriorated, the mounting should be renewed.

Renewal

2 Remove the engine undershield and support the engine under the sump using a block of wood between the jack and sump. Raise the jack to just take the load off the engine mountings.

17.7a Lift off the thrustwasher upper half . . .

3 Undo the nut and remove the two washers securing the mounting to the engine bracket.

4 Undo the two bolts securing the mounting to the chassis bracket.

5 Raise the engine sufficiently to allow the mounting to be withdrawn.

6 If necessary, remove the other mounting in the same way.

7 Refitting is a reversal of removal, but tighten the mountings to the specified torque.

19 Flywheel - removal, inspection and refitting

Removal

1 Remove the transmission as described in Chapter 7.

2 Undo the bolt securing the crankshaft sensor to the engine adaptor plate and withdraw the sensor.

3 To prevent the flywheel from turning, lock the ring gear teeth using a screwdriver inserted through the starter motor aperture (starter motor removed) and engaged with the flywheel ring gear. Alternatively, make up a tool from a strip of steel with a hooked end to

17.7b . . . and lower half

engage with the ring gear, and drilled so as to be suitably bolted to the rear of the cylinder block **(see illustration 19.4a)**.

4 Undo the six bolts and remove the flywheel. Remove the O-ring from the rear of the flywheel, noting that a new O-ring will be required for refitting **(see illustrations)**.

Inspection

5 If the flywheel's clutch mating surface is deeply scored, cracked or otherwise damaged, the flywheel must be renewed. However, it may be possible to have it surface-ground; seek the advice of a Vauxhall dealer or engine reconditioning specialist. If the ring gear is badly worn or has missing teeth, flywheel renewal will also be necessary.

Refitting

6 Locate a new O-ring in position on the flywheel, then fit the flywheel to the crankshaft.

7 Refit the retaining bolts and tighten the bolts in diagonal sequence in two stages as given in the Specifications.

8 Refit the crankshaft sensor to the adaptor plate.

9 Refit the transmission as described in Chapter 7.

2E

19.4a Undo the flywheel retaining bolts . . .

19.4b . . . lift off the flywheel . . .

19.4c . . . and remove the O-ring

Notes

Chapter 2 Part F
2.8 litre diesel engine in-car repair procedures

Contents

Camshaft and crankshaft oil seals - renewal 15
Compression test - description and interpretation 2
Crankshaft pulley - removal and refitting 6
Cylinder head - removal and refitting 11
Cylinder head cover - removal and refitting 5
Engine oil and filter renewal . . . . .See Chapter 1B
Engine oil level check . . . . .See Chapter 1B
Engine/transmission mountings - inspection and renewal 17
Flywheel - removal, inspection and refitting 16
General engine checks . . . . .See Chapter 1B
General information 1

Oil cooler - removal and refitting 14
Oil pump - removal, inspection and refitting 13
Rocker arms and pushrods - removal, inspection and
    refitting 10
Sump - removal and refitting 12
Timing belt - removal and refitting 8
Timing belt covers - removal and refitting 7
Timing belt sprockets, tensioner and idler pulleys -
    removal and refitting 9
Top dead centre (TDC) for No 1 piston - locating 3
Valve clearance - adjustment 4

Degrees of difficulty

Easy, suitable for novice with little experience		**Fairly easy,** suitable for beginner with some experience		**Fairly difficult,** suitable for competent DIY mechanic		**Difficult,** suitable for experienced DIY mechanic		**Very difficult,** suitable for expert DIY or professional	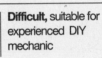

Specifications

General

Engine type	Four-cylinder, overhead valve (OHV) in-line, water-cooled
Manufacturer's engine code*	4JB1T
Bore	93 mm
Stroke	102 mm
Capacity	2771 cc
Firing order	1-3-4-2 (No 1 cylinder at timing belt end of engine)
Direction of crankshaft rotation	Clockwise (viewed from timing belt end of engine)
Compression ratio	17.9:1

Note: *The engine code forms the first five digits of the engine number (see Vehicle identification section of this manual)*

Valve clearances

Engine cold - inlet and exhaust valves	0.4 mm

Rocker arms and pushrods

Rocker shaft diameter	18.900 to 19.000 mm
Rocker arm bore internal diameter	19.036 to 19.100 mm
Rocker arm-to-shaft clearance	0.01 to 0.20 mm
Rocker shaft runout	Less than 0.3 mm
Pushrod runout	Less than 0.3 mm

Lubrication system

Oil pump type	Gear-type
Minimum permissible oil pressure at idle speed, with engine at operating temperature (oil temperature of at least 80°C)	1.0 bar (15 psi)
Oil pump clearances:	
Gear teeth-to-housing clearance	0.14 to 0.20 mm
Gear endfloat	0.06 to 0.15 mm
Drive gear shaft-to-housing clearance	0.04 to 0.20 mm
Driven gear-to-shaft clearance	0.05 to 0.15 mm

Torque wrench settings

	Nm	lbf ft
Camshaft oil seal retainer bolts	19	14
Camshaft sprocket bolts:		
Hub-to-camshaft bolt	64	47
Sprocket-to-hub bolts	8	6
Connecting rod big-end bearing cap bolt	83	61
Crankshaft pulley bolts:		
Hub-to-crankshaft bolt	186	137
Pulley-to-hub bolt	19	14
Cylinder block mounting plate bolts	83	61
Cylinder head bolts*:		
Stage 1	49	36
Stage 2	Angle-tighten a further 60°	
Stage 3	Angle-tighten a further 60°	
Cylinder head cover nuts	13	10
Engine-to-transmission unit bolts:		
M12 bolts	87	64
M10 bolts	40	30
Flywheel bolts	118	87
Injection pump sprocket nut	64	47
Main bearing cap bolts	167	123
Oil cooler:		
Housing mounting nuts and bolts	19	14
Matrix centre bolt	19	14
Oil pump bolts:		
Retaining bolts	19	14
Cover/strainer bolts	16	12
Outlet pipe union nut	25	19
Rocker arm shaft pedestal bolts	54	40
Valve clearance adjusting screw locknut	15	11
Sump retaining bolts:		
Upper section to cylinder block bolts	19	14
Lower section bolts	8	6
Timing belt backplate bolts	19	14
Timing belt cover bolts	8	6
Timing belt tensioner pulley bolt	76	56

* New bolts should be used

1 General information

How to use this Chapter

1 This Part of Chapter 2 describes those repair procedures that can reasonably be carried out on the 2.8 litre petrol engine while it remains in the car. If the engine has been removed from the car and is being dismantled as described in Part H, any preliminary dismantling procedures can be ignored.

2 Note that, while it may be possible physically to overhaul items such as the piston/connecting rod assemblies while the engine is in the car, such tasks are not normally carried out as separate operations. Usually, several additional procedures (not to mention the cleaning of components and of oilways) have to be carried out. For this reason, all such tasks are classed as major overhaul procedures, and are described in Part H of this Chapter.

3 Part H describes the removal of the engine unit from the vehicle, and the full overhaul procedures that can then be carried out.

Engine description

4 The 2.8 litre (2771 cc) diesel engine is a four-cylinder, overhead valve (OHV) in-line unit, mounted at the front of the car, with the clutch and transmission at the rear of the engine.

5 The crankshaft runs in five main bearings. Thrustwashers are fitted to the centre main bearing to control crankshaft endfloat.

6 The connecting rods rotate on horizontally-split bearing shells at their big-ends. The pistons are attached to the connecting rods by gudgeon pins, which are a sliding fit in the connecting rod small-end eyes and are retained by circlips. The aluminium-alloy pistons are fitted with three piston rings - two compression rings and an oil control ring.

7 The cylinder block houses the 'dry' cylinder liners which can be replaced if worn.

8 The inlet and exhaust valves are each closed by coil springs, and operate in guides pressed into the cylinder head.

9 The camshaft is driven by the crankshaft via a timing belt which also drives the fuel injection pump. The camshaft rotates directly in the cylinder block and operates the eight valves via a pushrod and rocker arm arrangement. Valve clearances are adjusted using a screw-and-locknut on each rocker arm.

10 Lubrication is by means of an oil pump, which is driven off the camshaft. It draws oil through a strainer located in the sump, and then forces it through an externally-mounted filter into galleries in the cylinder block/crankcase. From there, the oil is distributed to the crankshaft (main bearings) and camshaft. The big-end bearings are supplied with oil via internal drillings in the crankshaft, while the camshaft bearings and rocker arm shaft also receive a pressurised supply. The valves are lubricated by splash, as are all other engine components.

Repair operations possible with the engine in the car

11 The following work can be carried out with the engine in the car:

a) Compression pressure - testing.
b) Valve clearance - adjustment.
c) Cylinder head cover - removal and refitting.
d) Timing belt cover - removal and refitting.
e) Timing belt - removal and refitting.
f) Timing belt sprockets and tensioner - removal and refitting.
g) Rocker arms and pushrods - removal and refitting
h) Cylinder head - removal and refitting.

i)   Connecting rods and pistons - removal
     and refitting*.
j)   Sump - removal and refitting.
k)   Oil pump - removal, overhaul and refitting.
l)   Oil cooler - removal and refitting.
m)   Camshaft and crankshaft oil seals -
     renewal.
n)   Engine/transmission mountings -
     inspection and renewal.
o)   Flywheel - removal, inspection and
     refitting.

* Although the operation marked with an asterisk
can be carried out with the engine in the car after
removal of the sump, it is better for the engine to
be removed, in the interests of cleanliness and
improved access. For this reason, the procedure
is described in Chapter 2H.

2   Compression test - description and interpretation

Compression test

Note: *A compression tester specifically designed
for diesel engines must be used for this test.*

1 When engine performance is down, or if
misfiring occurs which cannot be attributed to
the fuel system, a compression test can
provide diagnostic clues as to the engine's
condition. If the test is performed regularly, it
can give warning of trouble before any other
symptoms become apparent.
2 A compression tester specifically intended
for diesel engines must be used, because of
the higher pressures involved. The tester is
connected to an adaptor which screws into the
glow plug hole. It is unlikely to be worthwhile
buying such a tester for occasional use, but it
may be possible to borrow or hire one - if not,
have the test performed by a garage.
3 Unless specific instructions to the contrary
are supplied with the tester, observe the
following points:
a)   The battery must be in a good state of
     charge, the air filter must be clean, and
     the engine should be at normal operating
     temperature.
b)   All the glow plugs should be removed
     before starting the test (see Chapter 5C).
c)   Unscrew the retaining nut and disconnect
     the wiring connector from the fuel injection
     pump fuel cut-off solenoid (see Chapter
     4B) to prevent fuel from being discharged.
4 Due to the nature of the quick-warming-up
system, it is necessary to detach the system
throttle valve from the manifold for the
compression check to be accurate. To do
this, slacken the retaining clips and remove
the duct linking the throttle housing assembly
to the intercooler metal pipe. Disconnect the
vacuum hoses from the housing, noting each
hoses correct fitted location, then slacken the
retaining clip securing the housing duct to the
manifold. Undo the retaining bolts then free
the housing assembly from the inlet manifold
and remove it from the engine, taking care not
to lose its rubber mountings.

5 Fit the adaptor to the first cylinder and
attach the compression gauge. Crank the
engine on the starter motor; after one or two
revolutions, the compression pressure should
build up to a maximum figure, and then
stabilise. Record the highest reading obtained.
6 Repeat the test on the remaining cylinders,
recording the pressure in each.
7 All cylinders should produce very similar
pressures; a difference of more than 2 bar
between any two cylinders indicates a fault.
Note that the compression should build up
quickly in a healthy engine; low compression
on the first stroke, followed by gradually-
increasing pressure on successive strokes,
indicates worn piston rings. A low
compression reading on the first stroke, which
does not build up during successive strokes,
indicates leaking valves or a blown head
gasket (a cracked head could also be the
cause). Deposits on the undersides of the
valve heads can also cause low compression.
Note: *The cause of poor compression is less
easy to establish on a diesel engine than on a
petrol one. The effect of introducing oil into
the cylinders (wet testing) is not conclusive,
because there is a risk that the oil will sit in the
swirl chamber or in the recess on the piston
crown instead of passing to the rings.*
8 Although Vauxhall do not specify exact
compression pressures, as a guide, any cylinder
pressure of below 20 bar can be considered as
less than healthy. Refer to a Vauxhall dealer or
other specialist if in doubt as to whether a
particular pressure reading is acceptable.
9 On completion of the test, reconnect the
injection pump fuel cut-off solenoid wiring
connector then refit the glow plugs. Refit the
quick-warming-up system throttle housing
assembly making sure the intake ducts and
vacuum hoses are correctly and securely
reconnected (see Chapter 4B and 5C).

Leakdown test

10 A leakdown test measures the rate at
which compressed air fed into the cylinder is
lost. It is an alternative to a compression test,

and in many ways it is better, since the
escaping air provides easy identification of
where pressure loss is occurring (piston rings,
valves or head gasket).
11 The equipment needed for leakdown
testing is unlikely to be available to the home
mechanic. If poor compression is suspected,
have the test performed by a suitably-
equipped garage.

3   Top dead centre (TDC) for No 1 piston - locating

1 In its travel up and down its cylinder bore,
Top Dead Centre (TDC) is the highest point
that each piston reaches as the crankshaft
rotates. While each piston reaches TDC both
at the top of the compression stroke and
again at the top of the exhaust stroke, for the
purpose of timing the engine, TDC refers to
the piston position (usually number 1) at the
top of its compression stroke.
2 Number 1 piston (and cylinder) is at the
front (timing belt) end of the engine, and its
TDC position is located as follows. Note that
the crankshaft rotates clockwise when viewed
from the front of the vehicle.
3 Disconnect the battery negative terminal.
To improve access to the crankshaft pulley,
unbolt the undercover and remove it from
underneath the engine.
4 Undo the retaining bolts and remove the
timing belt upper cover to expose the injection
pump timing belt sprocket. Take care not to
lose the sealing strip from the rear of the cover.
5 Using a socket and extension bar on the
crankshaft pulley bolt, rotate the crankshaft until
the TDC notch on the pulley rim is correctly
aligned with the pointer on the cover retaining
bolt. Note that there are several notches on the
pulley rim with the TDC notch being the largest;
the other notches are used when setting the
injection pump timing (see Chapter 4B). With the
TDC notch correctly aligned with the pointer,
No 1 and 4 pistons are at TDC **(see illustration)**.

2F

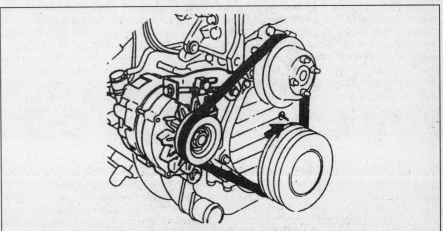

**3.5 Align the crankshaft pulley TDC notch with the pointer (arrowed) to
position No 1 and 4 pistons at TDC**

6 To determine which piston is at TDC on its compression stroke, check the position of injection pump sprocket timing hole. If the hole is visible on the left-hand side of the sprocket then No 1 piston is at TDC on its compression stroke. If the timing hole is not visible then No 4 cylinder is at TDC on its compression stroke; rotate the crankshaft through a further complete turn (360°) to bring No 1 cylinder to TDC on its compression stroke.

7 With No 1 cylinder at TDC on its compression, the engine can be locked in position by inserting a M8 bolt through the injection pump sprocket timing hole and screwing it into the threaded hole in the backplate.

4 Valve clearance - adjustment

Note: *The engine must be cold when checking and adjusting the valve clearances.*

1 The importance of having the valve clearances correctly adjusted cannot be overstressed, as they vitally affect the performance of the engine. If the clearances are too big, the engine will be noisy (characteristic rattling or tapping noises) and engine efficiency will be reduced, as the valves open too late and close too early. A more serious problem arises if the clearances are too small, however. If this is the case, the valves may not close fully when the engine is hot, resulting in serious damage to the engine (eg, burnt valve seats and/or cylinder head warping/cracking).

2 Remove the cylinder head cover as described in Section 5.

3 Position No 1 cylinder at TDC on its compression stroke as described in Section 3.

4 With the engine in this position, check the clearances of the No 1, 2, 3 and 6 valves (number 1 valve is at the front of the engine and 8 at the rear) **(see illustration)**.

5 Clearances are checked by inserting a feeler gauge of the correct thickness between the rocker arm and valve stem. The feeler gauge should be a light, sliding fit. If adjustment is necessary, slacken the locknut then rotate the rocker arm screw. Once the clearance is correctly set, hold the adjustment screw stationary and tighten the locknut to the specified torque.

6 Once all four valves are correctly adjusted, rotate the crankshaft a complete turn (360°) to bring No 4 cylinder to TDC and realign the TDC notch on the crankshaft pulley with the pointer.

7 With the engine in this position, the clearances of No 4, 5, 7 and 8 valves should be checked and adjusted as described in paragraph 5.

8 Once all the valve clearances have been checked, refit the cylinder head cover as described in Section 5.

9 Refit the timing belt cover, taking care not to lose the sealing strip, then refit the engine undercover.

5 Cylinder head cover - removal and refitting

Removal

1 Disconnect the battery negative terminal.

2 Slacken the retaining clips and remove the duct linking the quick-warm-up system throttle housing assembly to the intercooler metal pipe. Disconnect the vacuum hoses from the housing, noting each hoses correct fitted location, then slacken the retaining clip securing the housing duct to the manifold. Undo the retaining bolts then free the housing assembly from the inlet manifold and remove it from the engine, taking care not to lose its rubber mountings.

3 Disconnect the breather hose from the cylinder head cover.

4 Unscrew the retaining nuts and bolts securing the exhaust gas recirculation (EGR) pipe to the manifolds then remove the pipe from the engine. Recover the gasket from each end of the pipe and discard them; new ones should be used on refitting.

5 Remove the oil filler cap then unscrew the retaining bolts and lift the insulation cover off from the cylinder head cover.

6 Slacken and remove the retaining nuts and their sealing washers then lift the cylinder head cover and its seal away from the engine. Inspect the seal and sealing washers for signs of damage or deterioration and renew if necessary.

Refitting

7 Prior to refitting, examine the inside of the cover for a build-up of oil sludge or any other contamination, and if necessary clean the cover with paraffin, or a water-soluble solvent. Dry the cover thoroughly before refitting.

8 Ensure the cover is clean and dry and fit the seal to the cover. Refit the cover to the cylinder head, ensuring the seal remains correctly seated. Refit the sealing washers and retaining nuts and tighten them to the specified torque.

9 Ensure the grommets are correctly fitted then refit the insulation cover, tightening its retaining bolts securely. Reconnect the breather hose.

10 Ensure the mating surfaces are clean and dry then fit new gaskets to EGR pipe flanges. Refit the EGR pipe and securely tighten its retaining nuts and bolts.

11 Refit the quick-warm-up system throttle housing, ensuring its rubber mountings are correctly positioned, and securely tighten its retaining bolts. Ensure the vacuum hoses are correctly and securely reconnected then securely tighten the duct retaining clips.

12 Reconnect the battery negative terminal.

6 Crankshaft pulley - removal and refitting

Removal

1 Remove the cooling fan and coupling as described in Chapter 3.

2 Remove the auxiliary drivebelts as described in Chapter 1B.

3 Slacken and remove the four bolts securing the crankshaft pulley to its hub and remove

4.4 Valve clearance adjustment sequence

A   *Adjust with No 1 cylinder at TDC on its compression stroke*
B   *Adjust with No 4 cylinder at TDC on its compression stroke*

the pulley from the vehicle. If the locating pin is a loose fit, remove it and store it with the pulley for safe-keeping.

Refitting

4 Ensure the locating pin is in position then refit the pulley, aligning it with the pin. Refit the four retaining bolts and tighten securely.

5 Refit the auxiliary drivebelts as described in Chapter 1B.

6 Refit the cooling fan as described in Chapter 3.

7 Timing belt covers - removal and refitting

Upper cover

Removal

1 Unbolt the undercover from underneath the engine unit and remove it from the vehicle.

2 Slacken and remove the retaining bolts then remove the upper cover from the engine, along with its sealing strip. Inspect the sealing strip for signs of wear or damage and renew if necessary.

Refitting

3 Refitting is the reverse of removal, ensuring the sealing strip is correctly positioned. Tighten the cover retaining bolts to the specified torque.

Lower (main) cover

Removal

4 Remove the cooling fan as described in Chapter 3.

5 Remove the crankshaft pulley as described in Section 6.

6 Remove the upper cover (see paragraph 2) then unbolt the lower cover and remove it from the engine complete with sealing strip. Inspect the sealing strip for signs of damage or deterioration and renew if necessary.

Refitting

7 Ensure the sealing strip is correctly located in the cover groove then apply a smear of sealant to the upper run of the sealing strip which is located in the area underneath the coolant pump.

8 Refit the lower cover to the engine, ensuring the sealing strip remains correctly seated, and tighten its retaining bolts to the specified torque.

9 Refit the upper cover and sealing strip and tighten its retaining bolts to the specified torque.

10 Refit the crankshaft pulley as described in Section 6.

11 Refit the cooling fan as described in Chapter 3.

8 Timing belt - removal and refitting

Note: *The timing belt must be removed and refitted with the engine cold. A spring balance or 9 kg weight will be required to tension the belt correctly.*

Removal

1 Position No 1 cylinder at TDC on its compression stroke as described in Section 3.

2 Remove the crankshaft pulley as described in Section 6.

3 Remove the timing belt lower cover as described in Section 7.

4 Lock the camshaft and injection pump sprockets in position by inserting M8 bolts through the sprocket timing holes and screwing them into the threaded holes in the backplate. Check that the crankshaft pulley hub hole/pin is correctly aligned with the TDC pointer on the backplate **(see illustration)**.

5 Undo the retaining screws and remove the timing belt guide plates from the camshaft and injection pump sprockets **(see illustration)**.

6 Loosen the timing belt tensioner pulley retaining bolt and pivot the pulley away from the belt.

7 Slide the timing belt from its sprockets and remove it from the engine. If the belt is to be re-used, use white paint or similar to mark the direction of rotation on the belt. **Do not** rotate the crankshaft until the timing belt has been refitted.

8 Check the timing belt carefully for any signs of uneven wear, splitting or oil contamination, and renew it if there is the slightest doubt about its condition. If the engine is undergoing an overhaul and has covered 40 000 miles or it was more than 4 years since the belt was fitted, renew the belt as a matter of course, regardless of its apparent condition. If signs of oil contamination are found, trace the source of the oil leak and rectify it, then wash down the engine timing belt area and all related components to remove all traces of oil.

Refitting

9 On reassembly, thoroughly clean the timing belt sprockets and tensioner/idler pulleys.

10 Ensure that the camshaft and injection pump sprockets are still locked in position and make sure the crankshaft pulley hub hole/pin is still correctly aligned with the TDC pointer.

11 Fit the timing belt over the crankshaft and camshaft sprockets then around the idler

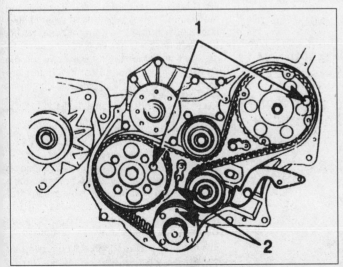

8.4 With No 1 cylinder at TDC on its compression stroke, lock the camshaft and injection pump sprockets in position with M8 bolts (1) and check the crankshaft pulley hub mark is aligned with the pointer (2)

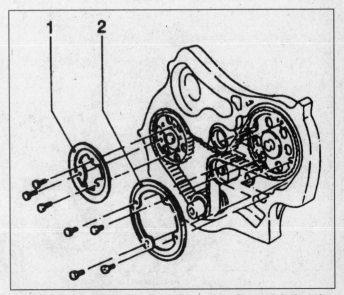

8.5 Undo the retaining screws and remove the camshaft and injection pump sprocket timing belt guides (1 and 2)

2F

pulley and over the injection pump sprocket. Ensure the belt is kept taut between the crankshaft, camshaft and injection pump sprockets (ie, so that all slack on the tensioner side of the belt) then fit the belt over the tensioner pulley. Do not twist the belt sharply while refitting it. Ensure that the belt teeth are correctly seated centrally in the sprockets, and that the timing marks remain in alignment. If a used belt is being refitted, ensure that the arrow mark made on removal points in the normal direction of rotation.

12 Free the tensioner lever and move the tensioner pulley towards the timing belt to remove all slack. Lightly tighten the pulley retaining bolt.

13 Ensure the crankshaft pulley hub mark is still correctly aligned with the TDC pointer then unscrew the locking bolts from the camshaft and injection pump sprockets.

14 Attach the spring balance/weight (as applicable) to the hole in the end of the tensioner pulley lever. With a load of 9 kg applied to the lever hole, slacken the tensioner pulley retaining bolt then securely retighten it **(see illustration)**.

15 Using a socket on the crankshaft pulley hub bolt, rotate the crankshaft 45° in anti-clockwise direction to ensure that all slack is on the tensioner side of the timing belt. With a load of 9 kg applied to the to the hole on the end of the tensioner lever, slacken the tensioner pulley retaining bolt again then retighten it to the specified torque setting.

16 Remove the spring balance/weight from the tensioner lever then rotate the crankshaft back to TDC. Check the pulley hub pin/hole is correctly aligned with the TDC pointer and that both the camshaft and injection pump sprocket bolts can be screwed into position. If adjustment is necessary, release the tensioner then disengage the belt from the sprockets and make any necessary adjustments before retensioning the belt again.

17 Once the timing belt is correctly tensioned, secure the tensioner lever back in position.

18 Refit the guide plates to the camshaft and injection pump sprockets, tightening their retaining bolts securely.

19 Ensure the sprocket locking bolts have been removed then refit the timing belt covers and crankshaft pulley as described in Sections 6 and 7.

9 Timing belt sprockets, tensioner and idler pulleys - removal and refitting

Camshaft sprocket

Note: *It is likely that a puller will be required to draw the sprocket off the camshaft.*

Removal

1 Remove the timing belt as described in Section 8.

2 Using the sprocket locking bolt to prevent rotation, slacken and remove the centre bolt securing the sprocket hub to the camshaft.

3 Remove the locking bolt then remove the sprocket and hub assembly from the end of the camshaft. If necessary, draw the sprocket off using a suitable puller which engages with the holes in the sprocket. If the Woodruff key is a loose fit in the camshaft end, remove it and store it with the sprocket for safe-keeping.

Refitting

4 Prior to refitting check the oil seal for signs of damage or leakage. If necessary, renew as described in Section 15.

5 Ensure the Woodruff key is in position in the camshaft end.

6 Refit the sprocket assembly, ensuring the hub slot is correctly aligned with the key. Take great care not to damage the oil seal lip as the sprocket is slid into position.

7 Align the sprocket timing hole with the threaded hole in the backplate and screw in the locking bolt. Refit the sprocket hub retaining bolt and washer and tighten it to the specified torque.

8 Refit the timing belt as described in Section 8.

Fuel injection pump sprocket

Note: *It is likely that a puller will be required to draw the sprocket off the pump shaft.*

Removal

9 Remove the timing belt as described in Section 8.

10 Using the sprocket locking bolt to prevent rotation, slacken and remove the sprocket retaining nut and washer.

11 Unscrew the locking bolt then remove the sprocket from the injection pump shaft. If necessary, draw the sprocket off using a suitable puller which engages with the holes in the sprocket. If the Woodruff key is a loose fit, remove it and store it with the sprocket for safe-keeping.

Refitting

12 Ensure the Woodruff key is in position in the pump shaft.

13 Refit the sprocket assembly, aligning its slot with the key, then refit the washer and retaining nut. Align the sprocket timing hole with the threaded hole in the backplate and screw in the locking bolt. The sprocket retaining nut can then be tightened to the specified torque.

14 Refit the timing belt as described in Section 8.

Crankshaft sprocket

Note: *It is likely that a puller will be required to draw the sprocket off the crankshaft.*

Removal

15 Remove the timing belt as described in Section 8.

16 Slacken the crankshaft pulley hub retaining bolt. To prevent crankshaft rotation, have an assistant select top gear and apply the brakes firmly. If the engine is removed from the vehicle it will be necessary to lock the flywheel (see Section 16).

17 Unscrew the retaining bolt and remove the crankshaft pulley hub from the end of the crankshaft.

18 Remove the sprocket off from the crankshaft, noting which way around it is fitted; if the sprocket is a tight fit, use a puller to draw it off. If the Woodruff key is a loose fit, remove it and store it with the sprocket.

Refitting

19 Prior to refitting check the oil seal for signs of damage or leakage. If necessary, renew as described in Section 15.

20 Ensure the Woodruff key is in position then slide on the crankshaft sprocket, making sure the sprocket flange is innermost.

21 Refit the crankshaft pulley hub, engaging it with the Woodruff key, and refit the retaining bolt. Lock the crankshaft by the method used on removal and tighten the sprocket retaining bolt to the specified torque setting.

22 Refit the timing belt as described in Section 8.

Tensioner assembly

Removal

23 Remove the timing belt as described in Section 8.

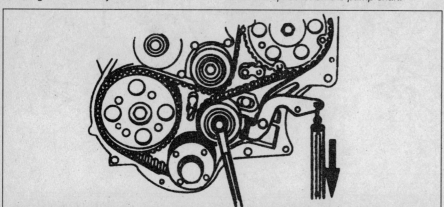

8.14 Apply a load of 9 kg to the tensioner pulley lever and securely tighten the pulley bolt

24 Slacken and remove the retaining bolt and remove the tensioner assembly from the backplate.

Refitting

25 Fit the tensioner to the engine, making sure that its cutout is correctly engaged with the backplate pin. Ensure the tensioner is correctly seated then refit the retaining bolt, tightening by hand only at this stage.

26 Refit the timing belt as described in Section 8.

Idler pulley

Removal

27 Remove the timing belt as described in Section 8.

28 Slacken and remove the retaining bolt and remove the idler pulley from the backplate.

Refitting

29 Refit the idler pulley and securely tighten its retaining bolt.

30 Refit the timing belt as described in Section 8.

---

10 Rocker arms and pushrods - removal, inspection and refitting

Removal

1 Remove the cylinder head cover as described in Section 5.

2 Slacken the locknuts and back off the rocker arm valve adjusting screws to minimise valve spring pressure on the rocker arms.

3 Starting from the centre and working outwards, go around and slacken the rocker arm shaft retaining bolts by a quarter of a turn at a time to gradually relieve the valve spring pressure from the rocker arms. Once all the bolts are loose they can be fully unscrewed from the cylinder head; do not remove the bolts from the pedestals, as they engage with cutouts in the rocker shaft and keep all the rocker shaft components correctly positioned.

4 Lift the rocker shaft assembly from the top of the cylinder head and remove it from the engine.

5 If the pushrods are also to be removed, withdraw them and store them in order, so that they can be refitted in their original locations. The pushrods can be stored by pushing them through a clearly-marked cardboard template.

6 To dismantle the rocker arm assembly, carefully prise off the circlip from the front end of the rocker shaft; retain the rocker arm to prevent it being sprung off the end of the shaft. Slide the various components off the end of the shaft, keeping all components in their correct fitted order. Make a note of each component's correct fitted position and orientation as it is removed, to ensure it is

fitted correctly on reassembly. Leave the circlip on the rear end of the shaft to identify its correct fitted orientation.

Inspection

7 Examine the rocker arm bearing surfaces which contact the camshaft lobes for wear ridges and scoring. Renew any rocker arms on which these conditions are apparent. If a rocker arm bearing surface is badly scored, also examine the corresponding lobe on the camshaft for wear, as it is likely that both will be worn. Renew worn components as necessary. The rocker arm assembly can be dismantled as described in paragraph 6.

8 Inspect the ends of the (valve clearance) adjusting screws for signs of wear or damage, and renew as required.

9 If the rocker arm assembly has been dismantled, examine the rocker arm and shaft bearing surfaces for wear ridges and scoring. If there are obvious signs of wear, the relevant rocker arm(s) and/or the shaft must be renewed. If the necessary measuring equipment is available, wear can be assessed by direct measurement (see Specifications).

10 Ensure the caps are securely fitted to the ends of the rocker shaft and the shaft oilways are clean and unblocked. If not, the oil supply to the rocker arms will be affected leading to premature wear of components.

11 Check all pushrods for signs of damage and check them for straightness by rolling them along a flat surface. If any rod shows signs of damage or exceeds the specified runout limit it must be renewed.

Refitting

12 If the rocker arm assembly was dismantled, apply a smear of clean engine oil to the shaft. Ensure that the rear circlip is securely fitted to the shaft groove then slide on all removed components, ensuring each is correctly fitted in its original position. Note

that the rocker shaft is not symmetrical; ensure that the shaft is assembled so that the larger shaft oilway is situated at the front end **(see illustration)**. Align the pedestal retaining bolt holes with the cutouts in the rockers arm shaft and insert the retaining bolts to hold them in position. Once all components are in position on the shaft, compress the front rocker arm spring and refit the circlip, ensuring it is correctly located in its groove.

13 Refit all the pushrods in their original locations ensuring that the lower end of each rod is correctly engaged with its camshaft follower.

14 Ensure all rocker arm adjusting screws are backed right off then refit the rocker arm assembly to the top of the cylinder head.

15 Tighten all retaining bolts by hand, then go around and tighten each bolt a quarter of a turn at time in sequence to draw to gradually impose the pressure of the valve springs on the rocker arms. Once the rocker shaft pedestals are all in contact with the cylinder head, go around and tighten the retaining bolts evenly and progressively to the specified torque.

16 Adjust the valve clearances as described in Section 4 then refit the cylinder head cover as described in Section 5.

---

11 Cylinder head - removal and refitting

Removal

Note: *The engine must be cold when removing the cylinder head. New cylinder head bolts must be used on refitting.*

Removal

1 Disconnect the battery negative lead.

2F

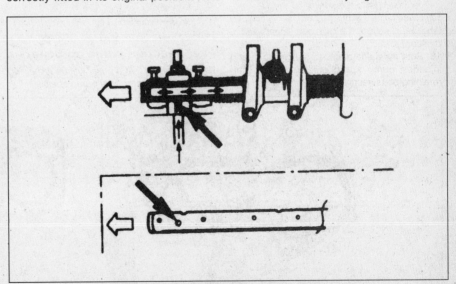

10.12 Ensure the rocker shaft is assembled so that its larger oilway (arrowed) is at the front

2 Drain the cooling system as described in Chapter 1B.

3 Working as described in Chapter 4B, carry out the following procedures.
a) Remove the exhaust manifold.
b) Slacken the union nuts and remove the metal injector pipes connecting the injection pump to the injectors.
c) Disconnect the fuel return pipe from the injector.
d) Remove the metal pipe and duct linking the intercooler to the quick-warm-up throttle housing.

4 Remove the auxiliary drivebelts as described in Chapter 1B.

5 Referring to Chapter 11, unbolt the power steering pump from its mountings and position it clear of the cylinder head, noting that there is no need to disconnect the hydraulic hoses from the pump.

6 On models with air conditioning, referring to Chapter 3, unbolt the compressor from its mounting bracket and position it clear of the engine with its refrigerant pipes still connected; do not open the refrigerant circuit. Unbolt the compressor mounting bracket from the side of the engine.

7 Remove the rocker arms and pushrods as described in Section 10.

8 Unscrew the retaining nut and disconnect the main supply lead from the glow plug.

9 Slacken the retaining clips and disconnect the coolant hoses from the thermostat housing. Also disconnect the heater and oil cooler hoses from the cylinder head.

10 Disconnect the wiring connector from the coolant temperature which is screwed into the thermostat housing.

11 Make a final check to ensure that all relevant hoses, pipes and wires, etc, have been disconnected.

12 Working in the sequence shown, progressively slacken the cylinder head bolts by a third of a turn at a time until all bolts can be unscrewed by hand (see illustration). Remove each bolt in turn and discard them; new ones must be used on refitting.

13 Lift the cylinder head from the cylinder block. If necessary, tap the cylinder head gently with a soft-faced mallet to free it from the block, but do not lever at the mating faces. Note the fitted positions of the two locating dowels, and remove them for safe-keeping if they are loose.

14 Recover the cylinder head gasket. Keep the head gasket for identification purposes (see paragraph 21).

15 If the cylinder head is to be dismantled for overhaul, then refer to Part H of this Chapter.

Preparation for refitting

16 The mating faces of the cylinder head and cylinder block/crankcase must be perfectly clean before refitting the head. Use a hard plastic or wood scraper to remove all traces of gasket and carbon; also clean the piston crowns. Take particular care, as the surfaces are damaged easily. Also, make sure that the carbon is not allowed to enter the oil and water passages - this is particularly important for the lubrication system, as carbon could block the oil supply to any of the engine's components. Using adhesive tape and paper, seal the water, oil and bolt holes in the cylinder block/crankcase. To prevent carbon entering the gap between the pistons and bores, smear a little grease in the gap. After cleaning each piston, use a small brush to remove all traces of grease and carbon from the gap, then wipe away the remainder with a clean rag. Clean all the pistons in the same way.

17 Check the mating surfaces of the cylinder block/crankcase and the cylinder head for nicks, deep scratches and other damage. If slight, they may be removed carefully with a file, but if excessive, machining may be the only alternative to renewal.

18 Ensure that the cylinder head bolt holes in the crankcase are clean and free of oil. Syringe or soak up any oil left in the bolt holes. This is most important in order that the correct bolt tightening torque can be applied and to prevent the possibility of the block being cracked by hydraulic pressure when the bolts are tightened.

19 The cylinder head bolts must be discarded and renewed, regardless of their apparent condition.

20 If warpage of the cylinder head gasket surface is suspected, use a straight-edge to check it for distortion. Refer to Part H of this Chapter if necessary.

21 On this engine, the cylinder head-to-piston clearance is controlled by fitting different thickness head gaskets. The gasket thickness can be determined by looking at the number of notches cut in its identification tab (see illustration).

Notches in gasket	Gasket thickness
One notches	1.50mm
Two notches	1.55 mm
Three notches	1.60mm

The correct thickness of gasket required is selected by measuring the piston protrusions as follows.

22 Rotate the crankshaft to bring pistons 1 and 4 to TDC and align the crankshaft pulley notch with the pointer. Ensure the crankshaft is accurately positioned then mount a dial test indicator securely on the block so that its pointer can be easily pivoted between the piston crown and block mating surface. Zero the dial test indicator on the gasket surface of the cylinder block then carefully move the indicator over No 1 piston and measure its protrusion. Take the measurements on the

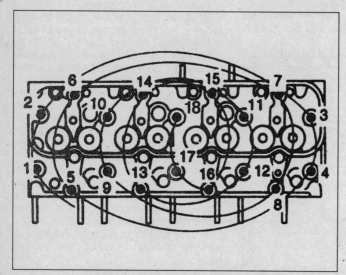

11.12 Cylinder head bolt loosening sequence

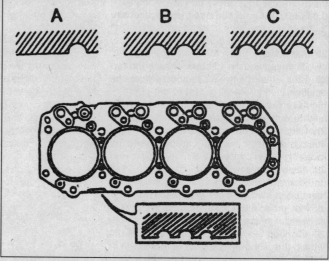

11.21 Cylinder head gasket thickness identification markings

A 1.50 mm thick   B 1.55 mm thick   C 1.60 mm thick

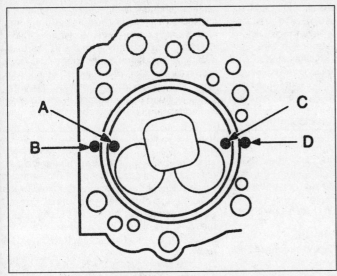

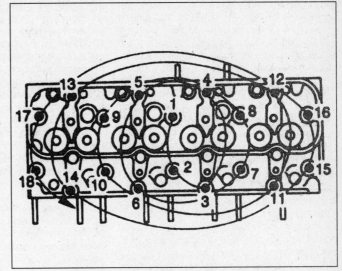

11.22 Measure the piston protrusion both at the front (A to B) and rear (C to D) edge of each piston, in line with the gudgeon pin axis

11.29 Cylinder head bolt tightening sequence

2F

front and rear edge of the piston, in line with the gudgeon pin axis **(see illustration)**. Repeat this procedure on No 4 piston.

23 Rotate the crankshaft half-a-turn (180°) to bring No 2 and 3 pistons to TDC. Ensure the crankshaft is accurately positioned then measure the protrusions of No 2 and 3 pistons; eight measurements in total should now have been taken.

24 Add the eight protrusion measurements together to find the total and then divide the total by eight to find the average (mean) protrusion measurement. Using this average measurement, select the correct thickness of head gasket required using the following table.

Average piston protrusion measurement	Head gasket thickness required
0.758 to 0.812 mm	1.50 mm (one notch)
0.813 to 0.858 mm	1.55 mm (two notches)
0.859 to 0.914 mm	1.60 mm (three notches)

Refitting

25 Wipe clean the mating surfaces of the cylinder head and cylinder block/crankcase.

26 Check that the two locating dowels are in position then fit a new gasket to the cylinder block, ensuring it is fitted the correct way around with its TOP mark uppermost.

27 With the aid of an assistant, carefully refit the cylinder head assembly to the block and locate the head on the dowels.

28 Apply a smear of oil to the threads and the underside of the heads of the new cylinder head bolts then carefully enter each bolt into its relevant hole (*do not drop them in*). Screw all bolts in, by hand only, until finger-tight.

29 Working in the specified sequence, tighten the cylinder head bolts to their stage 1 torque setting, using a torque wrench and suitable socket **(see illustration)**.

30 Once all bolts have been tightened to the

stage 1 torque, working again in the specified sequence, go around and tighten all bolts through the specified stage 2 angle. It is recommended that an angle-measuring gauge is used to ensure accuracy. If a gauge is not available, use white paint to make alignment marks prior to tightening; the marks can then be used to check that the bolt has been rotated through the correct angle.

31 Finally go around again in the specified sequence and tighten all bolts through the specified stage 3 angle.

32 Refit the pushrods and rocker arms as described in Section 10.

33 Adjust the valve clearances then refit the cylinder head cover as described in Sections 4 and 5.

34 Reconnect the wiring to the coolant temperature sender unit and glow plug.

35 Reconnect the coolant hoses to the thermostat housing and cylinder head, securing them in position with their retaining clips.

36 Working as described in Chapter 4B, refit the exhaust manifold and the injector pipes then reconnect the return pipe to the injector and refit the intake duct.

37 Refit the power steering pump and (where necessary) the air conditioning compressor (see Chapters 3 and 11) then refit the auxiliary drivebelts as described in Chapter 1B.

38 Refill the cooling system as described in Chapter 1B.

39 Reconnect the battery then start the engine and check for signs of leaks.

---

12 Sump - removal and refitting

Note: *An engine hoist or support bar will be required for this procedure.*

Removal

1 Disconnect the battery negative terminal.

2 Firmly apply the handbrake then jack up the front of the car and support it on axle stands.

3 Undo the retaining bolts and remove the engine undercover.

4 Drain the engine oil as described in Chapter 1B, then fit a new sealing washer and refit the drain plug, tightening it securely. If the engine is nearing its service interval when the oil and filter are due for renewal, it is recommended that the filter is also removed and a new one fitted. After reassembly, the engine can then be refilled with fresh engine oil.

5 Referring to Chapter 9, unbolt the front axle assembly from the chassis and lower it slightly to gain the necessary clearance required to remove the sump castings. **Note:** *This is not necessary if only the lower section of the sump is to be removed.*

6 Progressively slacken and remove the bolts securing the lower section of the sump to main casting. Break the joint by striking the lower section with the palm of the hand, then lower it away from the engine. Remove the gasket and discard it.

7 Withdraw the engine oil dipstick from the tube. Undo the dipstick tube retaining bolts then ease the tube out from the sump main casting and remove it from the engine. Discard the sealing rings from the lower end of the tube; new ones should be used on refitting.

8 Unscrew the retaining nuts securing the turbocharger oil return pipe to the sump main casting and free the pipe from the casting. Recover the gasket and discard it; a new one should be used on refitting.

9 Release the retaining clip and disconnect the vacuum pump oil return hose from the sump.

10 Slacken and remove the bolts securing the transmission unit to the rear of the sump casting.

11 Progressively slacken and remove the bolts securing the main section of the sump to the cylinder block. Break the joint by striking the lower section with the palm of the hand, then lower the main sump casting away from the engine, disengaging it from the oil pump.

12 With the sump removed, check the sealing strips on the front and rear main bearing caps for signs of damage and deterioration and renew if necessary. Also check the oil pump pick-up strainer for signs of damage or debris and clean/renew, if necessary.

Refitting

13 Remove all traces of dirt and oil from the mating surfaces of the sump castings and cylinder block.

14 Apply a bead of sealing compound to the mating surface of the sump main casting. Position the bead in the centre of the surface between each retaining bolt hole and around the inside of all bolt holes **(see illustration)**.

15 Ensure the sealing strips are correctly fitted to the front and rear main bearing cap grooves then manoeuvre the casting into position. Refit the retaining bolts and tighten them all by hand. Working in a diagonal sequence, from the centre outwards, go around and tighten all the retaining bolts to the specified torque setting.

16 Refit the bolts securing the transmission housing to the sump and tighten them securely.

17 Ensure the mating surfaces are clean and dry then fit a new gasket to the turbocharger oil return pipe union on the sump. Reconnect the pipe and securely tighten its retaining nuts.

18 Reconnect the vacuum pump oil return hose, securing it in position with the retaining clip.

19 Fit new sealing rings to the base of the dipstick tube and lubricate them with a smear of engine oil to aid installation. Ease the dipstick tube into position and securely tighten its retaining bolts. Refit the dipstick.

20 Ensure the mating surface is clean and dry then apply a bead of sealing compound to the mating surface of the sump lower section. Position the bead in the groove of the surface between each retaining bolt hole and around the inside of all bolt holes.

21 Fit a new gasket to the top of the sump lower section and refit it to the main casting. Refit the retaining bolts, tightening them all by hand, then go around and tighten them to the specified torque setting.

22 Refit the front axle as described in Chapter 9.

23 Refit the undercover then lower the vehicle to the ground.

24 Fill the engine with fresh oil, with reference to Chapter 1B and reconnect the battery.

13 Oil pump - removal, inspection and refitting

Removal

1 Remove the sump as described in Section 12.

2 Unscrew the retaining bolts securing the pump assembly to the base of the cylinder block then ease the pump assembly out of position. Remove the sealing ring from the oil pump outlet pipe and discard it; a new one should be used on refitting.

Inspection

3 Unbolt the pick-up strainer from the base of the pump then undo the retaining bolts and remove the cover from the pump housing. Remove the driven gear from the pump.

4 Unscrew the union nut and remove the outlet pipe from the pump body. Extract the split pin and remove the end cap, spring and pressure relief valve piston from the pump, noting which way around the piston is fitted.

5 Clean the components, and carefully examine the gears, pump body and valve piston for any signs of scoring or wear. Renew any component which shows signs of wear or damage; if the pump housing is marked then the complete pump assembly will have to be renewed.

6 If the pump components appear to be satisfactory, insert the driven gear back into the housing and, using feeler blades, check the gear teeth-to-housing clearance. Place a straight edge across the base of the housing and measure the endfloat of each gear. Compare the results to those given in the Specifications, if the gears are worn beyond the specified limits they must be renewed.

7 Fit the driven gear to the pump housing and lubricate it with clean engine oil. Ensure the mating surfaces are clean and dry then refit the pump cover and the pick-up strainer, tighten their retaining bolts to the specified torque.

8 Fit the pressure relief valve piston to the pump, ensuring it is fitted the correct way around, then refit the spring and end cap. Compress the end cap sufficiently and secure it in position using a new split pin.

9 Refit the outlet pipe to the pump tightening its union nut by hand only at this stage.

Refitting

10 Ensure the pump and cylinder block mating surfaces are clean and dry then fit a new sealing ring to the end of the outlet pipe. Apply a smear of engine oil to the sealing ring to aid installation.

11 Ease the pump into position then refit the retaining bolts, tightening them to the specified torque. With the pump in position, tighten the outlet pipe union nut to the specified torque (where necessary).

12 Refit the sump as described in Section 12.

14 Oil cooler - removal and refitting

Removal

1 Undo the retaining screws and remove the undercover from beneath the engine.

2 Drain the cooling system as described in Chapter 1B.

3 Referring to Chapter 1B, unscrew the oil filter and remove it from the base of the oil cooler. If the filter is damaged on removal, which is likely, a new filter must be used on refitting. If this is the case, drain the engine oil and refill the engine with fresh oil at the same time.

4 Unscrew the retaining bolts and remove the heatshield from the turbocharger exhaust flange.

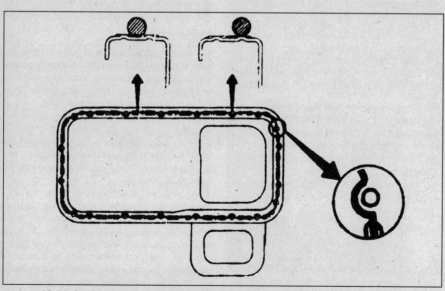

12.14 Apply a bead of sealant to the sump main casting surface as shown

5 Release the retaining clips and disconnect the coolant hoses from the oil cooler.

6 Slacken and remove the retaining nuts and bolts securing the oil cooler housing to the cylinder block then manoeuvre the assembly out of position. Recover the housing seal and discard it; a new one should be used on refitting.

7 With the assembly on the bench, unscrew the centre bolt and sealing washer securing the cooler matrix to the housing then separate the cooler from the housing. Remove the sealing ring from the base of the cooler. Discard the sealing ring and washer; new ones should be used on refitting.

8 If necessary, unscrew the bolt from the base of the housing and remove the thermostatic valve assembly, noting each components correct fitted location. Inspect the valve components for signs of wear or damage and renew as necessary.

Refitting

9 Refit the thermostatic valve assembly components (where removed) to the base of the housing, ensuring all items are correctly fitted, and securely tighten the end bolt.

10 Ensure all mating surfaces are clean and dry then fit the new sealing ring to the base of the cooler matrix and a new sealing washer to the centre bolt.

11 Fit the matrix to the housing, ensuring the sealing ring remains correctly seated, then refit the centre bolt. Ensure the matrix is correctly positioned in relation to the housing then tighten the centre bolt to the specified torque.

12 Fit a new seal and refit the oil cooler assembly to the cylinder block. Refit the cooler retaining nuts and bolts and tighten them to the specified torque setting.

13 Reconnect the coolant hoses to the cooler, securing them in position with the retaining clips.

14 Refit the heatshield to the turbocharger flange and securely tighten its retaining bolts.

15 Referring to Chapter 1B, fit the new oil filter to the oil cooler and (where necessary) fill the engine with fresh oil.

16 Refit the undercover then refill the cooling system as described in Chapter 1B.

15 Camshaft and crankshaft oil seals - renewal

Camshaft oil seal

1 Remove the camshaft sprocket as described in Section 9.

2 Using a flat-bladed screwdriver, carefully lever the oil seal out of position taking care not to damage the camshaft or housing.

3 Clean the seal housing and polish off any burrs or raised edges which may have caused the seal to fail in the first place.

4 Lubricate the lips of the new seal with clean engine oil and press/tap it squarely into

position. If necessary, a suitable tubular drift, such as a socket, which bears only on the hard outer edge of the seal can be used to tap the seal into position.

5 Wash off any traces of oil, then refit the camshaft sprocket as described in Section 9.

Crankshaft front oil seal

6 Remove the crankshaft sprocket as described in Section 9.

7 Carefully punch or drill two small holes opposite each other in the oil seal. Screw a self-tapping screw into each and pull on the screws with pliers to extract the seal.

8 Clean the seal housing and polish off any burrs or raised edges which may have caused the seal to fail in the first place.

9 Lubricate the lips of the new seal with clean engine oil. Ease the seal onto the end of the crankshaft and press it squarely into position (Vauxhall state that the seal should protrude by 0.9 ± 0.3 mm). If necessary, a suitable tubular drift, such as a socket, which bears only on the hard outer edge of the seal can be used to tap the seal into position. Take great care not to damage the seal lips during fitting and ensure that the seal lips face inwards.

10 Refit the crankshaft sprocket as described in Section 9.

Crankshaft rear oil seal

11 Remove the flywheel as described in Section 16.

12 Renew the seal as described in paragraphs 7 to 9 noting the Vauxhall state the oil seal should protrude by 1.25 ± 0.3 mm.

13 Refit the flywheel as described in Section 16.

16 Flywheel - removal, inspection and refitting

Removal

1 Remove the transmission as described in Chapter 7 then remove the clutch assembly as described in Chapter 6.

2 Prevent the flywheel from turning by locking the ring gear teeth with a similar arrangement to that shown **(see illustration)**. Alternatively,

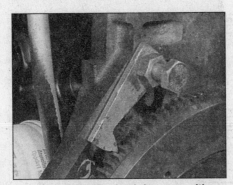

16.2 Lock the flywheel ring gear with a suitable tool

bolt a strap between the flywheel and the cylinder block/crankcase. Make alignment marks between the flywheel and crankshaft.

3 Slacken and remove the retaining bolts, along with the retaining plate, then remove the flywheel. Do not drop it, as it is very heavy.

Inspection

4 Examine the flywheel for wear or chipping of the ring gear teeth. Renewal of the ring gear is possible but is not a task for the home mechanic; renewal requires the new ring gear to be heated (up to 200ºC) to allow it to be fitted.

5 Examine the flywheel for scoring of the clutch face. If the clutch face is scored, the flywheel may be surface-ground, but renewal is preferable.

6 If there is any doubt about the condition of the flywheel, seek the advice of a Vauxhall dealer or engine reconditioning specialist. They will be able to advise if it is possible to recondition it or whether renewal is necessary.

Refitting

7 Clean the mating surfaces of the flywheel and crankshaft and remove all traces of dirt from the retaining bolt and crankshaft threads.

8 Offer up the flywheel, locating it on the dowel, then refit the retaining plate and insert the bolts. Tighten all bolts by hand.

9 Lock the flywheel using the method employed on dismantling then, working in a diagonal sequence, evenly and progressively tighten the retaining bolts to the specified torque setting.

10 Refit the clutch as described in Chapter 6 then remove the locking tool and refit the transmission as described in Chapter 7.

17 Engine/transmission mountings - inspection and renewal

Inspection

1 If improved access is required, raise the front of the car and support it securely on axle stands. Where necessary, undo the retaining bolts and remove the undercover from beneath the engine/transmission unit.

2 Check the mounting rubber to see if it is cracked, hardened or separated from the metal at any point; renew the mounting if any such damage or deterioration is evident.

3 Check that all the mounting fasteners are securely tightened.

4 Using a large screwdriver or a pry bar, check for wear in the mounting by carefully levering against it to check for free play; where this is not possible, enlist the aid of an assistant to move the engine/transmission unit back and forth, or from side-to-side, while you watch the mounting. While some free play is to be expected even from new components, excessive wear should be

2F

obvious. If excessive free play is found, check first that the fasteners are correctly secured, then renew any worn components as described below.

Renewal

Left- and right-hand side mountings

5 Slacken and remove the bolts securing both the left- and right-hand mountings to the chassis and unscrew the nuts securing each mounting to its engine bracket.

6 Attach an engine hoist to the lifting brackets on the cylinder head and raise the engine slightly until there is sufficient clearance to manoeuvre the mountings out of position.

7 Refitting is the reverse of removal, tightening the mounting nuts and bolts securely.

Rear mounting

8 Slacken and remove the nuts securing the mounting to the crossmember then undo the bolts securing the mounting plate to the underside of the transmission housing.

9 Position a jack beneath the rear of the transmission and raise the transmission unit slightly to gain the necessary clearance required to manoeuvre the mounting assembly out of position.

10 With the mounting assembly on a bench, undo the retaining nuts and separate the mounting from its mounting plate.

11 Refitting is the reverse of removal, tightening all nuts and bolts securely.

Chapter 2 Part G
Petrol engine removal and overhaul procedures

Contents

Crankshaft - inspection 13
Crankshaft - refitting and main bearing running clearance check . . 17
Crankshaft - removal 10
Cylinder block - cleaning and inspection 11
Cylinder head - dismantling 6
Cylinder head - reassembly 8
Cylinder head and valves - cleaning and inspection 7
Engine - initial start up after overhaul 19
Engine - removal and refitting 4
Engine overhaul - dismantling sequence 5

Engine overhaul - general information 2
Engine overhaul - reassembly sequence 15
Engine removal - methods and precautions 3
General information 1
Main and big-end bearings - inspection 14
Piston rings - refitting 16
Piston/connecting rod assembly - inspection 12
Piston/connecting rod assembly - refitting and big-end running
   clearance check 18
Piston/connecting rod assembly - removal 9

Degrees of difficulty

2G

Easy, suitable for novice with little experience	Fairly easy, suitable for beginner with some experience	Fairly difficult, suitable for competent DIY mechanic	Difficult, suitable for experienced DIY mechanic	Very difficult, suitable for expert DIY or professional

Specifications

Note: *Where specifications are given as N/A, no information was available at the time of writing. Refer to your Vauxhall dealer for the latest information available.*

Cylinder head

2.0 litre engine

Maximum gasket face distortion	0.05 mm
Cylinder head height	96.00 ± 0.25 mm
Valve seat width:	
Inlet	1.0 to 1.5 mm
Exhaust	1.7 to 2.2 mm

2.2 litre engine

Maximum gasket face distortion	0.025 mm
Cylinder head height	95.75 to 96.25 mm
Valve seat width:	
Inlet	1.2 ± 0.2 mm
Exhaust	1.6 ± 0.2 mm

2.4 litre engine

Maximum gasket face distortion	0.05 mm
Cylinder head height	102.45 to 102.95 mm
Valve seat width:	
Inlet	1.25 to 1.50 mm
Exhaust	1.60 to 1.85 mm

Valves and guides

2.0 litre engine

Valve stem diameter*:

Inlet:

Standard (K)	6.998 to 7.012 mm
1st oversize (0.075 mm - K1)	7.073 to 7.087 mm
2nd oversize (0.150 mm - K2)	7.148 to 7.162 mm
3rd oversize (0.250 mm - A)	7.248 to 7.262 mm

Exhaust:

Standard (K)	6.978 to 6.992 mm
1st oversize (0.075 mm - K1)	7.053 to 7.067 mm
2nd oversize (0.150 mm - K2)	7.128 to 7.142 mm
3rd oversize (0.250 mm - A)	7.228 to 7.242 mm

Valve stem runout	Less than 0.03 mm

Valve guide height in cylinder head:

Pre 1995 (C20NE) engines	83.50 to 83.80 mm
1995 on (X20SE) engines	83.25 to 84.05 mm

Valve guide bore diameter*:

Standard (K)	7.030 to 7.050 mm
1st oversize (0.075 mm - K1)	7.105 to 7.125 mm
2nd oversize (0.150 mm - K2)	7.180 to 7.200 mm
3rd oversize (0.250 mm - A)	7.280 to 7.300 mm

Stem-to-guide clearance:

Inlet	0.018 to 0.052 mm
Exhaust	0.038 to 0.072 mm

Valve length:

Inlet:

New	104.2 mm
Service limit	103.8 mm

Exhaust:

New	104.0 mm
Service limit	103.6 mm

Valve stem fitted height	17.85 to 18.25 mm

Valve head diameter:

Inlet	41.8 mm
Exhaust	36.5 mm

2.2 litre engine

Valve stem diameter*:

Inlet:

Standard (K)	5.995 to 5.970 mm
1st oversize (0.075 mm - K1)	6.030 to 6.045 mm
2nd oversize (0.150 mm - K2)	6.105 to 6.120 mm

Exhaust:

Standard (K)	5.945 to 5.960 mm
1st oversize (0.075 mm - K1)	6.020 to 6.035 mm
2nd oversize (0.150 mm - K2)	6.095 to 6.110 mm

Valve stem runout	Less than 0.03 mm
Valve guide height in cylinder head	13.70 to 14.00 mm

Valve guide bore diameter*:

Standard (K)	6.000 to 6.012 mm
1st oversize (0.075 mm - K1)	6.075 to 6.090 mm
2nd oversize (0.150 mm - K2)	6.150 to 6.165 mm

Stem-to-guide clearance:

Inlet	0.030 to 0.057 mm
Exhaust	0.040 to 0.067 mm

Valve length:

Inlet:

New	102.0 mm
Service limit	101.7 mm

Exhaust:

New	92.0 mm
Service limit	91.8 mm

Valve stem fitted height	39.2 to 40.2 mm

Valve head diameter:

Inlet	32 ± 0.1 mm
Exhaust	29 ± 0.1 mm

2.4 litre engine

Valve stem diameter**:	
Inlet:	
Standard (no colour)	8.977 to 8.990 mm
1st oversize (0.075 mm - white)	9.052 to 9.065 mm
2nd oversize (0.150 mm - green)	9.127 to 9.140 mm
3rd oversize (0.300 mm - no colour)	9.277 to 9.290 mm
Exhaust:	
Standard (no colour)	8.965 to 8.980 mm
1st oversize (0.075 mm - white)	9.040 to 9.055 mm
2nd oversize (0.150 mm - green)	9.115 to 9.130 mm
3rd oversize (0.300 mm - no colour)	9.265 to 9.280 mm
Valve stem runout:	
Inlet	Less than 0.04 mm
Exhaust	Less than 0.03 mm
Valve guide height in cylinder head	N/A
Valve guide bore diameter**:	
Standard (no colour)	9.025 to 9.050 mm
1st oversize (0.075 mm - white)	9.100 to 9.125 mm
2nd oversize (0.150 mm - green)	9.175 to 9.200 mm
3rd oversize (0.300 mm - no colour)	9.325 to 9.350 mm
Stem-to-guide clearance:	
Inlet	0.035 to 0.073 mm
Exhaust	0.045 to 0.085 mm
Valve length:	
Inlet	123.0 mm
Exhaust	123.7 mm
Valve stem fitted height	N/A
Valve head diameter:	
Inlet	45 mm
Exhaust	40 mm

*Identification marking in brackets
**Identification colour code

Cylinder block

2.0 litre engine

Maximum gasket face distortion	0.05 mm
Cylinder bore diameter:	
Pre 1995 (C20NE) engines:	
Standard:	
.Size group 8	85.97 to 85.98 mm
.Size group 99	85.98 to 85.99 mm
.Size group 00	85.99 to 86.00 mm
.Size group 01	86.00 to 86.01 mm
.Size group 02	86.01 to 86.02 mm
Oversize (0.5 mm) - size group 7 + 0.5	86.46 to 86.47 mm
1995 on (X20SE) engines:	
Standard:	
.Size group 8	85.975 to 85.985 mm
.Size group 99	85.985 to 85.995 mm
.Size group 00	85.995 to 86.005 mm
.Size group 01	86.005 to 86.015 mm
.Size group 02	86.015 to 86.025 mm
Oversize (0.5 mm):	
.Size group 7 + 0.5	86.465 to 86.475 mm
.Size group 8 + 0.5	86.475 to 86.485 mm
.Size group 9 + 0.5	86.485 to 86.495 mm
.Size group 0 + 0.5	86.495 to 86.505 mm
Maximum cylinder bore ovality	0.013 mm
Maximum cylinder bore taper	0.013 mm

2.2 litre engine

Maximum gasket face distortion	0.05 mm
Cylinder bore diameter:	
Standard:	
Size group 8	85.975 to 85.985 mm
Size group 99	85.985 to 85.995 mm
Size group 00	85.995 to 86.005 mm
Size group 01	86.005 to 86.015 mm
Size group 02	86.015 to 86.025 mm

2G

Cylinder block (continued)

2.2 litre engine

Cylinder bore diameter: (continued)
  Oversize (0.5 mm):
    Size group 7 + 0.5 .... 86.465 to 86.475 mm
    Size group 8 + 0.5 .... 86.475 to 86.485 mm
    Size group 9 + 0.5 .... 86.485 to 86.495 mm
    Size group 0 + 0.5 .... 86.495 to 86.505 mm
Maximum cylinder bore ovality .... 0.013 mm
Maximum cylinder bore taper .... 0.013 mm

2.4 litre engine

Maximum gasket face distortion .... 0.05 mm
Cylinder bore diameter:
  Standard:
    Size group 5 .... 94.95 mm
    Size group 6 .... 94.96 mm
    Size group 7 .... 94.97 mm
    Size group 8 .... 94.98 mm
    Size group 99 .... 94.99 mm
    Size group 0 .... 95.00 mm
    Size group 01 .... 95.01 mm
    Size group 02 .... 95.02 mm
    Size group 03 .... 95.03 mm
    Size group 04 .... 95.04 mm
    Size group 05 .... 95.05 mm
    Size group 06 .... 95.06 mm
    Size group 07 .... 95.07 mm
    Size group 08 .... 95.08 mm
    Size group 09 .... 95.09 mm
  Oversize (0.5 mm):
    Size group 7 + 0.5 .... 95.47 mm
    Size group 8 + 0.5 .... 95.48 mm
    Size group 9 + 0.5 .... 95.49 mm
    Size group 0 + 0.5 .... 95.50 mm
Maximum cylinder bore ovality .... 0.005 mm
Maximum cylinder bore taper .... 0.005 mm

Pistons and rings

2.0 litre engine

Piston diameter:
  Pre 1995 (C20NE) engines:
    Standard:
      Size group 8 .... 85.95 to 85.96 mm
      Size group 99 .... 85.96 to 85.97 mm
      Size group 00 .... 85.97 to 85.98 mm
      Size group 01 .... 85.98 to 85.99 mm
      Size group 02 .... 85.99 to 86.00 mm
    Oversize (0.5 mm) - size group 7 + 0.5 .... 86.44 to 86.45 mm
  1995 on (X20SE) engines:
    Standard:
      Size group 8 .... 85.955 to 85.965 mm
      Size group 99 .... 85.965 to 85.975 mm
      Size group 00 .... 85.975 to 85.985 mm
      Size group 01 .... 85.985 to 85.995 mm
      Size group 02 .... 85.995 to 86.005 mm
    Oversize (0.5 mm):
      Size group 7 + 0.5 .... 86.445 to 86.455 mm
      Size group 8 + 0.5 .... 86.455 to 86.465 mm
      Size group 9 + 0.5 .... 86.465 to 86.475 mm
      Size group 0 + 0.5 .... 86.475 to 86.485 mm
Piston-to-bore clearance .... 0.02 to 0.04 mm
Piston ring end gaps (fitted in bore):
  Top and second compression rings .... 0.3 to 0.5 mm
  Oil control ring .... 0.4 to 1.4 mm
Piston ring thickness:
  Top and second compression ring .... 1.5 mm
  Oil control ring .... 3.0 mm

2.2 litre engine

Piston diameter:

Standard:

Size group 8	85.955 to 85.965 mm
Size group 99	85.965 to 85.975 mm
Size group 00	85.975 to 85.985 mm
Size group 01	85.985 to 85.995 mm
Size group 02	85.995 to 86.005 mm

Oversize (0.5 mm):

Size group 7 + 0.5	86.445 to 86.455 mm
Size group 8 + 0.5	86.455 to 86.465 mm
Size group 9 + 0.5	86.465 to 86.475 mm
Size group 0 + 0.5	86.475 to 86.485 mm
Piston-to-bore clearance	0.02 to 0.04 mm

Piston ring end gaps (fitted in bore):

Top and second compression rings	0.3 to 0.5 mm
Oil control ring	0.4 to 1.4 mm

Piston ring thickness:

Top and second compression ring	1.5 mm
Oil control ring	3.0 mm

2.4 litre engine

Piston diameter:

Standard:

Size group 5	94.91 mm
Size group 6	94.92 mm
Size group 7	94.93 mm
Size group 8	94.94 mm
Size group 99	94.95 mm
Size group 00	94.96 mm
Size group 01	94.97 mm
Size group 02	94.98 mm
Size group 03	94.99 mm
Size group 04	95.00 mm
Size group 05	95.01 mm
Size group 06	95.02 mm
Size group 07	95.03 mm
Size group 08	95.04 mm
Size group 09	95.05 mm

Oversize (0.5 mm):

Size group 7 + 0.5	95.43 mm
Size group 8 + 0.5	95.44 mm
Size group 9 + 0.5	95.45 mm
Size group 0 + 0.5	95.46 mm
Piston-to-bore clearance	0.02 to 0.05 mm

Piston ring end gaps (fitted in bore):

Top and second compression rings	0.40 to 0.65 mm
Oil control ring	0.20 to 0.60 mm

Piston ring thickness:

Top and second compression ring	1.478 to 1.490 mm
Oil control ring	2.975 to 2.990 mm

Gudgeon pins

2.0 litre engine

Diameter	21 mm
Length	61.5 mm

Gudgeon pin-to-piston clearance:

Pre 1995 (C20NE) engine	0.011 to 0.014 mm
1995 on (X20SE) engine	0.003 to 0.010 mm

2.2 litre engine

Diameter	21 mm
Length	61.5 mm
Gudgeon pin-to-piston clearance	0.003 to 0.010 mm

2.4 litre engine

Diameter	22 mm
Length	65 mm

Gudgeon pin clearance:

Pin-to-piston clearance	0.006 to 0.013 mm
Pin-to-connecting rod clearance	0.005 to 0.016 mm

2G

Connecting rod

2.0 litre engine

Big-end side clearance . . . .   0.07 to 0.24 mm

2.2 litre engine

Big-end side clearance . . . .   0.07 to 0.24 mm

2.4 litre engine

Big-end side clearance . . . .   0.11 to 0.24 mm

Crankshaft

2.0 litre engine

Endfloat . . . .   0.05 to 0.15 mm

Main bearing journal diameter:

  Standard:

    Pre 1995 (C20NE) engines . . . .   57.982 to 57.995 mm

    1995 on (X20SE) engines . . . .   57.974 to 57.995 mm

  1st (0.25 mm) undersize . . . .   57.732 to 57.745 mm

  2nd (0.50 mm) undersize . . . .   57.482 to 57.495 mm

Big-end bearing journal (crankpin) diameter:

  Standard . . . .   48.970 to 48.988 mm

  1st (0.25 mm) undersize . . . .   48.720 to 48.738 mm

  2nd (0.50 mm) undersize . . . .   48.470 to 48.488 mm

Journal out-of round . . . .   0.04 mm

Journal taper . . . .   N/A

Crankshaft runout . . . .   Less than 0.03 mm

Main bearing running clearance . . . .   0.015 to 0.040 mm

Big-end bearing (crankpin) running clearance . . . .   0.006 to 0.031 mm

2.2 litre engine

Endfloat . . . .   0.05 to 0.15 mm

Main bearing journal diameter:

  Standard . . . .   57.974 to 57.995 mm

  1st (0.25 mm) undersize . . . .   57.732 to 57.745 mm

  2nd (0.50 mm) undersize . . . .   57.482 to 57.495 mm

Big-end bearing journal (crankpin) diameter:

  Standard . . . .   48.970 to 48.988 mm

  1st (0.25 mm) undersize . . . .   48.720 to 48.738 mm

  2nd (0.50 mm) undersize . . . .   48.470 to 48.488 mm

Journal out-of round . . . .   0.04 mm

Journal taper . . . .   N/A

Crankshaft runout . . . .   Less than 0.03 mm

Main bearing running clearance . . . .   0.015 to 0.040 mm

Big-end bearing (crankpin) running clearance . . . .   0.006 to 0.031 mm

2.4 litre engine

Endfloat . . . .   0.05 to 0.15 mm

Main bearing journal diameter:

  Standard . . . .   57.997 to 58.003 mm

  1st (0.25 mm) undersize . . . .   57.737 to 57.753 mm

  2nd (0.50 mm) undersize . . . .   57.487 to 57.503 mm

Big-end bearing journal (crankpin) diameter:

  Standard . . . .   51.971 to 51.990 mm

  1st (0.25 mm) undersize . . . .   51.721 to 51.740 mm

  2nd (0.50 mm) undersize . . . .   51.471 to 51.490 mm

Journal out-of round . . . .   0.004 mm

Journal taper . . . .   0.005 mm

Crankshaft runout . . . .   Less than 0.03 mm

Main bearing running clearance . . . .   0.020 to 0.060 mm

Big-end bearing (crankpin) running clearance . . . .   0.034 to 0.079 mm

Torque wrench settings

2.0 litre engine

Refer to Chapter 2A Specifications

2.2 litre engine

Refer to Chapter 2B Specifications

2.4 litre engine

Refer to Chapter 2C Specifications

1 General information

1 Included in this Part of Chapter 2 are details of removing the engine from the vehicle and general overhaul procedures for the cylinder head, cylinder block and all other engine internal components.

2 The information ranges from advice concerning preparation for an overhaul and the purchase of replacement parts, to detailed step-by-step procedures covering removal, inspection, renovation and refitting of engine internal components.

3 After Section 5, all instructions are based on the assumption that the engine has been removed from the car. For information concerning in-car engine repair, as well as the removal and refitting of those external components necessary for full overhaul, refer to the relevant in-car repair procedure section (Chapter 2A to 2C) of this Chapter and to Section 5. Ignore any preliminary dismantling operations described in the relevant in-car repair sections that are no longer relevant once the engine has been removed from the car.

4 Apart from torque wrench settings, which are given at the beginning of the relevant in-car repair procedure Chapter (2A to 2C), all specifications relating to engine overhaul are at the beginning of this Part of Chapter 2.

2 Engine overhaul - general information

1 It is not always easy to determine when, or if, an engine should be completely overhauled, as a number of factors must be considered.

2 High mileage is not necessarily an indication that an overhaul is needed, while low mileage does not preclude the need for an overhaul. Frequency of servicing is probably the most important consideration. An engine which has had regular and frequent oil and filter changes, as well as other required maintenance, should give many thousands of miles of reliable service. Conversely, a neglected engine may require an overhaul very early in its life.

3 Excessive oil consumption is an indication that piston rings, valve seals and/or valve guides are in need of attention. Make sure that oil leaks are not responsible before deciding that the rings and/or guides are worn. Perform a compression test, as described in the relevant Part A to C of this Chapter, to determine the likely cause of the problem.

4 Check the oil pressure with a gauge fitted in place of the oil pressure switch, and compare it with that specified (Chapter 2A to 2C). If it is extremely low, the main and big-end bearings, and/or the oil pump, are probably worn out.

5 Loss of power, rough running, knocking or metallic engine noises, excessive valve gear noise, and high fuel consumption may also point to the need for an overhaul, especially if they are all present at the same time. If a complete service does not remedy the situation, major mechanical work is the only solution.

6 An engine overhaul involves restoring all internal parts to the specification of a new engine. During an overhaul, the pistons and the piston rings are renewed. New main and big-end bearings are generally fitted; if necessary, the crankshaft may be renewed, to restore the journals. The valves are also serviced as well, since they are usually in less-than-perfect condition at this point. While the engine is being overhauled, other components, such as the starter and alternator, can be overhauled as well. The end result should be an as-new engine that will give many trouble-free miles. **Note:** *Critical cooling system components such as the hoses, thermostat and coolant pump should be renewed when an engine is overhauled. The radiator should be checked carefully, to ensure that it is not clogged or leaking. Also, it is a good idea to renew the oil pump whenever the engine is overhauled.*

7 Before beginning the engine overhaul, read through the entire procedure, to familiarise yourself with the scope and requirements of the job. Overhauling an engine is not difficult if you carefully follow all of the instructions, have the necessary tools and equipment, and pay close attention to all specifications. It can, however, be time-consuming. Plan on the car being off the road for a minimum of two weeks, especially if parts must be taken to an engineering works for repair or reconditioning. Check on the availability of parts and make sure that any necessary special tools and equipment are obtained in advance. Most work can be done with typical hand tools, although a number of precision measuring tools are required for inspecting parts to determine if they must be renewed. Often the engineering works will handle the inspection of parts and offer advice concerning reconditioning and renewal. As a general rule, time is the primary cost of an overhaul, so it does not pay to fit worn or sub-standard parts. **Note:** *Always wait until the engine has been completely dismantled, and until all components (especially the cylinder block and the crankshaft) have been inspected, before deciding what service and repair operations must be performed by an engineering works. The condition of these components will be the major factor to consider when determining whether to overhaul the original engine, or to buy a reconditioned unit. Do not, therefore, purchase parts or have overhaul work done on other components until they have been thoroughly inspected.*

8 As a final note, to ensure maximum life and minimum trouble from a reconditioned engine, everything must be assembled with care, in a spotlessly-clean environment.

3 Engine removal - methods and precautions

1 If you have decided that the engine must be removed for overhaul or major repair work, several preliminary steps should be taken.

2 Locating a suitable place to work is extremely important. Adequate work space, along with storage space for the car, will be needed. If a workshop or garage is not available, at the very least, a flat, level, clean work surface is required.

3 Cleaning the engine compartment and engine/transmission before beginning the removal procedure will help keep tools clean and organised.

4 An engine hoist or A-frame will also be necessary. Make sure the equipment is rated in excess of the weight of the engine. Safety is of primary importance, considering the potential hazards involved in lifting the engine out of the vehicle.

5 If this is the first time you have removed an engine, an assistant should ideally be available. Advice and aid from someone more experienced would also be helpful. There are many instances when one person cannot simultaneously perform all of the operations required when lifting the engine out of the vehicle.

6 Plan the operation ahead of time. Before starting work, arrange for the hire of or obtain all of the tools and equipment you will need. Some of the equipment necessary to perform engine/transmission removal and installation safely and with relative ease (in addition to an engine hoist) is as follows: a heavy duty trolley jack, complete sets of spanners and sockets as described in *Tools and Working facilities* at the rear of this manual, wooden blocks, and plenty of rags and cleaning solvent for mopping-up spilled oil, coolant and fuel. If the hoist must be hired, make sure that you arrange for it in advance, and perform all of the operations possible without it beforehand. This will save you money and time.

7 Plan for the car to be out of use for quite a while. An engineering works will be required to perform some of the work which the do-it-yourselfer cannot accomplish without special equipment. These places often have a busy schedule, so it would be a good idea to consult them before removing the engine, in order to accurately estimate the amount of time required to rebuild or repair components that may need work.

8 Always be extremely careful when removing and refitting the engine/transmission. Serious injury can result from careless actions. Plan ahead and take your time, and a job of this nature, although major, can be accomplished successfully.

2G

4 Engine - removal and refitting

Removal

1 Park the vehicle on firm, level ground then remove the battery (see Chapter 5A).

2 Remove the bonnet as described in Chapter 12.

3 Remove the radiator as described in Chapter 3.

4 Referring to Chapter 11, unbolt the power steering pump and position it clear of the engine unit with its hoses still attached.

5 Referring to Chapter 4, carry out the following procedures.

a) *Remove the intake duct connecting the air cleaner housing to the throttle housing.*

b) *Unbolt the exhaust front pipe from the manifold.*

c) *Disconnect the fuel feed and return hoses from the fuel rail.*

d) *Disconnect the accelerator cable and position it clear of the engine.*

e) *Disconnect the brake servo hose and various vacuum hoses and from the inlet manifold and exhaust manifolds, noting each hoses correct fitted location.*

f) *Disconnect the wiring connectors from the fuel and emission system components and free the wiring so it can be positioned clear of the engine unit.* **Note:** *On 1995 onwards 2.0 litre models (X20SE engine) and 2.2 litre engine models, it maybe found that it is easier to trace the engine wiring back to the connectors near the bulkhead and front of the engine compartment, disconnect the connectors then free the wiring harness so that it is free to be removed with the engine.*

6 Referring to Chapter 3, carry out the following procedures.

a) *Release the retaining clips and disconnect the various coolant hoses from the cylinder head and the block.*

b) *On models with air conditioning, unbolt the compressor and position it clear of the engine.* **Do not** *open the refrigerant circuit.*

c) *Release the coolant/air-conditioning hoses/pipes (as applicable) from any relevant clips and ties and position them clear of the engine unit.*

7 Referring to Chapter 5, disconnect the wiring from the starter motor, alternator and oil pressure warning light switch. Unbolt any relevant earth leads from the cylinder block then unbolt/unclip the wiring from the engine unit and position it clear.

8 On 1995 onwards 2.0 litre models (X20SE engine) and all 2.2 litre models, wipe clean the area around the oil cooler pipe unions on the oil filter housing. Slacken and remove the union bolts then disconnect both pipes from the engine and recover the sealing washers. Position the pipes clear of the engine and

discard the sealing washers; new one should be used on refitting. Plug/cover the pipe ends and housing ports to prevent the entry of dirt into the lubrication system.

9 Referring to Chapter 6, unbolt the clutch slave cylinder and position it clear of the transmission with its hydraulic hose still attached.

Caution: Do not depress the clutch pedal whilst the cylinder is removed.

10 Manoeuvre the engine hoist into position, and attach it to the lifting brackets bolted onto the engine. Raise the hoist until it is supporting the weight of the engine.

11 Slacken and remove the bolts securing both the left- and right-hand mountings to the chassis and unscrew the nut securing each mounting to its engine bracket. Raise the engine slightly until there is sufficient clearance to manoeuvre the mountings out of position, noting the correct fitted position of the mounting rubber heatshield (fitted on the exhaust manifold side).

12 Make a final check that any components which would prevent the removal of the engine from the car have been removed or disconnected. Ensure all wiring/hoses are secured so that they cannot be damaged on removal.

13 Work around the transmission bellhousing and slacken and remove the bolts securing the transmission unit to the engine. Note each bolt's correct fitted location (not all bolts are the same) and the locations of any brackets/clips retained by the bolts.

14 Move the hoist forwards and free the engine from the transmission unit. Once the engine is clear of the transmission, raise it carefully upwards and away from the engine compartment, making sure that nothing is trapped. Enlist the help of an assistant during this procedure, as it may be necessary to tilt the engine slightly to clear the body panels. Great care must be taken to ensure that no components are trapped and damaged during the removal procedure.

15 Lower the engine onto a suitable work area and detach the hoist.

Refitting

16 Refitting is the reverse of removal, noting the following.

a) *Prior to refitting, check the clutch release mechanism as described in Chapter 6.*

b) *Carefully align the transmission input shaft with the clutch as the engine and transmission are joined. Ensure the weight of the engine is not allowed to hang on the shaft at any time.*

c) *Tighten all bolts to their specified torque settings (where given).*

d) *Ensure that all wiring is correctly routed and retained by all the relevant retaining clips and that all connectors are correctly and securely reconnected.*

e) *Ensure that all disturbed hoses are correctly reconnected, and securely retained by their retaining clips.*

f) *Adjust the accelerator cable as described in the Chapter 4A.*

g) *Refill the engine with oil as described in Chapter 1A and also refill the cooling system.*

5 Engine overhaul - dismantling sequence

1 It is much easier to dismantle and work on the engine if it is mounted on a portable engine stand. These stands can often be hired from a tool hire shop. Before the engine is mounted on a stand, the flywheel should be removed, so that the stand bolts can be tightened into the end of the cylinder block.

2 If a stand is not available, it is possible to dismantle the engine with it blocked up on a sturdy workbench, or on the floor. Be extra-careful not to tip or drop the engine when working without a stand.

3 If you are going to obtain a reconditioned engine, all the external components must be removed first, to be transferred to the replacement engine (just as they will if you are doing a complete engine overhaul yourself). These components include the following:

a) *Inlet and exhaust manifolds (Chapter 4A).*

b) *Alternator/power steering pump/air conditioning compressor bracket(s) (as applicable).*

c) *Coolant pump (Chapter 3).*

d) *Fuel system components (Chapter 4A).*

e) *Wiring harness and all electrical switches and sensors.*

f) *Oil filter (Chapter 1A).*

g) *Flywheel (relevant Part of Chapter 2A to 2C).*

Note: *When removing the external components from the engine, pay close attention to details that may be helpful or important during refitting. Note the fitted position of gaskets, seals, spacers, pins, washers, bolts, and other small items.*

4 If you are obtaining a 'short' engine (which consists of the engine cylinder block, crankshaft, pistons and connecting rods all assembled), then the cylinder head, sump, oil pump, and timing belt/chains (as applicable) will also have to be removed.

5 If you are planning a complete overhaul, the engine can be dismantled, and the internal components removed, in the order given below, referring to the relevant Part of this Chapter unless otherwise stated.

a) *Inlet and exhaust manifolds (Chapter 4A).*

b) *Timing belt, sprockets and (where fitted) tensioner - 2.0 and 2.2 litre engine*

c) *Cylinder head.*

d) *Flywheel.*

e) *Sump.*

f) *Oil pump - 2.0 and 2.2 litre engine.*

g) *Timing chain and sprockets - 2.4 litre engine.*

h) *Piston/connecting rod assemblies.*

i) *Crankshaft.*

6 Before beginning the dismantling and overhaul procedures, make sure that you have all of the correct tools necessary. Refer to the *Tools and Working facilities* Section of this manual for further information.

6 Cylinder head - dismantling

Note: *New and reconditioned cylinder heads are available from the manufacturer, and from engine overhaul specialists. Be aware that some specialist tools are required for the dismantling and inspection procedures, and new components may not be readily available. It may therefore be more practical and economical for the home mechanic to purchase a reconditioned head, rather than dismantle, inspect and recondition the original head.*

1 On 2.0 litre engines, referring to Part A of this Chapter, remove the cylinder head from the engine then lift the camshaft followers, thrust pads and hydraulic tappets out from the cylinder head.

2 On 2.2 litre engines, remove the camshafts and followers as described in Part B of this Chapter then remove the cylinder head from the engine.

3 On 2.4 litre engines, referring to Part C of this Chapter, remove the cylinder head from the engine then remove the rocker arms, hydraulic valve lifters and camshaft from the head.

4 On all engines, using a valve spring compressor, compress each valve spring in turn until the split collets can be removed **(see illustration)**. Release the compressor, and lift off the spring retainer and spring. Using a pair of pliers, carefully extract the valve stem seal from the top of the guide then slide off the spring seat. **Note:** *On 2.4 litre engines spring seats are only fitted to the exhaust valves, and on some engines valve stem oil seals are only fitted to the inlet valve guides.*

5 If, when the valve spring compressor is screwed down, the spring retainer refuses to free and expose the split collets, gently tap the top of the tool, directly over the retainer, with a light hammer. This will free the retainer.

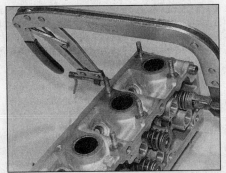
6.4 Valve spring compressor fitted to No 1 exhaust valve - 2.0 litre engine

If the components are to be refitted, place each valve and its associated components in a labelled polythene bag or similar small container, and mark the bag/container with the valve number to ensure that it is refitted in its original location

6 Withdraw the valve through the combustion chamber. It is essential that each valve is stored together with its collets, retainer, spring, and (where fitted) spring seat **(see Haynes Hint)**. The valves should also be kept in their correct sequence, unless they are so badly worn that they are to be renewed.

7 Cylinder head and valves - cleaning and inspection

1 Thorough cleaning of the cylinder head and valve components, followed by a detailed inspection, will enable you to decide how much valve service work must be carried out during the engine overhaul. **Note:** *If the engine has been severely overheated, it is best to assume that the cylinder head is warped - check carefully for signs of this.*

Cleaning

2 Scrape away all traces of old gasket material from the cylinder head.

3 Scrape away the carbon from the combustion chambers and ports, then wash the cylinder head thoroughly with paraffin or a suitable solvent.

4 Scrape off any heavy carbon deposits that may have formed on the valves, then use a power-operated wire brush to remove deposits from the valve heads and stems.

Inspection

Note: *Be sure to perform all the following inspection procedures before concluding that the services of a machine shop or engine overhaul specialist are required. Make a list of all items that require attention.*

Cylinder head

5 Inspect the head very carefully for cracks, evidence of coolant leakage, and other damage. If cracks are found, a new cylinder head should be obtained.

6 Use a straight-edge and feeler gauge blade to check that the cylinder head surface is not distorted. If it is, it may be possible to resurface it, provided that the cylinder head is not reduced to less than the minimum specified height.

7 Examine the valve seats in each of the combustion chambers. If they are severely pitted, cracked or burned, then they will need to be re-cut by an engine overhaul specialist. If they are only slightly pitted, this can be removed by grinding-in the valve heads and seats with fine valve-grinding compound, as described below.

8 If the valve guides are worn (indicated by a side-to-side motion of the valve, and accompanied by excessive blue smoke in the exhaust when running) new guides must be fitted. Measure the diameter of the existing valve stems (see below) and the bore of the guides, then calculate the clearance and compare the result with the specified value. If the clearance is not within the specified limits, renew the valves and/or guides as necessary.

9 The renewal of valve guides is best carried out by an engine overhaul specialist. If the work is to be carried out at home, however, use a stepped, double-diameter drift to drive out the worn guide towards the combustion chamber. On fitting the new guide, place it first in a deep-freeze for one hour, then drive it into its cylinder head bore from the camshaft side until it projects the specified amount above the cylinder head surface (where no measurement is given seek the advice of a Vauxhall dealer).

10 If the valve seats are to be re-cut this must be done only after the guides have been renewed.

Valves

11 Examine the head of each valve for pitting, burning, cracks and general wear, and check the valve stem for scoring and wear ridges. Rotate the valve, and check for any obvious indication that it is bent. Look for pitting and excessive wear on the tip of each valve stem. Renew any valve that shows any such signs of wear or damage.

12 If the valve appears satisfactory at this stage, measure the valve stem diameter at several points using a micrometer **(see illustration)**. Any significant difference in the

7.12 Using a micrometer to measure valve stem diameter

2G

7.15 Grinding-in a valve

8.1 Lubricate the valve stem with engine oil and insert the valve into the correct guide

8.2a Fit the spring seat . . .

8.2b . . . then fit the seal protector (where supplied) to the valve and install the new valve guide oil seal . . .

8.2c . . . pressing it onto the valve guide with a suitable socket

readings obtained indicates wear of the valve stem. Should any of these conditions be apparent, the valve(s) must be renewed.

13 If the valves are in satisfactory condition, they should be ground (lapped) into their respective seats, to ensure a smooth gas-tight seal. If the seat is only lightly pitted, or if it has been re-cut, fine grinding compound **only** should be used to produce the required finish. Coarse valve-grinding compound should **not** be used unless a seat is badly burned or deeply pitted; if this is the case, the cylinder head and valves should be inspected by an expert to decide whether seat re-cutting is required.

14 Valve grinding is carried out as follows. Place the cylinder head upside-down on a bench.

15 Smear a trace of the appropriate grade of valve-grinding compound on the seat face, and press a suction grinding tool onto the valve head. With a semi-rotary action, grind the valve head to its seat, lifting the valve occasionally to redistribute the grinding compound **(see illustration)**. A light spring placed under the valve head will greatly ease this operation.

16 If coarse grinding compound is being used, work only until a dull, matt even surface is produced on both the valve seat and the valve, then wipe off the used compound and repeat the process with fine compound. When a smooth unbroken ring of light grey matt finish is produced on both the valve and seat, the grinding operation is complete. **Do not** grind in the valves any further than absolutely necessary, or the seat will be prematurely sunk into the cylinder head.

17 When all the valves have been ground-in, carefully wash off all traces of grinding compound using paraffin or a suitable solvent before reassembly of the cylinder head.

Valve components

18 Examine the valve springs for signs of damage and discoloration; if possible; also compare the existing spring free length with new components.

19 Stand each spring on a flat surface, and check it for squareness. If any of the springs are damaged, distorted or have lost their

tension, obtain a complete new set of springs.

20 On pre 1995 2.0 litre models (C20NE engine) and 2.4 litre engine models, the exhaust valve spring seats incorporate a bearing; the bearing rotates the valve which helps to keep the valve seat clean. If any spring seat bearing shows signs of wear or does not rotate smoothly then the seat should be renewed.

8 Cylinder head - reassembly

1 Lubricate the stems of the valves, and insert them into their original locations. If new

valves are being fitted, insert them into the locations to which they have been ground **(see illustration)**.

2 Working on the first valve, refit the spring seat (where fitted). Dip the new valve stem seal in fresh engine oil, then carefully locate it over the valve and onto the guide. Take care not to damage the seal as it is passed over the valve stem. Use a suitable socket or metal tube to press the seal firmly onto the guide. **Note:** *If genuine seals are being fitted, use the oil seal protector which is supplied with the seals; the protector fits over the valve stem and prevents the oil seal lip being damaged on the valve* **(see illustrations)**.

3 Fit the valve spring and seat the spring retainer on the top of the valve **(see illustration)**.

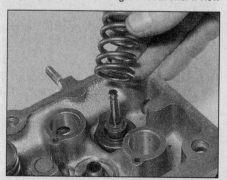

8.3a Refit the valve spring . . .

8.3b . . . and fit the spring retainer

8.4 Compress the valve and locate the collets in the recess on the valve stem

4 Compress the valve spring, and locate the split collets in the recess in the valve stem **(see illustration)**. Release the compressor, then repeat the procedure on the remaining valves **(See Haynes Hint)**.

5 With all the valves installed, place the cylinder head flat on the bench and, using a hammer and interposed block of wood, tap the end of each valve stem to settle the components.

6 On 2.0 litre engines, working as described in Part A, refit the hydraulic tappets, thrust pads and followers to the head then refit the cylinder head.

7 On 2.2 litre engines, working as described in Part B, refit the cylinder head to the engine and install the followers and camshafts.

8 On 2.4 litre engines, working as described in Part C, refit the camshaft to the cylinder head then refit the head to the engine and install the valve lifters and rocker arms.

9 Piston/connecting rod assembly - removal

Note: *On 2.0 and 2.2 litre engines new connecting rod big-end cap bolts will be needed on refitting*

1 Referring to Part A, B or C (as applicable) of this Chapter, remove the cylinder head and sump then unbolt the pick-up/strainer.

9.4 Checking connecting rod big-end side clearance

HAYNES HINT

Use a little dab of grease to hold the collets in position on the valve stem while the spring compressor is released

2 On 2.2 litre engines and later 2.0 litre engines (X20SE), evenly and progressively slacken the retaining bolts and remove the main bearing ladder casting and (where fitted) baffle plate from the base of the block.

3 On all engines, if there is a pronounced wear ridge at the top of any bore, it may be necessary to remove it with a scraper or ridge reamer, to avoid piston damage during removal. Such a ridge indicates excessive wear of the cylinder bore.

4 Prior to removal, using feeler blades, measuring the connecting rod big-end side clearance of each rod **(see illustration)**. If any rod exceeds the specified clearance, it must be renewed.

5 Using a hammer and centre-punch, paint or similar, mark each connecting rod and its bearing cap with its cylinder number on the flat machined surface provided; if the engine has been dismantled before, note carefully any identifying marks made previously **(see illustration)**. Note that No 1 cylinder is at the front (timing belt/chain) end of the engine.

6 Turn the crankshaft to bring pistons 1 and 4 to BDC (bottom dead centre).

9.5 Prior to removal, make identification markings on the connecting rods and bearing caps (circled). Note that lug on the bearing cap (arrowed) faces towards the flywheel end of the engine

7 Unscrew the bolts from No 1 piston big-end bearing cap. Take off the cap and recover the bottom half bearing shell **(see illustration)**. If the bearing shells are to be re-used, tape the cap and the shell together.

8 Using a hammer handle, push the piston up through the bore, and remove it from the top of the cylinder block. Recover the bearing shell, and tape it to the connecting rod for safe-keeping.

9 Loosely refit the big-end cap to the connecting rod, and secure with the bolts - this will help to keep the components in their correct order.

10 Remove No 4 piston assembly in the same way.

11 Turn the crankshaft through 180° to bring pistons 2 and 3 to BDC (bottom dead centre), and remove them in the same way.

10 Crankshaft - removal

Note: *On 2.0 and 2.2 litre engines new main bearing cap bolts will be required on refitting.*

1 On 2.0 and 2.2 litre engines, referring to Part A or B (as applicable) of this Chapter, remove the oil pump and flywheel from the engine.

2 On 2.4 litre engines, referring to Part C of this Chapter, remove the timing chain and sprockets and flywheel from the engine.

3 On all engines, remove the piston and connecting rod assemblies as described in Section 9. If no work is to be done on the pistons and connecting rods, unbolt the caps and push the pistons far enough up the bores that the connecting rods are positioned clear of the crankshaft journals.

4 Check the crankshaft endfloat as described in Section 13, then proceed as follows.

5 The main bearing caps should be numbered 1 to 5 from the front (timing belt/chain) end of the engine and all identification numbers should be the right way up when read from the right-hand side of the

2G

9.7 Unbolt and remove the bearing cap

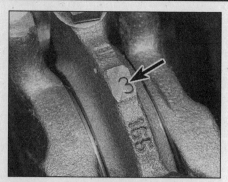

10.5 Main bearing cap identification marking (arrowed)

cylinder block **(see illustration)**. **Note:** *On some engines the rear bearing cap (flywheel end - number 5) may not be numbered but is easily identified anyway.* If the bearing caps are not marked, using a hammer and punch or a suitable marker pen, number the caps from 1 to 5 and mark each cap to indicate its correct fitted direction to avoid confusion on refitting.

6 Working in a diagonal sequence, evenly and progressively slacken the ten main bearing cap retaining bolts by half a turn at a time until all bolts are loose. Remove all bolts.

7 Carefully remove each cap from the cylinder block, ensuring that the lower main bearing shell remains in position in the cap.

8 Carefully lift out the crankshaft, taking care not to displace the upper main bearing shells. Remove the rear oil seal and discard it.

9 Recover the upper bearing shells from the cylinder block, and tape them to their caps for safe-keeping.

11 Cylinder block - cleaning and inspection

Cleaning

1 Remove all external components and electrical switches/sensors from the block. For complete cleaning, the core plugs should, ideally, be removed. Drill a small hole in the plugs, then insert a self-tapping screw into the hole. Pull out the plugs by pulling on the screw with a pair of grips, or by using a slide hammer.

2 Scrape all traces of gasket from the cylinder block, and from the main bearing casting (where fitted), taking care not to damage the gasket/sealing surfaces.

3 Remove all oil gallery plugs (where fitted). The plugs are usually very tight - they may have to be drilled out, and the holes re-tapped. Use new plugs when the engine is reassembled.

4 If any of the castings are extremely dirty, all should be steam-cleaned.

5 After the castings are returned, clean all oil holes and oil galleries one more time. Flush all

internal passages with warm water until the water runs clear. Dry thoroughly, and apply a light film of oil to all mating surfaces, to prevent rusting. Also oil the cylinder bores. If you have access to compressed air, use it to speed up the drying process, and to blow out all the oil holes and galleries.

 Warning: Wear eye protection when using compressed air!

6 If the castings are not very dirty, you can do an adequate cleaning job with hot (as hot as you can stand!), soapy water and a stiff brush. Take plenty of time, and do a thorough job. Regardless of the cleaning method used, be sure to clean all oil holes and galleries very thoroughly, and to dry all components well. Protect the cylinder bores as described above, to prevent rusting.

7 All threaded holes must be clean, to ensure accurate torque readings during reassembly. To clean the threads, run the correct-size tap into each of the holes to remove rust, corrosion, thread sealant or sludge, and to restore damaged threads. If possible, use compressed air to clear the holes of debris produced by this operation. A good alternative is to inject aerosol-applied water-dispersant lubricant into each hole, using the long spout usually supplied.

 Warning: Wear eye protection when cleaning out these holes in this way!

8 Apply suitable sealant to the new oil gallery plugs, and insert them into the holes in the block. Tighten them securely.

9 If the engine is not going to be reassembled right away, cover it with a large plastic bag to keep it clean; protect all mating surfaces and the cylinder bores as described above, to prevent rusting.

Inspection

10 Visually check the castings for cracks and corrosion. Look for stripped threads in the threaded holes. If there has been any history of internal water leakage, it may be worthwhile having an engine overhaul specialist check the cylinder block/crankcase with special equipment. If defects are found, have them repaired if possible, or renew the assembly.

11 Check the bore of each cylinder for scuffing and scoring.

12 Measure the diameter of each cylinder bore at the top (just below the wear ridge), centre and bottom of the bore, both parallel to the crankshaft axis and at right angles to it, so that a total of six measurements are taken. Note that there are various size groups of bore diameter to allow for manufacturing tolerances; the size group markings are stamped on the cylinder block (and also on the piston crowns).

13 Compare the results with the Specifications at the beginning of this Chapter; if any measurement exceeds the

service limit specified, the cylinder block must be rebored if possible, or renewed and new piston assemblies fitted.

14 If the cylinder bores are badly scuffed or scored, or if they are excessively worn, out-of-round or tapered, or if the piston-to-bore clearances is excessive (see Section 12), the cylinder block must be rebored (if possible) or renewed and new pistons fitted.

15 If the bores are in reasonably good condition and not worn beyond the specified limits, then the piston rings should be renewed. If this is the case, the bores should be honed to allow the new rings to bed in correctly and provide the best possible seal. The conventional type of hone has spring-loaded stones, and is used with a power drill. You will also need some paraffin (or honing oil) and rags. The hone should be moved up and down the bore to produce a crosshatch pattern, and plenty of honing oil should be used. Ideally, the crosshatch lines should intersect at approximately a 60° angle. Do not take off more material than is necessary to produce the required finish. If new pistons are being fitted, the piston manufacturers may specify a finish with a different angle, so their instructions should be followed. Do not withdraw the hone from the bore while it is still being turned – stop it first. After honing a bore, wipe out all traces of the honing oil. If equipment of this type is not available, or if you are not sure whether you are competent to undertake the task yourself, an engine overhaul specialist will carry out the work at moderate cost.

12 Piston/connecting rod assembly - inspection

1 Before the inspection process can begin, the piston/connecting rod assemblies must be cleaned, and the original piston rings removed from the pistons.

2 Carefully expand the old rings over the top of the pistons. The use of two or three old feeler blades will be helpful in preventing the rings dropping into empty grooves **(see illustration)**. Be careful not to scratch the

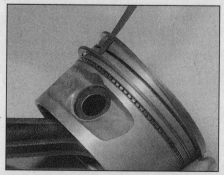

12.2 Using a feeler blade to aid removal of a piston ring

piston with the ends of the ring. The rings are brittle, and will snap if they are spread too far. They're also very sharp - protect your hands and fingers. Note that the third (oil control) ring consists either of a spacer and two side rails or an expander and ring. Always remove the rings from the top of the piston. Keep each set of rings with its piston if the old rings are to be re-used.

3 Scrape away all traces of carbon from the top of the piston. A hand-held wire brush (or a piece of fine emery cloth) can be used, once the majority of the deposits have been scraped away. The piston identification markings should now be visible.

4 Remove the carbon from the ring grooves in the piston, using an old ring. Break the ring in half to do this (be careful not to cut your fingers - piston rings are sharp). Be careful to remove only the carbon deposits - do not remove any metal, and do not nick or scratch the sides of the ring grooves.

5 Once the deposits have been removed, clean the piston/connecting rod assembly with paraffin or a suitable solvent, and dry thoroughly. Make sure that the oil return holes in the ring grooves are clear.

6 If the cylinder bores are not damaged or worn excessively, and if the cylinder block does not need to be rebored (see Section 11), check the pistons as follows.

7 Carefully inspect each piston for cracks around the skirt, around the gudgeon pin holes, and at the piston ring 'lands' (between the ring grooves).

8 Look for scoring and scuffing on the piston skirt, holes in the piston crown, and burned areas at the edge of the crown. If the skirt is scored or scuffed, the engine may have been suffering from overheating, and/or abnormal combustion which caused excessively high operating temperatures. The cooling and lubrication systems should be checked thoroughly. Scorch marks on the sides of the pistons show that blow-by has occurred. A hole in the piston crown, or burned areas at the edge of the piston crown, indicates that abnormal combustion (pre-ignition, knocking, or detonation) has been occurring. If any of the above problems exist, the causes must be investigated and corrected, or the damage will occur again. The causes may include incorrect ignition timing, or a faulty injector.

9 Corrosion of the piston, in the form of pitting, indicates that coolant has been leaking into the combustion chamber and/or the crankcase. Again, the cause must be corrected, or the problem may persist in the rebuilt engine.

10 Measure the piston diameter at right angles to the gudgeon pin axis; compare the results with the Specifications at the beginning of this Chapter. Note that there are various size groups of piston to allow for manufacturing tolerances; the size group markings are stamped on the piston crown.

11 To measure the piston-to-bore clearance, either measure the bore (see Section 11) and

piston skirt as described and subtract the skirt diameter from the bore measurement, or insert each piston into its original bore, then select a feeler gauge blade and slip it into the bore along with the piston. The piston must be aligned exactly in its normal attitude, and the feeler gauge blade must be between the piston and bore, on one of the thrust faces, just up from the bottom of the bore. If the clearance is excessive, a new piston will be required. If the piston binds at the lower end of the bore and is loose towards the top, the bore is tapered. If tight spots are encountered as the piston/feeler gauge blade is rotated in the bore, the bore is out-of-round.

12 Repeat this procedure for the remaining pistons and cylinder bores. Any piston which is worn beyond the specified limits must be renewed.

13 Examine each connecting rod carefully for signs of damage, such as cracks around the big-end and small-end bearings. Check that the rod is not bent or distorted. Damage is highly unlikely, unless the engine has been seized or badly overheated. Detailed checking of the connecting rod assembly can only be carried out by a Vauxhall dealer or engine repair specialist with the necessary equipment.

14 On 2.0 and 2.2 litre engines the gudgeon pins are an interference fit in the connecting rod small-end bearing. Therefore, piston and/or connecting rod renewal should be entrusted to a Vauxhall dealer, or engine repair specialist, who will have the necessary tooling to remove and install the gudgeon pins. If new pistons are to be fitted, ensure that the correct size pistons are fitted to each bore. **Note:** *Vauxhall state that the piston/connecting rod assemblies should not be disassembled. If any components requires renewal, then the complete assembly must be renewed. Do not fit a new piston to an old connecting rod or vice versa.*

15 On 2.4 litre engines, the gudgeon pins are of the floating type, secured in position by two circlips. On this engine, the pistons and connecting rods can be separated as follows.

16 Using a small flat-bladed screwdriver, prise out the circlips, and push out the gudgeon pin. Hand pressure should be sufficient to remove the pin. Identify the piston

and rod to ensure correct reassembly. Discard the circlips - new ones *must* be used on refitting.

17 Examine the gudgeon pin and connecting rod small-end bearing for signs of wear or damage **(see illustration)**. Wear will require the renewal of both the pin and connecting rod.

18 Where applicable, assemble the piston and connecting rod so that the timing mark (either a notch or an arrow) on the piston crown will face towards the front (timing chain) end of the engine and the raised mark which is cast onto the side of the connecting rod will face towards the rear (flywheel) end of the engine; the oil hole in the connecting rod will face towards the right-hand (manifold) side of the engine **(see illustration)**. Apply a smear of clean engine oil to the gudgeon pin. Slide it into the piston and through the connecting rod small-end. Check that the piston pivots freely on the rod, then secure the gudgeon pin in position with two new circlips, ensuring that each circlip is correctly located in its groove in the piston.

13 Crankshaft - inspection

Checking crankshaft endfloat

1 If the crankshaft endfloat is to be checked, this must be done when the crankshaft is still installed in the cylinder block, but is free to move.

2 Check the endfloat using a dial gauge in contact with the end of the crankshaft. Push the crankshaft fully one way, and then zero the gauge. Push the crankshaft fully the other

2G

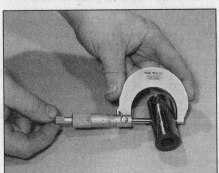

12.17 Measuring gudgeon pin diameter with a micrometer

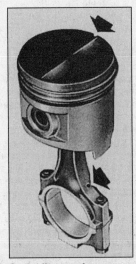

12.18 On 2.4 litre engines assemble the piston and connecting rod so that the piston timing mark is facing the front of the engine and connecting rod oil hole is on the right-hand side

13.2 Check the crankshaft endfloat using a dial gauge . . .

13.3 . . . or a feeler gauge

13.10 Using a micrometer to measure a crankshaft main bearing journal diameter

way, and check the endfloat (see illustration). The result can be compared with the specified amount, and will give an indication as to whether new main bearing shells are required.

3 If a dial gauge is not available, feeler gauges can be used. First push the crankshaft fully towards the flywheel/driveplate end of the engine, then use feeler gauges to measure the gap between the web of the crankpin and the side of thrustwasher (see illustration). The thrustwashers are incorporated into the centre (No 3) main bearing shells on 2.0 litre and 2.2 litre engine, and the rear (No 5) main bearing shell on 2.4 litre engines.

Inspection

4 Clean the crankshaft using paraffin or a suitable solvent, and dry it, preferably with compressed air if available. Be sure to clean the oil holes with a pipe cleaner or similar probe, to ensure that they are not obstructed.

 Warning: Wear eye protection when using compressed air.

5 Check the main and big-end bearing journals for uneven wear, scoring, pitting and cracking.

6 Big-end bearing wear is accompanied by distinct metallic knocking when the engine is running (particularly noticeable when the engine is pulling from low speed) and some loss of oil pressure.

7 Main bearing wear is accompanied by severe engine vibration and rumble - getting progressively worse as engine speed increases - and again by loss of oil pressure.

8 Check the bearing journal for roughness by running a finger lightly over the bearing surface. Any roughness (which will be accompanied by obvious bearing wear) indicates that the crankshaft requires regrinding (where possible) or renewal.

9 Check for burrs around the crankshaft oil holes (the holes are usually chamfered, so burrs should not be a problem unless regrinding has been carried out carelessly). Remove any burrs with a fine file or scraper, and thoroughly clean the oil holes as described previously.

10 Using a micrometer, measure the

diameter of the main and big-end bearing journals, and compare the results with the Specifications (see illustration). By measuring the diameter at a number of points around each journal's circumference, you will be able to determine whether or not the journal is out-of-round. Take the measurement at each end of the journal, near the webs, to determine if the journal is tapered. Compare the results obtained with those given in the Specifications.

11 Check the oil seal contact surfaces at each end of the crankshaft for wear and damage. If the seal has worn a deep groove in the surface of the crankshaft, consult an engine overhaul specialist; repair may be possible, but otherwise a new crankshaft will be required.

12 Set the crankshaft up in V-blocks, and position a dial gauge on the top of the crankshaft number 1 main bearing journal. Zero the dial gauge, then slowly rotate the crankshaft through two complete revolutions, noting the journal run-out. Repeat the procedure on the remaining four main bearing journals, so that a run-out measurement is available for all main bearing journals. If the run-out of any journal exceeds the service limit given in the Specifications, the crankshaft must be renewed.

13 Undersize big-end and main bearing shells are produced by Vauxhall for all engines. If the crankshaft journals have not already been reground, it may be possible to have the crankshaft reconditioned, and to fit undersize shells.

14 Main and big-end bearings - inspection

1 Even though the main and big-end bearings should be renewed during the engine overhaul, the old bearings should be retained for close examination, as they may reveal valuable information about the condition of the engine (see illustration).

2 Bearing failure can occur due to lack of lubrication, the presence of dirt or other foreign particles, overloading the engine, or

corrosion. Regardless of the cause of bearing failure, the cause must be corrected (where applicable) before the engine is reassembled, to prevent it from happening again.

3 When examining the bearing shells, remove them from the cylinder block, the main bearing caps, the connecting rods and the connecting rod big-end bearing caps. Lay them out on a clean surface in the same general position as their location in the engine. This will enable you to match any bearing problems with the corresponding crankshaft journal.

4 Dirt and other foreign matter gets into the engine in a variety of ways. It may be left in the engine during assembly, or it may pass through filters or the crankcase ventilation system. It may get into the oil, and from there into the bearings. Metal chips from machining operations and normal engine wear are often present. Abrasives are sometimes left in engine components after reconditioning, especially when parts are not thoroughly cleaned using the proper cleaning methods. Whatever the source, these foreign objects often end up embedded in the soft bearing

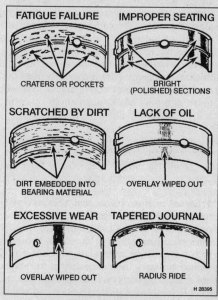

14.1 Typical bearing failures

material, and are easily recognised. Large particles will not embed in the bearing, and will score or gouge the bearing and journal. The best prevention for this cause of bearing failure is to clean all parts thoroughly, and keep everything spotlessly-clean during engine assembly. Frequent and regular engine oil and filter changes are also recommended.

5 Lack of lubrication (or lubrication breakdown) has a number of interrelated causes. Excessive heat (which thins the oil), overloading (which squeezes the oil from the bearing face) and oil leakage (from excessive bearing clearances, worn oil pump or high engine speeds) all contribute to lubrication breakdown. Blocked oil passages, which usually are the result of misaligned oil holes in a bearing shell, will also oil-starve a bearing, and destroy it. When lack of lubrication is the cause of bearing failure, the bearing material is wiped or extruded from the steel backing of the bearing. Temperatures may increase to the point where the steel backing turns blue from overheating.

6 Driving habits can have a definite effect on bearing life. Full-throttle, low-speed operation (labouring the engine) puts very high loads on bearings, tending to squeeze out the oil film. These loads cause the bearings to flex, which produces fine cracks in the bearing face (fatigue failure). Eventually, the bearing material will loosen in pieces, and tear away from the steel backing.

7 Short-distance driving leads to corrosion of bearings, because insufficient engine heat is produced to drive off the condensed water and corrosive gases. These products collect in the engine oil, forming acid and sludge. As the oil is carried to the engine bearings, the acid attacks and corrodes the bearing material.

8 Incorrect bearing installation during engine assembly will lead to bearing failure as well. Tight-fitting bearings leave insufficient bearing running clearance, and will result in oil starvation. Dirt or foreign particles trapped behind a bearing shell result in high spots on the bearing, which lead to failure.

9 As mentioned at the beginning of this Section, the bearing shells should be renewed as a matter of course during engine overhaul; to do otherwise is false economy.

15 Engine overhaul - reassembly sequence

1 Before reassembly begins, ensure that all new parts have been obtained, and that all necessary tools are available. Read through the entire procedure to familiarise yourself with the work involved, and to ensure that all items necessary for reassembly of the engine are at hand. In addition to all normal tools and materials, thread-locking compound will be needed. A good quality tube of liquid sealant

will also be required for the joint faces that are fitted without gaskets.

2 In order to save time and avoid problems, engine reassembly can be carried out in the following order:

a) Crankshaft.
b) Piston/connecting rod assemblies.
c) Timing chain and sprockets - 2.4 litre engine.
d) Oil pump - 2.0 and 2.2 litre engine.
e) Sump.
f) Flywheel.
g) Cylinder head.
h) Timing belt sprockets and belt - 2.0 and 2.2 litre engine.
i) Inlet and exhaust manifolds (Chapter 4A).
j) Engine external components.

3 At this stage, all engine components should be absolutely clean and dry, with all faults repaired. The components should be laid out (or in individual containers) on a completely clean work surface.

16 Piston rings - refitting

1 Before fitting new piston rings, the ring end gaps must be checked as follows.

2 Lay out the piston/connecting rod assemblies and the new piston ring sets, so that the ring sets will be matched with the same piston and cylinder during the end gap measurement and subsequent engine reassembly.

3 Insert the top ring into the first cylinder, and push it down the bore using the top of the piston. This will ensure that the ring remains square with the cylinder walls. Push the ring down into the bore until it is positioned 15 to 20 mm down from the top edge of the bore, then withdraw the piston.

4 Measure the end gap using feeler gauges, and compare the measurements with the figures given in the Specifications (see illustration).

5 If the gap is too small (unlikely if genuine Vauxhall parts are used), it must be enlarged, or the ring ends may contact each other during engine operation, causing serious

damage. Ideally, new piston rings providing the correct end gap should be fitted. As a last resort, the end gap can be increased by filing the ring ends very carefully with a fine file. Mount the file in a vice with soft jaws, slip the ring over the file with the ends contacting the file face, and slowly move the ring to remove material from the ends. Take care, as piston rings are sharp, and are easily broken.

6 With new piston rings, it is unlikely that the end gap will be too large. If the gaps are too large, check that you have the correct rings for your engine and for the particular cylinder bore size.

7 Repeat the checking procedure for each ring in the first cylinder, and then for the rings in the remaining cylinders. Remember to keep rings, pistons and cylinders matched up.

8 Once the ring end gaps have been checked and if necessary corrected, the rings can be fitted to the pistons as follows.

2.0 and 2.2 litre engines

9 Fit the piston rings using the same technique as for removal. Fit the bottom (oil control) spacer first then install both the side rails, noting that both the spacer and side rails can be installed either way up.

10 The second and top compression rings are different and can be identified by their cross-sections; the top ring is square whilst the second ring is tapered. Fit the second and top compression rings ensuring that each ring is fitted the correct way up with its identification (TOP) mark uppermost (see illustration). Note: Always follow any instructions supplied with the new piston ring sets - different manufacturers may specify different procedures. Do not mix up the top and second compression rings. On some engines the top ring will not have an identification marking and can be fitted either way up.

11 With the piston rings correctly installed, check that each ring is free to rotate easily in

16.4 Measuring a piston ring end gap using a feeler gauge

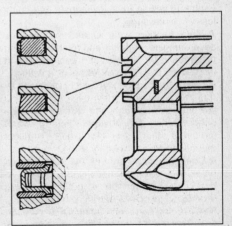

16.10 Sectional view of piston rings - 2.0 and 2.2 litre engines

2G

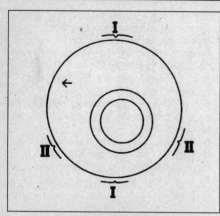

16.11 Piston ring end gap positions - 2.0 and 2.2 litre engines

I *Top and second compression rings*
II *Oil control ring side rails*

its groove then position the ring end gaps as shown **(see illustration)**.

2.4 litre engines

12 Fit the oil control ring expander first then fit the ring, position the expander ring end gap 180° (opposite) away from the control ring end gap.

13 The second and top rings are different and can be identified by their cross-sections and markings. The top ring has a more rounded profile and has the identification

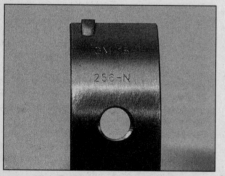

17.1 Typical main bearing shell identification markings

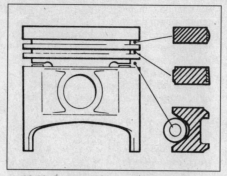

16.13 Sectional view of piston rings - 2.4 litre engines

marking TOP KL whereas the second rings has a tapered profile and has the identification marking TOP. Fit both compression rings ensuring that each ring is fitted the correct way up with its identification marking uppermost **(see illustration)**. Note: *Always follow any instructions supplied with the new piston ring sets - different manufacturers may specify different procedures. Do not mix up the top and second compression rings.*

14 Check that each ring is free to rotate easily in its groove, then position all the ring end gaps so each are approximately 120° apart.

---

17 Crankshaft - refitting and main bearing running clearance check

Note: *It is recommended that new main bearing shells are fitted regardless of the condition of the original ones.*
Note: *New main bearing cap bolts should be used on 2.0 and 2.2 litre engines.*

Selection of bearing shells

1 All replacement bearing shells sold are of the same grade **(see illustration)**. Vauxhall supply both standard size bearing shells and undersize shells for use when the crankshaft has been reground. The required size of shell required can be determined by measuring the crankshaft journals (see Section 13).

Main bearing running clearance check

2 Clean the backs of the bearing shells and the bearing locations in both the cylinder block and the main bearing caps.

3 Press the bearing shells into their locations, ensuring that the tab on each shell engages in the notch in the cylinder block or main bearing cap. Ensure the shells with the thrustwashers are fitted to the centre (No 3) main bearing on 2.0 and 2.2 litre engines, and the rear (No 5) main bearing on 2.4 litre engines. If the original bearing shells are being used for the check ensure they are refitted in their original locations **(see illustrations)**. The clearance can be checked in either of two ways.

4 One method (which will be difficult to achieve without a range of internal micrometers or internal/external expanding calipers) is to refit the main bearing caps to the cylinder block, with bearing shells in place. With the cap retaining bolts correctly tightened (on 2.0 and 2.2 litre engines use the original bolts for the check, not the new ones), measure the internal diameter of each assembled pair of bearing shells. If the diameter of each corresponding crankshaft journal is measured and then subtracted from the bearing internal diameter, the result will be the main bearing running clearance.

5 The second (and more accurate) method is to use a product known as Plastigauge. This consists of a fine thread of perfectly round plastic which is compressed between the bearing shell and the journal. When the shell is removed, the plastic is deformed and can be measured with a special card gauge supplied with the kit. The running clearance is determined from this gauge. Plastigauge is sometimes difficult to obtain but enquiries at one of the larger specialist quality motor factors should produce the name of a stockist in your area. The procedure for using Plastigauge is as follows.

6 With the main bearing upper shells in place, carefully lay the crankshaft in position. Do not use any lubricant; the crankshaft journals and bearing shells must be perfectly clean and dry.

17.3a Fit the bearing shells, making sure their tabs are correctly located in the slots in the bearing cap/block

17.3b On 2.0 and 2.2 litre engines the main bearing with the thrustwashers is fitted in the centre . . .

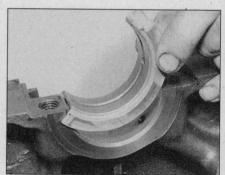

17.3c . . . and on 2.4 litre engines it is fitted at the rear

17.7 Plastigauge in place on a crankshaft main bearing journal

17.9 Measure the width of the deformed Plastigauge using the scale on the card

17.16 Lubricate the upper bearing shells with clean engine oil then fit the crankshaft

7 Cut several lengths of the appropriate size Plastigauge (they should be slightly shorter than the width of the main bearings) and place one length on each crankshaft journal axis **(see illustration)**.

8 With the main bearing lower shells in position, refit the main bearing caps, using the identification marks to ensure each one is correctly positioned. Refit the (original) retaining bolts and tighten them to the specified torque (2.4 litre engine - see paragraph 31) or to the specified stage 1 torque and then through the stage 2 and (where necessary) stage 3 angles (2.0 and 2.2 litre engines - see paragraphs 20 to 22). Take care not to disturb the Plastigauge and **do not** rotate the crankshaft at any time during this operation. Evenly and progressively slacken and remove the main bearing cap bolts then lift off the caps again, taking great care not to disturb the Plastigauge or rotate the crankshaft.

9 Compare the width of the crushed Plastigauge on each journal to the scale printed on the Plastigauge envelope to obtain the main bearing running clearance **(see illustration)**. Compare the clearance measured with that given in the Specifications at the start of this Chapter.

10 If the clearance is significantly different from that expected, the bearing shells may be the wrong size (or excessively worn if the

original shells are being re-used). Before deciding that the crankshaft is worn, make sure that no dirt or oil was trapped between the bearing shells and the caps or block when the clearance was measured. If the Plastigauge was wider at one end than at the other, the crankshaft journal may be tapered.

11 Before condemning the components concerned, seek the advice of your Vauxhall dealer or suitable engine repair specialist. They will also be able to inform as to the best course of action or whether renewal will be necessary.

12 Where necessary, obtain the correct size of bearing shell and repeat the running clearance checking procedure as described above.

13 On completion, carefully scrape away all traces of the Plastigauge material from the crankshaft and bearing shells using a fingernail or other object which is unlikely to score the bearing surfaces.

Final crankshaft refitting

2.0 and 2.2 litre engines

14 Carefully lift the crankshaft out of the cylinder block once more.

15 Place the bearing shells in their locations as described above in paragraphs 2 and 3. If new shells are being fitted, ensure that all

traces of the protective grease are cleaned off using paraffin. Wipe dry the shells and caps with a lint-free cloth.

16 Lubricate the upper shells with clean engine oil then lower the crankshaft into position **(see illustration)**.

17 Ensure the bearing shells are correctly located in the caps and refit the caps No 1 to 4 to the cylinder block. Ensure the caps are fitted in their correct locations, number 1 cap is at the front (timing belt/chain) end, and are fitted the correct way around so that all the numbers are the correct way up when read from the right-hand side of the cylinder block **(see illustration)**.

18 Ensure the rear (No 5) bearing cap is clean and dry. Apply a smear of sealant (Vauxhall recommend the use of sealant 15004200 - part no 08983368 - available from your Vauxhall dealer) to the cylinder block mating surface of the cap and fill the groove on each side of the cap with sealing compound (Vauxhall recommend the use of sealant 1503294 - part no 90001851 - available from your Vauxhall dealer) **(see illustrations)**. Fit the cap to the engine, ensuring it is fitted the correct way around.

19 Apply a smear of clean engine to oil to the threads and underneath the heads of the new main bearing cap bolts. Fit the bolts tightening them all by hand.

20 Working in a diagonal sequence from the

17.17 Lubricate the crankshaft journals then refit bearing caps number 1 to 4, ensuring each one is fitted in its original location

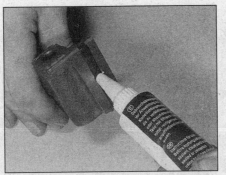

17.18a On 2.0 and 2.2 litre engines, fill the side grooves of the rear (No 5) bearing cap with sealant

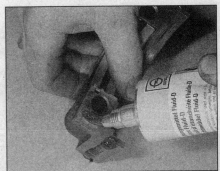

17.18b ... and apply sealant to the cap mating surfaces

2G

17.20 Fit the new main bearing cap bolts tightening them to the specified stage 1 torque setting . . .

17.21 . . . and then through the specified stage 2 and (where necessary) stage 3 angle - see text

17.29 On 2.4 litre engines fill the rear (No 5) bearing cap outer cutouts with sealant and apply sealant to the cap mating surface

centre outwards, tighten the main bearing cap bolts to the specified Stage 1 torque setting **(see illustration)**.

21 Once all bolts are tightened to the specified Stage 1 torque, go around again and tighten all bolts through the specified Stage 2 angle. It is recommended that an angle-measuring gauge is used during to ensure accuracy **(see illustration)**. If a gauge is not available, use white paint to make alignment marks between the bolt head and cap prior to tightening; the marks can then be used to check that the bolt has been rotated through the correct angle.

22 On 1995 onwards 2.0 litre engines (X20SE) and all 2.2 litre engines, go around again and tighten all bolts through the specified stage 3 angle.

23 On all engines, once all the bolts have been tightened, inject more sealant down the grooves in the rear main bearing cap until sealant is seen to be escaping through the joints. Once you are sure the cap grooves are full of sealant, wipe off all excess sealant using a clean cloth.

24 Check that the crankshaft is free to rotate smoothly; if excessive pressure is required to turn the crankshaft, investigate the cause before proceeding further.

25 Check the crankshaft endfloat as described in Section 13.

26 Refit/reconnect the piston connecting rod

assemblies to the crankshaft as described in Section 18.

27 Referring to Part A or B (as applicable), fit a new rear oil seal to the crankshaft then refit the flywheel, oil pump, cylinder head, timing belt sprockets and fit a new timing belt.

2.4 litre engine

28 Fit the bearing shells and crankshaft as described in paragraphs 14 to 18.

29 Ensure the rear (No 5) bearing cap is clean and dry. Apply a smear of sealant (Vauxhall recommend the use of sealant 15004200 - part no 08983368 - available from your Vauxhall dealer) to the cylinder block mating surface of the cap and fill the outer cutout on each side of the cap with sealing compound (Vauxhall recommend the use of sealant 1503294 - part no 90001851 - available from your Vauxhall dealer) **(see illustration)**. Fit the cap to the engine, ensuring it is fitted the correct way around.

30 Apply a smear of clean engine to oil to the threads and underneath the heads of the main bearing cap bolts. Refit the bolts tightening them all by hand.

31 Working in a diagonal sequence from the centre outwards, tighten the main bearing cap bolts evenly and progressively to the specified torque setting **(see illustration)**.

32 Once all the bolts have been tightened, Ensure the rear main bearing cap cutouts are

filled and wipe off excess sealant using a clean cloth.

33 Check that the crankshaft is free to rotate smoothly; if excessive pressure is required to turn the crankshaft, investigate the cause before proceeding further.

34 Check the crankshaft endfloat as described in Section 13.

35 Refit/reconnect the piston connecting rod assemblies to the crankshaft as described in Section 18.

36 Referring to Part C, fit a new rear oil seal to the crankshaft then refit the flywheel, timing chain and sprockets, timing chain cover and cylinder head.

18 Piston/connecting rod assembly - refitting and big-end running clearance check

Note: *It is recommended that new piston rings and big-end bearing shells are fitted regardless of the condition of the original ones.*

Note: *New big-end bearing cap bolts should be used on 2.0 and 2.2 litre engines.*

Selection of bearing shells

1 All replacement bearing shells sold are of the same grade. Vauxhall supply both standard size bearing shells and undersize shells for use when the crankshaft has been reground. The required size of shell required can be determined by measuring the crankshaft journals (see Section 13).

Big-end bearing running clearance check

2 Clean the backs of the bearing shells and the bearing locations in both the connecting rod and bearing cap.

3 Press the bearing shells into their locations, ensuring that the tab on each shell engages in the notch in the connecting rod and cap **(see illustration)**. If the original bearing shells are being used for the check ensure they are refitted in their original locations. The clearance can be checked in either of two ways.

17.31 Tighten the main bearing cap bolts evenly and progressively to the specified torque

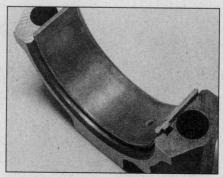

18.3 Fit the bearing shells making sure their tabs are correctly located in the connecting rod/cap groove

4 One method is to refit the big-end bearing cap to the connecting rod, with bearing shells in place. With the cap retaining bolts (on 2.0 and 2.2 litre engines use the original bolts for the check) correctly tightened, use an internal micrometer or vernier caliper to measure the internal diameter of each assembled pair of bearing shells. If the diameter of each corresponding crankshaft journal is measured and then subtracted from the bearing internal diameter, the result will be the big-end bearing running clearance.

5 The second method is to use Plastigauge as described in Section 17, paragraphs 7 to 13. Place a strand of Plastigauge on each (cleaned) crankpin journal and refit the (clean) piston/connecting rod assemblies, shells and big-end bearing caps. Tighten the bolts correctly taking care not to disturb the Plastigauge. Dismantle the assemblies without rotating the crankshaft and use the scale printed on the Plastigauge envelope to obtain the big-end bearing running clearance. On completion of the measurement, carefully scrape off all traces of Plastigauge from the journal and shells using a fingernail or other object which will not score the components.

Final piston/connecting rod assembly refitting

6 Ensure the bearing shells are correctly refitted as described above in paragraphs 2 and 3. If new shells are being fitted, ensure that all traces of the protective grease are cleaned off using paraffin. Wipe dry the shells and connecting rods with a lint-free cloth.

7 Lubricate the bores, the pistons and piston rings then lay out each piston/connecting rod assembly in its respective position.

8 Starting with assembly number 1, make sure that the piston rings are still spaced as described in Section 16, then clamp them in position with a piston ring compressor.

9 Insert the piston/connecting rod assembly into the top of cylinder No 1, ensuring that the

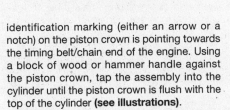

18.9a Insert the piston connecting rod into the correct bore and tap it gently into the bore using handle of a hammer . . .

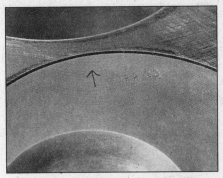

18.9b . . . ensuring the identification marking on the piston crown (arrow shown) is pointing towards the timing belt/chain end of the engine

identification marking (either an arrow or a notch) on the piston crown is pointing towards the timing belt/chain end of the engine. Using a block of wood or hammer handle against the piston crown, tap the assembly into the cylinder until the piston crown is flush with the top of the cylinder **(see illustrations)**.

10 Taking care not to mark the cylinder bore, liberally lubricate the crankpin and both bearing shells, then pull the piston/connecting rod assembly down the bore and onto the crankpin. Refit the big-end bearing cap using the markings to ensure it is fitted the correct way around (the lug on the bearing cap base should be facing the rear/flywheel end of the engine) and screw in the retaining bolts. New bolts must be used on 2.0 and 2.2 litre engines.

11 On pre 1995 2.0 litre engines (C20NE), tighten both bearing cap bolts to the specified Stage 1 torque setting and then tighten them through the specified Stage 2 angle. It is recommended that an angle-measuring gauge is used to ensure accuracy **(see illustrations)**. If a gauge is not available, use white paint to make alignment marks between the bolt head and cap prior to tightening; the

marks can then be used to check that the bolt has been rotated through the correct angle.

12 On 1995 onwards 2.0 litre engines (X20SE) and all 2.2 litre engines, tighten both bearing cap bolts to the specified Stage 1 torque setting then tighten them through the specified Stage 2 angle, and finally through the specified Stage 3 angle. It is recommended that an angle-measuring gauge is used during the final stages of the tightening, to ensure accuracy. If a gauge is not available, use white paint to make alignment marks between the bolt head and cap prior to tightening; the marks can then be used to check that the bolt has been rotated through the correct angle.

13 On 2.4 litre engines tighten both bearing cap bolts evenly and progressively to the specified torque setting.

14 On all engines, refit the remaining three piston and connecting rod assemblies in the same way.

15 Rotate the crankshaft, and check that it turns freely, with no signs of binding or tight spots.

16 On 2.2 litre engines and later 2.0 litre engines (X20SE), ensure the bearing cap and

2G

18.11a On 2.0 and 2.2 litre engines tighten the big-end bearing cap bolts to the specified stage 1 torque . . .

18.11b . . . and then through the specified angle(s) - see text

main bearing ladder casting surfaces are clean and dry. Refit the casting to the engine and (where fitted) the baffle plate and refit the retaining bolts. Working in a diagonal sequence from the centre outwards go around and securely tighten all the retaining bolts

17 On all engines, refit the oil pump strainer, sump and the cylinder head as described in Part A, B or C (as applicable) of this Chapter.

19 Engine - initial start up after overhaul

1 With the engine refitted in the vehicle, double-check the engine oil and coolant levels. Make a final check that everything has been reconnected, and that there are no tools or rags left in the engine compartment.

2 Disable the ignition system by disconnecting the wiring connector(s) from the ignition coil/DIS module (as applicable - see Chapter 5B) and the fuel system by removing the fuel pump fuse (see Chapter 13). Turn the engine on the starter until the oil pressure warning light goes out then stop. Reconnect the wiring and refit the fuse.

3 Start the engine as normal, noting that this may take a little longer than usual, due to the fuel system components having been disturbed.

4 While the engine is idling, check for fuel, water and oil leaks. Don't be alarmed if there are some odd smells and smoke from parts getting hot and burning off oil deposits.

5 Assuming all is well, keep the engine idling until hot water is felt circulating through the top hose, then switch off the engine. On 2.4 litre engines, perform the final stage of the cylinder head bolt tightening sequence while the engine is still warm (see Part C of this Chapter).

6 Allow the engine to cool then recheck the oil and coolant levels as described in *Weekly checks*, and top-up as necessary.

7 If new pistons, rings or crankshaft bearings have been fitted, the engine must be treated as new, and run-in for the first 500 miles (800 km). *Do not* operate the engine at full-throttle, or allow it to labour at low engine speeds in any gear. It is recommended that the oil and filter be changed at the end of this period.

Chapter 2 Part H
Diesel engine removal and overhaul procedures

Contents

Camshaft and tappets (2.5 litre engine) - removal, inspection
   and refitting 9
Camshaft and tappets (2.8 litre engine) - removal, inspection
   and refitting 10
Crankshaft - inspection 15
Crankshaft - main bearing clearance check and refitting 18
Crankshaft - removal 12
Cylinder block/crankcase and bores - cleaning and inspection 13
Cylinder head - dismantling 6
Cylinder head - reassembly 8
Cylinder head and valves - cleaning, inspection and renovation . . . 7
Engine - initial start-up after overhaul 20
Engine - removal and refitting 4
Engine overhaul - dismantling sequence 5
Engine overhaul - general information 2
Engine overhaul - reassembly sequence 17
Engine removal - methods and precautions 3
General information 1
Main and big-end bearings - inspection 16
Piston/connecting rods - big-end bearing clearance check
   and refitting 19
Piston/connecting rod assemblies - inspection and reassembly . . . 14
Piston/connecting rod assemblies - removal 11

Degrees of difficulty

| Easy, suitable for novice with little experience | 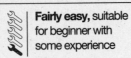 | Fairly easy, suitable for beginner with some experience | | Fairly difficult, suitable for competent DIY mechanic | | Difficult, suitable for experienced DIY mechanic | | Very difficult, suitable for expert DIY or professional | |

2H

Specifications

2.3 litre engines

Cylinder head

Maximum gasket face distortion	0.04 mm
Minimum cylinder head height	99.8 mm
Valve recess from gasket face	0.97 to 1.37 mm
Swirl chamber projection	0 to 0.04 mm
Valve seat width:	
Inlet	1.3 to 2.0 mm
Exhaust	1.4 to 2.0 mm

Inlet valves

Head diameter	42.0 mm
Stem diameter (standard)	7.99 to 8.0 mm
Stem-to-guide clearance	0.020 to 0.060 mm
Length . . 127.23 mm	
Valve seat angle	46.0°

Exhaust valves

Head diameter	34.5 mm
Stem diameter (standard)	7.98 to 7.99 mm
Stem-to-guide clearance	0.029 to 0.069 mm
Length . . 127.23 mm	
Valve seat angle	46.0°

Valve springs

Free length	N/A

2.3 litre engines (continued)

Cylinder bores
Diameter and classification .... N/A
Permissible oversize after rebore .... 0.5 to 1.0 mm
Maximum cylinder bore taper .... 0.013 mm
Maximum cylinder bore ovality .... 0.013 mm
Piston protrusion above top face .... 0.40 to 0.70 mm

Pistons
Diameter:
  Classification:
    6 .... 91.95 to 91.96 mm
    8 .... 91.97 to 91.98 mm
    00 .... 91.99 to 92.00 mm
    02 .... 92.01 to 92.02 mm
    04 .... 92.03 to 92.04 mm
    06 .... 92.05 to 92.06 mm
    08 .... 92.07 to 92.08 mm
Piston-to-bore clearance .... 0.05 to 0.07 mm

Piston rings
Thickness:
  Compression rings .... 1.978 to 1.990 mm
  Oil control .... 3.978 to 3.990 mm
End gap (measured in cylinder) .... 0.20 to 0.45 mm

Gudgeon pins
Diameter .... 30.0 -0.004 mm
Length .... 74.0 -0.3 mm
Fit in connecting rod and piston .... Floating

Crankshaft
Run-out .... 0.03 mm max
Endfloat .... 0.03 to 0.13 mm
Main bearing journal diameter (standard) .... 57.987 to 58.000 mm
Main bearing running clearance .... 0.02 to 0.07
Main bearing journal out-of-round .... 0.006 mm max
Main bearing journal taper .... 0.01 mm max
Big-end bearing journal diameter (standard) .... 53.967 to 53.971 mm
Big-end bearing running clearance .... 0.03 to 0.08 mm
Big-end bearing out-of-round .... 0.006 mm max
Big-end rod bearing taper .... 0.01 mm max

2.5 litre engines

Cylinder head
Maximum gasket face distortion .... N/A
Cylinder head height .... 89.95 to 90.05 mm
Valve recess from gasket face .... N/A
Swirl chamber depression .... N/A
Valve seat width:
  Inlet .... 1.8 to 2.2 mm
  Exhaust .... 1.65 to 2.05 mm
Valve seat angle:
  Inlet .... 54.2 to 54.4°
  Exhaust .... 44.2 to 44.4°

Inlet valves
Head diameter .... N/A
Stem diameter (standard) .... 7.940 to 7.960 mm
Stem-to-guide clearance .... 0.040 to 0.075 mm
Length .... N/A

Exhaust valves
Head diameter .... N/A
Stem diameter (standard) .... 7.922 to 7.940 mm
Stem-to-guide clearance .... 0.060 to 0.093 mm

Valve springs
Free length .... 44.65 mm

2.5 litre engines (continued)

Camshaft

Journal diameters:
- Front .... 53.495 to 53.510 mm
- Centre .... 53.450 to 53.470 mm
- Rear .... 53.480 to 53.500 mm

Bearing running clearance:
- Front .... 0.030 to 0.095 mm
- Centre .... 0.070 to 0.140 mm
- Rear .... 0.040 to 0.110 mm

Run-out .... N/A
Endfloat .... N/A

Lobe height:
- Inlet .... 45.70 mm
- Exhaust .... 45.14 mm

Hydraulic tappets

Diameter .... 14.965 to 14.985 mm
Running clearance .... 0.025 to 0.070 mm

Cylinder liners

Bore diameter .... 92.00 to 92.010 mm
Maximum cylinder bore taper .... N/A
Maximum cylinder bore ovality .... N/A
Projection above cylinder block top face .... 0.01 to 0.06 mm

Pistons

Diameter .... 91.935 to 91.945 mm
Piston-to-bore clearance .... 0.055 to 0.075 mm

Piston rings

End gap (measured in cylinder):
- Compression rings .... 0.20 to 0.50 mm
- Oil control ring .... 0.04 to 0.07 mm

Ring-to-groove clearance:
- Top compression ring .... 0.08 to 0.125 mm
- Second compression ring .... 0.07 to 0.102 mm
- Oil control ring .... 0.025 to 0.58 mm

Gudgeon pins

Diameter .... 29.990 to 29.996 mm
Length . . N/A
Fit in connecting rod and piston .... Floating

Crankshaft

Run-out .... N/A
Endfloat .... 0.15 to 0.30 mm

Main bearing journal diameter (standard):
- Front .... 62.985 to 63.00 mm
- Centre (2, 3, 4) .... 63.005 to 63.020 mm
- Rear .... 69.980 to 70.000 mm

Main bearing internal diameter (standard):
- Front .... 63.043 to 63.088 mm
- Centre (2, 3, 4) .... 63.050 to 63.093 mm
- Rear .... 70.030 to 70.055 mm

Main bearing running clearance:
- Front .... 0.043 to 0.103 mm
- Centre (2, 3, 4) .... 0.030 to 0.88 mm
- Rear .... 0.050 to 0.85 mm

Main bearing journal out-of-round .... N/A
Main bearing journal taper .... N/A
Big-end bearing journal diameter (standard) .... 53.940 to 53.955 mm
Big-end bearing running clearance .... 0.030 to 0.064 mm
Big-end bearing out-of-round .... N/A
Big-end rod bearing taper .... N/A

2H

2.8 litre engines

Cylinder head

Maximum gasket face distortion	0.05 to 0.20 mm
Cylinder head height	91.55 to 92.05 mm
Valve recess from gasket face	1.1 to 1.6 mm
Swirl chamber depression	0 to 0.02 mm
Valve seat width:	
Inlet	1.7 to 2.2 mm
Exhaust	2.0 to 2.5 mm

Inlet valves

Head diameter	N/A
Stem diameter (standard)	7.946 to 7.961 mm
Stem-to-guide clearance	0.039 to 0.069 mm
Length	N/A
Valve seat angle	45.0°

Exhaust valves

Head diameter	N/A
Stem diameter (standard)	7.921 to 7.936 mm
Stem-to-guide clearance	0.064 to 0.093 mm
Valve seat angle	45.0°

Valve springs

Free length	47.1 to 48.0 mm

Camshaft

Run-out	0.02 to 0.10 mm
Endfloat	0.08 to 0.2 mm
Lobe height	41.65 to 42.06 mm
Journal diameter	49.6 to 49.97 mm
Bearing internal diameter	50.0 to 50.08
Bearing running clearance	0.05 to 0.12 mm

Tappets

Stem diameter	12.95 to 12.99 mm
Running clearance	0.03 to 0.10 mm

Cylinder bores

Diameter	93.021 to 93.100 mm
Maximum cylinder bore taper	0.013 mm
Maximum cylinder bore ovality	0.013 mm
Piston protrusion above top face	0.01 mm

Pistons

Diameter:	
Classification:	
A	92.985 to 93.004 mm
B	93.005 to 93.024 mm
Piston-to-bore clearance	0.025 to 0.045 mm

Piston rings

End gap (measured in cylinder):	
Compression rings	0.20 to 0.40 mm
Oil control ring	0.1 to 0.3 mm
Ring-to-groove clearance:	
Top compression ring	0.09 to 0.125 mm
Second compression ring	0.05 to 0.075 mm
Oil control ring	0.03 to 0.07 mm

Crankshaft

Run-out	0.05 to 0.08 mm
Endfloat	0.1 to 0.3 mm
Main bearing journal diameter (standard)	69.91 to 69.93 mm
Main bearing running clearance	0.031 to 0.110 mm
Main bearing journal out-of-round	0.006 mm max
Main bearing journal taper	0.08 mm max
Big-end bearing journal diameter (standard)	52.90 to 52.93 mm
Big-end bearing running clearance	0.029 to 0.100 mm
Big-end bearing out-of-round	0.006 mm max
Big-end rod bearing taper	0.08 mm max

2.8 litre engines (continued)

Gudgeon pins
Diameter . . . . 33.97 to 34.00 mm
Length . . . . N/A
Fit in connecting rod and piston . . . . Floating

Torque wrench settings

2.3 litre engines
Refer to Specifications in Chapter 2D.

2.5 litre engines
Refer to Specifications in Chapter 2E.

2.8 litre engines
Refer to Specifications in Chapter 2F.

2H

1 General information

1 Included in this part of Chapter 2 are details of removing the engine from the vehicle and general overhaul procedures for the cylinder head, cylinder block and internal engine components.
2 The information ranges from advice concerning preparation for an overhaul and the purchase of replacement parts, to detailed step-by-step procedures covering removal, inspection, renovation and refitting of internal engine parts.
3 The following Sections have been compiled based on the assumption that the engine has been removed from the car. For information concerning in-car engine repair, as well as the removal and refitting of the external components necessary for the overhaul, refer to Parts D, E and F of this Chapter, and to Section 5 of this Part.
4 Apart from torque wrench settings, which are given at the beginning of the relevant in-car repair procedure Chapter, all specifications relating to engine overhaul are at the beginning of this Part of Chapter 2.

2 Engine overhaul - general information

1 It is not always easy to determine when, or if, an engine should be completely overhauled, as a number of factors must be considered.
2 High mileage is not necessarily an indication that an overhaul is needed, while low mileage does not preclude the need for an overhaul. Frequency of servicing is probably the most important consideration. An engine which has had regular and frequent oil and filter changes, as well as other required maintenance, will most likely give many thousands of miles of reliable service. Conversely, a neglected engine may require an overhaul very early in its life.
3 Excessive oil consumption is an indication that piston rings, valve stem oil seals and/or valves and valve guides are in need of attention. Make sure that oil leaks are not responsible before deciding that the rings and/or guides are bad. Perform a cylinder compression check to determine the extent of the work required.
4 Check the oil pressure with a gauge fitted in place of the oil pressure switch. If it is extremely low, the main and big-end bearings and/or the oil pump are probably worn out.
5 Loss of power, rough running, knocking or metallic engine noises, excessive valve gear noise and high fuel consumption may also point to the need for an overhaul, especially if they are all present at the same time. If a complete tune-up does not remedy the situation, major mechanical work is the only solution.
6 An engine overhaul involves restoring the internal parts to the specifications of a new engine. During an overhaul, the pistons and rings are renewed, and the cylinder bores are reconditioned. New main bearings, connecting rod bearings and camshaft bearings are generally fitted and, if necessary, the crankshaft may be reground to restore the journals. The valves are also serviced as well, since they are usually in less-than-perfect condition at this point. While the engine is being overhauled, other components, such as the starter and alternator, can be overhauled as well. The end result should be a like-new engine that will give many trouble-free miles. **Note:** *Critical cooling system components such as the hoses, drivebelts, thermostat and water pump MUST be renewed when an engine is overhauled. The radiator should be checked carefully, to ensure that it is not clogged or leaking. Also, it is a good idea to renew the oil pump whenever the engine is overhauled.*
7 Before beginning the engine overhaul, read through the entire procedure to familiarise yourself with the scope and requirements of the job. Overhauling an engine is not difficult if you follow all of the instructions carefully, have the necessary tools and equipment, and pay close attention to all specifications; however, it can be time-consuming. Plan on the vehicle being tied up for a minimum of two weeks, especially if parts must be taken to an engineering works for repair or reconditioning.

Check on the availability of parts, and make sure that any necessary special tools and equipment are obtained in advance. Most work can be done with typical hand tools, although a number of precision measuring tools are required for inspecting parts to determine if they must be renewed. Often the engineering works will handle the inspection of parts, and offer advice concerning reconditioning and renewal. **Note:** *Always wait until the engine has been completely disassembled, and all components (especially the cylinder block and crankshaft) have been inspected before deciding what service and repair operations must be performed by an engineering works. The condition of these components will be the major factor to consider when determining whether to overhaul the original engine or buy a reconditioned unit, do not purchase parts or have overhaul work done on other components until they have been thoroughly inspected. As a general rule, time is the primary cost of an overhaul, so it does not pay to fit worn or substandard parts.*
8 As a final note, to ensure maximum life and minimum trouble from a reconditioned engine, everything must be assembled with care, and in a spotlessly-clean environment.

3 Engine removal - methods and precautions

If you have decided that an engine must be removed for overhaul or major repair work, several preliminary steps should be taken.

Locating a suitable place to work is extremely important. Adequate work space, along with storage space for the vehicle, will be needed. If a garage is not available, at the very least a flat, level, clean work surface is required.

Cleaning the engine compartment and engine before beginning the removal procedure will help keep tools clean and organised.

An engine hoist or A-frame will also be necessary. Make sure the equipment is rated in excess of the weight of the engine. Safety is of primary importance, considering the potential hazards involved in lifting the engine out of the vehicle.

If this is the first time you have removed an engine, an assistant should be available. Advice and aid from someone more experienced would also be helpful. There are many instances when one person cannot simultaneously perform all of the operations required when lifting the engine out of the vehicle.

Plan the operation ahead of time. Arrange for, or obtain, all of the tools and equipment you will need prior to beginning the job. Some of the equipment necessary to perform engine removal and installation safely and with relative ease are (in addition to an engine hoist) a heavy-duty floor jack, complete sets of spanners and sockets as described in the back of this manual, wooden blocks, and plenty of rags and cleaning solvent for mopping up spilled oil, coolant and fuel. If the hoist must be hired, make sure that you arrange for it in advance, and perform all of the operations possible without it beforehand. This will save you money and time.

Plan for the vehicle to be out of use for quite a while. An engineering works will be required to perform some of the work which the do-it-yourselfer cannot accomplish without special equipment. These places often have a busy schedule, so it would be a good idea to consult them before removing the engine, in order to accurately estimate the amount of time required to rebuild or repair components that may need work.

Always be extremely careful when removing and refitting the engine. Serious injury can result from careless actions. Plan ahead, take your time, and you will find that a job of this nature, although major, can be accomplished successfully.

4 Engine - removal and refitting

Note: *After first removing the transmission, the engine is then removed upwards from the engine compartment on its own.*

Removal

2.3 litre engines

1 Remove the battery as described in Chapter 5A.

2 Drain the cooling system as described in Chapter 1B.

3 Remove the transmission as described in Chapter 7.

4 Remove the bonnet as described in Chapter 12.

5 Refer to Chapter 4B and remove the air cleaner assembly and all air intake ducting.

6 Remove the radiator with reference to Chapter 3. Also disconnect the top hose from the thermostat housing, and the bottom hose from the water pump.

7 Remove the radiator cooling fan as described in Chapter 3.

8 Clean the area around the hydraulic fluid pressure pipe union and return hose connection on the power steering pump.

9 Place a suitable container under the power steering pump, disconnect the fluid pressure pipe union and return hose and allow the fluid to drain into the container. Cover the pipe ends and the pump orifices after disconnection.

10 Disconnect the wiring connectors at the following components:
a) *Alternator.*
b) *Starter motor.*
c) *Air conditioning compressor (where fitted).*
d) *Glow plugs.*
e) *Injection pump.*
f) *Engine sensors.*

11 Disconnect the vacuum hoses from the following components, noting the colour coding stripes to aid refitting:
a) *EGR valve.*
b) *Vacuum pump.*
c) *Brake servo.*
d) *Fuel injection pump.*

12 Disconnect the accelerator cable and idle speed control cable from the injection pump, with reference to Chapter 4B if necessary.

13 Remove all traces of dirt from around the fuel feed and return hoses at the fuel lift pump. Loosen the clips and disconnect the hoses from the pump. Cover the open ends of the hoses and pump to keep dirt out.

14 On models fitted with air conditioning, remove the compressor with reference to Chapter 3, but leave the hoses attached, and position the pump to one side. **Do not** open any refrigerant lines.

15 Undo the bolt securing the engine earth strap to the chassis.

16 Check that the engine wiring harness has been disconnected from all attachments and connectors into the body harness, and that all other wires, hoses, cables and fittings likely to impede engine removal are disconnected and moved clear.

17 Attach suitable lifting eyes to the engine and connect a hoist to the lifting eyes, so that, when raised, the front of the engine will be higher than the rear. Raise the hoist slightly to just take the weight of the engine assembly.

18 Undo the nuts and bolts each side securing the engine mountings to the chassis and engine.

19 With the help of an assistant, slowly lift the engine from the engine compartment, taking care not to damage any components on the surrounding panels. When high enough, lift the assembly over the front body panel, and lower to the ground.

2.5 litre engines

20 Remove the battery as described in Chapter 5A.

21 Drain the cooling system as described in Chapter 1B.

22 Remove the transmission as described in Chapter 7.

23 Remove the bonnet as described in Chapter 12.

24 Refer to Chapter 4B and remove the air cleaner assembly and all air intake ducting.

25 Remove the radiator with reference to Chapter 3. Also disconnect the top hose from the thermostat housing, and the bottom hose from the water pump.

26 Remove the radiator cooling fan as described in Chapter 3.

27 Slacken the clip and detach the crankcase ventilation hose from the oil separator.

28 Slacken the clips and disconnect the expansion tank hose and heater hose from the cylinder head water manifold, and the heater hose from the pipe above the turbocharger.

29 Undo the banjo union bolts and disconnect the oil cooler hose unions from the oil filter adaptor. Recover the copper washers from each side of the banjo unions.

30 Disconnect the vacuum hose from the EGR valve and the brake servo vacuum hose at the bulkhead connection.

31 Disconnect the engine wiring harness connectors at the rear of the engine.

32 Unscrew the locking collar and disconnect the injection pump main wiring plug from the harness socket.

33 Unscrew the pump wiring harness socket retaining ring and withdraw the socket from the harness bracket.

34 Disconnect the remaining wiring connectors at the harness bracket and detach the wiring sockets from the bracket.

35 Clean the area around the hydraulic fluid pressure pipe union, and return hose connection on the power steering pump.

36 Undo the fluid pressure pipe banjo union bolt and remove the washer. Withdraw the pressure pipe from the pump connection and recover the second copper washer.

37 Slacken the clip, detach the return hose from the pump and allow the fluid to drain into a container. Cover the pipe ends and the pump orifices after disconnection.

38 Slacken the clips and disconnect the two injection pump fuel hoses from the fuel return pipe, and the feed hose from the fuel feed pipe. Seal the ends of the pipes and hoses to keep dirt out.

39 On models fitted with air conditioning, remove the compressor with reference to Chapter 3, but leave the hoses attached, and position the pump to one side. **Do not** open any refrigerant lines.

40 Undo the bolt securing the engine earth strap to the chassis.

41 Check that the engine wiring harness has been disconnected from all attachments and connectors into the body harness, and that all other wires, hoses, cables and fittings likely to impede engine removal are disconnected and moved clear.

42 Connect a hoist to the engine lifting eyes,

4.44 2.5 litre engine removal

so that, when raised, the front of the engine will be higher than the rear. Raise the hoist slightly to just take the weight of the engine assembly.

43 Undo the two bolts each side securing the engine mountings to the chassis.

44 With the help of an assistant, slowly lift the engine from the engine compartment, taking care not to damage any components on the surrounding panels **(see illustration)**. When high enough, lift the assembly over the front body panel, and lower to the ground.

2.8 litre engines

45 Remove the battery as described in Chapter 5A.

46 Drain the cooling system as described in Chapter 1B.

47 Remove the transmission as described in Chapter 7.

48 Remove the bonnet as described in Chapter 12.

49 Refer to Chapter 4B and remove the air cleaner assembly and all air intake ducting.

50 Remove the radiator with reference to Chapter 3. Also disconnect the top hose from the thermostat housing, and the bottom hose from the water pump.

51 Remove the radiator cooling fan as described in Chapter 3.

52 Referring to Chapter 11, unbolt the power steering pump from the engine and move it to one side without disconnecting the fluid hoses.

53 Disconnect the wiring connectors at the following components:

a) Alternator.
b) Starter motor.
c) Air conditioning compressor (where fitted).
d) Glow plugs.
e) Injection pump.
f) Engine sensors.

54 Disconnect the vacuum hoses from the following components, noting the colour coding stripes to aid refitting:

a) EGR valves.
b) Vacuum pump.
c) Quick-warm up system components.
d) Brake servo.
e) Fast idle control system.

55 Referring to Chapter 4B if necessary,

disconnect the accelerator cable at the injection pump.

56 Slacken the clips and disconnect the injection pump fuel feed and return hoses. Seal the ends of the pipes and hoses to keep dirt out.

57 On models fitted with air conditioning, remove the compressor with reference to Chapter 3, but leave the hoses attached, and position the pump to one side. **Do not** open any refrigerant lines.

58 Undo the bolt securing the engine earth strap to the chassis.

59 Check that the engine wiring harness has been disconnected from all attachments and connectors into the body harness, and that all other wires, hoses, cables and fittings likely to impede engine removal are disconnected and moved clear.

60 Attach suitable lifting eyes to the engine and connect a hoist to the lifting eyes, so that, when raised, the front of the engine will be higher than the rear. Raise the hoist slightly to just take the weight of the engine assembly.

61 Undo the nuts and bolts each side securing the engine mountings to the chassis and engine.

62 With the help of an assistant, slowly lift the engine from the engine compartment, taking care not to damage any components on the surrounding panels. When high enough, lift the assembly over the front body panel, and lower to the ground.

Refitting

63 Refitting is a reversal of removal, noting the following additional points.

a) Tighten all nuts and bolts to the specified torque and use new copper washers on all banjo unions.
b) Refer to the applicable Chapters as for removal.
c) Fill the engine and transmission with oil and fit a new oil filter, with reference to Chapter 1B.
d) Fill the cooling system with reference to Chapter 1B.
e) Top up/refill the power steering fluid reservoir, and where applicable bleed the system as described in Chapter 11.
f) Prime and bleed the fuel system as described in Chapter 4B.

5 Engine overhaul - dismantling sequence

1 It is much easier to disassemble and work on the engine if it is mounted on a portable engine stand. These stands can often be hired from a tool hire shop. Before the engine is mounted on a stand, the flywheel/driveplate should be removed from the engine, so that the engine stand bolts can be tightened into the end of the cylinder block.

2 If a stand is not available, it is possible to disassemble the engine with it blocked up on

a sturdy workbench or on the floor. Be extra-careful not to tip or drop the engine when working without a stand.

3 If you are going to obtain a reconditioned engine, all the external components must come off first, in order to be transferred to the replacement engine (just as they will if you are doing a complete engine overhaul yourself). Check with the engine supplier for details. Normally these components include:

a) Alternator mounting bracket.
b) Fuel injection pump and mounting bracket, and fuel injectors and glow plugs.
c) Thermostat housing and cover.
d) Turbocharger.
e) Inlet and exhaust manifolds.
f) Engine lifting brackets, hose brackets and wiring brackets.
g) Ancillary (power steering pump, air conditioning compressor) brackets.
h) Oil pressure warning light switch and oil level sensor (where applicable).
i) Coolant temperature sensors.
j) Wiring harnesses and brackets.
k) Coolant pipes and hoses.
l) Oil filler tube and dipstick.
m) Clutch.

Note: *When removing the external components from the engine, pay close attention to details that may be helpful or important during refitting. Note the fitted position of gaskets, seals, spacers, pins, washers, bolts and other small items.*

4 If you are obtaining a 'short' motor (which, when available, consists of the engine cylinder block, crankshaft, pistons and connecting rods all assembled), then the cylinder head, sump, oil pump, and timing belt (where applicable) will have to be removed also.

5 If you are planning a complete overhaul, the engine can be disassembled and the internal components removed in the following order:

a) Fuel system components.
b) Inlet and exhaust manifolds.
c) Cylinder head(s).
d) Timing cover/case.
e) Timing belt/chain and sprockets/gears.
f) Camshaft (where applicable).
g) Flywheel.
h) Sump.
i) Oil pump.
j) Pistons/connecting rod assemblies.
k) Crankshaft.

6 Before beginning the disassembly and overhaul procedures, make sure that you have all of the correct tools necessary. Refer to the introductory pages at the beginning of this manual for further information.

6 Cylinder head - dismantling

Note: *New and reconditioned cylinder heads are available from the manufacturers and from engine overhaul specialists. Be aware that*

2H

6.4a Compress each valve spring until the split collets can be removed

6.4b Release the compressor and lift off the cap . . .

6.4c . . . the valve spring . . .

6.4d . . . and where applicable, the lower seat

some specialist tools are required for the dismantling and inspection procedures, and new components may not be readily available. It may be more practical and economical for the home mechanic to purchase a reconditioned head rather than dismantle, inspect and recondition the original head.

2.3 litre engines

1 Remove the cylinder head from the engine (Chapter 2D), then remove the camshaft (Chapter 2D), the fuel injectors (Chapter 4B), and the glow plugs (Chapter 5C). If the swirl chambers are loose, remove them from the cylinder head and number them so they can be refitted to their original locations.

2.5 litre engines

2 Remove the cylinder head from the engine (Chapter 2E), then remove the glow plugs (Chapter 5C).

2.8 litre engines

3 Remove the cylinder head from the engine

(Chapter 2F), then remove the thermostat housing (Chapter 3), fuel injectors (Chapter 4B), and the glow plugs (Chapter 5C).

All engines

4 Using a valve spring compressor, compress each valve spring in turn until the split collets can be removed. Release the compressor and lift off the cap, spring and, where applicable, the spring seat (see illustrations). If, when the valve spring compressor is screwed down, the valve spring cap refuses to free and expose the split collets, gently tap the top of the tool, directly over the cap, with a light hammer. This will free the cap.
5 Withdraw the oil seal from the top of the valve guide, then remove the valve through the combustion chamber (see illustration).
6 It is essential that the valves and associated components are kept in their correct sequence, unless they are so badly worn that they are to be renewed. If they are going to be kept and used again, place them in labelled polythene bags, or in a compartmented box.

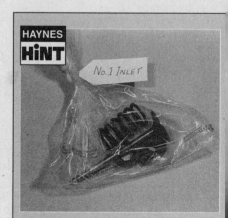

HAYNES HINT

No. 1 INLET

If the components are to be refitted, place each valve and its associated components in a labelled polythene bag or similar container, and mark the bag/container with the relevant valve number to ensure that it is refitted in its original location.

6.5 Withdraw the valve stem oil seal from the top of the guide

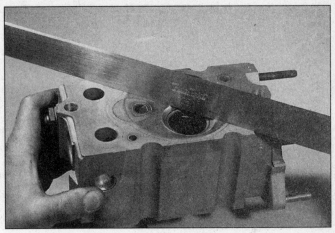

7.7 Checking the cylinder head surface for distortion

7 Cylinder head and valves - cleaning, inspection and renovation

1 Thorough cleaning of the cylinder head and valve components, followed by a detailed inspection, will enable you to decide how much valve service work must be carried out during the engine overhaul.

Cleaning

2 Scrape away all traces of old gasket material and sealing compound from the cylinder head. Take care not to damage the cylinder head surfaces.

3 Scrape away the carbon from the combustion chambers and ports, then wash the cylinder head thoroughly with paraffin or a suitable solvent.

4 Scrape off any heavy carbon deposits that may have formed on the valves, then use a power-operated wire brush to remove deposits from the valve heads and stems.

5 If the head is extremely dirty, it should be steam-cleaned. On completion, make sure that all oil holes and oil galleries are cleaned.

Inspection and renovation

Note: *Be sure to perform all the following inspection procedures before concluding that the services of an engine overhaul specialist are required. Make a list of all items that require attention.*

Cylinder head

6 Inspect the head very carefully for cracks, evidence of coolant leakage and other damage. If cracks are found, a new cylinder head should be obtained.

7 Use a straight-edge and feeler blade to check that the cylinder head surface is not distorted (see illustration). If the specified distortion limit is exceeded, machining of the gasket face may be possible. Consult a Vauxhall dealer as to the latest recommendations according to engine. If machining is not possible, the only course of action is to renew the cylinder head.

8 Examine the valve seats in each of the combustion chambers. If they are severely pitted, cracked or burned, then they will need to be renewed or recut by an engine overhaul specialist. If they are only slightly pitted, this can be removed by grinding the valve heads and seats together with coarse, then fine, grinding

paste as described below. Using a dial gauge or feeler blades, check that valve depth below the cylinder head gasket surface is within the limits given in the Specifications (see illustration).

9 If the valve guides are worn, indicated by a side-to-side motion of the valve in the guide, new guides must be fitted. A dial gauge may be used to determine the amount of side play of the valve. Recheck the fit using a new valve if in doubt, to decide whether it is the valve or the guide which is worn. If new guides are to be fitted, the valves must be renewed in any case. Valve guides may be renewed, but this work is best carried out by an engine overhaul specialist, since if it is not done skilfully, there is a risk of damaging the cylinder head.

Valves

10 Examine the head of each valve for pitting, burning, cracks and general wear, and check the valve stem for scoring and wear ridges. Rotate the valve, and check for any obvious indication that it is bent. Look for pits and excessive wear on the end of each valve stem. If the valve appears satisfactory at this stage, measure the valve stem diameter at several points using a micrometer (see illustration).

2H

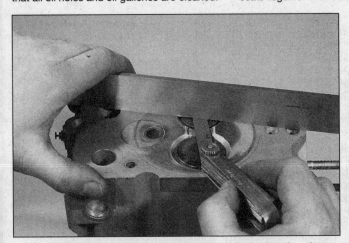

7.8 Checking the valve depth below the cylinder head surface

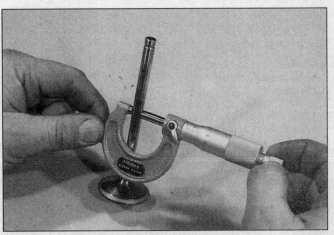

7.10 Checking the valve stem diameter

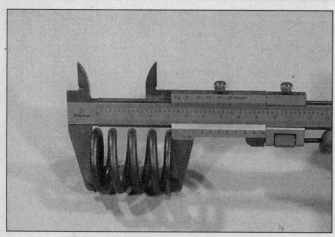

7.13 Checking the valve spring free length

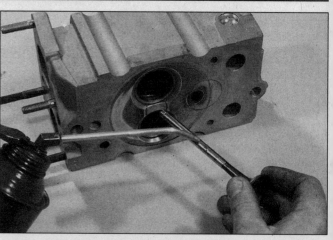

8.2 Lubricate the valve stems and insert the valves into their guides

Any significant difference in the readings obtained indicates wear of the valve stem. Should any of these conditions be apparent, the valve(s) must be renewed. If the valves are in satisfactory condition, or if new valves are being fitted, they should be ground (lapped) into their respective seats to ensure a smooth gas-tight seal.

11 Valve grinding is carried out as follows: Place the cylinder head upside-down on a bench, with a block of wood at each end to give clearance for the valve stems.

12 Smear a trace of coarse carborundum paste on the seat face, and press a suction grinding tool onto the valve head. With a semi-rotary action, grind the valve head to its seat, lifting the valve occasionally to redistribute the grinding paste. When a dull-matt even surface is produced on both the valve seat and the valve, wipe off the paste and repeat the process with fine carborundum paste. A light spring placed under the valve head will greatly ease this operation. When a smooth unbroken ring of light grey matt finish is produced on both the valve and seat, the grinding operation is complete. Be sure to remove all traces of grinding paste, using paraffin or a suitable solvent, before reassembly of the cylinder head.

Valve components

13 Examine the valve springs for signs of damage and discoloration, and also measure their free length using vernier calipers or a steel rule **(see illustration)** or by comparing the existing spring with a new component, where free length dimensions are not given.

14 Stand each spring on a flat surface, and check it for squareness. If any of the springs are damaged, distorted or have lost their tension, obtain a complete new set of springs. It is normal to renew the springs as a matter of course during a major overhaul.

8 Cylinder head - reassembly

1 On the 2.3 litre engine, if the swirl chambers have been removed, refit them to their original locations.

2 Lubricate the valve stems with clean engine oil and insert the valves into their original locations **(see illustration)**. If new valves are being fitted, insert them into the locations to which they have been ground.

3 Lubricate the valve stem oil seals then fit them by pushing into position in the cylinder head using a suitable socket or special tool **(see illustrations)**. Ensure that the seals are fully engaged with the valve guide.

4 Where applicable, locate the spring seat on the guide, followed by the spring and cap.

5 Compress the valve spring, and locate the split collets in the recess in the valve stem. Release the compressor, then repeat the procedure on the remaining valves. Use a little grease to hold the collets in place.

6 With all the valves installed, place the cylinder head on blocks so that there is clearance below the valves and, using a hammer and interposed block of wood, tap the end of each valve stem to settle the components.

7 The previously removed components can now be refitted with reference to Section 8.

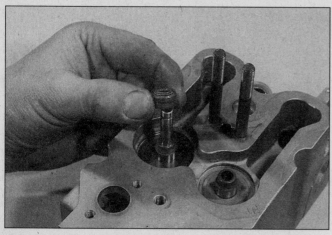

8.3a Locate the valve stem oil seals over the valve and guide . . .

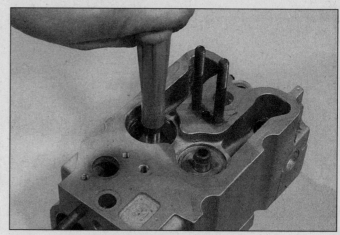

8.3b . . . and push them fully home using a socket or fitting tool

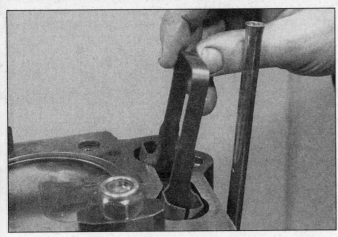

9.2 Extract the anti-rotation brackets from the tappet chest - 2.5 litre engine

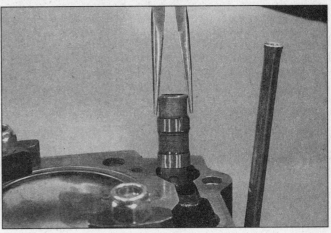

9.4 Using pliers, withdraw the hydraulic tappets - 2.5 litre engine

9 Camshaft and tappets (2.5 litre engine) - removal, inspection and refitting

Removal

1 Remove the timing cover and cylinder heads as described in Part E of this Chapter.
2 Extract the anti-rotation brackets from the tappet chest **(see illustration)**.
3 Obtain eight clean plastic containers or alternatively divide a larger container into compartments and fill the containers with clean engine oil. The container(s) must be deep enough to allow the tappets to remain upright and be completely submerged in the oil. Number the containers one to eight.
4 Using pointed-nose pliers, carefully withdraw the tappets using a slight twisting action and place it in its correct numbered container **(see illustration)**.
5 Working through the two holes in the camshaft sprocket, undo the camshaft thrust plate retaining bolts **(see illustration)**.
6 Withdraw the camshaft from the front of the engine, taking care not to nick the bearing with the sharp edges of the cam lobes **(see illustration)**.

Inspection

7 Examine the camshaft bearing surfaces and cam lobes for wear ridges, pitting or scoring. Renew the camshaft if evident.
8 Examine the camshaft bearing surfaces in the cylinder block. If deep scoring or other damage is evident, the bearings should be renewed by an engine reconditioning specialist.
9 Measure the cam lobe height and camshaft bearing journal diameters using a micrometer and compare the figures obtained with those given in the Specifications. Renew the camshaft or camshaft bearings if the figures obtained are outside the permitted tolerance.
10 Inspect the tappets for scoring, pitting and wear ridges. If any tappet shows signs of wear all eight should be renewed as a set.

Refitting

11 Set the engine to the TDC position for No 1 cylinder as described in Chapter 2E, Section 3.
12 Thoroughly lubricate the camshaft journals and bearings with clean engine oil and insert the camshaft into the cylinder block.
13 As the camshaft gear engages with the injection pump and vacuum pump gears, make sure that the timing marks on the gears are aligned. Refer to Chapter 2E, Section 15, for further information on the alignment of the timing marks.
14 Refit the camshaft thrust plate retaining bolts and tighten them to the specified torque.
15 Lubricate the tappet bores and refit the tappets to their original locations.
16 Refit the anti-rotation brackets and push them firmly into position so their tops are below the cylinder block face.
17 Refit the timing cover and cylinder heads as described in Part E of this Chapter.

2H

9.5 Undo the camshaft thrust plate retaining bolts (arrowed) - 2.5 litre engine

9.6 Withdraw the camshaft - 2.5 litre engine

11.3a Unscrew and remove the big-end bearing cap nuts or bolts as applicable

11.3b Withdraw the cap, complete with shell bearing, from the connecting rod

10 Camshaft and tappets (2.8 litre engine) - removal, inspection and refitting

Removal

1 Remove the rocker shaft and pushrods, timing belt, sump and oil pump as described in Part F of this Chapter.

2 Using a dial gauge, measure the camshaft endfloat, and compare with the value given in the Specifications. This will give an indication of the amount of wear present on the thrust surfaces.

3 Undo the camshaft sprocket centre retaining bolt and remove the bolt and washer. Prevent the camshaft from turning by holding the sprocket with a forked tool engaged with the sprocket holes, or by inserting a suitable bolt through the sprocket hole into a corresponding threaded hole in the cylinder block.

4 Withdraw the sprocket from the camshaft using a puller if it is tight.

5 Undo the bolts and remove the camshaft oil seal housing from the front of the cylinder block. Recover the O-ring from the rear of the housing.

6 To prevent the tappets from interfering with removal of the camshaft, turn the engine on its side, or preferably turn it right over.

7 Withdraw the camshaft from the front of the engine, taking care not to nick the bearing with the sharp edges of the cam lobes.

8 Lift out the tappets from within the crankcase. Keep the tappets in their correct order by placing them in a numbered compartment box or similar.

Inspection

9 Examine the camshaft bearing surfaces and cam lobes for wear ridges, pitting or scoring. Renew the camshaft if evident.

10 Renew the O-ring and the oil seal in the oil seal housing as a matter of course. Lubricate the lips of the new seal before fitting.

11 Examine the camshaft bearing surfaces in the cylinder block. If deep scoring or other damage is evident, the bearings should be renewed by an engine reconditioning specialist.

12 Measure the cam lobe height and camshaft bearing journal diameters using a micrometer and compare the figures obtained with those given in the Specifications. Renew the camshaft or camshaft bearings if the figures obtained are outside the permitted tolerance.

13 Inspect the tappets for scoring, pitting and wear ridges. If any tappet shows signs of wear all eight should be renewed as a set.

Refitting

14 Refitting is a reversal of removal ensuring that the camshaft, cam followers and bearings are lubricated with clean engine oil. Tighten all nuts and bolts to the specified torque

15 Refit the oil pump, sump timing belt, pushrods and rocker shaft as described in Part F of this Chapter.

11 Piston/connecting rod assemblies - removal

Piston/connecting rod removal

Note: *New micro-encapsulated connecting rod big-end cap bolts will be required on 2.3 litre engines for refitting.*

1 Remove the cylinder head(s), sump and oil pick-up pipe as described in the relevant Part of Chapter 2.

2 Rotate the crankshaft so that No 1 big-end cap is at the lowest point of its travel. If the big-end cap and rod are not already numbered, mark them with a centre-punch.

Mark both cap and rod to identify the cylinder they operate in.

3 Unscrew and remove the big-end bearing cap nuts or bolts as applicable. Withdraw the cap, complete with shell bearing, from the connecting rod **(see illustrations)**.

4 If only the bearing shells are being attended to, push the connecting rod up and off the crankpin, and remove the upper bearing shell. Keep the bearing shells and cap together in their correct sequence if they are to be refitted.

5 Push the connecting rod up, and remove the piston and rod from the bore. Note that if there is a pronounced wear ridge at the top of the bore there is a risk of damaging the piston as the rings foul the ridge. However, it is reasonable to assume that a rebore and new pistons will be required in any case if the ridge is so pronounced.

6 Repeat the procedure for the remaining piston/connecting rod assemblies. Ensure that the caps and rods are marked before removal, as described previously, and keep all components in order.

Cylinder liner removal (2.5 litre engines)

7 With the piston/connecting rod assemblies removed, the cylinder liners can be withdrawn. To do this it will be necessary to make up a tool consisting of a length of strip steel, of a diameter identical to that of the liner, and with a hole drilled in the centre to fit below the liner, another length of steel with a hole drilled in the centre to fit over the top of the cylinder block, and a length of threaded rod and two nuts to connect the two strips of steel. Locate the lower steel strip below the liner, engage the threaded rod and fit a nut to the rod. Place two blocks of wood on the cylinder block upper face, fit the second steel strip over the threaded rod, and screw a nut onto the rod. Tighten the upper nut to release the cylinder liner from its location **(see**

11.7 Using the tool described in the text to remove a cylinder liner - 2.5 litre engine

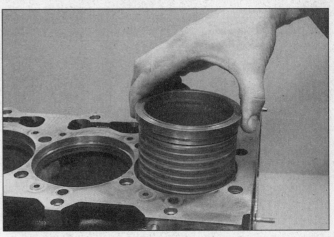

11.8 Removing the cylinder liner from the cylinder block - 2.5 litre engine

illustration). Note that the liners are not a tight fit in the cylinder block, but are secured by adhesive. The tool is necessary only to break the adhesive bond.

8 Once the adhesive bond is broken, remove the tool and withdraw the liner from the cylinder block **(see illustration)**. Collect the liner shims and mark the liner to identify its cylinder. Make sure that all the shims are collected and that none have remained in the cylinder block recess. Note the location of the O-rings in the liner grooves and also the colour coding of the O-rings which designates their thickness. Record the location and colour of the O-rings and remove them from the liners. Repeat this operation to remove the remaining liners.

12 Crankshaft - removal

Note: *All the preliminary component removal procedures described below are covered in the in-car engine repair procedures in Parts D to F of this Chapter, according to engine.*

2.3 litre engine

1 Remove the cylinder head, sump, oil pick-

up tube, timing case, timing chain and crankshaft sprocket and flywheel. The pistons/connecting rods must be free of the crankshaft journals, however it is not essential to remove them completely from the cylinder block.

2 Before the crankshaft is removed, check the endfloat using a dial gauge in contact with the end of the crankshaft. Push the crankshaft fully one way, and then zero the gauge. Push the crankshaft fully the other way, and check the endfloat. The result can be compared with the specified amount, and will give an indication as to whether new thrustwashers are required.

3 Identification numbers should already be cast onto the base of each main bearing cap. If not, number the cap and crankcase using a centre-punch, as was done for the connecting rods and caps.

4 Unscrew and remove the main bearing cap retaining bolts, and withdraw the caps, complete with bearing shells. Tap the caps with a wooden or copper mallet if they are stuck. Note that new main bearing cap retaining bolts will be required for reassembly.

5 Carefully lift the crankshaft from the crankcase.

6 Remove the bearing shell upper halves

from the crankcase. Place each shell with its respective bearing cap.

7 Remove the oil seal from the rear of the crankshaft.

2.5 litre engine

8 Remove the cylinder head, timing cover, sump, oil pick-up tube, and oil pump. The pistons/connecting rods must be free of the crankshaft journals, however it is not essential to remove them completely from the cylinder block.

9 Before the crankshaft is removed, check the endfloat using a dial gauge in contact with the edge of the flywheel **(see illustration)**. Push the crankshaft fully one way, and then zero the gauge. Push the crankshaft fully the other way, and check the endfloat. The result can be compared with the specified amount, and will give an indication as to whether new thrustwashers are required.

10 After checking the endfloat, remove the flywheel.

11 Undo the four bolts, six nuts and eight screws securing the engine rear adaptor plate to the cylinder block **(see illustration)**.

12 Remove the adaptor plate and recover the O-ring from the camshaft rear bearing location **(see illustration)**.

13 Remove the rear bearing carrier from the

2H

12.9 Checking the crankshaft endfloat - 2.5 litre engine

12.11 Rear adaptor plate retaining nuts, bolts and screws - 2.5 litre engine

12.12 Remove the adaptor plate and recover the O-ring from the camshaft rear bearing location - 2.5 litre engine

12.13a Remove the rear bearing carrier . . .

12.13b . . . and remove the O-ring - 2.5 litre engine

12.14a Unscrew the three crankshaft bearing carrier retainers (arrowed) . . .

12.14b . . . remove the retainers and recover the sealing washers - 2.5 litre engine

cylinder block and remove the O-ring (see illustrations).

14 Unscrew the three crankshaft bearing carrier retainers, identifying their locations for refitting, and recover the sealing washers (see illustrations).

15 With the help of an assistant to support the crankshaft at the front, withdraw the crankshaft and bearing carrier assembly from the rear of the cylinder block (see illustration).

16 With the crankshaft assembly removed, unscrew the bearing carrier retaining bolts and separate the two halves of each carrier (see illustrations). Suitably identify each bearing carrier half and its location on the crankshaft. Remove the bearing shell upper and lower halves from the carrier and place each shell with its respective carrier.

17 Removal and refitting of the front and rear one-piece main bearings entails the use of special tools to draw the bearing out of the cylinder block (front) or bearing carrier (rear) and to press the new bearings into place. If

12.15 Withdraw the crankshaft and bearing carrier assembly from the rear of the cylinder block - 2.5 litre engine

12.16a Unscrew the bearing carrier retaining bolts . . .

12.16b . . . and separate the two halves of each carrier - 2.5 litre engine

the checking procedures described later in this Chapter indicate that new bearings are required, have this work carried out by an engine reconditioning specialist.

2.8 litre engine

18 Remove the cylinder head, timing belt and sprockets, sump, oil pick-up tube, oil pump, timing case housing, flywheel and rear adaptor plate. The pistons/connecting rods must be free of the crankshaft journals, however it is not essential to remove them completely from the cylinder block.

19 Before the crankshaft is removed, check the endfloat using a dial gauge in contact with the end of the crankshaft. Push the crankshaft fully one way, and then zero the gauge. Push the crankshaft fully the other way, and check the endfloat. The result can be compared with the specified amount, and will give an indication as to whether new thrustwashers are required.

20 Identification numbers should already be cast onto the base of each main bearing cap. If not, number the cap and crankcase using a centre-punch, as was done for the connecting rods and caps.

21 Working in an anti-clockwise spiral sequence, starting with the right-hand rear main bearing cap bolt, unscrew and remove the retaining bolts, and withdraw the caps, complete with bearing shells. Tap the caps with a wooden or copper mallet if they are stuck.

22 Carefully lift the crankshaft from the crankcase.

23 Remove the bearing shell upper halves from the crankcase. Place each shell with its respective bearing cap.

13 Cylinder block/crankcase and bores - cleaning and inspection

Cleaning

1 Remove all external components and electrical switches/sensors from the block. For complete cleaning, the core plugs should be removed. Drill a small hole in them, then insert a self-tapping screw and pull out the plugs using a pair of grips or a slide-hammer. Also remove all external components and senders (if not already done), noting their locations. As applicable unbolt the drivebelt tensioner bracket, coolant pipe and oil cooler from the cylinder block.

2 Scrape all traces of gasket or sealant from the cylinder block, taking care not to damage the head and sump mating faces.

3 If the block is extremely dirty, it should be steam-cleaned.

4 After the block has been steam-cleaned, clean all oil holes and oil galleries one more time. Flush all internal passages with warm water until the water runs clear, dry the block thoroughly and wipe all machined surfaces

with a light rust-preventative oil. If you have access to compressed air, use it to speed up the drying process and to blow out all the oil holes and galleries.

> ⚠ **Warning: Wear eye protection when using compressed air!**

5 If the block is not very dirty, you can do an adequate cleaning job with hot soapy water and a stiff brush. Take plenty of time, and do a thorough job. Regardless of the cleaning method used, be sure to clean all oil holes and galleries very thoroughly, dry the block completely and coat all machined surfaces with light oil.

6 The threaded holes in the block must be clean to ensure accurate torque wrench readings during reassembly. Run the proper-size tap into each of the holes to remove rust, corrosion, thread sealant or sludge, and to restore damaged threads. If possible, use compressed air to clear the holes of debris produced by this operation. Now is a good time to clean the threads on the head bolts and the main bearing cap bolts as well.

7 After coating the mating surfaces of the new core plugs with suitable sealant, refit them in the cylinder block. Make sure that they are driven in straight and seated properly, or leakage could result. Special tools are available for this purpose, but a large socket, with an outside diameter that will just slip into the core plug, will work just as well.

8 Where applicable, check the gauze filters and the oil holes in the piston oil spray jets for blockage. Clean if necessary, then refit the jets and tighten the securing bolts.

9 If the engine is not going to be reassembled right away, cover it with a large plastic bag to keep it clean and prevent it rusting.

Inspection

10 Visually check the block for cracks, rust and corrosion. Look for stripped threads in the threaded holes. If there has been any history of internal water leakage, it may be worthwhile having an engine overhaul specialist check the block with special equipment. If defects are found, have the block repaired, if possible, or renewed.

11 Check the cylinder bores/liners for scuffing and scoring. Normally, bore wear will show up in the form of a wear ridge at the top of the bore. This ridge marks the limit of piston travel.

12 Measure the diameter of each cylinder at the top (just under the ridge area), centre and bottom of the cylinder bore, parallel to the crankshaft axis.

13 Next measure each cylinder's diameter at the same three locations across the crankshaft axis. If the difference between any of the measurements is greater than 0.20 mm, indicating that the cylinder is excessively out-of-round or tapered, then remedial action must be considered.

14 Repeat this procedure for the remaining cylinders.

15 If the cylinder walls are badly scuffed or scored, or if they are excessively out-of-round or tapered, have new sleeves or dry liners fitted by an engine reconditioning specialist (2.3 and 2.8 litre engines) or obtain new cylinder liners (2.5 litre engine). New pistons will also be required.

16 If the cylinders are in reasonably good condition, then it may only be necessary to renew the piston rings.

17 If this is the case, the bores should be honed in order to allow the new rings to bed in correctly and provide the best possible seal. The conventional type of hone has spring-loaded stones, and is used with a power drill. You will also need some paraffin or honing oil and rags. The hone should be moved up and down the cylinder to produce a crosshatch pattern, and plenty of honing oil should be used. Ideally, the crosshatch lines should intersect at approximately a 60° angle. Do not take off more material than is necessary to produce the required finish. If new pistons are being fitted, the piston manufacturers may specify a finish with a different angle, so their instructions should be followed. Do not withdraw the hone from the cylinder while it is still being turned, but stop it first. After honing a cylinder, wipe out all traces of the honing oil. If equipment of this type is not available, or if you are not sure whether you are competent to undertake the task yourself, an engine overhaul specialist will carry out the work at a moderate cost.

18 Before refitting the cylinder liners to the 2.5 litre engine, their fitted position in the cylinder block must be checked as follows, and new shims obtained to give the correct cylinder liner protrusion. Place a bare cylinder liner (all shims and O-rings removed) into the cylinder block, and press down and twist back and forth to make sure that it is seated correctly. Using the clamps from the cylinder head bolts, suitable studs and nuts, clamp the liner in position **(see illustration)**. Using a dial gauge, check the position of the liner in relation to upper surface of the cylinder block and select a shim to provide a protrusion of

13.18a Using the cylinder head bolt clamps, studs and nuts to clamp the liner in place - 2.5 litre engine

2H

13.18b Checking the cylinder liner protrusion - 2.5 litre engine

14.12a Extract the gudgeon pin retaining circlips . . .

0.01 to 0.06 mm above the top of the cylinder block face **(see illustration)**. Shims are available from Vauxhall parts stockists in various sizes. Check all of the liners in the same manner, and select shims for each.

19 Refit all external components and senders in their correct locations, as noted before removal.

---

14 Piston/connecting rod assemblies - inspection and reassembly

Inspection

1 Before the inspection process can begin, the piston/connecting rod assemblies must be cleaned, and the original piston rings removed from the pistons.

2 Carefully expand the old rings over the top of the pistons. The use of two or three old feeler blades will be helpful in preventing the rings dropping into empty grooves.

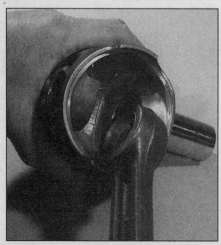

14.12b . . . and withdraw the gudgeon pin to separate the piston and connecting rods

3 Scrape away all traces of carbon from the top of the piston. A hand-held wire brush or a piece of fine emery cloth can be used once the majority of the deposits have been scraped away.

4 Remove the carbon from the ring grooves in the piston by cleaning them using an old ring. Break the ring in half to do this. Be very careful to remove only the carbon deposits; do not remove any metal, nor nick or scratch the sides of the ring grooves. Protect your fingers - piston rings are sharp.

5 Once the deposits have been removed, clean the piston/connecting rod assembly with paraffin or a suitable solvent, and dry thoroughly. Make sure the oil return holes in the ring grooves are clear.

6 If the pistons and cylinder bores are not damaged or worn excessively, and if the cylinder block does not need to be repaired, the original pistons can be re-used. Normal piston wear appears as even vertical wear on the piston thrust surfaces, and slight looseness of the top ring in its groove. New piston rings, however, should always be used when the engine is reassembled.

7 Carefully inspect each piston for cracks around the skirt, at the gudgeon pin bosses, and at the piston ring lands (between the piston ring grooves).

8 Look for scoring and scuffing on the sides of the skirt, holes in the piston crown, and burned areas at the edge of the crown. If the skirt is scored or scuffed, the engine may have been suffering from overheating and/or abnormal combustion, which caused excessively-high operating temperatures. The cooling and lubricating systems should be checked thoroughly. Scorch marks on the sides of the pistons show that blow-by has occurred and the rings are not sealing correctly. A hole in the piston crown is an indication that abnormal combustion (pre-ignition, knocking or detonation) has been occurring. If any of the above problems exist,

the causes must be corrected, or the damage will occur again.

9 Corrosion of the piston, in the form of small pits, indicates that coolant is leaking into the combustion chamber and/or the crankcase. Again, the cause must be corrected, or the problem may persist in the rebuilt engine.

10 If new rings are being fitted to old pistons, measure the piston ring-to-groove clearance by placing a new piston ring in each ring groove and measuring the clearance with a feeler blade. Check the clearance at three or four places around each groove. If no values are specified, but if the measured clearance is excessive - say greater than 0.10 mm - new pistons will be required. If the new ring is excessively tight, the most likely cause is dirt remaining in the groove.

11 Check the piston-to-bore/liner clearance by measuring the cylinder bore/liner and the piston diameter. Measure the piston across the skirt, at a 90¡ angle to the gudgeon pin, approximately half way down the skirt. Subtract the piston diameter from the bore/liner diameter to obtain the clearance.

12 Check the fit of the gudgeon pin by twisting the piston and connecting rod in opposite directions. Any noticeable play indicates excessive wear, which must be corrected. The gudgeon pins are secured by circlips, so the pistons and connecting rods can be separated without difficulty **(see illustrations)**. Note the position of the piston relative to the rod before dismantling, and use new circlips on reassembly.

13 Before refitting the rings to the pistons, check their end gaps by inserting each of them in their cylinder bores. Use the piston to make sure that they are square. Vauxhall rings are supplied pre-gapped; no attempt should be made to adjust the gaps by filing.

Reassembly

14 Install the new rings by fitting them over the top of the piston, starting with the oil control scraper ring and spring **(see**

14.14a Fit the oil control scraper ring spring . . .

14.14b . . . and scraper ring . . .

illustrations). Use feeler blades in the same way as when removing the old rings. Note that the second compression ring is tapered, and may additionally be stepped. Be careful when handling the compression rings; they will break if they are handled roughly or expanded too far. With all the rings in position, space the ring gaps at approximately 120° to each other on 2.3 litre engines, and as shown for 2.5 and 2.8 litre engines (see illustrations).

15 Crankshaft - inspection

1 Clean the crankshaft and dry it with compressed air if available.

 Warning: Wear eye protection when using compressed air! Be sure to clean the oil holes with a pipe cleaner or similar probe.

2 Check the main and big-end bearing journals for uneven wear, scoring, pitting and cracking.

3 If the crankshaft has been reground, check for burrs around the crankshaft oil holes (the holes are usually chamfered, so burrs should not be a problem unless regrinding has been carried out carelessly). Remove any burrs with a fine file or scraper, and thoroughly clean the oil holes as described previously.

4 Using a micrometer, measure the diameter of the main bearing and connecting rod journals, and compare the results with the

14.14c . . . then use feeler blades to assist with the fitting of the compression rings

2H

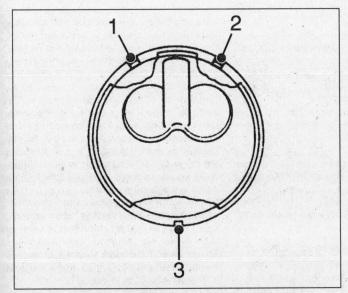

14.14d Correct positioning of the piston ring gaps on 2.5 litre engines

1   Oil control ring gap
2   Top compression ring gap
3   Second compression ring gap

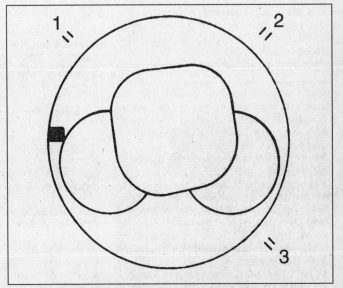

14.14e Correct positioning of the piston ring gaps on 2.8 litre engines

1   Second compression ring
2   Oil control ring
3   Top compression ring

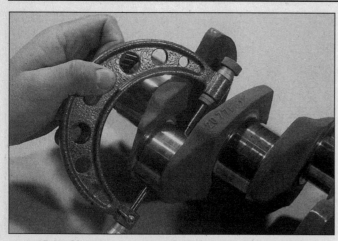

15.4a Checking the crankshaft big-end bearing journal diameters . . .

15.4b . . . and main bearing journal diameters

Specifications **(see illustrations)**. By measuring the diameter at a number of points around each journal's circumference, you will be able to determine whether or not the journal is out-of-round. Take the measurement at each end of the journal, near the webs, to determine if the journal is tapered. If any of the measurements vary by more than 0.025 mm, the crankshaft will have to be reground (where possible) and undersize bearings fitted.

5 Check the oil seal contact surfaces at each end of the crankshaft for wear and damage. If the seal has worn an excessive groove in the surface of the crankshaft, consult an engine overhaul specialist who will be able to advise whether a repair is possible or if a new crankshaft is necessary.

16 Main and big-end bearings - inspection

1 Even though the main and big-end bearings should be renewed during the engine overhaul, the old bearings should be retained for close examination, as they may reveal valuable information about the condition of the engine. The size of the bearing shells is stamped on the back metal, and this information should be given to the supplier of the new shells.

2 Bearing failure occurs because of lack of lubrication, the presence of dirt or other foreign particles, overloading the engine, and corrosion. Regardless of the cause of bearing failure, it must be corrected before the engine is reassembled, to prevent it from happening again **(see illustration)**.

3 When examining the bearings, remove them from the engine block, the main bearing caps or bearing carriers, the connecting rods and the rod caps, and lay them out on a clean surface in the same general position as their location in the engine. This will enable you to

match any bearing problems with the corresponding crankshaft journal.

4 Dirt and other foreign particles get into the engine in a variety of ways. Dirt may be left in the engine during assembly, or it may pass through filters or the crankcase ventilation system. It may get into the oil, and from there into the bearings. Metal chips from machining operations and normal engine wear are often present. Abrasives are sometimes left in engine components after reconditioning, especially when parts are not thoroughly cleaned using the proper cleaning methods. Whatever the source, these foreign objects often end up embedded in the soft bearing material, and are easily recognised. Large particles will not embed in the bearing, and will score or gouge the bearing and journal. The best prevention for this cause of bearing failure is to clean all parts thoroughly, and keep everything spotlessly clean during

FATIGUE FAILURE	IMPROPER SEATING
CRATERS OR POCKETS	BRIGHT (POLISHED) SECTIONS
SCRATCHED BY DIRT	LACK OF OIL
DIRT EMBEDDED INTO BEARING MATERIAL	OVERLAY WIPED OUT
EXCESSIVE WEAR	TAPERED JOURNAL
OVERLAY WIPED OUT	RADIUS RIDE

H 28395

16.2 Typical bearing failures

engine assembly. Frequent and regular engine oil and filter changes are also recommended.

5 Lack of lubrication (or oil breakdown) has a number of interrelated causes. Excessive heat (which thins the oil), overloading (which squeezes the oil from the bearing face) and oil leakage (from excessive bearing clearances, worn oil pump or high engine speeds) all contribute to lubrication breakdown. Blocked oil passages, which usually are the result of misaligned oil holes in a bearing shell, will also oil-starve a bearing and destroy it. When lack of lubrication is the cause of bearing failure, the bearing material is wiped or extruded from the steel backing of the bearing. Temperatures may increase to the point where the steel backing turns blue from overheating.

6 Driving habits can have a definite effect on bearing life. Full-throttle, low-speed operation (labouring the engine) puts very high loads on bearings, which tends to squeeze out the oil film. These loads cause the bearings to flex, which produces fine cracks in the bearing face (fatigue failure). Eventually, the bearing material will loosen in pieces and tear away from the steel backing. Short-trip driving leads to corrosion of bearings, because insufficient engine heat is produced to drive off the condensed water and corrosive gases. These products collect in the engine oil, forming acid and sludge. As the oil is carried to the engine bearings, the acid attacks and corrodes the bearing material.

7 Incorrect bearing installation during engine assembly will lead to bearing failure as well. Tight-fitting bearings leave insufficient bearing oil clearance, and will result in oil starvation. Dirt or foreign particles trapped behind a bearing shell result in high spots on the bearing which lead to failure.

8 If new bearings are to be fitted, the bearing running clearances should be measured before the engine is finally reassembled, to ensure that the correct bearing shells have been obtained. If the crankshaft has been reground,

18.6 Plastigauge in place on a main bearing journal

18.10 Measuring the width of the deformed Plastigauge using the card gauge supplied

the engineering works which carried out the work will advise on the correct size bearing shells to suit the work carried out. If there is any doubt as to which bearing shells should be used, seek advice from a Vauxhall dealer.

17 Engine overhaul - reassembly sequence

1 Before starting, ensure all new parts have been obtained, and all necessary tools are available. Read through the entire procedure to familiarise yourself with the work involved, and to ensure all items necessary for engine reassembly are at hand. In addition to all normal tools and materials, a thread-locking compound will be needed. A tube of RTV sealing compound will also be required for the joint faces that are fitted without gaskets and a tube of Loctite 275 will be required to bond the cylinder liners on 2.5 litre engines.

2 To save time and avoid problems, assembly can be carried out in the following order.
 a) Crankshaft.
 b) Pistons/connecting rod assemblies.
 c) Oil pump.
 d) Sump.
 e) Flywheel.
 f) Camshaft (where applicable).
 g) Timing belt/chain and sprockets/gears.
 h) Timing cover/case.
 i) Cylinder head(s).
 j) Engine external components.

18 Crankshaft - main bearing clearance check and refitting

Main bearing clearance check

2.3 and 2.8 litre engines

1 Clean the backs of the bearing shells and the bearing recesses in both the cylinder block and main bearing caps.

2 Press the bearing shells into the caps, ensuring that the tag on the shell engages in the notch in the cap/carrier. Note the following points.
 a) On the 2.3 litre engine, the shells without oil holes are located in the caps.
 b) On the 2.8 litre engine, the shells with grooves are located in the cylinder block and the shells without grooves are located in main bearing caps.

3 Press the bearing shells into the recesses in the cylinder block

4 Before the crankshaft can be permanently installed, the main bearing running clearance should be checked; this can be done in either of two ways. One method is to fit the main bearing caps to the cylinder block, with the bearing shells in place. With the cap retaining bolts tightened to the specified torque, measure the internal diameter of each assembled pair of bearing shells using a vernier dial indicator or internal micrometer. If the diameter of each corresponding crankshaft journal is measured and then subtracted from the bearing internal diameter, the result will be the main bearing running clearance. The second (and more accurate) method is to use a product known as Plastigauge. This consists of a fine thread of perfectly-round plastic which is compressed between the bearing cap and the journal. When the cap is removed, the deformation of the plastic thread is measured with a special card gauge supplied with the kit. The running clearance is determined from this gauge. The procedure for using Plastigauge is as follows.

5 With the upper main bearing shells in place, carefully lay the crankshaft in position. Do not use any lubricant; the crankshaft journals and bearing shells must be perfectly clean and dry.

6 Cut several pieces of the appropriate-size Plastigauge (they should be slightly shorter than the width of the main bearings), and place one piece on each crankshaft journal axis (see illustration).

7 With the bearing shells in position in the caps, fit the caps to their numbered or previously-noted locations. Take care not to disturb the Plastigauge.

8 Starting with the centre main bearing and working outward, tighten the main bearing cap bolts progressively to their specified torque setting. Don't rotate the crankshaft at any time during this operation.

9 Remove the bolts and carefully lift off the main bearing caps, keeping them in order. Don't disturb the Plastigauge or rotate the crankshaft. If any of the bearing caps are difficult to remove, tap them from side-to-side with a soft-faced mallet.

10 Compare the width of the crushed Plastigauge on each journal to the scale printed on the gauge to obtain the main bearing running clearance (see illustration).

11 If the clearance is not as specified, the bearing shells may be the wrong size (or badly worn if the original shells are being re-used). Before deciding that different size shells are needed, make sure no dirt or oil was trapped between the bearing shells and the caps or block when the clearance was measured. If the Plastigauge was wider at one end than at the other, the journal may be tapered.

12 Carefully scrape away all traces of the Plastigauge material from the crankshaft and bearing shells, using a fingernail or something similar which is unlikely to score the shells.

2.5 litre engines

13 Due to the one-piece front and rear main bearing arrangement on these engines, the main bearing running clearance can only be accurately checked using an internal micrometer as follows.

14 Press the bearing shells of Nos 2, 3 and 4 main bearings into the recesses in the bearing carriers. Assemble the two halves of the carriers, fit the retaining bolts and tighten the bolts to the specified torque. Measure the internal diameter of the front and rear main bearings and each assembled pair of bearing shells using an internal micrometer. If the

2H

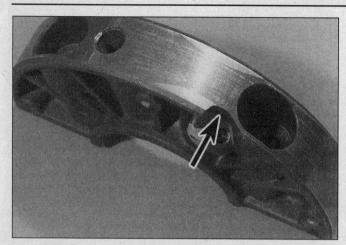

18.29 Fit the bearing carriers with the oil spray jet notch (arrowed) toward the front of the crankshaft - 2.5 litre engine

18.30 Align the holes in the bearing carriers (arrowed) with the centre of the cylinder block webs - 2.5 litre engine

diameter of each corresponding crankshaft journal is measured and then subtracted from the bearing internal diameter, the result will be the main bearing running clearance.

15 If the clearance is not as specified, the bearings or shells may be the wrong size (or badly worn if the original shells are being re-used). Before deciding that different size bearings are needed, make sure no dirt or oil was trapped between the bearing shells and the carriers when the clearance was measured.

16 After checking the clearance, unbolt and separate the bearing carriers.

Final refitting

2.3 litre engines

17 Carefully lift the crankshaft out of the cylinder block once more.

18 Press the main bearing shells into their locations in the cylinder block, making sure that the tags engage with the special grooves. Note that the rear shell incorporates thrust flanges.

19 Lubricate the shells with clean engine oil.

20 Carefully lower the crankshaft into the cylinder block. Rotate it several times and check that it is correctly seated by gently tapping the webs with a mallet.

21 Check that the crankshaft endfloat is as given in the Specifications by either using a feeler blade between the flanged main bearing shell and the crankshaft thrust face, or by using a dial test indicator on the crankshaft rear flange.

22 Clean the backs of the lower main bearing shells and the caps, then press them into position. Lubricate the shells with clean oil.

23 Apply a suitable sealant to the mating surface of the rear main bearing cap (Vauxhall recommend the use of GM spec 15 04 200 (Part No. 08 983 368) sealant - available from your dealer).

24 Fill the grooves on each outer edge of the rear main bearing cap with a bead of sealant approximately 6.0 mm in diameter

(Vauxhall recommend GM spec 15 03 294 (Part No. 90 001 851) sealant - available from your dealer).

25 Refit all the main bearing caps and install the new bearing cap bolts. Tighten the bolts by hand then tighten them evenly and progressively in stages to the specified torque setting, then through the specified angle. Check that the rear main bearing cap grooves are sufficiently sealed and wipe off any excess sealant.

26 Rotate the crankshaft and check that it turns freely with no binding or tight spots.

27 Lubricate the lips of the new crankshaft rear oil seal with grease. Ease the seal over the crankshaft end, making sure its sealing lip is facing inwards, and press it into the rear main bearing cap until flush.

28 Refit all the removed components with reference to the relevant Sections and Chapters as applicable.

2.5 litre engines

29 Lubricate the bearing shells in the bearing carriers, then fit the carrier halves on their correct crankshaft journals. Ensure that the carriers are positioned with the oil spray jet notch toward the front of the crankshaft **(see illustration)**. Refit the carrier retaining bolts and washers and tighten the bolts to the specified torque.

30 Lubricate the front main bearing in the cylinder block then with the help of an assistant to support the crankshaft at the front, guide the crankshaft and bearing carrier assembly in from the rear of the cylinder block. As the assembly is being fitted, align the holes in the bearing carriers with the centre of the cylinder block webs **(see illustration)**.

31 Using new sealing washers, fit the three crankshaft bearing carrier retainers to their previously noted locations, engaging their ends with the holes in the bearing carriers. Tighten the retainers to the specified torque.

32 Locate a new O-ring on the rear main bearing carrier and lubricate the bearing. Fit the carrier over the crankshaft and into position on the block, ensuring that the oil

hole in the carrier and corresponding hole in the block are aligned.

33 Place a new O-ring in the camshaft rear bearing location on the cylinder block then fit the engine adaptor plate ensuring the rear bearing carrier holes are aligned. Secure the adaptor plate with the four bolts, six nuts and eight screws tightened to the specified torque.

34 Refit all the removed components with reference to the relevant Sections and Chapters as applicable.

2.8 litre engines

35 Carefully lift the crankshaft out of the cylinder block once more.

36 Using a little grease, stick the thrust-washers to each side of the centre main bearing. Ensure that the oilway grooves on each thrustwasher face outwards from the bearing location, towards the crankshaft webs.

37 Liberally lubricate each bearing shell in the cylinder block, and lower the crankshaft into position.

38 Apply a suitable sealant to the mating surface of the rear main bearing cap (Vauxhall recommend the use of GM spec 15 04 200 (Part No. 08 983 368) sealant - available from your dealer). Locate a new sump upper seal in the groove of the rear main bearing cap.

39 Lubricate the bearing shells, then fit the bearing caps in their numbered or previously-noted locations.

40 Fit the main bearing cap bolts, and tighten them progressively to the specified torque. Tighten the bolts in a clockwise spiral sequence starting with the centre main bearing bolt on the left-hand side.

41 Check that the crankshaft is free to turn. Some stiffness is normal if new components have been fitted, but there must be no jamming or tight spots.

42 Check the crankshaft endfloat with reference to Section 12.

43 Refit all the removed components with reference to the relevant Sections and Chapters as applicable.

19.10a Place the shims on the cylinder liners . . .

19.10b . . . then fit the O-rings to the liner . . .

19 Piston/connecting rods - big-end bearing clearance check and refitting

2.3 and 2.8 litre engines

1 Clean the backs of the big-end bearing shells and the recesses in the connecting rods and big-end caps. If new shells are being fitted, ensure that all traces of the protective grease are cleaned off using paraffin. Wipe the shells and connecting rods dry with a lint-free cloth.

2 Press the big-end bearing shells into the connecting rods and caps in their correct positions. Make sure that the location tabs are engaged with the cut-outs in the connecting rods.

Big-end bearing clearance check

3 Lubricate No 1 piston and piston rings, and check that the ring gaps are spaced as described in Section 14.

4 Fit a ring compressor to No 1 piston, then insert the piston and connecting rod into No 1 cylinder. Ensure that the arrow or mark on the piston crown points towards the front of the engine. With No 1 crankpin at its lowest point, drive the piston carefully into the cylinder with the wooden handle of a hammer, at the same time guiding the connecting rod onto the crankpin.

5 To measure the big-end bearing running clearance, refer to the information contained in Section 18; the same general procedures apply. If the Plastigauge method is being used, ensure that the crankpin journal and the big-end bearing shells are clean and dry, then engage the connecting rod with the crankpin. Place the Plastigauge strip on the crankpin, fit the bearing cap in its previously-noted position, then tighten the nuts/bolts to the specified torque. Do not rotate the crankshaft during this operation. Remove the cap and check the running clearance by measuring the Plastigauge as previously described.

6 Repeat the above procedures on the remaining piston/connecting rod assemblies.

Final refitting

7 Having checked the running clearance of all the crankpin journals and taken any corrective action necessary, clean off all traces of Plastigauge from the bearing shells and crankpin.

8 Liberally lubricate the crankpin journals and big-end bearing shells. Refit the bearing caps once more, ensuring correct positioning as previously described. Tighten the bearing cap nuts/bolts to the specified torque, using new micro-encapsulated bolts on the 2.3 litre engine. Turn the crankshaft each time to make sure that it is free before moving on to the next assembly.

9 On completion, refit the oil pick-up pipe, sump and cylinder head as described in the relevant Part of Chapter 2.

2.5 litre engines

10 Place the previously selected liner protrusion shims on the liner followed by the O-rings. The O-rings should be positioned as follows (see illustrations).

   Top liner groove - one brown O-ring
   Centre liner grooves - two black O-rings
   Bottom liner groove - one brown O-ring

11 Lubricate the lower portion of the liner, below the ribbed area and the corresponding location in the cylinder block with clean

2H

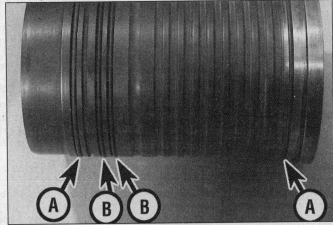

19.10c . . . and locate them in their correct grooves - 2.5 litre engine

A Brown O-ring   B Black O-rings

19.12a Apply Loctite 275 to the corner of the liner seat in the cylinder block . . .

19.12b . . . and to the side of the upper raised portion of the liner - 2.5 litre engine

19.14 Clamp all the liners in the cylinder block after fitting - 2.5 litre engine

engine oil. Lightly lubricate the O-rings also.

12 Apply Loctite 275 to the corner of the liner seat in the cylinder block, and uniformly to the side of the upper raised portion of the liner **(see illustrations)**.

13 Locate the liner in its cylinder bore and push it down until it is fully seated. Clamp the liner in position using the clamps from the cylinder head bolts, suitable studs and nuts.

19.16 Tap the piston and connecting rod into position - 2.5 litre engine

Wipe away any excess Loctite from the top of the liner and the cylinder block. Note that the liners must remained clamped for a minimum of 12 hours. If engine reassembly is to continue at this time, leave the liners clamped until the stage is reached where the cylinder heads are to be refitted.

14 Refit the remaining liners in the same way, ensuring each is securely clamped in place **(see illustration)**.

Big-end bearing clearance check

15 Lubricate No 1 piston and piston rings, and check that the ring gaps are spaced as described in Section 14.

16 Fit a ring compressor to No 1 piston, then insert the piston and connecting rod into No 1 cylinder. Ensure that the swirl chamber recess is towards the camshaft side of the engine. With No 1 crankpin at its lowest point, drive the piston carefully into the cylinder with the wooden handle of a hammer, at the same time guiding the connecting rod onto the crankpin **(see illustration)**.

17 To measure the big-end bearing running clearance, refer to the information contained in Section 18; the same general procedures

apply. If the Plastigauge method is being used, ensure that the crankpin journal and the big-end bearing shells are clean and dry, then engage the connecting rod with the crankpin. Place the Plastigauge strip on the crankpin, fit the bearing cap in its previously-noted position, then tighten the bolts to the specified torque. Do not rotate the crankshaft during this operation. Remove the cap and check the running clearance by measuring the Plastigauge as previously described.

18 Repeat the above procedures on the remaining piston/connecting rod assemblies.

Final refitting

19 Having checked the running clearance of all the crankpin journals and taken any corrective action necessary, clean off all traces of Plastigauge from the bearing shells and crankpin.

20 Liberally lubricate the crankpin journals and big-end bearing shells. Refit the bearing caps once more, ensuring correct positioning as previously described. Tighten the bearing cap bolts to the specified torque, then further through the specified angle **(see illustrations)**. Turn the crankshaft each time

19.20a Tighten the big-end bearing cap bolts to the specified torque . . .

19.20b . . . then further through the specified angle

to make sure that it is free before moving on to the next assembly.

21 On completion, refit the oil pick-up pipe, sump and cylinder head as described in the relevant Part of Chapter 2.

20 Engine - initial start-up after overhaul

1 With the engine refitted in the vehicle, double-check the engine oil and coolant levels. Make a final check that everything has been reconnected, and that there are no tools or rags left in the engine compartment.

2 Prime the fuel system as described in Chapter 4B.

3 Start the engine in the normal way. Additional cranking may be necessary to bleed the fuel system before the engine starts.

4 Once started, keep the engine running at fast tickover. Check that the oil pressure light goes out, then check that there are no leaks of oil, fuel and coolant. Where applicable, check the power steering pipe/hose unions for leakage. Do not be alarmed if there are some odd smells and smoke from parts getting hot and burning off oil deposits.

5 Keep the engine idling until hot coolant is felt circulating through the radiator top hose, indicating that the engine is at normal operating temperature, then stop the engine and allow it to cool.

6 Recheck the oil and coolant levels and top-up if necessary.

7 Check the fuel injection pump timing and the idle speed (where applicable) as described in Chapter 1B and 4B.

8 If new pistons, rings or bearings have been fitted, the engine must be run-in at reduced speeds and loads for the first 500 miles (800 km) or so. Do not operate the engine at full throttle, or allow it to labour in any gear during this period. It is beneficial to change the engine oil and filter at the end of this period.

2H

Notes

Chapter 3
Cooling, heating and air conditioning systems

Contents

Air conditioning auxiliary (compressor) drivebelt -
  checking and renewal . . . . .See Chapter 1
Air conditioning system - general information and precautions 12
Air conditioning system components - removal and refitting 13
Antifreeze mixture . . . . .See Chapter 1
Auxiliary electric cooling fan - removal and refitting 7
Coolant level check . . . . .See Weekly checks
Coolant pump - removal and refitting 9
Cooling system - draining . . . . .See Chapter 1
Cooling system - filling . . . . .See Chapter 1
Cooling system - flushing .See Chapter 1
Cooling system electrical switches and sensors -
  removal and refitting 8
Cooling system hoses - disconnection and renewal 2
General information and precautions 1
Heater/ventilation components - removal and refitting 11
Heating and ventilation system - general information 10
Radiator - removal, inspection and refitting 3
Radiator electric cooling fan - testing, removal and refitting 5
Radiator visco-clutch cooling fan - removal and refitting 6
Thermostat - removal, testing and refitting 4

3

Degrees of difficulty

| Easy, suitable for novice with little experience | Fairly easy, suitable for beginner with some experience | Fairly difficult, suitable for competent DIY mechanic | Difficult, suitable for experienced DIY mechanic | Very difficult, suitable for expert DIY or professional |

Specifications

Thermostat

Opening temperatures:
  Petrol engine models:
    Starts to open . . . . 92°C
    Fully open . . . . 107°C
  2.3 litre diesel engine models:
    Starts to open . . . . 92°C
    Fully open . . . . 107°C
  2.5 litre diesel engine models:
    Starts to open . . . . 78°C
    Fully open . . . . 82°C
  2.8 litre diesel engine models:
    Starts to open . . . . 92°C
    Fully open . . . . 95°C

Electric cooling fan operating temperature

Cooling fan on . . . . 100°C
Cooling fan off . . . . 95°C

Torque wrench settings

	Nm	lbf ft
2.0 and 2.2 litre petrol engine models:		
Coolant pump to cylinder block	25	18
Thermostat cover bolts	15	11
2.4 litre petrol engine models:		
Coolant pump to cylinder block	15	11
Thermostat cover to housing	6	4
2.3 litre diesel engine models:		
Coolant pump bolts	15	11
Thermostat cover to housing	8	6
Thermostat housing to cylinder head	22	16
Visco-clutch cooling fan centre bolt	26	19
2.5 litre diesel engine models:		
Coolant pump bolts	25	18
Coolant pump pulley bolts	27	20
Thermostat cover to housing	11	8
Visco-clutch cooling fan nut	55	41
2.8 litre diesel engine models:		
Coolant pump bolts/nuts	20	15
Thermostat cover bolts	19	14
Visco-clutch cooling fan hub nuts	8	6

1 General information and precautions

General information

The cooling system is of pressurised type, comprising a coolant pump (driven by the timing belt on petrol engines and the auxiliary drivebelt on diesel engines), a radiator, electric or visco-clutch cooling fan, a thermostat, heater matrix, and all associated hoses and switches.

The system functions as follows. Cold coolant in the bottom of the radiator passes through the bottom hose to the coolant pump, where it is pumped around the cylinder block and head passages, and through the oil cooler(s) (where fitted). After cooling the cylinder bores, combustion surfaces and valve seats, the coolant reaches the underside of the thermostat, which is initially closed. The coolant passes through the heater, and is returned via the cylinder block to the coolant pump.

When the engine is cold, the coolant circulates only through the cylinder block, cylinder head, and heater. When the coolant reaches a predetermined temperature, the thermostat opens, and the coolant passes through the top hose to the radiator. As the coolant circulates through the radiator, it is cooled by the inrush of air when the car is in forward motion. The airflow is supplemented by the action of the electric or visco-clutch cooling fan when necessary. Upon reaching the bottom of the radiator, the coolant has now cooled, and the cycle is repeated.

On diesel engine models, the coolant is also circulated through the engine oil cooler and around the turbocharger.

When the engine is at normal operating temperature, the coolant expands, and some of it is displaced into the expansion tank. Coolant collects in the tank, and is returned to the radiator when the system cools.

Precautions

 Warning: Do not attempt to remove the expansion tank filler cap, or to disturb any part of the cooling system, while the engine is hot, as there is a high risk of scalding. If the expansion tank filler cap must be removed before the engine and radiator have fully cooled (even though this is not recommended), the pressure in the cooling system must first be relieved. Cover the cap with a thick layer of cloth to avoid scalding, and slowly unscrew the filler cap until a hissing sound is heard. When the hissing has stopped, indicating that the pressure has reduced, slowly unscrew the filler cap until it can be removed; if more hissing sounds are heard, wait until they have stopped before unscrewing the cap completely. At all times, keep well away from the filler cap opening, and protect your hands.

 Warning: Do not allow antifreeze to come into contact with your skin, or with the painted surfaces of the vehicle. Rinse off spills immediately, with plenty of water. Never leave antifreeze lying around in an open container, or in a puddle in the driveway or on the garage floor. Children and pets are attracted by its sweet smell, and antifreeze can be fatal if ingested.

 Warning: If the engine is hot, the electric cooling fan may start rotating even if the engine is not running and the ignition is off. Be careful to keep your hands, hair, and any loose clothing well clear when working in the engine compartment.

 Warning: Refer to Section 12 for precautions to be observed when working on models equipped with air conditioning.

2 Cooling system hoses - disconnection and renewal

Note: *Refer to the warnings given in Section 1 of this Chapter before proceeding. Hoses should only be disconnected once the engine has cooled sufficiently to avoid scalding.*

1 If the checks described in Chapter 1 reveal a faulty hose, it must be renewed as follows.

2 First drain the cooling system (Chapter 1). If the coolant is not due for renewal, it may be re-used, providing it is collected in a clean container.

3 Release the hose clips from the hose concerned. Three types of clip are used: worm-drive, spring and crimped-type. The worm-drive clip is released by turning its screw anti-clockwise. The spring clip is released by squeezing its tags together with pliers, at the same time working the clip away from the hose stub. The crimped-type clip is not re-usable, and is best cut off with snips or side cutters and replaced with a standard worm-drive clip. Move the clips along the hose, and position them clear of the union.

4 Carefully work the hose free. The hoses can be removed with relative ease when new - on an older car, they may have stuck.

5 If a hose proves to be difficult to remove, try to release it by rotating its ends before attempting to free it. Gently prise the end of the hose with a blunt instrument (such as a flat-bladed screwdriver), but do not apply too much force, and take care not to damage the pipe stubs or hoses. Note in particular that the radiator inlet stub is fragile; do not use excessive force when attempting to remove the hose.

HAYNES HINT *If all else fails, cut the coolant hose with a sharp knife, then slit it so that it can be peeled off in two pieces. Although this may prove expensive if the hose is otherwise undamaged, it is preferable to buying a new radiator.*

6 When fitting a hose, first slide the clips onto the hose, then work the hose into position. If crimped-type clips were originally fitted, use standard worm-drive clips when refitting the hose. If the hose is stiff, use a little soapy water as a lubricant, or soften the hose by soaking it in hot water. Do not use oil or grease, which may attack the rubber.

7 Work the hose into position, checking that it is correctly routed, then slide each clip back along the hose until it passes over the flared end of the relevant inlet/outlet, before securing it in position with the retaining clips.

8 Refill the cooling system with reference to Chapter 1.

9 Check thoroughly for leaks as soon as possible after disturbing any part of the cooling system.

3 Radiator - removal, inspection and refitting

Note: *If leakage is the reason for removing the radiator, bear in mind that minor leaks can often be cured using a radiator sealant with the radiator in situ.*

2.0 litre (C20NE) and 2.4 litre petrol engine models

Removal

1 Disconnect the battery negative lead.

2 Drain the cooling system as described in Chapter 1.

3 Release the retaining clips and disconnect the coolant hoses from the radiator.

4 On early models, undo the bolts securing the fan shroud to the radiator. Lift the shroud off the radiator and rest it on the fan.

5 Slacken and remove the nuts and bolts securing the radiator upper mounting brackets to the front body panel **(see illustration)**.

6 Check that all pipes and wiring are released, then lift the radiator out from the engine compartment, taking care not to lose the radiator lower mounting rubbers.

Inspection

7 If the radiator has been removed due to suspected blockage, reverse-flush it as described in Chapter 1. Clean dirt and debris from the radiator fins, using an air line (in which case, wear eye protection) or a soft brush. Be careful, as the fins are sharp, and easily damaged.

8 If necessary, a radiator specialist can perform a flow test on the radiator, to establish whether an internal blockage exists.

9 A leaking radiator must be referred to a specialist for permanent repair. Do not attempt to weld or solder a leaking radiator, as damage to the plastic components may result.

10 In an emergency, minor leaks from the radiator can be cured by using a suitable radiator sealant, in accordance with its manufacturer's instructions, with the radiator in situ.

11 Inspect the condition of the radiator mounting rubbers, and renew them if necessary.

Refitting

12 Refitting is a reversal of removal, ensuring that all the mounting rubbers are correctly positioned, and that the upper mounting brackets are correctly engaged with the radiator. On completion, refill the cooling system as described in Chapter 1.

2.0 litre (X20SE) and 2.2 litre petrol engine models

Removal

13 Disconnect the battery negative lead.

14 Drain the cooling system as described in Chapter 1.

15 Release the retaining clips and disconnect the coolant hoses from the radiator. On 2.2 litre models, disconnect the air hoses from the air intake resonator attached to the fan shroud.

16 Disconnect the electric cooling fan and fan thermo-switch wiring harness plug(s) and release the wiring from any retaining cable ties.

17 Undo the two bolts securing the radiator upper retaining clamp to the body crossmember.

18 Check that all pipes and wiring are released, then lift the radiator and cooling fan assembly out from the engine compartment, taking care not to lose the radiator lower mounting rubbers.

Inspection

19 Refer to paragraphs 7 to 11 above.

Refitting

20 Refitting is a reversal of removal, ensuring that all the mounting rubbers are correctly positioned. On completion, refill the cooling system as described in Chapter 1.

2.3 litre diesel engine models

Removal

21 Disconnect the battery negative lead.

22 Drain the cooling system as described in Chapter 1.

23 Release the retaining clips and disconnect the coolant hoses from the radiator. For improved access, refer to Chapter 4B and remove the intake air ducts over the top of the radiator as necessary.

24 Extract the upper clips securing the fan shroud to the radiator. Lift the shroud off the radiator and rest it on the fan.

25 Slacken and remove the nuts and bolts securing the radiator upper mounting brackets to the front body panel.

26 Check that all pipes and wiring are released, then lift the radiator out from the engine compartment, taking care not to lose the radiator lower mounting rubbers.

Inspection

27 Refer to paragraphs 7 to 11 above.

Refitting

28 Refitting is a reversal of removal, ensuring that all the mounting rubbers are correctly positioned. On completion, refill the cooling system as described in Chapter 1.

2.5 and 2.8 litre diesel engine models

Removal

29 Disconnect the battery negative lead.

3

3.5 Radiator upper mounting bracket and fan shroud attachments - 2.0 litre (C20NE) petrol engine

3.32 Removing the fan shroud upper spring clips - 2.5 litre diesel engine

3.34 . . . and lift out the radiator - 2.5 litre diesel engine

30 Drain the cooling system as described in Chapter 1.

31 Release the retaining clips and disconnect the coolant hoses from the radiator. For improved access, refer to Chapter 4B and remove the intake air ducts over the top of the radiator as necessary.

32 Extract the two upper spring clips securing the fan shroud to the radiator **(see illustration)**. Lift the shroud upwards to disengage the two lower mounting lugs and rest it on the fan.

33 Undo the two bolts securing the radiator upper retaining clamp to the body crossmember **(see illustration)**.

34 Check that all pipes and wiring are released, then lift the radiator out from the engine compartment, taking care not to lose

3.33 Remove the radiator upper retaining clamp . . .

the radiator lower mounting rubbers **(see illustration)**.

Inspection

35 Refer to paragraphs 7 to 11 above.

Refitting

36 Refitting is a reversal of removal, ensuring that all the mounting rubbers are correctly positioned. On completion, refill the cooling system as described in Chapter 1.

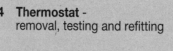

4 Thermostat -
removal, testing and refitting

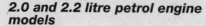

2.0 and 2.2 litre petrol engine models

Removal

1 Disconnect the battery negative lead.

2 Drain the cooling system as described in Chapter 1.

3 Disconnect the radiator top hose from the thermostat cover.

4 Unscrew and remove the thermostat cover securing bolts, and withdraw the cover complete with thermostat. Recover the O-ring or rubber seal from the cover **(see illustrations)**.

5 Note that if it is necessary to renew the thermostat, the complete cover and thermostat must be renewed as an assembly, as the two cannot be separated.

Testing

6 A rough test of the thermostat may be made by suspending it with a piece of string in a container full of water. Heat the water to bring it to the boil - the thermostat must open by the time the water boils. If not, renew it.

7 If a thermometer is available, the precise opening temperature of the thermostat may be determined; compare with the figures given in the Specifications **(see illustration)**. The opening temperature is also marked on the thermostat.

8 A thermostat which fails to close as the water cools must also be renewed.

Refitting

9 Refitting is a reversal of removal. Use a new O-ring or rubber seal as applicable on the thermostat cover and tighten the retaining bolts to the specified torque. Refill the cooling system as described in Chapter 1 on completion.

2.4 litre petrol engine models

Removal

10 Disconnect the battery negative lead.

11 Drain the cooling system as described in Chapter 1.

12 Disconnect the radiator top hose from the thermostat cover.

13 Unscrew the four bolts and remove the thermostat cover.

14 Lift out the thermostat and remove the rubber sealing ring from the edge of the thermostat.

Testing

15 Refer to paragraphs 6 to 8 inclusive.

Refitting

16 Refitting is a reversal of removal, bearing in mind the following points:
a) Use a new rubber sealing ring and make sure it is located squarely over the edge of the thermostat.
b) Fit the thermostat with the spring and capsule end facing into the engine.
c) Tighten the cover bolts to the specified torque and fill the cooling system as described in Chapter 1 on completion.

4.4a Withdraw the thermostat cover complete with thermostat . . .

4.4b . . . and recover the O-ring - 2.0 litre petrol engine

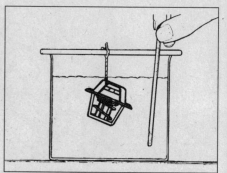

4.7 Testing the opening temperature of a typical thermostat

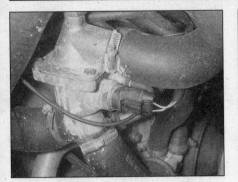

4.20 Temperature sensor and top hose attachment on the thermostat cover - 2.3 litre diesel engine

4.29 Remove the four bolts and thermostat cover . . .

2.3 litre diesel engine models

Removal

17 Disconnect the battery negative lead.

18 Drain the cooling system as described in Chapter 1.

19 For improved access, refer to Chapter 4B and remove the intake air ducts over the top of the radiator and thermostat housing as necessary.

20 Disconnect the temperature sensor wiring connector and radiator hose from the thermostat cover (see illustration).

21 Unscrew the four bolts and remove the thermostat cover.

22 Lift out the thermostat and remove the rubber sealing ring from the edge of the thermostat.

Testing

23 Refer to paragraphs 6 to 8 inclusive.

Refitting

24 Refitting is a reversal of removal, bearing in mind the following points:

a) Use a new rubber sealing ring and make sure it is located squarely over the edge of the thermostat.

b) Fit the thermostat with the spring and capsule end facing into the engine.

c) Tighten the cover bolts to the specified torque and fill the cooling system as described in Chapter 1 on completion.

2.5 litre diesel engine models

Removal

25 Disconnect the battery negative lead.

26 Drain the cooling system as described in Chapter 1.

27 Refer to Chapter 4B and remove the intake air ducts over the top of the radiator and thermostat housing.

28 Disconnect the radiator top hose from the thermostat cover.

29 Unscrew the four bolts and remove the thermostat cover (see illustration).

30 Lift out the thermostat and remove the rubber sealing ring from the edge of the thermostat (see illustrations).

Testing

31 Refer to paragraphs 6 to 8 inclusive.

Refitting

32 Refitting is a reversal of removal, bearing in mind the following points:

a) Use a new rubber sealing ring and make sure it is located squarely over the edge of the thermostat.

b) Fit the thermostat with the spring and capsule end facing into the engine and with the air bleed hole on the thermostat body uppermost.

c) Tighten the cover bolts to the specified torque and fill the cooling system as described in Chapter 1 on completion.

2.8 litre diesel engine models

Removal

33 Disconnect the battery negative lead.

34 Drain the cooling system as described in Chapter 1.

35 Disconnect the wiring connectors for the two temperature sensors fitted to the thermostat cover (see illustration).

36 Disconnect the radiator top hose and turbocharger outlet hose from the thermostat cover.

37 Unscrew the two bolts, remove the thermostat cover and collect the gasket.

38 Lift the thermostat out of the housing.

Testing

39 Refer to paragraphs 6 to 8 inclusive.

Refitting

40 Refitting is a reversal of removal, bearing in mind the following points:

a) Ensure that the thermostat housing and cover mating faces are clean and use a new gasket.

b) Fit the thermostat with the spring and capsule end facing into the engine.

c) Tighten the cover bolts to the specified torque and fill the cooling system as described in Chapter 1 on completion.

---

5 Radiator electric cooling fan - testing, removal and refitting

Note: An electric cooling fan is used on 2.0 litre (X20SE) and 2.2 litre petrol engine models. All other models are fitted with a visco-clutch type fan.

Testing

1 Current supply to the cooling fan is via the ignition switch, relay(s) and a fuse (see Chapter 13). The circuit is completed by the cooling fan thermostatic switch, which is located in the radiator bottom hose.

2 If a fan does not appear to work, first check the fuse. Run the engine until normal operating temperature is reached, then allow it to idle. The fan should cut in within a few

3

4.30a . . . withdraw the thermostat . . .

4.30b . . . and remove the rubber sealing ring - 2.5 litre diesel engine

4.35 Disconnect the wiring connectors for the two temperature sensors on the thermostat cover - 2.8 litre diesel engine

minutes (before the temperature gauge needle enters the red section, or before the coolant temperature warning light comes on). If not, switch off the ignition and disconnect the wiring plug from the cooling fan switch. Bridge the two contacts in the wiring plug using a length of spare wire, and switch on the ignition. If the fan now operates, the switch is probably faulty, and should be renewed.

3 If the fan still fails to operate, check that battery voltage is available at the feed wire to the switch; if not, then there is a fault in the feed wire. If there is no problem with the feed, check that there is continuity between the switch earth terminal and a good earth point on the body; if not, then the earth connection is faulty, and must be re-made.

4 If the switch and the wiring are in good condition, the fault must lie in the motor itself. The motor can be checked by disconnecting it from the wiring loom and connecting a 12-volt supply directly to it.

Removal

5 Remove the radiator as described in Section 3.

6 Unscrew the upper mounting bolts securing the fan shroud to the radiator. On 2.2 litre engine models, unscrew the additional bolt securing the air intake resonator to the shroud and remove the resonator. Carefully lift the fan and shroud from the two lower locating lugs and remove the assembly from the radiator.

7 Undo the three mounting nuts and withdraw the motor and fan from the shroud.

8 To remove the fan from the motor, extract the retaining clip from the motor spindle and withdraw the fan. If the motor is faulty, the complete unit must be renewed, as no spares are available.

Refitting

9 Refitting is a reversal of removal.

6 Radiator visco-clutch cooling fan - removal and refitting

Note: *An electric cooling fan is used on 2.0 litre (X20SE) and 2.2 litre petrol engine models, see Section 5.*

2.0 litre (C20NE) and 2.4 litre petrol engine models

Removal

1 Disconnect the battery negative lead.

2 Remove the auxiliary drivebelt(s) as described in Chapter 1.

3 If required, the cooling fan shroud may be moved out of the way. Undo the bolts securing the shroud to the radiator, then lift it off and rest it on the fan blades.

4 Using an open-ended spanner, hold the visco-clutch hub stationary, then using a wrench and hex bit, slacken and withdraw the

Allen bolt from the centre of the hub noting that it has a **left-hand thread**. **Note:** *Spanners specifically designed for the removal of visco-clutch fans may be purchased from automobile accessory shops.*

5 Remove the fan and hub assembly from the pulley spindle and manoeuvre it out from behind the shroud. The visco-clutch unit may be removed from the fan by slackening and removing the retaining screws.

Refitting

6 Refitting is a reversal of removal, tightening the centre hub bolt securely. Refit the auxiliary drivebelt as described in Chapter 1.

2.3 litre diesel engine models

Removal

7 Disconnect the battery negative lead.

8 Refer to Chapter 4B and remove the intake air ducts over the top of the radiator as necessary.

9 Drain the cooling system as described in Chapter 1, then slacken the clips and remove the radiator top hose.

10 Extract the upper clips securing the fan shroud to the radiator. Lift the shroud off the radiator and rest it on the fan blades.

11 Using an open-ended spanner, hold the visco-clutch hub stationary, then using a wrench and hex bit, slacken and withdraw the Allen bolt from the centre of the hub noting that it has a **left-hand thread**. **Note:** *Spanners specifically designed for the removal of visco-clutch fans may be purchased from automobile accessory shops.*

12 Remove the fan and hub assembly from the pulley spindle and manoeuvre it out from behind the shroud. The visco-clutch unit may be removed from the fan by slackening and removing the retaining screws.

Refitting

13 Refitting is a reversal of removal, tightening the centre hub bolt to the specified torque. Refill the cooling system as described in Chapter 1 on completion.

2.5 litre diesel engine models

Removal

14 Refer to Chapter 4B and remove the intake air ducts over the top of the radiator.

6.15a Using two open-ended spanners, unscrew the visco-clutch fan hub . . .

15 Using two open-ended spanners, hold the pulley hub stationary then unscrew the visco-clutch hub, noting that it has a conventional right-hand thread (see illustration). Remove the cooling fan and visco-clutch assembly (see illustration). **Note:** *Spanners specifically designed for the removal of visco-clutch fans may be purchased from automobile accessory shops.*

16 The visco-clutch unit may be removed from the fan by slackening and removing the retaining screws.

Refitting

17 Refitting is a reversal of removal.

2.8 litre diesel engine models

Removal

18 Disconnect the battery negative lead.

19 Remove the auxiliary drivebelt(s) as described in Chapter 1. Refer to Chapter 4B and remove the intercooler hose from the inlet manifold and intercooler.

20 Extract the two upper spring clips securing the fan shroud to the radiator. Lift the shroud upwards to disengage the two lower mounting lugs and rest it on the fan.

21 Unscrew the four nuts securing the fan visco-clutch hub and coolant pump pulley to the pump spindle.

22 Remove the fan and hub assembly from the pump spindle and manoeuvre it out from behind the shroud. The visco-clutch unit may be removed from the fan by slackening and removing the retaining screws.

Refitting

23 Refitting is a reversal of removal, tightening the four retaining nuts to the specified torque. Refit the auxiliary drivebelt as described in Chapter 1.

7 Auxiliary electric cooling fan - removal and refitting

Note: *On vehicles equipped with air conditioning, auxiliary cooling fan(s) are mounted behind the radiator grille, in front of the air conditioning condenser unit.*

6.15b . . . then remove the fan from the pulley hub - 2.5 litre diesel engine

8.6 Typical coolant temperature gauge sender location (arrowed) on petrol engines

8.11 Disconnecting the coolant temperature gauge sender wiring connector - 2.5 litre diesel engine

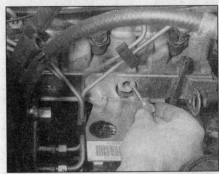

8.24 Engine coolant temperature sensor removal - 2.5 litre diesel engine

Removal

1 Disconnect the battery negative lead.
2 Remove the radiator grille as described in Chapter 12.
3 Disconnect the wiring for the auxiliary cooling fan(s) at the wiring harness connectors and release any retaining cable ties.
4 Undo the retaining bolt each side securing the fan assembly to the mounting brackets.
5 Undo the single upper bolt and two lower bolts and remove the centre vertical support stay.
6 Carefully manoeuvre the fan assembly out from between the mounting brackets.

Refitting

7 Refitting is a reversal of removal.

| 8 | Cooling system electrical switches and sensors - removal and refitting |

Electric cooling fan thermo-switch

Removal

1 The switch is located in the radiator bottom hose.
2 Drain the cooling system as described in Chapter 1.
3 Disconnect the wiring plug from the switch.
4 Carefully unscrew the switch and recover the sealing ring.

Refitting

5 Refitting is a reversal of removal using a new sealing ring. Tighten the switch securely and refill the cooling system as described in Chapter 1.

Coolant temperature gauge sender

Removal - petrol engine models

6 The coolant temperature gauge sender is located in the thermostat housing on all petrol engine models (see illustration).
7 Drain the cooling system as described in Chapter 1.

8 Disconnect the wiring connector from the sender terminal, then unscrew the sender from its location.

Removal - diesel engine models

9 The coolant temperature gauge sender is located in the side of the thermostat housing on 2.3 and 2.8 litre engines, and on the left-hand side of the cylinder head at the front on 2.5 litre engines.
10 Drain the cooling system as described in Chapter 1.
11 Disconnect the wiring connector from the sender terminal, then unscrew the sender from its location (see illustration).

Refitting - all engines

12 On all engines, refitting is a reversal of removal, but coat the sender threads with sealant before refitting. Tighten the sender securely and refill the cooling system as described in Chapter 1.

Engine coolant temperature sensor

Note: *On petrol engine models and 2.5 litre diesel engine models, the Motronic engine management ECU (petrol models) or the EDC (Electronic Diesel Control) ECU (diesel models) receive information on engine temperature from the coolant temperature sensor. Details of the temperature sensors used with the QOS (Quick On Start) and QWS (Quick Warm-up System) fitted to 2.8 litre diesel models is contained in Chapter 4B.*

Removal - 2.0 and 2.2 litre petrol engine models

13 The sensor is located on the right-hand side of the thermostat housing, just below the alternator upper mounting bracket (2.0 litre engines), or on the front right-hand side of the cylinder head (2.2 litre engines).
14 Disconnect the battery negative lead.
15 Referring to the procedures contained in Chapter 1, drain the cooling system then remove the auxiliary drivebelt.
16 Remove the air intake hose between the air cleaner and throttle body as described in Chapter 4A.
17 Undo the bolts securing the alternator front and rear upper mounting brackets to the

alternator. Slacken all the remaining alternator mountings and swing the alternator away from the engine.
18 Disconnect the wiring connector from the coolant temperature sensor, then unscrew the sensor from its location.

Removal - 2.4 litre petrol engine models

19 The sensor is located in the top of the thermostat housing body.
20 Drain the cooling system as described in Chapter 1.
21 Disconnect the wiring connector from the coolant temperature sensor, then unscrew the sensor from the thermostat housing.

Removal - 2.5 litre diesel engine models

22 The sensor is located on the rear left-hand side of the cylinder head.
23 Drain the cooling system as described in Chapter 1.
24 Disconnect the wiring connector from the coolant temperature sensor, then unscrew the sensor from the cylinder head (see illustration).

Refitting - all engines

25 On all engines, refitting is a reversal of removal. Where a copper washer is used to seal the sensor, use a new washer when refitting. Alternatively, where a washer is not used, coat the sensor threads with sealant before refitting. Tighten the sensor securely then refill the cooling system as described in Chapter 1. On 2.0 and 2.2 litre petrol models, refit the components disturbed for access with reference to the Chapters indicated in the removal procedure.

| 9 | Coolant pump - removal and refitting |

2.0 and 2.2 litre petrol engine models

Removal

1 Disconnect the battery negative lead.
2 Drain the cooling system, as described in Chapter 1.

3

9.5 Coolant pump securing bolt (arrowed) - 2.0 litre petrol engine

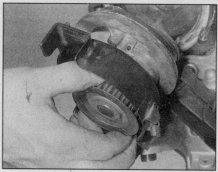

9.6a Withdraw the coolant pump . . .

9.6b . . . and recover the O-ring - 2.0 litre petrol engine

3 Remove the timing belt as described in Chapter 2.

4 Remove timing belt tension roller from the oil pump, where applicable. On early models, undo the small bolt securing the rear timing belt cover to the engine.

5 Unscrew and remove the coolant pump securing bolts **(see illustration)**.

6 Withdraw the coolant pump from the cylinder block, and recover the O-ring **(see illustrations)**. It may be necessary to tap the pump lightly with a plastic-faced hammer to free it from the cylinder block.

7 No overhaul of the coolant pump is possible, and if faulty, the unit must be renewed.

Refitting

8 Ensure that the pump and cylinder block mating surfaces are clean and apply a smear of silicone grease to the pump mating surface in the cylinder block.

9 Fit a new O-ring to the pump and install the pump on the cylinder block. Refit the retaining bolts but do not fully tighten the bolts until the timing belt has been refitted and tensioned (see Chapter 2).

10 Refit the tension roller (where applicable) and timing belt, as described in Chapter 2.

11 Refill the cooling system as described in Chapter 1, then reconnect the battery.

2.4 litre petrol and 2.3 litre diesel engine models

Removal

12 Disconnect the battery negative lead.

13 Drain the cooling system, as described in Chapter 1.

14 Remove the auxiliary drivebelts as described in Chapter 1.

15 Remove the visco-clutch cooling fan as described in Section 6, and remove the radiator fan shroud.

16 Refer to Chapter 2 and remove the crankshaft pulley.

17 Slacken the clips and detach the hoses from the coolant pump ports and thermostat housing, carefully noting their fitted positions.

18 Progressively slacken and remove the coolant pump retaining bolts. Note that the bolts are of different lengths; make a note of

the fitted position of each bolt to ensure correct refitting.

19 Lift the coolant pump away from the engine and recover the gasket.

20 No overhaul of the coolant pump is possible, and if faulty, the unit must be renewed.

Refitting

21 Thoroughly clean the mating surfaces of the coolant pump and cylinder block, then using a new gasket, locate the pump on the cylinder block.

22 Insert and then tighten the coolant pump retaining bolts progressively to the specified torque.

23 Refit the coolant hoses and tighten the clips securely, taking care not to overtighten them. Ensure that the hoses are connected to the correct ports on the coolant pump, according to the notes made during removal.

24 Refit the crankshaft pulley as described in Chapter 2.

25 Locate the radiator fan shroud over the visco-clutch cooling fan, then refit the fan as described in Section 6.

26 Referring to the procedures contained in Chapter 1, refit and tension the auxiliary drivebelts, then refill the cooling system and reconnect the battery.

2.5 litre diesel engine models

Removal

27 Disconnect the battery negative lead.

28 Refer to Chapter 4B and remove the air

9.32 Undo the three bolts and remove the coolant pump pulley - 2.5 litre diesel engine

intake hose from the air cleaner and turbocharger, the intercooler hose from the inlet manifold and intercooler pipe, and the intercooler pipe from the radiator fan shroud.

29 Drain the cooling system, as described in Chapter 1.

30 Remove the auxiliary drivebelt as described in Chapter 1.

31 Although it is possible to remove the pump without disturbing the radiator cooling fan, access is improved if the visco-clutch cooling fan is removed as described in Section 6.

32 Undo the three bolts and remove the coolant pump pulley **(see illustration)**. To prevent the pulley turning as the bolts are undone, use a suitable strap wrench, or an old auxiliary drivebelt or similar.

33 Progressively slacken and remove the coolant pump retaining bolts. Lift the coolant pump away from the housing and where fitted, disconnect the small hose at the base of the pump body **(see illustration)**.

34 Remove the sealing O-ring from the groove on the rear face of the pump.

35 No overhaul of the coolant pump is possible, and if faulty, the unit must be renewed.

Refitting

36 Thoroughly clean the mating surfaces of the coolant pump and pump housing, then fit a new O-ring to the pump groove.

37 Position the pump on the housing, connecting the small hose, where applicable, as the pump is fitted. Insert and tighten the

9.33 Undo the four bolts and remove the coolant pump from the housing - 2.5 litre diesel engine

pump retaining bolts progressively to the specified torque.

38 Refit the pump pulley and secure with the three bolts tightened to the specified torque.

39 If removed for access, refit the visco clutch cooling fan as described in Section 6.

40 Referring to the procedures contained in Chapter 1, refit and tension the auxiliary drivebelts then refill the cooling system.

41 Refit the intercooler pipe and hose and the air intake hose as described in Chapter 4B, then reconnect the battery.

2.8 litre diesel engine models

Removal

42 Disconnect the battery negative lead.

43 Refer to Chapter 4B and remove the intercooler hose from the inlet manifold and intercooler.

44 Drain the cooling system, as described in Chapter 1.

45 Remove the auxiliary drivebelt(s) as described in Chapter 1.

46 Remove the visco-clutch cooling fan as described in Section 6, and lift out the radiator fan shroud.

47 Referring to the procedures in Chapter 2, remove the crankshaft damper pulley and the timing belt upper and lower covers.

48 Undo the five bolts and two nuts securing the coolant pump to the engine and withdraw the pump. Where fitted remove the sealing ring from the groove on the rear face of the pump.

49 No overhaul of the coolant pump is possible, and if faulty, the unit must be renewed.

Refitting

50 Thoroughly clean the mating surfaces of the coolant pump and then fit a new sealing ring to the pump groove. Note that on certain engines an RTV sealant is used instead of a rubber sealing ring. If the sealing ring is unavailable from Vauxhall parts stockists, apply a bead of RTV sealant to the pump groove and mating surface.

51 Locate the pump on the engine, refit the retaining bolts and nuts and tighten to the specified torque.

52 Refit the timing belt upper and lower covers and crankshaft damper pulley as described in Chapter 2.

53 Refit the visco-clutch cooling fan and fan shroud as described in Section 6.

54 Referring to the procedures contained in Chapter 1, refit and tension the auxiliary drivebelts then refill the cooling system.

55 Refit the intercooler hose as described in Chapter 4B, then reconnect the battery.

10 Heating and ventilation system - general information

The heating/ventilation system consists of a four-speed blower motor, face level vents in the centre and at each end of the facia, and air ducts to the front footwells.

The control unit is located in the facia, and the controls operate flap valves to deflect and mix the air flowing through the various parts of the heating/ventilation system. The flap valves are contained in the heater unit and blower housing and pass air to the various ducts and vents.

Cold air enters the system through the grille at the rear of the engine compartment. If required, the airflow is boosted by the blower, and then flows through the various ducts, according to the settings of the controls. Stale air is expelled through ducts at the rear of the vehicle. If warm air is required, the cold air is passed over the heater matrix, which is heated by the engine coolant.

A recirculation control enables the outside air supply to be closed off, while the air inside the vehicle is recirculated. This can be useful to prevent unpleasant odours entering from outside the vehicle, but should only be used briefly, as the recirculated air inside the vehicle will soon become stale.

11 Heater/ventilation components - removal and refitting

Heater/ventilation control unit

Removal

1 Disconnect the battery negative lead.

2 Remove the trim panels under the facia on the driver's and, where fitted, the passenger's side.

3 On 1997 models onward, remove the instrument panel cover as described in Chapter 13.

4 Set the heater/ventilation controls to the following positions:

a) *Air selector lever to Face Level (lever fully left)*

b) *Temperature control lever to Cold (lever fully left)*

c) *Air source selector lever to Recirculating (lever fully left)*

5 From under the facia, locate the control cables at their attachments on the heater unit. The air selector control cable is on the driver's side of the heater unit, the temperature control cable is on the front of the heater unit, and the air source control cable is on the blower housing on the passenger's side **(see illustrations)**.

6 Having located the cables, note the position of the control linkages on the heater and blower housing with the controls set as described above. Move the control levers through their range of travel, while at the same time noting the direction of movement of the linkages on the heater and blower housing. Return the controls to the positions described above and sketch or suitably note the positions of the linkages. This will enable the cables to be connected correctly when refitting. Finally, mark the position of each of the three outer cables in their respective retaining clips.

7 Using a small screwdriver, release the outer cables from the retaining clips, and disconnect the inner cable ends from the studs on the linkage.

8 Carefully pull the knobs off the heater/ventilation control levers.

9 Insert a small screwdriver or thin blade, between the control unit bezel and housing and carefully release the bezel clips. Withdraw the bezel from the housing.

10 Undo the four control unit retaining screws and withdraw the unit from its location in the facia. Disconnect the blower motor switch wiring multiplug and remove the control unit.

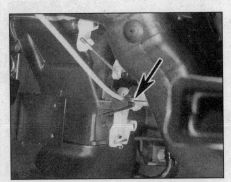

11.5a Heater air selector control cable and retaining clip (arrowed) . . .

11.5b . . . temperature control cable and retaining clip (arrowed) . . .

11.5c . . . and air source control cable (arrowed)

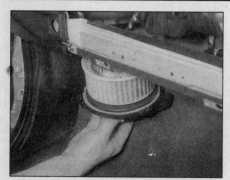

11.14 Removing the heater blower motor

11.20a Heater blower housing upper retaining bolt (arrowed) . . .

11.20b . . . and lower left-hand retaining bolt (arrowed)

11.21 Removing the heater blower housing

Refitting

11 Refitting is a reversal of removal. Before reconnecting the cables, set the control linkages on the heater and blower housing to the position noted during removal. Set the control levers to the positions indicated in paragraph 4, and reconnect the cables, aligning the marks made on removal with the retaining clips. Check the operation of the controls before refitting the facia trim panels.

Heater blower motor

Removal

12 Disconnect the battery negative lead.

13 Disconnect the blower motor wiring multiplug.

14 Undo the four screws securing the motor and carrier assembly to the underside of the blower housing and remove the motor and carrier (see illustration).

15 To remove the motor from the carrier, lift off the rubber seal then undo the screws securing the two halves of the carrier together. Separate the carrier and lift out the motor and fan.

Refitting

16 Refitting is a reversal of removal.

Heater blower housing

Removal

17 Remove the facia as described in Chapter 12.

18 Disconnect the wiring multiplug from the series resistor located in the air duct between the blower housing and heater unit.

19 Disconnect the blower motor wiring multiplug from the side of the motor.

20 Undo the single upper bolt and two lower bolts securing the housing to the bulkhead (see illustrations).

21 Lift the housing up and out of its location (see illustration). The air duct between the

blower housing and heater unit can be left in place or removed, together with the blower housing.

Refitting

22 Refitting is a reversal of removal.

Heater blower motor series resistor

Removal

23 Remove the glove compartment.

24 Disconnect the wiring multiplug from the series resistor located in the air duct between the blower housing and heater unit (see illustration).

25 Carefully ease the blower housing end of the air duct away from the blower housing and withdraw it through the glove compartment aperture. Take care not to damage the seal in the end of the duct.

26 Withdraw the end of the air duct from the heater unit and remove the duct from the vehicle.

27 Undo the two screws and withdraw the resistor from the air duct. From inside the air duct, collect the retaining plate which will drop off once the resistor screws are undone (see illustration).

11.24 Disconnect the wiring multiplug from the heater blower motor series resistor

11.27 Remove the series resistor and collect the retaining plate from inside the air duct

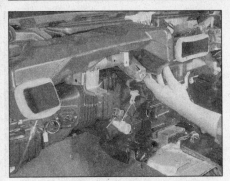

11.32 On 1997 models onward, undo the retaining screws and remove the ventilation ducting on the passenger's side

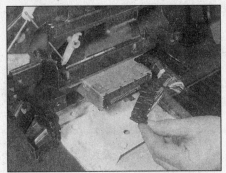

11.33 Disconnect the wiring harness connector at the anti-theft alarm control unit

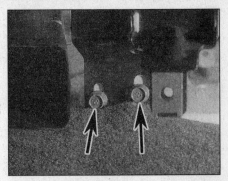

11.34a Undo the facia centre support stay lower retaining bolts (arrowed) on each side . . .

11.34b . . . and the two upper nuts . . .

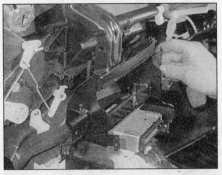

11.34c . . . then remove the centre support stay

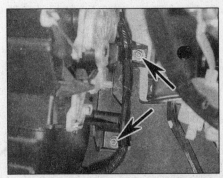

11.35 Undo the heater-to-bulkhead retaining nuts (arrowed) on each side . . .

Refitting

28 Refitting is a reversal of removal.

Heater unit

Removal

29 Drain the cooling system as described in Chapter 1.

30 From within the engine compartment, release the clips and disconnect the two heater hoses from the heater matrix pipe stubs.

31 Remove the facia as described in Chapter 12.

32 On 1997 models onward, undo the retaining screws and remove the ventilation ducting on the passenger's side (see illustration).

33 Where fitted, disconnect the wiring harness connector at the anti-theft alarm control unit (see illustration).

34 Undo the two lower bolts each side and the two upper nuts and remove the facia centre support stay (see illustrations).

35 Undo the two nuts each side securing the heater unit to the bulkhead (see illustration).

36 Carefully ease the heater unit clear of the bulkhead, and remove it from the vehicle (see illustration). As the heater is removed, try and keep the heater matrix unions uppermost, to prevent coolant spillage on the interior. Place absorbent rags around the housing as a precaution, and mop up any spilt coolant immediately with a damp cloth to prevent staining.

Refitting

37 Refitting is a reversal of removal. Refill the cooling system as described in Chapter 1 on completion.

Heater matrix

Removal

Note: If leakage is the reason for removing the matrix, bear in mind that minor leaks can often be cured using a radiator sealant with the matrix in situ.

38 Remove the heater unit as described previously.

39 Lift off the bulkhead seal from the matrix pipe stubs then undo the retaining screw and remove the abutment plate (see illustrations).

3

11.36 . . . and remove the heater unit

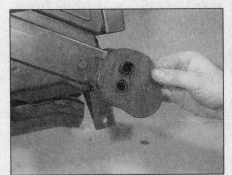

11.39a Lift off the bulkhead seal from the heater matrix pipe stubs . . .

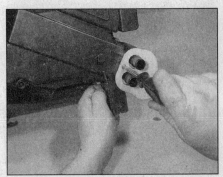

11.39b . . . then remove the abutment plate

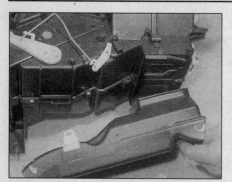

11.40 Remove the lower air duct from the heater unit

11.41a Undo the screws and separate the halves of the heater unit . . .

11.41b . . . then lift out the matrix

40 Remove the lower air duct from the heater unit **(see illustration)**.

41 Undo the nine retaining screws and separate the halves of the heater unit, then lift out the matrix **(see illustrations)**.

Refitting

42 Refitting is a reversal of removal. When assembling the heater, ensure that the air flap hinges engage with their locations in both halves of the unit.

Air nozzle inserts

Removal

43 Using a small screwdriver or thin blade, carefully lever the air nozzle from its location in the facia. Protect the facia with a cloth as the insert is being levered out.

Refitting

44 Engage the nozzle in its location and push it fully in until the retaining tags engage.

12 Air conditioning system - general information and precautions

General information

An air conditioning system is available as an option on later models. It enables the temperature of incoming air to be lowered, and also dehumidifies the air, which makes for rapid demisting and increased comfort.

The cooling side of the system works in the same way as a domestic refrigerator. Refrigerant gas is drawn into a belt-driven compressor, and passes into a condenser mounted on the front of the radiator, where it loses heat and becomes liquid. The liquid passes through an expansion valve to an evaporator, where it changes from liquid under high pressure to gas under low

pressure. This change is accompanied by a drop in temperature, which cools the evaporator. The refrigerant returns to the compressor, and the cycle begins again.

Air blown through the evaporator passes to the air distribution unit, where it is mixed with hot air blown through the heater matrix to achieve the desired temperature in the passenger compartment.

The heating side of the system works in the same way as on models without air conditioning (see Section 10).

The operation of the electric cooling fan(s), the compressor and the facia-mounted warning light is managed electronically by the control unit. Any problems with the system should be referred to a Vauxhall dealer.

Precautions

When an air conditioning system is fitted, it is necessary to observe special precautions whenever dealing with any part of the system, or its associated components. If for any reason the system must be disconnected, entrust this task to your Vauxhall dealer or a refrigeration engineer.

 Warning: The refrigeration circuit contains a liquid refrigerant (Freon). This refrigerant is potentially dangerous, and should only be handled by qualified persons. If it is splashed onto the skin, it can cause frostbite. It is not itself poisonous, but in the presence of a naked flame it forms a poisonous gas; inhalation of the vapour through a lighted cigarette could prove fatal. Uncontrolled discharging of the refrigerant is dangerous, and potentially damaging to the environment. It is therefore dangerous to disconnect any part of the system without specialised knowledge and equipment. If for any reason the system must be disconnected, entrust this task to

an authorised dealer or air conditioning specialist.
Caution: Do not operate the air conditioning system if it is known to be short of refrigerant, as this may damage the compressor.

13 Air conditioning system components - removal and refitting

 Warning: Do not attempt to open the refrigerant circuit. Refer to the precautions in Section 12.

1 The only operations which can be performed by the home mechanic are removal/refitting of the heater/ventilation control panel and cables, removal/refitting of the auxiliary cooling fan(s), and renewal of the auxiliary (compressor) drivebelt. Removal/refitting of the heater/ventilation control panel and cables can be carried out using the information given in Section 11. Procedures relating to the auxiliary electric cooling fan(s) are contained in Section 7, and renewal procedures for the auxiliary (compressor) drivebelt are contained in Chapter 1.

2 If necessary, the compressor can be unbolted and moved aside, without disconnecting its flexible hoses, after removing the drivebelt.

3 Removal/refitting of the remaining components will have to be entrusted to a Vauxhall dealer as no further operations are possible without discharging the air conditioning refrigerant. Therefore, the task should be entrusted to a Vauxhall dealer with access to the necessary equipment required to discharge/recharge the system safely (see Section 12).

Chapter 4 Part A
Fuel and exhaust systems - petrol engine models

Contents

Accelerator cable - removal and refitting 3
Accelerator pedal - removal and refitting 4
Air cleaner assembly - removal and refitting 2
Air cleaner filter element renewal .... See Chapter 1
Exhaust emission check .... See Chapter 1
Exhaust manifold - removal and refitting 15
Exhaust system - general information, removal and refitting 16
Fuel filter renewal .... See Chapter 1
Fuel gauge sender unit - removal and refitting 9
Fuel injection system - depressurisation 7

Fuel injection system - testing and adjustment 12
Fuel injection system components - removal and refitting 13
Fuel injection systems - general information 6
Fuel pump - removal and refitting 8
Fuel tank - removal and refitting 10
General information and precautions 1
Inlet manifold - removal and refitting 14
Throttle housing - removal and refitting 11
Unleaded petrol - general information and usage 5

Degrees of difficulty

| Easy, suitable for novice with little experience | Fairly easy, suitable for beginner with some experience | Fairly difficult, suitable for competent DIY mechanic | Difficult, suitable for experienced DIY mechanic | Very difficult, suitable for expert DIY or professional |

Specifications

System type

2.0 litre engines:	
Pre 1995 (C20NE) engines	Bosch Motronic M1.5
1995 on (X20SE) engines	Bosch Motronic M1.5.4
2.2 litre engines	Bosch Motronic M1.5.4
2.4 litre engines	Bosch Motronic M1.5

See Section 6 for further information

Fuel system data

Fuel pump type	Electric, immersed in tank
Fuel supply regulated pressure (approximate)	3.0 bar
Specified idle speed	Not adjustable - controlled by ECU
Idle mixture CO content	Not adjustable - controlled by ECU

Recommended fuel

Minimum octane rating	95 RON* unleaded (UK premium unleaded). Leaded fuel (UK 4-star) must **not** be used

91 RON unleaded fuel can be used but a slight power loss maybe noticeable - see Section 5.

Accelerator pedal

Stop bolt length:	
2.0 and 2.2 litre engines:	
Right-hand drive models	11 mm
Left-hand drive models	13 mm
2.4 litre engines:	
Right-hand drive models	8 mm
Left-hand drive models	11 mm

4A

Torque wrench settings

	Nm	lbf ft
Accelerator pedal stop bolt locknut	9	7
Braking system vacuum hose union nut	20	15
Camshaft sensor - 2.2 litre engine	6	4
Crankshaft sensor bolt	6	4
Exhaust system fasteners:		
Front pipe retaining clamp nut	20	15
Front pipe-to-manifold bolts:		
2.0 and 2.2 litre engines	20	15
2.4 litre engine	25	18
Front pipe-to-intermediate pipe bolts	20	15
Tailpipe clamping ring	18	13
Tailpipe-to-intermediate pipe nuts	45	33
Fuel rail bolts	8	6
Fuel tank:		
Mounting tray-to-chassis bolts	50	37
Retaining strap bolts	50	37
Inlet and exhaust manifold nuts and bolts:		
2.0 and 2.2 litre engines	22	16
2.4 litre engine	35	26
Knock sensor bolt - 2.0 litre (X20SE) and 2.2 litre engines	20	15
Spark plug heatshields - 2.0 litre engine (X20SE)	30	22

1 General information and precautions

1 The fuel system consists of a fuel tank (which is mounted under the rear of the car, with an electric fuel pump immersed in it), a fuel filter and the fuel feed and return lines. The fuel pump supplies fuel to the fuel rail, which acts as a reservoir for the four fuel injectors which inject fuel into the inlet tracts. In addition, there is an Electronic Control Unit (ECU) and various sensors, electrical components and related wiring.

2 Refer to Section 6 for further information on the operation of each fuel injection system, and to Section 16 for information on the exhaust system.

Note: *Residual pressure will remain in the fuel lines long after the vehicle was last used. Before disconnecting any fuel line, first depressurise the fuel system as described in Section 7.*

Warning: Many of the procedures in this Chapter require the removal of fuel lines and connections, which may result in some fuel spillage. Before carrying out any operation on the fuel system, refer to the precautions given in Safety first! at the beginning of this manual, and follow them implicitly. Petrol is a highly-dangerous and volatile liquid, and the precautions necessary when handling it cannot be overstressed. Also take great care to prevent dirt entering the fuel system.

2 Air cleaner assembly - removal and refitting

Removal

1 Ensure the ignition is switched off then disconnect the wiring connector from the airflow meter.

2 Slacken the retaining clip and disconnect the intake duct then release the retaining clips and remove the lid from the air cleaner housing. Remove the filter element.

3 Detach the intake duct from the front of the housing then remove the retaining clips and unclip the housing from its mounting brackets and remove it from the engine compartment.

Refitting

4 Refitting is the reverse of removal ensuring the housing is clipped securely in position.

3 Accelerator cable - removal and refitting

Removal

1 Working in the engine compartment, unclip the inner cable retaining clip (where fitted) then slide the clip out of the end fitting and release the cable from the throttle cam.

2 Free the accelerator outer cable from its mounting bracket, taking care not to lose the adjusting clip. Work back along the length of the cable, free it from any retaining clips or ties, noting its correct routing.

3 From inside the vehicle, reaching up behind the facia, unclip the accelerator inner cable from the top of the accelerator pedal

4 Return to the engine compartment then free the outer cable from the bulkhead and remove the cable and grommet from the vehicle, noting its correct routing.

5 Examine the cable for signs of wear or damage and renew if necessary.

Refitting

6 Feed the cable into position from the engine compartment, making sure it is correctly routed, and seat the outer cable in the bulkhead.

7 From inside the vehicle, clip the inner cable into position in the pedal end and check to make sure the outer cable is correctly located in the bulkhead.

8 From within the engine compartment, ensure the outer cable is correctly seated in the bulkhead, then work along the cable, securing it in position with the retaining clips and ties, and ensuring that the cable is correctly routed.

9 Connect the inner cable to the throttle cam and secure it in position with the retaining clip (where fitted). Clip the outer cable into its mounting bracket and adjust the cable as described below.

Adjustment

10 Working in the engine compartment, slide off the adjustment clip from accelerator outer cable.

11 With the clip removed, ensure that the throttle cam is fully against its stop. Gently pull the cable out of its grommet until all free play is removed from the inner cable.

12 With the cable held in this position, refit the spring clip to the last exposed outer cable groove in front of the rubber grommet. When the clip is refitted and the outer cable is released, there should be only a small amount of free play in the inner cable.

13 Have an assistant depress the accelerator pedal, and check that the throttle cam opens fully and returns smoothly to its stop.

4 Accelerator pedal - removal and refitting

Removal

1 Reaching up behind the facia, unclip the accelerator inner cable from the top of the accelerator pedal.

2 Unscrew the retaining bolts and remove the pedal assembly from the bulkhead.

3 Inspect the pedal assembly for signs of wear, paying particular attention to the pedal bushes. On left-hand-drive models the pedal assembly is only available as a complete unit; if any component is worn or damaged the complete assembly must be replaced. On right-hand-drive models, the assembly can be dismantled once the circlip has been removed from the pedal pivot; all components are available separately.

Refitting

4 Prior to refitting, check that the distance from the head of the accelerator pedal stop bolt to the bracket is as given in the Specifications. If adjustment is necessary, slacken the locknut then position the bolt as required before retightening the locknut to the specified torque.

5 Apply a smear of multi-purpose grease to the pedal pivot shaft then refit the pedal assembly, tightening its retaining bolts securely.

6 Clip the accelerator cable into position on the pedal then adjust the accelerator cable as described in Section 3.

5 Unleaded petrol - general information and usage

Note: *The information given in this Chapter is correct at the time of writing. If updated information is thought to be required, check with a Vauxhall dealer. If travelling abroad, consult one of the motoring organisations (or a similar authority) for advice on the fuel available.*

1 The fuel recommended by Vauxhall is given in the Specifications Section of this Chapter, followed by the equivalent petrol currently on sale in the UK.

2 All petrol engines are designed to run on fuel with a minimum octane rating of 95 (RON), however, lower octane fuel down to minimum of rating 91 (RON), can be safely used if necessary.

3 On pre 1995 2.0 litre engines (C20NE) and all 2.4 litre engines, it is necessary to ensure that the octane rating plug is correctly set to correspond to the minimum rating of fuel being used. The plug is located in the front right-hand corner of the engine compartment, behind the headlight. Free the octane plug from the body and check that the number which is visible on the retaining clip side of the plug, either 91 or 95, corresponds to the octane rating of the petrol being used. If adjustment is necessary, switch the ignition off then unclip the plug from the wiring connector and rotate it through 180° before reconnecting it. Once the plug is correctly set, clip it back into position on the body.

4 On 1995 on 2.0 litre engines (X20SE) and all 2.2 litre engines, the engine management system automatically adjusts the ignition timing to suit the octane rating of fuel being used (using the information supplied by the knock sensor). However, a slight power loss is likely if fuel with a octane rating of less than 95 (RON) is used.

5 Note that all models have a catalytic converter, and so must be run on unleaded fuel only. Under no circumstances should leaded fuel (UK 4-star) be used, as this will damage the converter.

6 Super unleaded petrol (98 octane) can also be used in all models if wished, though there is no advantage in doing so.

6 Fuel injection systems - general information

1 All petrol engine models are equipped with a Bosch Motronic engine management (fuel injection/ignition) system. Pre 1995 2.0 litre engine (C20NE) and all 2.4 litre engine models are equipped with a Motronic M1.5 system whereas later 1995 onwards 2.0 litre engine (X20SE) and 2.2 litre engine models have a Motronic M1.5.4 system. Both systems incorporate a closed-loop catalytic converter and an evaporative emission system and comply with the latest emission standards. The M1.5.4 system also incorporates an exhaust gas recirculation (EGR) system and a secondary air system to further improve emission levels (see Chapter 4C for details on emission control systems). The fuel injection side of the system operates as follows; refer to Chapter 5B for information on the ignition system.

2 The fuel pump, immersed in the fuel tank, pumps fuel from the fuel tank to the fuel rail, via a filter mounted underneath the rear of the vehicle. Fuel supply pressure is controlled by the pressure regulator which allows excess fuel to be returned to the tank.

3 The electrical control system consists of the ECU, along with the following sensors.

a) *Throttle potentiometer - informs the ECU of the throttle position, and the rate of throttle opening or closing.*

b) *Airflow meter - informs the ECU of the amount of air entering the inlet manifold*

c) *Coolant temperature sensor - informs the ECU of engine temperature.*

d) *Intake air temperature sensor (incorporated in the airflow meter on M1.5 system) - informs the ECU of the temperature of the air entering the manifold.*

e) *Oxygen sensor - informs the ECU of the oxygen content of the exhaust gases (explained in greater detail in Part C of this Chapter).*

f) *Crankshaft sensor - informs the ECU of engine speed and crankshaft position.*

g) *Knock sensor (M1.5.4 system only) - informs the ECU when pre-ignition (pinking) is occurring.*

h) *Camshaft sensor (2.2 litre engine only) - informs the ECU of speed and position of the exhaust camshaft.*

4 All the above information is analysed by the ECU and, based on this, the ECU determines the appropriate ignition and fuelling requirements for the engine. The ECU controls the fuel injector by varying its pulse width - the length of time the injector is held open - to provide a richer or weaker mixture, as appropriate. The mixture is constantly varied by the ECU, to provide the best setting for cranking, starting (with either a hot or cold engine), warm-up, idle, cruising, and acceleration.

5 The ECU also has full control over the engine idle speed, via an idle speed adjuster; on the later M1.5.4 system the adjuster is bolted onto the side of the throttle housing whereas on the earlier M1.5 system the adjuster is mounted away from manifold and is linked to the manifold/throttle housing by two hoses. The adjuster controls the opening of an air passage which bypasses the throttle valve. When the throttle valve is closed (accelerator pedal released), the ECU uses the adjuster to vary the amount of air entering the engine and so controls the idle speed.

6 The ECU also controls the exhaust and evaporative emission control systems, which are described in detail in Part C of this Chapter.

7 If there is an abnormality in any of the readings obtained from any sensor, the ECU enters its back-up mode. In this event, the ECU ignores the abnormal sensor signal, and assumes a pre-programmed value which will allow the engine to continue running (albeit at reduced efficiency). If the ECU enters this back-up mode, the warning light on the instrument panel will come on, and the relevant fault code will be stored in the ECU memory.

8 If the warning light comes on, the vehicle should be taken to a Vauxhall dealer at the earliest opportunity. A complete test of the engine management system can then be carried out, using a special electronic diagnostic test unit.

4A

7 Fuel injection system - depressurisation

⚠ **Warning: Refer to the warning note in Section 1 before proceeding. The following procedure will merely relieve the pressure in the fuel system - remember that fuel will still be present in the system components, and take precautions accordingly before disconnecting any of them.**

1 The fuel system referred to in this Section is defined as the tank-mounted fuel pump, the fuel filter, the fuel injectors and the pressure regulator, and the metal pipes and flexible hoses of the fuel lines between these components. All these contain fuel which will be under pressure while the engine is running, and/or while the ignition is switched on. The pressure will remain for some time after the ignition has been switched off, and it must be relieved in a controlled fashion when any of these components are disturbed for servicing work.

Pre 1995 2.0 litre engines (C20NE)

2 Disconnect the battery negative terminal then position a container and large rag beneath the connection or union to be disconnected.

3 Slowly loosen the connection or union (as applicable) to avoid a sudden release of pressure and position the rag around the connection to catch any fuel spray which may be expelled. Once the pressure is released, disconnect the fuel line and plug the pipe/hose ends to minimise fuel loss and prevent the entry of dirt into the system.

All other engines

4 Locate the valve assembly which is fitted to the fuel rail on the inlet manifold.

5 Unscrew the cap from the valve and position a container beneath the valve. Hold a wad of rag over the valve and relieve the pressure in the fuel system by depressing the valve core with a suitable screwdriver. Be prepared for the squirt of fuel as the valve core is depressed and catch it with the rag. Hold the valve core down until no more fuel is expelled from the valve.

6 Once all pressure is relieved, securely refit the valve cap.

8 Fuel pump - removal and refitting

⚠ **Warning: Refer to the warning note in Section 1 before proceeding.**

Note: *A new fuel pump cover sealing ring will be required on refitting.*

Removal

1 Remove the fuel tank as described in Section 10.

2 Unscrew the locking ring and remove it from the tank. This is best accomplished by using a screwdriver on the raised ribs of the locking ring. Carefully tap the screwdriver to turn the ring anti-clockwise until it can be unscrewed by hand.

3 Carefully lift the fuel pump/gauge unit out from the tank, taking great care not to damage the float arm. Recover the sealing ring and discard it, a new one must be used on refitting.

4 Release the retaining clips and remove the pump cover from the base of the unit. Check the pump filter for signs of clogging or damage and, if necessary, unclip the filter and clean/renew it. The pump can be separated from the bracket once the wiring connector and fuel hose has been disconnected and its retaining screws removed. **Note:** *Vauxhall do not supply the fuel pump separately only as part of the complete pump/gauge assembly.*

Refitting

5 Where necessary, reassemble the pump and housing components, ensuring the wiring and fuel hose are correctly and securely reconnected. Securely tighten the pump retaining screws. Ensure the filter is securely fitted to the base of the pump then carefully refit the pump cover, making sure it clips securely into position.

6 Fit a new sealing ring to the tank.

7 Manoeuvre the fuel pump/gauge unit into the tank, taking great care not to bend the float arm.

8 Ensure the fuel pump unions are facing the front of the fuel tank then refit the locking ring and tighten it securely.

9 Refit the fuel tank as described in Section 10.

9 Fuel gauge sender unit - removal and refitting

1 The fuel gauge sender unit is an integral part of the fuel pump/gauge unit. Refer to Section 8 for removal and refitting details.

10 Fuel tank - removal and refitting

⚠ **Warning: Refer to the warning note in Section 1 before proceeding.**

Removal

1 Disconnect the battery negative terminal.

2 Before removing the fuel tank, all fuel must be drained from the tank. Since a fuel tank drain plug is not provided, it is therefore preferable to carry out the removal operation when the tank is nearly empty. The remaining fuel can then be syphoned or hand-pumped from the tank.

3 Slacken the retaining clips and disconnect the filler neck and vent hoses from the right-hand side of the tank.

4 Place a trolley jack beneath the tank. Position a large piece of wood between the jack and tank to spread the load of the fuel tank, then raise the jack until it is supporting the weight of the tank.

5 Slacken and remove the four bolts securing the fuel tank mounting tray to the chassis.

6 Slowly lower the tank, taking care not to strain any of the fuel/breather hoses, until access can be gained to the fuel pump/gauge cover which is situated at the front of the tank.

7 Make alignment marks between the fuel hoses and pump/gauge cover. Referring to Section 7, depressurise the fuel system and disconnect both hoses from the cover. Plug the hose ends and cover unions to minimise fuel loss and prevent the entry of dirt into the system. Also disconnect the wiring connector from the cover.

8 Slacken the retaining clip and disconnect the fuel vapour hose from the vent valve T-piece connector.

9 Slowly lower the fuel tank out of position, disconnecting any other relevant vent pipes as they become accessible, and remove the tank from underneath the vehicle.

10 If necessary, slacken and remove the retaining nuts and bolts then separate the fuel tank from its mounting tray and straps.

11 If the tank is contaminated with sediment or water, remove the fuel pump/gauge unit (Section 8), and swill the tank out with clean fuel. The tank is injection-moulded from a synthetic material - if seriously damaged, it should be renewed. However, in certain cases, it may be possible to have small leaks or minor damage repaired. Seek the advice of a specialist before attempting to repair the fuel tank.

Refitting

12 Refitting is the reverse of the removal procedure, noting the following points:
a) When lifting the tank back into position, take care to ensure that none of the hoses/wiring become trapped between the tank and vehicle body. Ensure the tank is correctly located then tighten the bolts to the specified torque.
b) Ensure all pipes and hoses are correctly routed and all hoses unions are securely joined.
c) On completion, refill the tank with a small amount of fuel, and check for signs of leakage prior to taking the vehicle out on the road.

11 Throttle housing - removal and refitting

Removal

1 Disconnect the battery negative terminal.
2 Slacken the retaining clips then disconnect the air intake duct from the throttle housing, air cleaner and (where necessary) resonator. Unclip the wiring harness from the duct and position clear the duct clear of the throttle housing.
3 Unclip the accelerator inner cable retaining clip (where fitted) then slide the clip out of the end fitting and release the cable from the throttle cam. Free the outer cable from its mounting bracket, taking care not to lose the adjusting clip, and position it clear of the throttle housing. On 2.0 litre engines unhook the throttle linkage spring from the accelerator cable bracket and housing and remove it from the engine.
4 Depress the retaining clips and disconnect the wiring connector(s) from the throttle potentiometer and the idle speed adjuster valve.
5 Make a note of the correct fitted location of each hose then slacken the retaining clips (where fitted) and disconnect all the vacuum and breather hoses from the throttle housing. On some engines, coolant is circulated around the throttle housing to help warm it up on cold starts; on these engines plug/clamp the coolant hoses to minimise coolant and rinse off any spilt coolant immediately using cold water.
6 Slacken and remove the retaining nuts and washers then remove the throttle housing from the manifold. Discard the gasket, a new one should be used on refitting.

Refitting

7 Refitting is the reverse of removal, bearing in mind the following points.
a) *Ensure the mating surfaces are clean and dry and use a new throttle housing gasket.*
b) *Ensure all wiring and hoses and are correctly and securely reconnected.*
c) *On completion adjust the accelerator cable as described in Section 3.*

12 Fuel injection system - testing and adjustment

Testing

1 If a fault appears in the fuel injection system, first ensure that all the system wiring connectors are securely connected and free of corrosion. Ensure that the fault is not due to poor maintenance; ie, check that the air cleaner filter element is clean, the spark plugs are in good condition and correctly gapped, the cylinder compression pressures are correct, and that the engine breather hoses are

clear and undamaged, referring to Chapters 1, 2 and 5 for further information (as applicable).
2 If these checks fail to reveal the cause of the problem, the vehicle should be taken to a Vauxhall dealer or suitably-equipped garage for testing. They should have access to an electronic diagnostic tester which can be plugged into the system (see Section 6). The tester will locate the fault quickly and simply, alleviating the need to test all the system components individually, which is a time-consuming operation that carries a risk of damaging the ECU.

Adjustment

3 Experienced home mechanics with a considerable amount of skill and equipment (including a tachometer and an accurately calibrated exhaust gas analyser) may be able to check the exhaust CO level and the idle speed. However, if these are found to be in need of adjustment, the car will have to be taken to a Vauxhall dealer or suitably-equipped garage who has access to the necessary diagnostic equipment required to test and (where possible) adjust the settings.

13 Fuel injection system components - removal and refitting

Fuel rail and injectors

⚠️ **Warning: Refer to the warning note in Section 1 before proceeding.**

Note: *If a faulty injector is suspected, before condemning the injector, it is worth trying the effect of one of the proprietary injector-cleaning treatments.*

1 Disconnect the battery negative terminal and continue as described under the relevant sub-heading.

Pre 1995 2.0 litre engines (C20NE)

2 Remove the idle speed adjuster as described in this Section.
3 Disconnect the vacuum hose from the fuel pressure regulator then slacken the union nut and disconnect the braking system servo unit vacuum hose from the manifold.
4 Referring to Section 7, slacken the retaining clips and disconnect the fuel feed and return hoses from the fuel rail.
5 Disconnect the wiring connector from each injector.
6 Using a flat-bladed screwdriver, carefully prise out the retaining clip securing the fuel rail to the top of each injector.
7 Slacken and remove the fuel rail retaining bolts then carefully ease the fuel rail off from the top of the injectors and remove it from the engine. The injectors can then be eased out of position and removed from the manifold. Discard all injector sealing rings; new ones must be used on refitting.

8 Refitting is a reversal of the removal procedure, noting the following points.
a) *Renew all disturbed sealing rings and apply a smear of engine oil to them to aid installation.*
b) *Ease the injectors into the manifold, ensuring that the sealing ring(s) remain correctly seated, and position the injector wiring connectors correctly*
c) *On refitting the fuel rail ensure that all sealing rings remain in position. Once the fuel rail is correctly seated, tighten its retaining bolts to the specified torque then refit the injector retaining clips.*
d) *Ensure all hoses are correctly and securely reconnected.*
e) *On completion start the engine and check for fuel leaks.*

1995 on 2.0 litre engines (X20SE)

9 Depressurise the fuel system as described in Section 7.
10 Slacken and remove the union bolts securing the fuel feed and return hoses to either end of the fuel rail. Disconnect both hoses and discard the sealing washers; new ones must be used on refitting. Note that the union bolts are different and should not be interchanged.
11 Disconnect the accelerator cable from the throttle housing then unbolt the cable mounting bracket from the manifold and position it clear.
12 Disconnect the vacuum hoses from the fuel pressure regulator and the manifold chamber.
13 Disconnect the wiring connectors from the fuel injectors.
14 Undo the retaining nut and disconnect the earth lead and hose bracket from the front end of the fuel rail.
15 Slacken and remove the retaining bolts then carefully ease the fuel rail and injector assembly out of position and remove it from the manifold. Remove the lower sealing rings from the injectors and discard them; they must be renewed whenever they are disturbed.
16 Slide off the relevant retaining clip and withdraw the injector from the fuel rail. Remove the upper sealing ring from the injector and discard it; all disturbed sealing rings must be renewed **(see illustrations)**.

13.16a Withdraw the retaining clip . . .

4A

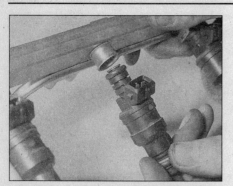

13.16b . . . and remove the injector from the fuel rail

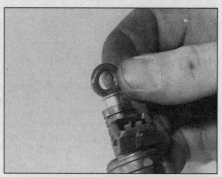

13.17 Renew all injector sealing rings prior to refitting

17 Refitting is a reversal of the removal procedure, noting the following points.

a) *Renew all disturbed sealing rings and apply a smear of engine oil to them to aid installation* **(see illustration)**.

b) *Ease the injector(s) into the fuel rail, ensuring that the sealing ring(s) remain correctly seated, and secure in position with the retaining clips.*

c) *On refitting the fuel rail, take care not to damage the injectors and ensure that all sealing rings remain in position. Once the fuel rail is correctly seated, securely tighten its retaining bolts.*

d) *Position a new sealing washer on each side of the fuel hose unions and securely tighten the unions bolts.*

e) *Adjust the accelerator cable as described in Section 3.*

f) *On completion start the engine and check for fuel leaks.*

2.2 litre engine

18 Disconnect the wiring connectors from the airflow meter and intake air temperature sensor then unclip the wiring harness from the intake duct.

19 Slacken the retaining clips securing the intake duct to the airflow meter, resonator and throttle housing and remove the duct from the engine compartment.

20 Disconnect the breather hoses from the camshaft cover and position them clear of the fuel rail.

21 Disconnect the wiring connectors from the throttle valve potentiometer and idle speed adjuster valve then unscrew the retaining nut and disconnect the earth lead from the fuel rail.

22 Disconnect the vacuum hose from the fuel pressure regulator.

23 Slacken the union nuts and disconnect the fuel feed and return pipes from the fuel rail. As the union nuts are slackened, retain the adapters with an open-ended spanner to prevent any excess strain being placed on the fuel rail.

24 Disconnect the accelerator cable from the throttle housing and position it clear of the fuel rail.

25 Release the retaining clips securing the wiring connectors to injectors No 1 and 4 then

lift the wiring cover squarely away from the top of the injectors; the wiring connectors are an integral part of the cover.

26 Slacken and remove the retaining bolts then carefully ease the fuel rail and injector assembly out of position and remove it from the manifold. Remove the lower sealing rings from the injectors and discard them; they must be renewed whenever they are disturbed.

27 Slide off the relevant retaining clip and withdraw the injector from the fuel rail. Remove the upper sealing ring from the injector and discard it; all disturbed sealing rings must be renewed.

28 Refitting is a reversal of the removal procedure, noting the following points.

a) *Renew all disturbed sealing rings and apply a smear of engine oil to them to aid installation.*

b) *Ease the injector(s) into the fuel rail, ensuring that the sealing ring(s) remain correctly seated, and secure in position with the retaining clips.*

c) *On refitting the fuel rail, take care not to damage the injectors and ensure that all sealing rings remain in position. Once the fuel rail is correctly seated, securely tighten its retaining bolts.*

d) *Adjust the accelerator cable as described in Section 3.*

e) *On completion start the engine and check for fuel leaks.*

2.4 litre engine

29 Depressurise the fuel system as described in Section 7.

30 Slacken the union nut and disconnect the fuel feed pipe from the fuel rail. As the nut is slackened, retain the adaptor with an open-ended spanner to prevent and excess strain being placed on the fuel rail.

31 Slacken and remove the union bolt securing the fuel return pipe to the fuel rail and recover the sealing washer from each side of the union. Discard the washers, new ones must be used on refitting.

32 Disconnect the vacuum hose from the fuel pressure regulator.

33 Slacken and remove the retaining bolts then carefully ease the fuel rail and injector assembly out of position and remove it from

the manifold. Remove the lower sealing rings from the injectors and discard them; they must be renewed whenever they are disturbed.

34 Slide off the relevant retaining clip and withdraw the injector from the fuel rail. Remove the upper sealing ring from the injector and discard it; all disturbed sealing rings must be renewed.

35 Refitting is a reversal of the removal procedure, noting the following points.

a) *Renew all disturbed sealing rings and apply a smear of engine oil to them to aid installation.*

b) *Ease the injector(s) into the fuel rail, ensuring that the sealing ring(s) remain correctly seated, and secure in position with the retaining clips.*

c) *On refitting the fuel rail, take care not to damage the injectors and ensure that all sealing rings remain in position. Once the fuel rail is correctly seated, securely tighten its retaining bolts.*

d) *Position a new sealing washer on each side of the fuel return hose union and securely tighten the unions bolt.*

e) *On completion start the engine and check for fuel leaks.*

Fuel pressure regulator

Warning: Refer to the warning note in Section 1 before proceeding.

Pre 1995 2.0 litre engines (C20NE)

36 Disconnect the battery negative terminal then disconnect the vacuum hose from the fuel pressure regulator.

37 Referring to Section 7, slacken the retaining clips then free the regulator from the fuel hoses and remove it from the engine.

38 On refitting ensure the hoses are correctly and securely reconnected.

1995 on 2.0 litre engines (X20SE) and all 2.2 litre engines

39 Disconnect the battery negative terminal then depressurise the fuel system as described in Section 7.

40 Disconnect the vacuum hose from the pressure regulator then slacken and remove the regulator retaining clamp. Ease the regulator out of position and remove it from the fuel rail, noting the correct fitted locations of the sealing rings. Renew the sealing rings if they show signs of damage.

41 On refitting ensure the sealing rings are correctly located then ease the regulator into position, making sure the vacuum union is correctly positioned. Refit the retaining clamp, tightening it securely, and reconnect the vacuum hose.

2.4 litre engines

42 Depressurise the fuel system as described in Section 7 then disconnect the battery negative terminal.

43 Disconnect the vacuum hose from the regulator.

13.49 Disconnect the wiring connector . . .

13.50 . . . then undo the retaining screws (arrowed) and remove the idle speed adjuster - 2.0 litre engine (X20SE)

13.54a On 2.0 litre (C20NE) and 2.4 litre engines, slacken and remove the outer retaining bolt . . .

44 Undo the retaining screws and remove the regulator from the fuel rail, noting the correct fitted location of the sealing rings. Renew the sealing rings if they show signs of damage.

45 On refitting ensure the sealing rings are correctly located then refit the regulator to the fuel rail and securely tighten its retaining screws.

Idle speed adjuster

Pre 1995 2.0 litre engines (C20NE) and all 2.4 litre engines

46 Ensure the ignition is switched off then disconnect the wiring connector from the idle speed adjuster, which is located above the injectors.

47 Slacken the retaining clips then disconnect the adjuster from its hoses and remove it from the engine.

48 On refitting, ensure the hoses and wiring connector are securely reconnected.

1995 on 2.0 litre engines (X20SE) and all 2.2 litre engines

49 Ensure the ignition is switched off then disconnect the wiring connector from the idle speed adjuster which is mounted onto the side of the throttle housing (see illustration). On 2.2 litre engines to improve access to the adjuster, remove the intake duct as described in paragraphs 18 and 19.

50 Slacken and remove the retaining bolts then remove the adjuster from the throttle housing (see illustration). Discard the gasket, a new one must be used on refitting.

51 On refitting, ensure the mating surfaces are clean and dry and use a new gasket. Securely tighten the retaining bolts then reconnect the wiring connector. On 2.2 litre, if necessary, refit the intake duct.

Airflow meter

Pre 1995 2.0 litre engines (C20NE) and all 2.4 litre engines

52 Ensure the ignition is switched off then disconnect the wiring connector from the airflow meter which is mounted on the air cleaner housing.

53 Slacken the retaining clip and disconnect the intake duct from the air cleaner housing. Unclip the housing lid and it from the engine compartment.

54 Slacken and remove the meter retaining bolts and plates from inside the lid and the single bolt from outside then separate the meter and lid (see illustrations). Recover the seal from the meter; the seal must be renewed if it shows signs of damage or deterioration.

55 Refitting is the reverse of removal ensuring the seal remains correctly seated. Apply thread locking compound to all the retaining bolts and tighten them securely.

1995 on 2.0 litre engines (X20SE) and all 2.2 litre engines

56 Ensure the ignition is switched off then disconnect the wiring connector from the airflow meter which is mounted on the air cleaner housing (see illustration).

57 Slacken the retaining clip and disconnect the intake duct then undo the retaining bolts and remove the airflow meter from the air cleaner housing lid. Recover the sealing ring from the meter; the seal must be renewed if it shows signs of damage or deterioration.

58 Refitting is the reverse of removal ensuring the sealing ring is correctly seated.

Throttle potentiometer

59 Ensure the ignition is switched off then disconnect the wiring connector from the throttle potentiometer (see illustration).

60 Undo the retaining screws and remove the potentiometer from the side of the housing.

61 On refitting, make sure the potentiometer is correctly engaged with the throttle valve spindle and securely tighten its retaining screws.

Coolant temperature sensor

62 Refer to Chapter 3 for removal and refitting details.

4A

13.54b . . . and the inner bolts and retaining plates, then separate the airflow meter from the housing lid

13.56 Disconnecting the airflow meter wiring connector - 2.0 litre engine (X20SE)

13.59 Disconnecting the throttle potentiometer wiring connector - 2.0 litre engine (X20SE)

Crankshaft sensor

2.0 litre engine

63 The crankshaft sensor is located on the front, left-hand side of the cylinder block. To enable access to the sensor to be gained from below, undo the retaining bolts and remove the undercover from beneath the engine.

64 Ensure the ignition is switched off then trace the wiring back from the sensor to its connector. Free the wiring from all the relevant clips then disconnect the connector.

65 Remove all traces of dirt from around the sensor then unscrew the retaining bolt and remove the sensor from the engine. Remove the sealing ring from the sensor and discard it; a new one should be used on refitting.

66 Refitting is the reverse of removal using a new sealing ring. Ensure the sensor wiring is correctly routed and retained by all the necessary clips.

2.2 litre engine

67 The crankshaft sensor is located on the front, left-hand side of the cylinder block. To enable access to the sensor to be gained from below, undo the retaining bolts and remove the undercover from beneath the engine.

68 Slacken the retaining clips and disconnect the breather hoses from the right-hand side of the camshaft cover.

69 Ensure the ignition is switched off. Lift the front end of the injector harness wiring cover then release the retaining clip and disconnect the crankshaft sensor wiring connector from the underside of the cover. If necessary, to improve access disconnect the cover from the injectors (see paragraph 25).

70 Free the wiring from all the relevant clips and remove all traces of dirt from around the sensor.

71 Unscrew the retaining bolt and remove the sensor from the engine. Remove the sealing ring from the sensor and discard it; a new one should be used on refitting.

72 Refitting is the reverse of removal using a new sealing ring. Ensure the sensor wiring is correctly routed and retained by all the necessary clips.

2.4 litre engine

73 The crankshaft sensor is mounted onto

13.82 Disconnecting the intake air temperature wiring connector - 2.0 litre engine (X20SE)

the base of timing chain cover. To enable access to the sensor to be gained from below, undo the retaining bolts and remove the undercover from beneath the engine.

74 Trace the wiring back from the sensor, freeing it from all clips, to its connector which is located near the throttle housing. Disconnect the wiring connector so that the wiring is free to be removed with the sensor.

75 Unscrew the retaining bolt and remove the sensor from the engine.

76 Refitting is the reverse of removal, ensuring the sensor tip is clean and the wiring is correctly routed and retained by all the necessary clips.

Electronic control unit (ECU)

77 The ECU is located behind the driver's side footwell trim panel, except on some early models where it can be found behind the passenger side footwell trim panel.

78 Disconnect the battery negative terminal then remove the fasteners and unclip the footwell side trim panel from the body.

79 Undo the retaining nuts and free the ECU from the body then release the retaining clip and disconnect the wiring connector. Remove the ECU from the vehicle.

80 Refitting is the reverse of removal ensuring the wiring connector is securely reconnected.

Intake air temperature sensor

1995 on 2.0 litre engines (X20SE) and all 2.2 litre engines

81 The intake air temperature sensor is mounted in the intake duct which connects the air cleaner housing to the inlet manifold.

82 Ensure the ignition is switched off, then disconnect the wiring connector from the sensor **(see illustration)**.

83 Carefully ease the sensor out of position taking care not to damage the intake duct. If the intake duct shows signs of damage or deterioration it should be renewed.

84 Refitting is the reverse of removal ensuring the sensor is correctly located in the duct.

Knock sensor

1995 on 2.0 litre engines (X20SE) and all 2.2 litre engines

85 The knock sensor is mounted onto the right-hand side of the cylinder block where it is situated between No 2 and 3 cylinders.

86 Ensure the ignition is switched off then release the retaining and disconnect the wiring connector from the sensor. On models where the wiring is an integral part of the sensor trace the wiring back to its connector, freeing it from its retaining clips, and disconnect the connector so that the wiring is free to be removed with the sensor. **Note:** On 2.2 litre engines the connector is connected to the underside of the injector wiring harness cover, between No 3 and 4 injectors. If necessary, to improve access to the

connector unclip the cover from injectors (see paragraph 25).

87 Slacken and remove the retaining bolt and remove the sensor from the engine.

88 On refitting ensure the mating surfaces are clean and dry then fit the sensor and tighten its retaining bolt to the specified torque. Ensure the wiring is correctly routed and securely reconnected.

Camshaft sensor

2.2 litre engine

89 Undo the retaining screws and remove the spark plug cover from the top of the cylinder head cover.

90 Ensure the ignition is switched off then disconnect the wiring connector from the camshaft sensor.

91 Remove the timing belt outer cover as described in Chapter 2B.

92 Unscrew the retaining bolt and remove the camshaft sensor from the top of the cylinder head.

93 Refitting is the reverse of removal tightening the sensor retaining bolt to the specified torque.

---

14 Inlet manifold - removal and refitting

⚠️ **Warning: Refer to the warning note in Section 1 before proceeding.**

Pre 1995 2.0 litre engines (C20NE)

Removal

1 Disconnect the battery negative terminal.

2 Remove the auxiliary drivebelt then drain the cooling system as described in Chapter 1A.

3 Slacken the retaining clips and disconnect the intake duct from the throttle housing.

4 Disconnect the wiring connector from the idle speed adjuster. Slacken the retaining clips securing the adjuster hoses to the manifold and throttle housing then remove the adjuster, complete with hoses.

5 Unclip the accelerator cable from the throttle cam then free the outer cable from its mounting bracket, taking care not to lose the adjusting clip.

6 Unscrew the union nut and disconnect the braking system servo unit vacuum hose from the manifold.

7 Make a note of the correct fitted location of each hose then slacken the retaining clips (where fitted) and disconnect all the vacuum, breather and coolant hoses from the throttle housing and manifold.

8 Disconnect the wiring connectors from the throttle potentiometer and the injectors and position the wiring clear of the manifold.

9 Referring to Section 7, slacken the retaining clips and disconnect the fuel feed and return

hoses from the fuel rail. Plug the hose ends to minimise fuel loss.

10 Slacken and remove the bolt securing the alternator upper mounting bracket to the inlet manifold.

11 Check that all the necessary vacuum/breather hoses have been disconnected then slacken and remove the manifold retaining nuts.

12 Remove the manifold from the engine and recover the manifold gasket, noting which way around it is fitted.

Refitting

13 Refitting is the reverse of removal bearing in mind the following points.
a) *Prior to refitting, check the manifold studs and renew any that are worn or damaged.*
b) *Ensure the manifold and cylinder mating surfaces are clean and dry and fit the new gasket. Refit the manifold and tighten the retaining nuts evenly and progressively to the specified torque.*
c) *Ensure that all relevant hoses are reconnected to their original positions, and are securely held (where necessary) by their retaining clips.*
d) *Refit the auxiliary drivebelt and refill the cooling system as described in Chapter 1A.*
e) *On completion, adjust the accelerator cable as described in Section 3.*

1995 on 2.0 litre engines (X20SE)

Removal

14 Disconnect the battery negative terminal then depressurise the fuel system as described in Section 7. To improve access, undo the retaining bolts and free the wiring harness tray from the camshaft housing cover.

15 Remove the auxiliary drivebelt then drain the cooling system as described in Chapter 1A.

16 Disconnect the wiring connectors from the airflow meter and intake air temperature sensor then unclip the wiring harness from the intake duct.

17 Slacken the retaining clips securing the intake duct to the airflow meter and throttle housing, and remove the duct from the engine compartment.

18 Unclip the accelerator cable from the throttle cam then free the outer cable from its mounting bracket, taking care not to lose the adjusting clip.

19 Unscrew the union nut and disconnect the braking system servo unit vacuum hose from the manifold.

20 Disconnect the wiring connectors from the throttle potentiometer, idle speed adjuster, exhaust gas recirculation (EGR) valve and the evaporative emission system purge valve. Also disconnect the wiring connectors from the injectors and ignition system DIS module then unbolt the earth lead from the front of the camshaft housing and position all wiring clear of the inlet manifold.

21 Slacken and remove the union bolts securing the fuel feed and return hoses to either end of the fuel rail. Disconnect both hoses and discard the sealing washers; new ones must be used on refitting. Note that the union bolts are different and should not be interchanged.

22 Make a note of the correct fitted location of each hose then slacken the retaining clips (where fitted) and disconnect all the vacuum, breather and coolant hoses from the throttle housing, manifold and associated components.

23 Unbolt the alternator upper mounting brackets and remove them from the engine.

24 Undo the retaining bolts and remove the support bracket from the underside of the manifold.

25 Check that all the necessary vacuum/breather hoses have been disconnected then slacken and remove the manifold retaining nuts.

26 Remove the manifold from the engine and recover the manifold gasket, noting which way around it is fitted. **Note:** *In order to gain the clearance required to remove the manifold, it may be necessary to unbolt the power steering pump (there is no need to disconnect the hydraulic lines from the pump) in order to allow the component to be pivoted away sufficiently (see Chapter 11).*

Refitting

27 Refitting is the reverse of removal bearing in mind the following points.
a) *Prior to refitting, check the manifold studs and renew any that are worn or damaged.*
b) *Ensure the manifold and cylinder mating surfaces are clean and dry and fit the new gasket. Refit the manifold and tighten the retaining nuts evenly and progressively to the specified torque.*
c) *Ensure that all relevant hoses are reconnected to their original positions, and are securely held (where necessary) by their retaining clips.*
d) *Position a new sealing washer on each side of the fuel hose unions and securely tighten the unions bolts.*
e) *Refit the auxiliary drivebelt and refill the cooling system as described in Chapter 1A.*
f) *On completion, adjust the accelerator cable as described in Section 3.*

2.2 litre engines

Removal

28 Disconnect the battery negative terminal then depressurise the fuel system as described in Section 7.

29 Remove the auxiliary drivebelt then drain the cooling system as described in Chapter 1A.

30 Disconnect the wiring connectors from the airflow meter and intake air temperature sensor then unclip the wiring harness from the intake duct.

31 Slacken the retaining clips securing the intake duct to the airflow meter and throttle

housing, and remove the duct from the engine compartment.

32 Unclip the accelerator cable from the throttle cam then free the outer cable from its mounting bracket, taking care not to lose the adjusting clip.

33 Unscrew the union nut and disconnect the braking system servo unit vacuum hose from the manifold.

34 Disconnect the wiring connectors from the throttle potentiometer and the idle speed adjuster. Unscrew the retaining nut and free the earth lead from the fuel rail.

35 Slacken the retaining clips and disconnect the breather hoses from the camshaft cover.

36 Release the retaining clips securing the wiring connectors to injectors No 1 and 4 then lift the wiring cover squarely away from the top of the injectors; the wiring connectors are an integral part of the cover. Disconnect the knock sensor wiring connector (situated between No 3 and 4 injectors) and position the wiring cover clear of the manifold.

37 Slacken the union nuts and disconnect the fuel feed and return pipes from the fuel rail. As the union nuts are slackened, retain the adapters with an open-ended spanner to prevent any excess strain being placed on the fuel rail. Slacken and remove the fuel pipe clamp retaining bolt then remove the clamp and position both hoses clear of the manifold.

38 Make a note of the correct fitted location of each hose then slacken the retaining clips (where fitted) and disconnect all the vacuum, breather and coolant hoses from the throttle housing, manifold and associated components.

39 Unbolt the alternator upper mounting brackets and remove them from the engine.

40 Undo the retaining bolts and remove the support bracket from the underside of the manifold.

41 Check that all the necessary vacuum/breather hoses have been disconnected then slacken and remove the manifold retaining nuts and bolts.

42 Remove the manifold from the engine and recover the manifold gasket, noting which way around it is fitted. **Note:** *In order to gain the clearance required to remove the manifold, it maybe necessary to unbolt the power steering pump (there is no need to disconnect the hydraulic lines from the pump) in order to allow the component to be pivoted away sufficiently (see Chapter 11).*

Refitting

43 Refitting is the reverse of removal bearing in mind the following points.
a) *Prior to refitting, check the manifold studs and renew any that are worn or damaged.*
b) *Ensure the manifold and cylinder mating surfaces are clean and dry and fit the new gasket. Refit the manifold and tighten the retaining nuts and bolts evenly and progressively to the specified torque.*
c) *Ensure that all relevant hoses are reconnected to their original positions,*

4A

and are securely held (where necessary) by their retaining clips.

d) *Refit the auxiliary drivebelt and refill the cooling system as described in Chapter 1A.*

e) *On completion, adjust the accelerator cable as described in Section 3.*

2.4 litre engines

Note: *The inlet and exhaust manifolds share the same gasket and are retained by the same bolts. Therefore both manifolds will need to be removed to allow the gasket to renewed.*

Removal

44 Disconnect the battery negative terminal then depressurise the fuel system as described in Section 7.

45 Slacken the retaining clips and remove the intake duct connecting the air cleaner to the throttle housing.

46 Trace the wiring back from the oxygen sensor, which is screwed into the exhaust manifold, freeing it from all the relevant clips. Disconnect the wiring connector so the sensor is free to be removed with the manifold.

47 Unscrew the retaining bolts securing the exhaust front pipe to the manifold. Recover the gasket and discard it; a new one should be used on refitting.

48 Disconnect the wiring connector from the idle speed adjuster. Slacken the retaining clips securing the adjuster hoses to the manifold and throttle housing then remove the adjuster, complete with hoses.

49 Unclip the accelerator cable from the throttle cam then free the outer cable from its mounting bracket, taking care not to lose the adjusting clip.

50 Unscrew the union nut and disconnect the braking system servo unit vacuum hose from the manifold.

51 Make a note of the correct fitted location of each hose then slacken the retaining clips (where fitted) and disconnect all the vacuum, breather and coolant hoses from the throttle housing and manifold. Clamp/plug the coolant hoses to minimise coolant loss and wash off any spilt coolant with cold water.

52 Disconnect the wiring connectors from the throttle potentiometer and the injectors and position the wiring clear of the manifold.

53 Locate the fuel feed and return hoses at their unions to the fuel rail pipes. Make alignment marks between the pipes and hoses, to avoid confusion on refitting, then slacken the retaining clips and disconnect both hoses. Plug the hose ends to minimise fuel loss.

54 Undo the retaining bolts and remove the support bracket from the underside of the inlet manifold.

55 Unscrew the retaining bolts and remove the heatshield from in between the manifolds.

56 Check that all the necessary vacuum/breather hoses have been disconnected then

slacken and remove the manifold retaining bolts.

57 Remove both manifolds from the engine and recover the manifold gasket, noting which way around it is fitted.

Refitting

58 Refitting is the reverse of removal bearing in mind the following points.

a) *Remove all traces of locking compound from the manifold bolt threads. Apply a drop of fresh locking compound (Vauxhall recommend the use of 1510177 - part no 90167347 - available from your Vauxhall dealer) to the threads of each bolt prior to refitting.*

b) *Ensure the manifold and cylinder mating surfaces are clean and dry and fit the new gasket. Refit the manifolds and tighten the retaining bolts evenly and progressively to the specified torque.*

c) *Ensure that all relevant hoses are reconnected to their original positions, and are securely held (where necessary) by their retaining clips.*

d) *On completion, adjust the accelerator cable as described in Section 3.*

15 Exhaust manifold - removal and refitting

2.0 litre engines

Note: *New manifold retaining nuts are required on refitting.*

Removal

1 Disconnect the battery negative terminal. To improve access, undo the retaining bolts and remove the undercover from beneath the engine unit.

2 Trace the wiring back from the oxygen sensor, freeing it from all the relevant clips, and disconnect it at the connector.

3 Unbolt the exhaust front pipe from manifold and remove the gasket. Discard the gasket, a new one must be used on refitting.

4 On 1995 on engines (X20SE), remove the engine oil dipstick and pull the plug caps off from the centre (No 2 and 3) spark plugs. Unscrew the centre spark plug heatshields and remove them from the manifold (a special socket, number KM-834, is available to ease removal of the heatshields).

5 On all engines, undo the retaining screws and remove the heatshield from the manifold.

6 Undo the retaining nuts securing the manifold to the head. Manoeuvre the manifold out of the engine compartment, complete with the gasket. Discard the retaining nuts and gasket, new ones must be used on refitting.

Refitting

7 Examine all the exhaust manifold studs for signs of damage and corrosion; remove all traces of corrosion, and repair or renew any damaged studs.

8 Ensure that the manifold and cylinder head sealing faces are clean and flat, and fit the new gasket.

9 Refit the manifold then fit the new retaining nuts and tighten them to the specified torque.

10 On 1995 on engines (X20SE), apply a smear of high-temperature grease (Vauxhall recommend the use of Molycote paste 1948525 - part no 90513211 - available from your Vauxhall dealer) to the threads of the spark plug heatshields then refit the shields and tighten them to the specified torque. Reconnect the plug caps and refit the dipstick.

11 On all engines, refit the heatshield to the manifold and securely tighten its retaining bolts.

12 Ensure the mating surfaces are clean then fit a new gasket to the exhaust front pipe joint. Refit the front pipe-to-manifold bolts and tighten them to the specified torque.

13 Reconnect the oxygen sensor wiring connector making sure the wiring is correctly routed and retained by all the necessary clips. Refit the undercover and reconnect the battery.

2.2 litre engine

14 Carry out the operations described in paragraphs 1 to 3 of this Section.

15 Remove the secondary air system non-return valve and metal pipe as described in Chapter 4C.

16 Slacken the retaining clip securing the crankcase ventilation hose to the rear of the cylinder head cover then undo the retaining bolts securing the ventilation pipe to the cylinder block. Remove the pipe and hose assembly from the engine and discard its gasket; a new gasket will be needed on refitting.

17 Undo the retaining nuts securing the manifold to the head. Manoeuvre the manifold out of the engine compartment, complete with the gasket. Discard the retaining nuts and gasket, new ones must be used on refitting.

Refitting

18 Examine all the exhaust manifold studs for signs of damage and corrosion; remove all traces of corrosion, and repair or renew any damaged studs.

19 Ensure that the manifold and cylinder head sealing faces are clean and flat, and fit the new gasket.

20 Refit the manifold then fit the new retaining nuts and tighten them to the specified torque.

21 Ensure the mating surfaces of the crankcase ventilation tube and block are clean and dry and fit a new gasket. Refit the ventilation tube and hose to the engine, tighten its retaining bolts and clip securely.

22 Refit the secondary air system metal pipe and valve as described in Chapter 4C.

23 Reconnect the front pipe to the manifold as described in paragraphs 12 and 13.

2.4 litre engine

24 Both the exhaust manifold and inlet manifold share the same retaining bolts and gasket and must therefore both be removed/refitted together. See Section 14 for removal and refitting details.

16 Exhaust system - general information, removal and refitting

General information

1 On pre 1995 2.0 litre engines (C20NE) and all 2.4 litre engines, the exhaust system consists of four sections: the front pipe, the catalytic converter, the intermediate pipe and silencer, and the tailpipe. On later 1995 on 2.0 litre engines (X20SE) and all 2.2 litre engines, the exhaust system is split into three sections; the system is similar to that described above except that the catalytic converter is incorporated into the front pipe assembly. The system is suspended throughout its entire length by rubber mountings.

Removal

2 Each exhaust section can be removed individually as follows. To improve access, first jack up the front or rear of the car and support it securely on axle stands. Alternatively, position the car over an inspection pit or on car ramps.

Front pipe - pre 1995 2.0 litre engines (C20NE) and all 2.4 litre engines

3 Undo the retaining bolts and remove the undercover from beneath the engine unit.
4 Trace the wiring back from the oxygen sensor, noting its correct routing, and disconnect its wiring connector. Free the wiring from any clips so the sensor is free to be removed with the front pipe.
5 Slacken and remove the nuts securing the front pipe flange joint to the catalytic converter.

6 Unscrew the retaining nut then unhook the retaining clamp from the front pipe support bracket which is located just in front of the catalytic converter joint.
7 Undo the bolts securing the front pipe to the manifold and remove the pipe from underneath the vehicle. Recover the gasket from the pipe-to-manifold joint.

Front pipe and catalytic converter - 1995 on 2.0 litre engines (X20SE) and all 2.2 litre engines

8 Carry out the operations described in paragraphs 3 and 4.
9 Slacken and remove the bolts and springs securing the front pipe joint to the intermediate pipe.
10 Unscrew the retaining nut then unhook the retaining clamp from the front pipe support bracket which is located just in front of the intermediate pipe joint.
11 Undo the bolts securing the front pipe to the manifold and remove the pipe from underneath the vehicle. Recover the gaskets from the pipe joints.

Catalytic converter - pre 1995 2.0 litre engines (C20NE) and all 2.4 litre engines

12 Unscrew the nuts securing the catalytic converter to the front pipe and intermediate pipe.
13 Separate the flange joints and remove the catalytic converter from the vehicle. Recover the gasket from the intermediate pipe joint.

Intermediate pipe - pre 1995 2.0 litre engines (C20NE) and all 2.4 litre engines

14 Slacken and remove the nuts securing the intermediate pipe to the catalytic converter.
15 Slacken the clamping ring then free the intermediate pipe from the converter and tailpipe and remove it from underneath the vehicle. Recover the gasket from the catalytic converter joint.

Intermediate pipe - 1995 on 2.0 litre engines (X20SE) and all 2.2 litre engines

16 Slacken and remove the bolts and springs securing the front pipe to the intermediate pipe.
17 Unscrew the nuts securing the tailpipe to the intermediate pipe.
18 Slacken and remove the nuts and washers securing the intermediate pipe silencer to its mounting rubber.
19 Free the intermediate pipe from its mounting and joints and remove it from underneath the vehicle. Recover the gaskets from the pipe joints.

Intermediate pipe - pre 1995 2.0 litre engines (C20NE) and all 2.4 litre engines

20 Slacken the clamping ring securing the tailpipe to the intermediate pipe then free it from its mounting rubbers and remove it from underneath the vehicle.

Tailpipe - 1995 on 2.0 litre engines (X20SE) and all 2.2 litre engines

21 Unscrew the nuts securing the tailpipe to the intermediate pipe.
22 Unhook the tailpipe from its mounting rubbers and remove it from underneath the vehicle. Recover the gasket from the joint.

Refitting

23 Each section is refitted by reversing the removal sequence, noting the following points:
a) Ensure that all traces of corrosion have been removed from the flanges and renew all necessary gaskets.
b) Inspect the rubber mountings for signs of damage or deterioration, and renew as necessary.
c) Where no gasket is fitted to a joint, apply a smear of exhaust system jointing paste to ensure a gas-tight seal.
d) Prior to tightening the exhaust system fasteners, ensure that all rubber mountings are correctly located, and that there is adequate clearance between the exhaust system and vehicle underbody.

4A

Notes

Chapter 4 Part B
Fuel and exhaust systems - diesel engine models

Contents

Accelerator cable - removal, refitting and adjustment 5
Accelerator pedal - removal and refitting 6
Air cleaner assembly and intake ducts - removal and refitting 2
Air cleaner element renewal .See Chapter 1B
Electronic Diesel Control (EDC) components
  (2.5 litre models) - removal and refitting 8
Exhaust manifold - removal and refitting 16
Exhaust system - general information and component renewal 20
Fuel filter renewal . . . . .See Chapter 1B
Fuel filter water draining . . . . .See Chapter 1B
Fuel gauge sender unit - removal and refitting 3
Fuel injection pump - removal and refitting 11
Fuel injectors - removal and refitting 14

Fuel lift pump (2.3 litre models) - removal and refitting 10
Fuel system - priming and bleeding 7
Fuel tank - removal and refitting 4
General information 1
Idle speed and exhaust emission check . . . . .See Chapter 1B
Injection timing - checking and adjustment 13
Injection timing - general 12
Inlet manifold - removal and refitting 15
Intercooler - removal and refitting 19
Quick Warm-up System components (2.8 litre models) -
  removal and refitting 9
Turbocharger - description and precautions 17
Turbocharger - removal and refitting 18

Degrees of difficulty

Easy, suitable for novice with little experience		Fairly easy, suitable for beginner with some experience		Fairly difficult, suitable for competent DIY mechanic		Difficult, suitable for experienced DIY mechanic		Very difficult, suitable for expert DIY or professional	

Specifications

General
System type:

2.3 litre models	Indirect injection system with distributor fuel injection pump, fuel lift pump, turbocharger, intercooler, exhaust gas recirculation system and catalytic converter on later models.
2.5 litre models	Indirect injection system incorporating electronically controlled fuel injection pump, turbocharger, intercooler, exhaust gas recirculation system and catalytic converter.
2.8 litre models	Direct injection system with distributor fuel injection pump, turbocharger, intercooler, exhaust gas recirculation system and catalytic converter.

Adjustment data
Idle speed:

2.3 litre models:	
With air conditioning	770 to 800 rpm
Without air conditioning	720 to 740 rpm
2.5 litre models	750 to 800 rpm (controlled by ECU)
2.8 litre models	700 to 800 rpm
Maximum speed:	
2.3 litre models	4900 to 5000 rpm
2.5 litre models	Controlled by ECU
2.8 litre models	4500 to 4700 rpm

Injection pump

Pump timing (static):

  2.3 litre models:

    Engine position . . . . No 1 piston at TDC (see Section 13)

    Pump timing measurement . . . . 0.85 ± 0.05 mm

  2.5 litre models:

    Engine position . . . . No 1 piston at TDC (see Section 13)

    Pump timing measurement . . . . 0.65 mm

  2.8 litre models:

    Engine position . . . . No 1 piston at 12° BTDC (see Section 13)

    Pump timing measurement . . . . 0.5 mm

Injectors

Opening pressure;

  2.3 litre models . . . . 135 to 143 bars

  2.5 litre models . . . . 150 to 158 bars

  2.8 litre models . . . . 181 bars

Recommended fuel

All engines . . . . Commercial diesel fuel for road vehicles (DERV)

Torque wrench settings

	Nm	lbf ft
2.3 litre models		
Fuel injectors to cylinder head	70	52
Fuel pipe union nuts	25	18
Inlet/exhaust manifold bolts:		
M8 hexagon-head bolts	25	18
M8 12-point socket-head bolts	20	15
Turbocharger to exhaust manifold:		
Stage 1	45	33
Stage 2	Angle-tighten a further 30°	
2.5 litre models		
Air mass meter to air cleaner	7	5
Alternator mounting bracket bolts	83	61
Crankshaft sensor retaining bolt	3	2
EGR air pipe union nut	69	51
Electronic control unit mounting bracket bolts	10	7
Exhaust front pipe to turbocharger	67	49
Exhaust manifold heatshield bolts	11	8
Exhaust manifold to cylinder head	32	24
Fuel injection pump drive gear nut	88	65
Fuel injection pump mounting nuts	27	20
Fuel injection pump overflow valve	22	16
Fuel injector to cylinder head	69	51
Fuel pipe union nuts	23	17
Heater pipe-to-support stud nut	20	15
Inlet manifold to cylinder head	32	24
Intake elbow to inlet manifold	11	8
Oil feed pipe to turbocharger	27	20
Turbocharger heatshield bolts	22	16
Turbocharger to exhaust manifold	32	24
2.8 litre models		
EGR air pipe nuts	24	18
Exhaust front pipe to turbocharger	67	49
Exhaust manifold to cylinder head	26	19
Fuel injector clamp bolt	37	27
Fuel pipe union nuts	29	21
Inlet manifold to cylinder head	26	19
Oil feed pipe to cylinder block	29	21
Oil feed pipe to turbocharger	22	16
Plenum chamber to cylinder head cover	13	10
Turbocharger coolant pipe unions	39	29
Turbocharger oil return pipe bolts	8	6
Turbocharger to exhaust manifold	26	19

1 General information

⚠️ **Warning:** *It is necessary to take certain precautions when working on the fuel system components, particularly the fuel injectors. Before carrying out any operations on the fuel system, refer to the precautions given in Safety first! at the beginning of this manual, and to any additional warning notes at the start of the relevant Sections.*

Caution: *Do not operate the engine if any of the air intake ducts are disconnected or the filter element removed. Any debris entering the engine will cause severe damage to the turbocharger.*

Caution: *To prevent damage to the turbocharger, do not race the engine immediately after start-up, especially if it is cold. Allow it to idle smoothly to give the oil a few seconds to circulate around the turbocharger bearings. Always allow the engine to return to idle speed before switching it off - do not blip the throttle and switch off, as this will leave the turbo spinning without lubrication.*

Caution: *Observe the recommended intervals for oil and filter changing, and use a reputable oil of the specified quality. Neglect of oil changing, or use of inferior oil, can cause carbon formation on the turbo shaft, leading to subsequent failure.*

2.3 litre models

1 The fuel system consists of a rear-mounted fuel tank, a fuel filter with integral water separator, a fuel injection pump, injectors, turbocharger, intercooler and associated components. Before passing through the filter, the fuel is heated by an electric heating element which is fitted to the filter housing. The exhaust system is conventional, but incorporates an exhaust gas recirculation (EGR) system and, on later models, an unregulated catalytic converter to reduce exhaust gas emissions (see Chapter 4C for further details).

2 Fuel is drawn from the fuel tank to the fuel injection pump by a mechanical fuel pump mounted on the front of the engine. Before reaching the pump the fuel passes through a fuel filter where foreign matter and water are removed. Excess fuel lubricates the moving components of the injection pump and is then returned to the tank.

3 The fuel injection pump is gear-driven by a driveshaft which meshes with a gear on the front of the crankshaft. The high pressure required to inject the fuel into the compressed air in the swirl chambers is achieved by a cam plate acting on a single piston. The fuel passes through a central rotor with a single outlet drilling which aligns with ports leading to the injector pipes.

4 Fuel metering is controlled by a centrifugal governor which reacts to accelerator pedal position and engine speed. The governor is linked to a metering valve which increases or decreases the amount of fuel delivered at each pumping stroke.

5 Basic injection timing is determined when the pump is fitted. When the engine is running it is varied automatically to suit the prevailing engine speed by a mechanism which turns the cam plate or ring.

6 The four fuel injectors produce a spray of fuel into the swirl chambers located in the cylinder head. The injectors are calibrated to open and close at critical pressures to provide efficient and even combustion. Each injector needle is lubricated by fuel which accumulates in the spring chamber and is channelled to the injection pump return hose by leak-off pipes.

7 Cold starting is assisted by pre-heater or 'glow' plugs fitted to each swirl chamber (see Chapter 5C for further details).

8 A stop solenoid cuts the fuel supply to the injection pump rotor when the ignition is switched off, and there is also a hand-operated stop lever for use in an emergency.

9 Provided that the specified maintenance is carried out, the fuel injection equipment will give long and trouble-free service. The injection pump itself may well outlast the engine. The main potential cause of damage to the injection pump and injectors is dirt or water in the fuel.

10 Servicing of the injection pump and injectors is very limited for the home mechanic, and any dismantling or adjustment other than that described in this Chapter must be entrusted to a Vauxhall dealer or fuel injection specialist.

2.5 litre models

11 The fuel system consists of a rear-mounted fuel tank, a fuel filter with integral water separator, a fuel injection pump, injectors, turbocharger, intercooler and associated components. Before passing through the filter, the fuel is heated by an electric heating element which is fitted to the filter housing. The exhaust system is conventional, but incorporates an exhaust gas recirculation (EGR) system and an unregulated catalytic converter to reduce exhaust gas emissions (see Chapter 4C for further details).

12 Fuel is drawn from the fuel tank by the fuel injection pump. Before reaching the pump the fuel passes through a fuel filter where foreign matter and water are removed. Excess fuel lubricates the moving components of the injection pump and is then returned to the tank.

13 The fuel injection pump is driven by the crankshaft via a series of timing gears. The high pressure required to inject the fuel into the compressed air in the swirl chambers is achieved by a radial piston pump.

14 The injection pump is electronically controlled to meet the latest emission standards. The Electronic Diesel Control (EDC) system consists of the injectors, injection pump electronic control unit (ECU) and the following sensors.

a) *Accelerator pedal position sensor - informs the ECU of accelerator pedal position.*

b) *Coolant temperature sensor - informs the ECU of engine temperature.*

c) *Air mass meter - informs the ECU of the amount of air passing through the intake duct.*

d) *Crankshaft sensor - informs the ECU of engine speed and crankshaft position.*

e) *Needle movement sensor - informs the ECU of the fuel injector needle position and the start of injection.*

15 Information on fuel temperature and injection pump control valve position are provided by sensors which are an integral part of the injection pump. Additional information is also sent to the ECU by the control units associated with the ABS, air conditioning and anti-theft systems, where fitted.

16 All the above information is analysed by the ECU and, based on this, the ECU determines the appropriate injection requirements for the engine. The ECU controls the injection pump timing to provide the best setting for cranking, starting (with either a hot or cold engine), warm-up, idle, cruising and acceleration.

17 The ECU also controls the turbocharger boost pressure wastegate, the exhaust gas recirculation (EGR) system (see Chapter 4C) and the pre-heating system (see Chapter 5C).

18 The four fuel injectors produce a spray of fuel directly into the cylinders. The injectors are calibrated to open and close at critical pressures to provide efficient and even combustion. Each injector needle is lubricated by fuel which accumulates in the spring chamber and is channelled to the injection pump return hose by leak-off pipes.

19 If there is an abnormality in any of the sensor signals, the ECU enters its back-up mode. In this event, the ECU ignores the abnormal sensor signal and assumes a pre-programmed value which in most cases will allow the engine to continue running (albeit at reduced performance and efficiency). If the ECU enters this back-up mode, the warning light on the instrument panel will illuminate, and the relevant fault code will be stored in the ECU memory.

20 If the warning light illuminates, the vehicle should be taken to a Vauxhall dealer at the earliest opportunity. A complete test of the injection system can then be carried out, using a special electronic diagnostic test unit which is simply plugged into the system's diagnostic connector. The connector is located behind the footwell trim panel on the passenger's side.

2.8 litre models

21 The fuel system consists of a rear-mounted fuel tank, a fuel filter with integral

4B

water separator, a fuel injection pump, injectors, turbocharger, intercooler and associated components. Before passing through the filter, the fuel is heated by an electric heating element which is fitted to the filter housing. The exhaust system is conventional, but incorporates an exhaust gas recirculation (EGR) system and an unregulated catalytic converter to reduce exhaust gas emissions (see Chapter 4C for further details).

22 Fuel is drawn from the fuel tank by the fuel injection pump. Before reaching the pump the fuel passes through a fuel filter where foreign matter and water are removed. Excess fuel lubricates the moving components of the injection pump and is then returned to the tank.

23 The fuel injection pump is driven by the timing belt from the engine crankshaft. The high pressure required to inject the fuel into the compressed air in the swirl chambers is achieved by a cam plate acting on a single piston. The fuel passes through a central rotor with a single outlet drilling which aligns with ports leading to the injector pipes.

24 Fuel metering is controlled by a centrifugal governor which reacts to accelerator pedal position and engine speed. The governor is linked to a metering valve which increases or decreases the amount of fuel delivered at each pumping stroke.

25 Basic injection timing is determined when the pump is fitted. When the engine is running it is varied automatically to suit the prevailing engine speed by a mechanism which turns the cam plate or ring.

26 The four fuel injectors produce a spray of fuel into the swirl chambers located in the cylinder head. The injectors are calibrated to open and close at critical pressures to provide efficient and even combustion. Each injector needle is lubricated by fuel which accumulates in the spring chamber and is channelled to the injection pump return hose by leak-off pipes.

27 Cold starting is assisted by pre-heater or 'glow' plugs fitted to each swirl chamber and controlled by the Quick-On Start (QOS) pre-heating control unit (see Chapter 5C for further details). A cold start solenoid on the injection pump is used to advance the injection pump timing during cold start conditions.

28 A Quick Warm-up System (QWS) is also fitted to allow the engine to quickly reach normal operating temperature after a cold start. The system is driver operated by a switch on the instrument panel and consists of two vacuum-operated throttle valves, one in the inlet manifold and one in the exhaust system, together with their vacuum actuators and sensors. When the system is in operation the throttle valves are closed by the vacuum actuators so that both the intake air entering the engine and the exhaust gas passage to atmosphere are restricted. This creates a choking effect on the engine leading to increased temperature and a quick warm-up. The system only operates below pre-determined engine and ambient air temperatures, and when the engine is at idle or part throttle. A vacuum-controlled actuator at the injection pump increases the engine idle speed slightly when the system is in operation to compensate for the intake air and exhaust gas restrictions created by the throttle valves.

29 A stop solenoid cuts the fuel supply to the injection pump rotor when the ignition is switched off, and there is also a hand-operated stop lever for use in an emergency.

30 Provided that the specified maintenance is carried out, the fuel injection equipment will give long and trouble-free service. The injection pump itself may well outlast the engine. The main potential cause of damage to the injection pump and injectors is dirt or water in the fuel.

31 Servicing of the injection pump and injectors is very limited for the home mechanic, and any dismantling or adjustment other than that described in this Chapter must be entrusted to a Vauxhall dealer or fuel injection specialist.

2 Air cleaner assembly and intake ducts - removal and refitting

Removal

2.3 and 2.8 litre models

1 Slacken the clip and disconnect the turbocharger air intake hose from the elbow on the air cleaner cover **(see illustration)**. Similarly disconnect the crankcase ventilation hose from the elbow.

2 Withdraw the air intake duct from the side of the air cleaner body and from the wheel arch intake.

3 Using pliers, compress the legs of the two spring clips securing the air cleaner rubber mountings to the support bracket, and remove the clips.

4 Lift the air cleaner assembly upwards while at the same time releasing it from the rubber mounting at the rear then remove the unit from the engine compartment.

5 The remaining ducts linking the turbocharger, intercooler and inlet manifold can be removed once their retaining clips and (where necessary) mounting bracket bolts have been removed.

2.5 litre models

6 Slacken the clips and disconnect the air

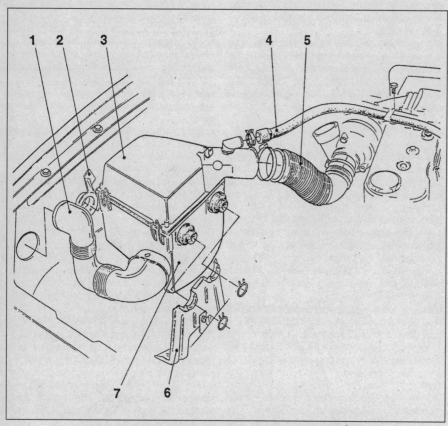

2.1 Air cleaner and intake duct attachments - 2.8 litre models

1 *Air intake duct*	4 *Crankcase ventilation hose*
2 *Rear mounting*	5 *Turbocharger air intake hose*
3 *Air cleaner lid*	

6 *Support bracket*
7 *Air cleaner body*

2.6 Disconnect the air duct from the intercooler plastic pipe - 2.5 litre models

2.7 Disconnect the hose from the crankcase ventilation valve - 2.5 litre models

2.8 Remove the intake hose, with the crankcase ventilation valve, from the air mass meter and turbocharger - 2.5 litre models

duct from the intercooler plastic pipe and the inlet manifold **(see illustration)**.

7 Compress the clip legs and disconnect the vent hose from the crankcase ventilation valve **(see illustration)**.

8 Slacken the clips securing the intake air hose to the air mass meter and turbocharger, and remove the hose complete with crankcase ventilation valve **(see illustration)**.

9 Disconnect the wiring multiplug from the air mass meter and release the coolant hose from the clips on the air cleaner cover.

10 Withdraw the air intake duct from the side of the air cleaner body and from the wheel arch intake.

11 Using pliers, compress the legs of the two spring clips securing the air cleaner rubber mountings to the support bracket, and remove the clips.

12 Lift the air cleaner assembly upwards while at the same time releasing it from the rubber mounting at the rear, then remove the unit from the engine compartment.

13 The remaining ducts linking the turbocharger, intercooler and inlet manifold can be removed once their retaining clips and (where necessary) mounting bracket bolts have been removed.

Refitting

14 Refitting is a reversal of removal, ensuring that all intake ducts are properly reconnected and their retaining clips securely tightened.

3 Fuel gauge sender unit - removal and refitting

1 Refer to Section 9 of Chapter 4A, noting that there is no fuel pump incorporated in the fuel gauge sender unit.

4 Fuel tank - removal and refitting

1 Refer to Section 10 of Chapter 4A.

5 Accelerator cable - removal, refitting and adjustment

2.3 and 2.8 litre models

Removal

1 Working in the engine compartment, operate the accelerator lever on the injection pump, and release the inner cable from the lever. Alternatively, on models with a press-fit balljoint cable end fitting, pull the cable end from the lever.

2 Extract the retaining clip and withdraw the outer cable end fitting from the grommet on the injection pump bracket.

3 Working inside the vehicle, remove the lower trim panel from under the facia. Disconnect the inner cable end from the slot on the accelerator pedal.

4 Return to the engine compartment, release the outer cable from the bulkhead and from the retaining clips and remove the cable from the engine compartment.

Refitting and adjustment - 2.3 litre models

5 Prior to refitting the cable, check the accelerator pedal position as follows:

6 Locate the accelerator pedal stop bolt on the pedal bracket under the facia and, where fitted, remove the rubber pad from the head of the stop bolt.

7 Measure the distance from the head of the stop bolt to the face of the bracket **(see illustration)**. The correct dimension according to vehicle should be as follows:

18.0 ± 0.5 mm (right-hand drive)
19.0 ± 0.5 mm (left-hand drive)

8 If the dimension is not as specified, slacken the stop bolt locknut and turn the stop bolt as necessary. When the correct setting is obtained, tighten the locknut and refit the rubber pad.

9 Refit the cable to the vehicle and connect the inner cable to the accelerator pedal.

4B

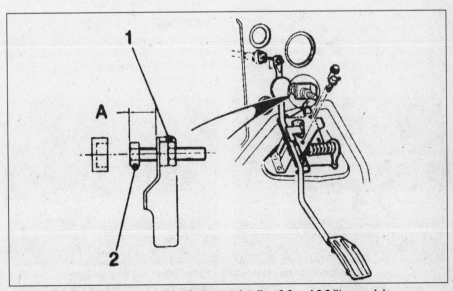

5.7 Accelerator pedal adjustment details - 2.3 and 2.8 litre models

1 Pedal stop bolt locknut   *2 Pedal stop bolt*   *A Stop bolt setting dimension (see text)*

10 Route the cable through the engine compartment to the injection pump and secure with the relevant retaining clips. Insert the outer cable through the pump bracket and connect the inner cable end to the pump lever.

11 With the accelerator pedal released and the injection pump lever in the closed position, pull the outer cable away from the pump to just take up any slack, then insert the retaining clip into the slot nearest to the cable grommet.

12 Check that the accelerator lever on the injection pump moves to the maximum speed position with the accelerator pedal fully depressed, and returns to the idle position with the pedal released. Refit the trim panel under the facia on completion.

Refitting and adjustment - 2.8 litre models

13 Refit the cable to the vehicle and connect the inner cable to the accelerator pedal.

14 Route the cable through the engine compartment to the injection pump and secure with the relevant retaining clips. Insert the outer cable through the pump bracket and connect the inner cable end to the pump lever.

15 With the accelerator pedal released and the injection pump lever in the closed position, pull the outer cable away from the pump to just take up any slack, then insert the retaining clip into the slot nearest to the cable grommet.

16 Locate the accelerator pedal stop bolt on the pedal bracket under the facia and, where fitted, remove the rubber pad from the head of the stop bolt.

17 Slacken the stop bolt locknut and turn the stop bolt to obtain a dimension of 19.0 ± 0.5 mm from the head of the stop bolt to the face of the bracket. Refit the rubber pad to the stop bolt.

18 Depress the pedal fully so that the accelerator lever on the injection pump is against the maximum speed stop screw. Hold the pedal in this position and adjust the stop bolt to contact the pedal. Tighten the locknut.

19 Check that the accelerator lever on the injection pump moves to the maximum speed position with the accelerator pedal fully depressed, and returns to the idle position with the pedal released. Refit the trim panel under the facia on completion.

2.5 litre models

20 On 2.5 litre models there is no accelerator cable. The injection pump is electronically controlled by the Electronic Diesel Control ECU. The accelerator pedal is connected to a position sensor which informs the ECU of pedal position (see Sections 1 and 8).

6 Accelerator pedal - removal and refitting

Removal

1 Remove the lower trim panel from under the facia.

2 On 2.3 and 2.8 litre models, disconnect the inner cable end from the slot on the accelerator pedal.

3 On 2.5 litre models, ensure that the ignition is switched off then disconnect the wiring connector for the pedal position sensor.

4 Undo the bolts securing the pedal bracket to the bulkhead and remove the pedal and bracket assembly (see illustration).

5 Examine the pedal and pivot bushes for signs of wear and renew as necessary. The pedal can be released from the bracket and bushes by extracting the circlip from the end of the pedal shaft. On 2.5 litre models, do not disturb the position of the pedal stop bolt on the pedal bracket. If the stop bolt setting is altered, it will be necessary to take the vehicle to a Vauxhall dealer to have the pedal position sensor setting adjusted using special electronic testing equipment.

Refitting

6 Refitting is a reversal of removal. On 2.3 and 2.8 litre models, check the adjustment of the accelerator cable and pedal as described in Section 5.

7 Fuel system - priming and bleeding

> ⚠️ **Warning: Refer to the warning note in Section 1 before proceeding.**

1 After disconnecting part of the fuel supply system or running out of fuel, it is necessary to prime the system and bleed off any air which may have entered the system components.

2 To prime the system, loosen the bleed screw located on the top of the fuel filter housing, then depress and release the hand pump on the filter housing several times until fuel, free from air bubbles, emerges from the bleed screw (see illustration).

3 Retighten the bleed screw and continue pumping until firm resistance is felt.

4 Attempt to start the engine at this stage by fully depressing the accelerator pedal and operating the starter motor. Do not operate the heater plugs. If it refuses to start after 15 seconds, operate the heater plugs as normal then attempt to start the engine again.

5 If a large amount of air has entered the injection pump, place a wad of rag around the bleeder plug in the centre of the pump between the four injector fuel pipe unions (to absorb spilt fuel), then slacken the plug (see illustration). Operate the priming hand pump (with the ignition switched on to activate the stop solenoid) until fuel, free from air bubbles, emerges from the bleeder plug. Tighten the plug and mop up spilt fuel.

6 If air has entered the injector pipes, place wads of rag around the injector pipe unions at the injectors (to absorb spilt fuel), then slacken the unions. Crank the engine on the starter motor until fuel emerges from the unions, then stop cranking the engine and retighten the unions. Mop up spilt fuel.

> ⚠️ **Warning: Be prepared to stop the engine if it should start to run, to avoid fuel spray and spillage.**

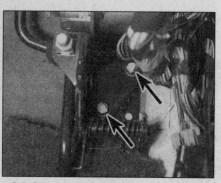

6.4 Accelerator pedal bracket retaining bolts (arrowed) - 2.5 litre models

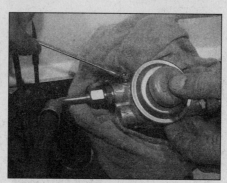

7.2 To prime the fuel system, loosen the bleed screw then operate the hand pump until fuel, free from air bubbles, emerges from the bleed screw

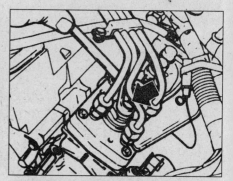

7.5 To bleed the injection pump, unscrew the bleeder plug (arrowed) then operate the hand pump until fuel, free from air bubbles, emerges - 2.3 litre models

8.3 Accelerator pedal position sensor connecting link balljoint (arrowed) - 2.5 litre models

8.7 Air mass meter wiring connector (arrowed) - 2.5 litre models

7 Attempt to start the engine by fully depressing the accelerator pedal and operating the starter motor. Initially do not operate the heater plugs, however, if it refuses to start after 15 seconds, operate the heater plugs as normal then start the engine.

8 Electronic Diesel Control (EDC) components (2.5 litre models) - removal and refitting

Accelerator pedal position sensor

Removal

1 Remove the lower trim panel from under the facia.
2 Ensure that the ignition is switched off then disconnect the wiring connector for the pedal position sensor.
3 Release the press-fit balljoint and disconnect the pedal connecting link from the sensor lever (see illustration).
4 Undo the two screws securing the sensor

to the pedal bracket, and remove the sensor from the bracket.

Refitting

5 Refitting is a reversal of removal.

Coolant temperature sensor

6 Refer to the procedures contained in Chapter 3, Section 8.

Air mass meter

Removal

7 Ensure that the ignition is switched off then disconnect the wiring connector at the air mass meter located on the air cleaner cover (see illustration).
8 Slacken the clip securing the intake air hose to the air mass meter and disconnect the hose.
9 Undo the two bolts securing the air mass meter to the air cleaner cover. Withdraw the unit from its location and collect the sealing O-ring.

Refitting

10 Refitting is a reversal of removal, but use a

new sealing O-ring and tighten the retaining bolts to the specified torque.

Crankshaft sensor

Removal

11 Locate the crankshaft sensor wiring harness connector at the cable support bracket on the right-hand side of the engine (see illustration). Ensure that the ignition is switched off, then release the harness from the bracket and disconnect the crankshaft sensor wiring connector from the engine wiring harness.
12 Undo the bolt securing the crankshaft sensor to the engine adaptor plate and withdraw the sensor (see illustration).

Refitting

13 Refitting is a reversal of removal.

Needle movement sensor

14 The needle movement sensor is an integral part of No 1 cylinder fuel injector. Refer to Section 14 for fuel injector removal and refitting procedures.

4B

8.11 Crankshaft sensor wiring harness connector location (arrowed) - 2.5 litre models

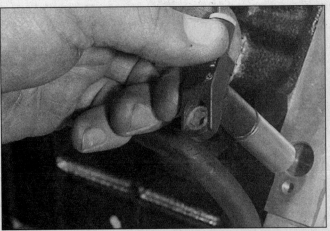

8.12 Undo the bolt and withdraw the sensor from the adaptor plate - 2.5 litre models

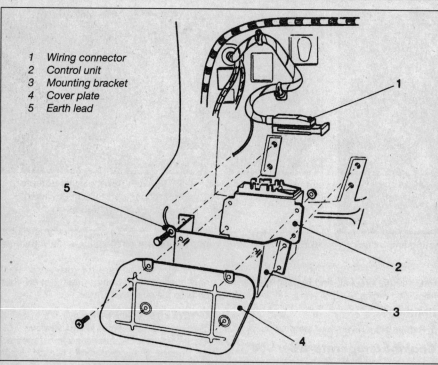

1 Wiring connector
2 Control unit
3 Mounting bracket
4 Cover plate
5 Earth lead

8.17 Electronic control unit attachments - 2.5 litre models

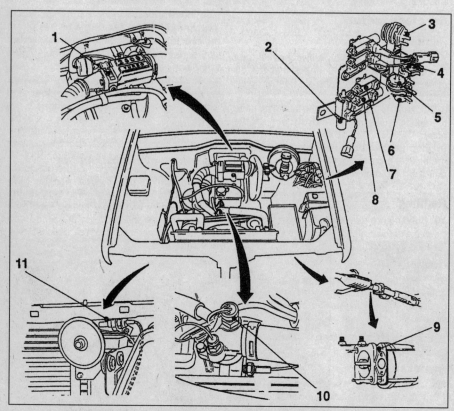

9.2 Quick Warm-up System component locations - 2.8 litre models

1 Intake throttle valve	6 Vacuum control valve	10 Coolant temperature
2 Vacuum switching valve 1	7 Vacuum switching valve 2	sensor
3 Vacuum regulating valve	8 Vacuum switching valve 3	11 Ambient air temperature
4 Delay valve 1	(fast idle control)	sensor
5 Delay valve 2	9 Exhaust throttle valve	

Electronic control unit

Removal

15 The electronic control unit is located inside the vehicle in the footwell on the passenger's side.

16 Disconnect the battery negative lead.

17 Undo the four screws and remove the cover plate from the control unit mounting bracket **(see illustration)**.

18 Release the retaining clip and disconnect the wiring connector from the top of the control unit.

19 Undo the four mounting bracket bolts noting the earth lead fitted under one of the bolt heads. Withdraw the bracket and control unit from the footwell, then undo the four nuts and separate the control unit from the bracket.

Refitting

20 Refitting is a reversal of removal, but ensure that the earth lead is fitted under the relevant mounting bracket bolt.

9 Quick Warm-up System components (2.8 litre models) - removal and refitting

Coolant temperature sensor

Removal

Note: *Two coolant temperature sensors are located in the thermostat cover. The larger of the two (coloured red) is used by the Quick Warm-up System, the smaller of the two (coloured white) is used by the Quick On Start pre-heating system. The following procedures are applicable to both sensors.*

1 Drain the cooling system as described in Chapter 1.

2 Disconnect the sensor wiring at the harness connector, then unscrew the sensor from the thermostat housing **(see illustration)**.

Refitting

3 Refitting is a reversal of removal, but coat the sensor threads with sealant before refitting. Tighten the sensor securely then refill the cooling system as described in Chapter 1.

Ambient air temperature sensor

Removal

4 Refer to Chapter 12 and remove the radiator grille.

5 Disconnect the sensor wiring at the harness connector.

6 Undo the screw securing the sensor mounting bracket to the body panel and remove the sensor and bracket.

7 If necessary, unscrew the sensor from the bracket.

Refitting

8 Refitting is a reversal of removal.

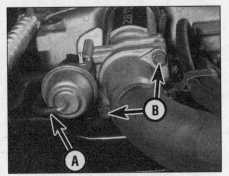

9.22 Intake throttle valve actuator vacuum hose (A) and throttle valve retaining bolts (B) - 2.8 litre models

9.26 Hose clip attachment (arrowed) at the air intake elbow - 2.8 litre models

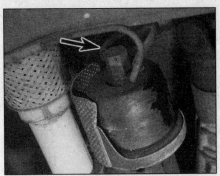

9.33 Exhaust throttle valve actuator vacuum hose connection (arrowed) - 2.8 litre models

Vacuum switching valves

Removal

9 Three vacuum switching valves are used in the system and are located on the left-hand side of the engine compartment, at the rear.

10 Disconnect the wiring connectors from the relevant valves, noting the colour coding.

11 Identify the vacuum hoses for correct refitting then disconnect the hoses from the valves.

12 Undo the two retaining bolts and remove the valve assembly mounting bracket from its location. Undo the screws and remove the relevant valve from the bracket.

Refitting

13 Refitting is a reversal of removal. Ensure that the vacuum hoses and wiring connectors are fitted correctly.

Vacuum regulating valve

Removal

14 The vacuum regulating valve is located on the left-hand side of the engine compartment at the rear, adjacent to the vacuum switching valves.

15 Identify the vacuum hoses for correct refitting then disconnect the hoses from the valve.

16 Lift the valve up and out of the mounting bracket.

Refitting

17 Refitting is a reversal of removal. Ensure that the vacuum hoses are fitted correctly.

Vacuum control and delay valves

Removal

18 The vacuum control valve and the two vacuum delay valves are located on the left-hand side of the engine compartment at the rear, adjacent to the vacuum switching valves.

19 Identify the vacuum hoses for correct refitting then disconnect the hoses from the relevant valve.

20 Lift the valve up and out of the mounting bracket.

Refitting

21 Refitting is a reversal of removal. Ensure that the vacuum hoses are fitted correctly.

Intake throttle valve actuator

Removal

22 Disconnect the vacuum hose from the valve actuator pipe stub (see illustration).

23 Undo the two bolts securing the actuator mounting bracket to the side of the throttle valve.

24 Disengage the actuator operating rod from the throttle valve lever and remove the actuator and bracket.

Refitting

25 Refitting is a reversal of removal.

Intake throttle valve

Removal

26 Undo the nut and bolt securing the hose clip to the throttle valve air intake elbow (see illustration). Lift away the clip and move the hoses to one side.

27 Slacken the clip and disconnect the air intake hose from the intake elbow.

28 Disconnect the vacuum hose from the throttle valve actuator pipe stub.

29 Undo the two bolts securing the intake elbow and throttle valve to the plenum chamber. Lift off the intake elbow and remove the throttle valve assembly.

30 Collect and discard the gaskets on each side of the throttle valve - new gaskets must be used for refitting.

Refitting

31 Refitting is a reversal of removal, but ensure that all the flange mating faces are clean and use a new gasket on each side of the throttle valve.

Exhaust throttle valve and actuator

Removal

32 Chock the rear wheels then jack up the front of the vehicle and support it on axle stands (see Jacking and Vehicle Support).

33 Disconnect the vacuum hose from the pipe stub at the rear of the valve actuator (see illustration).

34 Undo the two nuts and bolts securing the throttle valve between the exhaust front pipe and intermediate pipe flanges. Ease the

exhaust intermediate pipe rearwards slightly and withdraw the throttle valve from between the two flanges.

35 Collect and discard the gaskets on each side of the throttle valve - new gaskets must be used for refitting.

Refitting

36 Refitting is a reversal of removal, but ensure that all the flange mating faces are clean and use a new gasket on each side of the throttle valve.

10 Fuel lift pump (2.3 litre models) - removal and refitting

Note: Refer to the precautions given in Section 1 of this Chapter before proceeding.

Removal

1 Chock the rear wheels then jack up the front of the vehicle and support it on axle stands (see Jacking and Vehicle Support).

2 Mark the pump inlet and outlet hoses for identification purposes then slacken both retaining clips. Place wads of rag beneath the hose unions to catch any spilled fuel, then disconnect both hoses from the pump and plug the hose ends to minimise fuel loss (see illustration).

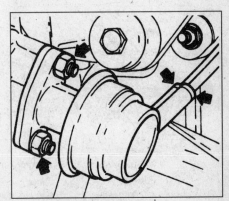

10.2 Fuel lift pump fuel hose connections and mounting nuts (arrowed) - 2.3 litre models

4B

3 Unscrew and remove the pump mounting nuts and withdraw the pump from the timing cover. Recover the spacer/gasket

Refitting

4 Refitting is a reversal of removal, but fit a new spacer/gasket. On completion, bleed the fuel system as described in Section 7.

11 Fuel injection pump - removal and refitting

Note: *Refer to the precautions given in Section 1 of this Chapter before proceeding. Be careful not to allow dirt into the pump or injector pipes during this procedure. New sealing rings should be used on the fuel pipe banjo unions when refitting.*

2.3 litre models

Removal

1 Disconnect the battery negative lead.
2 Referring to the procedures contained in Chapter 2D, remove the cylinder head cover and turn the crankshaft to bring No 1 piston to TDC on the compression stroke. The mark on the flywheel must be aligned with the pointer in the bellhousing and the mark on the camshaft sprocket must be at the top.
3 Disconnect the accelerator cable and idle speed control cable from the injection pump, with reference to Section 5 if necessary.
4 Disconnect the vacuum hose from the pump and the wiring connector from the injection pump solenoid (see illustration).
5 Remove all traces of dirt and make identification marks between the fuel feed and return hoses and their pump unions. Loosen the clips or undo the banjo unions, as applicable, and disconnect the hoses from the injection pump. Recover the sealing washers from the banjo unions, where applicable. Cover the open ends of the hoses or pipes, and plug the opening in the injection pump to keep dirt out.

6 Unscrew the union nuts securing the injector pipes to the injection pump and injectors. Counterhold the unions on the pump, when unscrewing the pipe-to-pump union nuts. Remove the pipes as a set. Cover open unions to keep dirt out, using small plastic bags or fingers cut from rubber gloves. Note that the leak-off hoses will have to be removed from the fuel injectors to enable the injectors to be covered.
7 Make a final check to ensure that all relevant pipes, hoses and wires have been disconnected to facilitate pump removal.
8 Make alignment marks between the pump and the mounting flange. This will aid pump timing on refitting.
9 Unscrew the injection pump flange mounting nuts, and withdraw the pump from its location.
Caution: Never attempt to dismantle the pump assembly. If there is a problem, take the pump to a Vauxhall dealer or diesel injection specialist for testing/repair.

Refitting

10 Manoeuvre the pump into position and loosely fit the flange mounting nuts.
11 Where applicable, align the marks made on the pump and the mounting flange before removal. If a new pump is being fitted, transfer the mark from the old pump to give an approximate setting.
12 Adjust the injection timing as described in Section 13, then tighten the pump mounting nuts securely.
13 Refit the cylinder head cover as described in Chapter 2D.
14 Refit and reconnect the injector fuel pipes, and tighten the unions. Counterhold the unions on the pump when tightening the pipe-to-pump union nuts.
15 Reconnect all relevant wiring to the pump.
16 Reconnect the fuel supply and return pipes and hoses, and tighten the unions, as applicable. Use new sealing washers on the banjo unions.

17 Reconnect and adjust the accelerator cable as described in Section 5.
18 Reconnect the battery negative lead.
19 Prime and bleed the fuel system as described in Section 7.
20 Start the engine, warm it up to normal operating temperature, and check the idle speed adjustment as described in Chapter 1B.

2.5 litre models

Removal

Note: *The following procedure entails the use of Vauxhall special tool KM-8076 to release the pump shaft from the drive gear, and to retain the drive gear in position within the timing cover while the pump is removed. If this tool, or a suitable alternative cannot be obtained, it is recommended that this task be entrusted to a Vauxhall dealer or suitably-equipped garage.*

21 Disconnect the battery negative lead.
22 Referring to the procedures contained in Chapter 2E, turn the crankshaft to bring No 1 piston to TDC on the compression stroke. Now turn the crankshaft anti-clockwise approximately 30° from TDC to set the injection pump away from the high cam lobe position
23 Disconnect the air ducts from the intercooler plastic pipe, then undo the bolts and remove the pipe from the top of the radiator.
24 Remove the alternator as described in Chapter 5A.
25 Slacken the clip and disconnect the vacuum pump oil drain hose from the adaptor on the front of the timing cover (see illustration). Unscrew the oil drain hose adaptor from the timing cover and recover the gasket.
26 Undo the two bolts and washers and remove the alternator mounting bracket and idler pulley assembly.
27 Unscrew the locking collar and disconnect the injection pump main wiring plug from the harness socket (see illustration).

11.4 Wiring connector, fuel hose and injector pipe union attachments (arrowed) at the injection pump - 2.3 litre models

11.25 Disconnect the vacuum pump oil drain hose (arrowed) from the timing cover adaptor - 2.5 litre models

11.27 Disconnect the injection pump main wiring plug from the harness socket - 2.5 litre models

28 Unscrew the pump wiring harness socket retaining ring and withdraw the socket from the harness bracket **(see illustration)**.

29 Disconnect the injection pump secondary wiring from the harness connector(s).

30 Clean the area around the hydraulic fluid pressure pipe union on the power steering pump and place a suitable container below the pipe union.

31 Undo the fluid pressure pipe banjo union bolt and remove the washer. Withdraw the pressure pipe from the pump connection, recover the second copper washer and allow the power steering fluid to drain into the container. Cover the pipe end and the pump orifice after disconnection.

32 Slacken the clips and disconnect the two fuel hoses from the fuel return pipe, and the feed hose from the fuel feed pipe. Seal the ends of the pipes and hoses to keep dirt out.

33 Unscrew the union nuts securing the injector pipes to the injection pump and injectors. Counterhold the unions on the pump, when unscrewing the pipe-to-pump union nuts. Remove the pipes as a set. Cover open unions to keep dirt out, using small plastic bags or fingers cut from rubber gloves. Note that the leak-off hoses will have to be removed from the fuel injectors to enable the injectors to be covered.

34 Working through the oil drain hose adaptor aperture on the timing cover, unscrew the injection pump drive gear retaining nut and remove the washer. Take care not to allow the washer to fall into the timing cover.

35 Insert the adaptor part of special tool KM-8076 into the timing cover aperture, then screw the puller part into the adaptor. Insert the drive bolt part of the tool into the puller, but do not tighten the drive bolt at this stage.

36 Make a final check to ensure that all relevant pipes, hoses and wires have been disconnected to facilitate pump removal.

37 Make alignment marks between the pump and the mounting flange to aid pump timing on refitting **(see illustration)**.

38 Unscrew the injection pump flange mounting nuts and remove the washers **(see illustration)**.

39 While supporting the pump, tighten the

11.28 Unscrew the retaining ring and withdraw the socket from the bracket - 2.5 litre models

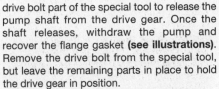

drive bolt part of the special tool to release the pump shaft from the drive gear. Once the shaft releases, withdraw the pump and recover the flange gasket **(see illustrations)**. Remove the drive bolt from the special tool, but leave the remaining parts in place to hold the drive gear in position.

Caution: Never attempt to dismantle the pump assembly. If there is a problem, take the pump to a Vauxhall dealer or diesel injection specialist for testing/repair.

Refitting

40 Check that the engine is still positioned as described in paragraph 22.

41 Clean the mating faces of the injection pump and engine, then position a new gasket over the mounting studs.

42 Position the injection pump shaft so that the Woodruff key is at the 11 o'clock position (viewed from the front). Slide the pump over the studs while at the same time engaging the shaft and key with the drive gear. Loosely fit the flange mounting nuts and washers.

43 Where applicable, align the marks made on the pump and the mounting flange before removal. If a new pump is being fitted, transfer the mark from the old pump to give an approximate setting.

44 Remove the special tool from the timing cover then refit the drive gear retaining nut and washer. Tighten the nut to the specified torque.

11.37 Make alignment marks between the injection pump and mounting flange - 2.5 litre models

45 Refit the oil drain hose adaptor to the timing cover using a new gasket. Reconnect the oil drain hose and secure with the clip.

46 Reconnect the two fuel hoses to the fuel return pipe, and the feed hose to the fuel feed pipe and tighten the clips securely.

47 Adjust the injection timing as described in Section 13, then tighten the pump mounting nuts to the specified torque.

48 Refit and reconnect the injector fuel pipes, and tighten the unions. Counterhold the unions on the pump when tightening the pipe-to-pump union nuts.

49 Reconnect the hydraulic fluid pressure pipe union on the power steering pump using new copper washers.

50 Refit the pump wiring harness socket to the harness bracket and secure with the retaining ring. Connect the pump wiring plug and tighten the locking collar.

51 Reconnect the injection pump secondary wiring harness connector(s).

52 Refit the alternator mounting bracket and idler pulley assembly, then refit the alternator as described in Chapter 5A.

53 Refit the intercooler plastic pipe and air ducts.

54 Reconnect the battery negative lead.

55 Prime and bleed the fuel system as described in Section 7, and bleed the power steering hydraulic system as described in Chapter 11.

4B

11.38 Unscrew the pump mounting flange nuts and remove the washers - 2.5 litre models

11.39a Withdraw the injection pump . . .

11.39b . . . and recover the gasket - 2.5 litre models

2.8 litre models

Removal

56 Refer to Chapter 2F and remove the timing belt and the injection pump sprocket.

57 Disconnect the accelerator cable from the injection pump, with reference to Section 5 if necessary. If not already done, remove the plenum chamber and throttle valve components as described in Section 14, paragraphs 33 to 37.

58 Remove all traces of dirt and make identification marks between the fuel feed and return hoses and their pump unions. Loosen the clips or undo the banjo unions, as applicable, and disconnect the hoses from the injection pump. Recover the sealing washers from the banjo unions, where applicable. Cover the open ends of the hoses or pipes, and plug the opening in the injection pump to keep dirt out.

59 Unscrew the union nuts securing the injector pipes to the injection pump and injectors. Counterhold the unions on the pump, when unscrewing the pipe-to-pump union nuts. Remove the pipes as a set. Cover open unions to keep dirt out, using small plastic bags or fingers cut from rubber gloves. Note that the leak-off hoses will have to be removed from the fuel injectors to enable the injectors to be covered.

60 Disconnect the wiring connectors and harness attachments from the injection pump, noting their locations for refitting.

61 Make a final check to ensure that all relevant pipes, hoses and wires have been disconnected to facilitate pump removal.

62 Make alignment marks between the injection pump front mounting flange and the mounting bracket. This will aid pump timing on refitting.

63 Undo the bolts securing the injection pump rear mounting bracket to the pump and cylinder block and remove the bracket.

64 Unscrew the injection pump front flange mounting nuts, and withdraw the pump from its location.

Caution: Never attempt to dismantle the pump assembly. If there is a problem, take the pump to a Vauxhall dealer or diesel injection specialist for testing/repair.

Refitting

65 Manoeuvre the pump into position and loosely fit the flange mounting nuts and the rear mounting bracket bolts.

66 Where applicable, align the marks made on the pump and the mounting flange before removal. If a new pump is being fitted, transfer the mark from the old pump to give an approximate setting.

67 Refit the injection pump sprocket and timing belt as described in Chapter 2F.

68 Adjust the injection timing as described in Section 13, then securely tighten the pump mounting nuts and mounting bracket bolts.

69 Refit and reconnect the injector fuel pipes, and tighten the unions. Counterhold the unions on the pump when tightening the pipe-to-pump union nuts.

70 Reconnect all relevant wiring to the pump.

71 Reconnect the fuel supply and return pipes and hoses, and tighten the unions, as applicable. Use new sealing washers on the banjo unions.

72 Reconnect and adjust the accelerator cable as described in Section 5. Refit the plenum chamber and throttle valve components using the reverse of the removal procedure.

73 Reconnect the battery negative lead.

74 Prime and bleed the fuel system as described in Section 7.

75 Start the engine, warm it up to normal operating temperature, and check the idle speed adjustment as described in Chapter 1B.

12 Injection timing - general

1 Checking the injection timing is not a routine operation. It is only necessary after the injection pump has been disturbed.

2 Dynamic timing equipment does exist, but it is unlikely to be available to the home mechanic. The equipment works by converting pressure pulses in an injector pipe into electrical signals. If such equipment is available, use it in accordance with its maker's instructions.

3 Static timing as described in this Chapter gives good results if carried out carefully. A dial gauge will be needed, with probes and adaptors appropriate to the type of injection pump **(see illustration)**. Read through the procedures before starting work to find out what is involved.

13 Injection timing - checking and adjustment

Caution: Some of the injection pump settings and access plugs may be sealed by the manufacturers at the factory using paint or locking wire and lead seals. Do

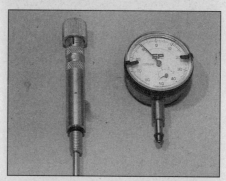

12.3 Dial gauge and adaptor needed to check the injection timing

not disturb the seals if the vehicle is still within the warranty period, otherwise the warranty will be invalidated. Also do not attempt the timing procedure unless accurate instrumentation is available. Suitable special tools for carrying out pump timing are available from motor factors, and a dial test indicator will be required regardless of the method used. Refer to the precautions given in Section 1 of this Chapter before proceeding.

2.3 litre models

1 Disconnect the battery negative lead.

2 Referring to the procedures contained in Chapter 2D, remove the cylinder head cover and turn the crankshaft to bring No 1 piston to TDC on the compression stroke. The mark on the flywheel must be aligned with the pointer in the bellhousing and the mark on the camshaft sprocket must be at the top.

3 Unscrew the bleeder plug from the end of the injection pump between the injector pipe connections. Be prepared for the loss of some fuel.

4 A dial test indicator will now be required, along with a special probe and adaptor to screw into the bleeder plug hole in the rear of the pump (designed specifically for the Bosch pump and available from motor factors).

5 Screw the adaptor into the bleeder plug hole and mount the dial gauge in the adaptor. Position the dial gauge so that its plunger is at the mid-point of its travel and securely tighten the adaptor locking nut.

6 Turn the engine crankshaft in the opposite direction to normal rotation until the dial gauge needle no longer moves, and zero the dial gauge.

7 Turn the crankshaft slowly in the direction of normal rotation until No 1 piston is again at the TDC position (flywheel mark aligned with bellhousing pointer).

8 The reading now obtained on the dial gauge should correspond to the static timing value given in the Specifications.

9 If the reading is not as specified, proceed as follows.

10 Slacken the pump mounting nuts and slowly rotate the pump body until the point is found where the specified reading is obtained on the dial gauge. When the pump is correctly positioned, tighten the mounting nuts, ensuring that the reading on the dial gauge does not change as the fixings are tightened.

11 Rotate the crankshaft through one and three quarter turns in the normal direction of rotation. Check that the dial test indicator is reading zero.

12 Continue to slowly rotate the crankshaft until No 1 piston is back to TDC. Recheck the timing measurement.

13 If further adjustment is necessary, slacken the pump mounting nuts and repeat the operations described in paragraphs 10 to 12.

14 When the timing is correct, remove the dial gauge and adaptor and refit the bleeder plug and washer.

15 Refit the remainder of the removed components, lower the vehicle to the ground and reconnect the battery negative lead.

16 Bleed the fuel system as described in Section 7.

17 Check and if necessary adjust the idle speed as described in Chapter 1.

2.5 litre models

18 Disconnect the battery negative lead.

19 Referring to the procedures contained in Chapter 2E, turn the crankshaft to bring No 1 piston to TDC on the compression stroke.

20 Disconnect the air ducts from the intercooler plastic pipe, then undo the bolts and remove the pipe from the top of the radiator.

21 Remove the alternator as described in Chapter 5A.

22 Undo the two bolts and washers and remove the alternator mounting bracket and idler pulley assembly.

23 Clean the area around the hydraulic fluid pressure pipe union on the power steering pump and place a suitable container below the pipe union.

24 Undo the fluid pressure pipe banjo union bolt and remove the washer. Withdraw the pressure pipe from the pump connection, recover the second copper washer and allow the power steering fluid to drain into the container. Cover the pipe end and the pump orifice after disconnection.

25 If the injection pump timing is being checked with the pump in position on the engine, rather than as part of the pump refitting procedure, the residual fuel pressure within the pump must be released. To do this, place absorbent rags beneath the fuel return pipe banjo union nut on the injection pump, then unscrew the union nut. Lift off the banjo union and the two copper washers noting that new washers will be required for refitting. Now unscrew the overflow valve, located behind the banjo union, and remove it from the pump, together with the remaining copper washer.

26 Unscrew the union nuts securing the injector pipes to the injection pump and injectors. Counterhold the unions on the pump, when unscrewing the pipe-to-pump union nuts. Remove the pipes as a set. Cover open unions to keep dirt out, using small plastic bags or fingers cut from rubber gloves. Note that the leak-off hoses will have to be removed from the fuel injectors to enable the injectors to be covered.

27 Unscrew the bleeder plug from the end of the injection pump between the injector pipe connections **(see illustration)**. Be prepared for the loss of some fuel.

28 A dial test indicator will now be required, along with a special probe and adaptor to screw into the bleeder plug hole in the rear of the pump (designed specifically for the Bosch pump and available from motor factors).

29 Screw the adaptor into the bleeder plug hole and mount the dial gauge in the adaptor **(see illustration)**. Position the dial gauge so

that its plunger is at the mid-point of its travel and securely tighten the adaptor locking nut.

30 Check that No 1 piston is still at TDC then set the dial gauge pointer to zero. Turn the crankshaft anti-clockwise (viewed from the front) until the dial gauge pointer stops moving. Do not rotate the crankshaft further beyond the point where the needle stops moving.

31 Set the dial gauge pointer to zero again and slowly turn the crankshaft clockwise (viewed from the front) until No 1 piston is once again at the TDC position. The reading now obtained on the dial gauge should correspond to the static timing value given in the Specifications.

32 If the reading is not as specified, proceed as follows.

33 Slacken the pump mounting nuts, rotate the pump body anti-clockwise (viewed from the front) until the gauge reads zero. Slowly rotate the pump clockwise until the point is found where the specified reading is obtained on the dial gauge. When the pump is correctly positioned, tighten the mounting nuts, ensuring that the reading on the dial gauge does not change as the fixings are tightened. Note that the final movement of the injection pump must be in a clockwise direction. If the pump is turned too far and the specified reading on the gauge is exceeded, turn the pump back so that the gauge reads zero again, then slowly turn the pump clockwise once more until the desired reading is indicated.

34 Rotate the crankshaft through one and three quarter turns in the normal direction of rotation. Continue to slowly rotate the crankshaft until No 1 piston is back to TDC. Recheck the timing measurement.

35 If further adjustment is necessary, slacken the pump mounting nuts and repeat the operations described in paragraphs 33 and 34.

36 When the timing is correct, remove the dial gauge and adaptor and refit the bleeder plug and washer.

37 If the fuel return pipe union was previously removed, refit the overflow valve and fuel return pipe banjo union to the pump using new copper washers. Tighten the union nut to the specified torque.

38 Refit and reconnect the injector fuel pipes, and tighten the unions. Counterhold the unions on the pump when tightening the pipe-to-pump union nuts.

39 Reconnect the hydraulic fluid pressure pipe union on the power steering pump using new copper washers.

40 Refit the alternator mounting bracket and idler pulley assembly, then refit the alternator as described in Chapter 5A.

41 Refit the intercooler plastic pipe and air ducts.

42 Reconnect the battery negative lead.

43 Prime and bleed the fuel system as described in Section 7, and bleed the power steering hydraulic system as described in Chapter 11.

2.8 litre models

44 Disconnect the battery negative lead.

45 Remove the plenum chamber and throttle valve components as described in Section 14, paragraphs 33 to 37.

46 Unscrew the union nuts securing the injector pipes to the injection pump and injectors. Counterhold the unions on the pump, when unscrewing the pipe-to-pump union nuts. Remove the pipes as a set. Cover open unions to keep dirt out, using small plastic bags or fingers cut from rubber gloves. Note that the leak-off hoses will have to be removed from the fuel injectors to enable the injectors to be covered.

47 Referring to the procedures contained in Chapter 2F, turn the crankshaft to bring No 1 piston to TDC on the compression stroke.

48 Unscrew the bleeder plug from the end of the injection pump between the injector pipe connections. Be prepared for the loss of some fuel.

49 A dial test indicator will now be required, along with a special probe and adaptor to screw into the bleeder plug hole in the rear of the pump (designed specifically for the Bosch pump and available from motor factors).

50 Screw the adaptor into the bleeder plug hole and mount the dial gauge in the adaptor. Position the dial gauge so that its plunger is at the mid-point of its travel and securely tighten the adaptor locking nut.

4B

13.27 Unscrew the bleeder plug from the end of the injection pump - 2.5 litre models

13.29 Screw the adaptor into the bleeder plug hole and mount the dial gauge - 2.5 litre models

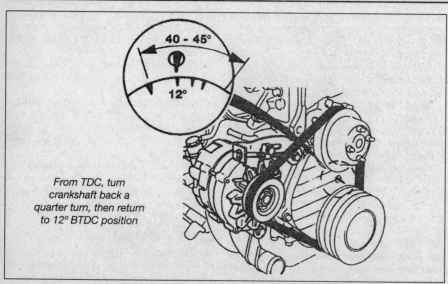

40 - 45°

12°

From TDC, turn crankshaft back a quarter turn, then return to 12° BTDC position

13.51 Crankshaft positioning diagram for injection timing - 2.8 litre models

51 With the crankshaft still set at TDC, turn the crankshaft backwards (ie in the opposite direction to normal rotation) approximately a quarter of a turn. Set the dial gauge to zero, then turn the crankshaft slightly in both directions to check that the dial gauge pointer remains at zero. Turn the crankshaft slowly in the direction of normal rotation until the 12° BTDC mark on the crankshaft pulley is aligned with the pointer on the timing cover **(see illustration)**.

52 The reading now obtained on the dial gauge should correspond to the static timing value given in the Specifications.

53 If the reading is not as specified, proceed as follows.

54 Slacken the pump mounting nuts and rear mounting bracket bolts and slowly rotate the pump body until the point is found where the specified reading is obtained on the dial gauge. When the pump is correctly positioned, tighten the mounting nuts and bolts, ensuring that the reading on the dial gauge does not change as the fixings are tightened.

55 Rotate the crankshaft through one and three quarter turns in the normal direction of rotation. Check that the dial test indicator is reading zero.

56 Continue to slowly rotate the crankshaft until the 12° BTDC mark on the pulley and the timing cover pointer are once again aligned. Recheck the timing measurement.

57 If further adjustment is necessary, slacken the pump mounting nuts and bolts and repeat the operations described in paragraphs 54 to 56.

58 When the timing is correct, remove the dial gauge and adaptor and refit the bleeder plug and washer.

59 Refit and reconnect the injector fuel pipes, and tighten the unions. Counterhold the unions on the pump when tightening the pipe-to-pump union nuts.

60 Refit the plenum chamber and throttle valve components using the reverse of the removal procedure.

61 Reconnect the battery negative lead, then bleed the fuel system as described in Section 7.

62 Check and if necessary adjust the idle speed as described in Chapter 1.

14 Fuel injectors - removal and refitting

Warning: Exercise extreme caution when working on the fuel injectors. Never expose the hands or any part of the body to injector spray, as the high working pressure can cause the fuel to penetrate the skin, with possibly fatal results. You are strongly advised to have any work which involves testing the injectors under pressure carried out by a dealer or fuel injection specialist. Refer to the precautions given in Section 1 of this Chapter before proceeding.

Caution: Be careful not to allow dirt into the injection pump, injectors or pipes during this procedure.

Caution: Take care not to drop the injectors, or allow the needles at their tips to become damaged. The injectors are precision-made to fine limits, and must not be handled roughly. In particular, never mount them in a bench vice.

2.3 litre models

Removal

1 Disconnect the battery negative lead, then carefully clean around the injectors and injector pipe union nuts.

2 Pull the leak-off pipes from the injectors.

3 Unscrew the union nuts securing the injector pipes to the fuel injection pump. Counterhold the unions on the pump when unscrewing the nuts. Cover open unions to keep dirt out, using small plastic bags or fingers cut from rubber gloves.

4 Unscrew the union nuts and disconnect the pipes from the injectors. If necessary the injector pipes may be completely removed. Note the locations of any clips attached to the pipes. Cover the ends of the injectors to prevent dirt ingress.

5 Unscrew the injectors using a deep socket or box spanner (27 mm across flats) and remove them from the cylinder head

Caution: Ensure you unscrew each injector holder from the cylinder head and remove the complete injector assembly rather than unscrewing the injector body from the holder. If the body is unscrewed from the holder, the small internal components of the injector will be disturbed and it will be necessary to take them to a specialist to have them reassembled and tested prior to refitting.

6 Recover the copper washers and fire seal washers from the injector/cylinder head and discard; new ones must be used on refitting. Also recover the sleeves if they are loose. Do not attempt to dismantle the injectors any further.

7 Testing of the injectors requires the use of special equipment. If any injector is thought to be faulty have it tested and, if necessary, reconditioned by a diesel injection specialist or Vauxhall dealer.

Refitting

8 Obtain new copper washers and fire seal washers. Also renew the sleeves if they are damaged.

9 Commence refitting by inserting the sleeves (if removed) into the cylinder head.

10 Fit the new fire seal washers to the cylinder head. Note that the fire seal washers must be fitted with the convex side downwards (towards the cylinder head).

11 Fit the copper washers to the cylinder head.

12 Insert the injectors and tighten them to the specified torque.

13 Refit the injector pipes and tighten the union nuts. Position any clips attached to the pipes as noted before removal.

14 Reconnect the leak-off pipes.

15 Reconnect the battery and start the engine. If difficulty is experienced, bleed the fuel system, referring to Section 7.

2.5 litre models

Removal

Note: To remove No 1 cylinder injector (fitted with the needle movement sensor) a suitable slotted socket will be required to allow clearance for the sensor wire. These sockets are available from Vauxhall dealers (as a special tool) or from retail accessory outlets specialising in diesel injection equipment.

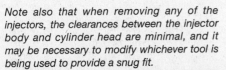

14.18 Pull the leak-off pipes from the fuel injectors - 2.5 litre models

14.21 Unscrew the injectors and remove them from the cylinder head - 2.5 litre models

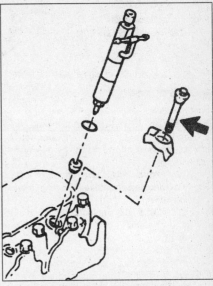

14.41 Fuel injector, injector clamp and clamp bolt (arrowed) - 2.8 litre models

Note also that when removing any of the injectors, the clearances between the injector body and cylinder head are minimal, and it may be necessary to modify whichever tool is being used to provide a snug fit.

16 Disconnect the battery negative lead, then carefully clean around the injectors and injector pipe union nuts.

17 If removing No 1 cylinder injector, disconnect the needle movement sensor wiring at the harness connector.

18 Pull the leak-off pipes from the injectors **(see illustration)**.

19 Unscrew the union nuts securing the injector pipes to the fuel injection pump. Counterhold the unions on the pump, when unscrewing the nuts. Cover open unions to keep dirt out, using small plastic bags or fingers cut from rubber gloves.

20 Unscrew the union nuts and disconnect the pipes from the injectors. If necessary the injector pipes may be completely removed. Note the locations of any clips attached to the pipes. Cover the ends of the injectors to prevent dirt ingress.

21 Unscrew the injectors using a deep socket or box spanner (27 mm across flats, suitably modified as necessary), and remove them from the cylinder head **(see illustration)**. *Caution: Ensure you unscrew each injector holder from the cylinder head and remove the complete injector assembly rather than unscrewing the injector body from the holder. If the body is unscrewed from the holder, the small internal components of the injector will be disturbed and it will be necessary to take them to a specialist to have them reassembled and tested prior to refitting.*

22 Recover the copper washers and fire seal washers from the injector/cylinder head and discard; new ones must be used on refitting. Also recover the sleeves if they are loose. Do not attempt to dismantle the injectors any further.

23 Testing of the injectors requires the use of special equipment. If any injector is thought to be faulty have it tested and, if necessary, reconditioned by a diesel injection specialist or Vauxhall dealer.

Refitting

24 Obtain new copper washers and fire seal washers. Also renew the sleeves if they are damaged.

25 Commence refitting by inserting the sleeves (if removed) into the cylinder head.

26 Fit the new fire seal washers to the cylinder head. Note that the fire seal washers must be fitted with the convex side downwards (towards the cylinder head).

27 Fit the copper washers to the cylinder head.

28 Insert the injectors and tighten them to the specified torque.

29 Refit the injector pipes and tighten the union nuts. Position any clips attached to the pipes as noted before removal.

30 Reconnect the leak-off pipes and where applicable the needle movement sensor wiring connector.

31 Reconnect the battery and start the engine. If difficulty is experienced, bleed the fuel system, referring to Section 7.

2.8 litre models

Removal

32 Disconnect the battery negative lead.

33 Slacken the clip and disconnect the air intake hose from the intake elbow over the top of the engine.

34 Undo the nut and bolt securing the hose clip to the throttle valve air intake elbow. Lift away the clip and move the hoses to one side.

35 Disconnect the vacuum hose from the throttle valve actuator pipe stub.

36 Slacken the clip securing the short plenum chamber connecting hose to the inlet manifold.

37 Disconnect the vacuum hose at the base of the plenum chamber, then undo the two bolts and remove the plenum chamber and throttle valve assembly from the cylinder head cover.

38 Carefully clean around the injectors and injector pipe union nuts. Pull the leak-off pipes from the injectors.

39 Unscrew the union nuts securing the injector pipes to the fuel injection pump.

Counterhold the unions on the pump, when unscrewing the nuts. Cover open unions to keep dirt out, using small plastic bags or fingers cut from rubber gloves.

40 Unscrew the union nuts and disconnect the pipes from the injectors. If necessary the injector pipes may be completely removed. Note the locations of any clips attached to the pipes. Cover the ends of the injectors to prevent dirt ingress.

41 Unscrew the injector clamp retaining bolt and remove the bolt and clamp **(see illustration)**.

42 Remove the injector(s) from the cylinder head and collect the gasket seal and O-ring. Note that new seals and O-rings will be required for refitting. Do not attempt to dismantle the injectors any further.

43 Testing of the injectors requires the use of special equipment. If any injector is thought to be faulty have it tested and, if necessary, reconditioned by a diesel injection specialist or Vauxhall dealer.

Refitting

44 Obtain new gasket seals and O-rings for each removed injector and fit the O-ring to the injector groove.

45 Using a new seal, locate the injector(s) in the cylinder head and secure with the clamp and retaining bolt tightened to the specified torque.

46 Refit the injector pipes and tighten the union nuts. Position any clips attached to the pipes as noted before removal.

47 Reconnect the leak-off pipes.

48 Refit the plenum chamber and throttle valve components using the reverse of the removal procedure.

49 Reconnect the battery and start the engine. If difficulty is experienced, bleed the fuel system, referring to Section 7.

4B

15 Inlet manifold - removal and refitting

Note: *New gasket(s) must be used on refitting.*

2.3 litre models

Removal

1 Disconnect the battery negative lead.

2 Slacken the clip and disconnect the crankcase ventilation hose from the cylinder head cover.

3 Slacken the clips and disconnect the vacuum hose and air intake duct from the inlet manifold.

4 Undo the EGR valve corrugated pipe retaining clip and release the pipe end from the manifold.

5 Undo the bolt securing the turbocharger support bracket to the cylinder block.

6 Move aside all pipes and hoses likely to interfere with removal of the manifold, releasing any cable ties or clips as necessary.

7 Evenly and progressively slacken and remove the bolts securing both the inlet and exhaust manifolds to the cylinder head, noting the locations of the different bolt types, then lift away the inlet manifold.

8 Carefully ease the exhaust manifold away from the cylinder head slightly and collect the one-piece manifold gasket.

9 Thoroughly clean the mating faces of the cylinder head and both manifolds.

Refitting

10 Refitting is a reversal of removal using a new manifold gasket. Progressively tighten the manifold retaining bolts to the specified torque, working in a diagonal sequence.

2.5 litre models

Removal

11 Remove the exhaust manifold as described in Section 16.

12 Evenly and progressively slacken and remove the eight nuts securing the inlet manifold to the cylinder head. Lift away the inlet manifold and recover the four individual gaskets.

13 Thoroughly clean the mating faces of the cylinder head and manifold.

Refitting

14 Refitting is a reversal of removal using new manifold gaskets. Progressively tighten the manifold retaining nuts to the specified torque, working in a diagonal sequence, then refit the exhaust manifold as described in Section 16.

2.8 litre models

Note: *Refer to the precautions given in Section 1 of this Chapter before proceeding.*

Removal

15 Disconnect the battery negative lead.

16 Slacken the clip and disconnect the air intake hose from the intake elbow over the top of the engine.

17 Undo the nut and bolt securing the hose clip to the throttle valve air intake elbow. Lift away the clip and move the hoses to one side.

18 Disconnect the vacuum hose from the throttle valve actuator pipe stub.

19 Slacken the clip securing the short plenum chamber connecting hose to the inlet manifold.

20 Disconnect the vacuum hose at the base of the plenum chamber, then undo the two bolts and remove the plenum chamber and throttle valve assembly from the cylinder head cover.

21 Carefully clean around the injectors and injector pipe union nuts. Pull the leak-off pipes from the injectors.

22 Unscrew the union nuts securing the injector pipes to the fuel injection pump. Counterhold the unions on the pump, when unscrewing the nuts. Cover open unions to keep dirt out, using small plastic bags or fingers cut from rubber gloves.

23 Unscrew the union nuts and disconnect the pipes from the injectors. Remove the pipe assemblies from the engine and cover the ends of the injectors to prevent dirt ingress.

24 Remove the engine oil dipstick from the dipstick tube and cover the open end of the tube.

25 Disconnect the vacuum hoses from the two EGR valves on the inlet manifold.

26 Undo the two nuts securing the air pipe flange to the EGR valve adaptor. Release the air pipe from the support clips on the manifold and carefully separate the pipe flange from the EGR valve adaptor. Recover the gasket.

27 Undo the bolts securing the coolant pipe assembly to the inlet manifold.

28 Check that all relevant pipes, hoses and wires have been disconnected to facilitate removal of the manifold.

29 Evenly and progressively slacken and remove the nuts and bolts securing the inlet manifold to the cylinder head, then lift away the manifold, complete with EGR valves. Recover the manifold gasket.

30 If necessary the EGR valves can be removed from the manifold as described in Chapter 4C.

31 Thoroughly clean the mating faces of the cylinder head, inlet manifold, and EGR pipe flange and adaptor.

Refitting

32 Position the new gasket on the cylinder head studs then locate the manifold in position. Fit the retaining bolts and nuts and tighten progressively, in a diagonal sequence to the specified torque.

33 Using a new gasket, refit the EGR valve air pipe to the valve adaptor and secure with the two nuts tightened to the specified torque. Reconnect the vacuum hoses to the EGR valves.

34 Refit the coolant pipe assembly to the manifold, and insert the engine oil dipstick.

35 Refit and reconnect the injector fuel pipes, and tighten the unions. Counterhold the unions on the pump when tightening the pipe-to-pump union nuts.

36 Locate the plenum chamber and throttle valve assembly on the cylinder head cover, with the connecting hose engaged over the inlet manifold air intake. Refit and tighten the plenum chamber mounting bolts and secure the hose with the clip.

37 Refit and secure the hose clip to the side of the throttle valve air intake elbow. Reconnect the remaining air and vacuum hoses to the plenum chamber assembly.

38 Reconnect the battery negative lead then prime and bleed the fuel system as described in Section 7.

16 Exhaust manifold - removal and refitting

Note: *New gasket(s) must be used on refitting.*

2.3 litre models

Removal

Note: *The exhaust manifold is removed with the turbocharger as an assembly.*

1 Disconnect the battery negative lead.

2 Chock the rear wheels then jack up the front of the vehicle and support it on axle stands (see *Jacking and Vehicle Support*). Remove the engine undershield.

3 Slacken and remove the nuts and bolts, then free the exhaust front pipe from the turbocharger and recover the gasket.

4 Undo the bolt securing the support bracket to the base of the turbocharger.

5 Undo the union and disconnect the oil return hose from the turbocharger. Suitably cover the end of the hose and the turbocharger union to prevent dirt entry, then tie the hose to one side.

6 Lower the vehicle to the ground.

7 Slacken the clip and disconnect the crankcase ventilation hose from the cylinder head cover.

8 Slacken the clips and disconnect the vacuum hose and air intake duct from the inlet manifold.

9 Undo the EGR valve corrugated pipe retaining clip and release the pipe end from the manifold.

10 Disconnect the vacuum hose at the EGR valve and the oil feed hose union at the turbocharger. Suitably cover the end of the hose and the turbocharger inlet to prevent dirt entry.

11 Move aside all pipes and hoses likely to interfere with removal of the manifolds, releasing any cable ties or clips as necessary.

12 Evenly and progressively slacken and remove the bolts securing both the inlet and exhaust manifolds to the cylinder head, noting the locations of the different bolt types. Lift away the inlet manifold, followed by the

16.22 Disconnect the coolant hose from the heater pipe - 2.5 litre models

16.23a Undo the nut (arrowed) . . .

16.23b . . . remove the washer and release the pipe from the stud - 2.5 litre models

exhaust manifold and turbocharger. Recover the gasket.

13 Thoroughly clean the mating faces of the cylinder head and both manifolds.

Refitting

14 Refitting is a reversal of removal bearing in mind the following points:

a) *Use a new gasket and progressively tighten the manifold retaining bolts to the specified torque, working in a diagonal sequence.*

b) *Use a new exhaust front pipe-to-turbocharger gasket and securely tighten the nuts and bolts.*

c) *Check and if necessary top up the engine oil on completion (see Weekly checks).*

2.5 litre models

Removal

Note: *The exhaust manifold is removed with the turbocharger as an assembly.*

15 Disconnect the battery negative lead.

16 Drain the cooling system as described in Chapter 1B.

17 Slacken the clip and disconnect the expansion tank hose from the cylinder head water manifold.

18 Slacken the clips and disconnect the air duct from the intercooler plastic pipe and the inlet manifold.

19 Compress the clip legs and disconnect the vent hose from the crankcase ventilation valve.

20 Slacken the clips securing the intake air hose to the air mass meter and turbocharger and remove the hose, complete with crankcase ventilation valve.

21 Slacken the clips and disconnect the remaining intake air hose from the turbocharger and intercooler.

22 Compress the clip legs and disconnect the coolant hose from the heater pipe connection at the front of the engine **(see illustration).**

23 Undo the nut securing the heater pipe to the support stud on the exhaust manifold **(see illustration).** Remove the washer, ease the pipe off the stud and move it to one side **(see illustration).**

24 Undo the two bolts securing the

turbocharger heat shield to the exhaust manifold **(see illustration).**

25 Remove the heat shield and recover the large flat washer from the heater pipe support stud **(see illustrations).** Unscrew the support stud from the manifold.

26 Unscrew the EGR air pipe union nut at the rear of the exhaust manifold.

27 Disconnect the vacuum hose from the EGR valve.

28 Undo the four bolts securing the intake elbow to the inlet manifold. Lift off the elbow, complete with upper hose bracket and EGR valve, while at the same time releasing the EGR air pipe from the exhaust manifold **(see illustrations).**

29 Undo the two bolts, remove the large flat

16.24 Undo the two turbocharger heat shield retaining bolts (arrowed) . . .

16.25a . . . remove the heat shield . . .

16.25b . . . and recover the large flat washer - 2.5 litre models

16.28a Remove the intake elbow from the inlet manifold . . .

16.28b . . . while at the same time releasing the EGR air pipe from the exhaust manifold - 2.5 litre models

4B

washers and lift off the exhaust manifold heat shield **(see illustration)**.

30 Chock the rear wheels then jack up the front of the vehicle and support it on axle stands (see *Jacking and Vehicle Support*). Remove the engine undershield.

31 Slacken and remove the nuts and bolts, then free the exhaust front pipe from the turbocharger and recover the gasket.

32 Slacken the clip and disconnect the turbocharger oil return hose from the cylinder block. Be prepared for oil spillage and have a suitable container handy. Cover the cylinder block pipe stub and the end of the hose to prevent dirt entry.

33 Lower the vehicle to the ground.

34 Undo the banjo union securing the oil feed pipe to the turbocharger and recover the two copper washers **(see illustration)**. Note that new washers will be required for refitting. Cover the turbocharger orifice to prevent dirt entry.

35 Slacken the clips and disconnect the radiator top hose from the thermostat cover and radiator. Similarly disconnect the bypass hose between the coolant pump and thermostat housing.

36 Undo the four nuts, collect the washers and remove the thermostat housing from the water manifold. Recover the gasket.

37 Undo the eight exhaust manifold retaining nuts and remove the washers. Remove the lifting bracket from the rear of the manifold then carefully slide the manifold and turbocharger assembly off the mounting studs. Recover the four manifold-to-cylinder head gaskets.

38 Thoroughly clean the mating faces of the cylinder head, manifold and thermostat housing.

Refitting

39 Refitting is a reversal of removal bearing in mind the following points:

a) *Use new gaskets and progressively tighten the manifold retaining bolts to the specified torque, working in a diagonal sequence.*

b) *Use new gaskets on all remaining sealing faces and tighten all fastenings to the specified torque, where given.*

c) *Use new copper washers on the turbocharger oil feed pipe banjo union.*

d) *Refill the cooling system as described in Chapter 1B, and check and if necessary top up the engine oil (see Weekly checks).*

2.8 litre models

Removal

Note: *It is preferable to remove the exhaust manifold complete with turbocharger as an assembly. If desired, however, the turbocharger can be removed first, as described in Section 18.*

40 Disconnect the battery negative lead.

41 Drain the cooling system as described in Chapter 1B.

42 Slacken the clip and disconnect the air intake hose from the intake elbow over the top of the engine.

43 Undo the nut and bolt securing the hose clip to the throttle valve air intake elbow. Lift away the clip and move the hoses to one side.

44 Disconnect the vacuum hose from the throttle valve actuator pipe stub.

45 Slacken the clip securing the short plenum chamber connecting hose to the inlet manifold.

46 Disconnect the vacuum hose at the base of the plenum chamber, then undo the two bolts and remove the plenum chamber and throttle valve assembly from the cylinder head cover.

47 Slacken the clips and disconnect the remaining air intake ducts from the turbocharger.

48 Undo the nuts securing the air pipe flange to the EGR valve adaptor and exhaust manifold. Release the air pipe from the support clips on the manifold and remove the pipe from the engine. Recover the gaskets.

49 Remove the engine oil dipstick from the dipstick tube and cover the open end of the tube.

50 Chock the rear wheels then jack up the front of the vehicle and support it on axle

stands (see *Jacking and Vehicle Support*). Remove the engine undershield.

51 Slacken and remove the nuts and bolts, then free the exhaust front pipe from the turbocharger and recover the gasket.

52 Undo the banjo unions securing the oil feed pipe to the turbocharger and cylinder block and recover the two copper washers at each union. Note that new washers will be required for refitting. Undo the pipe support bracket bolt and remove the oil feed pipe from the engine. Cover the open unions to prevent dirt entry.

53 Undo the nuts and disconnect the oil return pipe flanges from the sump and turbocharger. Remove the pipe and recover the gaskets. Be prepared for oil spillage and have a suitable container handy. Cover the sump orifice and the turbocharger outlet to prevent dirt entry.

54 Lower the vehicle to the ground.

55 Disconnect the vacuum hose from the turbocharger wastegate, and the coolant hoses from the turbocharger outlets.

56 Undo the bolts and remove the heat shield from the turbocharger.

57 Undo the bolts securing the two heat shields to the exhaust manifold and remove the heat shields.

58 Check that all relevant pipes, hoses and wires have been disconnected to facilitate removal of the manifold.

59 Evenly and progressively slacken and remove the six bolts and two nuts securing the exhaust manifold to the cylinder head. Undo the lower support bracket attachments and withdraw the exhaust manifold, turbocharger and support bracket from the cylinder head.

60 Thoroughly clean the mating faces of the cylinder head and exhaust manifold.

Refitting

61 Refitting is a reversal of removal bearing in mind the following points:

a) *Use a new gasket and progressively tighten the manifold retaining bolts to the specified torque, working in a diagonal sequence.*

b) *Use a new exhaust front pipe-to-turbocharger gasket and tighten the nuts and bolts to the specified torque.*

c) *Use new copper washers and new gasket on the turbocharger oil feed and return pipes.*

d) *Refill the cooling system as described in Chapter 1B, and check and if necessary top up the engine oil (see Weekly checks).*

17 Turbocharger - description and precautions

Description

1 A turbocharger is fitted to all diesel engines. It increases engine efficiency by raising the

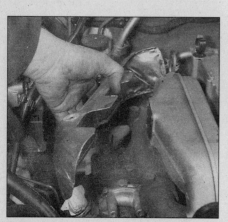

16.29 Remove the exhaust manifold heat shield - 2.5 litre models

16.34 Undo the turbocharger oil feed pipe banjo union (arrowed) - 2.5 litre models

pressure in the inlet manifold above atmospheric pressure; instead of the air simply being sucked into the cylinders, it is forced in. Additional fuel is supplied by the injection pump in proportion to the increased air intake.

2 Energy for the operation of the turbocharger comes from the exhaust gas. The gas flows through a specially-shaped housing (the turbine housing) and spins the turbine wheel. The turbine wheel is attached to a shaft, at the end of which is another vaned wheel known as the compressor wheel. The compressor wheel spins in its own housing and compresses the inducted air on the way to the inlet manifold.

3 Between the turbocharger and the inlet manifold, the compressed air passes through an intercooler. This is an air-to-air heat exchanger, mounted in front of the radiator, and supplied with cooling air directly through the radiator grille. The purpose of the intercooler is to remove some of the heat gained in being compressed from the inducted air. Because cooler air is denser, removal of this heat further increases the amount of air inducted and engine efficiency.

4 Boost pressure (the pressure in the inlet manifold) is limited by a wastegate, which diverts the exhaust gas away from the turbine wheel in response to a pressure-sensitive actuator.

5 The turbo shaft is pressure-lubricated by an oil feed pipe from the main oil gallery. The shaft floats on a cushion of oil. A drain pipe returns the oil to the sump.

Precautions

6 The turbocharger operates at extremely high speeds and temperatures. Certain precautions must be observed to avoid premature failure of the turbo or injury to the operator.

7 Do not race the engine immediately after start-up, especially if it is cold. Give the oil a few seconds to circulate.

8 Always allow the engine to return to idle speed before switching it off - do not blip the throttle and switch off, as this will leave the turbo spinning without lubrication.

9 Allow the engine to idle for several minutes before switching off after a high-speed run.

10 Observe the recommended intervals for oil and filter changing, and use a reputable oil of the specified quality. Neglect of oil changing, or use of inferior oil, can cause carbon formation on the turbo shaft and subsequent failure.

 Warning: Do not operate the turbo with any parts exposed. Foreign objects falling onto the rotating vanes could cause excessive damage and (if ejected) personal injury.

18 Turbocharger - removal and refitting

2.3 and 2.5 litre models

Removal

1 Remove the exhaust manifold complete with turbocharger as described in Section 16.

2 With the manifold on the bench, undo the bolts/nuts securing the turbocharger flange to the manifold. Lift off the turbocharger and recover the gasket.

3 On 2.3 litre models, the exhaust outlet elbow can be removed, if necessary, after undoing the nuts securing the elbow to the turbocharger.

4 Do not attempt to dismantle the turbocharger any further. If the unit is thought to be faulty, take it to a turbo specialist or Vauxhall dealer for testing and examination.

Refitting

5 Refitting is a reversal of removal using new gaskets. Ensure that all mating faces are clean before refitting and tighten all fastenings to the specified torque, where given. Refit the manifold and turbocharger assembly as described in Section 16.

2.8 litre models

Removal

6 Disconnect the battery negative lead.

7 Drain the cooling system as described in Chapter 1B.

8 Slacken the clip and disconnect the air intake hose from the intake elbow over the top of the engine.

9 Undo the nut and bolt securing the hose clip to the throttle valve air intake elbow. Lift away the clip and move the hoses to one side.

10 Disconnect the vacuum hose from the throttle valve actuator pipe stub.

11 Slacken the clip securing the short plenum chamber connecting hose to the inlet manifold.

12 Disconnect the vacuum hose at the base of the plenum chamber, then undo the two bolts and remove the plenum chamber and throttle valve assembly from the cylinder head cover.

13 Slacken the clips and disconnect the remaining air intake ducts from the turbocharger.

14 Chock the rear wheels then jack up the front of the vehicle and support it on axle stands (see *Jacking and Vehicle Support*). Remove the engine undershield.

15 Slacken and remove the nuts and bolts, then free the exhaust front pipe from the turbocharger and recover the gasket.

16 Undo the banjo unions securing the oil feed pipe to the turbocharger and cylinder block and recover the two copper washers at each union. Note that new washers will be required for refitting. Undo the pipe support

bracket bolt and remove the oil feed pipe from the engine. Cover the open unions to prevent dirt entry.

17 Undo the nuts and disconnect the oil return pipe flanges from the sump and turbocharger. Remove the pipe and recover the gaskets. Be prepared for oil spillage and have a suitable container handy. Cover the sump orifice and the turbocharger outlet to prevent dirt entry.

18 Lower the vehicle to the ground.

19 Disconnect the vacuum hose from the turbocharger wastegate, and the coolant pipes from the turbocharger outlets.

20 Undo the bolts and remove the heat shield from the turbocharger.

21 Undo the bolts securing the turbocharger flange to the manifold. Lift off the turbocharger and recover the gasket.

22 If necessary, the exhaust outlet elbow can be removed after undoing the nuts securing the elbow to the turbocharger.

23 Do not attempt to dismantle the turbocharger any further. If the unit is thought to be faulty, take it to a turbo specialist or Vauxhall dealer for testing and examination.

Refitting

24 Refitting is a reversal of removal bearing in mind the following points:

a) *Ensure that all mating faces are clean and use new gaskets.*

b) *Tighten all fastenings to the specified torque, where given.*

c) *Use new copper washers and new gaskets on the turbocharger oil feed and return pipes.*

d) *Before reconnecting the oil feed pipe to the turbocharger, inject 100 cc of clean engine oil into the oil feed port on the turbocharger and rotate the turbine shaft by hand to lubricate the bearings.*

e) *Refill the cooling system as described in Chapter 1B, and check and if necessary top up the engine oil (see Weekly checks).*

19 Intercooler - removal and refitting

Removal

Note: *On vehicles equipped with air conditioning, it will be necessary to unbolt and move aside the components mounted in the vicinity of the intercooler. Do not disconnect any refrigerant pipes or hoses when doing this. Depending on model, year, and optional equipment fitted, it may not be possible to move the air conditioning components sufficiently clear without disconnecting the refrigerant pipes. If this is the case, entrust removal and refitting of the intercooler to your Vauxhall dealer.*

1 The intercooler is located at the front of the vehicle, behind the radiator grille.

4B

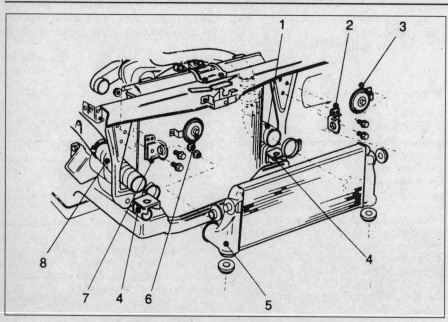

19.3 Intercooler components and attachments

1	Air duct	4	Lower mounting bracket	7	Upper mounting bracket
2	Upper mounting bracket	5	Intercooler	8	Air duct
3	Horn	6	Horn		

2 Remove the radiator grille as described in Chapter 12.

3 Slacken the clips and disconnect the two air ducts from the intercooler **(see illustration)**.

4 Disconnect the horn wiring connectors.

5 Undo the bolts and move the bonnet lock vertical stay to one side.

6 Undo the nuts and bolts securing the two upper intercooler mounting brackets and horn mounting brackets to the front body panel and remove the two horns.

7 Lift the intercooler upwards to disengage the lower mountings from the brackets and remove the intercooler from the vehicle.

8 Withdraw the upper mountings from the intercooler lugs and check the condition of all mounting bushes. Renew any that show signs of deterioration.

Refitting

9 Refitting is a reversal of removal.

20 Exhaust system - general information and component renewal

General information

1 The exhaust system consists of three sections; the front pipe (which incorporates the catalytic converter on later models), the intermediate pipe and silencer, and the tailpipe. On 2.8 litre models, an exhaust throttle valve is located between the front pipe and intermediate pipe joint flanges. The throttle valve is part of the Quick Warm-up System which is described in Section 1.

2 The system is suspended throughout its entire length by a combination of clamping brackets and rubber mountings.

Removal

3 To remove a part of the system, first jack up the front or rear of the vehicle, and support it on axle stands (see *Jacking and vehicle support*). Alternatively, position the vehicle over an inspection pit, or on car ramps. Where fitted, remove the engine undershield.

Front pipe (and catalytic converter)

4 Undo the nuts/bolts securing the front pipe to the turbocharger or turbocharger elbow, as applicable.

5 Release the front pipe at the transmission support bracket. This can be done by undoing the nut and removing the upper part of the front pipe clamp, or by undoing the nuts and bolts securing the complete bracket assembly to the transmission. On 2.5 litre models, undo the nut and bolt and release the front pipe from the additional support bracket on the bellhousing.

6 Undo and remove the flange nuts/bolts, and disconnect the front pipe from the intermediate pipe. On 2.8 litre models, lift away the exhaust throttle valve as the front pipe-to-intermediate pipe joint is separated. On 2.3 litre models, collect the tension springs (where fitted) from the bolts. Withdraw the front pipe from under the vehicle and collect the gaskets and/or seal rings.

Intermediate pipe - 2.3 litre models

7 Undo the tail pipe to intermediate pipe clamp bolt and nut and slide the clamp away from the joint. Apply a liberal amount of penetrating oil to the joint.

8 Undo and remove the flange nuts/bolts, disconnect the intermediate pipe from the front pipe and collect the tension springs (where fitted) from the bolts. Recover the gasket or seal ring.

9 Release the intermediate pipe from the tail pipe using a twisting motion, disengage the rubber support ring and remove the pipe from under the vehicle.

Intermediate pipe - 2.5 and 2.8 litre models

10 Undo and remove the flange bolts, and disconnect the intermediate pipe from the front pipe. Recover the gasket. Similarly disconnect the tail pipe from the intermediate pipe.

11 Undo the nuts securing the silencer rubber mountings to the mounting bracket and remove the pipe from under the vehicle.

Tailpipe

12 On 2.3 litre models, undo the tail pipe-to-intermediate pipe clamp bolt and nut and slide the clamp away from the joint. Apply a liberal amount of penetrating oil to the joint. On 2.5 and 2.8 litre models, undo and remove the flange bolts, and disconnect the tail pipe from the intermediate pipe.

13 Release the tail pipe from the intermediate pipe using a twisting motion (2.3 litre models), disengage the rubber support rings and remove the pipe from under the vehicle.

Heat shield(s)

14 The heat shields are secured to the underside of the body by various nuts and bolts. Each shield can be removed separately once the relevant exhaust section has been removed. If a shield is being removed to gain access to a component located behind it, it may prove sufficient in some cases to remove the retaining nuts and/or bolts, and simply lower the shield, without disturbing the exhaust system.

Refitting

15 Each section is refitted by reversing the removal sequence, noting the following points:

a) Ensure that all traces of corrosion have been removed from the flanges, and renew all necessary gaskets.

b) Inspect the rubber mountings for signs of damage or deterioration, and renew as necessary.

c) Prior to tightening the exhaust system fasteners, ensure that all rubber mountings are correctly located, and that there is adequate clearance between the exhaust system and vehicle underbody.

Chapter 4 Part C
Emission control systems

Contents

Catalytic converter - general information and precautions 4
Diesel engine emission control systems - testing and
   component renewal 3
General information and precautions 1
Petrol engine emission control systems - testing and
   component renewal 2

Degrees of difficulty

Easy, suitable for novice with little experience		**Fairly easy,** suitable for beginner with some experience		**Fairly difficult,** suitable for competent DIY mechanic		**Difficult,** suitable for experienced DIY mechanic		**Very difficult,** suitable for expert DIY or professional	

Specifications

Torque wrench settings	Nm	lbf ft
Air pipe to EGR valve (2.5 litre diesel models)	27	20
EGR valve to manifold (2.5 litre diesel models)	11	8
Oxygen sensor (petrol models)	30	22
Secondary air injection system:		
Air injection valve mounting bolts	7	5
Air pump bracket mounting bolts	9	6
Metal pipe flanges to engine	20	15
Solenoid valve mounting bolts	7	5

4C

1 General information and precautions

1 All petrol engine models use unleaded petrol and also have various other features built into the fuel system to help minimise harmful emissions. All models are equipped with a crankcase emission-control system, a catalytic converter, an evaporative emission control system and, on 2.0 litre (X20SE) and 2.2 litre (X22XE) engines, an exhaust gas recirculation (EGR) system, to keep fuel vapour/exhaust gas emissions down to a minimum. In addition, 2.2 litre (X22XE) engines are also equipped with a secondary air injection system to further improve the exhaust gas emissions during warm-up.

2 All diesel engine models are also designed to meet strict emission requirements and are also equipped with a crankcase emission control system. In addition to this, later models are fitted with a catalytic converter to reduce harmful exhaust emissions. To further reduce emissions, an exhaust gas recirculation (EGR) system is fitted.

3 The emission control systems function as follows.

Petrol models

Crankcase emission control

4 To reduce the emission of unburned hydrocarbons from the crankcase into the atmosphere, the engine is sealed and the blow-by gases and oil vapour are drawn from inside the crankcase, through a wire mesh oil separator, into the inlet tract to be burned by the engine during normal combustion.

5 Under conditions of high manifold depression (idling, deceleration) the gases will be sucked positively out of the crankcase. Under conditions of low manifold depression (acceleration, full-throttle running), the gases are forced out of the crankcase by the (relatively) higher crankcase pressure; if the engine is worn, the raised crankcase pressure (due to increased blow-by) will cause some of the flow to return under all manifold conditions.

Exhaust emission control

6 To minimise the amount of pollutants which escape into the atmosphere, all models are fitted with a catalytic converter in the exhaust system. The system is of the closed-loop type, in which an oxygen sensor in the exhaust system provides the fuel-injection/ignition system ECU with constant feedback, enabling the ECU to adjust the mixture to provide the best possible conditions for the converter to operate.

7 The oxygen sensor has a heating element built-in that is controlled by the ECU through the sensor relay to quickly bring the sensor's tip to an efficient operating temperature. The sensor's tip is sensitive to oxygen and sends the ECU a varying voltage depending on the amount of oxygen in the exhaust gases; if the inlet air/fuel mixture is too rich, the exhaust gases are low in oxygen so the sensor sends a low-voltage signal, the voltage rising as the mixture weakens and the amount of oxygen rises in the exhaust gases. Peak conversion efficiency of all major pollutants occurs if the inlet air/fuel mixture is maintained at the chemically-correct ratio for the complete combustion of petrol of 14.7 parts (by weight) of air to 1 part of fuel (the stoichiometric ratio). The sensor output voltage alters in a large step at this point, the ECU using the signal change as a reference point and correcting the inlet air/fuel mixture accordingly by altering the fuel injector pulse width.

Evaporative emission control

8 To minimise the escape into the atmosphere of unburned hydrocarbons, an evaporative emissions control system is also fitted to all models. The fuel tank filler cap is sealed and a charcoal canister is mounted on the left-hand side of the engine compartment. The canister collects the petrol vapours generated in the tank when the vehicle is parked and stores them until they can be cleared from the canister (under the control of the fuel-injection/ignition system ECU) via the purge valve into the inlet tract to be burned by the engine during normal combustion.

9 To ensure that the engine runs correctly when it is cold and/or idling and to protect the catalytic converter from the effects of an over-rich mixture, the purge control valve is not opened by the ECU until the engine has warmed up, and the engine is under load; the valve solenoid is then modulated on and off to allow the stored vapour to pass into the inlet tract.

Exhaust gas recirculation (EGR) system - 2.0 litre (X20SE) and 2.2 litre (X22XE) engine models

10 This system is designed to recirculate small quantities of exhaust gas into the inlet tract, and therefore into the combustion process. This reduces the level of unburnt hydrocarbons present in the exhaust gas before it reaches the catalytic converter. The system is controlled by the fuel-injection/ignition ECU, using the information from its various sensors, via the EGR valve. The EGR valve assembly is mounted on the cylinder head at the rear. The valve assembly contains the vacuum operated valve and the electrical solenoid valve which is used to switch the valve on and off.

Secondary air injection system - 2.2 litre (X22XE) engine models

11 The purpose of the secondary air injection system is to decrease exhaust gas emissions when the engine is cold. The system achieves this by raising the temperature of the exhaust gasses which has the effect of quickly warming the catalytic converter up to its normal operating temperature. Once the catalytic converter is up to temperature, the air injection system is switched off.

12 The system consists of the pump, the air injection valve and the solenoid valve and is controlled by the fuel-injection/ignition ECU. When the engine is cold, the solenoid valve switches the air injection valve to open and the pump injects a controlled amount of air into the cylinder head exhaust ports. The air then mixes with the exhaust gasses, causing any unburned particles of the fuel in the mixture to be burnt in the exhaust port/manifold which effectively raises the temperature of the exhaust gasses. Once the catalytic converter is up to temperature, the

solenoid valve closes the air injection valve and the pump is switched off. A non-return valve prevents the exhaust gasses passing through the air injection valve.

Diesel models

Crankcase emission control

13 Refer to paragraphs 4 and 5.

Exhaust emission control

14 To minimise the amount of pollutants which escape into the atmosphere, an unregulated catalytic converter is fitted in the exhaust system of later models. The catalytic converter operates remotely in the exhaust system, and there is no oxygen sensor as fitted to the petrol engines.

Exhaust gas recirculation (EGR) system

15 The system is designed to recirculate small quantities of exhaust gas into the inlet tract, and therefore into the combustion process. This reduces the level of unburnt hydrocarbons present in the exhaust gas before it reaches the catalytic converter (where fitted) or is released into the atmosphere, and also lowers the combustion temperature.

16 The volume of exhaust gas recirculated is controlled by vacuum supplied from the vacuum pump. On 2.3 litre models, vacuum is supplied directly to a vacuum regulator mounted on the injection pump. The vacuum regulator controls the EGR valve operation depending on engine speed and vacuum supply. On 2.5 litre models, the system is controlled by the injection system ECU, using information from its various sensors, via the EGR valve. The EGR valve is vacuum operated and is switched on and off by an electrically operated vacuum switching valve. On 2.8 litre models, the system is controlled by the EGR system control unit according to information received from various sensors, via two EGR valves. The EGR valves are vacuum operated and are switched on and off by two electrically operated vacuum switching valves.

2 Petrol engine emission control systems - testing and component renewal

Crankcase emission control

1 The components of this system require no attention other than to check that the hose(s) are clear and undamaged at regular intervals.

Evaporative emission control

Testing

2 If the system is thought to be faulty, disconnect the hoses from the charcoal canister and purge valve, and check that the hoses are clear by blowing through them. Full testing of the system can only be carried out using specialist electronic equipment which is

connected to the engine management system diagnostic wiring connector. If the purge valve or charcoal canister are thought to be faulty, they must be renewed.

Charcoal canister - renewal

3 The charcoal canister is located on the left-hand side of the engine compartment.

4 Compress the hose clamps, and disconnect the hoses from the top of the canister, noting their locations to ensure correct refitting.

5 Unscrew the canister clamp bolt, and withdraw the canister from the clamp bracket.

6 Fit the new canister using a reversal of the removal procedure. Make sure that the hoses are correctly reconnected, as noted before removal.

Purge valve - renewal

7 The purge valve is located on the right-hand side of the engine on 2.0 litre (X20SE) engines, at the rear of the cylinder head on 2.2 litre (X22XE) engines, or on a bracket adjacent to the power steering fluid reservoir on all other engines.

8 On X20SE engines, open the wiring loom trough on the side of the cylinder head, lift out the wiring harness then remove the trough. For improved access, disconnect the crankcase ventilation hose. On X22XE engines, remove the DIS module as described in Chapter 5B.

9 Disconnect the wiring plug from the valve, then disconnect the hoses noting their locations to ensure correct refitting.

10 Undo the retaining bolts and remove the purge valve and bracket from its location.

11 Refitting is a reversal of removal, ensuring that the hoses are reconnected correctly, as noted before removal.

Exhaust emission control

Testing

12 The performance of the catalytic converter can be checked only by measuring the exhaust gasses using a good quality, carefully-calibrated exhaust gas analyser.

13 If the CO level at the tailpipe is too rich, the vehicle should be taken to a Vauxhall dealer so that the complete fuel-injection and ignition systems, including the oxygen sensor, can be thoroughly checked using the special diagnostic equipment. Once these have been checked and are known to be free from faults, the fault must be in the catalytic converter which must be renewed.

Catalytic converter - renewal

14 Refer to Chapter 4A.

Oxygen sensor - renewal

Note: *The oxygen sensor is delicate and will not work if it is dropped or knocked, if its power supply is disrupted, or if any cleaning materials are used on it.*

15 Raise the front of the vehicle and support it on axle stands (see *Jacking and vehicle support*). Remove the engine undershield then

disconnect the oxygen sensor wiring, releasing it from the clips or cable ties where applicable.

16 Unscrew the sensor from the exhaust downpipe, and remove it.

17 Clean the threads in the exhaust pipe, and the threads of the sensor (if it is to be refitted).

18 Note that if the sensor wires are broken, the sensor must be renewed. No attempt should be made to repair them.

19 If the original oxygen sensor is being refitted, apply high-temperature anti-seize compound to the sensor threads (Vauxhall recommend the use of grease 19 48 602, part no. 90 295 397 - available from Vauxhall parts stockists). New sensors supplied by Vauxhall have there threads pre-coated and no additional compound should be applied. Screw the sensor in by hand, then tighten it fully to the specified torque.

20 Reconnect the sensor wiring, refit the undershield and lower the vehicle to the ground.

Exhaust gas recirculation

Testing

21 Comprehensive testing of the system can only be carried out using specialist electronic equipment which is connected to the engine management system diagnostic wiring connector. If the EGR valve is thought to be faulty, it must be renewed.

EGR valve - renewal

22 Ensure that the ignition is switched off then disconnect the wiring connector and vacuum hose from the EGR valve which is located at the rear of the cylinder head **(see illustration)**.

23 Undo the retaining screws and remove the valve and gasket.

24 Refitting is a reversal of removal, ensuring that the retaining bolts are securely tightened.

Secondary air injection system

Testing

25 Comprehensive testing of the system can only be carried out using specialist electronic equipment which is connected to the engine management system diagnostic wiring connector. If any component is thought to be faulty, it must be renewed.

Secondary air injection valve - renewal

26 The injection valve is mounted on a bracket above the secondary air pump on the right-hand side of the engine compartment **(see illustration)**.

27 Mark the location of the vacuum and air hoses before removing them from the valve.

28 After disconnecting the hoses undo the two mounting bolts, and remove the valve from the mounting bracket.

29 Refitting is a reversal of removal. Ensure that the hoses are fitted correctly.

Secondary air injection pump assembly - renewal

30 Disconnect the air injection pump and solenoid valve wiring connectors and release the wiring harness from the cable ties **(see illustration)**.

31 Disconnect the vacuum hose from the solenoid valve.

32 Disconnect the air hoses from the air injection pump and air injection valve.

33 Undo the two mounting bracket bolts and remove the air injection pump and mounting bracket assembly.

34 Refitting is a reversal of removal. Ensure that the hoses are fitted correctly.

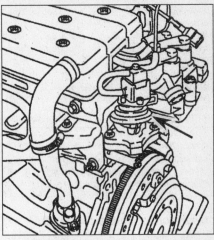

2.22 EGR valve location (arrowed) - 2.0 litre (X20SE) and 2.2 litre petrol engines

Secondary air injection metal pipe - renewal

35 Disconnect the air hose from the non-return valve on the end of the pipe.

36 Undo the two bolts securing the metal pipe bracket to the engine.

37 Undo the bolts and remove the exhaust manifold heat shield.

38 Undo the two bolts securing the metal pipe connecting flanges to the engine and remove the pipe. Recover the sealing washers from the pipe flanges.

39 Refitting is a reversal of removal, using new sealing washers and tightening the flange bolts to the specified torque.

Solenoid valve - renewal

40 The solenoid valve is mounted on a bracket above the secondary air injection

4C

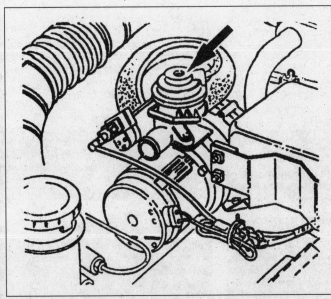

2.26 Secondary air injection valve (arrowed) - 2.2 litre petrol engines

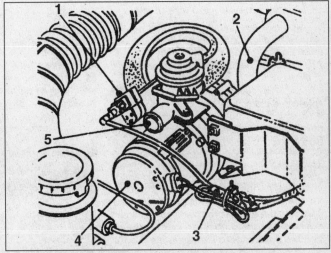

2.30 Secondary air injection pump attachments - 2.2 litre petrol engines

1 Solenoid valve
2 Air hose from air cleaner
3 Wiring connector
4 Secondary air injection pump
5 Injection valve hose outlet

pump on the right-hand side of the engine compartment.

41 Disconnect the solenoid valve wiring connector and the two vacuum hoses, identifying the hoses to aid refitting.

42 Undo the two bolts and remove the solenoid valve from its location.

43 Refitting is a reversal of removal. Ensure that the hoses are fitted correctly.

3 Diesel engine emission control systems - testing and component renewal

Crankcase emission control

1 The components of this system require no attention other than to check that the hose(s) are clear and undamaged at regular intervals.

Exhaust emission control

Testing

2 The performance of the catalytic converter can be checked only by measuring the exhaust gasses using a good quality, carefully-calibrated exhaust gas analyser.

3 If the catalytic converter is thought to be faulty, it is worth checking that the problem is not due to faulty injectors. Refer to your Vauxhall dealer for further information.

Catalytic converter - renewal

4 Refer to Chapter 4B.

Exhaust gas recirculation

Testing

5 Comprehensive testing of the system can only be carried out using specialist electronic equipment. If the EGR valve is thought to be faulty, it must be renewed.

EGR valve renewal - 2.3 litre models

6 The valve is located at the rear of the exhaust manifold and is connected to the inlet manifold via a corrugated metal pipe.

7 Disconnect the vacuum hose from the top of the valve.

8 Undo the clamp bolt and remove the corrugated pipe to manifold clamping ring.

9 Undo the two bolts securing the valve to the exhaust manifold. Lift off the valve and pipe and recover the flange gasket.

10 Refitting is a reversal of removal, using a new gasket.

EGR valve renewal - 2.5 litre models

11 The valve is bolted to the underside of the inlet manifold and is connected to the exhaust manifold via a metal pipe.

12 To gain access to the valve, remove the intercooler to inlet manifold air duct as described in Chapter 4B.

13 Disconnect the vacuum hose from the side of the valve **(see illustration)**.

14 Undo the two bolts securing the air pipe flange to the rear of the valve.

3.13 Disconnecting the vacuum hose from the EGR valve - 2.5 litre diesel engine

15 Undo the two bolts securing the valve to the manifold. Remove the valve and recover the gasket between the valve and manifold, and between the air pipe and valve.

16 Refitting is a reversal of removal, using new gaskets.

EGR valve renewal - 2.8 litre models

17 Two EGR valves are used in this system, bolted to the side of the inlet manifold and connected to the exhaust manifold via an adaptor and metal pipe **(see illustration)**.

18 Disconnect the vacuum hose from the valve to be removed.

19 Undo the two lower bolts securing the valve to the air pipe adaptor.

20 Undo the two nuts securing the valve to the manifold. Withdraw the valve from the manifold studs and recover the gasket between the valve and manifold, and between the air pipe adaptor and valve.

21 Refitting is a reversal of removal, using new gaskets.

EGR vacuum switching valve - 2.5 litre models

22 The vacuum switching valve is located on the right-hand side of the engine compartment, adjacent to the fuse/relay box **(see illustration)**.

23 Disconnect the wiring connector from the front of the valve.

24 Identify the vacuum hoses for correct refitting then disconnect the hoses from the valve.

3.22 EGR vacuum switching valve location (arrowed) - 2.5 litre diesel engine

3.17 Twin EGR valves located on the inlet manifold - 2.8 litre diesel engine

25 Undo the two retaining bolts and remove the valve from the mounting bracket.

26 Refitting is a reversal of removal. Ensure that the vacuum hoses are fitted correctly.

EGR vacuum switching valve renewal - 2.8 litre models

27 The two vacuum switching valves are located on the left-hand side of the engine compartment, at the rear **(see illustration)**.

28 Disconnect the wiring connectors from the front of both valves, noting the colour coding.

29 Identify the vacuum hoses for correct refitting then disconnect the hoses from the valves.

30 Undo the two retaining bolts and remove the valve assembly mounting bracket from its location.

31 Refitting is a reversal of removal. Ensure that the vacuum hoses and wiring connectors are fitted correctly.

EGR control unit renewal - 2.8 litre models

32 The EGR control unit is located in the front passenger compartment footwell on the driver's side behind the side trim kick panel.

33 Refer to Chapter 12 and remove the trim panel for access to the control unit.

34 The EGR control unit is the lower of the two control units located in the centre of the mounting bracket. Disconnect the wiring connector, undo the two screws and remove the unit from the mounting bracket.

35 Refitting is a reversal of removal

3.27 Twin vacuum switching valve location (arrowed) - 2.8 litre diesel engine

4 Catalytic converter - general information and precautions

1 The catalytic converter is a reliable and simple device which needs no maintenance in itself, but there are some facts of which an owner should be aware if the converter is to function properly for its full service life.

Petrol models

a) DO NOT use leaded petrol in a car equipped with a catalytic converter - the lead will coat the precious metals, reducing their converting efficiency and will eventually destroy the converter.

b) Always keep the ignition and fuel systems well-maintained in accordance with the manufacturer's schedule.

c) If the engine develops a misfire, do not drive the car at all (or at least as little as possible) until the fault is cured.

d) DO NOT push- or tow-start the car - this will soak the catalytic converter in unburned fuel, causing it to overheat when the engine does start.

e) DO NOT switch off the ignition at high engine speeds.

f) DO NOT use fuel or engine oil additives - these may contain substances harmful to the catalytic converter.

g) DO NOT continue to use the car if the engine burns oil to the extent of leaving a visible trail of blue smoke.

h) Remember that the catalytic converter operates at very high temperatures. DO NOT, therefore, park the car on dry undergrowth, over long grass or piles of dead leaves after a long run.

i) Remember that the catalytic converter is FRAGILE - do not strike it with tools during servicing work.

j) In some cases a sulphurous smell (like that of rotten eggs) may be noticed from the exhaust. This is common to many catalytic converter-equipped cars and once the car has covered a few thousand miles the problem should disappear.

k) The catalytic converter, used on a well-maintained and well-driven car, should last for between 50 000 and 100 000 miles - if the converter is no longer effective it must be renewed.

Diesel models

2 Refer to the information given in parts f, g, h, i and k of the petrol models information given above.

4C

Notes

Chapter 5 Part A
Starting and charging systems

Contents

Alternator - removal and refitting 7
Alternator - testing and overhaul 8
Alternator drivebelt - removal, refitting and tensioning 6
Battery - removal and refitting 4
Battery - testing and charging 3
Battery check ....See Weekly checks
Charging system - testing 5
Electrical fault finding - general information 2
Electrical system check ....See Chapter 1
General information and precautions 1
Ignition switch - removal and refitting 12
Starter motor - removal and refitting 10
Starter motor - testing and overhaul 11
Starting system - testing 9

Degrees of difficulty

Easy, suitable for novice with little experience 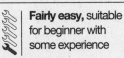	**Fairly easy,** suitable for beginner with some experience	**Fairly difficult,** suitable for competent DIY mechanic	**Difficult,** suitable for experienced DIY mechanic	**Very difficult,** suitable for expert DIY or professional

Specifications

System type .... 12-volt, negative earth

Battery
Charge condition:
Poor .... 12.5 volts
Normal .... 12.6 volts
Good .... 12.7 volts

Torque wrench settings

	Nm	lbf ft
Alternator mountings		
2.0 litre (C20NE) petrol engine	25	18
2.0 litre (X20SE) petrol engine:		
Lower mounting bolt	35	26
Rear support brace bolts	18	13
Upper mounting bracket bolts	18	13
2.2 litre (X22XE) petrol engine:		
Lower mounting bolt	35	26
Rear support brace bolts	18	13
Upper mounting bracket bolts	18	13
2.3 litre diesel engine	25	18
2.4 litre (C24NE) petrol engine	25	18
2.5 litre diesel engine:		
Lower mounting nut	47	35
Upper mounting bolt	25	18
2.8 litre diesel engine:		
Adjuster block bolt	19	14
Mounting bolt	40	30

Torque wrench settings (continued)

	Nm	lbf ft
Starter motor mountings		
2.0 litre (C20NE) petrol engine:		
Lower starter mounting bolt (engine side)	45	33
Support bracket to cylinder block	25	18
Upper starter mounting bolt (transmission side)	75	55
2.0 litre (X20SE) petrol engine:		
Starter mounting bolts	60	44
Support bracket to cylinder block	25	18
2.3 litre diesel engine	40	30
2.4 litre (C24NE) petrol engine	70	52
2.5 litre diesel engine:		
Exhaust front pipe elbow nuts and bolts	32	24
Heat shield bolts	9	7
Heat shield nuts	6	4
Starter mounting bolts	50	37
Support bracket to cylinder block	50	37
2.8 litre diesel engine:		
Clutch slave cylinder bolts	45	33
Starter mounting bolts	69	51

1 General information and precautions

General information

The engine electrical system consists mainly of the charging and starting systems. Because of their engine-related functions, these components are covered separately from the body electrical devices such as the lights, instruments, etc (which are covered in Chapter 13). On petrol engine models, refer to Part B for information on the ignition system, and on diesel engine models, refer to Part C for information on the pre-heating system.

The electrical system is of the 12-volt negative earth type.

The battery is of the low maintenance or 'maintenance-free' (sealed for life) type and is charged by the alternator, which is belt-driven from the crankshaft pulley.

The starter motor is of the pre-engaged type incorporating an integral solenoid. On starting, the solenoid moves the drive pinion into engagement with the flywheel ring gear before the starter motor is energised. Once the engine has started, a one-way clutch prevents the motor armature being driven by the engine until the pinion disengages from the flywheel.

Further details of the various systems are given in the relevant Sections of this Chapter. While some repair procedures are given, the usual course of action is to renew the component concerned. The owner whose interest extends beyond mere component renewal should obtain a copy of the *Automobile Electrical & Electronic Systems Manual*, available from the publishers of this manual.

Precautions

It is necessary to take extra care when working on the electrical system to avoid damage to semi-conductor devices (diodes and transistors), and to avoid the risk of personal injury. In addition to the precautions given in *Safety first!* at the beginning of this manual, observe the following when working on the system:

Always remove rings, watches, etc before working on the electrical system. Even with the battery disconnected, capacitive discharge could occur if a component's live terminal is earthed through a metal object. This could cause a shock or nasty burn.

Do not reverse the battery connections. Components such as the alternator, electronic control units, or any other components having semi-conductor circuitry could be irreparably damaged.

If the engine is being started using jump leads and a slave battery, connect the batteries *positive-to-positive* and *negative-to-negative* (see *Jump starting*). This also applies when connecting a battery charger.

Never disconnect the battery terminals, the alternator, any electrical wiring or any test instruments when the engine is running.

Do not allow the engine to turn the alternator when the alternator is not connected.

Never test for alternator output by 'flashing' the output lead to earth.

Never use an ohmmeter of the type incorporating a hand-cranked generator for circuit or continuity testing.

Always ensure that the battery negative lead is disconnected when working on the electrical system.

Before using electric-arc welding equipment on the car, disconnect the battery, alternator and components such as the engine management electronic control unit to protect them from the risk of damage.

Radio/cassette units are equipped with a built-in security code to deter thieves. If the power source to the unit is cut, the anti-theft system will activate. Even if the power source is immediately reconnected, the radio/cassette unit will not function until the correct security code has been entered. Therefore, if you do not know the correct security code for the radio/cassette unit **do not** disconnect the negative terminal of the battery or remove the radio/cassette unit from the vehicle. Refer to the Owner's Handbook, or your Vauxhall dealer for further information on security codes.

2 Electrical fault finding - general information

Refer to Chapter 13.

3 Battery - testing and charging

Traditional-style and low maintenance battery - testing

1 If the vehicle covers a small annual mileage, it is worthwhile checking the specific gravity of the electrolyte every three months to determine the state of charge of the battery. Use a hydrometer to make the check and compare the results with the following table.

	Ambient temperature above 25°C (77°F)	Ambient temperature below 25°C (77°F)
Fully-charged	1.210 to 1.230	1.270 to 1.290
70% charged	1.170 to 1.190	1.230 to 1.250
Fully-discharged	1.050 to 1.070	1.110 to 1.130

Note that the specific gravity readings assume an electrolyte temperature of 15°C (60°F); for every 10°C (18°F) below 15°C (60°F) subtract 0.007. For every 10°C (18°F) above 15°C (60°F) add 0.007.

2 If the battery condition is suspect, first check the specific gravity of electrolyte in each cell. A variation of 0.040 or more between any cells indicates loss of electrolyte or deterioration of the internal plates.

3 If the specific gravity variation is 0.040 or more, the battery should be renewed. If the cell variation is satisfactory but the battery is discharged, it should be charged as described later in this Section.

Maintenance-free battery - testing

4 In cases where a 'sealed for life' maintenance-free battery is fitted, topping-up and testing of the electrolyte in each cell is not possible. The condition of the battery can therefore only be tested using a battery condition indicator or a voltmeter.

5 Certain models may be fitted with a Delco-type maintenance-free battery, with a built-in charge condition indicator. The indicator is located in the top of the battery casing, and indicates the condition of the battery from its colour. If the indicator shows green, then the battery is in a good state of charge. If the indicator turns darker, eventually to black, then the battery requires charging, as described later in this Section. If the indicator shows clear/yellow, then the electrolyte level in the battery is too low to allow further use, and the battery should be renewed. **Do not** attempt to charge, load or jump start a battery when the indicator shows clear/yellow.

6 If testing the battery using a voltmeter, connect the voltmeter across the battery and compare the result with those given in the Specifications under 'charge condition'. The test is only accurate if the battery has not been subjected to any kind of charge for the previous six hours. If this is not the case, switch on the headlights for 30 seconds, then wait four to five minutes before testing the battery after switching off the headlights. All other electrical circuits must be switched off, so check that the doors and tailgate are fully shut when making the test.

7 If the voltage reading is less than 12.2 volts, then the battery is discharged, whilst a reading of 12.2 to 12.4 volts indicates a partially discharged condition.

8 If the battery is to be charged, remove it from the vehicle (Section 4) and charge it as described later in this Section.

Traditional-style and low maintenance battery - charging

Note: *The following is intended as a guide only. Always refer to the manufacturer's recommendations (often printed on a label attached to the battery) before charging a battery.*

9 Charge the battery at a rate of 3.5 to 4 amps and continue to charge the battery at this rate until no further rise in specific gravity is noted over a four hour period.

10 Alternatively, a trickle charger charging at the rate of 1.5 amps can safely be used overnight.

11 Especially rapid boost charges which are claimed to restore the power of the battery in 1 to 2 hours are not recommended, as they can cause serious damage to the battery plates through overheating.

12 While charging the battery, note that the temperature of the electrolyte should never exceed 37.8°C (100°F).

Maintenance-free battery - charging

Note: *The following is intended as a guide only. Always refer to the manufacturer's recommendations (often printed on a label attached to the battery) before charging a battery.*

13 This battery type takes considerably longer to fully recharge than the standard type, the time taken being dependent on the extent of discharge, but it can take anything up to three days.

14 A constant voltage type charger is required to be set, when connected, to 13.9 to 14.9 volts with a charger current below 25 amps. Using this method, the battery should be usable within three hours, giving a voltage reading of 12.5 volts, but this is for a partially discharged battery and, as mentioned, full charging can take considerably longer.

15 If the battery is to be charged from a fully discharged state (condition reading less than 12.2 volts), have it recharged by your Vauxhall dealer or local automotive electrician, as the charge rate is higher and constant supervision during charging is necessary.

4 Battery - removal and refitting

Note: *Make sure that you have a copy of the radio/cassette unit security code number before disconnecting the battery. Also, ensure that the unit is switched off before battery disconnection to avoid damage to the radio microprocessor circuitry.*

Removal

1 The battery is located at the front left-hand side of the engine compartment.

2 Slacken the clamp bolt and disconnect the clamp from the battery negative (earth) terminal **(see illustration)**.

3 Remove the insulation cover (where fitted) and disconnect the positive terminal lead(s) in the same way.

4 Unscrew the two nuts and remove the washers from the battery clamp tension rods. Remove the clamp then lift the battery out of the engine compartment.

Refitting

5 Refitting is a reversal of removal, but smear petroleum jelly on the terminals when reconnecting the leads, and always reconnect the positive lead first, and the negative lead last.

5 Charging system - testing

Note: *Refer to the warnings given in Safety first! and in Section 1 of this Chapter before starting work.*

1 If the ignition warning light fails to illuminate when the ignition is switched on, first check the alternator wiring connections for security. If satisfactory, check that the warning light bulb has not blown, and that the bulbholder is secure in its location in the instrument panel. If the light still fails to illuminate, check the continuity of the warning light feed wire from the alternator to the bulbholder. If all is satisfactory, the alternator is at fault and should be renewed or taken to an auto-electrician for testing and repair.

2 If the ignition warning light illuminates when the engine is running, stop the engine and check that the drivebelt is correctly tensioned (see Chapter 1) and that the alternator connections are secure. If all is so far satisfactory, have the alternator checked by an auto-electrician for testing and repair.

3 If the alternator output is suspect even though the warning light functions correctly, the regulated voltage may be checked as follows.

4 Connect a voltmeter across the battery terminals and start the engine.

5 Increase the engine speed until the voltmeter reading remains steady; the reading should be approximately 12 to 13 volts, and no more than 14 volts.

6 Switch on as many electrical accessories (eg, the headlights, heated rear window and heater blower) as possible, and check that the alternator maintains the regulated voltage at around 13 to 14 volts.

7 If the regulated voltage is not as stated, the fault may be due to worn brushes, weak brush springs, a faulty voltage regulator, a faulty diode, a severed phase winding or worn or damaged slip rings. The alternator should be renewed or taken to an auto-electrician for testing and repair.

5A

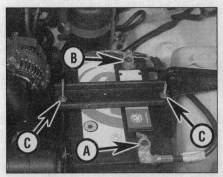

4.2 Battery negative terminal (A), positive terminal (B) and battery clamp tension rod nuts (C)

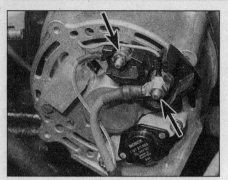

7.5 Wiring connections (arrowed) at rear of alternator - 2.0 litre petrol engine (C20NE)

7.6 Earth strap (arrowed) attached to top alternator mounting bolts - 2.0 litre petrol engine (C20NE)

7.11 Alternator mountings - 2.0 litre petrol engine (X20SE)

1   Rear support brace to engine
2   Upper mounting bracket to engine
3   Upper mounting bracket to alternator
4   Rear support brace to alternator

6 Alternator drivebelt - removal, refitting and tensioning

Refer to the procedure given for the auxiliary drivebelt(s) in Chapter 1.

7 Alternator - removal and refitting

Removal

1 Disconnect the battery negative lead.
2 Depending on the tools available, access to some of the alternator attachments and surrounding components may be improved from underneath the vehicle. If so, chock the rear wheels then jack up the front of the car and support it on axle stands (see *Jacking and Vehicle Support*). Remove the undershield beneath the engine.

2.0 litre (C20NE) and 2.4 litre (C24NE) petrol engines

3 Refer to Chapter 4A and remove the air cleaner assembly and air intake ducting as necessary for access to the alternator.
4 Remove the auxiliary drivebelts (alternator and power steering) as described in Chapter 1.
5 Disconnect the wiring plug, or disconnect the wires from their terminals on the rear of the alternator, noting their locations **(see illustration)**.
6 Unscrew the two mounting bolts and nuts and recover any washers and insulating bushes, noting their locations. Note the earth strap attached to the top mounting bolt on some models **(see illustration)**.
7 Withdraw the alternator, taking care not to knock or drop it.

2.0 litre (X20SE) and 2.2 litre (X22XE) petrol engines

8 Refer to Chapter 4A and remove the air cleaner assembly and air intake ducting as necessary for access to the alternator.

9 Remove the auxiliary drivebelt(s) as described in Chapter 1.
10 On models equipped with air conditioning, refer to Chapter 11 and remove the power steering pump for access to the alternator lower mounting. Note that it is not necessary to disconnect the power steering hoses, but just release the pump from its attachment to the engine.
11 Undo the two bolts and remove the alternator rear support brace **(see illustration)**.
12 Undo the two bolts and remove the alternator upper mounting bracket.
13 Slacken the alternator lower mounting bolt and swing the alternator away from the engine.
14 Disconnect the wires from their terminals on the rear of the alternator, noting their locations.
15 Undo the lower mounting bolt and lift the alternator up and off the engine, taking care not to drop it.

2.3 litre diesel engine

16 Release the auxiliary drivebelt (alternator) as described in Chapter 1 and disengage it from the alternator pulley.
17 Unscrew the oil feed and return hose banjo union bolts from the vacuum pump at the rear of the alternator and recover the two copper washers. Have ready a container and

7.23 Vacuum pump hose connections - 2.5 litre diesel engine

A   Oil return hose   C   Vacuum hose
B   Oil feed hose

rags to catch any spilled oil. Cover the open banjo unions with a piece of polythene and a rubber band to keep dirt out.
18 Disconnect the vacuum hose from the union on the vacuum pump.
19 Disconnect the wiring plug, or disconnect the wires from the alternator terminals, noting their locations.
20 Unscrew the alternator lower mounting nuts and bolts, and the bolt securing the adjuster block to the alternator. Recover any washers and insulating bushes, noting their locations.
21 Withdraw the alternator from the engine, taking care not to knock or drop it. Note that the alternator and vacuum pump are supplied as a complete assembly and are not available as separate individual components.

2.5 litre diesel engine

22 Release the auxiliary drivebelt as described in Chapter 1 and disengage it from the alternator pulley.
23 Slacken the clip and disconnect the oil return hose from the vacuum pump on the front of the alternator **(see illustration)**.
24 Unscrew the oil feed hose and vacuum hose banjo union bolts from the vacuum pump and recover the copper washer on each side of the banjo union **(see illustrations)**.

7.24a Unscrew the vacuum hose banjo union bolt and collect the upper copper washer . . .

7.24b . . . and the lower copper washer under the banjo union - 2.5 litre diesel engine

7.26a Alternator upper mounting bolt (arrowed) . . .

7.26b . . . and lower mounting bolt (arrowed) - 2.5 litre diesel engine

Cover the open banjo unions with a piece of polythene and a rubber band to keep dirt out.
25 Disconnect the wiring plug and the lead from the terminal stud at the rear of the alternator.
26 Unscrew the alternator upper and lower mounting nuts and bolts and recover any washers and insulating bushes, noting their locations **(see illustrations)**.
27 Withdraw the alternator from the engine, taking care not to knock or drop it. Note that the alternator and vacuum pump are supplied as a complete assembly and are not available as separate individual components.

2.8 litre diesel engine

28 Refer to Chapter 4B and remove the air cleaner assembly and air intake ducting as necessary for access to the alternator.
29 Release the auxiliary drivebelts (alternator, and where applicable, air conditioning) as described in Chapter 1 and disengage them from the air conditioning compressor and/or alternator pulleys.
30 On models equipped with air conditioning, refer to Chapter 3 and unbolt the air conditioning compressor from its mounting bracket. Do not disconnect the air conditioning refrigerant hoses, but just release the compressor from its attachment to the engine.
31 Unscrew the oil feed and return hose banjo union bolts from the vacuum pump and recover the two copper washers. Have a container and rags ready to catch any spilled oil. Cover the open banjo unions with a piece of polythene and a rubber band to keep dirt out.
32 Disconnect the vacuum hose from the union on the vacuum pump.
33 Disconnect the wiring plug, or disconnect the wires from the alternator terminals, noting their locations.
34 Unscrew the alternator mounting nuts and bolts, and the bolt securing the adjuster block to the alternator. Recover any washers and insulating bushes, noting their locations.
35 Withdraw the alternator from the engine, taking care not to knock or drop it. If a replacement alternator is to be fitted, remove the vacuum pump and transfer it to the new

unit. The vacuum pump is secured to the rear of the alternator with three screws.

Refitting

36 Refitting is a reversal of removal. Use new copper washers on all disturbed copper washers and refit and tension the auxiliary drivebelts as described in Chapter 1. If a new alternator and/or vacuum pump is being fitted to diesel engine models, prime the vacuum pump, through the oil feed union, with one or two strokes from an oil can filled with clean engine oil before fitting.

8 Alternator - testing and overhaul

If the alternator is thought to be suspect, it should be removed from the vehicle and taken to an auto-electrician for testing. Most auto-electricians will be able to supply and fit brushes at a reasonable cost. However, check on the cost of repairs before proceeding as it may prove more economical to obtain a new or exchange alternator.

9 Starting system - testing

Note: *Refer to the precautions given in Safety first! and in Section 1 of this Chapter before starting work.*
1 If the starter motor fails to operate when the ignition key is turned to the appropriate position, the following possible causes may be to blame.
a) *The battery is faulty.*
b) *The electrical connections between the switch, solenoid, battery and starter motor are failing to pass the necessary current from the battery through the starter to earth.*
c) *The solenoid is faulty.*
d) *The starter motor is mechanically or electrically defective.*
2 To check the battery, switch on the headlights. If they dim after a few seconds,

this indicates that the battery is discharged - recharge (see Section 3) or renew the battery. If the headlights glow brightly, operate the ignition switch and observe the lights. If they dim, then this indicates that current is reaching the starter motor, therefore the fault must lie in the starter motor. If the lights continue to glow brightly (and no clicking sound can be heard from the starter motor solenoid), this indicates that there is a fault in the circuit or solenoid - see following paragraphs. If the starter motor turns slowly when operated, but the battery is in good condition, then this indicates that either the starter motor is faulty, or there is considerable resistance somewhere in the circuit.
3 If a fault in the circuit is suspected, disconnect the battery leads (including the earth connection to the body), the starter/solenoid wiring and the engine/transmission earth strap. Thoroughly clean the connections, and reconnect the leads and wiring, then use a voltmeter or test lamp to check that full battery voltage is available at the battery positive lead connection to the solenoid, and that the earth is sound. Smear petroleum jelly around the battery terminals to prevent corrosion - corroded connections are amongst the most frequent causes of electrical system faults.
4 If the battery and all connections are in good condition, check the circuit by disconnecting the wire from the solenoid blade terminal. Connect a voltmeter or test lamp between the wire end and a good earth (such as the battery negative terminal), and check that the wire is live when the ignition switch is turned to the start position. If it is, then the circuit is sound - if not the circuit wiring can be checked as described in Chapter 13.
5 The solenoid contacts can be checked by connecting a voltmeter or test lamp between the battery positive feed connection on the starter side of the solenoid, and earth. When the ignition switch is turned to the start position, there should be a reading or lighted bulb, as applicable. If there is no reading or lighted bulb, the solenoid is faulty and should be renewed.

5A

6 If the circuit and solenoid are proved sound, the fault must lie in the starter motor. In this event, it may be possible to have the starter motor overhauled by a specialist, but check on the cost of spares before proceeding, as it may prove more economical to obtain a new or exchange motor.

10 Starter motor - removal and refitting

Removal

2.0 and 2.4 litre petrol engines

1 Disconnect the battery negative lead.
2 Disconnect the wiring connections from the starter motor solenoid noting their locations.
3 Where fitted, unbolt the starter motor rear support bracket from the engine.
4 Undo the two starter motor securing bolts, noting that the top bolt on some models is fitted from the transmission side and is longer than the lower bolt. Manoeuvre the unit from its location and remove it from the engine.

2.2 litre petrol engine

5 Disconnect the battery negative lead.
6 Refer to Chapter 1 and drain the cooling system.
7 Remove the alternator as described in Section 7.
8 Undo the retaining bolts and remove the support bracket from the underside of the inlet manifold.
9 Disconnect the coolant hoses from the water inlet manifold and remove the manifold.
10 Disconnect the wiring connector, undo the retaining bolt and remove the knock sensor from the side of the cylinder block.
11 Disconnect the wiring connections from the starter motor solenoid noting their locations.
12 Unbolt the starter motor rear support bracket from the engine.
13 Undo the two starter motor securing bolts, noting that the top bolt is fitted from the transmission side and is longer than the lower bolt. Manoeuvre the unit from its location and remove it from the engine.

2.3 litre diesel engine

14 Disconnect the battery negative lead.
15 Disconnect the wiring connections from the starter motor solenoid noting their locations.
16 Unbolt the starter motor rear support bracket from the engine.
17 Undo the starter motor securing bolts, releasing any cable or fuel line support brackets as applicable, noting their relevant positions for refitting. Manoeuvre the unit from its location and remove it from the engine.

2.5 litre diesel engine

18 Disconnect the battery negative lead.
19 Slacken the hose clips and remove the following hoses and ducts from the right-hand side of the engine:
a) Crankcase ventilation valve and hose from the air cleaner intake duct.
b) Intercooler upper hose from the inlet manifold and intercooler duct at the front of the engine.
c) Air cleaner intake duct from the air cleaner and turbocharger.
d) Intercooler lower hose from the turbocharger and intercooler duct on the right-hand side of the engine.
20 Undo the nut and release the coolant pipe located above the turbocharger heat shield, from the mounting stud. Move the pipe clear as far as the coolant hoses will allow.
21 Undo the two bolts, remove the washer and withdraw the turbocharger heat shield.
22 Chock the rear wheels then jack up the front of the vehicle and support it on axle stands (see *Jacking and Vehicle Support*). Remove the undershield beneath the engine.
23 Remove the front propeller shaft as described in Chapter 8.
24 Remove the exhaust system front pipe as described in Chapter 4B.
25 From under the vehicle, undo the two lower nuts and two upper nuts and remove the footwell heat shield from its mounting studs.
26 Undo the two bolts and three nuts and remove the exhaust front pipe elbow from the turbocharger. Recover the gasket.
27 Undo the two bolts and one nut and remove the starter motor heat shield.
28 Disconnect the wiring connections from the starter motor solenoid noting their locations.

29 Unbolt the starter motor rear support bracket from the engine.
30 Undo the starter motor securing bolts, manoeuvre the unit from its location and remove it from the engine.

2.8 litre diesel engine

31 Disconnect the battery negative lead.
32 Remove the engine oil dipstick then pull the dipstick tube out of its location in the cylinder block. Plug the dipstick tube orifice in the block after removal to prevent dirt ingress.
33 Unbolt the clutch slave cylinder and tie it to a suitable place on the chassis. Do not disconnect the hydraulic fluid hose.
34 Disconnect the wiring connections from the starter motor solenoid noting their locations.
35 Undo the starter motor securing nuts and bolts, manoeuvre the unit from its location and remove it from the engine.

Refitting

36 Refitting is a reversal of removal, tightening the retaining nuts and bolts to the specified torque (where given). On 2.2 litre petrol engines, refill the cooling system as described in Chapter 1 on completion. On 2.5 litre diesel engines, use a new gasket when refitting the exhaust front pipe elbow to the turbocharger.

11 Starter motor - testing and overhaul

If the starter motor is thought to be suspect, it should be removed from the vehicle and taken to an auto-electrician for testing. Most auto-electricians will be able to supply and fit brushes at a reasonable cost. However, check on the cost of repairs before proceeding as it may prove more economical to obtain a new or exchange motor.

12 Ignition switch - removal and refitting

Refer to Chapter 13, Section 4.

Chapter 5 Part B
Ignition system - petrol engine models

Contents

DIS module - removal and refitting 4
Distributor (2.0 litre C20NE engine) - removal and refitting 5
Distributor (2.4 litre C24NE engine) - removal and refitting 6
General information 1
Ignition HT coil - removal and refitting 3
Ignition system - testing 2
Ignition system check ....See Chapter 1
Ignition timing - checking and adjustment 7
Spark plug renewal ....See Chapter 1

Degrees of difficulty

Easy, suitable for novice with little experience	**Fairly easy,** suitable for beginner with some experience	**Fairly difficult,** suitable for competent DIY mechanic	**Difficult,** suitable for experienced DIY mechanic 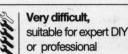	**Very difficult,** suitable for expert DIY or professional

Specifications

General
System type:

2.0 litre (C20NE) and 2.4 litre (C24NE) engines	Distributor system controlled by Bosch Motronic M 1.5 engine management ECU
2.0 litre (X20SE) and 2.2 litre (X22XE) engines	Distributorless (DIS) system controlled by Bosch Motronic M 1.5.4 engine management ECU
Firing order	1-3-4-2 (No. 1 cylinder at front (crankshaft pulley) end of engine

Spark plugs
Type .... See Chapter 1 Specifications

Torque wrench settings

	Nm	lbf ft
DIS module mounting bracket bolts (X20SE engine)	15	11
DIS module to mounting bracket	8	6

5B

1 General information

Note: *Refer to Chapter 4A and 4C for procedures relating to the engine management sensors and associated components not covered in this Chapter.*

The ignition system is responsible for igniting the air/fuel mixture in each cylinder at the correct moment, in relation to engine speed and load. The ignition system is integrated with the fuel injection system to form a combined engine management system under the control of a single electronic control unit (ECU).

The ignition system is based on feeding low tension voltage from the battery to the coil, where it is converted to high tension voltage. The high tension voltage is powerful enough to jump the spark plug gap in the cylinders many times a second under high compression pressures, providing that the system is in good condition. The low tension (or primary) circuit consists of the battery, the lead to the ignition switch, the lead from the ignition switch to the low tension coil windings, and also to the supply terminal on the ECU, and the lead from the low tension coil windings to the control terminal on the ECU. The high tension (or secondary) circuit consists of the high tension coil windings, the HT (high tension) lead from the coil to the distributor cap (where applicable), the rotor arm (where applicable), the HT leads to the spark plugs, and the spark plugs.

The system functions in the following manner. Current flowing through the low tension coil windings produces a magnetic field around the high tension windings. As the engine rotates, a sensor produces an electrical impulse that is amplified in the ECU and used to switch off the low tension circuit.

The subsequent collapse of the magnetic field over the high tension windings produces a high tension voltage, which is then fed to the relevant spark plug(s) either directly from the coil, or through the distributor cap and rotor arm, as applicable. The low tension circuit is automatically switched on again by the ECU, to allow the magnetic field to build up again before the firing of the next spark plug(s). The ignition is advanced and retarded automatically, to ensure that the spark occurs at the correct instant for the prevailing engine speed and load.

Motronic M1.5 system - 2.0 litre (C20NE) and 2.4 litre (C24NE) engines

The Motronic ECU receives information on engine operating conditions from a crankshaft speed/position sensor, an airflow meter, an intake air temperature sensor, an engine coolant temperature sensor, a throttle position sensor, a fuel octane coding plug and an exhaust gas oxygen sensor.

The primary electrical impulse that is required to initiate ignition is generated by the crankshaft speed/position sensor mounted at the front of the engine in close proximity to the crankshaft. The sensor consists of an inductive magnet that radiates a magnetic field, and is positioned just above a toothed disk mounted on the crankshaft. The disk theoretically comprises 60 teeth set around its circumference at 3° intervals, with two teeth omitted to provide a reference point. As the crankshaft turns, the teeth on the disk are rotated in the magnetic field and an electrical signal is generated and delivered to the ECU. The signal is used by the ECU to calculate speed of crankshaft rotation, and the gap left by the missing two teeth provides a TDC reference point enabling crankshaft position to be determined.

From this constantly-changing data, the ECU selects, and if necessary modifies, a particular ignition advance setting from a map of ignition characteristics stored in its memory.

With the firing point established, the ECU interrupts the primary current to the ignition coil, which induces a high-tension voltage in the coil secondary windings. This HT voltage is passed to the distributor cap, and then on to the spark plugs, via the distributor rotor arm and HT leads. The cycle is then repeated many times a second for each cylinder in turn.

Motronic M1.5.4 system - 2.0 litre (X20SE) and 2.2 litre (X22XE) engines

The Motronic 1.5.4 system is similar to the M1.5 system described previously, but with the following differences.

A DIS (Distributorless Ignition System) module is used in place of the distributor and coil. The DIS module consists of two ignition coils and an electronic control module housed in a cast casing. Each ignition coil supplies two spark plugs with HT voltage. One spark is provided in a cylinder with its piston on the compression stroke, and one spark is provided to a cylinder with its piston on the exhaust stroke. This means that a 'wasted spark' is supplied to one cylinder during each ignition cycle, but this has no detrimental effect. This system has the advantage that there are no moving parts (therefore there is no wear), and the system is largely maintenance-free.

Additionally, the Motronic M1.5.4 ECU receives information from a cylinder block-mounted knock sensor, which senses knocking (or pre-ignition) just as it begins to occur, enabling the module to retard the ignition timing, thus preventing engine damage.

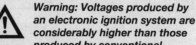

2 Ignition system - testing

> **Warning: Voltages produced by an electronic ignition system are considerably higher than those produced by conventional ignition systems. Extreme care must be taken when working on the system if the ignition is switched on. Persons with surgically-implanted cardiac pacemaker devices should keep well clear of the ignition circuits, components and test equipment.**

If a fault occurs in the engine management (fuel injection/ignition) system, first ensure that the fault is not due to a poor electrical connection or poor maintenance; ie, check that the air cleaner filter element is clean, the spark plugs are in good condition and correctly gapped, that the engine breather hoses are clear and undamaged, referring to Chapter 1 for further information. Also check that the accelerator cable is correctly adjusted as described in Chapter 4A. If the engine is running very roughly, check the compression pressures and (where applicable) the valve clearances as described in the relevant Part of Chapter 2.

If these checks fail to reveal the cause of the problem, the vehicle should be taken to a suitably-equipped Vauxhall dealer for testing. A wiring block connector is incorporated in the engine management circuit, into which a special electronic diagnostic tester can be plugged. The tester will locate the fault quickly and simply, alleviating the need to test all the system components individually, which is a time-consuming operation that carries a high risk of damaging the ECU. Alternatively, if suitable DIY diagnostic equipment is available (such as a fault code reader), it may be possible to isolate the problem to a specific part of the engine management system, thus allowing further investigations to be concentrated in that area. Refer to Chapter 4A for further details.

The only specific ignition system checks which can be carried out by the home mechanic are those described in Chapter 1 relating to the spark plugs. If necessary, the system wiring and wiring connectors can be checked as described in Chapter 13, ensuring that the ECU wiring connector is first disconnected with the ignition switched off.

3 Ignition HT coil - removal and refitting

Removal

1 On models with a distributor ignition system, the coil is mounted on the left-hand side of the engine compartment, in front of the suspension turret.

2 Disconnect the battery negative lead.

3 Disconnect the coil HT lead and the LT wiring connector.

4 Undo the bolts securing the coil mounting bracket and remove the assembly from the engine compartment **(see illustration)**.

5 Inspect the coil visually for cracks, leakage of insulating oil or other obvious damage. Renew it if such damage is evident.

Refitting

6 Refitting is a reversal of removal

4 DIS module - removal and refitting

Removal

1 Disconnect the battery negative lead.

2.0 litre (X20SE) engine

2 Disconnect the module wiring plug and release the wiring harness from the cable clip on the module mounting bracket.

3 Undo the two upper bolts and one lower bolt securing the module mounting bracket to the camshaft housing and cylinder head. Note that the upper right-hand bolt also secures the engine lifting bracket.

4 Lift the module and mounting bracket assembly upwards and around to the left-hand side of the engine.

5 Disconnect the HT leads from the module terminals noting their locations to ensure correct refitting. Note that the HT lead cylinder numbers are stamped on the module, next to each terminal, and similar numbers should appear on each HT lead.

6 Note the installed position of the DIS module on its mounting bracket, undo the four securing screws and separate the module from the bracket.

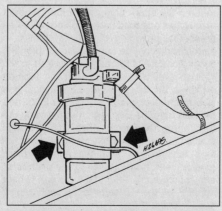

3.4 Ignition coil mounting bolts (arrowed)

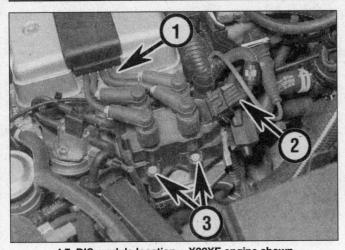

4.7 DIS module location - X22XE engine shown

1 HT leads   2 Wiring plug   3 Securing screws

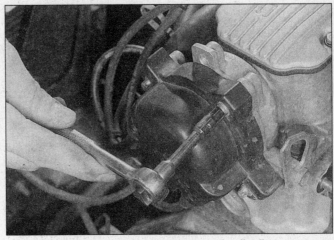

5.4 Undo the three screws and remove the distributor cap - C20NE engine

2.2 litre (X22XE) engine

7 Disconnect the module wiring plug and HT leads from the module terminals noting their locations to ensure correct refitting **(see illustration)**. Note that the HT lead cylinder numbers are stamped on the module, next to each terminal, and similar numbers appear on each HT lead.

8 Note the installed position of DIS module on its mounting bracket, undo the four securing screws and remove the module from the bracket.

Refitting

9 Refitting is a reversal of removal. Tighten the module securing screws to the specified torque and ensure that the HT leads are refitted to their correct numbered locations.

5 Distributor (2.0 litre C20NE engine) - removal and refitting

Removal

1 The distributor consists simply of a cap, plastic shield and rotor arm mounted on the end of the camshaft housing.

2 Disconnect the battery negative lead.

3 Identify each HT lead for position to aid correct refitting, then disconnect the leads from the spark plugs by pulling on the connectors, not on the leads. Similarly, disconnect the HT lead from the coil. Release the leads from their retaining clips.

4 Using a Torx socket, undo the three captive securing screws and withdraw the distributor cap (complete with HT leads) from the camshaft housing **(see illustration)**.

5 Withdraw the plastic shield from the camshaft housing. The shield is an interference fit in the housing via an O-ring seal located in a groove in its periphery. Ease out the shield taking care not to damage the rotor arm **(see illustration)**.

6 Using an Allen key, undo the two securing screws and withdraw the rotor arm, leaving the metal rotor hub in the housing **(see illustrations)**.

Refitting

7 Refitting is a reversal of removal bearing in mind the following points:

a)   *Examine the O-ring in the plastic shield and renew it if necessary.*

b)   *The rotor arm can only be fitted in one position. If necessary, turn the metal rotor*

hub so that the screw holes align with those in the rotor arm and the end of the camshaft.

c)   *Apply a suitable thread locking agent to the distributor cap retaining screw threads before refitting.*

d)   *Ensure that the HT leads are refitted to their correct numbered locations.*

6 Distributor (2.4 litre C24NE engine) - removal and refitting

Removal

1 Disconnect the battery negative lead.

2 Identify each HT lead for position to aid correct refitting, then disconnect the leads from the spark plugs by pulling on the connectors, not on the leads. Similarly, disconnect the HT lead from the coil. Release the leads from their retaining clips.

3 Release the two clips and lift off the distributor cap, complete with HT leads, from the distributor.

4 Withdraw the rotor arm and plastic shield from the distributor, then refit the rotor arm.

5B

5.5 Remove the plastic shield from the camshaft housing - C20NE engine

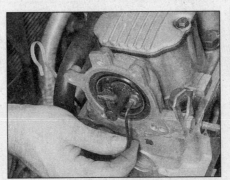

5.6a Undo the two screws . . .

5.6b . . . and withdraw the rotor arm - C20NE engine

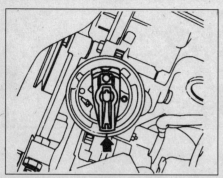

6.5a Turn the crankshaft to align the rotor arm with the notch on the distributor body . . .

6.5b . . . and the steel ball in the flywheel with the pointer in the flywheel housing - C24NE engine

5 Set the engine at TDC for No 1 cylinder on the firing stroke as follows. Using a socket or spanner on the crankshaft pulley, turn the engine over until the rotor arm is pointing toward the notch on the edge of the distributor body and the steel ball in the flywheel is aligned with the pointer in the flywheel housing inspection hole (see illustrations).

6 Undo the distributor clamp plate retaining bolt and remove the clamp plate.

7 Lift the distributor up and out of the timing cover and recover the gasket at the base of the distributor flange.

Refitting

8 Check that the engine is still at the TDC position with the steel ball in the flywheel aligned with the flywheel housing pointer.

9 As the distributor is lowered into position in the timing cover, the distributor shaft will rotate slightly as the drivegear on the distributor shaft engages with the drivegear on the crankshaft. To compensate for this, initially position the rotor arm so that it points to the distributor cap retaining clip, nearest to the notch on the edge of the distributor body. It will also be necessary to insert a long screwdriver down the opening in the timing cover and rotate the oil pump drivegear by a corresponding amount in the same direction.

10 Place a new gasket on the distributor flange base and while holding the distributor and shaft in the correct position, insert the assembly into the timing cover aperture.

11 When the distributor shaft has seated fully into the oil pump drivegear slot, check that the rotor arm is now pointing toward the notch on the edge of the distributor body. If, necessary turn the distributor body slightly then refit the clamp plate and secure with the retaining bolt.

12 Remove the rotor arm, refit the plastic shield then refit the rotor arm.

13 Refit the distributor cap and reconnect the HT leads ensuring that the leads are refitted to their correct spark plugs as noted during removal.

14 Reconnect the battery on completion.

7 Ignition timing - checking and adjustment

1 On all models, the ignition timing is constantly being monitored and adjusted by the engine management ECU, and nominal values cannot be given. Therefore it is not possible for the home mechanic to check the ignition timing.

2 The only way in which the ignition timing can be checked and (where possible) adjusted is by using special electronic test equipment connected to the engine management system diagnostic connector. Refer to your Vauxhall dealer for further information.

Chapter 5 Part C
Preheating system - diesel engine models

Contents

Glow plugs - removal, inspection and refitting 3
Preheating system - general information 1
Preheating system - testing 2
Preheating system components - removal and refitting 4

Degrees of difficulty

| **Easy,** suitable for novice with little experience | | **Fairly easy,** suitable for beginner with some experience | | **Fairly difficult,** suitable for competent DIY mechanic | | **Difficult,** suitable for experienced DIY mechanic | | **Very difficult,** suitable for expert DIY or professional | 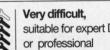 |

Specifications

Torque wrench settings	Nm	lbf ft
Glow plugs:		
2.3 litre models	20	15
2.5 litre models	15	11
2.8 litre models	23	17

1 Preheating system - general information

2.3 litre models

Each swirl chamber has a heater plug (commonly called a glow plug) screwed into it. The plugs are electrically-operated before, during, and a short time after start-up when the engine is cold. Electrical feed to the glow plugs is controlled by the preheating control unit.

A warning light in the instrument panel tells the driver that preheating is taking place. When the light goes out, the engine is ready to be started. If no attempt is made to start, the control unit cuts off the supply in order to avoid draining the battery and overheating the glow plugs.

The fuel filter is also fitted with a heating element to prevent the fuel 'waxing' in extremely cold conditions. The heating element is fitted between the filter and its housing and is controlled by the preheating system control unit, via the temperature switch in the filter housing and a relay. The heating element is switched on if the temperature of the fuel passing through the filter is less than 5°C (41°F) and switched off when the fuel temperature reaches 16°C (61°F).

2.5 litre models

The preheating system and fuel filter heating element fitted to 2.5 litre models operate on the same principle as described for 2.3 litre models except that the engine management ECU controls the operation of the system based on inputs received from the various engine sensors (see Chapter 4B for further information).

2.8 litre models

2.8 litre models are also equipped with preheating glow plugs and a fuel filter heating element as described previously for 2.3 litre models. The system fitted to these engines is known as the 'Quick On Start' (QOS) system and includes a QOS control unit, glow plug relay and coolant temperature sensor.

The glow plugs are electrically-operated before, during, and after start-up when the engine is cold. Electrical feed to the glow plugs is controlled by the QOS control unit which receives information on engine temperature from the coolant temperature sensor located in the thermostat housing. According to engine temperature at the time of starting, the QOS control unit maintains the electrical supply to the glow plugs until a pre-determined engine temperature is obtained.

The fuel filter heating element is also controlled by the QOS control unit.

2 Preheating system - testing

1 If the system malfunctions, testing is ultimately by substitution of known good units, but some preliminary checks may be made as follows.
2 Connect a voltmeter or 12 volt test lamp between the glow plug supply cable and earth (engine or vehicle metal). Make sure that the live connection is kept clear of the engine and bodywork.
3 Have an assistant switch on the ignition and check that voltage is applied to the glow plugs. Note the time for which the warning light is lit and the total time for which voltage is applied before the system cuts out. Switch off the ignition.
4 At an under-bonnet temperature of 20°C (68°F) typical times noted should be 3 to 5 seconds for warning light operation. Warning light time will increase with lower temperatures and decrease with higher temperatures.
5 If there is no supply at all, the control unit, relay or associated wiring is at fault.
6 To locate a defective glow plug, disconnect the main supply cable and the interconnecting wire or strap from the top of the glow plugs. Be careful not to drop the nuts and washers.
7 Use a continuity tester, or a 12 volt test

5C

lamp connected to the battery positive terminal, to check for continuity between each glow plug terminal and earth. The resistance of a glow plug in good condition is very low (less than 1 ohm), so if the test lamp does not light or the continuity tester shows a high resistance the glow plug is certainly defective.

8 If an ammeter is available, the current draw of each glow plug can be checked. After an initial surge of around 15 to 20 amps, each plug should draw around 10 amps. Any plug which draws much more or less than 10 amps is probably defective.

9 As a final check, the glow plugs can be removed and inspected as described in Section 3.

3 Glow plugs - removal, inspection and refitting

Caution: If the preheating system has just been energised, or if the engine has been running, the glow plugs may be very hot.

Removal

2.3 and 2.5 litre models

1 Disconnect the battery negative lead.

2 On 2.3 litre models, unscrew the nuts from the glow plug terminals, and recover the washers. Disconnect the wiring and electrical supply rail from the glow plug terminals. On 2.5 litre models, disconnect the wiring harness connector from the top of each glow plug.

3 Where applicable, carefully move any obstructing pipes or wires to one side to enable increased access to the glow plugs.

4 Unscrew the glow plugs and remove them from the cylinder head (see illustration).

2.8 litre models

5 Disconnect the battery negative lead.

6 Refer to Chapter 4B and remove the throttle body and plenum chamber.

7 Unscrew the nuts from the glow plug terminals, and recover the washers. Disconnect the wiring and electrical supply rail from the glow plug terminals.

8 Unscrew the glow plugs and remove them from the cylinder head.

Inspection

9 Inspect the glow plugs for physical damage. Burnt or eroded glow plug tips can be caused by a bad injector spray pattern. Have the injectors checked if this sort of damage is found.

10 If the glow plugs are in good physical condition, check them electrically using a 12 volt test lamp or continuity tester as described in the previous Section.

11 The glow plugs can be energised by applying 12 volts to them to verify that they heat up evenly and in the required time. Observe the following precautions:

a) Support the glow plug by clamping it carefully in a vice or self-locking pliers. Remember it will become red-hot.

b) Make sure that the power supply or test lead incorporates a fuse or overload trip to protect against damage from a short-circuit.

c) After testing, allow the glow plug to cool for several minutes before attempting to handle it.

12 A glow plug in good condition will start to glow red at the tip after drawing current for 5 seconds or so. Any plug which takes much longer to start glowing, or which starts glowing in the middle instead of at the tip, is defective.

Refitting

13 Refit by reversing the removal operations. Apply a smear of copper-based anti-seize compound to the plug threads and tighten the glow plugs to the specified torque. Do not overtighten, as this can damage the glow plug element.

4 Preheating system components - removal and refitting

2.3 litre models

Preheating system control unit

1 The unit is located at the left-hand rear of the engine compartment, behind the power steering fluid reservoir and vacuum tank. Lift

off the plastic cover for access (see illustration).

2 Disconnect the battery negative lead.

3 Unscrew the retaining bolt, and withdraw the mounting bracket from its location. Disconnect the wiring and release the unit from the mounting bracket.

4 Refitting is a reversal of removal, ensuring that the wiring connectors are correctly connected.

Fuel filter heating element

5 Remove the fuel filter as described in Chapter 1. If the filter is damaged on removal (which is likely), a new one should be used on refitting.

6 Disconnect the battery negative lead, then disconnect the wiring connector from the heating element.

7 Unscrew the centre bolt and remove the heating element from the filter housing. Recover the sealing ring and discard, a new one should be used on refitting.

8 Fit a new sealing ring to the heating element recess then refit the element to the filter housing and securely tighten the centre bolt.

9 Reconnect the wiring connector and battery negative lead then fit the fuel filter as described in Chapter 1.

Fuel filter heating element temperature switch

10 Disconnect the battery negative lead then disconnect the wiring connector from the temperature switch in the side of the fuel filter housing (see illustration).

11 Place absorbent rags beneath the filter housing then unscrew the switch and remove it from the housing. Plug the housing aperture to prevent dirt ingress and to minimise fuel loss.

12 Renew the switch sealing ring then refit the switch to the filter housing and tighten securely. Reconnect the wiring connector and the battery negative lead.

Relays and fuses

13 The fuel filter heating element relay and fuse are located adjacent to the preheating system control unit in the engine compartment. Refer to paragraphs 1 to 4 above.

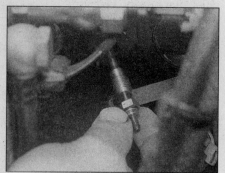

3.4 Removing a glow plug from the cylinder head - 2.3 litre models

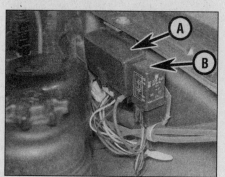

4.1 Preheating system control unit (A) and fuel filter heating element relay (B) - 2.3 litre models

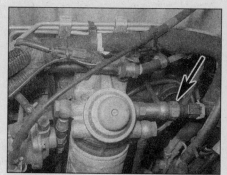

4.10 Fuel filter heating element temperature switch (arrowed) - 2.3 litre models

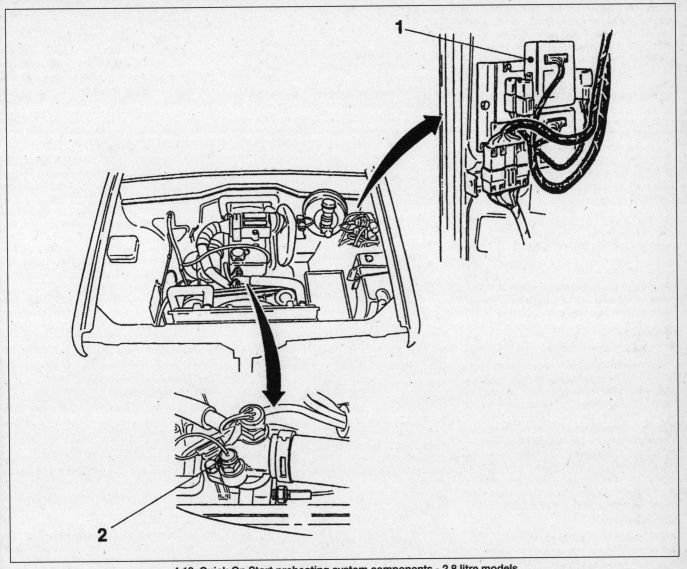

4.18 Quick On Start preheating system components - 2.8 litre models

1 QOS control unit (left-hand drive location shown)   2 Coolant temperature sensor

5C

Coolant temperature sensor

14 The coolant temperature sensor is screwed into the thermostat housing. Refer to Chapter 3 for removal and refitting details.

2.5 litre models

Preheating system control unit

15 The operation of the preheating system is controlled by the engine management ECU and its sensors. Refer to Chapter 4B for further information.

Fuel filter heating element temperature switch

16 Removal and refitting of the fuel filter heating element and temperature switch are as described previously for 2.3 litre models.

Relays and fuses

17 The preheating system relay is located on the left-hand side of the engine compartment on the inner wing panel. The engine management system fuses are located in the passenger compartment fusebox (see Chapter 13).

2.8 litre models

Preheating system control unit

18 The Quick On Start control unit is located in the front passenger compartment footwell on the driver's side behind the side trim kick panel **(see illustration)**.
19 Disconnect the battery negative lead.
20 Refer to Chapter 12 and remove the trim panel for access to the control unit.
21 The Quick On Start control unit is the upper of the two control units located in the centre of the mounting bracket. Disconnect the wiring connector, undo the two screws and remove the unit from the mounting bracket.
22 Refitting is a reversal of removal

Fuel filter heating element temperature switch

23 Removal and refitting of the fuel filter heating element and temperature switch are as described previously for 2.3 litre models.

Relays and fuses

24 The preheating system relay and fuel filter heating element relay are located at the rear right-hand side of the engine compartment.

Coolant temperature sensor

25 The coolant temperature sensor is screwed into the thermostat housing. Refer to Chapter 3 for removal and refitting details.

Notes

Chapter 6
Clutch

Contents

Clutch assembly - removal, inspection and refitting 8
Clutch fluid level check . . . . See *Weekly checks*
Clutch hydraulic damper - removal and refitting 6
Clutch hydraulic system - bleeding 7
Clutch master cylinder - removal and refitting 4
Clutch pedal - removal and refitting 3
Clutch pedal height and free play - adjustment 2
Clutch release bearing - removal, inspection and refitting 9
Clutch slave cylinder - removal and refitting 5
General information 1

Degrees of difficulty

Easy, suitable for novice with little experience		Fairly easy, suitable for beginner with some experience		Fairly difficult, suitable for competent DIY mechanic		Difficult, suitable for experienced DIY mechanic		Very difficult, suitable for expert DIY or professional	

Specifications

General
Clutch type . . . . Single dry plate, diaphragm spring, hydraulically-operated with automatic adjustment
Hydraulic fluid type . . . . See *Lubricants and fluids*

Clutch pedal adjustment (refer to illustration 2.7)
Clutch pedal height **H** (with carpets fitted):
  Right-hand-drive models . . . . 196 to 206 mm
  Left-hand-drive models . . . . 187 to 197 mm
Clutch pedal travel **H1** (with carpets fitted) . . . . 162 mm (minimum)
Clutch pedal free play **H2** . . . . 0.5 to 1.0 mm

Driven plate
Diameter:
  Petrol models:
    2.0 litre engine . . . . 216 mm
    2.2 and 2.4 litre engines . . . . 240 mm
  Diesel models:
    2.3 and 2.5 litre engines . . . . 240 mm
    2.8 litre engine . . . . 250 mm
Friction material thickness (new)
  Petrol models:
    2.0 and 2.4 litre engines . . . . 3.5 mm
    2.2 litre engine . . . . 3.6 mm
  Diesel models:
    2.3 and 2.8 litre engines . . . . 3.5 mm
    2.5 litre engine . . . . 2.8 mm

6

Torque wrench settings

	Nm	lbf ft
Hydraulic damper retaining nuts	8	6
Master cylinder mounting bolts	6	4
Pedal bracket mounting nuts	21	15
Pedal pivot bolt nut	35	26
Pedal push rod clevis locknut	28	21
Pedal stop bolt locknut	20	15
Pressure plate bolts:		
Petrol models:		
2.0 litre engine	15	11
2.2 and 2.4 litre engines:		
7 mm diameter bolts	15	11
8 mm diameter bolts	28	21
Diesel models:		
2.3 litre engine	15	11
2.5 litre engine	30	22
2.8 litre engine	20	15
Slave cylinder hydraulic hose banjo union bolt	35	26
Slave cylinder mounting bolts:		
Petrol models:		
2.0 litre engine	28	21
2.2 and 2.4 litre engines	45	33
Diesel models:		
2.3 and 2.5 litre engines	45	33
2.8 litre engine	87	64

1 General information

A single dry plate diaphragm spring clutch is fitted to all manual transmission models. The clutch is hydraulically operated via a master and slave cylinder.

The main components of the clutch are the pressure plate, the driven plate (sometimes called the friction plate or disc) and the release bearing. The pressure plate is bolted to the flywheel, with the driven plate sandwiched between them. The centre of the driven plate carries female splines which mate with the splines on the transmission input shaft. The release bearing is attached to the release fork and acts on the diaphragm spring fingers of the pressure plate.

When the engine is running and the clutch pedal is released, the diaphragm spring clamps the pressure plate, driven plate and flywheel firmly together. Drive is transmitted through the friction surfaces of the flywheel and pressure plate to the linings of the driven plate and thus to the transmission input shaft.

When the clutch pedal is depressed, the pedal movement is transmitted hydraulically to the release fork. The fork moves the bearing to press on the diaphragm spring fingers. Spring pressure on the pressure plate is relieved, and the flywheel and pressure plate spin without moving the driven plate. As the pedal is released, spring pressure is restored and the drive is gradually taken up.

The clutch hydraulic system consists of a master cylinder, a slave cylinder, and the associated pipes and hoses. Additionally, certain models are fitted with a hydraulic damper to assist in progressive take up of the drive **(see illustration)**.

Wear in the driven plate linings is compensated for automatically by the hydraulic system components and no adjustment (apart from clutch pedal height and free play) is necessary.

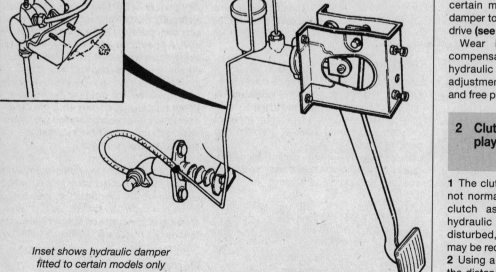

Inset shows hydraulic damper fitted to certain models only

1.5 Clutch hydraulic circuit components

2 Clutch pedal height and free play - adjustment

1 The clutch pedal height and free play will not normally require adjustment, but if the clutch assembly, pedal, or any of the hydraulic system components have been disturbed, the following initial adjustments may be required.

2 Using a tape measure or similar, measure the distance from the floor (with the carpets fitted) to the upper face of the clutch pedal's rubber pad, with the pedal in its normal resting position. This is the pedal height

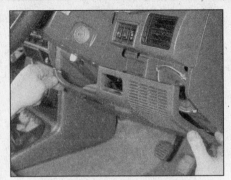

2.3a Removing the trim panel under the facia on a pre-1997 vehicle . . .

2.3b . . . and on a 1997 vehicle

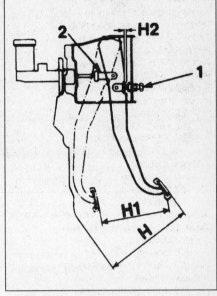

2.7 Clutch pedal height and free play adjustment details

1 Clutch pedal stop bolt
2 Master cylinder push rod
H Clutch pedal height
H1 Clutch pedal travel
H2 Clutch pedal free play

Refer to Specifications for dimensions H, H1 and H2

dimension and must be within the tolerance range given in the Specifications.

3 If adjustment is necessary, disconnect the battery negative lead then remove the trim panel under the facia on the driver's side **(see illustrations)**.

4 Remove the heater/ventilation duct over the top of the clutch pedal bracket assembly.

5 Slacken the locknut, then unscrew the clutch pedal stop bolt on the pedal bracket two or three turns **(see illustration 3.4)**.

6 Slacken the master cylinder push rod clevis locknut and turn the push rod as necessary until the correct pedal height dimension is obtained. Hold the pushrod and tighten the locknut.

7 With the pedal height correctly set, screw in the pedal stop bolt until the specified pedal free play is obtained. The pedal free play dimension is the amount of pedal movement (measured at the pedal stop bolt) from the at-rest position until resistance is met **(see illustration)**.

8 With the free play correctly adjusted, hold the stop bolt and tighten the locknut.

9 Again using the tape measure or similar, measure the distance from the centre of the clutch pedal's rubber pad to a fixed point on the steering wheel rim. The pedal must be hanging in its normal resting position. Repeat the measurement with the pedal fully depressed. Subtract the first measurement from the second to calculate the pedal travel which should be in accordance with the figures given in

the Specifications. If the pedal travel dimension cannot be obtained check, and if necessary repeat, the previous adjustment.

10 On completion, refit the heater duct and trim panel, then reconnect the battery.

3 Clutch pedal - removal and refitting

Removal

1 Disconnect the battery negative lead.

2 Remove the trim panel under the facia on the driver's side.

3 Remove the heater/ventilation duct over the top of the clutch pedal bracket assembly.

4 Extract the spring clip then withdraw the clevis pin securing the master cylinder pushrod to the clutch pedal **(see illustration)**.

5 Undo the four nuts securing the clutch pedal bracket to the bulkhead and remove the pedal bracket assembly from the vehicle.

6 Undo the nut and withdraw the pedal pivot bolt, then lift out the pedal and return spring from the pedal bracket.

7 With the pedal removed, check the condition of the pivot bushes and renew as necessary.

Refitting

8 Refit by reversing the removal operations, ensuring that the return spring is positioned correctly at the front of the pedal and its ends are located in the bracket. Tighten the pivot bolt nut and pedal bracket nuts to the specified torque.

9 On completion check, and if necessary adjust the clutch pedal height and free play as described in Section 2.

4 Clutch master cylinder - removal and refitting

 Warning: Hydraulic fluid is poisonous; wash off immediately and thoroughly in the case of skin contact, and

seek immediate medical advice if any fluid is swallowed or gets into the eyes. Certain types of hydraulic fluid are inflammable, and may ignite when allowed into contact with hot components; when servicing any hydraulic system, it is safest to assume that the fluid IS inflammable, and to take precautions against the risk of fire as though it is petrol that is being handled. Hydraulic fluid is also an effective paint stripper, and will attack plastics; if any is spilt, it should be washed off immediately, using copious quantities of clean water. Finally, it is hygroscopic (it absorbs moisture from the air) - old fluid may be contaminated and unfit for further use. When topping-up or renewing the fluid, always use the recommended type, and ensure that it comes from a freshly-opened sealed container.

Note: *Master cylinder internal components are not available separately and no repair or overhaul of the cylinder is possible. In the event of a hydraulic system fault, or any sign of visible fluid leakage on or around the master cylinder or clutch pedal, the unit should be renewed.*

Removal

1 Disconnect the battery negative lead.

2 From within the engine compartment, unscrew the hydraulic pipe union from the

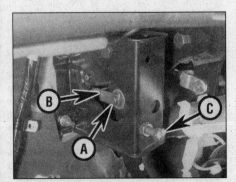

3.4 Master cylinder pushrod clevis pin (A)
B Push rod locknut   C Pedal stop bolt

6

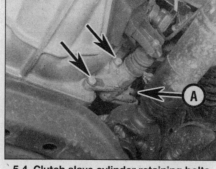
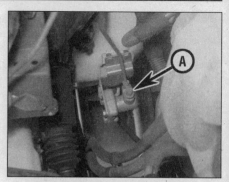

4.2 Unscrew the hydraulic pipe union from the clutch master cylinder

5.4 Clutch slave cylinder retaining bolts (arrowed)

A Bleed screw

6.2 The clutch hydraulic damper may be located on either side of the engine compartment

A Bleed screw

clutch master cylinder **(see illustration)**. Have a container and rags ready to catch the fluid which will spill. Cover the open pipe union with a piece of polythene and a rubber band to keep dirt out.
3 Remove the trim panel under the facia on the driver's side.
4 Remove the heater/ventilation duct over the top of the clutch pedal bracket assembly.
5 Extract the spring clip then withdraw the clevis pin securing the master cylinder pushrod to the clutch pedal.
6 Undo the four nuts securing the clutch pedal bracket to the bulkhead and remove the pedal bracket assembly from the vehicle.
7 Undo the two bolts which secure the master cylinder to the bulkhead.
8 Remove the master cylinder from the engine compartment, being careful not to drip fluid onto the paintwork.

Refitting

9 Refitting is a reversal of removal, noting the following points:
a) *Tighten the master cylinder retaining nuts to the specified torque.*
b) *Bleed the clutch hydraulic system (Section 7) and adjust the clutch pedal height and free play (Section 2).*

5 Clutch slave cylinder - removal and refitting

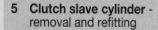

Note: *Slave cylinder internal components are not available separately and no repair or overhaul of the cylinder is possible. In the event of a hydraulic system fault, or any sign of visible fluid leakage on or around the slave cylinder push rod or rubber gaiter, the unit should be renewed.*

Removal

Note: *Refer to the warning at the beginning of Section 4 before proceeding.*
1 Working under the bonnet, remove the clutch master cylinder fluid reservoir cap, and secure a piece of polythene over the filler neck with a rubber band, or by refitting the

cap. This will reduce the loss of fluid during the following procedure.
2 Jack up the front of the vehicle, and securely support it on axle stands (see *Jacking and Vehicle Support*).
3 From under the vehicle, unscrew the hydraulic hose banjo union bolt and recover the two copper washers. Have a container and rags ready to catch any spilled fluid. Cover the open banjo union with a piece of polythene and a rubber band to keep dirt out.
4 Undo the two slave cylinder retaining bolts and withdraw the unit from the transmission and clutch release fork **(see illustration)**.

Refitting

5 Engage the slave cylinder pushrod with the clutch release fork, then locate the cylinder on the transmission. Refit the two retaining bolts and tighten to the specified torque.
6 Locate a new copper washer on each side of the hydraulic hose banjo union and position the union on the slave cylinder. Fit the union bolt and tighten to the specified torque. Ensure that the locating peg on the banjo union engages with the hole on the cylinder body.
7 Bleed the clutch hydraulic system (Section 7), then lower the vehicle to the ground and adjust the clutch pedal height and free play (Section 2).

6 Clutch hydraulic damper - removal and refitting

Note: *Refer to the warning at the beginning of Section 4 before proceeding.*

Removal

1 Remove the clutch master cylinder fluid reservoir cap, and secure a piece of polythene over the filler neck with a rubber band, or by refitting the cap. This will reduce the loss of fluid during the following procedure.
2 Trace the master cylinder hydraulic pipe down to the damper which may be located on either the right-hand or left-hand side of the engine compartment, according to engine and model **(see illustration)**.

3 Unscrew the two hydraulic pipe union nuts at the damper and carefully withdraw the pipes. Have a container and rags ready to catch any spilled fluid. Cover the open unions with a piece of polythene and a rubber band to keep dirt out.
4 Undo the two hydraulic damper mounting bracket retaining nuts and withdraw the unit from the vehicle.

Refitting

5 Refitting is a reversal of removal, noting the following points:
a) *Tighten the mounting bracket retaining nuts to the specified torque.*
b) *Bleed the clutch hydraulic system (Section 7) and adjust the clutch pedal height and free play (Section 2).*

7 Clutch hydraulic system - bleeding

Note: *Refer to the warning at the beginning of Section 4 before proceeding.*
1 Top-up the hydraulic fluid reservoir on the clutch master cylinder with fresh clean fluid of the specified type (see *Weekly checks*). Check the level frequently during the following procedure and keep the reservoir topped up.
2 Certain models are fitted with a damper in the hydraulic circuit between the master cylinder and slave cylinder **(see illustration 6.2)**. If a damper is fitted, this must be bled first, followed by the slave cylinder.
3 Remove the dust cover and fit a length of clear hose over the bleed screw on the damper (where applicable) or slave cylinder. Place the other end of the hose in a jar containing a small amount of hydraulic fluid.
4 Have an assistant depress the clutch pedal two or three times, then hold it down. Slacken the bleed screw and allow the fluid to flow into the container. Tighten the bleed screw while the pedal is still depressed, then have the assistant release the pedal.
5 Repeat the process until clean fluid, free of air bubbles, emerges from the bleed screw.

Tighten the screw at the end of a pedal downstroke and remove the hose and jar. Refit the dust cover.

6 If the vehicle is fitted with a hydraulic damper, repeat the above procedure at the slave cylinder.

7 Top-up the hydraulic fluid reservoir once more and refit the cap.

8 Clutch assembly - removal, inspection and refitting

⚠️ **Warning: Dust created by clutch wear and deposited on the clutch components may contain asbestos, which is a health hazard. DO NOT blow it out with compressed air, nor inhale any of it. DO NOT use petrol or petroleum-based solvents to clean off the dust. Brake system cleaner or methylated spirit should be used to flush the dust into a suitable receptacle. After the clutch components are wiped clean with rags, dispose of contaminated rags and cleaner in a sealed, marked container.**

Removal

1 Remove the transmission as described in Chapter 7.

2 Before disturbing the clutch, use paint or a marker pen to mark the relationship of the pressure plate assembly to the flywheel.

3 Working in a diagonal sequence, slacken the pressure plate bolts by half a turn at a time, until spring pressure is released and the bolts can be unscrewed by hand.

4 Prise the pressure plate assembly off its locating dowels, and collect the driven plate, noting which way round the driven plate is fitted **(see illustrations)**.

Inspection

Note: *Due to the amount of work necessary to remove and refit clutch components, it is usually considered good practice to renew the clutch driven plate, pressure plate assembly and release bearing as a matched set, even if only one of these is actually worn enough to require renewal.*

5 When cleaning clutch components, read first the warning at the beginning of this Section; remove any dust using a clean, dry cloth, and working in a well-ventilated atmosphere.

6 Check the driven plate facings for signs of wear, damage or oil contamination. If the friction material is cracked, burnt, scored or damaged, or if it is contaminated with oil or grease (shown by shiny black patches), the driven plate must be renewed. Check the depth of the rivets below the friction material surface; if the friction material is worn down to, or close to (less than approximately 0.5 mm) the rivet heads, then the driven plate must be renewed.

7 If the friction material is still serviceable, check that the centre boss splines are unworn, that the torsion springs (where applicable) are in good condition and securely fastened, and that all the rivets are tight. If any wear or damage is found, the driven plate must be renewed.

8 If the friction material is fouled with oil, this must be due to an oil leak from the crankshaft rear oil seal, from the sump-to-cylinder block joint, or from the transmission input shaft. Renew the seal or repair the joint, as appropriate, as described in the relevant Part of Chapter 2 or 7, before installing the new driven plate.

9 Check the pressure plate assembly for obvious signs of wear or damage; shake it to check for loose rivets or worn or damaged fulcrum rings, and check that the drive straps securing the pressure plate to the cover do not show signs of overheating (such as a deep yellow or blue discoloration). If the diaphragm spring is worn or damaged, or if its pressure is in any way suspect, the pressure plate assembly should be renewed.

10 Examine the machined bearing surfaces of the pressure plate and of the flywheel; they should be clean, completely flat, and free from scratches or scoring. If either is discoloured from excessive heat, or shows signs of cracks, it should be renewed - although minor damage of this nature can sometimes be polished away using emery paper.

11 Check that the release bearing contact surface rotates smoothly and easily, with no sign of noise or roughness. Also check that the surface itself is smooth and unworn, with no signs of cracks, pitting or scoring. If there is any doubt about its condition, the bearing must be renewed.

Refitting

12 On reassembly, ensure that the bearing surfaces of the flywheel and pressure plate are completely clean, smooth, and free from oil or grease. Use solvent to remove any protective grease from new components.

13 Fit the driven plate the correct way round as noted during removal. Original equipment components are marked 'Getriebeseite' (transmission side) to ensure correct positioning. If required at this stage, the driven plate may be held in position using a clutch aligning tool **(see illustration 8.16)**.

14 Refit the pressure plate assembly, aligning the arrow marks stamped on the pressure plate and flywheel, or the marks made on dismantling (if the original pressure plate is re-used), and locating the pressure plate on its locating dowels. Fit the pressure plate bolts, but tighten them only finger-tight, so that the driven plate can still be moved.

15 The driven plate must now be centralised, so that when the transmission is refitted, its input shaft will pass through the splines at the centre of the driven plate.

16 Centralisation can be achieved by passing a screwdriver or other long bar through the driven plate and into the hole in the crankshaft; the driven plate can then be moved around until it is centred on the crankshaft hole. Alternatively, a clutch-aligning tool can be used to eliminate the guesswork; these can be obtained from most accessory shops **(see illustration)**. A home-made aligning tool can be fabricated from a length of metal rod or wooden dowel which fits closely inside the crankshaft hole, and has insulating tape wound around it to match the diameter of the driven plate splined hole.

17 When the driven plate is centralised, tighten the pressure plate bolts evenly and in a diagonal sequence to the specified torque setting. Remove the centring tool.

18 Apply a thin smear of molybdenum

8.4a Remove the pressure plate from the flywheel locating dowels . . .

8.4b . . . and collect the driven plate

8.16 Using the clutch aligning tool

6

disulphide grease to the contact areas of the release bearing, guide tube and fork.

Caution: Do not apply too much grease, as there is a risk that it will contaminate the driven plate material.

19 Refit the transmission to the engine as described in Chapter 7.

9 Clutch release bearing - removal, inspection and refitting

Removal

1 Remove the transmission as described in Chapter 7.

2 Release the rubber gaiter from the bellhousing aperture and release fork **(see illustration)**.

3 Release the spring clip securing the release bearing carrier to the release fork then pull the release fork sideways off the pivot stud **(see illustration)**.

4 Slide the release bearing and carrier off the transmission input shaft guide tube.

5 Using a suitable puller, withdraw the release bearing from the bearing carrier.

Inspection

6 Check the release fork, bearing and rubber gaiters, renewing any component which is

9.2 Release the rubber gaiter from the bellhousing aperture and release fork

worn or damaged. Carefully check all bearing surfaces and points of contact.

7 When checking the release bearing itself, note that it is often considered worthwhile to renew it as a matter of course. Check that the contact surface rotates smoothly and easily, with no sign of noise or roughness, and that the surface itself is smooth and unworn, with no signs of cracks, pitting or scoring. If there is any doubt about its condition, the bearing must be renewed. **Note:** *Due to the amount of work necessary to remove and refit clutch components, it is usually considered good practice to renew the clutch driven plate, pressure plate assembly and release bearing as a matched set, even if only one of these is actually worn enough to require renewal.*

9.3 Pull the release fork sideways off the pivot stud

Refitting

8 Locate the release bearing on the bearing carrier then press the bearing fully into place on the carrier. This can be done using a bench vice with protected jaws, or with two pieces of wood placed between the vice jaws and the bearing and carrier.

9 Prior to refitting, smear molybdenum disulphide grease on the contact surfaces of the release bearing, release fork and pivot stud and the transmission input shaft guide tube **(see illustration)**.

Caution: Do not apply too much grease, as there is a risk that it will contaminate the driven plate material.

10 Slide the release bearing and carrier assembly onto the input shaft guide tube.

11 Insert the release fork through the aperture in the bellhousing, engage the fork ends with the release bearing carrier and at the same time engage the legs of the fork spring clip behind the pivot stud **(see illustration)**. This operation requires a lot of patience and will probably take two or three attempts to achieve success. It is all too easy for one of the spring clip legs to end up on the wrong side of the pivot stud.

12 Once the fork is correctly located, engage the spring clip on the bearing carrier with the release fork and refit the rubber gaiter to the bellhousing aperture. Check again that the release fork is correctly located and pivots freely.

13 Refit the transmission to the engine as described in Chapter 7.

9.9 Smear molybdenum disulphide grease on the pivot stud and all other contact areas before refitting the release fork

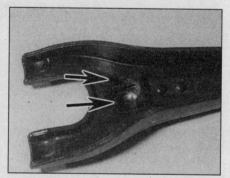

9.11 Ensure that the legs of the release fork spring clip (arrowed) engage behind the pivot stud

Chapter 7
Transmission

Contents

Gearchange lever - removal and refitting 2	Transfer change lever - removal and refitting 3
Gearchange quadrant box - removal, overhaul and refitting 4	Transmission - removal and refitting 8
General information 1	Transmission oil level check ....See Chapter 1
Oil seals - renewal 5	Transmission oil renewal ....See Chapter 1
Reversing light switch - testing, removal and refitting 6	Transmission overhaul - general information 9
Speedometer drive - removal and refitting 7	

Degrees of difficulty

Easy, suitable for novice with little experience	**Fairly easy,** suitable for beginner with some experience	**Fairly difficult,** suitable for competent DIY mechanic	**Difficult,** suitable for experienced DIY mechanic 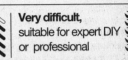	**Very difficult,** suitable for expert DIY or professional

Specifications

General

Type .... Manual with five forward speeds and reverse, all-synchromesh.
Integral transfer gearbox with selectable four-wheel drive

Designation:
   2.0 litre petrol engine models .... MSG
   All other models .... MUA

Lubrication
Oil type .... See *Lubricants and fluids*
Capacity .... See Chapter 1

Torque wrench settings

	Nm	lbf ft
MSG transmission		
Clutch slave cylinder mounting bolts	28	21
Crossmember to chassis members	80	59
Gearchange quadrant box mounting bolts	20	15
Input shaft cover plate bolts	20	15
Transfer gearbox protector plate bolts	47	35
Transmission bellhousing to engine:		
2.0 litre (C20NE) petrol engines	70	52
2.0 litre (X20SE) petrol engines:		
Primary bolts	68	50
Secondary bolts	41	30
Transmission mounting to crossmember	48	35
MUA transmission		
Clutch slave cylinder mounting bolts	28	21
Crossmember to chassis members	80	59
Gearchange quadrant box mounting bolts	20	15
Input shaft cover plate bolts	20	15
Output flange retaining nut	167	123
Transfer gearbox protector plate bolts	47	35
Transmission bellhousing to engine:		
2.4 litre petrol and 2.3 litre diesel engines	45	33
2.2 litre petrol engines	68	50
2.5 litre diesel engines:		
Primary bolts	78	58
Secondary bolts	22	16
2.8 litre diesel engines:		
Primary bolts	87	64
Secondary bolts	40	30
Transmission mounting to crossmember	50	37

7

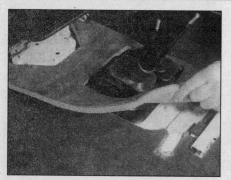

2.2a Lift out the sound insulation mat around the gearchange lever . . .

2.2b . . . then ease out the base of the gearchange lever rubber gaiter

1 General information

All Frontera models are equipped with an Isuzu 5-speed, all-synchromesh manual transmission, incorporating an integral 2-speed transfer gearbox for the part-time four-wheel drive system. Two transmission types are used; the MSG type is fitted to 2.0 litre petrol engines and the MUA type is fitted to all other engines. Both transmission types are similar in design and operation. The transmission is contained in a cast-aluminium alloy casing bolted to the rear of the engine,

and consists of the main gearbox with the transfer mechanism housed in the rear case of the assembly.

Main gear selection is via a floor-mounted lever and selector rod mechanism. A second lever, mounted alongside, controls the transfer mechanism and allows selection of two or four-wheel drive, and low or high ratio when four-wheel drive is selected.

2 Gearchange lever - removal and refitting

Removal

1 Remove the centre console as described in Chapter 12.
2 Where applicable, lift out the sound insulation mat then ease out the base of the gearchange lever rubber gaiter from the lip of the transmission tunnel aperture **(see illustrations)**. On some models it will be necessary to undo four screws and remove the rubber gaiter retaining plate before the gaiter can be released.
3 Withdraw the rubber gaiter up and off the gearchange and transfer change levers.
4 Slide the rubber dust cover upwards for access, then undo the three gearchange lever retaining plate bolts **(see illustration)**.

5 Withdraw the gearchange lever from the gearchange quadrant box **(see illustration)**.

Refitting

6 Lubricate the gearchange lever pivot ball and seat with clean engine oil then locate the lever in the quadrant box. Secure the gearchange lever retaining plate with the three bolts tightened securely.
7 Slide the rubber dust cover down into position, then refit the rubber gaiter and sound insulation mat (where fitted).
8 Refit the centre console as described in Chapter 12.

3 Transfer change lever - removal and refitting

Removal

1 Remove the centre console as described in Chapter 12.
2 Where applicable, lift out the sound insulation mat then ease out the base of the gearchange lever rubber gaiter from the lip of the transmission tunnel aperture. On some models it will be necessary to undo four screws and remove the rubber gaiter retaining plate before the gaiter can be released.
3 Withdraw the rubber gaiter up and off the gearchange and transfer change levers.
4 Undo the two retaining plate bolts and withdraw the transfer change lever from the gearchange quadrant box **(see illustration)**.

Refitting

5 Lubricate the transfer change lever pivot ball and seat with clean engine oil then locate the lever in the quadrant box. Secure the lever retaining plate with the two bolts tightened securely.
6 Slide the rubber dust cover down into position, then refit the rubber gaiter and sound insulation mat (where fitted).
7 Refit the centre console as described in Chapter 12.

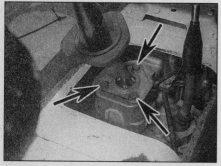

2.4 Undo the three gearchange lever retaining plate bolts (arrowed) . . .

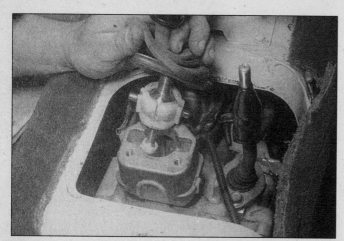

2.5 . . . and withdraw the gearchange lever from the quadrant box

3.4 Transfer change lever retaining plate bolts (arrowed)

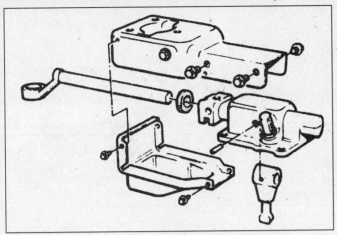
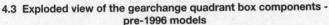

4.3 Exploded view of the gearchange quadrant box components - pre-1996 models

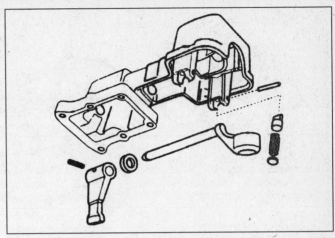

4.20 Exploded view of the gearchange quadrant box components - 1996 models onward

4 Gearchange quadrant box - removal, overhaul and refitting

Pre-1996 models

Removal

1 Remove the gearchange lever as described in Section 2.

2 Undo the four bolts and withdraw the quadrant box from the transmission. Recover the gasket.

Overhaul

3 Undo the three bolts and two screws and withdraw the remote control housing upper and lower halves from the quadrant box (see illustration).

4 Working through the front retaining bolt holes in the quadrant box, tap out the roll pin securing the shift finger to the selector rod, using a small punch. Remove the selector rod and shift finger from the quadrant box.

5 Using a suitable screwdriver, prise the selector rod oil seal from the quadrant box.

6 Undo the screws securing the upper and lower halves of the remote control housing together and separate the two parts.

7 Undo the two bolts and remove the two tension springs and centre shaft from the upper half of the remote control housing.

8 Check the condition of all the components and renew any which are suspect. The selector rod oil seal and the shift finger retaining roll pin must be renewed as a matter of course.

9 Commence reassembly by carefully tapping a new oil seal into the quadrant box.

10 Refit the tension springs and centre shaft to the remote control housing upper half, then reassemble the upper and lower housing halves.

11 Lubricate the selector rod and oil seal with multipurpose grease and insert the selector rod into the quadrant box. Fit the shift finger and secure by tapping in a new roll pin.

12 Refit the remote control housing to the quadrant box and secure with the retaining bolts and screws.

Refitting

13 Locate a new gasket in position on the transmission, refit the quadrant box assembly and secure with the four bolts, tightened to the specified torque.

14 Refit the gearchange lever as described in Section 2.

1996 models onward

Removal

15 Remove the gearchange lever as described in Section 2.

16 Disconnect the reversing light switch wiring connector and release the wiring harness from the cable clips.

17 Undo the four bolts, remove the wiring harness cable clips and withdraw the quadrant box from the transmission. Recover the gasket.

Overhaul

18 Unscrew the reversing light switch and collect the washer, spring and ball.

19 Release the clips and remove the plastic cover from the base of the unit.

20 Unscrew the blanking plug in the side of the quadrant box, then tap out the roll pin securing the shift finger to the selector rod, using a small punch. Remove the selector rod and shift finger from the quadrant box (see illustration).

21 Using a suitable screwdriver, prise out the selector rod oil seal.

22 Tap out the retaining roll pins and withdraw the retaining discs, springs and plungers from the posts on the underside of the unit.

23 Check the condition of all the components and renew any which are suspect. The selector rod oil seal and the shift finger retaining roll pin must be renewed as a matter of course.

24 Commence reassembly by carefully tapping in a new oil seal.

25 Refit the plungers, springs and retaining discs to the posts on the underside of the unit and secure by tapping in the roll pins.

26 Lubricate the selector rod and oil seal with multipurpose grease and insert the selector rod into the quadrant box. Fit the shift finger and secure by tapping in a new roll pin.

27 Refit the blanking plug to the side of the quadrant box.

28 Refit the plastic cover to the base of the unit.

29 Refit the reversing light switch ball, spring and washer then screw in the switch.

Refitting

30 Locate a new gasket in position on the transmission, refit the quadrant box assembly and secure with the four bolts, tightened to the specified torque.

31 Reconnect the reversing light switch wiring connector and secure the wiring harness with the cable clips.

32 Refit the gearchange lever as described in Section 2.

5 Oil seals - renewal

Transmission rear (output shaft) oil seal

1 Remove the rear propeller shaft as described in Chapter 8.

2 Using a suitable screwdriver, lever out the old seal, taking care not to damage the casing.

3 Lubricate the lips of the new seal with clean engine oil and position it on the casing.

4 Using a block of wood or tube of suitable diameter, tap the new seal fully into place, taking care to keep it square as it is being fitted.

5 Refit the rear propeller shaft as described in Chapter 8.

7

5.14 Input shaft cover plate and belleville spring washer as fitted to the MSG transmission

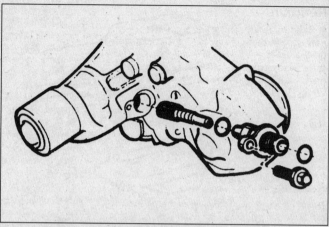

7.3 Speedometer drive components as fitted to the MUA transmission

Transfer gearbox front oil seal (MUA transmission)

6 Remove the front propeller shaft as described in Chapter 8.

7 Unscrew the transfer gearbox front output shaft flange retaining nut while preventing the flange rotating using a suitable forked tool engaged with the flange bolt holes.

8 Withdraw the flange from the output shaft then, using a suitable screwdriver, lever out the old seal, taking care not to damage the casing.

9 Lubricate the lips of the new seal with clean engine oil and position it on the casing.

10 Using a block of wood or tube of suitable diameter, tap the new seal fully into place, taking care to keep it square as it is being fitted.

11 Refit the output flange and retaining nut and tighten the nut to the specified torque.

Transfer gearbox front oil seal (MSG transmission)

12 It is not possible to renew the transfer gearbox front oil seal without first dismantling the transmission, which is beyond the scope of this manual. Front oil seal renewal should therefore be entrusted to a Vauxhall dealer or transmission overhaul specialist.

Input shaft oil seal

13 Remove the transmission as described in Section 8, and remove the clutch release mechanism as described in Chapter 6.

14 Unscrew the clutch release fork pivot stud and the bolts securing the input shaft cover plate and guide tube to the transmission casing (**see illustration**).

15 Withdraw the cover plate and gasket from the front of the transmission casing. On the MSG transmission, collect the belleville spring washer from inside the cover plate unless it remained in place on the transmission.

16 Carefully lever out the old oil seal from inside the cover plate taking care not to damage the plate.

17 Remove all traces of old gasket from the transmission and cover plate.

18 Lubricate the lips of the new seal with clean engine oil and position it inside the cover plate.

19 Using a block of wood or tube of suitable diameter, tap the new seal fully into place, taking care to keep it square as it is being fitted.

20 Place a new gasket on the cover plate and on the MSG transmission, position the belleville spring washer with its dished face toward the input shaft bearing.

21 Refit the cover plate and secure with the bolts tightened to the specified torque. On the MUA transmission, apply a suitable sealing compound to the cover plate bolt threads before refitting. Refit the clutch release fork pivot stud.

22 Refit the clutch release mechanism as described in Chapter 6, then refit the transmission as described in Section 8.

Gearchange quadrant selector rod oil seal

23 Refer to the procedures contained in Section 4.

6 Reversing light switch - testing, removal and refitting

1 The reversing light circuit is controlled by a plunger-type switch located on the left-hand side of the transmission. Depending on transmission type and model year, the switch will either be screwed into the left-hand side of the casing itself, or into the left-hand side of the gearchange quadrant box, just forward of the gearchange lever. Where switches are fitted to both of these locations, the reversing light switch is located in the casing and the switch in the quadrant box is a neutral position switch used by the engine management system.

Testing

2 If a fault develops in the circuit, first ensure that the circuit fuse has not blown.

3 To test the switch, disconnect the wiring connector, and use a multimeter (set to the resistance function) or a battery-and-bulb test circuit to check that there is continuity between the switch terminals only when reverse gear is selected. If this is not the case, and there are no obvious breaks or other damage to the wires, the switch is faulty, and must be renewed.

Removal

4 Firmly apply the handbrake, then jack up the front of the vehicle and support it on axle stands (see *Jacking and Vehicle Support*).

5 Disconnect the wiring connector, then unscrew the switch and collect the sealing washer, spring and ball.

Refitting

6 Fit a new sealing washer to the switch, fit the ball and spring, then screw the switch back into position and tighten it securely. Reconnect the wiring connector, and test the operation of the circuit. If any oil was lost when the switch was removed, check the oil level as described in Chapter 1 before lowering the vehicle to the ground.

7 Speedometer drive - removal and refitting

Removal

1 Firmly apply the handbrake, then jack up the front of the vehicle and support it on axle stands (see *Jacking and Vehicle Support*).

2 Disconnect the speedometer cable or wiring connector, as applicable, from the speedometer drive at the rear of the transmission casing.

3 Undo the drive housing retaining bolt and withdraw the housing, seals and driven gear assembly from the transmission casing (**see illustration**).

Refitting

4 Refitting is a reversal of removal, but use new seals if there is any sign of deterioration on the old seals. If any oil was lost when the drive was removed, check the oil level as described in Chapter 1 before lowering the vehicle to the ground.

8 Transmission - removal and refitting

Removal

Note: *Although the following procedure is not difficult, the transmission assembly is heavy and awkward to handle and suitable lifting and supporting equipment is essential. Read through the entire procedure to familiarise yourself with the work involved before proceeding. The front and rear of the vehicle will have to be raised and securely supported, and a transmission support fixture will be required to take the weight of the unit as it is removed from the engine. Suitable equipment of this nature is available from tool and equipment hire outlets. Alternatively (although less satisfactory) an engine hoist can be used to support the transmission from above, through the gearchange lever aperture in the passenger compartment. Throughout the following procedure, the help of an assistant will prove invaluable.*

1 Remove the gearchange and transfer change levers and the gearchange quadrant box as described in Sections 2, 3 and 4.

2 Jack up the front and rear of the vehicle and support it on axle stands (see *Jacking and Vehicle Support*). Note that the vehicle must be raised sufficiently to allow removal of the transmission from below.

3 Remove the undershield beneath the engine and the protector plate from beneath the transfer gearbox.

4 Refer to Chapter 1 and drain the transmission oil.

5 Remove the front and rear propeller shafts as described in Chapter 8.

6 Disconnect the speedometer cable, or speedometer transducer wiring connector, from the speedometer drive at the rear of the transmission.

7 On the left-hand side of the transmission, disconnect the reversing light wiring and, where applicable the neutral switch wiring at the harness connectors. Similarly, disconnect

the four-wheel-drive warning light switch wiring at the connector on the right-hand side of the transfer gearbox.

8 Undo the two clutch slave cylinder securing bolts, disengage the push rod from the release fork and support the cylinder clear of the transmission. Do not disconnect the hydraulic fluid hose.

9 With reference to the Note at the beginning of this Section, suitably support the transmission from below on a proprietary support fixture or from above, through the gearchange lever aperture, by means of slings attached to an engine hoist.

 Warning: Ensure that the transmission is adequately and safely supported before proceeding. Any attempt to remove the transmission without the use of mechanical assistance is likely to result in damage and personal injury.

10 With the transmission support in place, lift the transmission slightly to just take the weight off the rear crossmember.

11 Remove the exhaust system front downpipe and transmission attachment as described in Chapter 4.

12 Undo the nuts securing the transmission mounting to the crossmember, and the bolts securing the crossmember to the side chassis members. Remove the crossmember.

13 Working diagonally around the bellhousing, undo the bolts securing the transmission to the engine. Note that the transmission may move backwards from the engine once the bolts are removed - be prepared for this and do not allow the unit to move uncontrolled.

14 Support the rear of the engine by positioning a block of wood between the rear sump flange and front crossmember, or by using a suitable jack.

15 Carefully withdraw the transmission, taking care not to damage the clutch disc or transmission input shaft. Once the transmission is clear of the engine, lower it to the ground and slide it out from under the vehicle.

Refitting

16 Refitting is a reversal of removal, bearing in mind the following points:

a) *Clean the transmission and engine mating faces and lightly smear molybdenum disulphide grease on the contact surfaces of the clutch release bearing, transmission input shaft guide tube and input shaft splines.*

b) *Tighten the transmission-to-engine mounting bolts and the crossmember attachments to the specified torque.*

c) *Refit the exhaust front pipe, and propeller shafts with reference to the Chapters indicated.*

d) *Refit the gearchange quadrant box, gearchange lever and transfer change lever as described earlier in this Chapter.*

e) *Refill the transmission with oil as described in Chapter 1.*

f) *On completion, adjust the clutch pedal height and free play as described in Chapter 6.*

9 Transmission overhaul - general information

1 Overhauling a transmission is a difficult and involved job for the DIY home mechanic. In addition to dismantling and reassembling many small parts, clearances must be precisely measured and, if necessary, changed by selecting shims and spacers. Internal transmission components are also often difficult to obtain, and in many instances, extremely expensive. Because of this, if the transmission develops a fault or becomes noisy, the best course of action is to have the unit overhauled by a specialist repairer, or to obtain an exchange reconditioned unit.

2 Nevertheless, it is not impossible for the more experienced mechanic to overhaul the transmission, provided the special tools are available, and the job is done in a deliberate step-by-step manner, so that nothing is overlooked.

3 The tools necessary for an overhaul include internal and external circlip pliers, bearing pullers, a slide hammer, a set of pin punches, a dial test indicator, and possibly a hydraulic press. In addition, a large, sturdy workbench and a vice will be required.

4 During dismantling of the transmission, make careful notes of how each component is fitted, to make reassembly easier and more accurate.

5 Before dismantling the transmission, it will help if you have some idea what area is malfunctioning. Certain problems can be closely related to specific areas in the transmission, which can make component examination and replacement easier. Refer to the *Fault finding* Section at the rear of this manual for more information.

7

Notes

Chapter 8
Propeller shafts and driveshafts

Contents

Driveshaft - removal and refitting 9
Driveshaft CV joint - checking and renewal 10
Driveshaft CV joint gaiter check . . . . See Chapter 1
Driveshaft CV joint gaiters - renewal 11
Driveshafts - description 8
Front propeller shaft - removal and refitting 3
General information 1
Propeller shaft check and lubrication . . . . See Chapter 1
Propeller shaft universal joints - renewal 5
Propeller shafts - description 2
Rear propeller shaft - removal and refitting 4
Rear propeller shaft flexible coupling - removal and refitting 6
Rear propeller shaft support bearing - removal and refitting 7

Degrees of difficulty

Easy, suitable for novice with little experience	Fairly easy, suitable for beginner with some experience	Fairly difficult, suitable for competent DIY mechanic	Difficult, suitable for experienced DIY mechanic	Very difficult, suitable for expert DIY or professional

Specifications

Propeller shafts

Front propeller shaft . . . . Single-piece tubular with needle roller universal joints

Rear propeller shaft:
  3-door models . . . . Single-piece tubular with needle roller universal joints
  5-door models . . . . Two-piece tubular with needle roller universal joints, with front flexible rubber coupling and centre support bearing

Driveshafts

Type . . . . Equal length solid steel shafts with inner and outer ball and cage constant velocity (CV) joints

Lubricant type/specification . . . . Special grease - Vauxhall part number 19 41 521 (90 094 176) supplied with gaiter kits. Joints are otherwise pre-packed with grease and sealed

Torque wrench settings

	Nm	lbf ft
Mounting bracket to front axle:		
Pre-1996 models	82	61
1996 models onward	93	70
Propeller shaft flange bolts*:		
Front propeller shaft:		
Flange to front axle pinion	75	55
Flange to transfer gearbox:		
2.0 litre petrol engine models (MSG transmission)	35	26
All other models (MUA transmission)	75	55
Rear propeller shaft:		
Flange to rear axle pinion	75	55
Rear propeller shaft support bearing to chassis	33	24
Roadwheel nuts:		
Steel wheels	110	81
Alloy wheels	120	89

*New micro-encapsulated bolts must be used.

8

1 General information

The information in this Chapter deals with the driveline components from the transmission to the front and rear axles, and from the front axle to the front wheels. For the purposes of this Chapter, these components are grouped into the two categories, propeller shafts and driveshafts. Separate Sections within this Chapter provide descriptions and repair procedures for each group.

Refer to Chapter 9 for procedures specific to the front and rear axle components, and to Chapter 11 for suspension and steering component details.

2 Propeller shafts - description

Front propeller shaft

1 Drive is transmitted from the transmission transfer gearbox to the front axle by a single-piece tubular propeller shaft (see illustration).
2 To cater for slight movement of the engine/transmission assembly on its mountings, needle roller type universal joints are fitted at each end of the shaft. The universal joint flanges are bolted to the transfer gearbox output shaft flange and front axle pinion flange. A splined sliding sleeve is also used at one end of the propeller shaft to permit slight longitudinal movement of the power unit.

Single-piece rear propeller shaft

3 On 3-door models, drive is transmitted from the transmission to the rear axle by a single-piece tubular propeller shaft, incorporating needle roller type universal joints at each end (see illustration).
4 The front universal joint yoke is internally splined to engage with the transmission output flange, while at the rear, the universal joint flange is bolted to the rear axle pinion flange.

Two-piece rear propeller shaft

5 To cater for the longer vehicle wheelbase, 5-door models are equipped with a two-piece rear propeller shaft, transmitting the drive from the transmission to the rear axle (see illustration).
6 The forward end of the front shaft is bolted to a flexible rubber coupling which is in turn bolted to an internally splined yoke which engages with the transmission output shaft. The rear end of the front shaft incorporates a rubber-cushioned support bearing bolted to the underside of the vehicle chassis. The front and rear shafts are connected by a needle roller type universal joint, while a second universal joint is fitted at the rear and bolted to the rear axle pinion flange.

3 Front propeller shaft - removal and refitting

Removal

Note: *New bolts will be required to secure the propeller shaft coupling flange(s) when refitting.*
1 Chock the rear wheels then jack up the front of the vehicle and support it on axle stands (see *Jacking and Vehicle Support*).
2 If the original propeller shaft is to be refitted, make alignment marks between the universal joint flange and axle pinion flange at the front, and between the universal joint and transfer gearbox flanges at the rear.
3 Counterhold the nuts then unscrew the bolts securing the propeller shaft to the front axle pinion flange (see illustration). Note that the flange bolts are of the micro-encapsulated type and must be renewed when the propeller shaft is refitted. Support the shaft on an axle stand after disconnecting the flanges.
4 Similarly disconnect the rear of the shaft from the transfer gearbox output flange and remove the shaft from under the vehicle.

Refitting

5 Refitting is a reversal of removal bearing in mind the following points:
a) Ensure that the propeller shaft is refitted with the sliding joint towards the front of the vehicle (nearest the front axle).
b) If the original propeller shaft is being refitted, align the marks made on the flanges prior to removal, before inserting the flange bolts.
c) Use new encapsulated flange bolts and tighten them to the specified torque.

Front propeller shaft

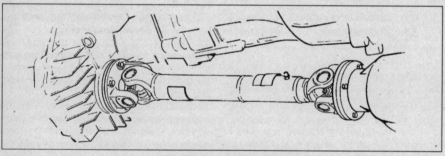

2.1 Front propeller shaft

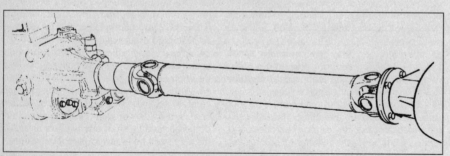

2.3 Single-piece rear propeller shaft

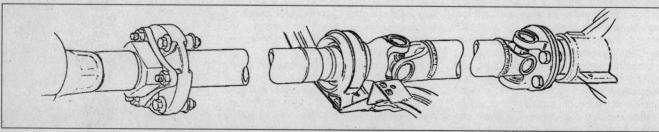

2.5 Two-piece rear propeller shaft

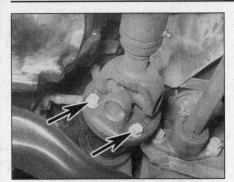

3.3 Front propeller shaft-to-axle pinion flange bolts (arrowed)

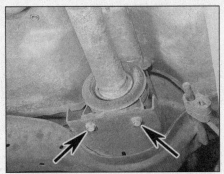

4.8 Two-piece rear propeller shaft support bearing mounting bolts (arrowed)

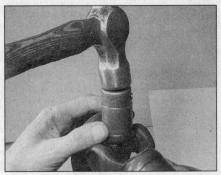

5.10 Tapping the uppermost bearing cup

4 Rear propeller shaft - removal and refitting

Note: *New bolts will be required to secure the propeller shaft coupling flange(s) when refitting.*

Removal

Note: *New bolts will be required to secure the propeller shaft coupling flange when refitting.*

Single-piece propeller shaft

1 Chock the front wheels then jack up the rear of the vehicle and support it on axle stands (see *Jacking and Vehicle Support*).

2 If the original propeller shaft is to be refitted, make alignment marks between the rear universal joint flange and axle flange.

3 Counterhold the nuts then unscrew the bolts securing the propeller shaft to the rear axle pinion flange. Note that the flange bolts are of the micro-encapsulated type and must be renewed when the propeller shaft is refitted.

4 Lower the rear of the propeller shaft and pull it rearwards to disengage it from the transmission output shaft. To prevent any loss of oil from the transmission, a plastic bag can be positioned on the transmission and retained with an elastic band.

Two-piece propeller shaft

5 Chock the front wheels then jack up the rear of the vehicle and support it on axle stands (see *Jacking and Vehicle Support*).

6 If the original propeller shaft is to be refitted, make alignment marks between the rear universal joint flange and axle flange.

7 Counterhold the nuts then unscrew the bolts securing the rear propeller shaft to the rear axle pinion flange. Note that the flange bolts are of the micro-encapsulated type and must be renewed when the propeller shaft is refitted. Support the rear shaft on an axle stand after disconnecting the flanges.

8 Undo the two bolts securing the centre bearing to the chassis crossmember **(see illustration)**.

9 Lower the rear of the propeller shaft and pull it rearwards to disengage it from the transmission output shaft. Withdraw the shaft over the centre support bearing crossmember

and remove it from under the vehicle. To prevent any loss of oil from the transmission, a plastic bag can be positioned on the transmission and retained with an elastic band.

Refitting

10 Refitting is a reversal of removal bearing in mind the following points:

a) If the original propeller shaft is being refitted, align the marks made on the flanges prior to removal, before inserting the flange bolts.

b) Use new encapsulated flange bolts and tighten them to the specified torque.

c) On completion, check, and if necessary top up the transmission oil as described in Chapter 1.

5 Propeller shaft universal joints - renewal

1 If the inspection procedures described in Chapter 1 indicate wear in the universal joint(s), the joint spider and bearings can be renewed as follows.

2 Remove the relevant propeller shaft from the vehicle as described in Section 3 or 4, as applicable.

3 If working on the front propeller shaft, release the clips securing the rubber gaiter over the sliding joint, and slide the gaiter towards the rear of the shaft.

4 Check that alignment marks are visible on the two halves of the shaft (normally two stamped arrows). If no marks can be found, scribe a line along the two halves of the shaft, to ensure that the two halves are reassembled in exactly the same position. This is vital, to ensure that the correct universal joint alignment and shaft balance is maintained.

5 Unscrew the dust cap, and withdraw the front section of the shaft from the splined end of the rear section.

6 Working on one of the universal joints, note the position of the grease nipple on the spider, in relation to the adjacent shaft yoke and coupling flange yoke (make alignment marks on the yokes). This is vital to ensure correct reassembly, and to ensure that the shaft balance is maintained.

7 Clean away all traces of dirt and grease from the circlips located on the ends of the joint spiders, and from the grease nipple.

8 Unscrew the grease nipple.

9 Using a suitable pair of circlip pliers, remove the four joint circlips. If a circlip proves difficult to remove, as a last resort, place a drift on the bearing cup, in the centre of the circlip, and tap the top of the bearing cup to ease the pressure on the circlip.

10 Support the end of the shaft in a vice, with the yoke in a vertical plane. Using a hammer and a suitable drift (a socket of appropriate size, for example), tap the uppermost bearing cup until the bottom bearing cup protrudes from the yoke **(see illustration)**.

11 Remove the shaft from the vice, then securely grip the protruding bearing cup in the vice jaws. Turn the shaft from side-to-side, at the same time lifting the shaft until the bearing cup comes free.

12 Refit the shaft to the vice, with the exposed spider uppermost. Tap the spider with the hammer and drift until the lower bearing cup protrudes, then remove the cup as described previously.

13 The coupling flange and the spider can now be removed from the shaft, and the remaining two bearing cups can be removed as described previously.

14 Where applicable, repeat the previous operations to remove the remaining joint from the shaft.

15 With the universal joint dismantled, carefully examine the needle rollers, bearing cups and spider for wear, scoring and pitting of the surface finish. If any wear is detected, the joint must be renewed **(see illustration)**.

5.15 Universal joint bearing components

8

5.25 Press the bearing cups into place using a vice and socket

5.26 Fit new circlips to retain the bearing cups

16 Where applicable, unscrew the sliding joint grease nipple, and thoroughly clean the nipple and its hole.

17 If working on the front propeller shaft, examine the condition of the sliding joint rubber gaiter, and renew if necessary.

18 Temporarily fit the front section of the shaft to the rear section, ensuring that the alignment marks are correctly positioned. Grip the front section of the shaft in a vice, and check for wear in the sliding joint splines.

19 If a new joint is being fitted, remove the bearing cups from the new spider. Check that all the needle rollers are present, and correctly positioned in the bearing cups.

20 Ensure that the bearing cups are one-third full of fresh grease (multi-purpose lithium based grease).

21 Fit the new spider, complete with seals, into the coupling flange yoke. Make sure that the grease nipple hole is aligned with the mark on the yoke made during dismantling, and note that the grease nipple hole must face away from the coupling flange.

22 Partially insert one of the bearing cups into the yoke, and enter the spider trunnion into the bearing cup, taking care not to dislodge the needle rollers.

23 Similarly, insert a bearing cup into the opposite yoke.

24 Using the vice, carefully press both bearing cups into place, ensuring that the spider trunnions do not dislodge any of the needle rollers.

25 Using a suitable tube or socket of a slightly smaller diameter than the bearing cups, press each cup into its respective yoke, until the top of the cup just reaches the lower land of the circlip groove (see illustration). Do not press the cups below this point, as damage may be caused to the cups and seals.

26 Fit the new circlips to retain the bearing cups (see illustration).

27 Engage the spider with the yokes on the relevant propeller shaft section, then partially fit both bearing cups to the yokes, taking care not to dislodge any of the needle rollers.

28 Press the bearing cups into position, and fit the new circlips, as described in paragraphs 24 to 26.

29 Screw the grease nipple into position in the joint spider.

30 Where applicable, repeat the operations described in paragraphs 19 to 29 to fit the remaining joint to the shaft.

31 Where applicable, screw the sliding joint grease nipple into position.

32 Smear the sliding joint splines on the end of the rear section of the shaft with grease, then slide the rear section of the shaft into the front section, ensuring that the marks made during dismantling are aligned. **Note:** *Do not pack grease into the open end of the shaft front section, as this may prevent the shaft from being pushed fully home.*

33 Where applicable, screw the sliding joint dust cap into position, followed by the rubber gaiter.

34 Refit the propeller shaft as described in Sections 3 or 4, then lubricate the joints using a grease gun applied to the grease nipples (see Chapter 1).

6 Rear propeller shaft flexible coupling - removal and refitting

Removal

1 Remove the propeller shaft as described in Section 4.

2 Before removal of the coupling, mark the relative fitted positions of the propeller shaft to the splined yoke.

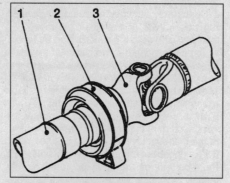

7.2 Rear propeller shaft support bearing removal

1 Propeller shaft   3 Universal
2 Support bearing   joint yoke

3 Fit a clamp, comprising of two worm-drive hose clips joined together, around the circumference of the flexible coupling and tighten it until it just begins to compress the rubber.

4 Undo the six nuts, remove the bolts and separate the coupling from the propeller shaft and splined yoke.

5 Carefully inspect the coupling for signs of deterioration and renew if necessary.

Refitting

6 Align the previously made marks on the propeller shaft and splined yoke, fit the joint and insert the bolts. Secure the assembly with the retaining nuts securely tightened.

7 If the original joint has been refitted, remove the clamp. If a new joint has been fitted, cut off and discard the metal retaining band.

8 Refit the propeller shaft as described in Section 4.

7 Rear propeller shaft support bearing - removal and refitting

Removal

1 Remove the propeller shaft as described in Section 4.

2 Undo the retaining bolt located in the centre of the universal joint, and separate the universal joint yoke from the front propeller shaft section (see illustration).

3 Remove the support bearing and housing assembly from the propeller shaft using a press or suitable puller.

Refitting

4 Stand the propeller shaft on end and drive the centre bearing home, using a hammer and tubular sleeve.

5 Reassemble the universal joint yoke to the shaft, aligning the master spline with the double width groove, and press them together.

6 Refit the universal joint retaining bolt and tighten securely.

7 Refit the propeller shaft as described in Section 4.

8 Driveshafts - description

1 Drive is transmitted from the front axle to the front wheels by means of two solid steel, equal length driveshafts equipped with constant velocity (CV) joints at their inner and outer ends (see illustration).

2 Ball-and-cage type CV joints are used at both the inner and outer ends of each driveshaft. Each joint has an outer member, which is externally splined to engage with the free-wheeling hub (outer joint) or differential

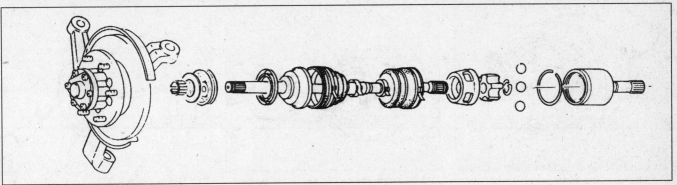

8.1 Exploded view of the driveshaft components

sun wheel (inner joint). Each joint contains six balls within a cage, which engage with joint the inner member. The complete assembly is protected by a flexible gaiter secured to the driveshaft and joint outer member.

3 The inner CV joints and the driveshaft joint gaiters are available as separate items, but the outer CV joints are only available as part of a complete driveshaft assembly (but without inner CV joint). Removal and refitting of the driveshafts and CV joints is a complicated procedure entailing removal of the complete front axle assembly. The driveshaft joint gaiters however, can be renewed with the front axle *in situ*.

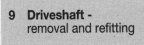

9 Driveshaft -
removal and refitting

Removal

Note: *New driveshaft retaining circlips and a new inner oil seal will be required for refitting.*
1 Remove the front axle assembly from the vehicle as described in Chapter 9.
2 If not already done as part of the front axle removal procedure, unscrew the axle oil drain plug and allow the oil to drain into a suitable container (refer to Chapter 1 if necessary). Refit the drain plug on completion.

3 Undo the four bolts and remove the relevant axle mounting bracket, together with the driveshaft, from the front axle **(see illustration)**. Be prepared for oil spillage as the driveshaft is withdrawn.
4 Using circlip pliers, extract the outer circlip from the driveshaft inner CV joint shaft, then remove the support bearing from the shaft **(see illustration)**.
5 Extract the inner circlip, withdraw the oil seal then remove the driveshaft from the axle mounting bracket **(see illustration)**.
6 Prior to refitting, obtain new inner and outer circlips and a new oil seal. Check the condition of the driveshaft support bearing and all disturbed components and renew as necessary.

Refitting

7 Slide the axle mounting bracket over the driveshaft inner CV joint shaft then place the new oil seal in position.
8 Fit the new inner circlip, the support bearing and the new outer circlip. Ensure that the circlips locate fully in their grooves.
9 Refit the driveshaft and mounting bracket assembly to the front axle and secure with the four bolts tightened to the specified torque.
10 Refit the front axle assembly to the vehicle as described in Chapter 9. On completion of the installation, refill the axle with oil as described in Chapter 1.

10 Driveshaft CV joint -
checking and renewal

Checking

1 Road test the vehicle and listen for a metallic clicking noise from the front as the vehicle is driven slowly in a circle on full lock. If evident, this indicates wear in the outer constant velocity joint which must be renewed.
2 To check for wear in the inner joint, chock the rear wheels then jack up the front of the vehicle and support it on axle stands (see *Jacking and Vehicle Support*). Attempt to move the inner end of the driveshaft up and down, then hold the joint with one hand and attempt to rotate the driveshaft with the other. If excessive wear is evident, the joint must be renewed.

Renewal

3 Depending on the extent of the wear detected, the following options are available when obtaining new components from Vauxhall parts stockists:
a) *Obtain a complete new driveshaft assembly complete with inner and outer CV joints.*
b) *Obtain a new outer CV joint which is*

8

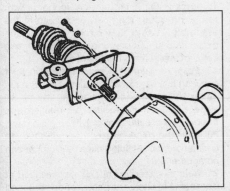

9.3 Remove the axle mounting bracket and driveshaft from the front axle

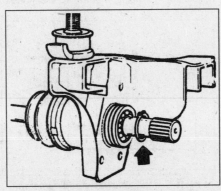

9.4 Extract the outer circlip (arrowed) from the driveshaft inner CV joint shaft

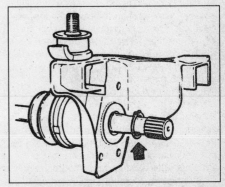

9.5 Extract the inner circlip (arrowed), withdraw the oil seal, then remove the driveshaft

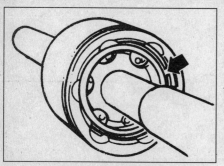

11.4 Extract the circlip (arrowed) securing the ball cage and inner member to the joint outer member

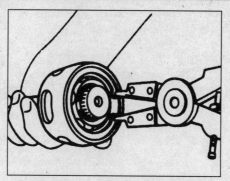

11.6 Extract the circlip securing the ball cage to the joint inner member

11.7 Using a screwdriver, carefully release the six balls from the ball cage

supplied complete with driveshaft but without the inner CV joint.

c) *Obtain a new inner CV joint and fit it to the existing driveshaft.*

4 If a new driveshaft is to be obtained, the removal and refitting procedures are contained in Section 9.

5 The procedures for fitting a new outer CV joint and driveshaft, or a new individual inner CV joint are the same and are part of the driveshaft CV joint gaiter renewal procedure given in Section 11.

11 Driveshaft CV joint gaiters - renewal

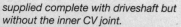

1 Chock the rear wheels then jack up the front of the vehicle and support it on axle stands (see *Jacking and Vehicle Support*). Remove the relevant roadwheel, then remove the undershield beneath the engine.

2 Remove the steering knuckle on the side being worked on as described in Chapter 11.

3 Cut off the inner CV joint gaiter retaining clips, then slide the gaiter down the shaft to expose the inner constant velocity joint components.

4 Extract the circlip securing the ball cage and inner member to the joint outer member **(see illustration)**. Withdraw the driveshaft,

ball cage and inner member assembly from the outer member.

5 Clean off as much old grease as possible from the inner CV joint components.

6 Extract the circlip securing the ball cage to the joint inner member **(see illustration)**.

7 Using a screwdriver, carefully release each of the six balls from the ball cage **(see illustration)**. Turn the ball cage so that the ball openings are positioned halfway between two ball tracks in the inner member, then slide the ball cage off the inner member toward the gaiter.

8 Extract the remaining circlip securing the inner member to the driveshaft and withdraw the inner member, ball cage and gaiter off the driveshaft **(see illustration)**.

9 If the outer CV joint gaiter is to be renewed also, cut off the gaiter retaining clips, then slide the gaiter off the inner end of the driveshaft.

10 Clean all the old grease off the dismantled inner joint components and carefully inspect the balls, ball cage, inner member and outer member for wear. If any wear ridges, scoring of the ball tracks or pitting of the balls are evident, the joint should be renewed. If the joint components are in a satisfactory condition, obtain new joint gaiters, retaining clips and a tube of the special grease as required. Note that all the circlips disturbed during dismantling must also be renewed.

11 If the outer joint gaiter is being renewed, half fill the new gaiter with the special grease,

and smear some of the grease on the exposed components of the joint itself.

12 Slide the new gaiter onto the shaft, ease it over the joint ensuring it is not twisted or distorted, then fit the new retaining clips. To fit a loop-type clip, locate it over the gaiter then squeeze the raised loop using pincers. To fit a lug and slot type clip, wrap it around the gaiter and while pulling the clip as tight as possible, engage the lug on the end of the clip with one of the slots. Use a screwdriver if necessary to push the clip as tight as possible before engaging the lug and slot. Finally tighten the clip by compressing the raised square portion of the clip with pliers, taking care not to cut the gaiter.

13 Fit the new inner joint gaiter to the driveshaft and slide it up the shaft as far as possible.

14 Locate the ball cage on the driveshaft with its smaller diameter towards the outer CV joint. Fit the inner member and secure with a new circlip.

15 Turn the ball cage so that the ball openings are positioned halfway between two ball tracks in the inner member, then slide the ball cage back into position on the inner member. Realign the ball cage openings with the tracks in the inner member.

16 Using finger pressure, carefully push the six balls into the ball cage.

17 Half fill the new gaiter with the special grease, and smear some of the grease on the exposed components of the joint itself.

18 Engage the inner joint components with the joint outer member and secure the assembly using a new circlip. Position the circlip so that its open ends are between two ball grooves in the outer member.

19 Ease the gaiter into position over the joint ensuring it is not twisted or distorted. Set the gaiter to the dimension shown, lifting one edge slightly if necessary, to release any trapped air **(see illustration)**.

20 With the gaiter correctly positioned, fit and secure the retaining clips as described in paragraph 12.

21 Refit the steering knuckle as described in Chapter 11, then refit the roadwheel and engine undershield before lowering the vehicle to the ground.

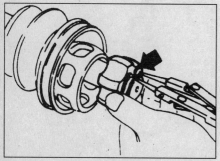

11.8 Extract the remaining circlip (arrowed) and withdraw the inner member, ball cage and gaiter off the driveshaft

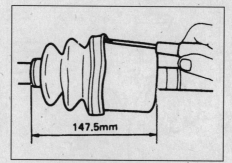

11.19 Set the gaiter to the dimension shown, lifting one edge to release any trapped air

147.5mm

Chapter 9
Front and rear axles

Contents

Front axle - removal and refitting 2
Front axle differential carrier - removal and refitting 4
Front axle drive pinion oil seal - renewal 3
Front axle oil level check ....See Chapter 1
Front axle oil renewal ....See Chapter 1
General information 1
Rear axle - removal and refitting 5
Rear axle drive pinion oil seal - renewal 6
Rear axle halfshaft - removal and refitting 7
Rear axle halfshaft bearings - renewal 8
Rear axle oil level check ....See Chapter 1
Rear axle oil renewal ....See Chapter 1

Degrees of difficulty

Easy, suitable for novice with little experience		**Fairly easy,** suitable for beginner with some experience		**Fairly difficult,** suitable for competent DIY mechanic		**Difficult,** suitable for experienced DIY mechanic		**Very difficult,** suitable for expert DIY or professional

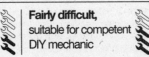

Specifications

Type

Front axle	Spiral bevel with external driveshafts and CV joints
Rear axle	Spiral bevel with semi-floating solid steel halfshafts

Torque wrench settings

	Nm	lbf ft
Front axle		
Axle mounting bolts/nuts	152	112
Centre tie-rod to steering gear drop arm	110	81
Centre tie-rod to steering idler pivot drop arm	59	44
Differential carrier to axle casing:		
3-door petrol engine models	28	21
All other models	54	40
Front suspension crossmember mounting bolts/nuts	75	55
Roadwheel nuts:		
Steel wheels	110	81
Alloy wheels	120	89
Rear axle (vehicles with leaf spring suspension)		
Axle U-bolt nuts	68	50
Differential housing cover bolts	24	18
Halfshaft bearing clamping plate/brake backplate to axle	95	70
Load sensing valve link rod nut	13	10
Shock absorber lower mounting nut	40	30
Roadwheel nuts:		
Steel wheels	110	81
Alloy wheels	120	89
Rear axle (vehicles with coil spring suspension)		
ABS wheel sensor bracket to centre link	26	19
ABS wiring connector bracket to underbody	26	19
Centre link to axle nut/bolt	165	122
Differential housing cover bolts	24	18
Halfshaft bearing holder/brake backplate to axle	74	55
Load sensing valve link rod nut	13	10
Panhard rod to axle nut	80	59
Roadwheel nuts:		
Steel wheels	110	81
Alloy wheels	120	89
Shock absorber lower mounting nut	80	59
Trailing link to axle nuts/bolts	165	122

1 General information

Front axle

1 The front axle assembly contains the final drive differential and pinion components which are housed in a detachable carrier bolted to the axle casing **(see illustration)**. The differential and pinion are supported on taper roller bearings within the casing and use selective shims to control differential bearing preload and gear backlash. Pinion bearing preload is controlled by a collapsible spacer located between the bearings.

2 The front axle is rigidly mounted to the vehicle via rubber insulation bushes. Suspension travel and steering movement is catered for by two driveshafts incorporating inner and outer constant velocity joints. The driveshaft inner constant velocity joints engage with the differential gears, thus transmitting drive to the front wheels when four-wheel-drive is selected.

3 Information and repair procedures relating to the driveshafts and front suspension and steering components are contained in Chapters 8 and 11 respectively.

Rear axle

4 The rear axle final drive and differential components are supported on taper roller bearings and are housed within the axle casing itself **(see illustration)**. Bearing preloads and gear backlash are controlled by a similar selective shim and collapsible spacer arrangement as used on the front axle.

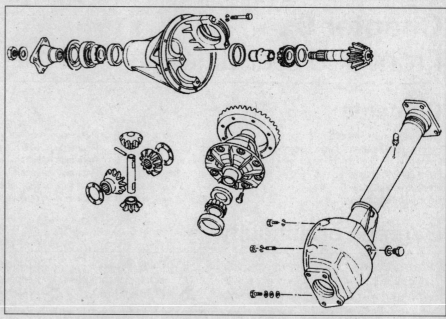

1.1 Exploded view of the front axle and differential components

5 Drive to the rear wheels is by two semi-floating solid steel halfshafts supported on ball bearings at their outer ends **(see illustration)**. Each bearing incorporates an integral oil seal and is retained on the halfshaft by an interference fit retaining ring.

6 The axle is supported on semi-elliptic, multi-leaf rear springs on all models up to mid 1995. On later vehicles, a four-link coil spring rear suspension arrangement is used.

7 Information and repair procedures relating to the rear suspension components are contained in Chapter 11.

2 Front axle - removal and refitting

Removal

1 Chock the rear wheels then jack up the front of the vehicle and support it on axle stands (see *Jacking and Vehicle Support*). Remove the undershield beneath the engine and both front roadwheels.

2 If further dismantling of the axle after removal is anticipated, refer to Chapter 1 and drain the axle oil.

3 Refer to Chapter 8 and remove the front propeller shaft.

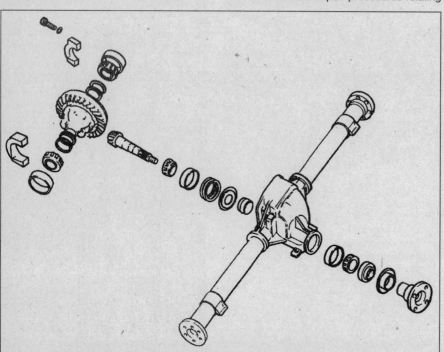

1.4 Exploded view of the rear axle and differential components

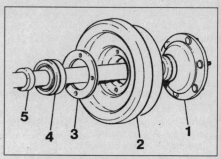

1.5 Rear axle halfshaft and bearing components (vehicles with leaf spring suspension shown, others similar)

1 Halfshaft
2 Brake backplate
3 Bearing clamping plate
4 Bearing
5 Bearing retaining ring

2.4 Front suspension crossmember left-hand side retaining bolts (arrowed)

2.6 Steering tie rod-to-idler pivot drop arm retaining nut and split pin (arrowed)

2.9a Front axle mounting bracket rear retaining bolt (arrowed) - left-hand side mounting shown

4 Undo the two nuts and bolts each side and remove the front suspension crossmember **(see illustration)**.

5 Refer to Chapter 11 and remove both front steering knuckles and both front suspension lower control arms.

6 Extract the split pin and unscrew the castellated nut securing the steering centre tie rod to the idler pivot assembly drop arm **(see illustration)**. Disconnect the balljoint from the centre tie rod using a suitable balljoint separator tool.

7 Similarly, extract the split pin and unscrew the castellated nut securing the steering centre tie rod balljoint to the steering gear drop arm. Disconnect the balljoint from the centre tie rod using a suitable balljoint separator tool. Move the centre tie rod clear of the axle front mounting bolts.

8 Position a trolley jack below and in contact with the axle differential housing. It is advisable to engage the help of an assistant at this stage to support the axle when the mounting nuts and bolts are removed.

9 Undo the rear bolt and washer, and front bolt, nut and washer each side, securing the axle mounting brackets to the chassis **(see illustrations)**. Support the axle and driveshafts, lower the unit to the ground and withdraw it from under the front of the vehicle.

10 With the axle removed, check the condition of the insulation bushes in the axle mounting brackets. If renewal is necessary, the old bushes can be removed by

driving them out using a hammer and suitable drift. Fit the new bushes by pressing them in or by using a threaded bar, nuts, washers and suitable tubing to draw them into place.

Refitting

11 Position the axle assembly on the trolley jack and guide it into position under the vehicle.

12 Raise the jack, locate the axle in position and fit the front and rear mounting bolts, washers and nuts. Fit all four mountings hand tight initially, then tighten them in a diagonal sequence to the specified torque.

13 Reconnect the steering centre tie-rod to the idler pivot drop arm and steering gear drop arm, fit the castellated nuts and tighten them to the specified torque. Align the split pin holes by tightening the nuts further slightly, if necessary, then secure the nuts using new split pins.

14 Refit the front suspension lower control arms and the steering knuckles as described in Chapter 11.

15 Refit the front suspension crossmember, tightening the nuts and bolts to the specified torque.

16 Refit the front propeller shaft as described in Chapter 8.

17 If the axle oil has been drained, fill the unit with fresh oil as described in Chapter 1.

18 Refit the engine undershield and the roadwheels, then lower the vehicle to the ground.

3 Front axle drive pinion oil seal - renewal

Note: *The axle is fitted with a collapsible spacer sleeve between the pinion shaft taper roller bearings to maintain the necessary bearing preload. A pre-load gauge will be needed to measure the pinion turning torque, and a new pinion nut must be fitted on reassembly. Do not attempt this procedure without the necessary tools as it is all too easy to overtighten the pinion nut during reassembly. If this happens it will be necessary to renew the collapsible spacer which entails complete overhaul of the differential assembly.*

1 To enable the driveshafts to turn with minimal resistance when measuring the pinion shaft turning torque, the vehicle must remain on its roadwheels and the free-wheeling hubs must be removed. If possible, raise the vehicle on a workshop hoist. Alternatively, drive it up on ramps at the front.

2 With the vehicle securely positioned as described, refer to Chapter 11 and remove the free-wheeling hubs on both sides.

3 Remove the front propeller shaft as described in Chapter 8.

4 Using a pre-load gauge, determine the torque required to turn the drive pinion and record it **(see illustration)**.

5 Using a suitable forked tool to engage in the pinion flange holes, hold the flange stationary and unscrew the locknut **(see illustration)**.

2.9b Front axle mounting bracket front retaining nut (arrowed) - right-hand side mounting shown

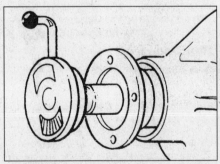

3.4 Using a pre-load gauge to determine the torque required to turn the axle drive pinion

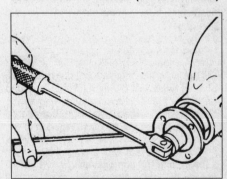

3.5 Hold the drive flange with a suitable tool and unscrew the pinion locknut

9

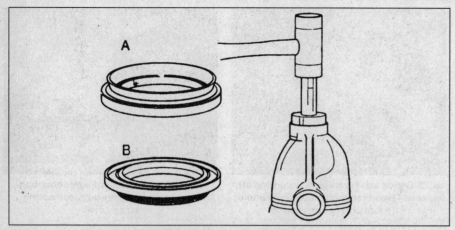

3.8 Pinion oil seal fitting details

A   *Oil seal used on vehicles manufactured up to mid 1995 (with leaf spring rear suspension)*
B   *Oil seal used on vehicles manufactured from mid 1995 onward (with coil spring rear suspension)*

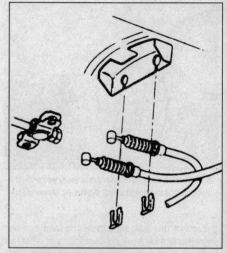

5.6 Handbrake cable to support bracket and compensator attachments

Note that a new locknut will be required when refitting.

6 Mark the position of the pinion flange in relation to the pinion shaft and remove the flange, using a puller if necessary.

7 Carefully prise free the old oil seal using a blunt screwdriver or similar implement, then clean out the oil seal location in the differential carrier.

8 Locate the new oil seal in the differential carrier having first greased the mating surfaces of the seal and the carrier. Ensure that the seal is fitted the correct way round **(see illustration)**.

9 Using a tube of suitable diameter, carefully drive the new oil seal into differential carrier recess until the face of the seal is flush with the carrier. Make sure that the end of the pinion shaft is not knocked during this operation.

10 Lubricate the oil seal lip and the running surface of the drive pinion flange then refit the flange to its original position on the pinion splines.

11 Fit a new locknut and progressively tighten it in small increments. Check the pinion turning torque, using the pre-load gauge, at regular intervals during tightening. Whilst tightening the nut, prevent the pinion flange from turning in the manner described in paragraph 5.

12 When the previously recorded pinion turning torque value is obtained, rotate the pinion to settle the bearing then further tighten the nut until the original turning torque value plus an additional 0.5 to 1.1 Nm is indicated on the gauge. This additional turning torque being the added value required to compensate for the additional friction of the new oil seal. For example, if the original value noted during removal (paragraph 4) was 2.2 Nm, and the compensating value for the new oil seal of 0.5 Nm is added to it, the total turning torque requirement in this instance will be 2.7 Nm. It is most important that the

required turning torque is not exceeded for the reasons outlined in the introductory paragraph at the start of this Section.

13 Refit the propeller shaft as described in Chapter 8, and the free-wheeling hubs as described in Chapter 11.

14 On completion, check and if necessary top up the front axle oil as described in Chapter 1.

4 Front axle differential carrier - removal and refitting

Removal

1 Remove the front axle from the vehicle as described in Section 2.

2 Remove both driveshafts from the axle as described in Chapter 8.

3 Unscrew the bolts which retain the differential carrier to the axle casing. Have a container handy to catch any remaining oil which will drip from the casing.

4 Withdraw the differential carrier and remove it from the axle casing.

5 Further dismantling of the differential unit is not recommended. If it is worn or damaged, its overhaul should be entrusted to a dealer with the necessary tools required for this task. Alternatively, obtain an exchange unit.

Refitting

6 Refitting the differential carrier is a reversal of removal, bearing in mind the following points:

a) *Thoroughly clean the mating faces of the differential carrier and axle casing and remove all traces of old sealant. Apply Vauxhall sealing compound 15 03 166 (90 094 714) to the mating faces prior to refitting.*

b) *Make sure that the differential carrier is fitted with the pinion to the bottom, and*

tighten the retaining bolts in a diagonal sequence in three or four stages.

c) *Refit the front axle to the vehicle as described in Section 2.*

d) *If a new differential unit has been installed, it should be run-in for 500 miles (800 km) to ensure that the new bearings bed in correctly.*

5 Rear axle - removal and refitting

Removal

Vehicles with leaf spring rear suspension

1 Unscrew the brake master cylinder reservoir fluid cap and place a piece of polythene over the filler neck. Secure the polythene with an elastic band ensuring that an airtight seal is obtained.

2 Chock the front wheels then jack up the rear of the vehicle and support it on axle stands (see *Jacking and Vehicle Support*). Remove the rear roadwheels.

3 If further dismantling of the axle after removal is anticipated, refer to Chapter 1 and drain the axle oil.

4 Refer to Chapter 8 and remove the rear propeller shaft.

5 Undo the two bolts each side and remove the bump stops from the chassis brackets.

6 Ensure that the handbrake is off then extract the spring clip securing each handbrake cable to the support bracket adjacent to the compensator yoke **(see illustration)**. Release the cable ends from the compensator yoke then withdraw the outer cables from the support bracket. If necessary, slacken the handbrake adjuster locknuts if it proves difficult to remove the cable ends from the compensator.

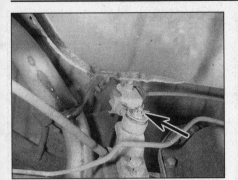

5.7 Brake load sensing valve link rod-to-axle retaining nut and split pin (arrowed)

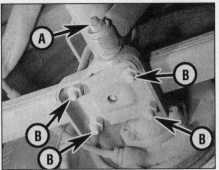

5.10 Shock absorber lower mounting (A) and axle U-bolt retaining nuts (B) - vehicles with leaf spring suspension

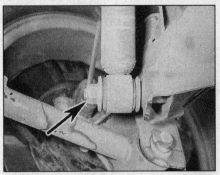

5.25 Shock absorber lower mounting (arrowed) - vehicles with coil spring suspension

7 Extract the split pin, then unscrew the nut securing the brake load sensing valve link rod to the axle bracket stud **(see illustration)**. Remove the washers and slide the link rod end fitting off the stud.

8 Thoroughly clean the area around the rear brake flexible hose-to-metal pipe union, then unscrew the pipe from the hose. Extract the clip and withdraw the hose end from the support bracket. Tape over the pipe and hose unions after disconnection to prevent dirt ingress.

9 Detach the rear axle breather hose from the axle.

10 Undo the nut, remove the washer and detach the shock absorber lower mountings from the rear spring clamp plates each side **(see illustration)**.

11 Support the weight of the rear axle with a trolley jack positioned beneath the differential housing.

12 Undo the retaining nuts and remove the spring to axle U-bolts and fittings each side. Check that the various axle fittings and attachments are disconnected and out of the way.

13 Raise the axle on the jack, move it sideways until clear of the rear springs then lower it to the ground.

Vehicles with coil spring rear suspension

14 Unscrew the brake master cylinder reservoir fluid cap and place a piece of

polythene over the filler neck. Secure the polythene with an elastic band ensuring that an airtight seal is obtained.

15 Chock the front wheels then jack up the rear of the vehicle and support it on axle stands (see *Jacking and Vehicle Support*). Remove the rear roadwheels.

16 If further dismantling of the axle after removal is anticipated, refer to Chapter 1 and drain the axle oil.

17 Refer to Chapter 8 and remove the rear propeller shaft.

18 Ensure that the handbrake is off, then extract the spring clip securing each handbrake cable to the support bracket adjacent to the compensator yoke **(see illustration 5.7)**. Release the cable ends from the compensator yoke then withdraw the outer cables from the support bracket. If necessary, slacken the handbrake adjuster locknuts if it proves difficult to remove the cable ends from the compensator.

19 Undo the clip retaining bolts, remove the clips and detach the handbrake cables from their support brackets on the underbody.

20 Extract the split pin, then unscrew the nut securing the brake load sensing valve link rod to the axle bracket stud. Remove the washers and slide the link rod end fitting off the stud.

21 Thoroughly clean the area around the rear brake flexible hose-to-metal pipe union, then unscrew the pipe from the hose. Extract the clip and withdraw the hose end from the

support bracket. Tape over the pipe and hose unions after disconnection to prevent dirt ingress.

22 Detach the rear axle breather hose from the axle.

23 Undo the nuts and disconnect the anti-roll bar lower links from the axle on each side.

24 Support the weight of the rear axle with a trolley jack positioned beneath the differential housing.

25 Undo the nut, remove the washer and detach the shock absorber lower mountings from the axle brackets each side **(see illustration)**.

26 Lower the axle on the trolley jack until all load is released from the rear coil springs. Lift away the two springs, together with their rubber insulators.

27 Undo the nut, remove the washer and slide the panhard rod off the mounting bracket stud on the axle **(see illustration)**.

28 On vehicles equipped with ABS, undo the bolt and release the bracket securing the rear wheel sensor cables to the axle centre link. Similarly, disconnect the cables at the wiring connector and release the support bracket from the underbody.

29 Undo the nut and remove the bolt securing the centre link to the axle.

30 Undo the nut and bolt each side securing the trailing links to the axle **(see illustration)**.

31 Check that the various axle fittings and attachments are disconnected and out of the way then lower the axle on the jack and remove it from under the vehicle.

Refitting

32 On all models, refitting the axle unit is basically a reversal of the removal procedure, but the following points should be noted:

a) *Tighten all nuts and bolts to the specified torque as outlined below.*

b) *On vehicles with leaf spring suspension, do not fully tighten the spring to axle U-bolt nuts until the weight of the vehicle is on the roadwheels.*

c) *On vehicles with coil spring suspension, tighten the nuts and bolts of all rubber bushings finger tight initially, then to the*

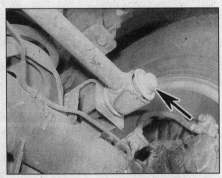

5.27 Panhard rod retaining nut and washer (arrowed) - vehicles with coil spring suspension

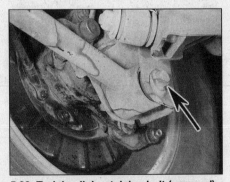

5.30 Training link retaining bolt (arrowed) - vehicles with coil spring suspension

specified torque when the weight of the vehicle is on the roadwheels.

d) *After reconnecting the cables, adjust the handbrake as described in Chapter 10.*

e) *Bleed the brake hydraulic system as described in Chapter 10.*

f) *On completion, check and if necessary top up the rear axle oil as described in Chapter 1.*

6 Rear axle drive pinion oil seal - renewal

Note: *The axle is fitted with a collapsible spacer sleeve between the pinion shaft taper roller bearings to maintain the necessary bearing preload. A pre-load gauge will be needed to measure the pinion turning torque, and a new pinion nut must be fitted on reassembly. Do not attempt this procedure without the necessary tools as it is all too easy to overtighten the pinion nut during reassembly. If this happens it will be necessary to renew the collapsible spacer which entails complete overhaul of the differential assembly.*

1 Remove the rear propeller shaft as described in Chapter 8.

2 Remove both rear axle halfshafts as described in Section 7.

3 Using a pre-load gauge, determine the torque required to turn the drive pinion and record it **(see illustration 3.4)**.

4 Using a suitable forked tool to engage in the pinion flange holes, hold the flange stationary and unscrew the locknut **(see illustration 3.5)**. Note that a new locknut will be required when refitting.

5 Mark the position of the pinion flange in relation to the pinion shaft and remove the flange, using a puller if necessary.

6 Carefully prise free the old oil seal using a blunt screwdriver or similar implement, then clean out the oil seal location in the pinion housing.

7 Locate the new oil seal in the pinion housing having first greased the mating surfaces of the seal and the housing. Ensure that the seal is fitted the correct way round **(see illustration 3.8)**.

8 Using a tube of suitable diameter, carefully drive the new oil seal into the housing recess until the face of the seal is flush with the housing. Make sure that the end of the pinion shaft is not knocked during this operation.

9 Lubricate the oil seal lip and the running surface of the drive pinion flange then refit the flange to its original position on the pinion splines.

10 Fit a new locknut and progressively tighten it in small increments. Check the pinion turning torque, using the pre-load gauge, at regular intervals during tightening. Whilst tightening the nut, prevent the pinion flange from turning in the manner described in paragraph 4.

11 When the previously recorded pinion turning torque value is obtained, rotate the pinion to settle the bearing then further tighten the nut until the original turning torque value plus an additional 0.5 to 1.1 Nm is indicated on the gauge. This additional turning torque being the added value required to compensate for the additional friction of the new oil seal. For example, if the original value noted during removal (paragraph 3) was 2.2 Nm, and the compensating value for the new oil seal of 0.5 Nm is added to it, the total turning torque requirement in this instance will be 2.7 Nm. It is most important that the required turning torque is not exceeded for the reasons outlined in the introductory paragraph at the start of this Section.

12 Refit the halfshafts as described in Section 7 and the propeller shaft as described in Chapter 8.

13 On completion, check and if necessary top up the rear axle oil as described in Chapter 1.

7 Rear axle halfshaft - removal and refitting

Removal

Vehicles with leaf spring rear suspension

1 Unscrew the brake master cylinder reservoir fluid cap and place a piece of polythene over the filler neck. Secure the polythene with an elastic band, or refit the cap, ensuring that an airtight seal is obtained.

2 Chock the front wheels then jack up the rear of the vehicle and support it on axle stands (see *Jacking and Vehicle Support*). Remove the rear roadwheels.

3 Refer to Chapter 1 and drain the axle oil.

4 Thoroughly clean the area around the brake pipe union on the rear wheel cylinder. Unscrew the union nut and carefully ease the pipe out of the cylinder. Tape over the pipe end and wheel cylinder to prevent dirt ingress.

5 Refer to Chapter 10 and remove the brake drum then disconnect the handbrake cable from the brake shoe and brake backplate.

6 Undo the bolts securing the brake backplate and halfshaft bearing clamping plate to the axle.

7 Withdraw the halfshaft, complete with the brake backplate, from the axle. If the halfshaft

bearing is tight in the axle, temporarily refit the brake drum the wrong way round and secure with the roadwheel nuts. Pull or tap on the brake drum using a soft-faced mallet, to withdraw the halfshaft. Alternatively, use a slide hammer with suitable adaptor.

Vehicles with coil spring rear suspension

8 Chock the front wheels then jack up the rear of the vehicle and support it on axle stands (see *Jacking and Vehicle Support*). Remove the rear roadwheels.

9 Refer to Chapter 1 and drain the axle oil.

10 Refer to Chapter 10 and remove the brake caliper (without disconnecting the hydraulic hose), the brake disc, the handbrake shoes and the handbrake cable from the brake backplate.

11 On vehicles equipped with ABS, undo the retaining bolt and withdraw the wheel sensor from the bearing housing.

12 Undo the four bolts/nuts securing the brake backplate and halfshaft bearing holder to the axle.

13 Withdraw the halfshaft complete with the brake backplate and bearing holder from the axle.

Refitting

14 On all models, refitting the halfshaft a reversal of the removal procedure, but the following points should be noted:

a) *On vehicles with leaf spring suspension, lubricate the bearing outer O-ring with axle oil prior to refitting the halfshaft.*

b) *On vehicles with coil spring suspension, apply a suitable sealant to the axle flange and bearing holder mating faces.*

c) *Tighten all nuts and bolts to the specified torque.*

d) *Refit all brake components with reference to Chapter 10.*

e) *Adjust the handbrake as described in Chapter 10.*

f) *On vehicles with leaf spring suspension, bleed the brake hydraulic system as described in Chapter 10.*

g) *On completion, refill the rear axle with oil as described in Chapter 1.*

8 Rear axle halfshaft bearings - renewal

On all vehicle types, the halfshaft bearing is retained on the halfshaft by an interference fit retaining ring (or by the ABS wheel sensor ring on models so equipped). Removal and refitting of the retaining ring and bearing entail the use of special pullers and press tools and should be left to a suitably-equipped dealer.

Chapter 10
Braking system

Contents

Anti-lock braking system (ABS) - general information 23
Anti-lock braking system (ABS) components - removal and refitting . . . 24
Brake pedal - removal and refitting 15
Front brake caliper - removal, overhaul and refitting 11
Front brake disc - inspection, removal and refitting 8
Front brake pad wear check . . . . See Chapter 1
Front brake pads - renewal 4
General information 1
Handbrake - adjustment 18
Handbrake cables - removal and refitting 20
Handbrake lever - removal and refitting 19
Handbrake shoes (rear disc brakes) - inspection,
    removal and refitting 7
Hydraulic fluid level check . . . . See Weekly checks
Hydraulic fluid renewal . . . . See Chapter 1
Hydraulic pipes and hoses - renewal 3
Hydraulic system - bleeding 2
Load-sensing/bypass valve - testing, removal and refitting 21
Master cylinder - removal, overhaul and refitting 14
Rear brake caliper - removal, overhaul and refitting 13
Rear brake disc - inspection, removal and refitting 10
Rear brake drum - removal, inspection and refitting 9
Rear brake pad wear check . . . . See Chapter 1
Rear brake pads - renewal 6
Rear brake shoe wear check . . . . See Chapter 1
Rear brake shoes - renewal 5
Rear wheel cylinder - removal, overhaul and refitting 12
Stop-light switch - removal and refitting 22
Vacuum hose check valve - testing and renewal 17
Vacuum pump (diesel engine models) - removal and refitting 25
Vacuum reservoir (diesel engine models) - removal and refitting . . . 26
Vacuum servo unit - testing, removal and refitting 16

Degrees of difficulty

Easy, suitable for novice with little experience 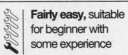	**Fairly easy,** suitable for beginner with some experience 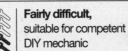	**Fairly difficult,** suitable for competent DIY mechanic 	**Difficult,** suitable for experienced DIY mechanic	**Very difficult,** suitable for expert DIY or professional 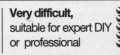

Specifications

Front brakes
Minimum disc thickness:
    Models with coil spring rear suspension . . . . 24.6 mm
    Models with leaf spring rear suspension . . . . 20.6 mm
Maximum disc run-out . . . . 0.13 mm
Brake pad lining minimum thickness . . . . 1.0 mm

Rear drum brakes
Drum internal diameter:
    New . . . . 254.0 mm
    Maximum diameter after machining . . . . 255.5 mm
Brake shoe lining minimum thickness . . . . 1.0 mm

Rear disc brakes
Minimum disc thickness . . . . 16.6 mm
Maximum disc run-out . . . . 0.13 mm
Brake pad lining minimum thickness . . . . 1.0 mm
Handbrake drum maximum diameter after machining . . . . 211.4 mm
Handbrake shoe minimum lining thickness . . . . 1.0 mm

Brake pedal
Pedal height (with carpets fitted):
    Right-hand drive models . . . . 198.0 mm
    Left-hand drive models . . . . 179.0 mm
Pedal free play . . . . 6.0 to 10.0 mm

Brake hydraulic fluid
Type/specification . . . . See Lubricants and fluids

10

Torque wrench settings

	Nm	lbf ft
ABS hydraulic modulator mounting nuts	9	7
ABS wheel sensor cable bracket bolts:		
Front:		
Lower bracket	27	20
Upper bracket	6	4
Rear	26	19
ABS wheel sensor retaining bolt:		
Front	9	7
Rear	22	16
Brake caliper guide pin bolts:		
Front:		
Vehicles with coil spring rear suspension	74	55
Vehicles with leaf spring rear suspension	32	24
Rear	44	32
Brake caliper mounting bracket to axle	104	77
Brake caliper mounting bracket to steering knuckle	212	156
Brake disk (front) to wheel hub	103	76
Brake hose banjo union bolt	35	26
Brake hose union nuts	16	12
Brake pedal pivot bolt	34	25
Handbrake lever mounting bolts	21	15
Load sensing/bypass valve connecting link to axle	13	10
Load sensing/bypass valve mounting nuts	12	9
Master cylinder mounting nuts	13	10
Master cylinder secondary piston stop bolt	8	6
Roadwheel nuts:		
Alloy wheels	120	89
Steel wheels	110	81
Vacuum servo unit to bulkhead:		
Vehicles with coil spring rear suspension	21	15
Vehicles with leaf spring rear suspension	26	19
Wheel cylinder to backplate	10	7

1 General information

The braking system is of the servo-assisted, dual-circuit hydraulic type. The arrangement of the hydraulic system is such that the primary circuit operates the front brakes and the secondary circuit operates the rear brakes from a tandem master cylinder. Under normal circumstances, both circuits operate in unison. However, in the event of hydraulic failure in one circuit, full braking force will still be available at two wheels.

A combined load-sensing/bypass valve is situated in the hydraulic circuit to the rear brakes. The valve is linked to the rear axle and regulates the hydraulic pressure applied to the rear brakes, according to the loading on the axle, and so helps prevent rear wheel lock-up during emergency braking. The valve has a second 'bypass' function whereby full hydraulic pressure is allowed to the rear brakes in the event of front brake hydraulic circuit failure.

All models are fitted with front disc brakes, with rear drum brakes on models with leaf spring rear suspension, and rear disc brakes on models with coil spring rear suspension. The front disc brakes (and rear disc brakes where applicable) are actuated by single piston sliding type calipers, which ensure that equal pressure is applied to each brake pad. The rear drum brakes incorporate leading and trailing shoes, which are actuated by twin-piston wheel cylinders. A self-adjust mechanism is incorporated, to automatically compensate for brake shoe wear.

The handbrake is cable-operated on the rear brakes by a lever mounted between the front seats. On rear disc brake models, the handbrake actuates separate handbrake shoes which act on a drum incorporated in the brake disc.

A 4-channel ABS (Anti-lock Braking System) is available as an option on models from mid-1995 onward.

On diesel engine models, since there is no throttling of the inlet manifold, the manifold is not a suitable source of vacuum to operate the vacuum servo unit. On 2.3 and 2.8 litre models the servo unit is therefore connected to a separate vacuum pump, attached to the alternator. On 2.5 litre models, the servo unit is connected to two interlinked vacuum pumps, one on the alternator and a second fitted within the engine timing cover and driven by the timing gears.

Warning: When servicing any part of the system, work carefully and methodically; also observe scrupulous cleanliness

when overhauling any part of the hydraulic system. Always renew components (in axle sets, where applicable) if in doubt about their condition, and use only genuine Vauxhall replacement parts, or at least those of known good quality. Note the warnings given in Safety first and at relevant points in this Chapter concerning the dangers of asbestos dust and hydraulic fluid.

2 Hydraulic system - bleeding

Warning: Hydraulic fluid is poisonous; wash off immediately and thoroughly in the case of skin contact, and seek immediate medical advice if any fluid is swallowed or gets into the eyes. Certain types of hydraulic fluid are inflammable, and may ignite when allowed into contact with hot components; when servicing any hydraulic system, it is safest to assume that the fluid is inflammable, and to take precautions against the risk of fire as though it is petrol that is being handled. Hydraulic fluid is also an effective paint stripper, and will attack plastics; if any is spilt, it should be washed off immediately,

using copious quantities of fresh water. Finally, it is hygroscopic (it absorbs moisture from the air) - old fluid may be contaminated and unfit for further use. When topping-up or renewing the fluid, always use the recommended type, and ensure that it comes from a freshly-opened sealed container.

General

1 The correct operation of any hydraulic system is only possible after removing all air from the components and circuit; this is achieved by bleeding the system.

2 During the bleeding procedure, add only clean, unused hydraulic fluid of the recommended type; never re-use fluid that has already been bled from the system. Ensure that sufficient fluid is available before starting work.

3 If there is any possibility of incorrect fluid being already in the system, the brake components and circuit must be flushed completely with uncontaminated, correct fluid, and new seals should be fitted to the various components.

4 If hydraulic fluid has been lost from the system, or air has entered because of a leak, ensure that the fault is cured before proceeding further.

5 Park the vehicle over an inspection pit or on car ramps. Alternatively, apply the handbrake then jack up the front and rear of the vehicle and support it on axle stands (see *Jacking and Vehicle Support*). For improved access with the vehicle jacked up, remove the roadwheels.

6 Check that all pipes and hoses are secure, unions tight and bleed screws closed. Clean any dirt from around the bleed screws.

7 Unscrew the master cylinder reservoir cap, and top the master cylinder reservoir up to the MAX level line; refit the cap loosely, and remember to maintain the fluid level at least above the MIN level line throughout the procedure, or there is a risk of further air entering the system.

8 There are a number of one-man, do-it-yourself brake bleeding kits currently available from motor accessory shops. It is recommended that one of these kits is used whenever possible, as they greatly simplify the bleeding operation, and also reduce the risk of expelled air and fluid being drawn back into the system. If such a kit is not available, the basic (two-man) method must be used, which is described in detail below.

9 If a kit is to be used, prepare the vehicle as described previously, and follow the kit manufacturer's instructions, as the procedure may vary slightly according to the type being used; generally, they are as outlined below in the relevant sub-section.

10 Whichever method is used, the same sequence must be followed (paragraph 13) to ensure the removal of all air from the system.

11 Note that with all the following methods, the engine should be running at idling speed. Depressing the brake pedal fully without the engine running can cause damage to the vacuum servo unit.

Bleeding sequence

12 If the system has been only partially disconnected, and suitable precautions were taken to minimise fluid loss, it should be necessary only to bleed that part of the system (ie the primary or secondary circuit).

13 If the complete system is to be bled, then it should be done by starting at the brake furthest from the master cylinder and finishing at the brake nearest to the master cylinder.

Bleeding - basic (two-man) method

Caution: On vehicles equipped with ABS, remove the ABS fuse from the fuse holder mounted on the battery tray to allow correct bleeding of the hydraulic modulator (see Chapter 13).

Caution: The engine should be running at idling speed. Depressing the brake pedal fully without the engine running can cause damage to the vacuum servo unit.

14 Collect a clean glass jar, a suitable length of plastic or rubber tubing which is a tight fit over the bleed screw, and a ring spanner to fit the screw. The help of an assistant will also be required.

15 Remove the dust cap from the first screw in the sequence **(see illustration)**. Fit the spanner and tube to the screw, place the other end of the tube in the jar, and pour in sufficient fluid to cover the end of the tube.

16 Ensure that the master cylinder reservoir fluid level is maintained at least above the MIN level line throughout the procedure.

17 Have the assistant fully depress the brake pedal several times to build up pressure, then maintain it on the final downstroke.

18 While pedal pressure is maintained, unscrew the bleed screw (approximately one turn) and allow the compressed fluid and air to flow into the jar. The assistant should maintain pedal pressure, following it down to the floor if necessary, and should not release it until instructed to do so. When the flow stops, tighten the bleed screw again, have the assistant release the pedal slowly, and recheck the reservoir fluid level.

19 Repeat the steps given in paragraphs 17 and 18 until the fluid emerging from the bleed

2.15 Dust cap on a bleed screw (arrowed)

screw is free from air bubbles. If the master cylinder has been drained and refilled, and air is being bled from the first screw in the sequence, allow approximately five seconds between cycles for the master cylinder passages to refill.

20 When no more air bubbles appear, tighten the bleed screw, remove the tube and spanner, and refit the dust cap. Do not overtighten the bleed screw.

21 Repeat the procedure on the remaining screws in the sequence, until all air is removed from the system and the brake pedal feels firm again.

Bleeding - using a one-way valve kit

Caution: On vehicles equipped with ABS, remove the ABS fuse from the fuse holder mounted on the battery tray to allow correct bleeding of the hydraulic modulator (see Chapter 13).

Caution: The engine should be running at idling speed. Depressing the brake pedal fully without the engine running can cause damage to the vacuum servo unit.

22 As their name implies, these kits consist of a length of tubing with a one-way valve fitted, to prevent expelled air and fluid being drawn back into the system; some kits include a translucent container, which can be positioned so that the air bubbles can be more easily seen flowing from the end of the tube.

23 The kit is connected to the bleed screw, which is then opened. The user returns to the driver's seat, depresses the brake pedal with a smooth, steady stroke, and slowly releases it; this is repeated until the expelled fluid is clear of air bubbles.

24 Note that these kits simplify work so much that it is easy to forget the master cylinder reservoir fluid level; ensure that this is maintained at least above the MIN level line at all times.

Bleeding - using a pressure-bleeding kit

Caution: On vehicles equipped with ABS, remove the ABS fuse from the fuse holder mounted on the battery tray to allow correct bleeding of the hydraulic modulator (see Chapter 13). On completion of bleeding, and with the engine switched off, refit the fuse.

25 These kits are usually operated by the reservoir of pressurised air contained in the spare tyre. However, note that it will probably be necessary to reduce the pressure to a lower level than normal; refer to the instructions supplied with the kit.

26 By connecting a pressurised, fluid-filled container to the master cylinder reservoir, bleeding can be carried out simply by opening each screw in turn (in the specified sequence - paragraph 13), and allowing the fluid to flow out until no more air bubbles can be seen in the expelled fluid.

10

27 This method has the advantage that the large reservoir of fluid provides an additional safeguard against air being drawn into the system during bleeding.

28 Pressure-bleeding is particularly effective when bleeding difficult systems, or when bleeding the complete system at the time of routine fluid renewal.

All methods

29 When bleeding is complete, and firm pedal feel is restored, wash off any spilt fluid, tighten the bleed screws and refit their dust caps.

30 Check the hydraulic fluid level in the master cylinder reservoir, and top-up if necessary (see *Weekly checks*).

31 Discard any hydraulic fluid that has been bled from the system; it will not be fit for re-use.

32 Check the feel of the brake pedal. If it feels at all spongy, air must still be present in the system, and further bleeding is required. Failure to bleed satisfactorily after a reasonable repetition of the bleeding procedure may be due to worn master cylinder seals.

3 Hydraulic pipes and hoses - renewal

Note: *Before starting work, refer to the note at the beginning of Section 2 concerning the dangers of hydraulic fluid.*

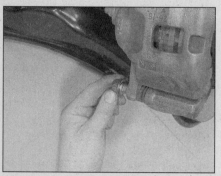

4.2a Slacken and remove the caliper lower guide pin bolt . . .

1 If any pipe or hose is to be renewed, minimise fluid loss by first removing the master cylinder reservoir cap, placing a piece of polythene over the reservoir and securing it with an elastic band to obtain an airtight seal. Alternatively, flexible hoses can be sealed, if required, using a proprietary brake hose clamp; metal brake pipe unions can be plugged (if care is taken not to allow dirt into the system) or capped immediately they are disconnected. Place a wad of rag under any union that is to be disconnected, to catch any spilt fluid.

2 If a flexible hose is to be disconnected, unscrew the brake pipe union nut before removing the spring clip which secures the hose to its mounting bracket. Where applicable, unscrew the banjo union bolt securing the hose to the caliper and recover the copper washers.

3 To unscrew the union nuts, it is preferable to obtain a brake pipe spanner of the correct size; these are available from most large motor accessory shops. Failing this, a close-fitting open-ended spanner will be required, though if the nuts are tight or corroded, their flats may be rounded-off if the spanner slips. In such a case, a self-locking wrench is often the only way to unscrew a stubborn union, but it follows that the pipe and the damaged nuts must be renewed on reassembly. Always clean a union and surrounding area before disconnecting it. If disconnecting a component with more than one union, make a careful note of the connections before disturbing any of them.

4 If a brake pipe is to be renewed, it can be obtained, cut to length and with the union nuts and end flares in place, from Vauxhall dealers. All that is then necessary is to bend it to shape, following the line of the original, before fitting it to the car. Alternatively, most motor accessory shops can make up brake pipes from kits, but this requires very careful measurement of the original, to ensure that the replacement is of the correct length. The safest answer is usually to take the original to the shop as a pattern.

5 On refitting, do not overtighten the union nuts. It is not necessary to exercise brute force to obtain a sound joint.

6 When refitting the hoses to the calipers, always use new copper washers and tighten the banjo union bolts to the specified torque. Make sure that the hoses are positioned so that they will not chafe on surrounding bodywork, suspension components or the roadwheels.

7 Ensure that the pipes and hoses are correctly routed, with no kinks, and that they are secured in the clips or brackets provided. After fitting, remove the polythene from the reservoir, and bleed the hydraulic system as described in Section 2. Wash off any spilt fluid, and check carefully for fluid leaks.

4 Front brake pads - renewal

⚠ Warning: Renew both sets of front brake pads at the same time - never renew the pads on only one wheel, as uneven braking may result. Note that the dust created by wear of the pads may contain asbestos, which is a health hazard. Never blow it out with compressed air, and don't inhale any of it. An approved filtering mask should be worn when working on the brakes. DO NOT use petrol or petroleum-based solvents to clean brake parts; use brake cleaner or methylated spirit only.

1 Chock the rear wheels then jack up the front of the vehicle and support it on axle stands (see *Jacking and Vehicle Support*). Remove the front roadwheels.

2 Slacken and remove the caliper lower guide pin bolt, then pivot the caliper upwards to allow access to the brake pads (see illustrations). Tie the caliper in the raised position from a suitable place under the wheel arch. Take care to avoid straining the flexible brake hose.

3 Remove the inner anti-rattle shim and shim retainer plate from the mounting bracket, followed by the inner brake pad (see illustrations).

4 Similarly remove the outer anti-rattle shim,

4.2b . . . then pivot the caliper upwards

4.3a Remove the inner anti-rattle shim and shim retainer plate . . .

4.3b . . . followed by the inner brake pad

4.4a Remove the outer anti-rattle shim and retainer plate . . .   **4.4b . . . followed by the outer brake pad**

retainer plate and brake pad **(see illustrations)**.

5 Remove the upper and lower spring clips from the mounting bracket **(see illustration)**.

6 Measure the thickness of the friction material on each brake pad. If either pad is worn at any point to the specified minimum thickness or less, all four pads must be renewed. The pads should also be renewed if any are fouled with oil or grease; note that there is no satisfactory way of degreasing friction material, once contaminated. If any of the brake pads are worn unevenly, or are fouled with oil or grease, trace and rectify the cause before reassembly.

7 If the brake pads are still serviceable, carefully clean them using a clean, fine wire brush or similar, paying particular attention to the sides and back of the metal backing. Clean out the grooves in the friction material, and pick out any large embedded particles of dirt or debris. Carefully clean the pad locations in the caliper mounting bracket.

8 Prior to fitting the pads, check that the lower guide pin bolt is free to slide easily in the caliper mounting bracket, and check that the rubber guide pin gaiters are undamaged. Brush the dust and dirt from the caliper and piston, but **do not** inhale it, as it is a health hazard. Inspect the dust seal around the

piston for damage, and the piston for evidence of fluid leaks, corrosion or damage. If attention to any of these components is necessary, refer to Section 11.

9 If new brake pads are to be fitted, the caliper piston must be pushed back into the cylinder to make room for them. Either use a proprietary piston retracting tool, a G-clamp or use suitable pieces of wood as levers; take care not to damage the piston seals **(see illustration)**. Provided that the master cylinder reservoir has not been overfilled with hydraulic fluid, there should be no spillage, but keep a careful watch on the fluid level while retracting the piston. If the fluid level rises above the MAX level line at any time, the surplus should be syphoned off.

> ⚠️ **Warning: Do not syphon the fluid by mouth, as it is poisonous; use a syringe or an old poultry baster.**

10 Locate the upper and lower spring clips in the mounting bracket, ensuring that they are properly seated.

11 Ensuring that the friction material of each pad is against the brake disc, fit the pads to the caliper mounting bracket noting that the pad with the wear indicator should be fitted as the inner pad.

12 Apply a little high-melting point copper

brake grease to the anti-rattle shims and shim retainer plates, then locate these components over the brake pad backing plates.

13 Pivot the caliper down into position over the pads and refit the guide pin bolt. Tighten the guide pin bolt to the specified torque.

14 Depress the brake pedal repeatedly, until the pads are pressed into firm contact with the brake disc, and normal (non-assisted) pedal pressure is restored.

15 Repeat the above procedure on the remaining front brake caliper.

16 Refit the roadwheels, then lower the vehicle to the ground.

17 Check the hydraulic fluid level in the master cylinder reservoir as described in *Weekly checks*.

> **HAYNES HiNT** *New pads will not give full braking efficiency until they have bedded in. Be prepared for this, and avoid hard braking as far as possible for the first hundred miles or so after pad renewal.*

5 Rear brake shoes - renewal

> ⚠️ *Warning: Brake shoes must be renewed on both rear wheels at the same time - never renew the shoes on only one wheel, as uneven braking may result. Also, the dust created by wear of the shoes may contain asbestos, which is a health hazard. Never blow it out with compressed air, and don't inhale any of it. An approved filtering mask should be worn when working on the brakes. DO NOT use petrol or petroleum-based solvents to clean brake parts; use brake cleaner or methylated spirit only.*

10

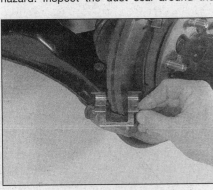

4.5 Remove the spring clips from the caliper mounting bracket

4.9 Using a piston retracting tool to push the piston back into the caliper

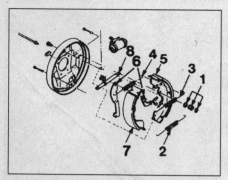

5.6 Exploded view of the rear brake shoe components

1 Retainer cups and spring
2 Lower brake shoe return spring
3 Adjuster lever tension spring
4 Upper brake shoe return spring
5 Leading brake shoe
6 Adjuster lever
7 Trailing brake shoe
8 Adjuster strut

1 Remove the brake drum as described in Section 9.

2 Working carefully, and taking the necessary precautions, remove all traces of brake dust from the brake drum, backplate and shoes.

3 Measure the thickness of the friction material on each brake shoe at several points; if either shoe is worn at any point to the specified minimum thickness or less, all four shoes must be renewed as a set. The shoes should also be renewed if any are fouled with oil or grease; there is no satisfactory way of degreasing friction material, once contaminated.

4 If any of the brake shoes are worn unevenly, or fouled with oil or grease, trace and rectify the cause before reassembly.

5 If all the components are in good condition, refit the brake drum as described in Section 9. To renew the brake shoes, proceed as follows.

6 Note the position of each shoe, and the location of each of the springs **(see illustration)**. Also make a note of the self-adjuster component locations, to aid refitting later.

7 Using a pair of pliers, remove the shoe retainer spring outer cups by depressing and turning them through 90° while holding the

retainer pins from the rear of the backplate. With the outer cups removed, lift off the springs and withdraw the inner cups and retainer pins.

8 Using suitable pliers, disconnect the tension spring from the adjuster lever.

9 Disconnect the lower brake shoe return spring and ease the shoes out one at a time from the lower pivot point.

10 Disconnect the upper return spring, lift off the leading shoe and collect the adjuster strut.

11 Lift off the trailing shoe and disconnect the handbrake cable end from the lever on the shoe. Do not depress the brake pedal until the brakes are reassembled; wrap a strong elastic band around the wheel cylinder pistons to retain them.

12 Clean the backplate and inspect the brake assembly components. Keep the sub-assemblies separate, as the right and left-hand assemblies are different and must not be interchanged.

13 Depending on the type of brake shoes being installed, it may be necessary to remove the handbrake lever from the original trailing shoe, and install it on the new shoe. Secure the lever in position with a new retaining clip. All return springs should be renewed, regardless of their apparent condition; spring kits are available from Vauxhall dealers.

14 Apply a smear of high melting-point copper grease to the shoe contact areas on the brake backplate, to the lower pivot and wheel cylinder pistons, and to the adjuster strut.

15 Refitting is a reversal of removal. Take care not to get grease or oil onto the brake friction linings or the drum friction surface. Ensure that all springs are correctly located and properly seated.

16 With the brake shoes correctly assembled, refit the brake drum as described in Section 9.

17 Repeat the operations on the remaining brake.

18 Once both sets of brake shoes have been renewed, with the handbrake fully released, operate the self-adjust mechanism by repeatedly depressing and releasing the brake pedal. Whilst depressing the pedal, have an assistant listen to the rear drums, to check the adjuster strut is functioning correctly; if so, a clicking sound will be heard as the pedal is

depressed. Continue depressing and releasing the brake pedal until the clicking stops, indicating that the shoe-to-drum clearance has been fully taken up by the self-adjust mechanism.

19 Check and if necessary, adjust the handbrake as described in Section 18.

20 On completion, check the hydraulic fluid level as described in *Weekly checks*.

 HAYNES HiNT *New shoes will not give full braking efficiency until they have bedded in. Be prepared for this, and avoid hard braking as far as possible for the first hundred miles or so after shoe renewal.*

6 Rear brake pads - renewal

 Warning: Renew both sets of rear brake pads at the same time - never renew the pads on only one wheel, as uneven braking may result. Note that the dust created by wear of the pads may contain asbestos, which is a health hazard. Never blow it out with compressed air, and don't inhale any of it. An approved filtering mask should be worn when working on the brakes. DO NOT use petrol or petroleum-based solvents to clean brake parts; use brake cleaner or methylated spirit only.

1 Chock the front wheels then jack up the rear of the vehicle and support it on axle stands (see *Jacking and Vehicle Support*). Remove the rear roadwheels.

2 Slacken and remove the caliper lower guide pin bolt, then pivot the caliper upwards to allow access to the brake pads **(see illustration)**. Tie the caliper in the raised position from a suitable place under the wheel arch. Take care to avoid straining the flexible brake hose.

3 Remove the inner anti-rattle shim and shim retainer plate from the mounting bracket, followed by the inner brake pad **(see illustrations)**.

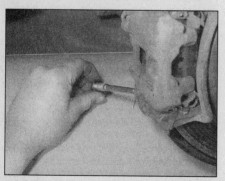

6.2 Remove the caliper lower guide pin bolt then pivot the caliper upwards

6.3a Remove the inner anti-rattle shim and shim retainer plate . . .

6.3b . . . followed by the inner brake pad

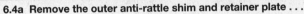
6.4a Remove the outer anti-rattle shim and retainer plate . . .

6.4b . . . followed by the outer brake pad

4 Similarly remove the outer anti-rattle shim, retainer plate and brake pad (see illustrations).
5 Remove the upper and lower spring clips from the mounting bracket.
6 Measure the thickness of the friction material on each brake pad. If either pad is worn at any point to the specified minimum thickness or less, all four pads must be renewed. The pads should also be renewed if any are fouled with oil or grease; note that there is no satisfactory way of degreasing friction material, once contaminated. If any of the brake pads are worn unevenly, or are fouled with oil or grease, trace and rectify the cause before reassembly.
7 If the brake pads are still serviceable, carefully clean them using a clean, fine wire brush or similar, paying particular attention to the sides and back of the metal backing. Clean out the grooves in the friction material, and pick out any large embedded particles of dirt or debris. Carefully clean the pad locations in the caliper mounting bracket.
8 Prior to fitting the pads, check that the lower guide pin bolt is free to slide easily in the caliper mounting bracket, and check that the rubber guide pin gaiters are undamaged. Brush the dust and dirt from the caliper and piston, but **do not** inhale it, as it is a health

hazard. Inspect the dust seal around the piston for damage, and the piston for evidence of fluid leaks, corrosion or damage. If attention to any of these components is necessary, refer to Section 13.
9 If new brake pads are to be fitted, the caliper piston must be pushed back into the cylinder to make room for them. Either use a proprietary piston retracting tool, a G-clamp or use suitable pieces of wood as levers; take care not to damage the piston seals (see illustration). Provided that the master cylinder reservoir has not been overfilled with hydraulic fluid, there should be no spillage, but keep a careful watch on the fluid level while retracting the piston. If the fluid level rises above the MAX level line at any time, the surplus should be syphoned off.

 Warning: Do not syphon the fluid by mouth, as it is poisonous; use a syringe or an old poultry baster.

10 Locate the upper and lower spring clips in the mounting bracket, ensuring that they are properly seated.
11 Ensuring that the friction material of each pad is against the brake disc, fit the pads to the caliper mounting bracket.
12 Apply a little high-melting point copper brake grease to the anti-rattle shims and shim retainer plates, then locate these components over the brake pad backing plates.
13 Pivot the caliper down into position over the pads and refit the guide pin bolt. Tighten the guide pin bolt to the specified torque.
14 Depress the brake pedal repeatedly, until the pads are pressed into firm contact with the brake disc, and normal (non-assisted) pedal pressure is restored.
15 Repeat the above procedure on the remaining rear brake caliper.
16 Refit the roadwheels, then lower the vehicle to the ground.
17 Check the hydraulic fluid level in the master cylinder reservoir as described in Weekly checks.

HAYNES HINT *New pads will not give full braking efficiency until they have bedded in. Be prepared for this, and avoid hard braking as far as possible for the first hundred miles or so after pad renewal.*

7 Handbrake shoes (rear disc brakes) - inspection, removal and refitting

6.9 Using a piston retracting tool to push the piston back into the caliper

⚠ *Warning: Handbrake shoes must be renewed on both rear wheels at the same time - never renew the shoes on only one wheel, as uneven braking may result. Also, the dust created by wear of the shoes may contain asbestos, which is a health hazard. Never blow it out with compressed air, and don't inhale any of it. An approved filtering mask should be worn when working on the brakes. DO NOT use petrol or petroleum-based solvents to clean brake parts; use brake cleaner or methylated spirit only.*

Inspection

1 On models fitted with rear disc brakes, the handbrake operates independently of the footbrake, using brake shoes on the inside of the disc, in a similar way to rear drum brake models.
2 Remove the rear brake disc as described in Section 10.
3 Working carefully, and taking the necessary precautions, remove all traces of brake dust from the brake disc, backplate and shoes.
4 Check that the friction material has not worn down to less than the specified minimum.
5 If any one of the shoes has worn below the specified limit, all four handbrake shoes must be renewed as a set. The shoes should also be renewed if any are fouled with oil or grease; there is no satisfactory way of

10

7.7a Remove the handbrake shoe retainer spring cups and springs . . .

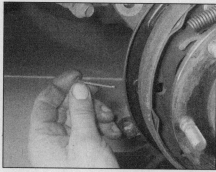

7.7b . . . followed by the retainer pins

7.8a Disconnect the upper return springs . . .

7.8b . . . then remove the retaining plate

7.9a Remove the adjuster . . .

7.9b . . . followed by the lower return spring

degreasing friction material, once contaminated.

6 If any of the brake shoes are worn unevenly, or fouled with oil or grease, trace and rectify the cause before reassembly.

Removal

7 Using a pair of pliers, remove the shoe retainer spring cups by depressing and turning them through 90° while holding the retainer pins from the rear of the backplate. With the cups removed, lift off the springs and withdraw the retainer pins **(see illustrations)**.

8 Disconnect the leading and trailing shoe upper return springs from the upper pivot point and shoes, then remove the retaining plate **(see illustrations)**.

9 Using a large screwdriver or similar tool, spread the shoes apart at their lower ends and remove the adjuster assembly, followed by the lower return spring **(see illustrations)**.

10 Lift off the leading brake shoe and collect the operating strut and spring.

11 Using pointed-nose pliers, disconnect the handbrake cable from the handbrake lever on the trailing shoe and remove the trailing shoe **(see illustration)**.

12 Clean the backplate and inspect the brake assembly components. If both brake assemblies are dismantled at the same time, take care not to mix them up

13 Before refitting, it will be necessary to remove the handbrake lever from the original

trailing shoe, and install it on the new shoe. Secure the lever in position with a new retaining clip **(see illustration)**. All return springs should be renewed, regardless of their apparent condition; spring kits are available from Vauxhall dealers.

Refitting

14 Apply a smear of high melting-point copper grease to the shoe contact areas on the brake backplate and to the threads of the adjuster wheel.

15 Reconnect the handbrake cable to the trailing shoe lever, ensuring that it seats fully in the slot in the lever **(see illustration)**.

16 Connect the lower return spring to both handbrake shoes with the spring ends located

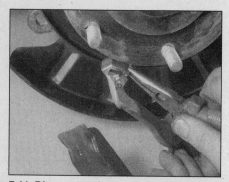

7.11 Disconnect the handbrake cable from the handbrake lever

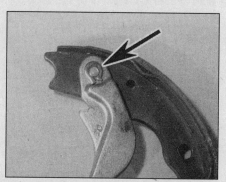

7.13 Handbrake lever pivot retaining clip (arrowed)

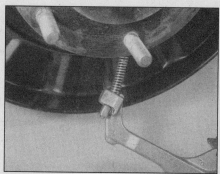

7.15 Ensure the handbrake cable is correctly located in the lever

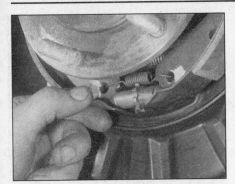

7.17 With the adjuster and spring in place, locate the handbrake shoes on the backplate

7.18 Fit the retaining plate and trailing shoe upper return spring

7.19 Locate the larger forked end of the strut (arrowed) over the trailing shoe and handbrake lever

behind the leading shoe and in front of the trailing shoe.

17 Fit the adjuster assembly between the lower ends of both brake shoes, then locate the shoes on the backplate **(see illustration)**.

18 With the trailing shoe in contact with the upper pivot on the backplate, fit the retaining plate, then engage the trailing shoe upper return spring with the shoe and upper pivot **(see illustration)**.

19 Fit the spring to the operating strut then locate the larger forked end of the strut over the trailing shoe and the handbrake lever **(see illustration)**.

20 Attach the leading shoe upper return spring to the shoe, guide the shoe onto the other end of the operating strut and connect the spring to the upper pivot **(see illustration)**. Ensure that the leading shoe upper return spring fits on top of the trailing shoe return spring on the upper pivot.

21 Refit the shoe retainer pins, springs and cups and secure the cups by turning them through 90°.

22 Temporarily refit the brake disc over the shoes to determine the adjustment, then if necessary use a screwdriver to turn the notched adjuster wheel until it is just possible to fit the disc over the shoes without them binding.

23 Refit the brake disc as described in Section 10.

24 Adjust the handbrake as described in Section 18.

25 Refit the roadwheels and lower the vehicle to the ground.

8 Front brake disc - inspection, removal and refitting

Note: *Before starting work, refer to the note at the beginning of Section 4 concerning the dangers of asbestos dust.*

Inspection

Note: *If either disc requires renewal, BOTH should be renewed at the same time, to ensure even and consistent braking. New brake pads should also be fitted.*

1 Chock the rear wheels then jack up the front of the vehicle and support it on axle stands (see *Jacking and Vehicle Support*). Remove the front roadwheels.

2 Slowly rotate the brake disc so that the full area of both sides can be checked; remove the brake pads if better access is required to the inboard surface. Light scoring is normal in the area swept by the brake pads, but if heavy scoring or cracks are found, the disc must be renewed.

3 It is normal to find a lip of rust and brake dust around the disc's perimeter; this can be scraped off if required. If, however, a lip has formed due to excessive wear of the brake

pad swept area, then the disc's thickness must be measured using a micrometer. Take measurements at several places around the disc, at the inside and outside of the pad swept area; if the disc has worn at any point to the specified minimum thickness or less, the disc must be renewed.

4 If the disc is thought to be warped, it can be checked for run-out. Either use a dial gauge mounted on any convenient fixed point, while the disc is slowly rotated, or use feeler blades to measure (at several points all around the disc) the clearance between the disc and a fixed point, such as the caliper mounting bracket. If the measurements obtained are at the specified maximum or beyond, the disc is excessively warped, and must be renewed; however, it is worth checking first that the hub bearings are correctly adjusted (Chapter 11).

5 Check the disc for cracks or any other wear or damage, and renew if necessary.

Removal

6 Remove the front hub assembly as described in Chapter 11.

7 Use chalk or paint to mark the relationship of the disc to the hub, then remove the six bolts securing the brake disc to the hub **(see illustration)**. Where fitted, remove the ABS wheel sensor ring, then remove the disc. If it is tight, lightly tap it off with a hide or plastic mallet.

Refitting

8 Refitting is the reverse of the removal procedure, noting the following points:

a) *Ensure that the mating surfaces of the disc and hub are clean and flat.*

b) *Align (if applicable) the marks made on removal, and tighten the disc retaining bolts to the specified torque.*

c) *If a new disc has been fitted, use a suitable solvent to wipe any preservative coating from the disc, before refitting the brake caliper.*

d) *Refit and adjust the front hub as described in Chapter 11.*

10

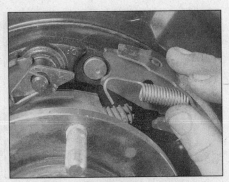

7.20 Guide the leading shoe onto the other end of the strut

8.7 Remove the six bolts securing the disc to the front hub

9 Rear brake drum - removal, inspection and refitting

Note: *Before starting work, refer to the note at the beginning of Section 5 concerning the dangers of asbestos dust.*

Removal

1 Chock the front wheels then jack up the rear of the vehicle and support it on axle stands (see *Jacking and Vehicle Support*). Remove the rear roadwheel.

2 Undo the brake drum retaining screws then withdraw the drum from the axle halfshaft flange.

3 It is quite likely that the drum will be stuck due to corrosion between the drum and halfshaft contact faces. If so, try to tap it off with a hide or plastic mallet. If this fails, liberally apply penetrating oil to the visible joint between the drum and halfshaft flange, and to the wheel studs where they protrude through the drum. Leave the penetrating oil to soak in for some time then try tapping the drum off once more. Continue this process until the drum eventually releases.

Inspection

4 Working carefully, remove all traces of brake dust from the drum, but *avoid inhaling the dust, as it is injurious to health.*

5 Scrub clean the outside of the drum, and check it for obvious signs of wear or damage, renewing the drum if necessary.

6 Examine carefully the inside of the drum. Light scoring of the friction surface is normal, but if heavy scoring is found, the drum must be renewed. It is usual to find a lip on the drum's inboard edge which consists of a mixture of rust and brake dust; this should be scraped away to leave a smooth surface which can be polished with fine (120 to 150 grade) emery paper. If the lip is due to the friction surface being recessed by wear, then the drum must be refinished (within the specified limits) or renewed.

7 If the drum is thought to be excessively worn or oval, its internal diameter must be measured at several points using an internal micrometer. Take measurements in pairs, the second at right-angles to the first, and compare the two to check for signs of ovality. Minor ovality can be corrected by machining; otherwise, renew the drum.

Refitting

8 If a new brake drum is to be installed, use a suitable solvent to remove any preservative coating that may have been applied to its interior.

9 Apply a smear of high melting point copper grease to the halfshaft flange and slide on the brake drum, being careful not to get grease onto the brake shoes or the friction surface of the drum.

10 Refit the drum retaining screws then depress the footbrake several times to operate the self-adjust mechanism.

11 On completion, refit the roadwheel and lower the vehicle to the ground.

10 Rear brake disc - inspection, removal and refitting

Note: *Before starting work, refer to the note at the beginning of Section 6 concerning the dangers of asbestos dust.*

Inspection

Note: *If either disc requires renewal, BOTH should be renewed at the same time, to ensure even and consistent braking. New brake pads should also be fitted.*

1 Chock the front wheels then jack up the rear of the vehicle and support it on axle stands (see *Jacking and Vehicle* Support). Remove the rear roadwheels.

2 Slowly rotate the brake disc so that the full area of both sides can be checked; remove the brake pads if better access is required to the inboard surface. Light scoring is normal in the area swept by the brake pads, but if heavy scoring or cracks are found, the disc must be renewed.

3 It is normal to find a lip of rust and brake dust around the disc's perimeter; this can be scraped off if required. If, however, a lip has formed due to excessive wear of the brake pad swept area, then the disc's thickness must be measured using a micrometer. Take measurements at several places around the disc, at the inside and outside of the pad swept area; if the disc has worn at any point to the specified minimum thickness or less, the disc must be renewed.

4 If the disc is thought to be warped, it can be checked for run-out. Temporarily refit two roadwheel nuts to hold the disc in place. Either use a dial gauge mounted on any convenient fixed point, while the disc is slowly rotated, or use feeler blades to measure (at several points all around the disc) the clearance between the disc and a fixed point, such as the caliper mounting bracket. If the measurements obtained are at the specified maximum or beyond, the disc is excessively warped, and must be renewed.

5 Check the disc for cracks or any other wear or damage, and renew if necessary.

Removal

6 Remove the roadwheel nuts used when checking the disc.

7 Undo the two bolts securing the brake caliper mounting bracket to the rear axle **(see illustration)**.

8 Slide the caliper, complete with pads, off the disc and tie it up from a convenient place under the wheel arch **(see illustration)**. Take care not to strain the flexible brake hose.

9 Using a hide or copper mallet, tap the rear of the disc, while rotating it until it frees from the axle hub. If the disc is very tight, it may be necessary to screw a suitable bolt into the threaded hole on the disc front face. Tighten the bolt to free the disc **(see illustration)**.

10 Once the disc is released, withdraw it off the axle and wheel studs **(see illustration)**.

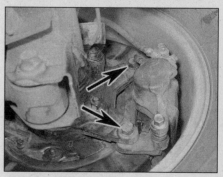

10.7 Rear brake caliper mounting bracket to axle bolts (arrowed)

10.8 Tie the caliper to a location under the wheel arch without straining the brake hose

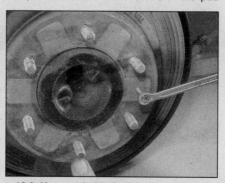

10.9 Use a suitable bolt to free the rear disc, if tight . . .

10.10 . . . then withdraw the disc from the axle

Refitting

11 Refitting is the reverse of the removal procedure, noting the following points:

a) Ensure that the mating surfaces of the disc and axle hub are clean and flat.

b) If a new disc has been fitted, use a suitable solvent to wipe any preservative coating from the disc, before refitting the brake caliper.

c) Tighten the brake caliper mounting bracket bolts to the specified torque.

11 Front brake caliper - removal, overhaul and refitting

Note: Before starting work, refer to the note at the beginning of Section 2 concerning the dangers of hydraulic fluid, and to the warning at the beginning of Section 4 concerning the dangers of asbestos dust.

Removal

1 Chock the rear wheels then jack up the front of the vehicle and support it on axle stands (see Jacking and Vehicle Support). Remove the front roadwheels.

2 Minimise fluid loss by first removing the master cylinder reservoir cap, and then tightening it down onto a piece of polythene, to obtain an airtight seal. Alternatively, use a brake hose clamp, a G-clamp or a similar tool to clamp the flexible hose.

3 Clean the area around the caliper hose union, then unscrew the union bolt and collect the two copper washers. Note that new copper washers will be required for refitting. Seal the end of the hose and the caliper orifice to prevent dirt ingress.

4 Slacken and remove the upper and lower caliper guide pin bolts and lift the caliper off the mounting bracket and brake disc. Note that the brake pads need not be disturbed, and can be left in position in the caliper mounting bracket.

Overhaul

5 With the caliper on the bench, wipe away all traces of dust and dirt, but avoid inhaling the dust, as it is injurious to health.

6 Carefully remove the retaining ring from the outside of the caliper dust seal (see illustration). Withdraw the piston from the caliper body, and remove the dust seal. If the piston cannot be withdrawn by hand, it can be pushed out by applying compressed air to the brake hose union hole. Only low pressure should be required, such as is generated by a foot pump. As the piston is expelled take great care not to trap your fingers between the piston and caliper.

7 Using a small screwdriver, extract the piston hydraulic seal, taking great care not to damage the caliper bore.

8 Thoroughly clean all components, using only methylated spirit, isopropyl alcohol or clean hydraulic fluid as a cleaning medium. Never use mineral-based solvents such as petrol or paraffin, as they will attack the hydraulic system's rubber components. Dry the components immediately, using compressed air or a clean, lint-free cloth. Use compressed air to blow clear the fluid passages.

9 Check all components, and renew any that are worn or damaged. Check particularly the cylinder bore and piston; these should be renewed (note that this means the renewal of the complete body assembly) if they are scratched, worn or corroded in any way. Similarly check the condition of the guide pin bolts and their gaiters, and the guide sleeve (where fitted). Both pins should be undamaged and (when cleaned) a reasonably tight sliding fit in the caliper bracket. If there is any doubt about the condition of any component, renew it.

10 If the assembly is fit for further use, obtain the appropriate repair kit; the components are available from Vauxhall dealers in various combinations. All rubber seals should be renewed as a matter of course; these must never be re-used.

11 On reassembly, ensure that all components are clean and dry.

12 Soak the piston and the new piston (fluid) seal in clean hydraulic fluid. Smear clean fluid on the cylinder bore surface.

13 Fit the new piston (fluid) seal, using only your fingers (no tools) to manipulate it into the cylinder bore groove.

14 Fit the new dust seal to the piston groove then carefully ease the piston squarely into the cylinder bore using a twisting motion. Press the piston fully into position then seat the outer lip of the dust seal on the caliper body and secure it in position with the retaining ring.

Refitting

15 Ensure that the brake pads are still correctly fitted in the caliper mounting bracket and locate the caliper over the pads. Fit the upper and lower guide pin bolts and tighten to the specified torque.

16 Using new copper washers on each side of the brake hose union, position the union on the caliper with the locating peg engaged with the hole in the caliper. Refit the union bolt, tighten to the specified torque then remove the brake hose clamp or polythene (where fitted).

17 Bleed the hydraulic system as described in Section 2. Note that, providing the precautions described were taken to minimise brake fluid loss, it should only be necessary to bleed the relevant front brake.

18 Refit the roadwheel, then lower the vehicle to the ground.

12 Rear wheel cylinder - removal, overhaul and refitting

Note: Before starting work, refer to the note at the beginning of Section 2 concerning the dangers of hydraulic fluid, and to the warning at the beginning of Section 5 concerning the dangers of asbestos dust.

Removal

1 Remove the rear brake shoes as described in Section 5.

2 Minimise fluid loss by first removing the master cylinder reservoir cap, and then tightening it down onto a piece of polythene, to obtain an airtight seal. Alternatively, use a brake hose clamp, a G-clamp or a similar tool to clamp the flexible hose at the nearest convenient point to the wheel cylinder.

3 Wipe away all traces of dirt around the brake pipe union at the rear of the wheel cylinder, and unscrew the union nut. Carefully ease the pipe out of the wheel cylinder, and plug or tape over its end to prevent dirt entry. Wipe off any spilt fluid immediately.

4 Unscrew the two wheel cylinder retaining bolts from the rear of the backplate, and remove the cylinder.

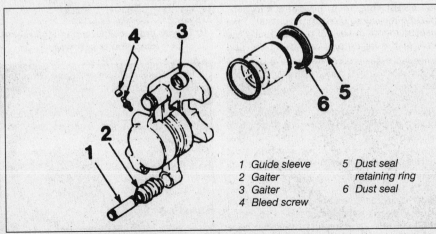

1 Guide sleeve
2 Gaiter
3 Gaiter
4 Bleed screw
5 Dust seal retaining ring
6 Dust seal

11.6 Exploded view of the brake caliper components

10

12.5 Exploded view of the wheel cylinder components

Overhaul

5 Clean the external surfaces of the cylinder, then pull free the dust cover from each end of the cylinder **(see illustration)**.

6 The pistons and seals will probably shake out, if not use a foot pump to apply air pressure through the hydraulic union and eject them. Recover the spring fitted between the pistons.

7 Note their fitted direction, then remove the seals from the pistons.

8 Clean the pistons and the cylinder by washing in fresh hydraulic fluid or methylated spirits (not petrol, paraffin or any other mineral-based fluid). Examine the surfaces of the pistons and the cylinder bores and look for any signs of rust, scoring or metal-to-metal rubbing, which if evident, will necessitate renewal of the wheel cylinder unit.

9 Reassemble by lubricating the first piston in clean hydraulic fluid then manipulating its new seal into position so that its raised lip faces away from the brake shoe bearing face of the piston.

10 Insert the piston into the cylinder from the opposite end of the cylinder body and push it through to its normal location in the bore.

11 Insert the spring into the cylinder, then fit the second new seal into position on the second piston (as described for the first) and fit the second piston into the wheel cylinder. Take care not to damage the lip of the seal as the piston is inserted into the cylinder - additional lubrication and a slight twisting action may help. Only use fingers to manipulate the piston and seal into position.

12 Fit the new dust covers to each end of the piston and cylinder body.

Refitting

13 Ensure that the backplate and wheel cylinder mating surfaces are clean and dry and locate the wheel cylinder in position on the backplate.

14 Engage the brake pipe, and screw in the union nut two or three turns to ensure that the thread has started.

15 Insert the two wheel cylinder retaining

bolts tightening them to the specified torque, then tighten the brake pipe union nut to the specified torque also.

16 Remove the clamp from the flexible brake hose, or the polythene from the master cylinder reservoir (as applicable).

17 Refit the brake shoes as described in Section 5.

18 Bleed the brake hydraulic system as described in Section 2. Providing suitable precautions were taken to minimise loss of fluid, it should only be necessary to bleed the relevant rear brake.

13 Rear brake caliper - removal, overhaul and refitting

Note: *Before starting work, refer to the note at the beginning of Section 2 concerning the dangers of hydraulic fluid, and to the warning at the beginning of Section 6 concerning the dangers of asbestos dust.*

Removal

1 Chock the front wheels then jack up the rear of the vehicle and support it on axle stands (see *Jacking and Vehicle Support*). Remove the rear roadwheels.

2 Minimise fluid loss by first removing the master cylinder reservoir cap, and then tightening it down onto a piece of polythene, to obtain an airtight seal. Alternatively, use a brake hose clamp, a G-clamp or a similar tool to clamp the flexible hose.

3 Clean the area around the caliper hose union, then unscrew the union bolt and collect the two copper washers. Note that new copper washers will be required for refitting. Seal the end of the hose and the caliper orifice to prevent dirt ingress.

4 Slacken and remove the upper and lower caliper guide pin bolts and lift the caliper off the mounting bracket and brake disc. Note that the brake pads need not be disturbed, and can be left in position in the caliper mounting bracket.

Overhaul

5 With the caliper on the bench, wipe away all traces of dust and dirt, but *avoid inhaling the dust, as it is injurious to health.*

6 Carefully remove the retaining ring from the outside of the caliper dust seal **(see illustration 11.6)**. Withdraw the piston from the caliper body, and remove the dust seal. If the piston cannot be withdrawn by hand, it can be pushed out by applying compressed air to the brake hose union hole. Only low pressure should be required, such as is generated by a foot pump. As the piston is expelled take great care not to trap your fingers between the piston and caliper.

7 Using a small screwdriver, extract the piston hydraulic seal, taking great care not to damage the caliper bore.

8 Thoroughly clean all components, using only methylated spirit, isopropyl alcohol or clean hydraulic fluid as a cleaning medium. Never use mineral-based solvents such as petrol or paraffin, as they will attack the hydraulic system's rubber components. Dry the components immediately, using compressed air or a clean, lint-free cloth. Use compressed air to blow clear the fluid passages.

9 Check all components, and renew any that are worn or damaged. Check particularly the cylinder bore and piston; these should be renewed (note that this means the renewal of the complete body assembly) if they are scratched, worn or corroded in any way. Similarly check the condition of the guide pin bolts and their gaiters, and the guide sleeve (where fitted). Both pins should be undamaged and (when cleaned) a reasonably tight sliding fit in the caliper bracket. If there is any doubt about the condition of any component, renew it.

10 If the assembly is fit for further use, obtain the appropriate repair kit; the components are available from Vauxhall dealers in various combinations. All rubber seals should be renewed as a matter of course; these must never be re-used.

11 On reassembly, ensure that all components are clean and dry.

12 Soak the piston and the new piston (fluid) seal in clean hydraulic fluid. Smear clean fluid on the cylinder bore surface.

13 Fit the new piston (fluid) seal, using only your fingers (no tools) to manipulate it into the cylinder bore groove.

14 Fit the new dust seal to the piston groove then carefully ease the piston squarely into the cylinder bore using a twisting motion. Press the piston fully into position then seat the outer lip of the dust seal on the caliper body and secure it in position with the retaining ring.

Refitting

15 Ensure that the brake pads are still correctly fitted in the caliper mounting bracket and locate the caliper over the pads. Fit the

14.1 Master cylinder reservoir location on the vacuum servo unit

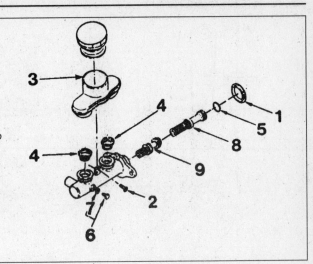

1 Dust seal
2 Reservoir retaining screw
3 Reservoir
4 Reservoir seals
5 Primary piston circlip
6 Stop bolt
7 Gasket
8 Primary piston assembly
9 Secondary piston assembly

14.7 Exploded view of the master cylinder components as fitted to pre-mid-1995 models

upper and lower guide pin bolts and tighten to the specified torque.

16 Using new copper washers on each side of the brake hose union, position the union on the caliper with the locating peg engaged with the hole in the caliper. Refit the union bolt, tighten to the specified torque then remove the brake hose clamp or polythene (where fitted).

17 Bleed the hydraulic system as described in Section 2. Note that, providing the precautions described were taken to minimise brake fluid loss, it should only be necessary to bleed the relevant front brake.

18 Refit the roadwheel, then lower the vehicle to the ground.

14 Master cylinder - removal, overhaul and refitting

Note: *Before starting work, refer to the warning at the beginning of Section 2 concerning the dangers of hydraulic fluid.*

Removal

1 Unscrew the master cylinder fluid reservoir cap and syphon the hydraulic fluid from the reservoir **(see illustration)**.

 Warning: Do not syphon the fluid by mouth, as it is poisonous; use a syringe or an old poultry baster.

2 Disconnect the low brake fluid warning light wiring at the connector on the side of the fluid reservoir or at the adjacent harness connector as applicable.

3 Wipe clean the area around the brake pipe unions on the side of the master cylinder, and place absorbent rags beneath the pipe unions to catch any surplus fluid. Make a note of the correct fitted positions of the unions, then unscrew the union nuts and carefully withdraw the pipes. Plug or tape over the pipe ends and master cylinder orifices, to minimise the loss of brake fluid, and to prevent the entry of dirt into the system. Wash off any spilt fluid immediately with cold water.

4 Undo the two nuts securing the master cylinder to the vacuum servo unit and remove the washers. Withdraw the master

cylinder from the vacuum servo unit, noting that on later models it will be necessary to carefully move aside the brake pipe and three-way connector support bracket first. Where fitted, remove the gasket and spacer from the end of the master cylinder body or servo unit.

Overhaul

5 The master cylinder fitted to mid-1995 models onward is a sealed unit and overhaul is not possible as replacement internal components are not available separately. If there is any doubt about the condition and function of the master cylinder, or if there is any visible sign of fluid leakage from the primary piston area, a new master cylinder should be obtained.

6 The following procedures are applicable only to the master cylinder fitted to models manufactured up to mid-1995.

7 Undo the fluid reservoir retaining screw and detach the reservoir by pulling it upwards from the cylinder and removing the rubber seals **(see illustration)**.

8 Mount the cylinder in a soft-jawed vice, then use a length of dowel rod to depress the primary piston. With the piston held down, locate and remove the stop bolt and gasket from the side of the cylinder body.

9 Remove the dust seal from the mouth of the cylinder, then extract the primary piston retaining circlip. Withdraw the internal components, placing them on a clean surface in the exact order of removal; tap the cylinder on a wooden block if necessary to remove the secondary piston assembly.

10 Wash all components in clean hydraulic fluid or methylated spirit. Examine the pistons and cylinder bore surfaces for scoring, scratches, or bright wear areas and if any are observed, renew the master cylinder as a complete unit. If the surfaces of the cylinder are in good condition, obtain a repair kit comprising primary and secondary piston assemblies.

11 With the piston assemblies well lubricated

with clean hydraulic fluid, fit them into the master cylinder bore, secondary piston first, followed by the primary piston.

12 Refit the circlip to the mouth of the cylinder, followed by the dust seal, then depress the primary piston and refit the secondary piston stop bolt and gasket.

13 Lubricate the reservoir seals with clean hydraulic fluid, refit the reservoir and secure with the retaining screw.

Refitting

14 Ensure that the mating surfaces are clean and dry then, where applicable, fit the gasket and spacer to the rear of the master cylinder.

15 Carefully fit the master cylinder to the servo unit, ensuring that the servo unit pushrod enters the master cylinder bore centrally. Locate the brake pipe and three-way connector support bracket in position on later models, then fit the retaining nuts and tighten to the specified torque.

16 Wipe clean the brake pipe unions and refit them to the master cylinder ports, tightening them to the specified torque.

17 Reconnect the warning light wiring then refill the master cylinder reservoir with new fluid (see *Weekly checks*). Bleed the complete hydraulic system as described in Section 2.

15 Brake pedal - removal and refitting

Removal

1 Disconnect the battery negative lead.
2 Remove the trim panel under the facia on the driver's side.
3 Remove the heater/ventilation duct over the top of the pedal bracket assembly.
4 Disconnect the wiring connector from the brake stop light switch on the pedal bracket. Turn the switch body through 90° and remove the switch from the pedal bracket.

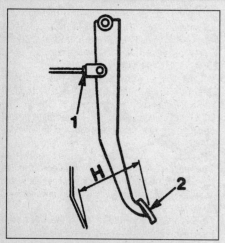

15.12 Brake pedal height adjustment

1 *Pushrod clevis locknut*
2 *Pedal rubber pad*
H *Pedal height dimension (see Specifications)*

5 Disconnect the return spring from the brake pedal and pedal bracket.

6 Extract the spring clip then withdraw the clevis pin securing the vacuum servo pushrod to the brake pedal.

7 Undo the nut, remove the washer and withdraw the pedal pivot bolt, then lift out the pedal from the pedal bracket.

8 With the pedal removed, check the condition of the pivot bushes and renew as necessary.

Refitting

9 Lubricate the pivot bolt with molybdenum disulphide grease, then locate the pedal in the pedal bracket and insert the pivot bolt.

10 Refit the pivot bolt retaining nut and washer and tighten to the specified torque.

11 Connect the vacuum servo pushrod to the pedal, insert the clevis pin and secure with the retaining clip. Reconnect the pedal return spring.

12 Using a tape measure or similar, check the brake pedal height by measuring the distance from the floor (with the carpets fitted) to the upper face of the brake pedal's rubber pad, with the pedal in its normal resting position (see illustration). Check that the pedal height dimension obtained is within the tolerance range given in the Specifications.

13 If adjustment is necessary, slacken the push rod clevis locknut and turn the push rod as necessary until the correct pedal height dimension is obtained. Hold the pushrod and tighten the locknut.

14 With the pedal height correctly set, check that the pedal free play is within the tolerance range given in the Specifications. The pedal free play dimension is the amount of pedal movement (measured at the pedal pad) from the at rest position until resistance is met. If insufficient free play exists, reduce the pedal height slightly.

15 Pull out the stop light switch plunger as far as it will go from the switch body. Depress the brake pedal, then fit the switch to the pedal bracket, turning it through 90° to secure. Release the brake pedal. The switch will automatically adjust to the correct setting when the pedal is released.

16 Reconnect the wiring connector to the stop light switch.

17 Refit the heater/ventilation duct over the top of the pedal bracket and refit the trim panel. Reconnect the battery on completion

16 Vacuum servo unit - testing, removal and refitting

Testing

1 To test the operation of the servo unit, depress the footbrake several times to exhaust the vacuum, then start the engine whilst keeping the pedal firmly depressed. As the engine starts, there should be a noticeable 'give' in the brake pedal as the vacuum builds up. Allow the engine to run for at least two minutes, then switch it off. If the brake pedal is now depressed it should feel normal, but further applications should result in the pedal feeling firmer, with the pedal stroke decreasing with each application.

2 If the servo does not operate as described, first inspect the vacuum hose check valve as described in Section 17. If the check valve is functioning correctly, renew the servo unit air filter as described below.

3 If the servo unit still fails to operate satisfactorily, the fault lies within the unit itself. Repairs to the unit are not possible - if faulty, the servo unit must be renewed.

Removal

Note: *On vehicles manufactured from mid-1995 onward, it will be necessary to have the servo unit master cylinder pushrod dimension checked and if necessary adjusted prior to refitting. As this entails the use of special tools, refer to your Vauxhall dealer for further information.*

4 Disconnect the battery negative lead.

5 Remove the master cylinder as described in Section 14.

6 Disconnect the vacuum hose from the front of the servo unit.

7 Remove the trim panel under the facia on the driver's side.

8 Remove the heater/ventilation duct over the top of the pedal bracket assembly.

9 Extract the spring clip then withdraw the clevis pin securing the vacuum servo pushrod to the brake pedal.

10 From inside the vehicle, slacken and remove the four retaining nuts then return to the engine compartment and manoeuvre the servo unit from its location. Recover the gasket and spacer fitted between the servo unit and the bulkhead.

11 If the servo unit is faulty it must be renewed; overhaul of the unit is not possible. The only items which are available separately are the servo unit air filter components which can be renewed as follows.

12 Count and record the number of exposed threads visible on the servo unit pushrod, up to the clevis locknut. This will give an initial pushrod setting when refitting.

13 Slacken the locknut then unscrew the clevis and locknut from the pushrod.

14 Remove the retaining clip, then slide the cover, silencer and air filter off the pushrod.

15 Obtain new components as necessary and refit them to the servo using the reversal of the removal procedures. Set the pushrod clevis and locknut in the position recorded during removal, then tighten the locknut.

Refitting

16 Prior to refitting, the servo unit master cylinder pushrod should be checked for correct adjustment. The checking and adjusting procedure for vehicles manufactured up to mid-1995 is described in the following paragraphs. The procedure for later vehicles entails the use of a vacuum pump, setting gauge and adjusting wrench all of which are Vauxhall special tools. Before refitting the servo unit have this setting checked and if necessary adjusted by a Vauxhall dealer.

17 To check the pushrod setting on pre-mid-1995 vehicles, measure the distance from the servo unit front mating surface to the end of the pushrod (see illustration). The dimension should be 18.0 to 18.2 mm (0.71 to 0.72 in). To adjust the length of the pushrod, slacken the locknut, rotate the pushrod end fitting as necessary to give the correct dimension, then tighten the locknut.

18 Ensure that all mating surfaces are clean and dry and fit the gasket and spacer to the rear of the servo unit. Manoeuvre the servo unit into position and locate it in the bulkhead.

19 From inside the vehicle, ensure that the pushrod clevis is correctly engaged with the

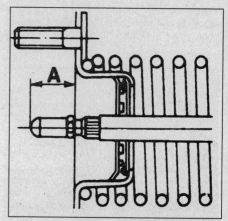

16.17 Vacuum servo unit pushrod setting dimension (A) on pre-mid-1995 models

See text for dimension A

brake pedal then refit the retaining nuts and tighten them to the specified torque.

20 Align the pushrod clevis with the brake pedal and slide in the clevis pin. Secure the pin in position with the retaining clip, ensuring it is correctly located in the pin groove.

21 Refer to Section 15, paragraphs 12 to 14 and check the brake pedal height dimension, adjusting as described if necessary.

22 Refit the heater duct and trim panel, under the facia.

23 From within the engine compartment, reconnect the vacuum hose to the servo unit.

24 Refit the master cylinder as described in Section 14 and reconnect the battery.

25 Bleed the complete hydraulic system as described in Section 2.

---

17 Vacuum hose check valve - testing and renewal

Testing

1 The check valve is located in the vacuum hose between the servo unit and inlet manifold (petrol engines) or between the servo unit and vacuum pump (diesel engines). On 2.5 litre diesel engines two check valves are fitted - one between the vacuum hose from the servo to the engine mounted vacuum pump, and one between the vacuum hose and alternator-mounted vacuum pump.

2 Disconnect the vacuum hose from the connection on the front of the servo unit. The valve may be tested by alternately blowing then sucking the disconnected end of the hose. Air should flow through the valve in one direction only - when blown through from the servo unit end of the valve. If this is not the case the valve should be renewed. If the valve is faulty it must be renewed.

Renewal

3 According to current information, the check valves are only supplied by Vauxhall parts stockists complete with the relevant vacuum hose as an assembly. In this case the hose

and valve assembly can be simply disconnected at both ends and removed from the locating clips and cable ties. Fit the new hose assembly in the same way, ensuring all connections are leak free.

4 On completion, start the engine and check the operation of the vacuum servo unit.

---

18 Handbrake - adjustment

Rear drum brake models

1 Chock the front wheels then jack up the rear of the vehicle and support it on axle stands (see *Jacking and Vehicle Support*).

2 Fully release the handbrake lever, then apply the footbrake several times to ensure that the rear brake shoe self-adjust mechanism is fully adjusted. Apply the handbrake lever to the 4th notch and check that both rear wheels are locked firmly by attempting to rotate them by hand. If adjustment is necessary, proceed as follows.

3 Set the handbrake lever to the 2nd notch then, from underneath the vehicle, slacken the locknut on the cable adjuster **(see illustration)**. Tighten the cable adjuster until the rear wheels can just be turned by hand.

4 Apply the handbrake lever to the 4th notch and check that both rear wheels are locked firmly. Now fully release the handbrake lever and check that both rear wheels are free to turn.

5 When the adjustment is correct, tighten the adjuster locknut and lower the vehicle to the ground.

Rear disc brake models

6 Chock the front wheels then jack up the rear of the vehicle and support it on axle stands (see *Jacking and Vehicle Support*). Fully release the handbrake lever.

7 Pull out the rubber plug from the handbrake shoe adjusting hole in the rear of the brake backplate **(see illustration)**.

8 Using a screwdriver inserted through the adjusting hole, turn the notched adjuster wheel downwards until the handbrake shoes contact the drum and the roadwheel is locked firmly **(see illustration)**.

9 Turn the adjuster wheel in the opposite direction until the roadwheel is free to turn without binding.

10 Refit the rubber plug to the adjusting hole and repeat the operation on the other rear brake.

11 With the handbrake shoes correctly adjusted, apply the handbrake lever to the 7th notch and check that both rear wheels are locked firmly. If adjustment is necessary, proceed as follows.

12 Set the handbrake lever to the 5th notch then, from underneath the vehicle, slacken the locknut on the cable adjuster **(see illustration 18.3)**. Tighten the cable adjuster until the rear wheels can just be turned by hand.

13 Apply the handbrake lever to the 7th notch and check that both rear wheels are locked firmly. Now fully release the handbrake lever and check that both rear wheels are free to turn.

14 When the adjustment is correct, tighten the adjuster locknut and lower the vehicle to the ground.

---

19 Handbrake lever - removal and refitting

Removal

1 Chock the front wheels then jack up the rear of the vehicle and support it on axle stands (see *Jacking and Vehicle Support*).

2 Fully release the handbrake lever, then from underneath the vehicle, unscrew and remove the locknut and cable adjuster from the handbrake lever primary rod.

3 Remove the centre console as described in Chapter 12.

4 Undo the four screws and remove the handbrake lever rubber boot retaining plate.

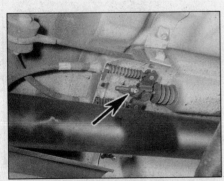

18.3 Handbrake cable adjuster locknut (arrowed)

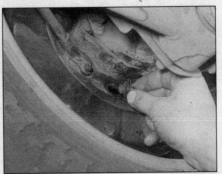

18.7 On rear disc brake models, pull out the rubber plug . . .

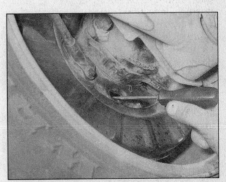

18.8 . . . and turn the adjuster wheel with a screwdriver through the hole

10

Lift the boot up and off the handbrake lever **(see illustrations).**

5 Disconnect the wiring connector from the handbrake warning light switch on the handbrake lever.

6 Undo the two mounting bolts and withdraw the handbrake lever from its location **(see illustration)**.

Refitting

7 Refitting is a reversal of removal, tightening the lever mounting bolts to the specified torque. Adjust the handbrake cable as described in Section 18 before lowering the vehicle to the ground.

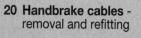

20 Handbrake cables - removal and refitting

Removal

1 The handbrake cable arrangement consists of two individual cables which connect the rear brakes to the handbrake lever via a compensating yoke. Each cable can be removed individually as follows.

2 Chock the front wheels then jack up the rear of the vehicle and support it on axle stands (see *Jacking and Vehicle Support*). Remove the rear roadwheels.

3 Fully release the handbrake lever, then from underneath the vehicle, slacken the locknut and cable adjuster on the handbrake lever primary rod.

4 Extract the retaining clip securing the cable to the support bracket located just to the rear of the primary rod. Withdraw the outer cable from the support bracket then release the inner cable end fitting from the compensator yoke.

5 Remove the rear brake shoes (rear drum brake models) or handbrake shoes (rear disc brake models) as described in Sections 5 or 7 respectively.

6 Remove the handbrake cable from the brake backplate by undoing the retaining bolt (where fitted) then withdrawing the outer cable abutment from the backplate **(see illustration)**.

7 Undo the bolts and remove the clips

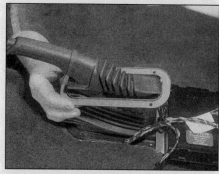

19.4a Remove the handbrake lever rubber boot retaining plate . . .

securing the cable to the rear axle or rear suspension trailing link, as applicable **(see illustration)**. Release the cable from any remaining cable clips or underbody straps and remove it from under the vehicle.

Refitting

8 Refitting is a reversal of removal ensuring that the cable is correctly routed and retained by all the relevant clips and ties. Adjust the handbrake as described in Section 18 on completion.

21 Load-sensing/bypass valve - testing, removal and refitting

Testing

1 A load-sensing/bypass valve is fitted into the hydraulic circuit to the rear brakes. The valve is mounted onto the underside of the rear of the vehicle and is attached to the rear axle by means of an operating rod and connecting link. The valve measures the load on the rear axle, via the movement of the axle, and regulates the hydraulic pressure being applied to the rear brakes to help prevent rear wheels locking up under hard braking.

2 Specialist equipment is required to check the performance of the valve, therefore if the valve is thought to be faulty the car should be taken to a suitably-equipped Vauxhall dealer

19.4b . . . and lift the boot off the lever

19.6 Handbrake lever mounting bolts (arrowed)

for testing. Repairs are not possible and, if faulty, the valve must be renewed.

Removal

Note: *Before starting work, refer to the warning at the beginning of Section 2 concerning the dangers of hydraulic fluid.*

3 Minimise fluid loss by first removing the master cylinder reservoir cap, placing a piece of polythene over the reservoir and securing it with an elastic band to obtain an airtight seal.

4 Chock the front wheels then jack up the rear of the vehicle and support it on axle stands (see *Jacking and Vehicle Support*). Remove the rear roadwheels.

5 Extract the split pin and unscrew the castellated nut securing the operating rod connecting link to the bracket on the rear axle **(see illustration)**. Lift off the dished washer

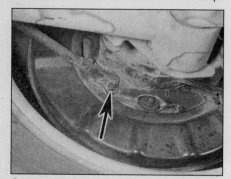

20.6 Handbrake cable to backplate retaining bolt (arrowed) on models with rear disc brakes

20.7 Handbrake cable-to-trailing link clip retaining bolt (arrowed) on models with rear disc brakes

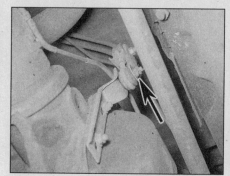

21.5 Load sensing/bypass valve connecting link castellated nut (arrowed)

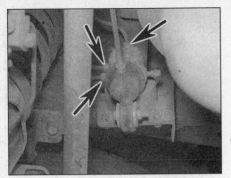

21.7 Brake pipe union connections (arrowed) on the load sensing/bypass valve

and slide the connecting link of the axle bracket stud.

6 Wipe clean the area around the brake pipe unions on the valve assembly, and place absorbent rags beneath the pipe unions to catch any surplus fluid. To avoid confusion on refitting, make identification marks on the pipes and valve assembly.

7 Slacken the union nuts and disconnect the brake pipes from the valve **(see illustration)**. Plug or tape over the pipe ends and valve orifices, to minimise the loss of brake fluid, and to prevent the entry of dirt into the system.

8 Undo the two nuts and remove the washers securing the valve to the chassis bracket. Withdraw the valve assembly off the studs and remove the valve, operating rod and connecting link from under the vehicle.

Refitting

9 Locate the valve assembly over the mounting studs, refit the washers and nuts and tighten the nuts to the specified torque.

10 Refit the brake pipes to their specific unions on the valve and tighten the union nuts to the specified torque.

11 Slide the connecting link onto the axle bracket stud and fit the dished washer with its convex side toward the connecting link rubber bush. Refit the castellated nut, tighten it to the specified torque and secure with a new split pin.

12 Bleed the complete hydraulic system as described in Section 2, then lower the vehicle to the ground.

13 If a new valve assembly has been fitted, it will be necessary to take the vehicle to a Vauxhall dealer for accurate adjustment.

22 Stop-light switch - removal and refitting

Removal

1 Remove the trim panel under the facia on the driver's side.

2 Remove the heater/ventilation duct over the top of the pedal bracket assembly.

3 Disconnect the wiring connector from the stop light switch which is located on the brake pedal bracket. Turn the switch body through 90° and remove the switch from the pedal bracket.

Refitting

4 Pull out the stop light switch plunger as far as it will go from the switch body.

5 Depress the brake pedal, then fit the switch to the pedal bracket, turning it through 90° to secure. Release the brake pedal. The switch will automatically adjust to the correct setting when the pedal is released.

6 Reconnect the wiring connector to the switch.

7 Refit the heater/ventilation duct over the top of the pedal bracket and refit the trim panel.

23 Anti-lock braking system (ABS) - general information

ABS is available as an option on vehicles manufactured from mid-1995 onwards. The system comprises a hydraulic modulator and the four roadwheel sensors. The hydraulic unit contains the electronic control unit (ECU), the eight hydraulic solenoid valves (two for each brake - one inlet and one outlet) and the electrically driven pump. The purpose of the system is to prevent the wheel(s) locking during heavy braking. This is achieved by automatic release of the brake on the relevant wheel, followed by re-application of the brake. In the case of the rear wheels both brakes are applied at the same time.

The solenoid valves are controlled by the ECU, which itself receives signals from the four wheel sensors (which are fitted to the wheel hubs), which monitor the speed of rotation of each wheel. By comparing these signals, the ECU can determine the speed at which the vehicle is travelling. It can then use this speed to determine when a wheel is decelerating at an abnormal rate, compared to the speed of the vehicle, and therefore predicts when a wheel is about to lock. During normal operation, the system functions in the same way as a non-ABS braking system.

If the ECU senses that a wheel is about to lock, it closes the relevant outlet solenoid valves in the hydraulic unit, which then isolates the relevant brake on the wheel which is about to lock from the master cylinder, effectively sealing-in the hydraulic pressure.

If the speed of rotation of the wheel continues to decrease at an abnormal rate, the ECU opens the inlet solenoid valves on the relevant brake(s) and operates the electrically-driven return pump which pumps the hydraulic fluid back into the master cylinder, releasing the brake. Once the speed of rotation of the wheel returns to an acceptable rate, the pump stops; the solenoid valves switch again, allowing the hydraulic

master cylinder pressure to return to the caliper/wheel cylinder (as applicable), which then re-applies the brake. This cycle can be carried out many times a second.

The action of the solenoid valves and return pump creates pulses in the hydraulic circuit. When the ABS system is functioning, these pulses can be felt through the brake pedal.

The operation of the ABS system is entirely dependent on electrical signals. To prevent the system responding to any inaccurate signals, a built-in safety circuit monitors all signals received by the ECU. If an inaccurate signal or low battery voltage is detected, the ABS system is automatically shut down, and the warning light on the instrument panel is illuminated, to inform the driver that the ABS system is not operational. Normal braking should still be available, however.

If a fault does develop in the ABS system, the vehicle must be taken to a Vauxhall dealer for fault diagnosis and repair.

24 Anti-lock braking system (ABS) components - removal and refitting

Hydraulic modulator and electronic control unit

Note: *Before starting work, refer to the warning at the beginning of Section 2 concerning the dangers of hydraulic fluid. Blanking plugs will be needed to seal the hydraulic modulator unions once the pipes have been disconnected.*

Removal

1 Unscrew the master cylinder fluid reservoir cap and syphon the hydraulic fluid from the reservoir.

 Warning: Do not syphon the fluid by mouth, as it is poisonous; use a syringe or an old poultry baster.

2 Release the retaining clip and disconnect the wiring harness connector from the top of the hydraulic modulator.

3 Mark the locations of the hydraulic fluid pipes to ensure correct refitting. Unscrew the union nuts, and disconnect the pipes from the modulator assembly, whilst being prepared for fluid spillage. Seal the modulator ports with the blanking plugs and plug the pipes to prevent dirt ingress and further fluid loss.

4 Slacken and remove the three nuts securing the modulator and control unit to the mounting bracket, then lift the assembly upwards and remove it from the engine compartment.

Refitting

5 Refitting is a reversal of removal, ensuring that the wiring connector is securely held in position with its retaining clip. On completion, bleed the hydraulic system as described in Section 2.

10

Front wheel sensor

Removal

6 Chock the rear wheels then jack up the front of the vehicle and support it on axle stands (see *Jacking and Vehicle Support*). Remove the front roadwheel.

7 Disconnect the sensor wiring connector under the wheel arch then undo the retaining bolts and detach the sensor cable brackets from the suspension upper control arm and inner wheel arch.

8 Slacken and remove the retaining bolt and withdraw the sensor from the steering knuckle.

Refitting

9 Ensure that the mating faces of the sensor and the steering knuckle are clean, then ease the sensor into position in the steering knuckle. Refit the retaining bolt and tighten it to the specified torque.

10 Work along the sensor wiring, making sure it is correctly routed, then secure the cable brackets with the retaining bolts. Reconnect the wiring connector, refit the roadwheel and lower the vehicle to the ground.

Rear wheel sensors

Removal

11 Chock the front wheels then jack up the rear of the vehicle and support it on axle stands (see *Jacking and Vehicle Support*). Remove the rear roadwheels.

12 Undo the bolt and release the bracket securing the wheel sensor cables to the rear suspension centre link. Similarly, disconnect the cables at the wiring connector and release the support bracket from the underbody.

13 Undo the bolt securing the wheel sensor cable bracket to the rear axle.

14 Undo retaining bolt each side securing the left-hand and right-hand wheel sensors to the axle. Withdraw both sensors from their locations and remove the sensors and cable harness from under the vehicle.

Refitting

15 Ensure that the mating faces of the sensors and the axle are clean then ease the sensors into position. Refit the retaining bolts and tighten them to the specified torque.

16 Work along the sensor wiring, making sure it is correctly routed, then secure the cable brackets with the retaining bolts. Reconnect the wiring connector, refit the roadwheels and lower the vehicle to the ground.

25 Vacuum pump (diesel engine models) - removal and refitting

Note: *All diesel engine models are equipped with a vacuum pump mounted on the alternator. However, in addition to the alternator vacuum pump, 2.5 litre models incorporate a second vacuum pump located inside the engine timing cover and driven by the timing gears. Removal and refitting procedures for the alternator-mounted vacuum pump on these engines are contained in this Section. Refer to Chapter 2E for procedures relating to the engine mounted vacuum pump.*

Removal

1 Remove the alternator from the engine as described in Chapter 5A.

2 Undo the bolts securing the vacuum pump to the front or rear face of the alternator, as applicable, taking note of any cable clips/supports fitted beneath them **(see illustration)**.

3 Withdraw the vacuum pump from the alternator and recover the O-ring, where fitted **(see illustration)**.

Refitting

4 Check the condition of the O-ring (where fitted) and renew if there is any sign of deterioration.

5 Refit the pump to the alternator and secure with the retaining bolts, tightened securely.

6 Refit the alternator to the engine as described in Chapter 5A.

26 Vacuum reservoir (diesel engine models) - removal and refitting

Note: *On vehicles manufactured up to mid-1995, the vacuum reservoir is located at the rear left-hand side of the engine compartment. On later vehicles the reservoir is located under the right-hand front wheel arch.*

Removal

Reservoir in engine compartment

1 Remove the retaining clip and disconnect the vacuum hose from the front of the reservoir.

2 Undo the front mounting bolt and rear mounting nut and remove the reservoir from the engine compartment.

Reservoir under wheel arch

3 Chock the rear wheels then jack up the front of the vehicle and support it on axle stands (see *Jacking and Vehicle Support*). Remove the right-hand front roadwheel.

4 Release the plastic fasteners and clips and remove the front section of the wheel arch liner for access to the reservoir **(see illustration)**.

5 From within the engine compartment, remove the retaining clip and disconnect the vacuum hose from the side of the reservoir.

6 Undo the three mounting bolts and remove the reservoir from under the wheel arch.

Refitting

7 Refitting is a reversal of removal.

25.2 Undo the bolts securing the vacuum pump to the alternator - 2.5 litre diesel model shown . . .

25.3 . . . then withdraw the vacuum pump from the alternator

26.4 Remove the wheel arch liner for access to the vacuum reservoir on later models

Chapter 11
Suspension and steering

Contents

Auxiliary drivebelt check and renewal . . . . .See Chapter 1
Centre tie rod - removal and refitting 29
Front anti-roll bar - removal and refitting 13
Front free-wheeling hubs - removal and refitting 3
Front hub assembly - removal, refitting and adjustment 4
Front hub bearing check and adjustment . . . . .See Chapter 1
Front hub bearing lubrication .See Chapter 1
Front hub bearings - renewal 5
Front shock absorber - removal and refitting 7
Front suspension lower control arm - removal and refitting 10
Front suspension trim height - checking and adjustment 2
Front suspension upper control arm - removal and refitting 8
Front torsion bar - removal and refitting 12
General information and precautions 1
Lower control arm balljoint - removal and refitting 11
Outer tie rod - removal and refitting 30
Outer tie rod balljoint - removal and refitting 31
Power steering hydraulic system - bleeding 26
Power steering fluid level check . . . . .See Weekly checks
Power steering pump - removal and refitting 25

Rear anti-roll bar - removal and refitting 20
Rear coil spring - removal and refitting 16
Rear leaf spring - removal and refitting 15
Rear shock absorber - removal and refitting 14
Rear suspension centre link - removal and refitting 18
Rear suspension panhard rod - removal and refitting 17
Rear suspension trailing link - removal and refitting 19
Steering - adjustment 23
Steering column - removal and refitting 22
Steering gear - removal and refitting 24
Steering gear and idler pivot drop arms - removal and refitting 28
Steering idler pivot - removal and refitting 27
Steering knuckle - removal and refitting 6
Steering wheel - removal and refitting 21
Suspension and steering check . . . . .See Chapter 1
Upper control arm balljoint - removal and refitting 9
Wheel alignment and steering angles -
    general information 32
Wheel and tyre maintenance, tyre pressures . . . . .See Weekly checks
Wheel nut tightness check . . . . .See Chapter 1

Degrees of difficulty

Easy, suitable for novice with little experience	Fairly easy, suitable for beginner with some experience	Fairly difficult, suitable for competent DIY mechanic	Difficult, suitable for experienced DIY mechanic	Very difficult, suitable for expert DIY or professional

Specifications

General

Front suspension type .... Independent, with unequal length upper and lower control arms, torsion bars, telescopic shock absorbers and anti-roll bar

Rear suspension type:

Up to mid-1995 .... Live axle with semi-eliptic multi-leaf springs and telescopic shock absorbers

Mid-1995 onwards .... Live axle with four link location, coil springs, gas-filled shock absorbers and anti-roll bar

Steering type .... Power assisted recirculating ball steering gear with centre tie rod and adjustable outer tie rod linkage

Front wheel alignment and steering angles

Note: *The following measurements are with the vehicle in an unladen condition and with the tyres at the correct pressures.*

Vehicles with leaf spring rear suspension

Camber .... +0°30' ± 1°
  Maximum difference between sides .... 30'
Castor .... +2°30' ± 1°
  Maximum difference between sides .... 45'
Steering axis inclination .... 10° ± 1°
Toe setting .... 2.0 mm ± 2.0 mm (toe-in)
Turn angles:
  Outer wheel set at .... 20°
  Inner wheel .... 21° 50' ± 1°

Vehicles with coil spring rear suspension

Camber .... 0° ± 1°
  Maximum difference between sides .... 45'
Castor .... +2°10' ± 1°
  Maximum difference between sides .... 35'
Steering axis inclination .... 12°30' ± 30'
Toe setting .... 0 mm ± 2.0 mm
Turn angles:
  Outer wheel set at .... 20°
  Inner wheel .... 21° 50' ± 1°

Front suspension trim height

Vehicles with leaf spring rear suspension .... 130.0 ± 2.0 mm
Vehicles with coil spring rear suspension .... 139.0 mm
Maximum difference between sides (all models) .... 5.0 mm

Steering

Ratio .... 15.8 : 1
Steering wheel free play .... 10 to 30 mm

Roadwheels

Type .... Pressed-steel or aluminium alloy (depending on model)

Tyres

Tyre pressures .... See end of *Weekly checks*

Torque wrench settings

	Nm	lbf ft
Rear suspension (leaf spring type)		
Axle-to-leaf spring U-bolt nuts	68	51
Leaf spring front mounting nut	160	118
Leaf spring shackle nuts	108	80
Shock absorber upper and lower mounting nuts	40	30
Rear suspension (coil spring type)		
ABS wheel sensor bracket to centre link	26	19
ABS wiring connector bracket to underbody	26	19
Anti-roll bar mounting clamp bolts	22	16
Centre link mounting nuts/bolts	165	122
Panhard rod-to-axle nut	80	59
Panhard rod-to-chassis bracket bolt/nut	165	122
Shock absorber lower mounting nut	80	59
Shock absorber upper mounting bolt	105	77
Trailing link mounting nuts/bolts	165	122

Torque wrench settings

	Nm	lbf ft
Front suspension		
Anti-roll bar link nuts:		
Vehicles with leaf spring rear suspension	10	7
Vehicles with coil spring rear suspension	51	38
Anti-roll bar mounting clamp bolts:		
Vehicles with leaf spring rear suspension	28	21
Vehicles with coil spring rear suspension	20	15
Automatic free-wheeling hub housing/cover to wheel hub	59	44
Lower control arm balljoint to control arm	105	77
Lower control arm balljoint to steering knuckle	140	103
Lower control arm front pivot bolt nut	160	118
Lower control arm rear pivot bolt nut	200	147
Manual free-wheeling hub body to wheel hub	59	44
Manual free-wheeling hub housing/clutch assembly to hub body	12	9
Shock absorber lower mounting to control arm	83	61
Shock absorber upper mounting to chassis	20	15
Torsion bar seat to lower control arm	116	86
Upper control arm balljoint to control arm:		
Balljoints with four bolt fastening	33	24
Balljoints with three bolt fastening	61	45
Upper control arm balljoint to steering knuckle	105	77
Upper control arm fulcrum shaft pivot bush nuts	108	80
Upper control arm fulcrum shaft to chassis	155	114
Steering		
Airbag-to-steering wheel screws	8	6
Centre tie-rod to steering gear drop arm	110	81
Centre tie-rod to steering idler pivot drop arm	59	44
Outer tie rod balljoint locknuts	120	88
Outer tie rod balljoint to centre tie rod	110	81
Outer tie rod balljoint to steering knuckle	110	81
Power steering pump attachments:		
2.0 litre (C20NE) petrol engine models:		
Mounting and adjuster bracket bolts	25	18
Pressure pipe union nut	20	14
2.0 litre (X20XE) and 2.2 litre petrol engine models:		
Front mounting bracket bolts	20	15
Pressure pipe union nut	20	14
Rear mounting bolts	25	18
2.4 litre petrol and 2.3 litre diesel engine models:		
Mounting and adjuster bracket bolts	25	18
Pressure pipe union nut	20	14
2.5 litre diesel engine models:		
Compressor coupling shaft bolts	16	12
Pressure pipe banjo union bolt	32	24
Pump mounting nuts	25	18
Pump pulley nut	166	123
2.8 litre diesel engine models:		
Mounting/adjuster bracket bolts	37	27
Pressure pipe union nut	20	14
Steering column base to floor	19	14
Steering column shaft coupling clamp bolt	25	18
Steering column upper mounting bracket bolts	17	13
Steering gear adjuster locknut	41	30
Steering gear drop arm nut	220	162
Steering gear hydraulic fluid pipe unions	45	32
Steering gear idler pivot drop arm nut	130	96
Steering gear-to-chassis bolts	48	35
Steering idler pivot to chassis	48	35
Steering wheel nut	35	26
Roadwheels		
Steel wheels	110	81
Alloy wheels	120	89

11

1 General information and precautions

General information

1 The front suspension is of independent type incorporating unequal length upper and lower control arms, torsion bars, telescopic shock absorbers, steering knuckles and an anti-roll bar **(see illustration)**. The control arms are attached to the chassis at their inner ends by means of metal and rubber bonded bushes and fulcrum shaft/pivot pins. Camber and castor angles are adjustable by means of spacers fitted to the upper control arm fulcrum pin. The steering knuckle which carries the hub, brake disc and caliper, is attached to the outer end of each control arm by means of an upper and lower balljoint. Adjustable taper roller bearings support the hub assembly on the steering knuckle. Manual or automatic free-wheeling hubs (according to model and/or options) are attached to the outer end of the hub assembly to transmit the drive from the front axle, via the driveshafts, when four-wheel-drive is selected. The longitudinal torsion bars are splined at each end and are connected to the lower control arms via an internally splined seat, and to the chassis brackets via trim height control arms. The anti-roll bar is mounted transversely on the chassis and connected to the lower control arms by vertical links. The telescopic shock absorbers are attached to the lower control arm and

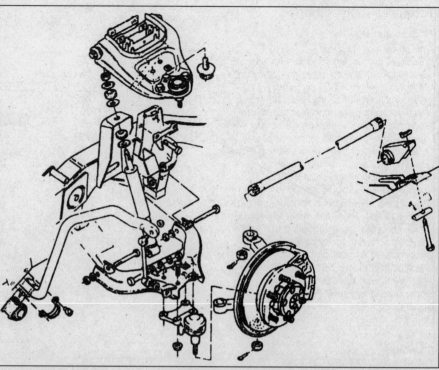

1.1 Exploded view of the front suspension components from mid-1995 onwards (earlier version similar)

chassis at their lower and upper ends respectively, through rubber bushes.

2 The rear suspension on vehicles manufactured prior to mid-1995 is of semi-eliptic multi-leaf spring type **(see illustration)**. The leaf springs are attached to the chassis

via rubber bushed eye bolts and shackles and to the rear axle by means of U-bolts and clamp plates. Telescopic shock absorbers are attached via rubber bushes to the rear spring clamp plates at their lower ends and to the chassis at their upper ends. The shock

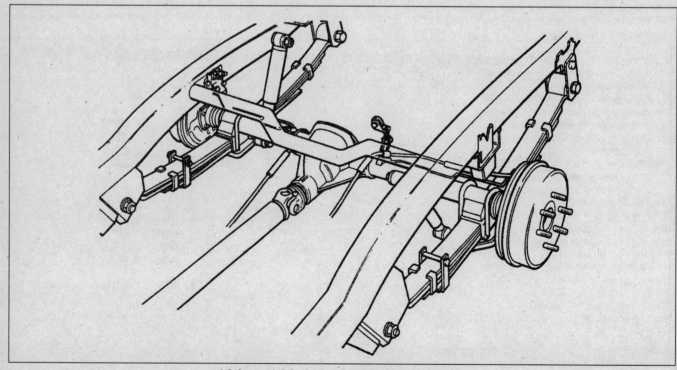

1.2 Layout of the leaf spring type rear suspension

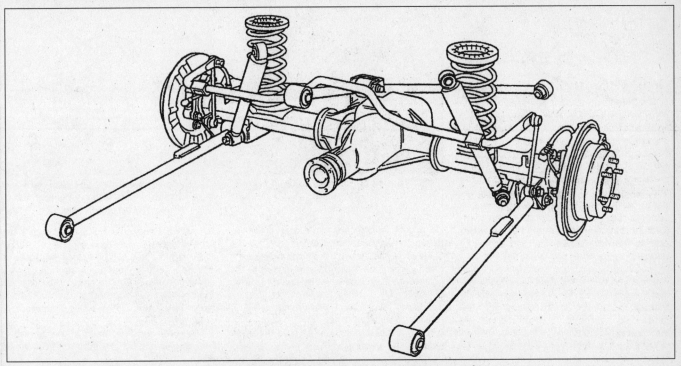

1.3 Layout of the four-link coil spring type rear suspension

absorbers are angled in opposite directions to resist axle tramp and wind-up.

3 On vehicles manufactured from mid-1995 onward, a four-link coil spring rear suspension arrangement is used **(see illustration)**. The rear axle is located longitudinally by two long lower trailing links and a short upper centre link. Lateral location is provided by a panhard rod attached to the left-hand side of the

chassis and to the right-hand side of the axle. The telescopic shock absorbers are gas-filled and angled inward at the top to provide increased lateral stability. A rear anti-roll bar is fitted to all vehicles with coil spring rear suspension and attached to the rear axle by vertical links.

4 Power assisted recirculating ball type steering gear, incorporating a collapsible

energy absorbing steering column is fitted to all models. The power steering pump is belt driven from the crankshaft pulley and is supplied by a remotely located hydraulic fluid reservoir. The steering linkage consists of a centre tie rod attached to the steering gear and idler pivot drop arms via balljoints **(see illustration)**. Two adjustable outer tie rods connect the centre tie rod to the steering

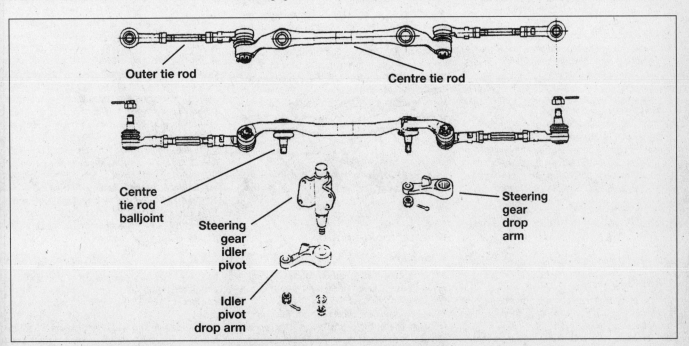

Outer tie rod

Centre tie rod

Centre
tie rod
balljoint

Steering
gear
idler
pivot

Steering
gear
drop
arm

Idler
pivot
drop
arm

1.4 Steering linkage component arrangement

11

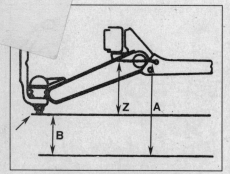

2.2 Subtract dimension B from dimension A to obtain front suspension trim height dimension Z

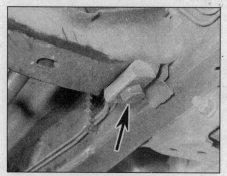

2.6 Torsion bar tension adjusting bolt (arrowed)

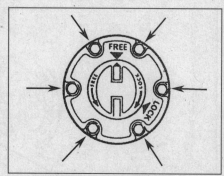

3.3 Undo the six outer bolts (arrowed) and remove the manual free-wheeling hub housing and clutch assembly

knuckles, each outer tie rod containing an inner and outer balljoint.

Precautions

5 An airbag is available as an option on later models. To ensure that it operates correctly should it ever be needed, and to avoid the risk of personal injury from it being accidentally triggered, the following precautions must be observed. Also refer to Chapter 13 for more information.

a) *Before carrying out any operations on the airbag system, disconnect the battery negative lead and wait at least 1 minute to ensure that the system back-up capacitor has been discharged.*

b) *Note that the airbag must not be subjected to temperatures in excess of 90ºC (194ºF). When the airbag is removed, ensure that it is stored with the pad facing upwards.*

c) *Do not allow any solvents or cleaning agents to contact the airbag assembly. The unit may be cleaned using only a damp cloth.*

d) *The airbag and control unit are both sensitive to impact. If either is dropped from a height of more than 50 cm (20 in), they must be renewed.*

e) *Disconnect the airbag control unit wiring plug prior to using arc-welding equipment on the vehicle.*

f) *On vehicles also fitted with a passenger side airbag, do not fit accessories in the airbag zone. Items like telephones, cassette storage boxes, additional mirrors, etc., can be ripped off and cause serious injury, if the airbag inflates.*

2 Front suspension trim height - checking and adjustment

Checking

1 Check and if necessary adjust the tyre pressures (see *Weekly Checks*), then position the vehicle on level ground.
2 Starting on one side of the vehicle, measure the distance from the torsion bar centreline to

the ground and record this measurement as dimension A **(see illustration)**.
3 Measure the distance from the base of the front suspension lower balljoint shank to the ground and record this measurement as dimension B.
4 Subtract dimension B from dimension A to give the trim height dimension Z.
5 Repeat these measurements on the other side of the vehicle and compare the trim height dimensions obtained with the figures given in the Specifications. If the trim height dimensions obtained, or the difference between sides are outside the tolerance range given, adjust the trim height as follows.

Adjustment

6 Adjustment of the trim height is carried out by increasing or decreasing the tension on the torsion bar on each side of the vehicle. This is done by turning the tension adjusting bolt, located at the end of each torsion bar, clockwise to increase the tension (increase the trim height), or anti-clockwise to decrease the tension (decrease the trim height) **(see illustration)**.
7 When making an adjustment, only turn the relevant adjusting bolt half a turn at a time, then bounce the front of the vehicle once or twice to settle the suspension. Re-check the trim height on both sides as described previously and continue the adjustment procedure until the correct dimensions are obtained.

3 Front free-wheeling hubs - removal and refitting

Manual locking hub

Removal

1 Place the transmission transfer change lever in the 2H position and set the free-wheeling hub to the FREE position.
2 Chock the rear wheels then jack up the front of the vehicle and support it on axle stands (see *Jacking and Vehicle Support*). Remove the relevant front roadwheel.

3 Undo the six outer bolts and remove the free-wheeling hub housing and clutch assembly from the hub body **(see illustration)**.
4 Using circlip pliers and/or a small screwdriver, extract the circlip then remove the shim(s) from the end of the driveshaft. Note that a new circlip will be required for refitting.
5 Undo the six inner bolts and remove the free-wheeling hub body from the front wheel hub.
6 Do not attempt to dismantle the free-wheeling hub body components or the housing and clutch assembly as individual parts are not available separately. If there is any doubt about the condition of the free-wheeling hub, a complete new unit should be obtained.

Refitting

7 Thoroughly clean the mating faces of the front wheel hub and the free-wheeling hub body and apply Vauxhall sealing compound 15 03 166 (90 094 714) to the two faces.
8 Locate the hub body in position and secure with the six inner bolts, tightened to the specified torque.
9 Temporarily refit the original circlip to the driveshaft groove, and screw a suitable bolt into the end of the driveshaft. Using the bolt, pull the driveshaft outwards then measure the clearance between the circlip and the free-wheeling hub body. Obtain new shims as necessary, to give a clearance of 0 to 0.30 mm. Note that shims are available from Vauxhall parts stockists in increments of 0.1 mm.
10 Extract the old circlip, fit the selected shims then fit the new retaining circlip. Ensure that the circlip fully enters the driveshaft groove by pulling the driveshaft outwards, by means of the bolt. Remove the bolt once the circlip is fully seated.
11 Thoroughly clean the mating faces of the free-wheeling hub body and the housing and clutch assembly, then apply Vauxhall sealing compound 15 03 166 (90 094 714) to the two faces.
12 Fit the housing and clutch assembly to the hub body, aligning the clutch outer teeth with the grooves in the hub body.

3.17 Remove the automatic free-wheeling hub cover and hub housing from the front wheel hub

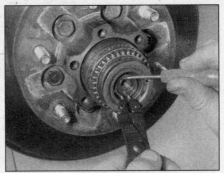

3.18a Extract the circlip from the end of the driveshaft . . .

3.18b . . . then remove the shim(s)

13 Refit the six outer retaining bolts and tighten them to the specified torque.

14 Refit the roadwheel, lower the vehicle to the ground, then tighten the wheel nuts to the specified torque.

Automatic locking hub

Note: *The following procedure describes removal and refitting of the free-wheeling hub where this is necessary to enable other work to be carried out on the front axle and/or suspension components. If a free-wheeling hub is to be renewed, this work entails the use of numerous Vauxhall special tools to determine the thickness of shims to be fitted behind the drive clutch retaining circlip. It is recommended that renewal of the free-wheeling hub be left to a suitably-equipped dealer. Read through the entire procedure to familiarise yourself with the work involved before starting.*

Removal

15 Place the transmission transfer change lever in the 2H position and move the vehicle forwards and backwards approximately 1 metre to disengage the free-wheeling hub assembly.

16 Chock the rear wheels then jack up the front of the vehicle and support it on axle stands (see *Jacking and Vehicle Support*). Remove the relevant front roadwheel.

17 Undo the six outer bolts and remove the free-wheeling hub cover and hub housing from the front wheel hub **(see illustration)**.

18 Using circlip pliers and/or a small screwdriver, extract the circlip then remove the shim(s) from the end of the driveshaft **(see illustrations)**. Note that a new circlip will be required for refitting.

19 Withdraw the drive clutch assembly and the inner cam from the driveshaft and front wheel hub **(see illustrations)**.

20 Do not attempt to dismantle the drive clutch assembly as individual parts are not available separately. If there is any doubt about the condition of the components, a complete new unit should be obtained.

Refitting

21 Clean away as much of the old grease as possible from the drive clutch assembly. hub cover and hub housing.

22 Locate the inner cam in position, ensuring that the lug on the cam engages with the groove in the steering knuckle and that the cam is in full contact with hub bearing lock washer.

23 Sparingly lubricate the inner cam and drive clutch assembly with Vauxhall special grease HD2 (94 171 686). Similarly lubricate the inner surfaces of the hub cover and hub housing, using 5.0 g of the grease in the cover and 8.0 g of the grease in the housing. Do not use excessive grease or the operation of the free-wheeling hub will be adversely affected.

24 Position a jack below the lower suspension arm and raise the arm until the driveshaft is in its normal running position.

25 Fit the drive clutch assembly, aligning the cut-out in the hold-out ring with the lug on the inner cam **(see illustration)**. Engage the drive clutch and inner cam teeth as the clutch assembly is fitted, by rotating the driveshaft.

26 Obtain a suitable bolt to screw into the end of the driveshaft. This will allow the driveshaft to be pulled out to ease fitting of the circlip.

27 Refit the shim(s) over the end of the driveshaft, then locate a new circlip in position using circlip pliers and a small screwdriver. Ensure that the circlip fully enters the driveshaft groove by pulling the driveshaft outwards, by means of the bolt, while at the same time easing the circlip into its groove with the screwdriver **(see illustration)**.

3.19a Withdraw the drive clutch assembly . . .

3.19b . . . followed by the inner cam

3.25 When refitting, align the inner cam lug (A) with the cut-out (B) in the drive clutch hold-out ring

3.27 Pull the driveshaft outwards with a suitable bolt when refitting the circlip

11

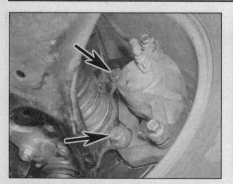

4.3 Brake caliper bracket to steering
knuckle retaining bolts (arrowed)

4.4a Undo the retaining screws . . .

4.4b . . . and remove the hub nut
lockwasher

Remove the bolt once the circlip is fully
seated.

28 Thoroughly clean the mating faces of the
front wheel hub, the free-wheeling hub
housing and the hub cover. Apply Vauxhall
sealing compound 15 03 166 (90 094 714) to
the two faces of the free-wheeling hub
housing.

29 Locate the housing and cover in position
and fit the six retaining bolts. Tighten the bolts
to the specified torque.

30 Rotate the hub housing checking for signs
of tightness. If it turns smoothly, the thickness
of the adjustment shim(s) fitted behind the
drive clutch circlip is correct. If the hub
housing does not turn freely, it is likely that the
shim(s) are too thick. If this is the case, the
following options are available:

a) *Take the vehicle to a Vauxhall dealer for
the correct shim thickness to be
determined using the manufacturer's
special tools.*

b) *Obtain an assortment of new shims in
various thicknesses (available from
Vauxhall parts stockists in increments of
0.1 mm). Remove the free-wheeling hub
components, fit a slightly thinner shim
and reassemble. Continue on a trial and
error basis until a satisfactory result is
obtained.*

31 Refit the roadwheel, lower the vehicle to
the ground, then tighten the wheel nuts to the
specified torque.

4 Front hub assembly - removal, refitting and adjustment

Removal

Note: *A Vauxhall special tool is required to
unscrew the hub retaining nut, however a
suitable alternative can be easily fabricated
and is described in the following procedure.*

1 Chock the rear wheels then jack up the
front of the vehicle and support it on axle
stands (see *Jacking and Vehicle Support*).
Remove the relevant front roadwheel.

2 Remove the front free-wheeling hub as
described in Section 3.

3 Undo the two bolts securing the brake
caliper bracket to the steering knuckle **(see
illustration)**. Slide the caliper, complete with
brake pads, off the disc and suspend it from a
suitable place under the wheel arch using
string or wire. Take care to avoid straining the
flexible brake hose.

4 Undo the retaining screws and remove the
hub nut lock washer **(see illustrations)**.

5 To unscrew the hub nut, insert a suitable
bolt into each of the two holes on the hub nut
face, then use a large screwdriver, or similar
tool, across the bolt shanks to undo the nut.
Alternatively, make up the special tool
described in paragraph 12.

6 Remove the hub nut, withdraw the outer

hub bearing and inner race, then lift off the
hub and brake disc assembly from the
steering knuckle **(see illustrations)**.

7 Examine the surfaces of the outer bearing
for signs of excessive wear and pitting. If new
bearings are required, renew the bearings and
bearing races as a pair. If the oil seal is
defective it must be renewed. To renew the
hub bearings and oil seal, proceed as
described in Section 5.

8 The brake disc can be removed from the
hub if necessary, as described in Chapter 10.

Refitting and adjustment

9 If removed, refit the brake disc to the hub
as described in Chapter 10.

10 Lubricate the hub bearings and oil seal
lips with Vauxhall Anti-Friction Bearing Grease
19 48 606 (90 510 336) or a suitable
alternative prior to refitting the hub onto the
stub axle.

11 Take care when refitting the hub assembly
not to damage the oil seal lips. Slide the unit
into position on the stub axle and then fit the
outer hub bearing and inner race followed by
the hub nut, but do not tighten the nut at this
stage.

12 To adjust the hub bearings it will be
necessary to make up a special tool to
engage with the two holes in the hub nut. The
tool can be made from a flat metal strip and
three nuts and bolts. Lay the hub nut on the
metal strip and mark the position of the two

4.6a Remove the hub nut . . .

4.6b . . . withdraw the outer hub bearing
and inner race . . .

4.6c . . . then lift off the hub and brake disc
assembly

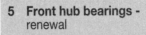
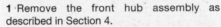

4.13 Using the tool and a torque wrench to tighten the hub nut and settle the bearings

4.14 Using a spring balance to obtain the correct hub bearing pre-load

TOOL TiP

Make up a simple tool like this to remove and refit the hub nut

holes. Drill the metal to accept two long bolts and drill a third hole in the centre. Insert the two long bolts and secure with two nuts. Insert a third bolt in the centre, secure with a nut then cut off the shank up to the edge of the nut **(see Tool tip)**.

13 Using the tool and a torque wrench, tighten the hub nut to 29.0 Nm (21.4 lbf ft) to settle the bearings, then fully slacken the nut **(see illustration)**.

14 Using a spring balance attached to one of the wheel studs, tighten the hub nut using the tool and a spanner to give the following bearing pre-load **(see illustration)**:

New hub bearings -
   20.0 to 24.0 N (4.5 to 5.4 lbf)
Used hub bearings -
   12.0 to 17.0 N (2.7 to 3.8 lbf)

15 Locate the hub nut lock washer over the stub axle with its lugs engaged with the steering knuckle grooves. Check that the retaining screw holes in the lock washer are aligned with the corresponding holes in the hub nut **(see illustration)**. If the holes are not aligned, turn the lockwasher through 180° and try again. If the holes still do not align, tighten the hub nut very slightly until alignment is obtained.

16 Refit the lockwasher retaining screws and tighten them fully. Ensure that the screw heads are below the surface of the lockwasher when tightened.

17 Refit the brake caliper to the steering knuckle and secure with the two bolts tightened to the specified torque (see Chapter 10).

18 Refit the front free-wheeling hub as described in Section 3.

5 Front hub bearings - renewal

1 Remove the front hub assembly as described in Section 4.

2 Withdraw the inner oil seal from the hub by levering it out with a suitable screwdriver or similar tool **(see illustration)**.

3 Lift out the inner bearing and inner race.

4 Remove the two bearing outer races by driving them out of the hub using a suitable soft metal drift **(see illustration)**. Take care not to damage the bore of the hub during this operation.

5 Thoroughly clean the hub bore ensuring that all traces of the old grease are removed.

6 Drive the new bearing outer races into the hub using a suitable tube drift, whilst supporting the hub assembly. Ensure that the races are driven fully home and in contact with their abutment faces in the hub.

7 Lubricate the new bearings and the hub bore with Vauxhall Anti-Friction Bearing Grease 19 48 606 (90 510 336) or a suitable alternative

8 Locate the inner bearing in position then drive a new oil seal into place in the hub on the inboard side. The outer bearing can be left until later for fitting if required (after the hub is refitted onto the stub axle).

4.15 Hub nut lockwasher retaining screw holes (arrowed) aligned with corresponding holes in the nut

9 Refit the front hub assembly as described in Section 4.

6 Steering knuckle - removal and refitting

Removal

1 Remove the front hub assembly as described in Section 4.

2 Measure and record the protruding length of the torsion bar tension adjusting bolt thread above the height control arm to enable an initial trim height setting to be achieved when refitting **(see illustration)**. Fully slacken the

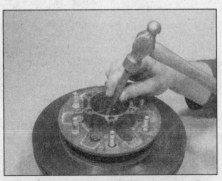

5.2 Withdraw the inner oil seal from the hub by levering it out with a suitable screwdriver

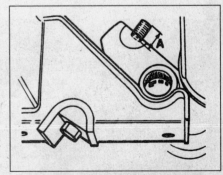

6.2 Measure and record the protruding length (A) of the torsion bar tension adjusting bolt thread

5.4 Remove the bearing outer races by driving them out of the hub using a soft metal drift

11

6.4 Remove the brake backplate from the steering knuckle

6.6a Extract the split pins securing the steering knuckle balljoint castellated nuts . . .

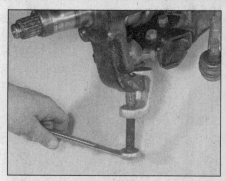

6.6b . . . unscrew the nuts and release the balljoint tapers using a separator tool

6.7 Disengage the balljoints and remove the steering knuckle from the driveshaft

torsion bar tension adjusting bolt until all tension is removed from the lower control arm and steering knuckle. Check that it is possible to lift the steering knuckle slightly without encountering any resistance from the torsion bar.

3 On vehicles fitted with ABS, undo the bolt and withdraw the ABS wheel sensor from the steering knuckle.

4 Undo the three bolts and remove the brake backplate from the steering knuckle **(see illustration)**.

5 Extract the split pin securing the outer tie rod outer balljoint to the steering knuckle arm.

Unscrew the castellated retaining nut then release the balljoint taper using a suitable balljoint separator.

6 Similarly, extract the split pins, unscrew the castellated nuts and release the upper and lower control arm balljoint tapers from the steering knuckle **(see illustrations)**.

7 Disengage the steering knuckle from the balljoint shanks and withdraw it from the end of the driveshaft **(see illustration)**.

8 Check the condition of the oil seal and support bearing in the steering knuckle and if necessary renew these components as follows.

9 Extract the oil seal by levering it out with a suitable screwdriver or similar tool **(see illustration)**. Collect the washer located behind the oil seal.

10 Extract the support bearing using a slide hammer and suitable adaptor **(see illustration)**.

Refitting

11 If the support bearing is being renewed, lubricate it with Vauxhall Anti-Friction Bearing Grease 19 48 606 (90 510 336) or a suitable alternative. Drive the new bearing into the hub using a suitable tube drift, whilst supporting the steering knuckle.

12 Place the washer over the bearing then

drive a new oil seal into place. Lubricate the oil seal lips with the bearing grease.

13 Ensure that the balljoint tapers are clean, then carefully engage the steering knuckle with the driveshaft, and the balljoint shanks.

14 Refit the upper and lower balljoint castellated retaining nuts and tighten them to the specified torque.

15 Secure the retaining nuts using new split pins. If necessary, tighten the nuts further to align the slots in the nuts with the split pin holes in the balljoint shanks.

16 Using the same procedure, reconnect the outer tie rod outer balljoint to the steering knuckle. Fit and tighten the castellated nut to the specified torque and secure with a new split pin.

17 Refit the brake backplate and secure with the three bolts, tightened securely.

18 Where applicable, refit the ABS wheel sensor and secure with the bolt tightened to the specified torque (see Chapter 10).

19 Tighten the torsion bar tension adjusting bolt until the same amount of thread protrudes as noted during removal.

20 Refit the front hub assembly as described in Section 4.

21 On completion of refitting and with the vehicle lowered to the ground, adjust the front suspension trim height as described in Section 2.

6.9 Extract the steering knuckle oil seal using a screwdriver

6.10 Using a slide hammer to remove the steering knuckle support bearing

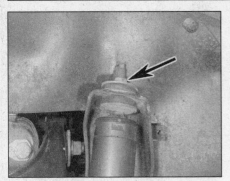

7.3 Shock absorber upper retaining nut (arrowed)

7.4 Shock absorber to control arm mounting bolt and nut (arrowed)

7 Front shock absorber - removal and refitting

Removal

1 Chock the rear wheels then jack up the front of the vehicle and support it on axle stands (see *Jacking and Vehicle Support*). Remove the relevant front roadwheel.

2 Position a jack under the suspension lower control arm and raise it to just support the weight of the arm.

3 Unscrew the shock absorber upper retaining nut, then withdraw the dished washers and rubber bush **(see illustration)**. Hold the end of the shock absorber piston with a suitable spanner while undoing the retaining nut.

4 Unscrew the nut, remove the washer and bolt and detach the shock absorber from the lower control arm bracket **(see illustration)**. Push the piston down to disengage the upper mounting then remove the unit from the lower control arm. Withdraw the remaining rubber bush and dished washer from the upper mounting.

5 To check the action of the shock absorber, mount it in a vice and then operate the piston rod a few times through its full stroke. If the action is noticeably weak or there is an uneven resistance, renewal is necessary. It is advisable to renew both front shock absorbers at the same time or the handling characteristics of the vehicle could be adversely affected.

6 Also check the condition of the upper and lower rubber bushes and renew as necessary. The upper bushes and dished washers are available individually, however the lower bush is only supplied with a new shock absorber.

Refitting

7 Locate the dished washer and rubber bush on the shock absorber piston with the concave side of the washer facing away from the shock absorber body.

8 Engage the lower mounting with the control arm and fit the bolt, washer and nut.

9 Engage the piston with the chassis mounting bracket and fit the dished washers

and rubber bush. The concave sides of the washers must face each other.

10 Refit the upper retaining nut then tighten the upper and lower nuts to the specified torque.

11 Remove the jack under the suspension lower control arm, refit the roadwheel, lower the vehicle to the ground, then tighten the wheel nuts to the specified torque.

8 Front suspension upper control arm - removal and refitting

Removal

1 Chock the rear wheels then jack up the front of the vehicle and support it on axle stands (see *Jacking and Vehicle Support*). Remove the relevant front roadwheel.

2 Position a jack under the suspension lower control arm and raise it to just support the weight of the arm.

3 Undo the bolt and detach the flexible brake hose support bracket from the upper control arm.

4 On vehicles equipped with ABS, undo the bolt and detach the ABS wheel sensor cable bracket from the control arm.

5 Extract the split pin, unscrew the castellated nut and release the upper control arm balljoint taper from the steering knuckle **(see illustration)**.

8.5 Lift the control arm upwards and disengage the balljoint shank from the steering knuckle

6 Undo the two bolts securing the upper control arm fulcrum shaft to the chassis.

7 Carefully withdraw the control arm and fulcrum shaft assembly from the vehicle, being careful to retain the camber and castor adjustment shims fitted over the bolts between the fulcrum shaft and chassis **(see illustration)**. It is most important to retain these shims in their original position during removal, otherwise the camber and castor settings will be lost. If this happens the front suspension geometry will have to be reset by a dealer with special optical alignment equipment. Once the control arm is removed from the vehicle, make a careful note of the number of shims used, and their fitted positions.

8 With the control arm removed, check the condition of the fulcrum shaft and the pivot bushes. If wear is evident on the bushes and/or fulcrum shaft, the control arm assembly should be taken to a Vauxhall dealer for overhaul. Special tools and a press are required to remove and refit the bushes and fulcrum shaft.

Refitting

9 Refitting the upper control arm is a reversal of removal, bearing in mind the following points:

a) *Position the fulcrum shaft so that the side with the projections will be facing the chassis when the arm is fitted. The projections are on the area of the shaft between the two bolt holes. Early models have one projection, later models have two.*

b) *Ensure that the castor and camber adjustment shims are positioned exactly as noted during removal.*

c) *Tighten the two mounting bolts and the upper balljoint castellated nut to the specified torque. Secure the castellated nut using a new split pin. If necessary, tighten the nut further to align the slots in the nut with the split pin hole in the balljoint shank.*

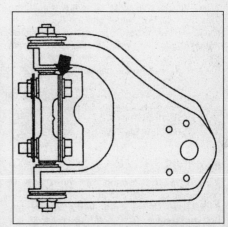

8.7 Location of the upper control arm camber and castor adjustment shims (arrowed)

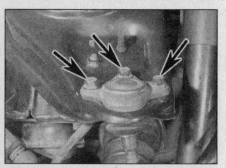

9.4 Upper control arm balljoint retaining bolts (arrowed). Later type balljoint shown - early type have four bolts

9 Upper control arm balljoint - removal and refitting

Removal

1 Chock the rear wheels then jack up the front of the vehicle and support it on axle stands (see *Jacking and Vehicle Support*). Remove the relevant front roadwheel.

2 Position a jack under the suspension lower control arm and raise it to just support the weight of the arm.

3 Extract the split pin, unscrew the castellated nut and release the upper control arm balljoint taper from the steering knuckle. Lift the control arm upwards and disengage the balljoint shank from the steering knuckle.

4 Undo the nuts and bolts securing the balljoint to the upper control arm (four nuts/bolts on early models, three on later models) **(see illustration)**.

5 Lift the balljoint up and out of the control arm and remove it from the vehicle.

6 Check the balljoint condition and renew it if there is any sign of damage or deterioration of the rubber dust cover, or excessive free play in the ball pin.

Refitting

7 Refitting is a reversal of removal ensuring that the retaining nuts/bolts are tightened to the specified torque. Secure the castellated nut using a new split pin. If necessary, tighten the nut further to align the slots in the nut with the split pin hole in the balljoint shank.

10 Front suspension lower control arm - removal and refitting

Removal

1 Remove the torsion bar on the side concerned as described in Section 12.

2 Unscrew the nut, remove the washer and bolt and detach the shock absorber from the lower control arm bracket.

3 Undo the nuts and disconnect the anti-roll bar connecting link from the lower control

10.6 Lower control arm front pivot bolt nut (arrowed)

arm. Where applicable, make a note the arrangement of washers and rubber bushes as a guide when refitting.

4 Extract the split pin, unscrew the castellated nut and release the lower control arm balljoint taper from the steering knuckle. Lift the control arm upwards and disengage the balljoint shank from the steering knuckle.

5 Undo the two nuts and bolts securing the torsion bar seat to the rear face of the control arm and remove the seat.

6 Undo the front and rear pivot bolt nuts, remove the pivot bolts and washers and withdraw the control arm from its location **(see illustration)**.

7 With the control arm removed, check the condition of the pivot bushes in the chassis mounting brackets. If renewal is necessary, the old bushes can be removed using a threaded bar, nuts, washers and suitable tubing to draw them out. Fit the new bushes in the same way ensuring that they are drawn fully into place and are central within the mounting brackets.

Refitting

8 Locate the control arm over the bushes and fit the pivot bolts, washers and nuts. Tighten the nuts finger tight only at this stage.

9 Refit the torsion bar seat to the control arm and secure with the two nuts and bolts tightened to the specified torque.

10 Engage the control arm balljoint shank with the steering knuckle, refit the castellated nut and tighten to the specified torque. Secure the nut using a new split pin. If

11.4a Undo the four lower control arm retaining nuts and bolts . . .

necessary, tighten the nut further to align the slots in the nut with the split pin hole in the balljoint shank.

11 Refit the anti-roll bar connecting link to the lower control arm and secure with the retaining nut tightened to the specified torque. Where applicable, arrange the washers and rubber bushes as noted during removal.

12 Refit the shock absorber lower mounting bolt and nut and tighten to the specified torque.

13 Refit the torsion bar as described in Section 12, paragraphs 8 to 10.

14 Position a jack under the lower control arm and raise the arm until the distance between the rubber bump stop and the bump stop contact point on the control arm is as follows:

> Vehicles with leaf spring rear suspension - 15.0 mm (0.6 in)
> Vehicles with coil spring rear suspension - 25.0 mm (1.0 in)

15 With the control arm correctly positioned, tighten the front and rear pivot bolt nuts to the specified torque.

16 Remove the jack under the suspension lower control arm, refit the roadwheel, lower the vehicle to the ground, then tighten the wheel nuts to the specified torque.

17 Check and adjust the front suspension trim height as described in Section 2.

11 Lower control arm balljoint - removal and refitting

Removal

1 Chock the rear wheels then jack up the front of the vehicle and support it on axle stands (see *Jacking and Vehicle Support*). Remove the relevant front roadwheel.

2 Position a jack under the suspension lower control arm and raise it to just support the weight of the arm.

3 Extract the split pin, unscrew the castellated nut and release the lower control arm balljoint taper from the steering knuckle. Lower the steering knuckle and upper control arm and disengage the balljoint shank.

4 Undo the four nuts and bolts and withdraw the balljoint from the control arm **(see illustrations)**.

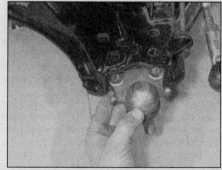

11.4b . . . and remove the balljoint from the control arm

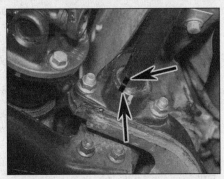

12.2 Mark the relationship of the torsion bar to the seat in the control arm (arrowed) using paint

5 Check the balljoint condition and renew it if there is any sign of damage or deterioration of the rubber dust cover, or excessive free play in the ball pin.

Refitting

6 Refitting is a reversal of removal ensuring that the retaining nuts/bolts are tightened to the specified torque. Secure the castellated nut using a new split pin. If necessary, tighten the nut further to align the slots in the nut with the split pin hole in the balljoint shank.

12 Front torsion bar - removal and refitting

Removal

1 Chock the rear wheels then jack up the front of the vehicle and support it on axle stands (see *Jacking and Vehicle Support*). Remove the relevant front roadwheel.
2 Using quick-drying paint, mark the fitted position of the torsion bar to the torsion bar seat on the lower control arm and to the height control arm at the rear of the torsion bar **(see illustration)**. Only use paint to make the mark, **do not** centre punch, scribe or chisel mark the torsion bar.
3 Measure and record the protruding length of the torsion bar tension adjusting bolt thread above the height control arm to enable an initial trim height setting to be achieved when refitting **(see illustration 6.2)**.
4 Unscrew and remove the torsion bar tension adjusting bolt then remove the height control arm from the torsion bar and chassis bracket **(see illustration)**.
5 Withdraw the torsion bar from the seat on the lower control arm and remove it from the vehicle.
6 Note that the torsion bars are handed and are marked on one end, L for the left-hand side and R for the right-hand side **(see illustration)**. If both torsion bars are to be removed, ensure that the identification marks are visible, or make your own identification markings using paint only.
7 Check the condition of the torsion bar over

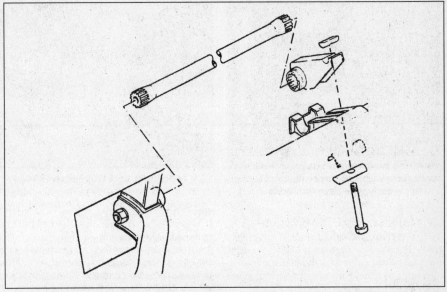

12.4 Exploded view of the torsion bar tension adjusting bolt and height control arm components

its entire surface. If there is any signs of wear on the locating splines or any visible damage on the surface of the bar, a new torsion bar should be fitted. Similarly check the condition of the splines in the torsion bar seat and height control arm and renew as necessary.

Refitting

8 Coat the splines of the torsion bar with multi-purpose grease and engage the end of the bar without the identification marks, with the torsion bar seat on the suspension lower control arm. If the original torsion bar is being refitted, make sure that the paint marks made during removal are aligned. In all cases make sure that the correct torsion bar (left or right) is being fitted to the relevant side of the vehicle.
9 Fit the height control arm to the other end of the torsion bar ensuring that the paint marks made during removal are aligned. If a new torsion bar is being fitted, position the height control arm on the torsion bar so that the arm lower face is parallel with the upper face of the chassis bracket.
10 Refit the torsion bar tension adjusting bolt and tighten the bolt until the same amount of thread protrudes as noted during removal.
11 Refit the roadwheel, lower the vehicle to the ground, then tighten the wheel nuts to the specified torque.

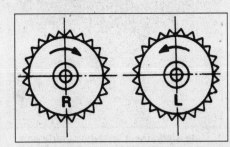

12.6 Torsion bar identification markings

12 Bounce the front of the vehicle two or three times to settle the suspension, then check and adjust the front suspension trim height as described in Section 2.

13 Front anti-roll bar - removal and refitting

Removal

1 Chock the rear wheels then jack up the front of the vehicle and support it on axle stands (see *Jacking and Vehicle Support*). Remove the front roadwheels and the undershield beneath the engine.
2 On vehicles with anti-roll bar links incorporating washers and rubber bushes, undo the upper and lower retaining nuts and lift off the upper and lower washers and rubber bushes. Remove the links and collect the remaining washers and rubber bushes noting their arrangement **(see illustration)**.

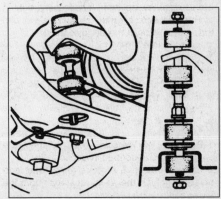

13.2 Anti-roll bar link attachment and bush arrangement on pre-mid 1995 vehicles

11

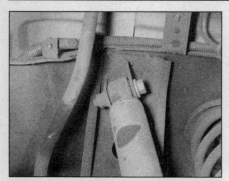

14.3 Rear shock absorber upper mounting attachment on vehicles with coil spring rear suspension

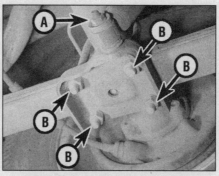

14.4a Rear shock absorber lower mounting (A) and axle U-bolt retaining nuts (B) on vehicles with leaf spring rear suspension

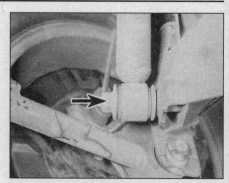

14.4b Rear shock absorber lower mounting (arrowed) on vehicles with coil spring rear suspension

3 On vehicles with straight anti-roll bar links with a ball pin at each end, undo the upper and lower ball pin nuts and remove the links. Collect the spacer fitted between the lower ball pin and suspension control arm.

4 Undo the bolts securing the anti-roll bar mounting clamps to the chassis. Remove the clamps and withdraw the anti-roll bar from under the vehicle. Remove the rubber mounting bushes from the anti-roll bar.

5 Carefully examine the anti-roll bar components for signs of wear, damage or deterioration, paying particular attention to the mounting bushes. Renew any worn components as necessary.

Refitting

6 Refitting is a reversal of removal tightening all nuts and bolts to the specified torque. On vehicles with straight anti-roll bar links, ensure that the spacer is fitted between the ball pin and control arm.

14 Rear shock absorber - removal and refitting

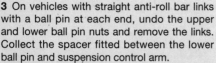

Removal

1 Chock the front wheels then jack up the rear of the vehicle and support it on axle stands (see *Jacking and Vehicle Support*).

2 Position a jack under the rear axle on the side being worked on and raise the axle to just take the load off the shock absorber.

3 Undo the nut or bolt as applicable, remove the washer and detach the upper mounting from the chassis bracket **(see illustration)**.

4 Similarly detach the shock absorber lower mounting from the rear spring clamp plate or axle bracket and remove the shock absorber from the vehicle **(see illustrations)**. Collect the spacers and rubber bushes from the lower mounting.

5 To check the action of the shock absorber, mount it in a vice and then operate the piston rod a few times through its full stroke. If the action is noticeably weak or there is an uneven resistance, renewal is necessary. It is advisable

to renew both rear shock absorbers at the same time or the handling characteristics of the vehicle could be adversely affected.

6 Also check the condition of the upper and lower rubber bushes and renew as necessary.

Refitting

7 Refitting is a reversal of removal. Tighten the mounting nuts/bolts finger tight initially, then to the specified torque when the weight of the vehicle is on the axle.

15 Rear leaf spring - removal and refitting

Removal

1 Chock the front wheels then jack up the rear of the vehicle and support it on axle stands (see *Jacking and Vehicle Support*). Remove the rear roadwheel.

2 Undo the nut, remove the washer and detach the shock absorber lower mounting from the rear spring clamp plate **(see illustration 14.4a)**.

3 Support the weight of the rear axle with a trolley jack positioned beneath the differential housing.

4 Undo the retaining nuts and remove the spring-to-axle U-bolts and clamp plate.

5 Raise the axle on the jack, until it is just clear of the spring.

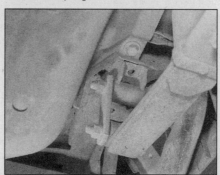

15.6 Rear leaf spring shackle pin attachments

6 Unscrew and remove the spring rear shackle retaining nuts and withdraw the plate and shackle pins, using a soft metal drift as necessary **(see illustration)**. Collect the rubber bushes from the spring eye and chassis bracket.

7 Unscrew and remove the front mounting retaining nut and washer **(see illustration)**. Drive out the mounting bolt with a soft metal drift and remove the spring from under the vehicle.

8 Examine the mounting bushes and the condition of the shackle U-bolts and spring leaves, and renew any worn or damaged components. The rear shackle mounting bushes should be renewed as a matter of course. To renew the front mounting bush it will be necessary to use a press and suitable mandrel of a diameter just slightly smaller than the spring eye. Press out the old bush then press the new bush into the eye until it is centrally positioned.

Refitting

9 Refitting is a reversal of removal bearing in mind the following points:
a) Lubricate the rear shackle bushes with rubber grease prior to fitting.
b) When lowering the axle onto the spring, ensure that the spring centre bolt engages in the axle housing.
c) Tighten all nuts and bolts finger tight initially, then to the specified torque when the weight of the vehicle is on the axle.

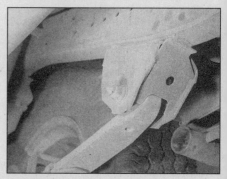

15.7 Rear leaf spring front mounting

17.2 Undo the nut, remove the washer and slide the panhard rod off the mounting bracket stud on the axle

19.3a Trailing link to chassis bracket attachment . . .

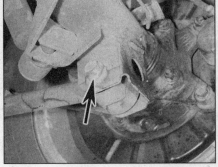

19.3b . . . and axle bracket mounting bolt (arrowed)

16 Rear coil spring - removal and refitting

Removal

1 Chock the front wheels then jack up the rear of the vehicle and support it on axle stands (see *Jacking and Vehicle Support*). Remove the rear roadwheel.
2 Undo the clip retaining bolt, remove the clip and detach the handbrake cable from the trailing link.
3 Undo the nut and disconnect the anti-roll bar lower link from the axle.
4 Support the weight of the rear axle with a trolley jack positioned beneath the differential housing.
5 Undo the nut, remove the washer and detach the shock absorber lower mounting from the axle bracket.
6 Lower the axle on the trolley jack until all load is released from the coil spring. Take care not to strain the flexible brake hose, axle breather hose or the handbrake cable when lowering the axle. Lift away the spring, together with the rubber insulator.

Refitting

7 Refitting is a reversal of removal bearing in mind the following points:
a) Ensure that the spring ends are correctly positioned in the axle and rubber insulator.
b) Tighten the nuts and bolts of all rubber bushings finger tight initially, then to the specified torque when the weight of the vehicle is on the axle.

17 Rear suspension panhard rod - removal and refitting

Removal

1 Chock the front wheels then jack up the rear of the vehicle and support it on axle stands (see *Jacking and Vehicle Support*).

2 Undo the nut, remove the washer and slide the panhard rod off the mounting bracket stud on the axle **(see illustration)**.
3 At the other end undo the nut and bolt, then withdraw the panhard rod from the chassis bracket and remove it from under the vehicle.
4 Check the rod and mounting bushes for damage, distortion or general wear and renew any components as necessary. To renew the mounting bushes it will be necessary to use a press and suitable mandrel of a diameter just slightly smaller than the rod eye. Press out the old bush then press the new bush into the eye until it is centrally positioned.

Refitting

5 Refitting is a reversal of removal but tighten the mounting nuts and bolts finger tight initially, then to the specified torque when the weight of the vehicle is on the axle.

18 Rear suspension centre link - removal and refitting

Removal

1 Chock the front wheels then jack up the rear of the vehicle and support it on axle stands (see *Jacking and Vehicle Support*).
2 On vehicles equipped with ABS, undo the bolt and release the bracket securing the rear wheel sensor cables to the axle centre link. Similarly, disconnect the cables at the wiring connector and release the support bracket from the underbody.
3 Undo the nut and remove the mounting bolt at each end of the centre link. Withdraw the link from the chassis and axle brackets and remove it from under the vehicle.
4 Check the link and mounting bushes for damage, distortion or general wear and renew any components as necessary. To renew the mounting bushes it will be necessary to use a press and suitable mandrel of a diameter just slightly smaller than the link eye. Press out the old bush then press the new bush into the eye until it is centrally positioned.

Refitting

5 Refitting is a reversal of removal but tighten

the mounting nuts and bolts finger tight initially, then to the specified torque when the weight of the vehicle is on the axle.

19 Rear suspension trailing link - removal and refitting

Removal

1 Chock the front wheels then jack up the rear of the vehicle and support it on axle stands (see *Jacking and Vehicle Support*).
2 Undo the clip retaining bolt, remove the clip and detach the handbrake cable from the trailing link.
3 Undo the nut and remove the mounting bolt at each end of the trailing link **(see illustrations)**. Withdraw the arm from the chassis and axle brackets and remove it from under the vehicle.
4 Check the arm and mounting bushes for damage, distortion or general wear and renew any components as necessary. To renew the mounting bushes it will be necessary to use a press and suitable mandrel of a diameter just slightly smaller than the arm eye. Press out the old bush then press the new bush into the eye until it is centrally positioned.

Refitting

5 Refitting is a reversal of removal ensuring that the arm is positioned with the handbrake cable clip mounting plate uppermost and nearest to the axle. Tighten the mounting nuts and bolts finger tight initially, then to the specified torque when the weight of the vehicle is on the axle.

20 Rear anti-roll bar - removal and refitting

Removal

1 Chock the front wheels then jack up the rear of the vehicle and support it on axle stands (see *Jacking and Vehicle Support*). Remove the rear roadwheels.

11

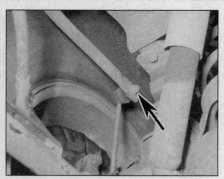

20.2 Rear anti-roll bar link upper attachment (arrowed)

20.3 Anti-roll bar to chassis right-hand mounting clamp

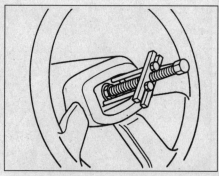

21.5 Using a two-legged puller to remove the steering wheel on pre-1997 models

2 Undo the nuts and disconnect the anti-roll bar links from the anti-roll bar and chassis brackets **(see illustration)**.

3 Undo the bolts securing the anti-roll bar mounting clamps to the chassis **(see illustration)**. Remove the clamps and withdraw the anti-roll bar from under the vehicle. Remove the rubber mounting bushes from the anti-roll bar.

4 Carefully examine the anti-roll bar components for signs of wear, damage or deterioration, paying particular attention to the mounting bushes. Renew any worn components as necessary.

Refitting

5 Refitting is a reversal of removal tightening the mounting clamp bolts to the specified torque.

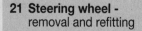

21 Steering wheel -
removal and refitting

Removal

Pre-1997 models

1 Centralise the front roadwheels so that they are in the straight-ahead position and release the steering lock by inserting the ignition key.

2 Prise free the centre pad with the horn button from the steering wheel.

3 Unscrew the steering wheel retaining nut and remove the lockwasher.

4 Make aligning marks between the steering wheel boss and the steering column shaft.

5 A two-legged puller will be required to free the steering wheel from the steering column splines. Locate the legs of the puller in the holes in the centre of the wheel and draw the wheel off the column splines **(see illustration)**.

1997 models onward without airbag

6 Centralise the front roadwheels so that they are in the straight-ahead position and release the steering lock by inserting the ignition key.

7 Undo the screw at the base of the steering wheel then prise free the centre trim pad **(see illustration)**.

8 Unscrew the steering wheel retaining nut and remove the lockwasher.

9 Make aligning marks between the steering wheel boss and the steering column shaft.

10 Vauxhall special tool KM-J-29752 will be required to draw the steering wheel off the steering column splines. If the Vauxhall tool is not available, a suitable alternative can be made from a flat strip of metal, three bolts and a nut. Obtain two suitable bolts to screw into the two holes in the centre of the steering wheel and a third bolt and nut to apply force to the steering column. Suitably mark and drill the metal strip to accept the bolts and make up the tool as shown **(see Tool tip)**.

11 Attach the tool to the steering wheel using

the two outer bolts, then turn the centre bolt while holding the nut until the steering wheel releases from the column splines **(see illustration)**. Once the wheel is free, disconnect the horn button wiring connector and remove the wheel.

1997 models onward with airbag

⚠️ *Warning: Before removing the steering wheel, observe the safety precautions given in Chapter 13 and in Section 1 of this Chapter.*

12 Disconnect the battery negative lead. *Caution: Wait at least 1 minute before proceeding. This is necessary to allow the airbag back-up capacitor to fully discharge.*

13 Set the front wheels in the straight-ahead position, then lock the steering column in this position after removing the ignition key.

14 Undo the four captive screws in the side of the steering wheel centre boss.

15 Carefully lift the airbag unit from the steering wheel and disconnect the wiring connector. Position the air bag unit in a safe place where it cannot be tampered with, making sure that the padded side is facing upwards.

16 Unscrew the steering wheel retaining nut and remove the lockwasher.

17 Make aligning marks between the steering wheel boss and the steering column shaft.

18 Vauxhall special tool KM-J-29752 will be required to draw the steering wheel off the

21.7 Removing the steering wheel centre trim pad on 1997 models onward without airbag

TOOL TiP

Make up a simple tool like this to remove the steering wheel on 1997 models onward

21.11 Using the home made tool to remove the steering wheel

22.5a Undo the retaining screws and remove the steering column lower . . .

22.5b . . . and upper shrouds

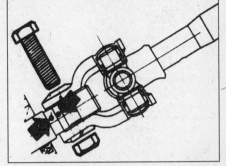

22.8 Make alignment marks (arrowed) on the steering column shaft coupling and steering gear worm shaft before removal

steering column splines. If the Vauxhall tool is not available, a suitable alternative can be made as described in paragraph 10 above.

19 Attach the tool to the steering wheel using the two outer bolts, then turn the centre bolt while holding the nut until the steering wheel releases from the column splines. Once the wheel is free, disconnect the horn button wiring connector and remove the wheel.

20 With the steering wheel removed, do not disturb the airbag contact unit on the steering column. If necessary hold it in position with tape.

Refitting

All models without airbag

21 Locate the steering wheel on the column shaft ensuring that the marks made on removal are aligned.

22 Push the wheel fully onto the splines then refit the lockwasher and steering wheel retaining nut. Tighten the nut to the specified torque and where applicable, reconnect the horn wiring.

23 Refit the steering wheel centre pad and secure with the retaining screw, where applicable.

All models with airbag

24 Check that the airbag contact unit is positioned with the arrows aligned with each other. If it has been disturbed, return it to its central position by depressing the detent and rotating it fully anti-clockwise then clockwise to determine the central position - instructions

are given on the unit. The arrows must be aligned with each other before refitting the steering wheel.

25 Locate the steering wheel on the column shaft ensuring that the marks made on removal are aligned. Feed the airbag wiring harness through the aperture in the steering wheel.

26 Push the wheel fully onto the splines then refit the lockwasher and steering wheel retaining nut. Tighten the nut to the specified torque.

27 Refit the airbag and reconnect the wiring. Secure the airbag with the four screws, tightened to the specified torque.

28 Release the steering lock then reconnect the battery.

22 Steering column - removal and refitting

Removal

1 Disconnect the battery negative lead.

2 Remove the steering wheel as described in Section 21.

3 On 1997 models onward, undo the two screws and detach the bonnet release lever from its location.

4 Remove the trim panel under the facia on the driver's side. On 1997 models onward, disconnect the wiring for the headlight range control when removing the trim panel.

5 Undo the retaining screws and remove the lower and upper column shrouds **(see illustrations)**.

6 On models fitted with an airbag, remove the steering column multi-function switch as described in Chapter 13.

7 Disconnect the wiring for the steering column switches at the wiring multiplugs on the column and under the facia as applicable. Cut off any cable ties as necessary to free the harness and allow removal of the column.

8 Undo the clamp bolt and nut securing the steering column shaft coupling to the steering gear worm shaft. Make alignment marks on the coupling and worm shaft to ensure correct refitting **(see illustration)**.

9 Undo the two bolts securing the base of the steering column to the floor **(see illustration)**.

10 Support the column assembly then undo the two bolts securing the column to the upper mounting bracket **(see illustration)**. Ease the column away from its location to disconnect the shaft coupling from the steering gear worm shaft. Do not use any force on the column - if necessary, ease removal by spreading the coupling slightly with a screwdriver.

11 Once the column is free, manoeuvre it out through the driver's door.

Refitting

12 Refitting is a reversal of removal bearing in mind the following points:

a) *Align the marks made on the column shaft coupling and steering gear worm shaft when reconnecting the coupling to the shaft.*

b) *Tighten all fastenings loosely initially, then to the specified torque in the order: column-to-floor panel bolts, upper mounting bolts, coupling clamp bolt.*

c) *On models with an airbag, refit the steering column multi-function switch as described in Chapter 13.*

d) *Ensure that all wiring loom connections are securely made and fit new cable ties as necessary. Check the operation of the various switches before refitting the column shrouds.*

e) *Refit the steering wheel as described in Section 21.*

22.9 Steering column to floor retaining bolts (arrowed)

22.10 Steering column right-hand upper retaining bolt (arrowed)

11

23 Steering - adjustment

1 With the engine running, the free play measured at the steering wheel should be within the tolerance given in the Specifications. If the free play is excessive, first check the condition of all steering and suspension linkages and components with reference to the procedures contained in Chapter 1. If the free play is still excessive after rectifying any problems found, check the adjustment at the steering gear as follows.

2 Locate the adjuster and locknut on the top of the steering gear (see illustration). For access, it may be necessary to remove surrounding components according to model.

3 Slacken the locknut then turn the adjuster clockwise to decrease the free play and anti-clockwise to increase it. Turn the adjuster a quarter of a turn initially then tighten the locknut. Start the engine and slowly turn the steering to full left and right lock checking for any signs of tightness. If any tightness is felt, slacken the locknut and back off the adjustment slightly. Continue this process until the correct adjustment is obtained without any tightness being felt when the steering is turned from lock to lock.

4 On completion of the adjustment, tighten the adjuster locknut to the specified torque and refit any components disturbed for access.

24 Steering gear - removal and refitting

Removal

1 Chock the rear wheels then jack up the front of the vehicle and support it on axle stands (see *Jacking and Vehicle Support*). Remove the undershield beneath the engine. According to model, it may also be necessary to remove surrounding components to allow access from above.

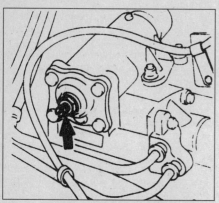

23.2 Steering wheel free play adjuster (arrowed) and locknut located on top of the steering gear

2 Clean the area around the hydraulic fluid pressure and return pipe unions on the steering gear and position a suitable container underneath to catch escaping fluid.

3 Unscrew the two pipe unions on the steering gear and allow the fluid to drain into the container. Cover the pipe ends and steering gear orifices after disconnection to prevent the ingress of foreign matter. Do not start the engine when the fluid has been drained otherwise damage will be caused to the power steering pump.

4 Extract the split pin and unscrew the castellated nut securing the steering centre tie rod balljoint to the steering gear drop arm. Disconnect the balljoint from the drop arm using a suitable balljoint separator tool.

5 Undo the clamp bolt and nut securing the steering column shaft coupling to the steering gear worm shaft (see illustration 22.8). Make alignment marks on the coupling and worm shaft to ensure correct refitting.

6 Undo the four nuts and bolts securing the steering gear to the chassis. Ease the steering gear from its location to disconnect the worm shaft from the steering column shaft coupling. Do not use any force - if necessary, ease removal by spreading the coupling slightly with a screwdriver. Once the coupling is released, remove the steering gear from under the vehicle.

Refitting

7 Refitting is a reversal of removal bearing in mind the following points:

a) Align the marks made on the column shaft coupling and steering gear worm shaft when reconnecting the shaft to the coupling. If a new steering gear unit is being fitted, set the steering gear in the centre position and the roadwheels in the straight-ahead position.

b) Do not use any force when connecting the steering gear worm shaft to the coupling. Spread the coupling slightly with a screwdriver if necessary.

c) Tighten all nuts and bolts and the hydraulic pipe unions to the specified torque.

d) Use a new split pin to secure the centre tie-rod balljoint castellated nut, tightening the nut further, if necessary, to align the split pin holes.

e) On completion, bleed the power steering hydraulic system as described in Section 26.

25 Power steering pump - removal and refitting

Note: *Depending on model type and optional equipment fitted, it may be beneficial to move aside additional components for access to the pump attachments. Refer to the applicable Chapters and Sections of this manual for details, where necessary.*

2.0 litre (C20NE) petrol engine models

Removal

1 Remove the power steering pump drivebelt as described in Chapter 1. Mark the drivebelt with the direction of travel to ensure correct refitting.

2 Clean the area around the hydraulic fluid pressure pipe union and return hose connection on the pump.

3 Place a suitable container under the power steering pump, disconnect the fluid pressure pipe union and return hose and allow the fluid to drain into the container. Cover the pipe ends and the pump orifices after disconnection.

4 Undo the bolt securing the drivebelt adjuster bracket to the pump and move the bracket clear.

5 Undo the pump lower mounting bolts and remove the pump from the engine.

Refitting

6 Locate the pump on the engine and refit the mounting bolts and drivebelt adjuster bracket bolt. Do not fully tighten the bolts at this stage.

7 Reconnect the pressure pipe and return hose to the pump. Tighten the pressure pipe union nut to the specified torque.

8 Refit and tension the power steering pump drivebelt as described in Chapter 1. Once the drivebelt is fitted and correctly tensioned, tighten the pump mounting bolts and adjuster bracket bolt to the specified torque.

9 Refit any components removed for access with reference to the relevant Chapters and Sections of this manual.

10 Fill the hydraulic fluid reservoir with fresh fluid and bleed the system as described in Section 26.

2.0 litre (X20XE) and 2.2 litre petrol engine models

Removal

11 Remove the auxiliary drivebelt as described in Chapter 1. Mark the drivebelt with the direction of travel to ensure correct refitting.

12 Clean the area around the hydraulic fluid pressure pipe union and return hose connection on the pump.

13 Place a suitable container under the power steering pump, disconnect the fluid pressure pipe union and return hose and allow the fluid to drain into the container. Cover the pipe ends and the pump orifices after disconnection.

14 Slacken the bolt securing the pump front mounting bracket to the engine, and undo the bolt securing the front mounting bracket to the pump.

15 Undo the two bolts securing the rear mounting bracket to the pump. Move the front mounting bracket upwards then lift the pump upwards and off the engine.

Refitting

16 Locate the pump on the engine and refit the rear mounting bolts and the bolt securing the front mounting bracket to the pump. Tighten the mounting bolts (including the previously slackened front mounting bracket - to-engine bolt) to the specified torque.

17 Reconnect the pressure pipe and return hose to the pump. Tighten the pressure pipe union nut to the specified torque.

18 Refit the auxiliary drivebelt as described in Chapter 1, then refit any components removed for access with reference to the relevant Chapters and Sections of this manual.

19 Fill the hydraulic fluid reservoir with fresh fluid and bleed the system as described in Section 26.

2.4 litre petrol and 2.3 litre diesel engine models

Removal

20 Remove the air conditioning compressor drivebelt (where fitted) and power steering pump drivebelt as described in Chapter 1. Mark the drivebelt(s) with the direction of travel to ensure correct refitting.

21 Clean the area around the hydraulic fluid pressure pipe union and return hose connection on the pump.

22 Place a suitable container under the power steering pump, disconnect the fluid pressure pipe union and return hose and allow the fluid to drain into the container. Cover the pipe ends and the pump orifices after disconnection.

23 Undo the nut and bolt securing the drivebelt adjuster nut clamp to the pump bracket.

24 Undo the pump lower mounting bolts and remove the pump from the engine.

Refitting

25 Locate the pump on the engine and refit the mounting bolts and drivebelt adjuster nut clamp bolt and nut. Do not fully tighten the nuts and bolts at this stage.

26 Reconnect the pressure pipe and return hose to the pump. Tighten the pressure pipe union nut to the specified torque.

27 Refit and tension the power steering pump drivebelt as described in Chapter 1.

25.38 Removing the power steering pump on a 2.5 litre diesel engine

Once the drivebelt is fitted and correctly tensioned, tighten the pump mounting bolts and adjuster nut clamp bolt and nut to the specified torque.

28 Refit any components removed for access with reference to the relevant Chapters and Sections of this manual.

29 Fill the hydraulic fluid reservoir with fresh fluid and bleed the system as described in Section 26.

2.5 litre diesel engine models

Removal

30 Remove the auxiliary drivebelt as described in Chapter 1. Mark the drivebelt with the direction of travel to ensure correct refitting.

31 Slacken the clip and disconnect the vacuum pump non-return valve hose from the pipe stub below the pump.

32 Clean the area around the hydraulic fluid pressure pipe union and return hose connection on the pump.

33 Undo the fluid pressure pipe banjo union bolt and remove the washer. Withdraw the pressure pipe from the pump connection and recover the second copper washer.

34 Slacken the clip, detach the return hose from the pump and allow the fluid to drain into the container. Cover the pipe ends and the pump orifices after disconnection.

35 Undo the nut securing the pulley to the steering pump shaft. Prevent the pump shaft from turning as the nut is undone using an Allen key or similar tool inserted into the end of the pump shaft.

36 Withdraw the pulley from the pump shaft, using a puller if the pulley is tight.

37 On models with air conditioning, undo the bolts and disconnect the compressor coupling shaft from the flange at the rear of the power steering pump.

38 Undo the two nuts and withdraw the pump and shaft rearwards from the pulley bearing housing **(see illustration)**.

Refitting

39 Engage the pump shaft with the pulley bearing housing and push the pump fully into place.

40 Refit the two pump mounting nuts and tighten to the specified torque.

41 Locate the pulley over the pump shaft, refit the retaining nut and tighten to the specified torque. Hold the pump shaft while the nut is tightened using the method employed for removal.

42 On models with air conditioning, attach the compressor coupling shaft and secure with the bolts tightened to the specified torque.

43 Refit the fluid return hose and secure with the clip.

44 Using a new copper washer on each side of the banjo union, locate the fluid pressure pipe on the pump, refit the union bolt and tighten to the specified torque.

45 Attach the vacuum pump non-return valve

hose to the pipe stub below the pump and secure with the clip.

46 Refit the auxiliary drivebelt as described in Chapter 1, then refit any components removed for access with reference to the relevant Chapters and Sections of this manual.

47 Fill the hydraulic fluid reservoir with fresh fluid and bleed the system as described in Section 26.

2.8 litre diesel engine models

Removal

48 Remove the power steering pump/air conditioning compressor drivebelt as described in Chapter 1. Mark the drivebelt with the direction of travel to ensure correct refitting.

49 Clean the area around the hydraulic fluid pressure pipe union and return hose connection on the pump then position a suitable container below the unions.

50 Undo the fluid pressure pipe union nut and remove the washer. Withdraw the pressure pipe banjo union from the pump connection. Slacken the clip, detach the return hose from the pump and allow the fluid to drain into the container. Cover the pipe ends and the pump orifices after disconnection.

51 Undo the nut securing the pump to the rear mounting/adjuster bracket.

52 Undo the two front mounting bracket bolts and withdraw the pump from the engine.

Refitting

53 Locate the pump on the engine and refit the front mounting bracket bolts and rear mounting/adjuster bracket nut. Do not fully tighten the nuts and bolts at this stage.

54 Reconnect the pressure pipe and return hose to the pump, using a new washer on the pressure pipe union. Tighten the pressure pipe union nut to the specified torque.

55 Refit and tension the power steering pump/air conditioning compressor drivebelt as described in Chapter 1. Once the drivebelt is fitted and correctly tensioned, tighten the pump mounting bolts/nut to the specified torque.

56 Refit any components removed for access with reference to the relevant Chapters and Sections of this manual.

57 Fill the hydraulic fluid reservoir with fresh fluid and bleed the system as described in Section 26.

26 Power steering hydraulic system - bleeding

1 This procedure will only be necessary when any part of the hydraulic system has been disconnected, or if air has entered because of leakage.

2 Remove the fluid reservoir filler cap, and top-up the fluid level to the maximum mark,

11

using only the specified fluid as described in *Weekly checks*. Allow the fluid to settle for at least two minutes before proceeding.

3 Without turning the steering wheel, start the engine, let it run for a few seconds, then switch it off. Check the fluid level in the reservoir and top up if necessary. Repeat this procedure until the fluid level remains constant after running the engine.

4 Chock the rear wheels then jack up the front of the vehicle and support it on axle stands (see *Jacking and Vehicle Support*). Ensure that the front wheels are clear of the ground.

5 Start the engine and slowly move the steering from lock-to-lock several times to expel any air remaining in the system. Top up the reservoir as necessary and repeat this procedure until bubbles cease to appear in the fluid reservoir.

6 Switch the engine off and lower the vehicle to the ground. Start the engine again and slowly move the steering from lock-to-lock several times. Switch the engine off and recheck the fluid level.

27 Steering idler pivot -
removal and refitting

Removal

1 Chock the rear wheels then jack up the front of the vehicle and support it on axle stands (see *Jacking and Vehicle Support*). Remove the undershield beneath the engine.

2 Extract the split pin and unscrew the castellated nut securing the steering centre tie rod balljoint to the idler pivot drop arm. Disconnect the balljoint from the drop arm using a suitable balljoint separator tool.

3 Undo the four nuts and bolts securing the idler pivot to the chassis and remove the pivot from under the vehicle **(see illustration)**.

Refitting

4 Refitting is a reversal of removal bearing in mind the following points:

a) *Tighten all nuts and bolts to the specified torque.*

b) *Use a new split pin to secure the centre tie-rod balljoint castellated nut, tightening the nut further, if necessary, to align the split pin holes.*

28 Steering gear and idler pivot drop arms -
removal and refitting

Removal

1 Chock the rear wheels then jack up the front of the vehicle and support it on axle stands (see *Jacking and Vehicle Support*). Remove the undershield beneath the engine.

2 Extract the split pin and unscrew the castellated nut securing the steering centre tie rod balljoint to the steering gear or idler pivot drop arm as applicable. Disconnect the balljoint from the drop arm using a suitable balljoint separator tool.

3 Unscrew and remove the nut securing the drop arm to the steering gear or idler pivot shaft. Using a suitable puller, extract the drop arm from the shaft.

Refitting

4 Align the master splines on the steering gear or idler pivot shaft and drop arm, then locate the arm on the shaft.

5 Refit the drop arm retaining nut and tighten to the specified torque.

6 Reconnect the steering centre tie-rod to the drop arm, fit the castellated nut and tighten to the specified torque. Align the split pin holes by tightening the nut further slightly, if necessary, then secure the nut using a new split pin.

7 Refit the engine undershield and lower the vehicle to the ground.

29 Centre tie rod -
removal and refitting

Removal

1 Chock the rear wheels then jack up the front of the vehicle and support it on axle

stands (see *Jacking and Vehicle Support*). Remove the undershield beneath the engine.

2 Extract the split pins and unscrew the castellated nuts securing the outer tie rod inner balljoints to the centre tie rod. Disconnect the two balljoints from the centre tie rod using a suitable balljoint separator tool.

3 Using the same procedure, disconnect the centre tie rod balljoints from the steering gear drop arm and idler pivot drop arm, then withdraw the tie rod from under the vehicle.

Refitting

4 Refitting is a reversal of removal. Tighten the balljoint castellated nuts to the specified torque and secure using new split pins. If necessary, tighten the nuts further slightly to align the split pin holes.

30 Outer tie rod -
removal and refitting

Removal

1 Chock the rear wheels then jack up the front of the vehicle and support it on axle stands (see *Jacking and Vehicle Support*). Remove the relevant roadwheel and the undershield beneath the engine.

2 Extract the split pin and unscrew the castellated nut securing the outer tie rod outer balljoint to the steering knuckle **(see illustration)**. Disconnect the balljoint from the steering knuckle using a suitable balljoint separator tool.

3 Using the same procedure, disconnect the inner balljoint from the centre tie rod and remove the outer tie rod assembly from the vehicle **(see illustration)**.

4 If the inner and outer balljoints are to be removed, refer to the procedures contained in Section 31.

Refitting

5 Refitting is a reversal of removal, bearing in mind the following points:

a) *The outer tie rod must be fitted with the left-hand threaded end (balljoint locknuts*

27.3 Steering idler pivot mounting bolt nuts (arrowed)

30.2 Extract the split pin and unscrew the nut securing the outer tie rod outer balljoint to the steering knuckle

30.3 Using the same procedure, disconnect the inner balljoint (arrowed) from the centre tie rod

marked with an L) facing the centre tie rod ie towards the centre of the vehicle.

b) *Tighten the balljoint castellated nuts to the specified torque and secure using new split pins. If necessary, tighten the nuts further slightly to align the split pin holes.*

31 Outer tie rod balljoint - removal and refitting

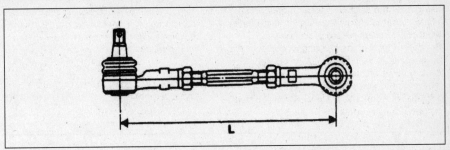

31.5 Outer tie rod setting dimension L measured through the ballpin centres

Removal

1 Remove the outer tie rod from the vehicle as described in Section 30.

2 Clamp the tie rod in a vice and slacken both locknuts securing the balljoints to the tie rod. Note that one of the locknuts will be marked with an L indicating it has a **left-hand thread.**

3 Unscrew the balljoint to be removed from the tie rod noting that the joint adjacent to the locknut marked with an L also has a left-hand thread.

Refitting

4 Screw the new balljoint onto the tie rod, up to the locknut.

5 With both balljoint locknuts slackened, measure the distance between the centres of the two ballpins **(see illustration)**.

6 Remove the tie rod from the vice and, while holding the balljoints, turn the tie rod until the following dimension is obtained between the centres of the ballpins. Note that there must also be the same number of exposed threads at each end of the tie rod when the correct dimension is obtained.

262.0 mm (10.32 in) for vehicles with leaf spring rear suspension

299.0 mm (11.78 in) for vehicles with coil spring rear suspension

7 Once the tie rod length is correctly set, tighten the locknuts to the specified torque.

8 Refit the tie rod to the vehicle as described in Section 30 then refer to Section 32 and check the front wheel toe setting.

32 Wheel alignment and steering angles - general information

1 Accurate front wheel alignment is essential to provide positive steering and prevent excessive tyre wear. Before considering the steering/suspension geometry, check that the tyres are correctly inflated, that the front wheels are not buckled, and that the steering linkage and suspension joints are in good order, without slackness or wear.

2 Wheel alignment consists of four factors:

Camber is the angle at which the roadwheels are set from the vertical when viewed from the front or rear of the vehicle. Positive camber is the amount (in degrees) that the wheels are tilted outward at the top from the vertical. Negative camber is the amount (in degrees) that the wheels are tilted inward at the top from the vertical. The camber angle is adjusted by adding or removing shims positioned between the suspension upper control arm fulcrum shaft and the chassis. The shims are slotted to locate over the two fulcrum shaft retaining bolts.

Castor is the angle between the steering axis and a vertical line when viewed from each side of the vehicle. Positive castor is when the steering axis is inclined rearward at the top. The castor angle is adjusted in the same way as the camber angle but by adding or removing shims at the front or rear retaining bolt only.

Steering axis inclination - also known as kingpin inclination is the angle (when viewed from the front or rear of the vehicle) between the vertical and an imaginary line drawn through the front suspension upper and lower control arm balljoints. This angle is not adjustable.

Toe setting is the amount by which the distance between the front inside edges of the roadwheel rims (measured at hub height) differs from that between the rear inside edges.

3 Owing to the need for optical alignment equipment and precision gauges to measure the small angles of the steering and suspension settings, it is essential that checking of the camber, castor and toe setting is left to a Vauxhall dealer or service station having the necessary equipment.

Notes

Chapter 12
Bodywork and fittings

Contents

Body exterior fittings - removal and refitting 25
Bonnet - removal, refitting and adjustment 9
Bonnet lock - removal and refitting 11
Bonnet release cable - removal and refitting 10
Bumpers - removal and refitting 6
Central locking components - removal and refitting 20
Centre console - removal and refitting 31
Doors - removal and refitting 12
Door handle and lock components - removal and refitting 14
Door inner trim panel - removal and refitting 13
Door window glass and regulator - removal and refitting 15
Electric window components - removal and refitting 21
Exterior mirrors and associated components - removal and refitting .. 22
Facia assembly - removal and refitting 32
General information 1
Hard top (3-door models) - removal and refitting 29

Interior trim - removal and refitting 28
Maintenance - bodywork and underframe 2
Maintenance - upholstery and carpets 3
Major body damage - repair 5
Minor body damage - repair 4
Nudge bar - removal and refitting 7
Radiator grille - removal and refitting 8
Roll over bar (3-door models) - removal and refitting 30
Seat belt components - removal and refitting 27
Seats - removal and refitting 26
Sliding sunroof - general information 24
Tailgate door - removal and refitting 18
Tailgate lock components - removal and refitting 19
Tailgate window - removal and refitting 16
Tailgate window support struts - removal and refitting 17
Windscreen and fixed window glass - general information 23

Degrees of difficulty

Easy, suitable for novice with little experience	Fairly easy, suitable for beginner with some experience	Fairly difficult, suitable for competent DIY mechanic	Difficult, suitable for experienced DIY mechanic	Very difficult, suitable for expert DIY or professional

Specifications

Torque wrench settings	Nm	lbf ft
Air dam-to-bumper bolts	9	7
Door hinge bolts	37	27
Bumpers:		
Front:		
Bumper bracket-to-chassis rail bolts	130	96
Bumper side extension nuts	16	12
Bumper-to-bumper bracket nuts	16	12
Rear:		
Bumper-to-chassis rail bolts	47	35
Hard top mounting bolts/nuts (3-door models)	26	19
Nudge bar mountings:		
Steel nudge bar-to-chassis rail bolts	50	37
'Soft feel' nudge bar-to-bumper bolts	20	15
'Soft feel' nudge bar-to-chassis bolts	25	18
Roof rail mounting bolts (3-door models)	13	10
Seat belt:		
Height adjuster mounting bolts	20	15
Inertia reel mounting bolts:		
Small bolt	20	15
Large bolt	40	30
Stalk and buckle mounting bolts	40	30
Upper and lower mountings	40	30

Torque wrench settings

	Nm	lbf ft
Seat mountings:		
Front:		
Seat belt rail front bolt (3-door models)	23	17
Seat belt rail rear bolt (3-door models)	57	42
Seat rail front bolts	57	42
Seat rail rear bolts	23	17
Rear:		
3-door models	27	20
5-door models	57	42
Tailgate hinge bolts	34	25

1 General information

The bodyshell is of 3-door or 5-door configuration, constructed of high-strength, low alloy pressed-steel sections. The sections are alloy-galvanized on one or both sides, depending on their position on the vehicle. Most components are welded together, but some use is made of structural adhesives and bolted joints. The complete bodyshell assembly is attached to a separate box-section chassis frame via a series of composite rubber-in-steel mountings.

5-door models are fitted with a two-piece tailgate, comprising drop down or side hinged-tailgate door, with separate lift-up hinged window. 3-door models feature a side hinged tailgate door fitted with removable glass window. The window is secured to the door by means of four knurl-headed bolts. A moulded plastic hard top is used on 3-door models, with an optional soft top being available on later models.

Extensive use is made of plastic materials, mainly in the interior, but also in exterior components. The radiator grille, hard top (3-door models) and various other components are moulded from a synthetic material which is very strong and yet light. Plastic components such as wheel arch liners are fitted to the underside of the vehicle, to improve corrosion resistance.

2 Maintenance - bodywork and underframe

The general condition of a vehicle's bodywork is the one thing that significantly affects its value. Maintenance is easy, but needs to be regular. Neglect, paticularly after minor damage can lead quickly to further deterioration and costly repair bills. It is important also to keep watch on those parts of the vehicle not immediately visible, for instance the underside, inside all the wheel arches, and the lower part of the engine compartment.

The basic maintenance routine for the bodywork is washing - preferably with a lot of water, from a hose. This will remove all the loose solids which may have stuck to the vehicle. It is important to flush these off in such a way as to prevent grit from scratching the finish. The wheel arches and underframe need washing in the same way, to remove any accumulated mud, which will retain moisture and tend to encourage rust. Paradoxically enough, the best time to clean the underframe and wheel arches is in wet weather, when the mud is thoroughly wet and soft. In very wet weather, the underframe is usually cleaned of large accumulations automatically, and this is a good time for inspection.

Periodically, except on vehicles with a wax-based underbody protective coating, it is a good idea to have the whole of the underframe of the vehicle steam-cleaned, engine compartment included, so that a thorough inspection can be carried out to see what minor repairs and renovations are necessary. Steam-cleaning is available at many garages, and is necessary for the removal of the accumulation of oily grime, which sometimes is allowed to become thick in certain areas. If steam-cleaning facilities are not available, there are some excellent grease solvents available which can be brush-applied; the dirt can then be simply hosed off. Note that these methods should not be used on vehicles with wax-based underbody protective coating, or the coating will be removed. Such vehicles should be inspected annually, preferably just prior to Winter, when the underbody should be washed down, and any damage to the wax coating repaired. Ideally, a completely fresh coat should be applied. It would also be worth considering the use of such wax-based protection for injection into door panels, sills, box sections, etc, as an additional safeguard against rust damage, where such protection is not provided by the vehicle manufacturer.

After washing paintwork, wipe off with a chamois leather to give an unspotted clear finish. A coat of clear protective wax polish will give added protection against chemical pollutants in the air. If the paintwork sheen has dulled or oxidised, use a cleaner/polisher combination to restore the brilliance of the shine. This requires a little effort, but such dulling is usually caused because regular washing has been neglected. Care needs to be taken with metallic paintwork, as special non-abrasive cleaner/polisher is required to avoid damage to the finish. Always check that the door and ventilator opening drain holes and pipes are completely clear, so that water can be drained out. Brightwork should be treated in the same way as paintwork. Windscreens and windows can be kept clear of the smeary film which often appears, by the use of proprietary glass cleaner. Never use any form of wax or other body or chromium polish on glass.

3 Maintenance - upholstery and carpets

Mats and carpets should be brushed or vacuum-cleaned regularly, to keep them free of grit. If they are badly stained, remove them from the vehicle for scrubbing or sponging, and make quite sure they are dry before refitting. Seats and interior trim panels can be kept clean by wiping with a damp cloth. If they do become stained (which can be more apparent on light-coloured upholstery), use a little liquid detergent and a soft nail brush to scour the grime out of the grain of the material. Do not forget to keep the headlining clean in the same way as the upholstery. When using liquid cleaners inside the vehicle, do not over-wet the surfaces being cleaned. Excessive damp could get into the seams and padded interior, causing stains, offensive odours or even rot.

> **HAYNES HiNT**
> *If the inside of the vehicle gets wet accidentally, it is worthwhile taking some trouble to dry it out properly, particularly where carpets are involved. Do not leave oil or electric heaters inside the vehicle for this purpose.*

4 Minor body damage - repair

Repairs of minor scratches in bodywork

If the scratch is very superficial, and does not penetrate to the metal of the bodywork, repair is very simple. Lightly rub the area of the scratch with a paintwork renovator, or a very fine cutting paste, to remove loose paint from the scratch, and to clear the surrounding bodywork of wax polish. Rinse the area with clean water.

Apply touch-up paint to the scratch using a fine paint brush; continue to apply fine layers of paint until the surface of the paint in the scratch is level with the surrounding paintwork. Allow the new paint at least two weeks to harden, then blend it into the surrounding paintwork by rubbing the scratch area with a paintwork renovator or a very fine cutting paste. Finally, apply wax polish.

Where the scratch has penetrated right through to the metal of the bodywork, causing the metal to rust, a different repair technique is required. Remove any loose rust from the bottom of the scratch with a penknife, then apply rust-inhibiting paint to prevent the formation of rust in the future. Using a rubber or nylon applicator, fill the scratch with bodystopper paste. If required, this paste can be mixed with cellulose thinners to provide a very thin paste which is ideal for filling narrow scratches. Before the stopper-paste in the scratch hardens, wrap a piece of smooth cotton rag around the top of a finger. Dip the finger in cellulose thinners, and quickly sweep it across the surface of the stopper-paste in the scratch; this will ensure that the surface of the stopper-paste is slightly hollowed. The scratch can now be painted over as described earlier in this Section.

Repairs of dents in bodywork

When deep denting of the vehicle's bodywork has taken place, the first task is to pull the dent out, until the affected bodywork almost attains its original shape. There is little point in trying to restore the original shape completely, as the metal in the damaged area will have stretched on impact, and cannot be reshaped fully to its original contour. It is better to bring the level of the dent up to a point which is about 3 mm below the level of the surrounding bodywork. In cases where the dent is very shallow anyway, it is not worth trying to pull it out at all. If the underside of the dent is accessible, it can be hammered out gently from behind, using a mallet with a wooden or plastic head. Whilst doing this, hold a suitable block of wood firmly against the outside of the panel, to absorb the impact from the hammer blows and thus prevent a large area of the bodywork from being 'belled-out'.

Should the dent be in a section of the bodywork which has a double skin, or some other factor making it inaccessible from behind, a different technique is called for. Drill several small holes through the metal inside the area - particularly in the deeper section. Then screw long self-tapping screws into the holes, just sufficiently for them to gain a good purchase in the metal. Now the dent can be pulled out by pulling on the protruding heads of the screws with a pair of pliers.

The next stage of the repair is the removal of the paint from the damaged area, and from an inch or so of the surrounding 'sound' bodywork. This is accomplished most easily by using a wire brush or abrasive pad on a power drill, although it can be done just as effectively by hand, using sheets of abrasive paper. To complete the preparation for filling, score the surface of the bare metal with a screwdriver or the tang of a file, or alternatively, drill small holes in the affected area. This will provide a really good 'key' for the filler paste.

To complete the repair, see the Section on filling and respraying.

Repairs of rust holes or gashes in bodywork

Remove all paint from the affected area, and from an inch or so of the surrounding 'sound' bodywork, using an abrasive pad or a wire brush on a power drill. If these are not available, a few sheets of abrasive paper will do the job most effectively. With the paint removed, you will be able to judge the severity of the corrosion, and therefore decide whether to renew the whole panel (if this is possible) or to repair the affected area. New body panels are not as expensive as most people think, and it is often quicker and more satisfactory to fit a new panel than to attempt to repair large areas of corrosion.

Remove all fittings from the affected area, except those which will act as a guide to the original shape of the damaged bodywork (eg headlight shells etc). Then, using tin snips or a hacksaw blade, remove all loose metal and any other metal badly affected by corrosion. Hammer the edges of the hole inwards, in order to create a slight depression for the filler paste.

Wire-brush the affected area to remove the powdery rust from the surface of the remaining metal. Paint the affected area with rust-inhibiting paint, if the back of the rusted area is accessible, treat this also.

Before filling can take place, it will be necessary to block the hole in some way. This can be achieved by the use of aluminium or plastic mesh, or aluminium tape.

Aluminium or plastic mesh, or glass-fibre matting, is probably the best material to use for a large hole. Cut a piece to the approximate size and shape of the hole to be filled, then position it in the hole so that its edges are below the level of the surrounding bodywork. It can be retained in position by several blobs of filler paste around its periphery.

Aluminium tape should be used for small or very narrow holes. Pull a piece off the roll, trim it to the approximate size and shape required, then pull off the backing paper (if used) and stick the tape over the hole; it can be overlapped if the thickness of one piece is insufficient. Burnish down the edges of the tape with the handle of a screwdriver or similar, to ensure that the tape is securely attached to the metal underneath.

Bodywork repairs - filling and respraying

Before using this Section, see the Sections on dent, deep scratch, rust holes and gash repairs.

Many types of bodyfiller are available, but generally speaking, those proprietary kits which contain a tin of filler paste and a tube of resin hardener are best for this type of repair. A wide, flexible plastic or nylon applicator will be found invaluable for imparting a smooth and well-contoured finish to the surface of the filler.

Mix up a little filler on a clean piece of card or board - measure the hardener carefully (follow the maker's instructions on the pack), otherwise the filler will set too rapidly or too slowly. Using the applicator, apply the filler paste to the prepared area; draw the applicator across the surface of the filler to achieve the correct contour and to level the surface. As soon as a contour that approximates to the correct one is achieved, stop working the paste - if you carry on too long, the paste will become sticky and begin to 'pick-up' on the applicator. Continue to add thin layers of filler paste at 20-minute intervals, until the level of the filler is just proud of the surrounding bodywork.

Once the filler has hardened, the excess can be removed using a metal plane or file. From then on, progressively-finer grades of abrasive paper should be used, starting with a 40-grade production paper, and finishing with a 400-grade wet-and-dry paper. Always wrap the abrasive paper around a flat rubber, cork, or wooden block - otherwise the surface of the filler will not be completely flat. During the smoothing of the filler surface, the wet-and-dry paper should be periodically rinsed in water. This will ensure that a very smooth finish is imparted to the filler at the final stage.

At this stage, the 'dent' should be surrounded by a ring of bare metal, which in turn should be encircled by the finely 'feathered' edge of the good paintwork. Rinse the repair area with clean water, until all of the dust produced by the rubbing-down operation has gone.

Spray the whole area with a light coat of primer - this will show up any imperfections in the surface of the filler. Repair these imperfections with fresh filler paste or bodystopper, and once more smooth the surface with abrasive paper. Repeat this

12

spray-and-repair procedure until you are satisfied that the surface of the filler, and the feathered edge of the paintwork, are perfect. Clean the repair area with clean water, and allow to dry fully.

HAYNES HINT

If bodystopper is used, it can be mixed with cellulose thinners to form a really thin paste which is ideal for filling small holes.

The repair area is now ready for final spraying. Paint spraying must be carried out in a warm, dry, windless and dust-free atmosphere. This condition can be created artificially if you have access to a large indoor working area, but if you are forced to work in the open, you will have to pick your day very carefully. If you are working indoors, dousing the floor in the work area with water will help to settle the dust which would otherwise be in the atmosphere. If the repair area is confined to one body panel, mask off the surrounding panels; this will help to minimise the effects of a slight mis-match in paint colours. Bodywork fittings (eg chrome strips, door handles etc) will also need to be masked off. Use genuine masking tape, and several thicknesses of newspaper, for the masking operations.

Before commencing to spray, agitate the aerosol can thoroughly, then spray a test area (an old tin, or similar) until the technique is mastered. Cover the repair area with a thick coat of primer; the thickness should be built up using several thin layers of paint, rather than one thick one. Using 400-grade wet-and-dry paper, rub down the surface of the primer until it is really smooth. While doing this, the work area should be thoroughly doused with water, and the wet-and-dry paper periodically rinsed in water. Allow to dry before spraying on more paint.

Spray on the top coat, again building up the thickness by using several thin layers of paint. Start spraying at one edge of the repair area, and then, using a side-to-side motion, work until the whole repair area and about 2 inches of the surrounding original paintwork is covered. Remove all masking material 10 to 15 minutes after spraying on the final coat of paint.

Allow the new paint at least two weeks to harden, then, using a paintwork renovator, or a very fine cutting paste, blend the edges of the paint into the existing paintwork. Finally, apply wax polish.

Plastic components

With the use of more and more plastic body components by the vehicle manufacturers (eg bumpers, spoilers, and in some cases major body panels), rectification of more serious damage to such items has become a matter

of either entrusting repair work to a specialist in this field, or renewing complete components. Repair of such damage by the DIY owner is not really feasible, owing to the cost of the equipment and materials required for effecting such repairs. The basic technique involves making a groove along the line of the crack in the plastic, using a rotary burr in a power drill. The damaged part is then welded back together, using a hot-air gun to heat up and fuse a plastic filler rod into the groove. Any excess plastic is then removed, and the area rubbed down to a smooth finish. It is important that a filler rod of the correct plastic is used, as body components can be made of a variety of different types (eg polycarbonate, ABS, polypropylene).

Damage of a less serious nature (abrasions, minor cracks etc) can be repaired by the DIY owner using a two-part epoxy filler repair material. Once mixed in equal proportions, this is used in similar fashion to the bodywork filler used on metal panels. The filler is usually cured in twenty to thirty minutes, ready for sanding and painting.

If the owner is renewing a complete component himself, or if he has repaired it with epoxy filler, he will be left with the problem of finding a suitable paint for finishing

which is compatible with the type of plastic used. At one time, the use of a universal paint was not possible, owing to the complex range of plastics encountered in body component applications. Standard paints, generally speaking, will not bond to plastic or rubber satisfactorily. However, it is now possible to obtain a plastic body parts finishing kit which consists of a pre-primer treatment, a primer and coloured top coat. Full instructions are normally supplied with a kit, but basically, the method of use is to first apply the pre-primer to the component concerned, and allow it to dry for up to 30 minutes. Then the primer is applied, and left to dry for about an hour before finally applying the special-coloured top coat. The result is a correctly-coloured component, where the paint will flex with the plastic or rubber, a property that standard paint does not normally possess.

5 Major body damage - repair

Where serious damage has occurred, or large areas need renewal due to neglect, it means that complete new panels will need

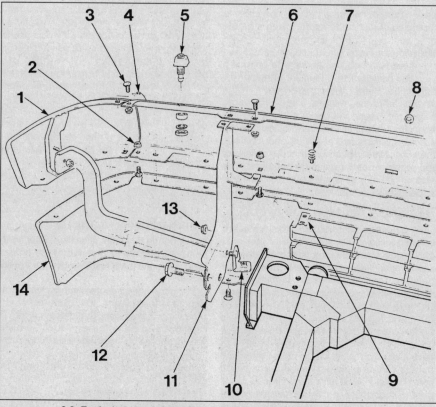

6.3 Exploded view of the front bumper and air dam components

1 *Bumper side extension*	6 *Bumper centre section*	11 *Bumper bracket*
2 *Nut*	7 *Screw*	12 *Bolt*
3 *Bolt*	8 *Nut*	13 *Nut*
4 *Finisher*	9 *Clip*	14 *Air dam*
5 *Headlight washer jet*	10 *Air dam support bracket*	

6.8 Rear bumper bracket-to-rear step mounting nut and bolt - 3-door models

7.6a Prise off the covers over the nudge bar lower mounting bolts . . .

7.6b . . . then undo the mounting bolts each side

welding-in, and this is best left to professionals. If the damage is due to impact, it will also be necessary to check completely the alignment of the bodyshell, and this can only be carried out accurately by a Vauxhall dealer using special jigs. If the body is left misaligned, it is primarily dangerous, as the car will not handle properly, and secondly, uneven stresses will be imposed on the steering, suspension and possibly transmission, causing abnormal wear, or complete failure, particularly to such items as the tyres.

---

6 Bumpers -
removal and refitting

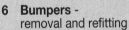

Front bumper and air dam

Removal

1 Where fitted, remove the nudge bar as described in Section 7.
2 On models equipped with headlight washer jets, disconnect the washer hoses from the jets.
3 Undo the two bolts each side securing the bumper brackets to the side of the chassis rails (see illustration). Withdraw the complete bumper and air dam forwards and remove it from the vehicle.
4 With the assembly removed, the individual components can each be unbolted and

removed separately as required. These components comprise the centre bumper, side bumpers, air dam, air grille and bumper brackets. Undo the relevant retaining nuts and bolts and remove the various components as necessary.

Refitting

5 Reassembly and refitting are the reversal of removal, but tighten the attachments to the specified torque.

Rear bumper

Removal (3-door models)

6 From behind the bumper, disconnect the rear light cluster wiring at the harness connector.
7 Undo the two bolts securing the left-hand bumper or right-hand bumper mounting bracket to the chassis rail.
8 Undo the nut and bolt securing the inner end of the bumper to the bracket on the rear step panel, then withdraw the relevant bumper from the vehicle (see illustration). If required, undo the nuts and remove the light cluster from the bumper.
9 To remove the step panel, undo the four bolts securing the panel to the rear of the chassis. Remove the panel and recover the two bumper inner mounting brackets.

Removal (5-door models)

10 Undo the two bolts each side securing the bumper brackets to the side of the chassis rails. Withdraw the bumper from the vehicle.

11 If necessary, the bumper brackets and the bumper side extensions can be unbolted from the bumper and removed separately.

Refitting (all models)

12 Refitting is the reversal of removal, but tighten the attachments to the specified torque.

---

7 Nudge bar -
removal and refitting

Removal

Steel nudge bar

1 Where fitted, disconnect the front fog light or long-range driving light wiring harnesses at the connectors located adjacent to the radiator.
2 Chock the rear wheels then jack up the front of the vehicle and support it on axle stands (see *Jacking and Vehicle Support*).
3 Have an assistant support the nudge bar as the mounting bolts are undone.
4 From under the front of the vehicle, undo the bolts securing the nudge bar lower mountings to the chassis rails each side, noting the position of any spacers that may be fitted. Withdraw the nudge bar and remove it from the front of the vehicle.

'Soft-feel' nudge bar

5 Where fitted, disconnect the front fog light or long-range driving light wiring harnesses at the connectors located adjacent to the radiator.
6 Using a screwdriver, prise off the covers over the lower mounting bolts each side and undo the two bolts (see illustrations).
7 Similarly, prise out the caps over the two upper bolts securing the nudge bar to the front bumper (see illustration).
8 With an assistant supporting the nudge bar, undo the two upper bolts and lift the nudge bar off the front of the vehicle (see illustration).
9 Refitting is the reversal of removal, but tighten the attachments to the specified torque.

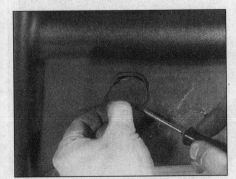

7.7 Prise out the caps over the nudge bar upper mounting bolts . . .

7.8 . . . and remove the two bolts (arrowed)

12

8.2 Undo the screw (arrowed) in the lower centre of the grille panel

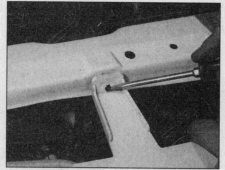

8.3a Push down the tag on the grille plastic retaining clips . . .

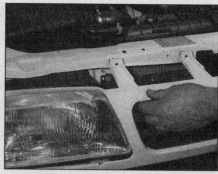

8.3b . . . and remove the grille

8 Radiator grille - removal and refitting

Removal

1 Where fitted, remove the nudge bar as described in Section 7.
2 Undo the screw in the lower centre of the grille panel **(see illustration)**.
3 Using a screwdriver, push down the tag on the upper plastic retaining clips to release the clips from the grille, then withdraw the grille from its location **(see illustrations)**.

Refitting

4 Withdraw the retaining clips from the body panel and refit them to the grille panel, ensuring that the tag on the clip locates fully in the slot on the grille **(see illustrations)**.
5 Locate the grille in position and engage the retaining clips with the openings in the body panel. Push the grille in until the clips lock into place.
6 Refit the centre retaining screw to secure the grille then, where applicable, refit the nudge bar as described in Section 7.

9 Bonnet - removal, refitting and adjustment

Removal

1 Open the bonnet and place a wad of rag underneath each corner of the bonnet to protect against possible damage should the bonnet slip.
2 Disconnect the windscreen washer hose.
3 Using a pencil or felt tip pen, mark the outline of each retaining bolt relative to the bonnet, to use as a guide on refitting.
4 With the aid of an assistant, slacken and remove the left- and right-hand hinge-to-bonnet bolts and carefully remove the bonnet from the vehicle.
5 Inspect the bonnet hinges for signs of wear and free play at the pivots, and if necessary renew; the hinges are secured in position by two bolts.

Refitting and adjustment

6 With the aid of an assistant, engage the bonnet with the hinges. Refit the retaining bolts and tighten them by hand only. Align the

bolts with the marks made on removal, then tighten them securely.
7 Close the bonnet, and check for alignment with the adjacent panels. If necessary, slacken the hinge bolts and re-align the bonnet; the height of the bonnet is altered by moving the rubber stops on the bonnet crossmember. Once the bonnet is correctly aligned, check that the bonnet fastens and releases satisfactorily.

10 Bonnet release cable - removal and refitting

Removal

1 Remove the bonnet lock as described in Section 11.
2 From inside the vehicle, unbolt the bonnet release lever from under the facia. Slide the release outer cable from the lever bracket and the inner cable from the lever.
3 Free the cable from all the necessary retaining clips and ties, then withdraw the cable into the engine compartment and remove it from the vehicle.

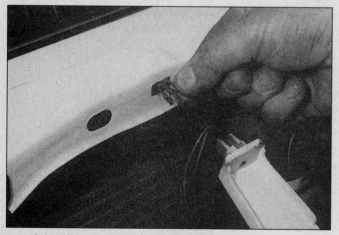

8.4a Withdraw the plastic clips from the body panel . . .

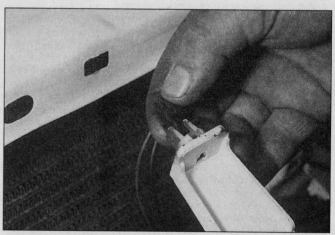

8.4b . . . and refit them to the grille

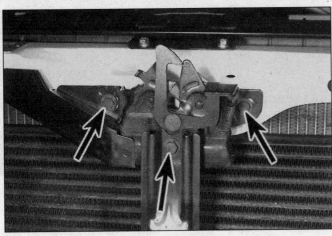

11.2 Bonnet lock mounting bolts (arrowed)

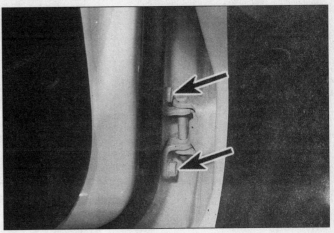

12.6 Door lower hinge retaining bolts (arrowed)

Refitting

4 Refitting is a reversal of removal, ensuring that the cable is correctly routed, and secured to all the relevant retaining clips. Prior to closing the bonnet, operate the release handle and have an assistant check that the lock hook moves easily and smoothly to its stop.

11 Bonnet lock - removal and refitting

Removal

1 Using a suitable marker pen, make alignment marks between the lock and body panel.
2 Undo the three mounting bolts and withdraw the lock from the panel (see illustration).
3 Slide the release outer cable from the lock bracket and the inner cable from the lever then remove the lock.

Refitting

4 Refitting is a reversal of removal, aligning the lock with the marks made prior to removal. Check the lock operation and lubricate it with multi-purpose grease.

12 Doors - removal and refitting

Front door

Removal

1 Disconnect the battery negative lead.
2 Release the front door tread plate on the side being worked on, then peel back the front door weatherstrip to allow removal of the footwell side kick panel. Undo the screw and remove the kick panel from the footwell.
3 From within the footwell side aperture,

disconnect the front door wiring harness at the cable connectors. Release the grommet in the A-pillar and withdraw the harness from the pillar.
4 Using a small punch, tap out the roll pin securing the door check strap to the A-pillar.
5 Using a suitable marker pen, make alignment marks between the door hinges and the door.
6 Have an assistant support the weight of the door then undo the two upper and lower hinge retaining bolts (see illustration). Carefully lift the door off the vehicle and recover the gaskets from behind the hinges.

Refitting

7 Locate the door in position, slide the gaskets behind the hinges and loosely secure the door with the hinge retaining bolts.
8 Reconnect the check strap and tap in the roll pin.
9 Feed the wiring harness into the A-pillar and locate the grommet in the A-pillar hole. Reconnect the harness connectors and refit the kick panel, weatherstrip and tread plate.
10 Align the hinges with the previously made marks and tighten the hinge bolts securely.
11 Close the door and check that it is positioned centrally within the body aperture. If necessary make small adjustments by repositioning the hinges slightly. After adjustment, make sure that the door lock engages correctly with the striker on the B-pillar. If necessary loosen the striker retaining bolts then reposition the striker and tighten the bolts (see illustration).
12 On completion, tighten the hinge retaining bolts to the specified torque and reconnect the battery.

Rear door (5-door models)

Removal

13 On models with electrical components in the door, disconnect the battery negative lead, then remove the front seat belt inertia reel assembly from the B-pillar as described in Section 27. From within the B-pillar aperture,

disconnect the rear door wiring harness at the cable connectors. Release the grommet in the B-pillar and withdraw the harness from the pillar.
14 Using a small punch, tap out the roll pin securing the door check strap to the B-pillar.
15 Using a suitable marker pen, make alignment marks between the door hinges and the door.
16 Have an assistant support the weight of the door then undo the two upper and lower hinge retaining bolts. Carefully lift the door off the vehicle and recover the gaskets from behind the hinges.

Refitting

17 Locate the door in position, slide the gaskets behind the hinges and loosely secure the door with the hinge retaining bolts.
18 Reconnect the check strap and tap in the roll pin.
19 Where applicable, feed the wiring harness into the B-pillar and locate the grommet in the B-pillar hole. Reconnect the harness connectors and refit the seat belt as described in Section 27.
20 Align the hinges with the previously made marks and tighten the hinge bolts securely.
21 Close the door and check that it is positioned centrally within the body aperture. If necessary make small adjustments by repositioning the hinges slightly. After

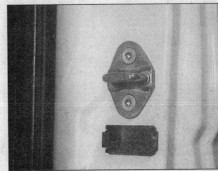

12.11 Door striker retaining bolts

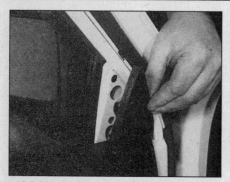

13.2 Unclip the exterior mirror inner trim

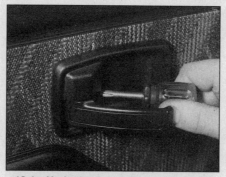

13.4a Undo the door inner handle bezel retaining screw . . .

13.4b . . . and remove the bezel from the handle

adjustment, make sure that the door lock engages correctly with the striker on the body pillar. If necessary loosen the striker retaining bolts then reposition the striker and tighten the bolts **(see illustration 12.11)**.

22 On completion, tighten the hinge retaining bolts to the specified torque and where applicable, reconnect the battery.

13 Door inner trim panel - removal and refitting

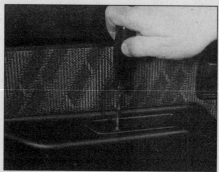
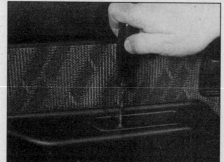

13.5 Undo the screws in the armrest pocket

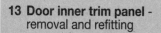

Removal

1 Disconnect the battery negative lead and proceed as described under the relevant sub-heading.

Front door

2 Unclip the exterior mirror inner trim panel from the front of the door **(see illustration)**.
3 On models with manual windows, close the window and note the fitted angle of the handle. Using a piece of cloth rag inserted behind the handle, release the clip then withdraw the handle from the splined shaft.
4 Undo the screw and remove the bezel from around the door inner handle **(see illustrations)**.
5 Where fitted, remove the trim caps from the screws at the base of the armrest pocket then

undo screws and lift the pocket out of position **(see illustration)**.
6 Undo the screw at each side of the door storage bin. On later models, lift up the trim caps to gain access to the screws **(see illustration)**.
7 Undo the two remaining screws at the base of the storage bin **(see illustration)**.
8 Using a wide-bladed screwdriver or trim removal tool, carefully prise the panel clips from the door. Unhook the top of the panel and remove it from the door. On 1997 models onward, disconnect the wiring for the tweeter speaker as the panel is lifted off.
9 For access to the door internal components, undo the trim panel support

13.6 Where fitted lift up the trim caps, then undo the screws at each side of the storage bin

bracket bolts and remove the bracket. Now carefully peel the protective plastic membrane from the door **(see illustrations)**.

Rear door

10 On models with manual windows, close the window and note the fitted angle of the handle. Using a piece of cloth rag inserted behind the handle, release the clip then withdraw the handle from the splined shaft.
11 Undo the screw and remove the bezel from around the door inner handle.
12 Where fitted, remove the trim caps from the screws at the base of the armrest pocket then undo the screws and lift the pocket out of position.

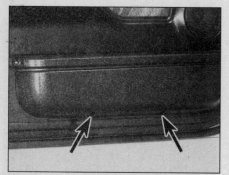

13.7 Undo the remaining screws (arrowed) at the base of the storage bin then remove the trim panel

13.9a For access to the door components, undo the screws (arrowed) and remove the support bracket . . .

13.9b . . . then peel back the plastic membrane

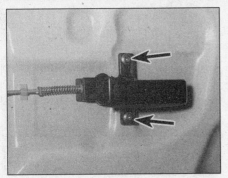

14.2 Door interior handle retaining screws (arrowed)

13 Using a wide-bladed screwdriver or trim removal tool, carefully prise the panel clips from the door. Unhook the top of the panel and remove it from the door. Where applicable, disconnect the wiring for the electric window switches as the panel is lifted off.

14 For access to the door internal components, carefully peel the protective plastic membrane from the door.

Refitting

15 Refitting of the trim panel is the reverse of removal, but where manual windows are fitted, align the window regulator handle as noted during removal.

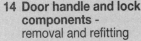

14 Door handle and lock components - removal and refitting

Removal

Door interior handle

1 Remove the door inner trim panel and locally peel back the protective plastic sheeting as described in Section 13.

2 Undo the two screws securing the handle to the door, then detach the handle assembly from the link rod and remove it from the vehicle (see illustration).

Front door exterior handle

3 Remove the door inner trim panel and

14.10 Remove the lock linkage guard

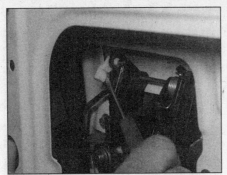

14.4 Prise free the link rod plastic securing clips

locally peel back the protective plastic sheeting as described in Section 13.

4 Using a small screwdriver, prise free the plastic clips securing the link rods to the lock cylinder and exterior handle (see illustration).

5 Using a socket and extension bar inserted through the access hole in door frame, undo the bolt securing the outer end of the handle to the door (see illustration).

6 Undo the remaining bolt securing the inner end of the handle to the door panel (see illustration).

7 Release the link rod ends from the handle and remove the handle from the door (see illustration).

Front door lock cylinder

8 Remove the door inner trim panel and

14.6 . . . and inner retaining bolt (arrowed) . . .

14.11 Undo the screw and remove the lock cylinder

14.5 Undo the door exterior handle outer retaining bolt . . .

locally peel back the protective plastic sheeting as described in Section 13.

9 Using a small screwdriver, prise free the plastic clips securing the link rod to the lock cylinder.

10 Slacken the lock cylinder retaining screw and remove the linkage guard (see illustration).

11 Unscrew the lock cylinder retaining screw, release the link rod end and remove the cylinder from the exterior handle (see illustration).

Front door lock assembly

12 Remove the door inner trim panel and locally peel back the protective plastic sheeting as described in Section 13.

13 Undo the three screws securing the lock assembly to the door (see illustration).

14.7 . . . then remove the handle from the door

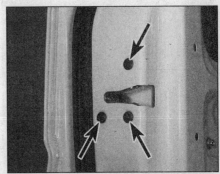

14.13 Undo the front door lock retaining screws (arrowed) . . .

12

14.15 . . . and remove the lock assembly

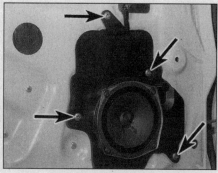

15.2 Loudspeaker housing retaining screws (arrowed)

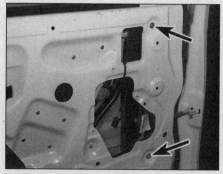

15.3 Window glass front guide channel retaining bolts (arrowed)

14 Lower the lock into the door aperture and prise free the plastic link rod securing clips.

15 Release the link rod ends and remove the lock assembly from the door **(see illustration)**.

Rear door exterior handle

16 Remove the door inner trim panel and locally peel back the protective plastic sheeting as described in Section 13.

17 Using a small screwdriver, prise free the plastic clips securing the link rods to the exterior handle.

18 Undo the two bolts securing the handle to the door.

19 Release the link rod ends from the handle and remove the handle from the door.

Rear door lock assembly

20 Remove the door inner trim panel and locally peel back the protective plastic sheeting as described in Section 13.

21 Undo the three screws securing the lock assembly to the door.

22 Lower the lock into the door aperture and prise free the plastic link rod securing clips.

23 Release the link rod ends and remove the lock assembly from the door.

Refitting

24 Refitting is the reverse of removal, ensuring that all link rods are clipped securely in position.

---

15 Door window glass and regulator -
removal and refitting

Front door window

Removal

1 Remove the inner trim panel and protective plastic sheeting from the door as described in Section 13.

2 Undo the four screws and remove the loudspeaker housing from the door panel **(see illustration)**.

3 Undo the two bolts securing the window glass front vertical guide channel to the door **(see illustration)**. On pre-1994 models also undo the screw securing the top of the channel to the door frame.

4 Carefully prise free and remove the window glass outer weathershield waist seal from the door.

5 Raise or lower the window as necessary until the two bolts securing the bottom of the glass to the regulator lifting channel are accessible through the door apertures **(see illustration)**. Support the glass and undo the two bolts.

6 Manipulate the glass free of the guide channels, tip it down at the front and withdraw it from the top of the door **(see illustration)**.

Refitting

7 Refitting is a reversal of removal.

Front door window regulator

Removal

Note: *The regulator is secured to the door with pop rivets which must be drilled out to allow removal of the regulator. New rivets will be required to secure the regulator when refitting.*

8 Remove the inner trim panel and protective plastic sheeting from the door as described in Section 13.

9 Undo the four bolts and remove the loudspeaker housing from the door panel.

10 Raise or lower the window as necessary until the two bolts securing the bottom of the glass to the regulator lifting channel are accessible through the door apertures **(see illustration 15.5)**.

11 Support the glass and undo the two glass-to-regulator retaining bolts. Raise the glass and tape it to the top of the door frame to hold it in the closed position.

12 Drill the heads off the seven rivets securing the regulator assembly to the door panel **(see illustration)**. Lower the regulator to the bottom of the door and manipulate it out of the door panel aperture. Where electric windows are fitted, disconnect the motor wiring connector when it becomes accessible.

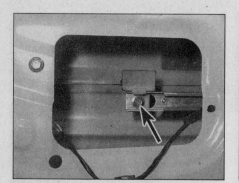

15.5 Window glass positioned to allow access to the lifting channel rear bolt (arrowed)

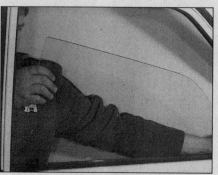

15.6 Removing the front door window glass

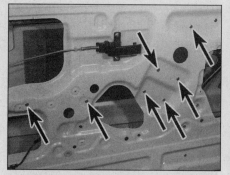

15.12 Front door window regulator securing rivet locations (arrowed)

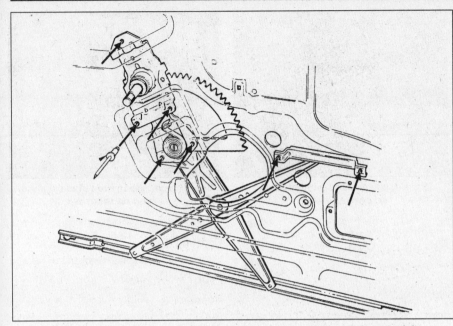

15.27 Rear door window regulator securing rivet locations - 5-door models

Refitting

13 Refitting is a reversal of removal, but use a pop rivet gun and new rivets to secure the regulator to the door.

Rear door fixed window (5-door models)

Removal

14 Remove the inner trim panel and protective plastic sheeting from the door as described in Section 13.

15 Fully lower the rear sliding window.

16 Undo the two upper screws and single lower bolt securing the sliding window rear vertical guide channel to the door.

17 Withdraw the guide channel from the door then carefully ease the fixed window from the door seal to remove.

Refitting

18 Refitting is a reversal of removal.

Rear door sliding window (5-door models)

Removal

19 Remove the rear door fixed window as described previously.

20 Carefully prise free and remove the window glass outer weathershield waist seal from the door.

21 Position the window so that the two bolts securing the base of the glass to the regulator lifting plate are accessible.

22 Undo the two bolts securing the glass to the lifting plate and withdraw the window from the door.

Refitting

23 Refitting is a reversal of removal.

Rear door window regulator (5-door models)

Removal

Note: *The regulator is secured to the door with pop rivets which must be drilled out to allow removal of the regulator. New rivets will be required to secure the regulator when refitting.*

24 Remove the inner trim panel and protective plastic sheeting from the door as described in Section 13.

25 Raise or lower the window as necessary until the two bolts securing the bottom of the glass to the regulator lifting plate are accessible through the door aperture.

26 Support the glass and undo the two glass-to-regulator retaining bolts. Raise the glass and tape it to the top of the door frame to hold it in the closed position.

27 Drill the heads off the seven rivets securing the regulator assembly to the door panel **(see illustration)**. Lower the regulator to the bottom of the door and manipulate it out of the door panel aperture. Where electric windows are fitted, disconnect the motor wiring connector when it becomes accessible.

Refitting

28 Refitting is a reversal of removal, but use a pop rivet gun and new rivets to secure the regulator to the door.

16 Tailgate window - removal and refitting

3-door models

Removal

1 Release the access panel in the tailgate trim and disconnect the wiring connectors located in the aperture **(see illustrations)**.

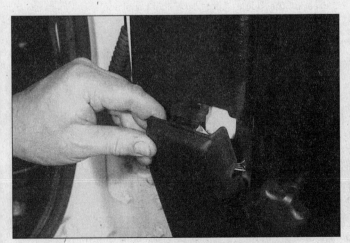

16.1a Release the access panel in the tailgate trim . . .

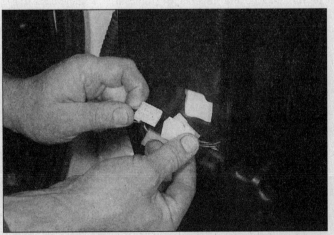

16.1b . . . and disconnect the wiring connectors - 3-door models

2 Undo the four hand bolts and lift the window off the tailgate door (see illustrations).

Refitting

3 Refitting is a reversal of removal, but ensure that the window is fully seated on the waist seal.

5-door models

Removal

4 Open the tailgate window and disconnect the wiring harness at the connectors, and the washer hose at the adaptor on the roof.

5 Undo the two bolts securing the air deflector to the tailgate window (see illustration).

6 Have an assistant support the tailgate, then disconnect the tops of the support struts by prising out the spring clips with a small screwdriver. Lower the struts to the body.

7 Undo the four nuts securing the tailgate window to the hinges. Remove the thrust pads and lift the tailgate window off the hinge studs.

Refitting

8 Refitting is a reversal of removal.

16.2a Undo the four hand bolts . . .

16.2b . . . and lift off the tailgate window -
3-door models

17 Tailgate window support struts - removal and refitting

Removal

1 Open the tailgate window and support it in the open position.

2 Using a small screwdriver, extract the

spring clips securing the lower end of the strut to the ball stud (see illustration). Withdraw the strut from the stud.

3 Similarly release the upper end of the strut from the stud on the tailgate window or from the side of the release wheel assembly. Withdraw the strut from the stud and remove it from the vehicle.

Refitting

4 Refitting is a reversal of removal.

18 Tailgate door - removal and refitting

3-door models

Removal

1 On hardtop models, remove the tailgate window as described in Section 16.

2 Remove the spare wheel from the carrier on the tailgate door.

3 Remove the tailgate inner trim panel as described in Section 28.

4 Disconnect the tailgate wiring harness at the door lock, number plate light and door switch connectors inside the tailgate. Release the cable ties and retaining clips securing the wiring harness, extract the grommet on the side of the tailgate door and withdraw the harness from the door.

5 Undo the bolt securing the tailgate door check link to the bracket on the body.

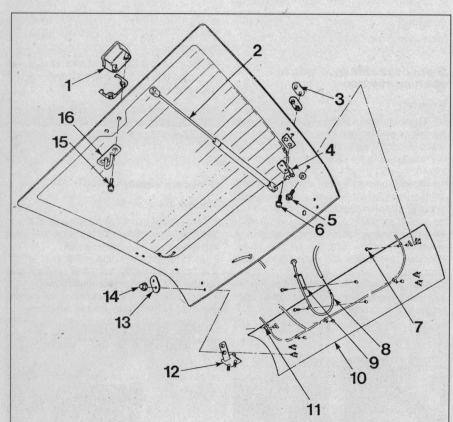

16.5 Exploded view of the tailgate window components - 5-door models

1 Fastener	6 Bolt	11 Clip
2 Support strut	7 Screw	12 Tailgate hinge
3 Support strut fastener	8 Washer nozzle assembly	13 Thrust pad
4 Support strut upper mounting bracket	9 Washer nozzle mounting bracket	14 Nut
5 Bolt	10 Air deflector	15 Screw
		16 Striker

17.2 Extract the spring clip to release the support strut from the ball stud

Recover the spacer washers, noting their locations.

6 Using a suitable marker pen, make alignment marks between the tailgate door hinges and the body.

7 Have an assistant support the weight of the tailgate door then undo the three upper and three lower hinge-to-body retaining bolts **(see illustration)**. Carefully lift the tailgate door off the vehicle and recover the gaskets from behind the hinges.

Refitting

8 Refitting is a reversal of removal, but check that the tailgate door is positioned centrally within the body aperture. If necessary make small adjustments by repositioning the hinges slightly. After adjustment, make sure that the door lock engages correctly with the striker and guide on the rear pillar **(see illustration)**. If necessary loosen the retaining bolts then reposition the striker and guide and tighten the bolts.

5-door models with drop-down tailgate

Removal

9 Remove the tailgate inner trim panel and locally peel back the protective plastic sheeting as described in Section 28.

10 Disconnect the tailgate wiring harness at the wiper motor, lock actuator and door switch connectors inside the tailgate. Release the cable ties and retaining clips securing the wiring harness, extract the grommet from the base of the tailgate and withdraw the harness.

11 Using a suitable marker pen, make alignment marks between the tailgate hinges and the body.

12 Have an assistant support the weight of the tailgate then undo the bolt each side securing the check straps to the tailgate. Recover the spacer collars located between the check strap and tailgate.

13 Undo the two nuts each side securing the tailgate hinges to the studs on the body. Carefully withdraw the tailgate from the vehicle. Note that the tailgate is under considerable tension from the counterbalance torsion bar and it will be necessary to support

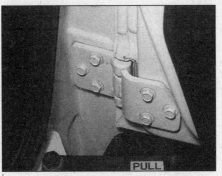

18.7 Tailgate door lower hinge retaining bolts - 3-door models

the hinges which will spring back as the tailgate is removed. With the tailgate removed, recover the gaskets from behind the hinges.

Refitting

14 Refitting is a reversal of removal, but check that the tailgate is positioned centrally within the body aperture. If necessary make small adjustments by repositioning the hinges slightly. After adjustment, make sure that the lock engages correctly with the striker on the rear pillar. If necessary loosen the retaining bolts then reposition the striker and tighten the bolts.

5-door models with side opening tailgate

Removal

15 Undo the four screws and withdraw the left-hand side rear light cluster from the body. Disconnect the wiring at the connector and remove the light cluster.

16 From within the light cluster aperture, disconnect the tailgate wiring at the harness connector. Release the grommet and withdraw the disconnected end of the harness from the body pillar.

17 Undo the bolt securing the tailgate door check link to the bracket on the body. Recover the spacer washers noting their locations.

18 Using a suitable marker pen, make alignment marks between the tailgate door hinges and the body.

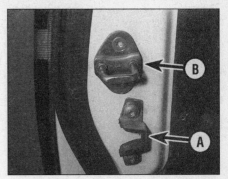

18.8 Tailgate door lock striker (A) and guide (B) - 3-door models

19 Have an assistant support the weight of the tailgate door then undo the three upper and three lower hinge-to-body retaining bolts. Carefully lift the tailgate door off the vehicle and recover the gaskets from behind the hinges.

Refitting

20 Refitting is a reversal of removal, but check that the tailgate door is positioned centrally within the body aperture. If necessary make small adjustments by repositioning the hinges slightly. After adjustment, make sure that the door lock engages correctly with the striker and guide on the rear pillar. If necessary loosen the retaining bolts then reposition the striker and guide and tighten the bolts.

19 Tailgate lock components - removal and refitting

Removal (3-door models)

Exterior handle

1 Remove the covers over the four number plate light hood assembly retaining nuts **(see illustration)**.

2 Undo the four nuts and withdraw the light and hood assembly from the tailgate and position it to one side **(see illustration)**.

3 Undo the two bolts securing the handle assembly to the tailgate **(see illustration)**.

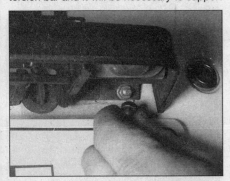

19.1 Remove the covers and undo the number plate light hood retaining nuts - 3-door models

19.2 Undo the nuts and withdraw the hood assembly - 3-door models

19.3 Undo the two bolts (arrowed) . . .

19.4 . . . and remove the tailgate lock exterior handle - 3-door models

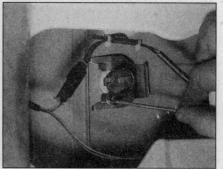

19.8 Prise free the plastic clip and disconnect the lock cylinder link rod - 3-door models

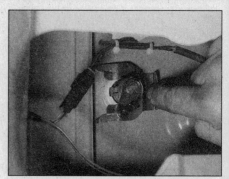

19.9 Extract the horseshoe shaped clip and remove the lock cylinder - 3-door models

4 Manipulate the handle assembly from its location and, where fitted, recover the spacer behind the handle **(see illustration)**.

Lock cylinder

5 On hardtop models, remove the tailgate window as described in Section 16.
6 Remove the spare wheel from the carrier on the tailgate door.
7 Remove the tailgate inner trim panel and locally peel back the protective plastic sheeting as described in Section 28.
8 Using a small screwdriver, prise free the plastic clips securing the link rod to the lock cylinder and release the rod from the lock cylinder lever **(see illustration)**.
9 Slide the horseshoe-shaped retaining clip from the rear of the cylinder then remove the cylinder from the tailgate **(see illustration)**.

Lock assembly

10 Remove the tailgate inner trim panel and locally peel back the protective plastic sheeting as described in Section 28.
11 Undo the three screws securing the lock assembly to the tailgate.
12 Lower the lock into the tailgate aperture and prise free the plastic link rod securing clips. Where applicable, disconnect the wiring at the harness connector.
13 Release the link rod ends and remove the lock assembly from the tailgate **(see illustration)**.

Refitting (3-door models)

Exterior handle

14 Refitting is a reversal of removal, but position the handle to allow approximately 1.5 mm of free play before the handle internal operating lever contacts the lock.

Lock cylinder

15 Refitting is a reversal of removal, ensuring that the link rod is clipped securely in position.

Lock assembly

16 Refitting is a reversal of removal, ensuring that all link rods are clipped securely in position.

Removal (5-door models with drop-down tailgate)

Exterior handle

17 Remove the tailgate inner trim panel and locally peel back the protective plastic sheeting as described in Section 28. Where fitted, undo the bolts and remove the tailgate inner cover panel(s).
18 Using a small screwdriver, prise free the plastic clips securing the link rods to the exterior handle and release the rods from the handle levers.
19 Undo the two retaining bolts and withdraw the handle from the tailgate.

Lock cylinder

20 Remove the tailgate inner trim panel and locally peel back the protective plastic

sheeting as described in Section 28. Where fitted, undo the bolts and remove the tailgate inner cover panel(s).
21 Using a small screwdriver, prise free the plastic clips securing the link rod to the lock cylinder and release the rod from the lock cylinder lever.
22 Slide the horseshoe-shaped retaining clip from the rear of the cylinder then remove the cylinder from the tailgate.

Lock assembly

23 Remove the tailgate inner trim panel and locally peel back the protective plastic sheeting as described in Section 28. Where fitted, undo the bolts and remove the tailgate inner cover panel(s).
24 Undo the three screws securing the lock assembly to the tailgate.
25 Lower the lock into the tailgate aperture and prise free the plastic link rod securing clips. Where applicable, disconnect the wiring at the harness connector.
26 Release the link rod ends and remove the lock assembly from the tailgate.

Refitting (5-door models with drop-down tailgate)

Exterior handle

27 Refitting is a reversal of removal.

Lock cylinder

28 Refitting is a reversal of removal, ensuring that the link rod is clipped securely in position.

Lock assembly

29 Refitting is a reversal of removal, ensuring that all link rods are clipped securely in position.

Removal (5-door models with side opening tailgate)

Exterior handle

30 Remove the tailgate inner trim panel and locally peel back the protective plastic sheeting as described in Section 28. Where fitted, undo the bolts and remove the tailgate inner cover panel(s).
31 Undo the bolt securing the lock cylinder to the rear of the interior handle **(see illustration)**.

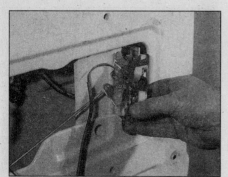

19.13 Removing the tailgate lock assembly - 3-door models

19.31 Tailgate lock cylinder retaining bolt (arrowed) - 5-door models

19.33 Tailgate lock exterior handle retaining bolts - 5-door models

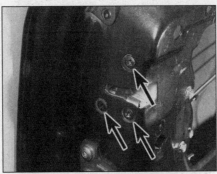

19.38 Tailgate lock retaining screws (arrowed) - 5-door models

19.42a Undo the two screws (arrowed) . . .

32 Using a small screwdriver, prise free the plastic clips securing the link rod to the exterior handle and release the rod from the handle lever.

33 Undo the two bolts securing the exterior handle to the tailgate **(see illustration)**. Push the lock cylinder out of the handle, and remove the handle from the tailgate.

Lock cylinder

34 Remove the tailgate inner trim panel and locally peel back the protective plastic sheeting as described in Section 28. Where fitted, undo the bolts and remove the tailgate inner cover panel(s).

35 Using a small screwdriver, prise free the plastic clip securing the link rod to the lock cylinder and release the rod from the lock cylinder lever.

36 Undo the bolt securing the lock cylinder to the rear of the interior handle and remove the cylinder from inside the tailgate.

Tailgate door lock

37 Remove the tailgate inner trim panel and locally peel back the protective plastic sheeting as described in Section 28. Where fitted, undo the bolts and remove the tailgate inner cover panel(s).

38 Undo the three screws securing the lock assembly to the tailgate **(see illustration)**.

39 Lower the lock into the tailgate aperture and prise free the plastic link rod securing clips.

40 Release the link rod ends and remove the lock assembly from the tailgate.

Tailgate window lock

41 Remove the tailgate inner trim panel and locally peel back the protective plastic sheeting as described in Section 28. Where fitted, undo the bolts and remove the tailgate inner cover panel(s).

42 Undo the two screws securing the lock outer bezel to the lock cover and withdraw the bezel **(see illustrations)**.

43 Undo the two small bolts securing the lock cover to the tailgate **(see illustration)**.

44 Undo the wiper motor mounting bracket upper bolt and slide the lock cover out from under the bracket **(see illustration)**.

45 Prise free the plastic link rod securing

clips and release the link rod ends from the lock levers.

46 Undo the two bolts securing the lock to the tailgate and withdraw the lock through the tailgate aperture **(see illustrations)**.

Tailgate window release button

47 Remove the tailgate inner trim panel and locally peel back the protective plastic sheeting as described in Section 28. Where fitted, undo the bolts and remove the tailgate inner cover panel(s).

48 Slide the horseshoe-shaped retaining clip from the rear of the cylinder.

49 Withdraw the cylinder from its location and detach the operating link from the plastic insert on the release button lever. Remove the release button from the tailgate.

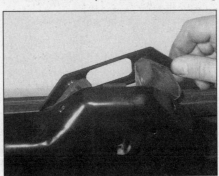

19.42b . . . and remove the tailgate window lock outer bezel - 5-door models

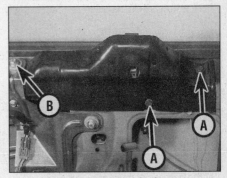

19.43 Undo the two lock cover bolts (A) and wiper motor mounting bracket bolt (B) . . .

19.44 . . . and slide the lock cover out from under the bracket - 5-door models

19.46a Undo the two bolts (arrowed) . . .

19.46b . . . and remove the window lock from the tailgate - 5-door models

12

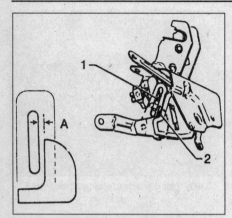

19.54a Tailgate window lock adjustment - 5-door models

1 *Operating bracket slot*
2 *Operating cam*
A = *1.0 to 2.0 mm (clearance between edge of operating cam and bracket slot)*

Refitting (5-door models with side opening tailgate)

Exterior handle

50 Refitting is a reversal of removal.

Lock cylinder

51 Refitting is a reversal of removal, ensuring that the link rod is clipped securely in position.

Lock assembly

52 Refitting is a reversal of removal, ensuring that all link rods are clipped securely in position.

Tailgate window lock

53 Refitting is the reverse of removal, but check the adjustment of the operating mechanism with the lock refitted as follows.
54 Check that the operating cam on the underside of the lock assembly is not obstructing the slot in the adjacent bracket. There should be a clearance of 1.0 to 2.0 mm between the edge of the cam and the side of the slot **(see illustration)**. If adjustment is required, prise free the plastic clip securing the upper lateral link rod to the exterior handle **(see illustration)**. Release the link rod from

19.54b Prise free the clip (A) securing the upper lateral link rod (B) to the exterior handle . . .

the handle lever and screw it in or out of the adjusting collar located at the other end of the rod **(see illustration)**. This has the effect of increasing or decreasing the length of the rod, depending on which way it is turned. Continue this procedure on a trial and error basis until the correct setting is achieved.
55 With the tailgate window in the locked position, adjust the lower lateral link rod until the lever at the rear of the tailgate window release button just touches the end of the release button shaft. Adjust the lower lateral link rod using the same procedure as for the upper rod but note that the adjusting collar is at the opposite end of the rod **(see illustration)**.

Tailgate window release button

56 Refitting is a reversal of removal.

20 Central locking components - removal and refitting

Removal

Door lock motor

1 Remove the door inner trim panel and locally peel back the protective plastic sheeting as described in Section 23.
2 Undo the two bolts securing the motor to the door panel **(see illustration)**.

19.54c . . . then screw the link rod in or out of adjusting collar (arrowed) as necessary - 5-door models

3 Withdraw the motor from its location and prise free the plastic link rod securing clip.
4 Release the link rod end, disconnect the wiring connector and remove the motor from the door **(see illustration)**.

Tailgate lock motor

5 Remove the tailgate inner trim panel and locally peel back the protective plastic sheeting as described in Section 28. Where fitted, undo the bolts and remove the tailgate inner cover panel(s).
6 Undo the two bolts securing the motor to the tailgate.
7 Withdraw the motor from its location and prise free the plastic link rod securing clip.
8 Release the link rod end, disconnect the wiring connector and remove the motor from the tailgate.

Driver's door switch

9 Remove the door lock motor as described previously.
10 Undo the two switch securing bolts, located just below the door lock motor.
11 Withdraw the switch from its location and prise free the plastic link rod securing clip.
12 Release the link rod end, disconnect the wiring connector and remove the switch.

Control unit

13 Release the front door tread plate on the passenger's side then peel back the front

19.55 Adjust lower lateral link rod by screwing in or out of adjusting collar (arrowed)

20.2 Undo the two door lock motor retaining bolts . . .

20.4 . . . and remove the motor from the door

door weatherstrip to allow removal of the footwell side kick panel. Undo the screw and remove the kick panel from the footwell.

14 Disconnect the wiring connector from the front face of the control unit located in the footwell.

15 Undo the mounting bracket bolt and remove the unit.

Refitting

16 Refitting is a reversal of removal.

21 Electric window components - removal and refitting

Removal

Centre console control switch

1 Carefully lever between the rear edge of the switch and the centre console using a small screwdriver.

2 Once the switch releases, withdraw the switch body fully, disconnect the wiring and remove the switch.

Rear door control switch

3 Remove the rear door inner trim panel as described in Section 13.

4 From the rear of the panel, press in the retaining tags on the side of the switch body and remove the switch from the panel.

Window regulator motor

5 Remove the window regulator as described in Section 15.

6 Undo the three retaining nuts and remove the motor from the regulator assembly.

Electronic control unit

7 Undo the screws and lift out the cassette storage box from the rear of the centre console.

8 Lift out the foam pad, then disconnect the two wiring multiplugs from the top of the control unit.

9 Undo the three screws and remove the control unit from the centre console.

Refitting

10 Refitting is a reversal of removal.

22.6 Exterior mirror retaining screws

22 Exterior mirrors and associated components - removal and refitting

Removal

Manually-adjusted mirror

1 Carefully unclip the top of the mirror inner trim panel from the door then free the trim panel and remove it from the door.

2 Undo the three screws and remove the mirror from the door. Recover the rubber seal which is fitted between the door and the mirror; if the seal is damaged it must be renewed.

Electrically-operated mirror

3 Carefully unclip the top of the mirror inner trim panel and remove the panel from the door.

4 Remove the door inner trim panel and locally peel back the protective plastic sheeting as described in Section 13.

5 Disconnect the motor wiring at the harness connector.

6 Undo the three screws and remove the mirror from the door **(see illustration)**. Recover the rubber seal which is fitted between the door and the mirror; if the seal is damaged it must be renewed.

Mirror glass

Note: *The mirror glass is clipped into position.*

22.7 Removing the exterior mirror glass

Removal of the glass is likely to result in breakage if carried out carelessly.

7 Tilt the mirror glass fully downwards and insert a wide plastic or wooden wedge in-between the centre of the mirror glass and the mirror housing **(see illustration)**. Carefully prise the glass from the motor/adjuster; take great care when removing the glass; do not use excessive force as the glass is easily broken.

8 Disconnect the wiring from the mirror heating element and remove the glass **(see illustration)**.

Mirror housing cover

9 Remove the mirror glass as described previously.

10 Using a small screwdriver, release the four retaining tags inside the housing and withdraw the housing cover **(see illustrations)**.

Mirror switch

11 Refer to Chapter 12.

Refitting

12 Refitting is a reversal of removal. When refitting the mirror glass, reconnect the wiring to the glass and clip the glass onto the motor/adjuster, taking great care not to break it. Ensure that the glass is clipped securely into position and adjust as necessary.

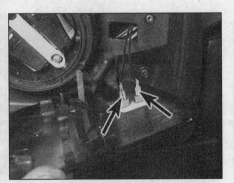

22.8 Mirror glass heating element wiring connectors (arrowed)

22.10a Release the four internal tags . . .

22.10b . . . and remove the mirror housing cover

12

23 Windscreen and fixed window glass - general information

These areas of glass are bonded in position with a special adhesive and require the use of specialist equipment for their removal and refitting. Renewal of such fixed glass is considered beyond the scope of the home mechanic. Owners are strongly advised to have this sort of work carried out by one of the many specialist windscreen fitters.

24 Sliding sunroof - general information

1 Due to the complexity of the sunroof mechanism, considerable expertise is needed to repair, replace or adjust the sunroof components successfully. Removal of the roof first requires the headlining to be removed, which is a complex operation, and not a task to be undertaken lightly. Therefore, any problems with the sunroof should be referred to a Vauxhall dealer.

2 On models with an electric sunroof, if the sunroof motor fails to operate, first check the relevant fuse. If the fault cannot be traced and rectified, the sunroof can be opened and closed manually using a screwdriver to turn the motor spindle. To gain access to the motor spindle, push the driver cover on the console to the rear until the motor spindle is visible. Using a screwdriver, compress the sprung central section of the spindle then rotate the spindle and move the sunroof to the required position.

25 Body exterior fittings - removal and refitting

Wheel arch liners and external plastic panels

Removal and refitting

1 These components are secured in position by a mixture of screws, nuts and retaining clips and removal will be fairly obvious on inspection. Work methodically around the panel removing its retaining screws and releasing its retaining clips until the panel is free and can be removed. Most clips used on the vehicle are simply prised out of position. Other clips can be released by unscrewing/prising out the centre pins and then removing the clip.

2 On refitting, renew any retaining clips that may have been broken on removal, and ensure that the panel is securely retained by all the relevant clips and screws.

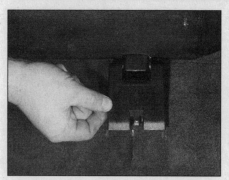

26.6a Remove the rear seat hinge trim covers . . .

Body trim strips and badges

Removal and refitting

3 The various body trim strips and badges are held in position with a special adhesive tape. Removal requires the trim/badge to be heated, to soften the adhesive, and then cut away from the surface. Due to the high risk of damage to the vehicle's paintwork during this operation, it is recommended that this task should be entrusted to a Vauxhall dealer.

26 Seats - removal and refitting

Front seat

Removal

1 On 3-door models, prise off the trim cap and undo the seat belt rail side retaining bolt located at the rear of the belt rail nearest to the centre console. At the front of the same rail, undo the remaining side retaining bolt and collect the washer.

2 On all models, slide the seat fully forward and undo the two inner bolts and single outer bolt securing the seat rails at the rear.

3 Slide the seat rearwards and undo the bolt at the front of each seat rail.

4 Lift the seat up and disconnect the seat heater wiring connectors (where fitted). Remove the seat from the vehicle.

Refitting

5 Refitting is a reversal of removal, but tighten the mounting bolts to the specified torque.

Rear seat (3-door models)

Removal

6 Remove the trim covers and undo the two seat base retaining bolts each side **(see illustrations)**.

7 Release the catches for the seat backrest and the rear of the seat base and remove the seat from the vehicle.

Refitting

8 Refitting is a reversal of removal, but tighten

26.6b . . . for access to the hinge retaining bolts - 3-door models

the mounting bolts to the specified torque. Ensure that the seat base rear catch is fully engaged and the release lever is parallel with the floor.

Rear seat (5-door models)

Removal

9 Fold the rear seat cushion forwards then remove the trim covers over the seat hinges.

10 Undo the hinge retaining bolts and remove the seat from the vehicle **(see illustration)**.

Refitting

11 Refitting is a reversal of removal but tighten the mounting bolts to the specified torque.

27 Seat belt components - removal and refitting

Front seat belt and reel (3-door models)

Removal

1 Remove the rear interior trim panel as described in Section 28.

2 The seat belt upper and lower mountings are detached as part of the interior trim removal procedure, leaving only the inertia reel still in place. Undo the inertia reel upper

26.10 Rear seat hinge retaining bolt - 5-door models

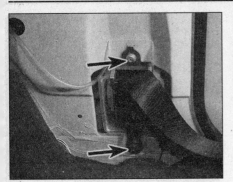

27.2 Front seat belt inertia reel mounting bolts (arrowed) - 3-door models

27.14 Remove the upper cover from the rear trim panel and slide the rear seat belt through the slot - 3-door models

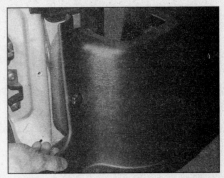

27:15 Remove the side trim detachable rear panel for access to the inertia reel - 3-door models

and lower mounting bolts and withdraw the reel from the B-pillar (see illustration).

Refitting

3 Refitting is a reversal of removal, but tighten the mounting bolts to the specified torque.

Front seat belt and reel (5-door models)

Removal

4 To improve access, remove the relevant front seat as described in Section 26.
5 Remove the trim cover then slacken and remove the seat belt upper mounting bolt at the height adjuster. Collect the spacer from the end of the bolt.
6 Release the tread plates from the door aperture then peel away the door seal weatherstrip from both sides of the B-pillar.
7 Remove the trim cover then slacken and remove the seat belt lower mounting bolt.
8 Unclip the B-pillar trim panel (starting at the top and working down). Release the seat belt access cover from the centre of the B-pillar trim panel and feed the seat belt through the slot in the cover.
9 Undo the inertia reel upper and lower mounting bolts and withdraw the reel from the B-pillar. Remove the seat belt and reel from the vehicle.

Refitting

10 Refitting is a reversal of removal, but tighten the mounting bolts to the specified torque.

Front seat belt stalk (all models)

Removal

11 To improve access, remove the relevant front seat as described in Section 26.
12 Remove the trim cap then undo the bolt securing the stalk to the seat. Remove the bolt noting the arrangement of washers and lift off the stalk.

Refitting

13 Refitting is a reversal of removal, but tighten the mounting bolts to the specified torque.

Rear seat belt and reel (3-door models)

Removal

14 Undo the screw or quick-release knob and lift off the upper cover from the side trim detachable rear panel (see illustration). Slide the seat belt through the slot in the cover and manipulate the cover around the roll over bar to remove.
15 Undo the screws or quick-release knobs

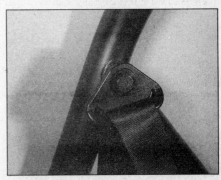

27.16 Remove the rear seat belt upper mounting at the roll over bar - 3-door models . . .

and remove the side trim detachable rear panel (see illustration).
16 Remove the trim cap then slacken and remove the seat belt upper mounting bolt at the roll over bar (see illustration). Collect the spacers from the end of the bolt.
17 Remove the trim cap then slacken and remove the seat belt lower mounting bolt noting the arrangement of washers (see illustration).
18 Undo the bolt securing the inertia reel to the roll over bar and remove the seat belt assembly from the vehicle (see illustration).

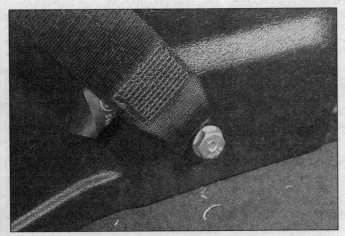

27.17 . . . and the lower mounting from the body - 3-door models

27.18 Undo the inertia reel mounting bolt at the roll over bar - 3-door models

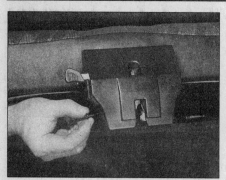

27.19 Undo the screws and remove the rear seat lock cover - 3-door models

19 Undo the screws and remove the cover over the rear seat locking assembly (see illustration).

20 Undo the seat belt buckle mounting bolts, remove the washers and withdraw the seat belts from the rear seat (see illustration).

Refitting

21 Refitting is a reversal of removal, but tighten the mounting bolts to the specified torque.

Rear seat belt and reel (5-door models)

Removal

22 Remove the rear interior trim panel as described in Section 28.

23 The seat belt upper and lower mountings are detached as part of the interior trim removal procedure, leaving only the inertia reel still in place. Undo the inertia reel upper and lower mounting bolts and withdraw the reel from the body aperture.

24 Identify the arrangement of the seat belt buckle mountings then undo the mounting bolts, collect the washers and remove the belt buckles.

Refitting

25 Refitting is a reversal of removal, but tighten the mounting bolts to the specified torque.

28 Interior trim - removal and refitting

1 The interior trim panels are secured using either screws or various types of trim fasteners, usually studs or clips. Removal and refitting is usually self-evident, noting that it may be necessary to remove or loosen surrounding panels to allow a particular panel to be removed. The following paragraphs describe the removal and refitting of the major panels in more detail.

Front footwell side trim panel

Removal

2 Open the front door and release the front of the tread plate.

27.20 Undo the two bolts (arrowed) securing the seat belt buckles to the lock - 3-door models

3 Peel back the weatherstrip sufficiently to allow removal of the footwell side trim panel.

4 Undo the screw and remove the panel from the footwell.

Refitting

5 Refitting is a reversal of removal.

B-pillar trim panel (5-door models)

Removal

6 To improve access, remove the relevant front seat as described in Section 26.

7 Remove the trim cover then slacken and remove the seat belt upper mounting bolt at the height adjuster. Collect the spacer from the end of the bolt.

8 Release the tread plates from the front and rear door apertures sufficiently to allow removal of the B-pillar trim panel.

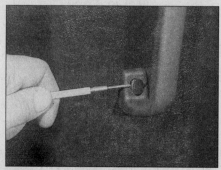

28.17a Prise up the trim caps, undo the two bolts . . .

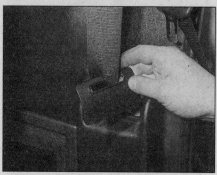

28.18 Release the front seat belt access cover from the trim panel - 3-door models

9 Peel away the door seal weatherstrip from both sides of the B-pillar.

10 Remove the trim cover then slacken and remove the seat belt lower mounting bolt.

11 Unclip the B-pillar trim panel (starting at the top and working down). Release the seat belt access cover from the centre of the trim panel and feed the seat belt through the slot in the cover.

Refitting

12 Refitting is a reversal of removal, but tighten the seat belt mounting bolts to the specified torque.

Rear interior trim panel (3-door models)

Removal

13 On hardtop models, remove the hardtop as described in Section 29.

14 Remove the roll over bar as described in Section 30.

15 Remove the rear seat as described in Section 26.

16 Remove the loudspeaker from the trim panel as described in Chapter 13.

17 Using a screwdriver, prise up the trim caps over the grab handle retaining bolts. Undo the two bolts and remove the grab handle (see illustrations).

18 Release the seat belt access cover from the trim panel and feed the seat belt through the slot in the cover (see illustration).

19 Remove the trim cap then slacken and remove the front seat belt lower mounting bolt (see illustration).

28.17b . . . and remove the grab handle from the rear trim panel - 3-door models

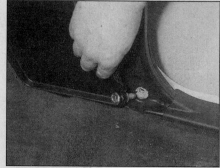

28.19 Undo the front seat belt lower mounting bolt - 3-door models

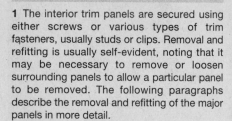

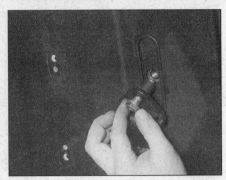

28.20 Undo the front seat belt upper mounting bolt at the height adjuster - 3-door models

28.21a Undo the upper screw securing the trim panel to the body . . .

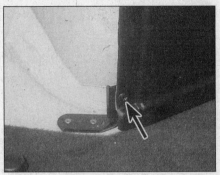

28.21b . . . and the lower screw (arrowed) securing the panel to the floor bracket - 3-door models

20 Remove the trim cap then slacken and remove the seat belt upper mounting bolt at the height adjuster **(see illustration)**. Collect the spacer from the end of the bolt.
21 Undo the upper screw securing the rear of the trim panel to the side of the body and the lower screw securing the panel to the floor bracket **(see illustrations)**.
22 Peel away the door seal weatherstrip from the rear of the front door aperture **(see illustration)**.
23 Pull the panel away from the body, starting at the front and working rearwards, to release the eight retaining clips **(see illustration)**. Remove the panel from the vehicle.

Refitting

24 Refitting is a reversal of removal, but tighten the seat belt mounting bolts to the specified torque.

Rear interior trim panel (5-door models)

Removal

25 Disconnect the battery negative lead.
26 If removing the left-hand side trim panel on vehicles having the spare wheel mounted internally in the luggage compartment, remove the wheel from the mounting bracket. Remove the trim, undo the four bolts and remove the mounting bracket from the vehicle.
27 Remove the rear seat as described in Section 26.

28 Remove the loudspeaker from the trim panel as described in Chapter 13.
29 Using a small screwdriver, carefully press in the end of the rear interior light lens to release the retaining lug. Pivot the lens downward to disengage the lugs at the other end and remove the lens.
30 Undo the two rear interior light retaining screws, withdraw the light from the rear header trim panel and disconnect the wiring.
31 Prise up the trim caps and undo the two rear header trim panel retaining screws. Remove the trim panel.
32 Release the seat belt access cover from the interior trim panel and feed the seat belt through the slot in the cover.
33 Remove the trim cap then slacken and remove the rear seat belt lower mounting bolt.
34 Remove the trim cap then slacken and remove the seat belt upper mounting bolt at the height adjuster. Collect the spacer from the end of the bolt.
35 Undo the screw securing the trim panel to the body.
36 Peel away the door seal weatherstrip from the rear door aperture.
37 Pull the panel away from the body, starting at the front and working rearwards, to release the eight retaining clips. Remove the panel from the vehicle.

Refitting

38 Refitting is a reversal of removal, but

tighten the seat belt mounting bolts to the specified torque.

Tailgate trim panel (3-door models)

Removal

39 Remove the tailgate window as described in Section 16.
40 Using a screwdriver, prise up the trim caps over the tailgate inner handle retaining screws **(see illustration)**. Undo the two screws and remove the inner handle.
41 Starting at the lower left-hand corner, pull the panel away from the tailgate to release the ten retaining clips, then remove the panel **(see illustration)**.

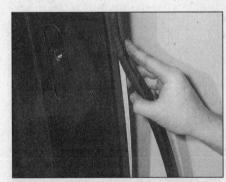

28.22 Peel away the weatherstrip from the door aperture - 3-door models

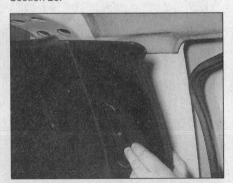

28.23 Pull the panel away from the body to release the clips - 3-door models

28.40 Prise up the trim caps and remove the tailgate handle retaining screws and handle - 3-door models

28.41 Pull the panel away to release the clips - 3-door models

12

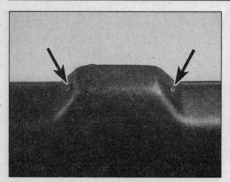

28.43 Tailgate trim panel retaining screws (arrowed) - 5-door models

29.3a Undo the quarter window hand bolt . . .

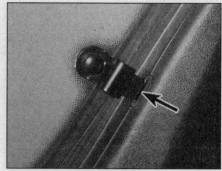

29.3b . . . and disengage the hinges (arrowed) to remove the window - 3-door models

Refitting

42 Refitting is a reversal of removal.

Tailgate trim panel (5-door models)

Removal

43 Undo the two upper screws securing the trim panel to the tailgate **(see illustration)**.
44 Starting at one corner, pull the panel away from the tailgate to release the ten retaining clips, then remove the panel.

Refitting

45 Refitting is a reversal of removal.

Carpets

46 The passenger compartment floor carpet

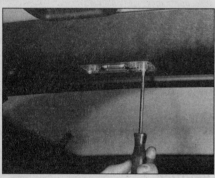

29.6a Undo the interior light retaining screws . . .

is in one piece and is secured at its edges by screws or clips, usually the same fasteners used to secure the various adjoining trim panels.
47 Carpet removal and refitting is reasonably straightforward but very time-consuming because all adjoining trim panels must be removed first, as must components such as the seats, the centre console and seat belt lower anchorages.

Headlining

48 The headlining is screwed and clipped to the roof and can be withdrawn only once all fittings such as the grab handles, sun visors, and related trim panels have been removed and the door, tailgate and sunroof aperture sealing strips have been prised clear.
49 Note that headlining removal requires considerable skill and experience if it is to be carried out without damage and is therefore best entrusted to an expert.

29 Hard top (3-door models) - removal and refitting

Removal

1 Disconnect the battery negative lead.

2 From inside the vehicle, release the four catches securing the detachable roof panel to the hard top. Engage the help of an assistant and lift the roof panel off the hard top.
3 Open the rear quarter windows and lock them in the open position. Undo the hand bolt and release the quarter window latch from the body. Support the window, pivot it outwards and disengage the hinges from their locating slots **(see illustrations)**.
4 On models fitted with roof rails, lift out the cover caps over the four mounting bolts using a small screwdriver. Undo the four bolts each side and remove the roof rails. Recover the spacers, O-rings and sponge seals, noting their arrangement.
5 Using a small screwdriver, carefully press in the end of the centre interior light lens to release the retaining lug. Pivot the lens downward to disengage the lugs at the other end and remove the lens.
6 Undo the two centre interior light retaining screws, withdraw the light from the header trim panel and disconnect the wiring **(see illustrations)**.
7 Undo the remaining screws securing the header trim panel to the roof. Lower the trim panel and, where fitted, disconnect the wiring for the anti-theft alarm sensor **(see illustrations)**.
8 Undo the five nuts now exposed, securing

29.6b . . . withdraw the light and disconnect the wiring - 3-door models

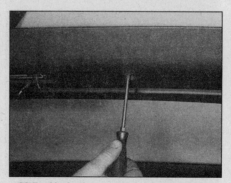

29.7a Undo the screws and remove the header trim panel . . .

29.7b . . . then disconnect the sensor wiring connector - 3-door models

29.8 Undo the nuts (arrowed) securing the hardtop to the roof panel - 3-door models

29.9a Remove the rear vent panels . . .

29.9b . . . and the vapour barriers - 3-door models

29.10 Disconnect the tailgate washer hose - 3-door models

29.13 Lift the hard top up and off the vehicle

b) Feed the washer hose up through the left-hand vent panel aperture in the hard top as it is fitted, and take care not to trap or kink the hose.
c) Tighten the retaining nuts and screws to the specified torque.

30 Roll over bar (3-door models) - removal and refitting

Removal

1 Remove the rear seat belts as described in Section 27.
2 On hard top models, remove the hard top as described in Section 29. On soft top models, remove the side and rear windows.
3 Lift off the detachable covers from the inner trim panels for access to the roll over bar front mountings (see illustration).
4 Undo the four front mounting bolts and three rear mounting bolts each side securing the roll over bar to the floor (see illustrations).
5 With the help of an assistant, lift the roll over bar upwards to clear the trim panel, then remove it from the rear of the vehicle.

Refitting

6 Refitting is a reversal of removal.

the front edge of the hard top to the roof panel (see illustration).
9 Undo the three screws securing the left-hand rear vent panel to the hard top. Lift off the panel and remove the inner plastic vapour barrier (see illustrations). Remove the right-hand rear vent panel in the same way.
10 Disconnect the tailgate washer hose at the connector located in the left-hand rear vent panel aperture (see illustration).
11 Undo the two screws each side located in the rear vent panel apertures securing the hard top to the body. Recover the washers.
12 Peel away the rear quarter window weatherstrip from the body on both sides sufficiently to allow removal of the hard top.
13 With the help of an assistant, lift the rear of the hard top upwards on both sides to

release it from the rubber seal (see illustration). Similarly lift the front of the hard top to release the seal and the five retaining studs from the roof attachment. Lift the hard top to clear the roll over bar and remove it off the rear of the vehicle.
14 With the hard top removed, check the condition of the rubber seals at all the contact areas and renew any that show signs of deterioration.

Refitting

15 Refitting is a reversal of removal, bearing in mind the following points:
a) Ensure that the rubber seals are in position and that the hard top locates squarely and evenly on them as it is lowered into position.

30.3 Lift off the detachable covers from the interior trim panels - 3-door models

30.4a Roll over bar front mounting bolts . . .

30.4b . . . and rear mounting bolts - 3-door models

12

31.10 Unscrew the knobs from the shift levers

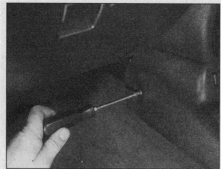

31.13 Undo the screws securing the front console to the facia

31.14 Lift the console up and remove over the shift levers

31 Centre console - removal and refitting

Removal

Note: *A front console is fitted as standard equipment to all models, with a rear console being available as an option.*

Front console - pre-1997 models

1 Disconnect the battery negative lead.
2 If a rear console is fitted, remove the rear console first as described below.
3 Unscrew the knobs from the transmission shift levers.
4 Release the blanking plate from the front of the console and undo the two screws located in the aperture.
5 On models without a rear console, undo the four screws and remove the finisher panel from the rear edge of the console.
6 Undo the screw securing the rear of the console to the floor mounting bracket, and where fitted the additional screw each side securing the front of the console to the facia.
7 Lift the console up at the rear, slide it away from the facia and withdraw it up and off the transmission shift levers.

Front console - 1997 models onward

8 Disconnect the battery negative lead.
9 If a rear console is fitted, remove the rear console first as described below.

10 Unscrew the knobs from the transmission shift levers **(see illustration)**.
11 On models without a rear console, undo the screws and remove the finisher panel from the rear edge of the console.
12 Undo the screw(s) securing the rear of the console to the floor mounting bracket.
13 Undo the screw on each side securing the console to the facia bracket **(see illustration)**.
14 Lift the console up at the rear and slide it away from the facia. Where fitted, disconnect the wiring from the heated seat switches. Withdraw the console up and off the transmission shift levers **(see illustration)**.

Rear console - all models

15 Where electric windows are fitted, carefully lever between the rear edge of the operating switches and the centre console using a small screwdriver. Withdraw the switches fully and disconnect the wiring.
16 Lift up the console lid, undo the screw at the centre rear of the cassette tape storage box and lift out the box **(see illustration)**.
17 Remove the foam insulation from the bottom of the console **(see illustration)**.
18 Undo the two screws and lift off the storage box mounting bracket **(see illustration)**.
19 From the base of the storage box aperture, undo the three console mounting bracket screws **(see illustration)**.
20 Lift off the rubber mat and undo the two screws beneath the mat and the two small screws securing the rear console to the front console **(see illustrations)**.

31.16 Remove the storage box from the rear console . . .

31.17 . . . and lift out the foam insulation

31.18 Remove the storage box mounting bracket

31.19 Undo the three screws (arrowed) in the storage box aperture

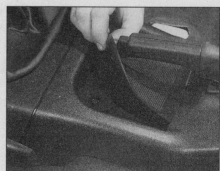

31.20a Lift off the rubber mat . . .

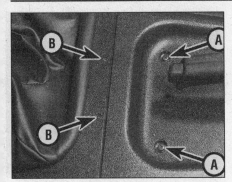

31.20b . . . and undo the two screws (A) and two screws (B)

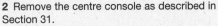

31.21 Lift the rear console up and slide over the handbrake lever

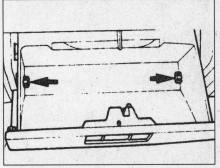

32.7 Extract the glove compartment pivot clips (arrowed) - pre-1997 models

21 Pull the handbrake lever up as far as it will go, lift the console up at the rear, then slide it forward and off the handbrake lever (see illustration).

Refitting

22 Refitting is the reverse of removal, ensuring all wiring is correctly routed and all fasteners are securely tightened.

32 Facia assembly - removal and refitting

Removal

> **HAYNES HINT**
> Attach an identification label to each wiring connector as it is disconnected. The labels can then be used on refitting to help ensure that all wiring is correctly routed through the relevant facia apertures.

Pre-1997 models

1 Disconnect the battery negative lead.

2 Remove the centre console as described in Section 31.
3 Remove the radio/cassette player, facia loudspeakers, clock, and instrument panel as described in Chapter 13.
4 Remove the heater/ventilation control unit as described in Chapter 3.
5 Remove the steering column as described in Chapter 11.
6 Undo the two screws and remove the radio console.
7 Extract the two pivot clips and withdraw the glove compartment from the facia (see illustration).
8 Disconnect the wiring connectors from the heater blower motor and stop light switch.
9 Undo the two nuts and bolts and release the fusebox from the facia (see illustration).
10 Undo the two screws and detach the bonnet release handle from under the facia.
11 Undo the six radio console support retaining bolts.
12 Undo the two facia side retaining bolts and the three upper retaining nuts (see illustration).
13 Disconnect all the remaining wiring block connectors and heater ducts likely to interfere with removal of the facia.

14 Undo the bolt securing the facia to the steering column support bracket.
15 Check that all fastenings have been detached and all wiring released from the relevant connectors and cable ties then carefully withdraw the facia from the bulkhead. Note the routing of the wiring as the facia is withdrawn then remove the assembly from the vehicle.

1997 models onward

16 Disconnect the battery negative lead.

> ⚠ **Warning: On models fitted with an airbag, wait for at least 1 minute after disconnecting the battery to allow the airbag control system capacitor to discharge.**

17 Remove the steering wheel as described in Chapter 11.
18 Undo the two screws securing the bonnet release handle to the trim panel under the facia on the driver's side
19 Undo the six screws securing the driver's side trim panel under the facia and ease the panel from its location. Disconnect the wiring for the headlight range control switch and remove the panel.

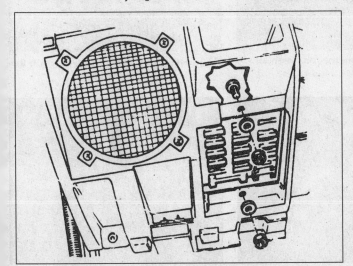

32.9 Undo the two fusebox retaining nuts and bolts - pre-1997 models

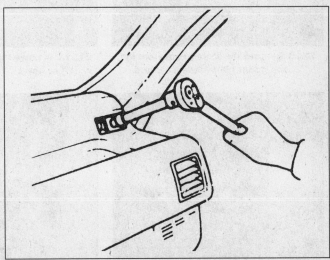

32.12 Undo the retaining bolts on each side of the facia - pre-1997 models

12

32.28a Release the wiring connector . . .

32.28b . . . and remove the reinforcing bracket - 1997 models onward

32.31a Withdraw the ashtray housing . . .

20 Undo the seven screws and remove the steering column upper and lower shrouds.
21 Disconnect the multi-function switch wiring and, where fitted, the airbag wiring at the multiplugs on the steering column and under the facia, as applicable. Cut off any cable ties as necessary to free the harness.
22 Undo the four screws securing the switch assembly to the top of the steering column and remove the switch.
23 Remove the centre console as described in Section 31.
24 Remove the front footwell side trim panels on both sides as described in Section 28.
25 Undo the two screws and remove the glove compartment.
26 On models fitted with a passenger's side

airbag, remove the airbag unit as described in Chapter 13.
27 Remove the radio/cassette player, clock, and instrument panel as described in Chapter 13.
28 Release the wiring connector from the reinforcing bracket on the driver's side, then undo the bolts and remove the reinforcing bracket **(see illustrations)**.
29 Undo the two bolts securing the base of the steering column to the floor.
30 Support the column assembly, then undo the two bolts securing the column to the upper mounting bracket. Lower the column slightly so it is clear of the facia and support it on a suitable block.
31 Undo the screws and withdraw the ashtray housing from the facia. Disconnect

the ashtray illumination and cigarette lighter wiring connectors and remove the housing **(see illustrations)**.
32 Undo the four screws, release the clips and remove the glove compartment upper cover from the facia **(see illustration)**.
33 From the passenger's side of the facia, undo the three screws and remove the lower side cover **(see illustration)**.
34 Disconnect the radio aerial at the in-line connector and the facia wiring harness at the adjacent block connector **(see illustrations)**.
35 Disconnect the heater/ventilation control cables as described in Chapter 3.
36 Using a small screwdriver, carefully lever out the demister vent from the top of the facia on the passenger's side **(see illustration)**.

32.31b . . . and disconnect the wiring connectors - 1997 models onward

32.32 Remove the glove compartment upper cover - 1997 models onward

32.33 Remove the lower side cover on the passenger's side . . .

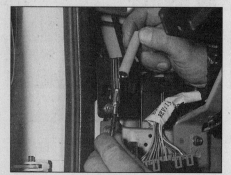

32.34a . . . disconnect the aerial connector . . .

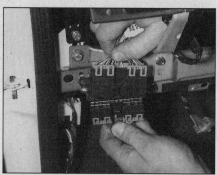

32.34b . . . and the wiring harness block connector - 1997 models onward

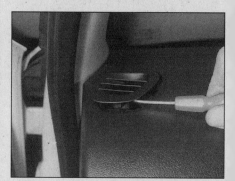

32.36 Lever out the passenger's side demister vent - 1997 models onward

32.37 Undo the screw (arrowed) on each side of the centre reinforcing bracket - 1997 models onward

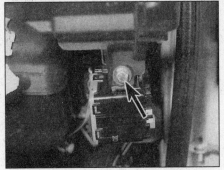

32.38a Undo the bolt (arrowed) above the fusebox . . .

32.38b . . . the nut on the right-hand side of the instrument panel aperture . . .

37 Undo the screw on each side of the centre reinforcing bracket **(see illustration)**.

38 Undo the nuts and bolts at the following locations **(see illustrations)**.

a) *Above the fusebox.*

b) *On both sides of the instrument panel aperture.*

c) *In the passenger's side demister vent aperture.*

39 Undo the two reinforcing bar retaining

bolts under the facia on the passenger's side **(see illustrations)**.

40 From above the heater unit on the passenger's side, undo the bolts securing the facia to the bulkhead cross tube **(see illustration)**.

41 Check that all fastenings have been detached and all wiring released from the relevant connectors and cable ties then carefully withdraw the facia from the bulkhead

(see illustration). Note the routing of the wiring as the facia is withdrawn then remove the assembly from the vehicle.

Refitting

42 Refitting is the reverse of removal, referring to the relevant Chapters where necessary. Ensure that all wiring is correctly routed and all fasteners are securely tightened.

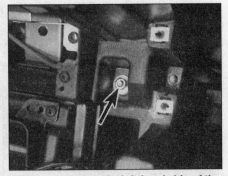

32.38c . . . and on the left-hand side of the aperture . . .

32.38d . . . and the bolt in the demister vent aperture - 1997 models onward

32.39a Undo the reinforcing bar bolt adjacent to the door aperture . . .

32.39b . . . and in the centre of the facia - 1997 models onward

32.40 Undo the bolts (arrowed) securing the facia to the bulkhead cross tube above the heater - 1997 models onward

32.41 Withdraw the facia assembly from the bulkhead - 1997 models onward

12

Notes

Chapter 13
Body electrical system

Contents

Airbag system - general information and precautions 22
Airbag system components - removal and refitting 23
Anti-theft alarm and engine immobiliser - general information 21
Battery - removal and refitting ....See Chapter 5A
Battery check and maintenance ....See Weekly checks
Bulbs (exterior lights) - renewal 5
Bulbs (interior lights) - renewal 6
Clock - removal and refitting 12
Electrical fault finding - general information 2
Exterior light units - removal and refitting 7
Fuses and relays - general information 3
General information and precautions 1
Headlight beam alignment - general information 8
Headlight range control motor - removal and refitting 9
Horn(s) - removal and refitting 13

Instrument panel - removal and refitting 10
Instrument panel components - removal and refitting 11
Loudspeakers - removal and refitting 19
Radio aerial - removal and refitting 20
Radio/cassette player - removal and refitting 18
Reversing light switch - testing, removal and refitting ..See Chapter 7
Stop light switch - removal and refitting ....See Chapter 10
Switches - removal and refitting 4
Tailgate wiper motor - removal and refitting 16
Windscreen wiper blade check and renewal ......See Weekly checks
Windscreen wiper motor and linkage - removal and
  refitting 15
Windscreen/tailgate/headlight washer system
  components - removal and refitting 17
Wiper arm - removal and refitting 14

Degrees of difficulty

Easy, suitable for novice with little experience	**Fairly easy,** suitable for beginner with some experience	**Fairly difficult,** suitable for competent DIY mechanic	**Difficult,** suitable for experienced DIY mechanic	**Very difficult,** suitable for expert DIY or professional

Specifications

System type	12-volt negative earth	
Torque wrench settings	**Nm**	**lbf ft**
Airbag control unit earth lead bolt	8	6
Airbag control unit mounting bolts	10	7
Airbag-to-steering wheel screws	8	6
Passenger's airbag mounting bolts/nuts	8	6

1 General information and precautions

 Warning: Before carrying out any work on the electrical system, read through the precautions given in Safety first! at the beginning of this manual and Chapter 5A.

The electrical system is of the 12-volt negative earth type. Power for the lights and all electrical accessories is supplied by a lead/acid type battery which is charged by the alternator.

This Chapter covers repair and service procedures for the various electrical components not associated with the engine. Information on the battery, alternator and starter motor can be found in Chapter 5A.

It should be noted that prior to working on any component in the electrical system, the battery negative terminal should first be disconnected to prevent the possibility of electrical short circuits and/or fires.

At regular intervals, carefully check the routing of the wiring harnesses, ensuring that they are correctly secured by the clips and cable ties provided so that chafing against other components cannot occur. If evidence is found of a harness chafing against other components, repair the damage and ensure that the harness is secured or protected so that the problem cannot occur again.

Caution: If the radio/cassette player fitted to the vehicle is one with an anti-theft security code, refer to Radio/cassette player anti-theft system - precaution, in the Reference Section of this manual before disconnecting the battery.

13

2 Electrical fault finding - general information

Note: *Refer to the precautions given in Safety first! and in Section 1 of this Chapter before starting work. The following tests relate to testing of the main electrical circuits, and should not be used to test delicate electronic circuits (such as engine management or anti-lock braking systems), particularly where an electronic control unit (ECU) is used.*

General

1 A typical electrical circuit consists of an electrical component, any switches, relays, motors, fuses, fusible links or circuit breakers related to that component, and the wiring and connectors which link the component to both the battery and the chassis. To help to pinpoint a problem in an electrical circuit, wiring diagrams are included at the end of this Manual.

2 Before attempting to diagnose an electrical fault, first study the appropriate wiring diagram to obtain a complete understanding of the components included in the particular circuit concerned. The possible sources of a fault can be narrowed down by noting if other components related to the circuit are operating properly. If several components or circuits fail at one time, the problem is likely to be related to a shared fuse or earth connection.

3 Electrical problems usually stem from simple causes, such as loose or corroded connections, a faulty earth connection, a blown fuse, a melted fusible link, or a faulty relay (refer to Section 3 for details of testing relays). Visually inspect the condition of all fuses, wires and connections in a problem circuit before testing the components. Use the wiring diagrams to determine which terminal connections will need to be checked in order to pinpoint the trouble spot.

4 The basic tools required for electrical fault finding include the following:
a) A circuit tester or voltmeter (a 12-volt bulb with a set of test leads can also be used for certain tests).
b) A self-powered test light (sometimes known as a continuity tester).
c) An ohmmeter (to measure resistance).
d) A battery.
e) A set of test leads.
f) A jumper wire, preferably with a circuit breaker or fuse incorporated, which can be used to bypass suspect wires or electrical components.

Before attempting to locate a problem with test instruments, use the wiring diagram to determine where to make the connections.

5 To find the source of an intermittent wiring fault (usually due to a poor or dirty connection, or damaged wiring insulation), a 'wiggle' test can be performed on the wiring. This involves wiggling the wiring by hand to see if the fault occurs as the wiring is moved. It should be possible to narrow down the source of the fault to a particular section of wiring. This method of testing can be used in conjunction with any of the tests described in the following sub-sections.

6 Apart from problems due to poor connections, two basic types of fault can occur in an electrical circuit - open circuit, or short circuit.

7 Open circuit faults are caused by a break somewhere in the circuit, which prevents current from flowing. An open circuit fault will prevent a component from working, but will not cause the relevant circuit fuse to blow.

8 Short circuit faults are caused by a 'short' somewhere in the circuit, which allows the current flowing in the circuit to 'escape' along an alternative route, usually to earth. Short circuit faults are normally caused by a breakdown in wiring insulation, which allows a feed wire to touch either another wire, or an earthed component such as the bodyshell. A short circuit fault will normally cause the relevant circuit fuse to blow.

9 Before carrying out any electrical fault finding or when carrying out electrical repairs, note the following wire insulation colour-codes.

Black = Earth
Brown = Live
Red = Live - unfused direct from the battery (mid-1995 models onward)
White = Live - fused (mid-1995 models onward)
White = Live - unfused with the ignition on (1997 models onward)

Finding an open circuit

10 To check for an open circuit, connect one lead of a circuit tester or voltmeter to either the negative battery terminal or a known good earth.

11 Connect the other lead to a connector in the circuit being tested, preferably nearest to the battery or fuse.

12 Switch on the circuit, bearing in mind that some circuits are live only when the ignition switch is moved to a particular position.

13 If voltage is present (indicated either by the tester bulb lighting or a voltmeter reading, as applicable), this means that the section of the circuit between the relevant connector and the battery is problem-free.

14 Continue to check the remainder of the circuit in the same fashion.

15 When a point is reached at which no voltage is present, the problem must lie between that point and the previous test point with voltage. Most problems can be traced to a broken, corroded or loose connection.

Finding a short circuit

16 To check for a short circuit, first disconnect the load(s) from the circuit (loads are the components which draw current from a circuit, such as bulbs, motors, heating elements, etc).

17 Remove the relevant fuse from the circuit, and connect a circuit tester or voltmeter to the fuse connections.

18 Switch on the circuit, bearing in mind that some circuits are live only when the ignition switch is moved to a particular position.

19 If voltage is present (indicated either by the tester bulb lighting or a voltmeter reading, as applicable), this means that there is a short circuit.

20 If no voltage is present, but the fuse still blows with the load(s) connected, this indicates an internal fault in the load(s).

Finding an earth fault

21 The battery negative terminal is connected to earth- the metal of the engine/transmission and the car body - and most systems are wired so that they only receive a positive feed, the current returning through the metal of the car body. This means that the component mounting and the body form part of that circuit. Loose or corroded mountings can therefore cause a range of electrical faults, ranging from total failure of a circuit, to a puzzling partial fault. In particular, lights may shine dimly (especially when another circuit sharing the same earth point is in operation), motors (eg, wiper motors or the radiator cooling fan motor) may run slowly, and the operation of one circuit may have an apparently unrelated effect on another. Note that on many vehicles, earth straps are used between certain components, such as the engine/transmission and the body, usually where there is no metal-to-metal contact between components due to flexible rubber mountings, etc.

22 To check whether a component is properly earthed, disconnect the battery and connect one lead of an ohmmeter to a known good earth point. Connect the other lead to the wire or earth connection being tested. The resistance reading should be zero; if not, check the connection as follows.

23 If an earth connection is thought to be faulty, dismantle the connection and clean back to bare metal both the bodyshell and the wire terminal or the component earth connection mating surface. Be careful to remove all traces of dirt and corrosion, then use a knife to trim away any paint, so that a clean metal-to-metal joint is made. On reassembly, tighten the joint fasteners securely; if a wire terminal is being refitted, use serrated washers between the terminal and the bodyshell to ensure a clean and secure connection. When the connection is remade, prevent the onset of corrosion in the future by applying a coat of petroleum jelly or silicone-based grease.

3.3a Facia fusebox cover and fuses - pre-1997 models

3.3b Facia fusebox cover and fuses - 1997 models onward

3.3b Engine compartment fuse/relay box - all models

3 Fuses and relays - general information

Fuses

1 Fuses are designed to break a circuit when a pre-determined current is reached, to protect the components and wiring which could be damaged by excessive current flow. Any excessive current flow will be due to a fault in the circuit, usually a short circuit (see Section 2).

2 The majority of fuses are located in the fusebox situated on the driver's side of the facia with additional fuses being located in the fuse/relay box on the right-hand side of the engine compartment. On later models, one or three additional, higher-rated fuses can be found in the engine compartment, next to the battery. On models with a single fuse next the battery, this fuse protects the ABS electrical circuits. Where three fuses are fitted, the two next to the battery protect the alternator charging circuit and the fuse furthest away from the battery protects the ABS electrical circuits.

3 To gain access to the facia fusebox, open up the cover. To gain access to the fuses in the engine compartment fuse/relay box, simply unclip the cover **(see illustrations)**.

4 The circuits protected by the various fuses and relays are marked on the fusebox cover.

5 To remove a fuse, first switch off the circuit concerned (or the ignition), then pull the fuse out of its terminals. The wire within the fuse should be visible; if the fuse is blown it will be broken or melted.

6 Always renew a fuse with one of an identical rating; never use a fuse with a different rating from the original or substitute anything else. Never renew a fuse more than once without tracing the source of the trouble. The fuse rating is stamped on top of the fuse; note that the fuses are also colour-coded for easy recognition.

7 If a new fuse blows immediately, find the cause before renewing it again; a short to earth as a result of faulty insulation is most likely. Where a fuse protects more than one circuit, try to isolate the defect by switching on each circuit in turn (if possible) until the fuse blows again. Always carry a supply of spare fuses of each relevant rating on the vehicle, a spare of each rating should be clipped into the base of the fusebox.

Relays

8 A relay is an electrically-operated switch, which is used for the following reasons:

a) *A relay can switch a heavy current remotely from the circuit in which the current is flowing, allowing the use of lighter gauge wiring and switch contacts.*

b) *A relay can receive more than one control input, unlike a mechanical switch.*

c) *A relay can have a timer function - for example an intermittent wiper delay.*

9 The majority of relays are located in the engine compartment fusebox, or behind the trim/kick panel in the passenger's side front footwell. Depending on engine, model year, equipment and options fitted, additional individual relays may be located in the engine compartment and in various places around the vehicle.

10 If a circuit or system controlled by a relay develops a fault and the relay is suspect, operate the system; if the relay is functioning it should be possible to hear it click as it is energised. If this is the case the fault lies with the components or wiring of the system. If the relay is not being energised then either the relay is not receiving a main supply or a switching voltage, or the relay itself is faulty. Testing is by the substitution of a known good unit but be careful; some relays are identical in appearance and in operation, others look similar but perform different functions.

11 To renew a relay first ensure that the ignition switch is off. The relay and then simply be pulled out from the socket and the new relay pressed in.

4 Switches - removal and refitting

Note: *Disconnect the battery negative lead before removing any switch, and reconnect the lead after refitting the switch.*

Pre-1997 models

Ignition switch/steering column lock

1 Undo the four screws securing the trim panel under the facia on the driver's side. Pull the upper part of the panel away from the facia to disengage the upper locating lugs and remove the panel **(see illustrations)**.

4.1a Undo the four facia trim panel retaining screws . . .

4.1b . . . and pull the panel away to disengage the upper locating lugs - pre-1997 models

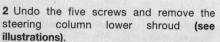

4.2a Undo the five screws . . .

4.2b . . . and remove the steering column lower shroud - pre-1997 models

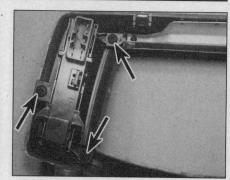

4.17a Undo the three screws (arrowed) . . .

2 Undo the five screws and remove the steering column lower shroud **(see illustrations)**.

3 Remove the steering wheel as described in Chapter 11.

4 Undo the two screws securing the multi-function switch assembly to the top of the steering column and lift the switch off the column.

5 Insert the ignition key and turn it to position I.

6 Using a small screwdriver or pin punch, depress the locking pin through the hole in the front of column, then withdraw the lock cylinder using the key **(see illustration 4.49)**.

7 To refit the lock cylinder, push the assembly into the lock housing, until the locking pin engages, then turn the ignition key to position 0 and withdraw the key.

8 Refit the components removed for access using the reversal of removal.

9 To remove the ignition switch contact plate, remove the lock cylinder as previously described.

10 Disconnect the switch wiring at the harness connector, undo the switch retaining screw and remove the switch from the steering column.

11 Refitting is a reversal of removal.

Steering column multi-function switch assembly

12 Undo the four screws securing the trim panel under the facia on the driver's side. Pull the upper part of the panel away from the facia to disengage the upper locating lugs and remove the panel.

13 Undo the five screws and remove the steering column lower shroud.

14 Remove the steering wheel as described in Chapter 11.

15 Disconnect the switch wiring at the harness connector, undo the two screws securing the switch assembly to the top of the steering column and lift the switch off the column.

16 Refitting is a reversal of removal.

Instrument panel pushbutton switches

17 Remove the instrument panel cover as described in Section 10. Undo the three screws securing the switch assembly to the instrument panel cover and remove the assembly from the cover **(see illustrations)**.

18 Refitting is a reversal of removal.

Facia switches

19 Using a small screwdriver, carefully prise the relevant switch from its location in the facia **(see illustration)**. Withdraw the switch fully, disconnect the wiring plug and remove the switch.

20 To refit, connect the wiring plug and push the switch fully into position until the retaining lugs engage.

Heater blower motor switch

21 Refer to Chapter 3.

4.17b . . . and remove the switch assembly from the instrument panel cover - pre-1997 models

Stop light switch

22 Refer to Chapter 10.

Electrically-operated window switches

23 To remove the switches located in the centre console, carefully lever between the rear edge of the switch and the centre console using a small screwdriver **(see illustration)**.

24 Once the switch releases, withdraw the switch body fully, disconnect the wiring and remove the switch **(see illustration)**.

25 To refit, connect the wiring plug and push the switch fully into position until the retaining lugs engage.

4.19 Using a small screwdriver, carefully prise out the facia switches - pre-1997 models

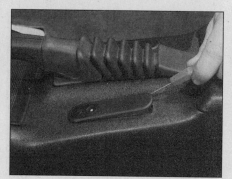

4.23 Lift up the centre console switches at the rear . . .

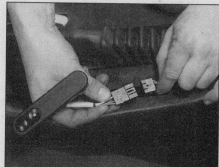

4.24 . . . then withdraw the switch and disconnect the wiring - pre-1997 models

4.41 Undo the two screws and release the bonnet release handle - 1997 models onward

4.42 Undo the six screws and remove the facia trim panel - 1997 models onward

4.43 Remove the steering column upper and lower shrouds - 1997 models onward

26 To remove the switches located in the rear door trim panels (4-door models), remove the trim panel as described in Chapter 12.

27 From the rear of the panel, press in the retaining tags on the side of the switch body and remove the switch from the panel.

28 Refitting is a reversal of removal.

Handbrake 'on' warning light switch

29 Where fitted, remove the centre console as described in Chapter 12.

30 Undo the four screws and remove the handbrake lever rubber boot retaining plate. Lift the boot up and off the handbrake lever.

31 Undo the two mounting bolts and withdraw the handbrake lever from its location.

32 Undo the nut securing the switch to the handbrake lever, disconnect the wiring connector and remove the switch.

33 Refitting is a reversal of removal.

Courtesy light switch

34 Undo the retaining screw and ease the switch out from the door pillar. Disconnect the wiring connector and tie a piece of string to the wiring to prevent it falling back into the door pillar.

35 Refitting is a reversal of removal.

Horn push pad switch

36 Undo the screw securing the base of the horn push pad to the steering wheel lower spoke.

37 Withdraw the push pad in an upward direction to release the two upper retaining clips from the top of the steering wheel.

38 Lift off the push pad and disconnect the wiring connector.

39 Refitting is a reversal of removal, but ensure that the two upper clips fully engage with the steering wheel.

1997 models onward

Steering column multi-function switch assembly

40 Remove the steering wheel as described in Chapter 11.

41 Undo the two screws securing the bonnet release handle to the trim panel under the facia on the driver's side (see illustration).

42 Undo the six screws securing the driver's side trim panel under the facia and ease the panel from its location (see illustration). Disconnect the wiring for the headlight range control switch and remove the panel.

43 Undo the seven screws and remove the steering column upper and lower shrouds (see illustration).

44 Disconnect the multi-function switch wiring, and where fitted, the airbag wiring at the multiplugs on the steering column and under the facia as applicable. Cut off any cable ties as necessary to free the harness.

45 Undo the four screws securing the switch assembly to the top of the steering

column and remove the switch (see illustrations).

46 Refitting is a reversal of removal, but ensure that the wiring harness is secured to the steering column with new cable ties where necessary.

Ignition switch/steering column lock

47 Remove the steering column multi-function switch assembly as described previously.

48 Insert the ignition key and turn it to position I.

49 Using a small screwdriver or pin punch, depress the locking pin through the hole in the front of column, then withdraw the lock cylinder using the key (see illustration).

50 To refit the lock cylinder, push the assembly into the lock housing, until the locking pin engages, then turn the ignition key to position 0 and withdraw the key.

51 Refit the components removed for access using the reversal of removal.

52 To remove the ignition switch contact plate, remove the lock cylinder as previously described.

53 Disconnect the switch wiring at the harness connector, undo the switch retaining screw and remove the switch from the steering column.

54 Refitting is a reversal of removal.

Headlight and fog light switches

55 Using a small screwdriver, carefully lever

4.45a Undo the four multi-function switch retaining screws . . .

4.45b . . . and withdraw the switch from the steering column - 1997 models onward

4.49 Depress the locking pin to remove the lock cylinder - 1997 models onward

13

4.55 Carefully prise free the headlight/foglight switch panel

4.56 Withdraw the switch panel and disconnect the wiring - 1997 models onward

4.59a Using a small screwdriver, carefully prise out the facia switches . . .

the headlight/fog light switch bezel from the instrument panel cover (see illustration).

56 Once the bezel releases, withdraw the assembly fully and disconnect the switch wiring multiplugs (see illustration).

57 To remove the switches from the bezel, depress the retaining lugs on the side of the switch body and remove the relevant switch.

58 Refitting is a reversal of removal.

Facia pushbutton switches

59 Using a small screwdriver, carefully prise the relevant switch from its location in the facia. Withdraw the switch fully, disconnect the wiring plug and remove the switch (see illustrations).

60 To refit, connect the wiring plug and push the switch fully into position until the retaining lugs engage.

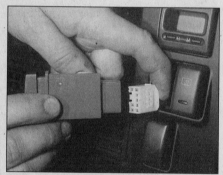

4.59b . . . then disconnect the wiring and remove the switch - 1997 models onward

Headlight range control switch

61 Using a small screwdriver, carefully lever the range control switch bezel from the facia (see illustration).

62 Pull the knob off the switch, then depress the clips and push the switch out of the bezel.

63 Refitting is a reversal of removal.

Heater blower motor switch

64 Refer to Chapter 3.

Stop light switch

65 Refer to Chapter 10.

Electrically-operated window switches

66 To remove the switches located in the centre console, carefully lever between the rear edge of the switch and the centre console using a small screwdriver (see illustration 4.23).

67 Once the switch releases, withdraw the switch body fully, disconnect the wiring and remove the switch.

68 Refitting is a reversal of removal.

Handbrake 'on' warning light switch

69 Remove the centre console as described in Chapter 12.

70 Undo the four screws and remove the handbrake lever rubber boot retaining plate. Lift the boot up and off the handbrake lever.

71 Undo the two mounting bolts and withdraw the handbrake lever from its location.

72 Undo the nut securing the switch to the handbrake lever, disconnect the wiring connector and remove the switch.

73 Refitting is a reversal of removal.

Courtesy light switch

74 Undo the retaining screw and ease the switch out from the door pillar. Disconnect the wiring connector and tie a piece of string to the wiring to prevent it falling back into the door pillar.

75 Refitting is a reversal of removal.

Horn push switches

76 On models without an airbag, undo the screw at the base of the steering wheel then prise free the centre trim pad.

77 On models with an airbag, remove the airbag from the steering wheel as described in Section 23.

78 Undo the screw securing the switch bracket to the steering wheel frame, disconnect the wiring connector and remove the switch (see illustrations).

79 Refitting is a reversal of removal. On models with an airbag, refit the airbag unit as described in Section 23.

Heated seat switches

80 Remove the centre console as described in Chapter 12.

81 Depress the clips on the switch body and push the switch out of the centre console front section.

82 Refitting is a reversal of removal.

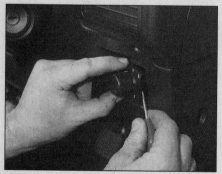

4.61 Removing the headlight range control switch - 1997 models onward

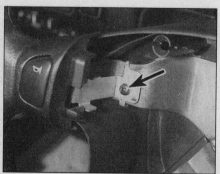

4.78a Undo the horn switch bracket retaining screw (arrowed) . . .

4.78b . . . disconnect the wiring and remove the switch - 1997 models onward

5 Bulbs (exterior lights) - renewal

1 Whenever a bulb is renewed, note the following points.

a) *Remember that if the light has just been in use the bulb may be extremely hot.*

b) *Always check the bulb contacts and holder, ensuring that there is clean metal-to-metal contact between the bulb and its live(s) and earth. Clean off any corrosion or dirt before fitting a new bulb.*

c) *Always ensure that the new bulb is of the correct rating and that it is completely clean before fitting it; this applies particularly to headlight/foglight bulbs (see below).*

Headlight

2 Disconnect the wiring connector from the rear of the bulb and remove the rubber dust cover **(see illustrations)**.

3 If the bulb is secured by a plastic retaining ring, turn the ring anti-clockwise and remove it from the light unit. If the bulb is secured by a spring clip, unhook and release the ends of the clip and release it from the rear of the light unit **(see illustration)**.

4 Carefully withdraw the bulb from the light unit **(see illustration)**.

5 When handling the new bulb, use a tissue or clean cloth to avoid touching the glass with the fingers; moisture and grease from the skin can cause blackening and rapid failure of this type of bulb. If the glass is accidentally touched, wipe it clean using methylated spirit.

6 Install the new bulb, ensuring that its locating tabs are correctly located in the light cutouts, and secure it in position with the retaining ring or clip.

7 Reconnect the dust cover, and reconnect the wiring connector making sure it is securely fitted.

Front sidelight

8 The sidelight bulbholder is located in the base of the headlight unit.

9 Rotate the sidelight bulbholder and release

5.2a Disconnect the headlight wiring connector . . .

5.2b . . . and remove the dust cover

5.3 Release the headlight bulb retaining clip

5.4 Carefully withdraw the bulb from the light unit

it from the headlight unit. The bulb is of the capless (push-fit) type and can be removed by simply pulling it out of the bulbholder **(see illustrations)**.

10 Refitting is a reversal of removal.

Front direction indicator

11 Undo the three screws securing the direction indicator light unit to the front wing **(see illustration)**.

12 Withdraw the light unit, rotate the bulbholder anti-clockwise and remove it from the base of the light unit. The bulb is a bayonet fit in the holder and can be removed by pressing it and twisting in an anti-clockwise direction.

13 Refitting is a reversal of removal.

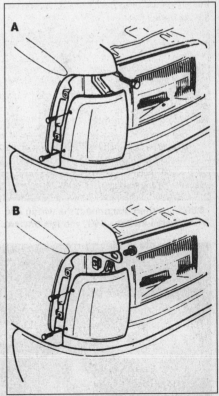

5.11 Front direction indicator retaining screw locations

A Early type light unit   B Later type light unit

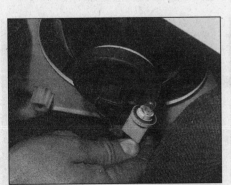

5.9a Release the sidelight bulbholder from the headlight . . .

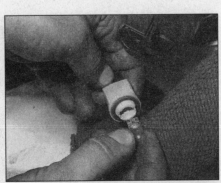

5.9b . . . then pull out the capless bulb

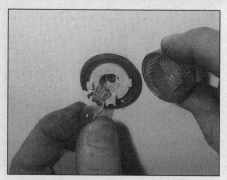

5.14 Removing the front direction indicator side repeater bulb

5.24 Undo the four screws and remove the body-mounted rear light cluster lens

5.25 Press and turn the relevant bulb to remove

Front direction indicator side repeater

14 Remove the side repeater lens by pushing it in and turning anti-clockwise. The bulb is of the capless (push-fit) type and can be removed by simply pulling it out of the bulbholder (see illustration).

15 Refitting is a reversal of removal.

Long-range driving light

16 Support the lens unit then undo the screw and remove the clamp plate at the base of the lens. Withdraw the lens unit from the light body.

17 Unhook and release the ends of the bulb retaining clip and release it from the rear of the lens unit. Disconnect the wiring connector and withdraw the bulb.

18 When handling the new bulb, use a tissue or clean cloth to avoid touching the glass with the fingers; moisture and grease from the skin can cause blackening and rapid failure of this type of bulb. If the glass is accidentally touched, wipe it clean using methylated spirit.

19 Install the new bulb, ensuring that its locating tabs are correctly located in the lens cutouts, and secure it in position with the retaining clip. Reconnect the bulb wiring.

20 Locate the lens unit in the light body and secure with the clamp plate and screw.

Front foglight

21 Undo the two screws, recover the

retaining plates and remove the lens unit from the light body.

22 Renew the bulb using the same procedure as described previously for long-range driving lights.

23 With the new bulb in place, locate the lens unit in the light body and secure with the screws and retaining plates.

Body-mounted rear light cluster

24 Undo the four screws and remove the lens from the light unit (see illustration).

25 All bulbs have bayonet fittings. The relevant bulb can be removed by pressing in and rotating anti-clockwise (see illustration).

26 Refitting is a reversal of removal.

Bumper-mounted rear light cluster

27 Undo the two screws and remove the lens from the light unit.

28 All bulbs have bayonet fittings. The relevant bulb can be removed by pressing in and rotating anti-clockwise (see illustration).

29 Refitting is a reversal of removal.

Number plate light

30 Undo the two screws and withdraw the lens. The bulb is of the capless (push-fit) type and can be removed by simply pulling it out of the bulbholder.

31 Refitting is a reversal of removal.

6 Bulbs (interior lights) - renewal

1 Whenever a bulb is renewed, note the following points.

a) Remember that if the light has just been in use the bulb may be extremely hot.
b) Always check the bulb contacts and holder, ensuring that there is clean metal-to-metal contact between the bulb and its live(s) and earth. Clean off any corrosion or dirt before fitting a new bulb.
c) Always ensure that the new bulb is of the correct rating and that it is completely clean before fitting.

Front interior light

2 Close the front doors so that the light is not live then using a small screwdriver, carefully prise the lens from the light unit.

3 Remove the courtesy light bulb by pressing it sideways towards the spring clips and withdraw the bulb. Remove the reading light bulbs by pulling them from their holders.

4 Refitting is the reverse of removal.

Centre and rear interior light

5 Using a small screwdriver, carefully press in the end of the lens to release the retaining lug. Pivot the lens downward to disengage the lugs at the other end and remove the lens (see illustrations).

5.28 Bulb removal from the bumper-mounted rear light cluster

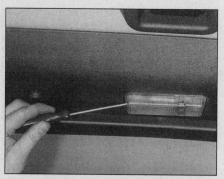

6.5a Release the lug at the end of the interior light lens using a screwdriver . . .

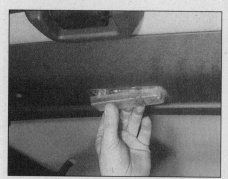

6.5b . . . pivot the lens down and lift off

6.9a Twist the instrument panel bulbholders to remove . . .

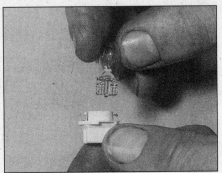

6.9b . . . then, where possible, pull the capless bulbs from the holders

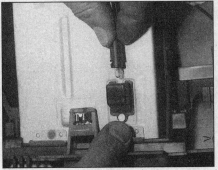

6.12a Remove the ashtray illumination bulbholder . . .

6 Push the bulb sideways towards the spring clips and remove the bulb.

7 Fit the new bulb, engage the lugs at one end of the lens with the light body and push the other end into place.

Instrument panel illumination/warning lights

8 Remove the instrument panel as described in Section 10.

9 Twist the relevant bulbholder anti-clockwise and withdraw it from the rear of the panel, then where possible remove the bulb from the bulbholder **(see illustrations)**. Note that some bulbs cannot be removed from their bulbholders. Be very careful to ensure that the new bulbs are of the correct rating, the same as those removed; this is especially important in the case of the ignition/battery charging warning light.

10 Refit the bulbholder to the rear of the instrument panel then refit the instrument panel as described in Section 10.

Cigarette lighter and ashtray illumination

11 Access to these bulbs is a complicated operation entailing the removal of most of the facia and surrounding panels. Refer to the facia removal and refitting procedures

contained in Chapter 12 to gain access to the rear of the cigarette lighter and ashtray mounting panels.

12 Once access is gained, the ashtray illumination bulbholder can be withdrawn from the ashtray frame. The bulb is of the capless (push-fit) type and can be removed by simply pulling it out of the bulbholder **(see illustrations)**.

13 The cigarette lighter illumination bulb can be renewed by releasing the bulb hood from the lighter body then withdrawing the bulbholder from the hood. The bayonet fitting bulb can be removed by pressing in and rotating anti-clockwise **(see illustrations)**.

14 Fit the new bulb(s) and bulbholders to their locations, then refit the facia components as described in Chapter 12.

Switch illumination bulbs

15 All of the switches are fitted with illuminating bulbs; some are also fitted with a bulb to show when the circuit concerned is operating. On some switches, these bulbs can be removed by simply twisting the bulbholder through 90° once access has been gained to the rear of the switch. However, on some switches, it will be found that the bulbs are an integral part of the switch assembly and cannot be obtained separately. Bulb replacement will therefore require the renewal of the complete switch assembly.

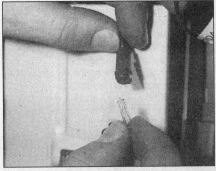

6.12b . . . and withdraw the capless bulb from the holder

7 Exterior light units - removal and refitting

Headlight

1 Switch on the headlights, set the headlight range control switch to the 0 position then switch the headlights off.

2 Disconnect the battery negative lead. Note that for improved access it is beneficial to remove the battery completely if working on the left-hand headlight, and to remove the air cleaner assembly if working on the right-hand headlight. Refer to Chapters 5A and 4A or 4B

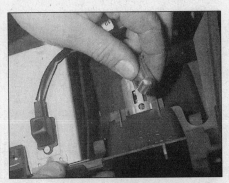

6.13a Release the cigarette lighter bulb hood from the lighter body . . .

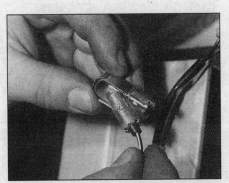

6.13b . . . withdraw the bulbholder from the hood . . .

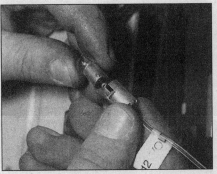

6.13c . . . and remove the bulb from the holder

13

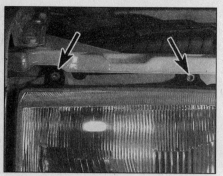

7.6 Undo the two bolts (arrowed) securing the headlight mounting frame to the body panel

7.7 Pull the headlight and mounting frame outwards to release the two lower lugs

Body-mounted rear light cluster

21 Undo the four screws and remove the lens from the light unit.
22 Withdraw the light unit from the body and disconnect the wiring connector at the rear of the unit.
23 Refitting is a reversal of removal.

Bumper-mounted rear light cluster

24 Working behind the rear bumper, undo the two nuts securing the light cluster to the bumper.
25 Withdraw the light cluster from its location, disconnect the wiring connector and remove the cluster.
26 Refitting is a reversal of removal.

Number plate light

27 Undo the two screws and withdraw the light unit from its location.
28 Pull the wiring out through the entry hole in the tailgate until the connector is accessible then disconnect the wiring connector and remove the light unit.
29 Refitting is a reversal of removal.

for battery and air cleaner removal procedures.
3 Remove the radiator grille as described in Chapter 12.
4 Remove the headlight range control motor as described in Section 9.
5 Disconnect the wiring connectors at the headlight and sidelight bulbs.
6 Undo the two bolts securing the top of the headlight mounting frame to the front body panel (see illustration).
7 Pull the headlight and mounting frame outwards to release the two lower lugs on the frame from the retaining sockets, then remove the headlight and frame assembly from the vehicle (see illustration).
8 To remove the frame, pull the headlight adjusters out of their locating sockets and lift off the frame (see illustration).
9 Refitting is a reversal of removal, but ensure that the two lugs on the headlight frame engage fully with the retaining sockets on the body panel. On completion, have the headlight beam alignment checked at the earliest opportunity.

Front direction indicator light

10 Undo the three screws securing the direction indicator light unit to the front wing (see illustration 5.11).
11 Withdraw the light unit, rotate the bulbholder anti-clockwise and remove it from the base of the light unit.
12 Refitting is a reversal of removal.

Front direction indicator side repeater

13 Chock the rear wheels then jack up the front of the vehicle and support it on axle stands (see *Jacking and Vehicle Support*). Remove the relevant front roadwheel.
14 Release the plastic fasteners and remove the wheel arch liner in the area of the side repeater.
15 Trace the side repeater wiring harness back to the connector in the engine compartment and disconnect the wiring connector.
16 Depress the retaining tags on the side repeater body and push the unit out from its location in the wing.
17 Refitting is a reversal of removal.

Long-range driving light and front foglight

18 On vehicles equipped with a 'soft-feel' nudge bar, remove the nudge bar as described in Chapter 12. From the rear of the nudge bar, unscrew the retaining nut, remove the washer and withdraw the light unit from the nudge bar (see illustration).
19 On vehicles with a solid nudge bar, disconnect the driving light wiring at the connector located next to the radiator. Unscrew the retaining nut, remove the washer and withdraw the light unit from the nudge bar.
20 Refitting is a reversal of removal.

---

8 Headlight beam alignment - general information

1 Accurate adjustment of the headlight beam is only possible using optical beam setting equipment and this work should therefore be carried out by a Vauxhall dealer or suitably-equipped workshop.
2 For reference the headlights can be adjusted by rotating the adjuster screws located at the bottom of each headlight and accessible through cut-outs in the radiator grille.
3 All models have an electrically-operated headlight beam adjustment range control system, operated via a switch on the facia. The recommended settings are as follows:
0   Front seat(s) occupied
1   All seats occupied
2   All seats occupied and load in the luggage compartment
3   5-door models only: Driver's seat occupied and load in the luggage compartment
Note: *When adjusting the headlight aim, ensure that the switch is set to position 0.*

---

9 Headlight range control motor - removal and refitting

Removal

1 Switch on the headlights, set the headlight range control switch to the 0 position then switch the headlights off.
2 Disconnect the battery negative lead. Note that for improved access it is beneficial to

7.8 To remove the frame, pull the headlight adjusters out of their locating sockets

7.18 Long range driving light retaining nut (arrowed) viewed from the underside of the 'soft-feel' nudge bar

9.5 Removing a headlight range control motor

10.3a Undo the screw each side securing the instrument panel cover to the facia . . .

10.3b . . . then pull the cover outwards to disengage the upper clips - pre-1997 models

remove the battery completely if working on the left-hand unit, and to remove the air cleaner assembly if working on the right-hand unit. Refer to Chapters 5A and 4A or 4B for battery and air cleaner removal procedures.

3 Disconnect the range control motor wiring at the harness connector.

4 Rotate the motor body 45° clockwise (left-hand motor) or 45° anti-clockwise (right-hand motor) to release the mounting attachment.

5 Pull the actuating rod out of the socket on the headlight and remove the motor from the body panel **(see illustration)**.

Refitting

6 Refitting is a reversal of removal, but ensure that the actuating rod is fully located in the headlight socket. On completion, have the headlight beam alignment checked at the earliest opportunity.

---

10 Instrument panel - removal and refitting

Removal

Pre-1997 models

1 Disconnect the battery negative lead.
2 On vehicles with a tiltable steering column,

set the column to its lowest position. On vehicles with a fixed steering column, remove the steering wheel as described in Chapter 11.

3 Undo the two screws securing the instrument panel cover to the facia, then pull the cover outwards at the top to disengage the upper retaining clips **(see illustrations)**.

4 Disconnect the wiring multiplugs from the rear of the switch assemblies then remove the cover **(see illustration)**.

5 Undo the screws and lift off the lower and upper steering column shrouds **(see illustration)**.

6 Undo the two upper and two lower screws securing the instrument panel to the facia. The upper screws are located on each side of the instrument panel and the lower screws are located on each side of the steering column **(see illustrations)**.

7 Carefully withdraw the instrument panel from its location as far as the wiring harness and speedometer cable will allow. Reach behind the panel, depress the clip on the end fitting and disconnect the speedometer cable **(see illustration)**. It may be necessary to release the cable from its clips in the engine compartment to allow sufficient access to the rear of the instrument panel.

10.4 Disconnect the switch wiring multiplugs and remove the cover - pre-1997 models

10.5 Undo the screws and lift off the steering column shrouds - pre-1997 models

10.6a Undo the upper screws (arrowed) located on each side of the instrument panel . . .

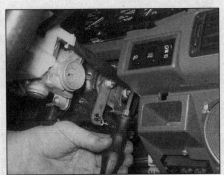

10.6b . . . and the lower screws on each side of the steering column - pre-1997 models

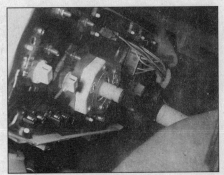

10.7 Depress the clip on the end fitting and disconnect the speedometer cable - pre-1997 models

10.8 Disconnect the wiring multiplugs and remove the instrument panel - pre-1997 models

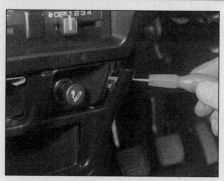

10.14a Carefully ease the upper part of the facia lower centre moulding away from its location . . .

10.14b . . . and with the three clips (arrowed) released, remove the moulding - 1997 models onward

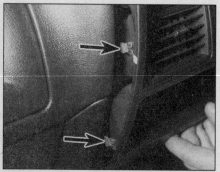

10.16a Ease the instrument panel cover from its location to release the retaining clips (arrowed) located along each side . . .

10.16b . . . disconnect the wiring from the rear and remove the cover - 1997 models onward

8 Disconnect the wiring multiplugs from the rear of the instrument panel and remove the unit **(see illustration)**.

1997 models onward

9 Disconnect the battery negative lead.
10 Undo the two screws securing the bonnet release handle to the trim panel under the facia on the driver's side.
11 Undo the six screws securing the driver's side trim panel under the facia and ease the panel from its location. Disconnect the wiring for the headlight range control switch and remove the panel.
12 Undo the seven screws and remove the steering column upper and lower shrouds.
13 Where fitted, remove the radio/cassette player as described in Section 18.
14 Remove the ashtray then, using a small screwdriver, carefully ease the upper part of the facia lower centre moulding away from its location. The moulding is secured by three retaining clips, one on each side of the cigarette lighter housing, and one at the passenger's side edge of the moulding. Once the clips are released, ease the moulding away at the top and lift up to disengage the lower retaining lugs **(see illustrations)**.
15 Undo the two screws at the top of the instrument panel aperture securing the instrument panel cover to the facia. Undo the third screw located above the radio aperture.
16 Carefully ease the instrument panel cover from its location to release the retaining clips located along each side **(see illustrations)**. Reach behind the cover and disconnect the radio and switch assembly wiring connectors, then remove the cover from the vehicle.
17 Undo the two screws each side securing the instrument panel to the facia **(see illustration)**.
18 Carefully withdraw the instrument panel from its location as far as the wiring harness will allow. Reach behind the panel, disconnect the wiring multiplugs and remove the unit **(see illustration)**.

Refitting

19 Refitting is a reversal of removal.

10.17 Undo the four screws (arrowed) securing the instrument panel to the facia (steering wheel removed for clarity) - 1997 models onward

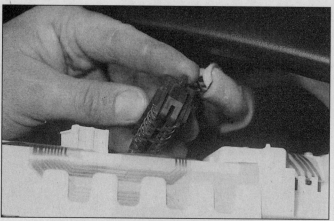

10.18 Disconnect the wiring multiplugs and remove the instrument panel - 1997 models onward

11.5 Separate the cover and lens from the instrument panel by depressing the retaining tags (arrowed) around the periphery of the cover

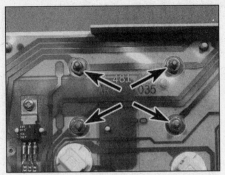

11.6 Instrument panel gauge assembly retaining nuts (arrowed)

11.8 Speedometer retaining screws (arrowed)

11 Instrument panel components - removal and refitting

Removal

1 Remove the instrument panel from the vehicle as described in Section 10.

Panel illumination and warning lights

2 Make a note of the location of the various bulbholders, and particularly of the vacant locations in the instrument panel.
3 Twist the bulbholders anti-clockwise and withdraw them from the rear of the panel.

Gauge assembly

4 From the front of the panel, carefully pull off the odometer reset knob.
5 Separate the cover and lens from the instrument panel by depressing the retaining tags around the periphery of the cover (see illustration).
6 Undo the four nuts at the rear of the panel and withdraw the gauge assembly from the front (see illustration).

Speedometer

7 Separate the cover and lens from the

instrument panel as described in paragraphs 4 and 5.
8 Undo the four screws at the rear of the panel and withdraw the speedometer from the front (see illustration).

Voltage stabiliser

9 Undo the screw securing the voltage stabiliser to the rear of the panel (see illustration).
10 Disconnect the voltage stabiliser from the plug contacts and lift it off the printed circuit.

Tachometer

11 Separate the cover and lens from the instrument panel as described in paragraphs 4 and 5.
12 From the front of the instrument panel, undo the two diagonally opposite screws and withdraw the tachometer from the front of the panel.

Printed circuit

13 Remove all the components from the instrument panel as described in the previous paragraphs.
14 Very carefully release the printed circuit from the locating pegs on the rear of the instrument panel. Take care when doing this as the printed circuit is fragile and it is very

easy to damage the circuit tracks. Withdraw the multiplug contacts from their apertures and lift off the printed circuit.

Refitting

15 Refitting is a reversal of removal, but ensure that the contact pins on the various components are fully engaged in the sockets on the panel and in the printed circuit.

12 Clock - removal and refitting

Removal

Pre-1997 models

1 Using a small screwdriver, carefully ease the clock surround trim from the facia.
2 Undo the two screws and withdraw the clock from its location. Disconnect the wiring connector and remove the unit.

1997 models onward

3 Using a small screwdriver, carefully ease the clock from the facia aperture (see illustration).

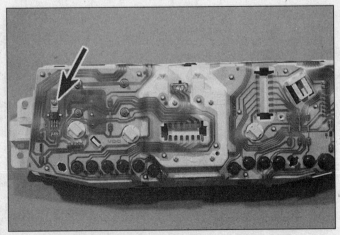

11.9 Voltage stabiliser retaining screw (arrowed)

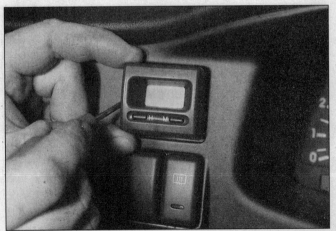

12.3 Using a small screwdriver to ease the clock from the facia aperture - 1997 models onward

13.4 Right-hand horn bracket retaining bolt (arrowed)

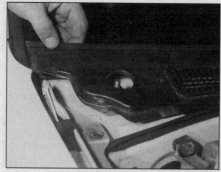

15.3 Remove the ventilation grille panel at the base of the windscreen

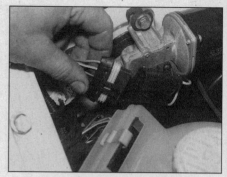

15.4a Disconnect the wiper motor wiring multiplug . . .

4 Disconnect the wiring connector and remove the unit.

Refitting

5 Refitting is a reversal of removal.

13 Horn(s) - removal and refitting

Note: *Refer to Section 21 for the anti-theft alarm horn.*

Removal

1 The horns are located behind the radiator grille, one on each side of the radiator.
2 Remove the radiator grille as described in Chapter 12.
3 Disconnect the wiring connectors from the horn terminals.
4 Undo the horn bracket retaining bolt and remove the horn and bracket **(see illustration)**.

Refitting

5 Refitting is a reversal of removal.

14 Wiper arm - removal and refitting

Removal

1 Operate the wiper motor then switch it off so that the wiper arm returns to the at-rest position.
Stick a piece of masking tape on the windscreen or tailgate glass along the edge of the wiper blade to use as an alignment aid on refitting.
2 Lift the wiper arm retaining nut cover then slacken and remove the nut. Where fitted, remove the washer located under the nut.
3 Lift the blade off the glass and pull the wiper arm off the spindle using a large, flat-bladed screwdriver. If the arm is very tight, free it from the spindle using a suitable puller.

Refitting

4 Ensure that the wiper and spindle are clean and dry then refit the arm to the spindle and

15.4b . . . then undo the wiper motor mounting bolts

align the blade with the previously noted rest position. Refit the washer (where applicable) and spindle nut, securely tighten the nut and refit the cover.

15 Windscreen wiper motor and linkage - removal and refitting

Wiper motor

Removal

1 Remove the wiper arms as described in Section 14.
2 Extract the retaining clip and release the cooling system expansion tank from the support bracket.
3 Undo the five screws and remove the ventilation grille panel at the base of the windscreen **(see illustration)**.
4 Disconnect the wiper motor wiring multiplug, then undo the four bolts securing the motor to the bulkhead **(see illustrations)**.
5 Withdraw the motor from the bulkhead until there is sufficient clearance to gain access to the linkage connection through the bulkhead aperture.
6 Using a large screwdriver, carefully prise the linkage balljoint off the motor bellcrank stud, then remove the motor from the engine compartment.

15.9 Wiper arm spindle retaining nuts (arrowed)

Refitting

7 Refitting is a reversal of removal, but ensure that the linkage balljoint is pushed fully onto the motor bellcrank stud.

Wiper linkage

Removal

8 Remove the wiper motor as described previously.
9 Undo the two nuts securing each wiper arm spindle to the scuttle panel **(see illustration)**.
10 Slide the linkage assembly sideways then manoeuvre the linkage out through the scuttle panel aperture.
11 The linkage rods can be separated from the spindles by prising off the balljoints using a screwdriver.

Refitting

12 Refitting is a reversal of removal, but ensure that the linkage balljoints are pushed fully onto the spindle bellcrank studs.

16 Tailgate wiper motor - removal and refitting

3-door models

Removal

1 Remove the wiper arm as described in Section 14.

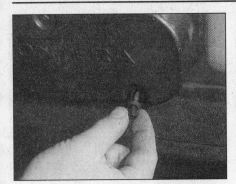

16.2 Undo the screws, withdraw the inserts and remove the tailgate wiper motor cover - 3-door models

16.3 Disconnect the wiper motor wiring multiplug - 3-door models

16.4a From the inside, undo the support bracket retaining screw and remove the spacer and grommet . . .

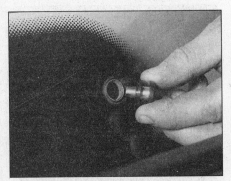

16.4b . . . then collect the nut and collar from the outside - 3-door models

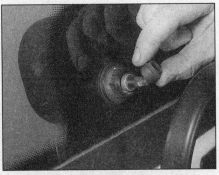

16.5a Remove the dust cover from the spindle . . .

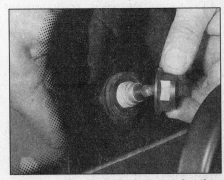

16.5b . . . then undo the nut securing the tailgate motor to the glass - 3-door models

2 Undo the retaining screws, remove the plastic screw inserts and lift off the wiper motor inner cover panel **(see illustration)**.

3 Disconnect the wiring harness at the multiplug on the side of the motor **(see illustration)**.

4 From the inside of the tailgate glass, undo the motor support bracket retaining screw and remove the spacer and rubber grommet. Remove the nut and plastic collar from the outside of the glass **(see illustrations)**.

5 Remove the dust cover from the motor spindle and undo the nut securing the motor body to the glass **(see illustrations)**.

6 Lift off the washer and outer rubber seal,

withdraw the motor from the inside of the glass and collect the inner rubber seal **(see illustrations)**.

Refitting

7 Refitting is a reversal of removal.

5-door models

Removal

Note: *On pre-mid 1995 models, the tailgate wiper is operated by the motor via a linkage arrangement. On later models the wiper is driven directly by the motor. The removal and refitting procedure is virtually the same for both arrangements, but if working on the later*

version, ignore all references to wiper linkage.

8 Remove the wiper arm as described in Section 14.

9 Remove the tailgate inner trim panel as described in Chapter 12.

10 Where fitted, undo the bolts and remove the tailgate inner cover panel for access to the wiper motor and linkage.

11 Disconnect the wiring harness at the multiplug on the motor and linkage mounting bracket.

12 Remove the dust cover from the motor/linkage spindle and undo the nut securing the spindle to the tailgate. Lift off the washer and outer rubber seal.

16.6a Lift off the washer . . .

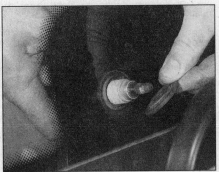

16.6b . . . and outer rubber seal . . .

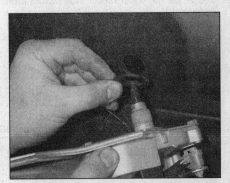

16.6c . . . then withdraw the motor and collect the inner rubber seal - 3-door models

13

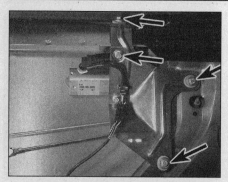
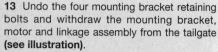

16.13 Later type tailgate wiper motor mounting bracket retaining bolts (arrowed) - 5-door models

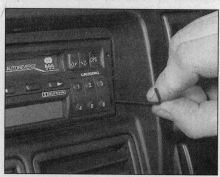

18.1 Undo the grub screws from the front of the radio

18.2 Using the DIN removal tools to remove the radio from the frame

13 Undo the four mounting bracket retaining bolts and withdraw the mounting bracket, motor and linkage assembly from the tailgate **(see illustration)**.

14 To separate the motor from the linkage, mark the position of the motor bellcrank on the motor shaft then undo the retaining nut. Remove the washer and withdraw the bellcrank from the motor shaft.

15 Undo the three mounting bolts and remove the motor from the mounting bracket.

16 Where fitted, the linkage components can be further dismantled by separating the linkage arm balljoints from the spindles and undoing the relevant attachment nuts and bolts.

Refitting

17 Refitting is a reversal of removal.

17 Windscreen/tailgate/headlight washer system components - removal and refitting

Washer fluid reservoir

1 Unscrew the two nuts and remove the washers from the battery clamp tension rods, then lift off the battery clamp.

2 Suitably identify the washer hoses at the pump connections to avoid confusion when refitting. Place a suitable container beneath the washer fluid reservoir and disconnect the hoses from the pumps. Allow the washer fluid to drain into the container.

3 Disconnect the wiring at the pump connections, then undo the mounting bolts and remove the reservoir from the engine compartment.

4 Refitting is a reversal of removal, ensuring that the hoses are securely reconnected. Refill the reservoir and check for leakage.

Washer pumps

5 Two washer pumps are located at the lower front of the reservoir, one for the windscreen and one for the tailgate. Where a headlight washer system is fitted, a third pump is

located in the upper front part of the reservoir, above the other two pumps.

6 Suitably identify the washer hoses at the pump connections to avoid confusion when refitting. Place a suitable container beneath the washer fluid reservoir and disconnect the hoses from the pumps. Allow the washer fluid to drain into the container.

7 If the windscreen or tailgate washer pumps are to be removed, withdraw the support strap from the top of the pumps and the reservoir.

8 Disconnect the wiring at the pump connections, then carefully lever the pumps out of their rubber grommets on the reservoir. If necessary remove the grommet from the reservoir.

9 Check the condition of the grommet and renew if necessary.

10 Refitting is a reversal of removal, ensuring that the hoses are securely reconnected. Refill the reservoir and check for leakage.

Windscreen washer jet

11 With the bonnet open, disconnect the washer hose from the relevant jet, and if the jet is of the heated type, disconnect the wiring connector.

12 Release the jet from the bonnet and remove it upwards.

13 Refitting is a reversal of removal.

Tailgate washer jet

14 The location of the tailgate washer jet and its hose attachments varies considerably according to model, year and optional equipment fitted. Locate the jet and remove any trim panels as necessary for access.

15 Withdraw the jet from its grommet or panel location, disconnect the washer hose and remove the jet.

16 Refitting is a reversal of removal.

Headlight washer jet

17 Remove the front bumper as described in Chapter 12.

18 Undo the jet retaining nut, remove the washer and withdraw the jet from the top of the bumper.

19 Refitting is a reversal of removal.

18 Radio/cassette player - removal and refitting

Note: *On models with a security-coded radio/cassette player, once the battery has been disconnected, or the radio removed, the unit cannot be re-activated until the appropriate security code has been entered. Do not remove the unit unless the appropriate code is known. The following information applies to radio/cassette players fitted by Vauxhall and having standard DIN fixings. Two DIN removal tools will be required for this operation.*

Removal

1 Using an Allen key, undo the grub screws from the four holes in each corner of the radio front face **(see illustration)**.

2 Insert the two DIN removal tools into the holes on each side of the radio/cassette player until they are felt to engage with the retaining strips **(see illustration)**.

3 Carefully withdraw the unit from its frame in the facia.

Refitting

4 Remove the DIN tools, then push the radio/cassette player into the frame until the sockets at the rear of the unit engage with the plugs in the frame, and the retaining strips lock into place.

5 On completion, enter the security code.

19 Loudspeakers - removal and refitting

Facia loudspeakers

Removal

1 Undo the four screws (driver's side) or single screw (passenger's side) securing the trim panel or loudspeaker cover panel under the facia. Pull the upper part of the panel away from the facia to disengage the upper locating lugs and remove the panel.

19.2 Facia-mounted loudspeaker retaining screws

19.6 Undo the four screws securing the door mounted loudspeaker to the housing

19.7 Withdraw the loudspeaker and disconnect the wiring

2 Undo the four screws and withdraw the loudspeaker from the facia (see illustration).
3 Disconnect the wiring and remove the loudspeaker.

Refitting

4 Refitting is a reversal of removal.

Front door low frequency loudspeakers

Removal

5 Remove the front door inner trim panel as described in Chapter 12.
6 Undo the four screws securing the loudspeaker to the door panel housing (see illustration).
7 Disconnect the wiring and remove the loudspeaker (see illustration).

Refitting

8 Refitting is a reversal of removal.

Front door high frequency (tweeter) loudspeakers

Removal

9 Remove the front door inner trim panel as described in Chapter 12.
10 From the rear of the trim panel, turn the tweeter locking ring anti-clockwise using pointed-nose pliers, and remove the locking ring (see illustrations). Withdraw the tweeter from the front of the trim panel.

19.13 Undo the four screws . . .

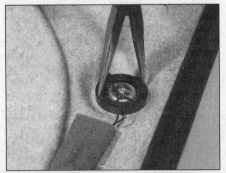

19.10a Turn the tweeter locking ring anti-clockwise . . .

Refitting

11 Locate the tweeter in the trim panel and fit the locking ring. Turn the locking ring clockwise at least two clicks, to secure the tweeter.
12 Refit the inner trim panel as described in Chapter 12.

Rear loudspeakers

Removal

13 Undo the four screws securing the loudspeaker and grille to the trim panel (see illustration).
14 Withdraw the loudspeaker and disconnect the wiring (see illustration).

Refitting

15 Refitting is a reversal of removal.

19.14 . . . then withdraw the rear loudspeaker and disconnect the wiring

19.10b . . . then remove the ring and withdraw the tweeter from the trim panel

20 Radio aerial - removal and refitting

Removal

1 Disconnect the battery negative lead.
2 Peel back the front door weatherstrip on the passenger's side sufficiently to allow removal of the windscreen A-pillar inner trim.
3 Carefully pull the trim from the A-pillar to release the retaining clips.
4 Using a small screwdriver, release the front interior light(s) from their location in the headlining.
5 On pre-1997 models, remove the facia loudspeaker on the passenger's side as described in Section 19.
6 On 1997 models onward, release the front door tread plate on the passenger's side then further peel back the front door weatherstrip to allow removal of the footwell side kick panel. Undo the screw and remove the kick panel from the footwell.
7 Undo the screws and remove the sun visors and holders from the headlining.
8 Undo the screws and remove the grab handle on the passenger's side.
9 Ease the front of the headlining down and release the aerial lead from the retaining clips in the roof and down the A-pillar. Trace the aerial lead down to the connector located in the loudspeaker aperture (pre-1997 models) or in the aperture behind the previously removed kick panel (1997 models onward).

13

10 Lift off the plastic cap and undo the screw securing the aerial base to the roof. Withdraw the aerial and lead from the roof.

Refitting

11 Refitting is a reversal of removal, but ensure that the aerial lead is securely retained by the clips and not likely to be trapped when the headlining is refitted.

21 Anti-theft alarm and engine immobiliser - general information

Anti-theft alarm

1 Later models may be equipped with an anti-theft alarm system and engine immobiliser as an option. The anti-theft alarm system monitors the doors, tailgate, bonnet, radio, ignition, starter and, on some models, the passenger compartment. On early versions the system is activated and de-activated by means of the ignition key. On later versions the central locking system remote control transmitter is used to activate and de-activate the system. The control unit for the system is located behind the passenger's side facia trim panel on pre-1997 models and in the centre of the facia, in front of the centre console, on 1997 models onward. The ultrasonic sensors (where fitted) that monitor the passenger compartment are located at the top of each B-pillar and the alarm horn is located under the right-hand side front wheel arch.

2 To remove the control unit, remove the trim panel from the front of the facia on the passenger's side (early models) or remove the centre console (later models). Disconnect the wiring connector and remove the unit from its mounting.

3 To remove an ultrasonic sensor, carefully prise off the sensor cover and undo the two retaining screws. Disconnect the wiring and remove the sensor.

4 To remove the alarm horn, chock the rear wheels then jack up the front of the vehicle and support it on axle stands (see *Jacking and Vehicle Support*). Remove the right-hand front roadwheel. Release the plastic fasteners and clips and remove the front section of the wheel arch liner. Disconnect the wiring, undo the mounting bolts and remove the horn.

5 Refitting of the components is a reversal of the removal procedure.

Engine immobiliser

6 The engine immobiliser prevents the engine from being started when the ignition key is removed from the steering lock. On diesel models, the fuel system is shut off and, on petrol models, both the ignition and fuel systems are rendered inoperative. On early versions, the system is de-activated by passing a special key fob over a sensor located in the steering column cowl. On later

versions de-activation is carried out by inserting the ignition key into the steering lock and turning it to the 'on' position.

7 To remove the sensor used on early versions, remove the steering column lower cowl and extract the sensor retaining clip. Disconnect the wiring connector and remove the sensor from the cowl. To remove the sensor located around the steering lock on later versions, remove the steering column cowls and undo the screw securing the sensor to the steering lock. Disconnect the wiring connector and remove the sensor.

8 To remove the control unit on pre-mid 1995 models, remove the instrument panel (Section 10) then undo the bolt securing the unit to the facia cross brace. Disconnect the wiring connector and remove the control unit. To remove the control unit on later models, remove the facia (Chapter 12) then undo the bolts securing the control unit to the facia cross brace adjacent to the steering column mounting. Disconnect the wiring connectors and remove the unit.

9 Refitting of the components is a reversal of the removal procedure.

22 Airbag system - general information and precautions

General information

Both a driver and passenger's airbag are available as optional equipment on 1997 models onward. Models fitted with a driver's side airbag have the word AIRBAG stamped on the airbag unit, which is fitted to the centre of the steering wheel. Models also equipped with a passenger side airbag also have the word AIRBAG stamped on the glove compartment. The airbag system comprises the airbag unit(s) (complete with gas generators), the control unit (with an integral impact sensor) and a warning light in the instrument panel.

The airbag system is triggered in the event of a heavy frontal impact above a predetermined force; depending on the point of impact. The airbag is inflated within milliseconds and forms a safety cushion between the driver and steering wheel and (where fitted) the passenger and facia. This prevents contact between the upper body and wheel/facia and therefore greatly reduces the risk of injury. The airbag then deflates almost immediately.

Every time the ignition is switched on, the airbag control unit performs a self-test and during the test the warning light in the instrument panel flashes seven times. After the self-test has been completed the warning light should go out. If the warning light fails to come on, remains illuminated after the initial period, or comes on at any time when the vehicle is being driven, there is a fault in the airbag system. The vehicle should be taken to

a Vauxhall dealer for examination at the earliest possible opportunity.

Precautions

⚠ *Warning: The following precautions must be observed when working on vehicles equipped with an airbag system, to prevent the possibility of personal injury.*

The following precautions **must** be observed when carrying out work on a vehicle equipped with an airbag.

a) *Do not disconnect the battery with the engine running.*

b) *Before carrying out any work in the vicinity of the airbag, removal of any of the airbag components, or any welding work on the vehicle, de-activate the system as described in the following sub-section.*

c) *Do not attempt to test any of the airbag system circuits using test meters or any other test equipment.*

d) *If the airbag warning light comes on, or any fault in the system is suspected, consult a Vauxhall dealer without delay.* **Do not** *attempt to carry out fault diagnosis, or any dismantling of the components.*

Precautions to be taken when handling an airbag unit

a) *Transport the airbag by itself, bag upward.*

b) *Do not put your arms around the airbag.*

c) *Carry the airbag close to the body, bag outward.*

d) *Do not drop the airbag or expose it to impacts.*

e) *Do not attempt to dismantle the airbag unit.*

f) *Do not connect any form of electrical equipment to any part of the airbag circuit.*

g) *Do not allow any solvents or cleaning agents to contact the airbag assembly. The unit may be cleaned using* **only** *a damp cloth.*

Precautions to be taken when storing an airbag unit

a) *Store the unit in a cupboard with the airbag upward.*

b) *Do not expose the airbag to temperatures above 90°C.*

c) *Do not expose the airbag to flames.*

d) *Do not attempt to dispose of the airbag; consult a Vauxhall dealer.*

e) *Never refit an airbag which is known to be faulty or damaged.*

De-activation of airbag system

The system must be deactivated as follows, before carrying out any work on the airbag components or surrounding area.

a) *Switch off the ignition.*

b) *Remove the ignition key.*

c) *Switch off all electrical equipment.*

d) Disconnect the battery negative lead (see Chapter 5A).

e) Insulate the battery negative terminal and the end of the battery negative lead to prevent any possibility of contact.

f) Wait for at least one minute before carrying out any further work. This will allow the system capacitor to discharge.

23 Airbag system components - removal and refitting

Driver's side airbag unit

Warning: Refer to the precautions given in Section 22 before attempting to carry out work on the airbag components.

Removal

1 The airbag unit is an integral part of the steering wheel centre pad.

2 De-activate the airbag system as described in Section 22.

3 Set the front wheels in the straight-ahead position, then lock the steering column in this position after removing the ignition key.

4 Undo the four captive screws in the side of the steering wheel centre boss.

5 Carefully lift the airbag unit from the steering wheel and disconnect the wiring connector. Position the air bag unit in a safe place where it cannot be tampered with, making sure that the padded side is facing upwards.

Refitting

6 Refitting is a reversal of removal, but make sure that the wiring connector is securely reconnected and tighten the retaining screws to the specified torque.

Passenger's side airbag

Warning: Refer to the precautions given in Section 22 before attempting to carry out work on the airbag components.

Removal

7 De-activate the airbag system as described in Section 22.

8 Undo the two lower screws and remove the glove compartment from the facia.

9 Undo the four screws, disengage the two clips and remove the cover from the top of the glove compartment aperture.

10 Undo the four bolts and two nuts and withdraw the airbag unit from its mounting. Disconnect the wiring connector and remove the unit from under the facia.

Refitting

11 Refitting is a reversal of removal, but make sure that the wiring connector is securely reconnected and tighten the retaining screws to the specified torque.

Airbag contact unit (on steering column)

Removal

Note: *The contact unit is an integral part of the steering column multi-function switch.*

12 Remove the driver's airbag unit as described earlier in this Section.

13 Remove the steering wheel as described in Chapter 11.

14 Undo the two screws securing the bonnet release handle to the trim panel under the facia on the driver's side.

15 Undo the six screws securing the driver's side trim panel under the facia and ease the panel from its location. Disconnect the wiring for the headlight range control switch and remove the panel.

16 Undo the seven screws and remove the steering column upper and lower shrouds.

17 Disconnect the multi-function switch wiring, and airbag wiring at the multiplugs on the steering column and under the facia as applicable. Cut off any cable ties as necessary to free the harness.

18 Undo the four screws securing the switch assembly and contact unit to the top of the steering column and remove the switch.

Refitting

19 Check that the contact unit is positioned with the arrows aligned with each other. If it has been disturbed, return it to its central position by depressing the detent and rotating it fully anti-clockwise until resistance is felt. Now turn it 2.5 turns clockwise and align the arrows on the outer edge.

20 If a new unit is being fitted, remove the transit plug.

21 Locate the multi-function switch and contact unit over the steering column and secure with the four screws.

22 Reconnect the wiring connectors and secure with new cable ties where necessary.

23 Refit the steering column shrouds, facia trim panel and bonnet release handle.

24 Refit the steering wheel as described in Chapter 11.

25 Refit the airbag unit as described earlier.

Airbag control unit

Removal

26 De-activate the airbag system as described in Section 22.

27 Remove the centre console as described in Chapter 12 to gain access to the control unit which is mounted under the centre of the facia.

28 Withdraw the red tag from the end of the wiring connector, depress the top of the connector to release the locking arrangement and disconnect the connector.

29 Unscrew the three control unit retaining bolts and the earth lead terminal retaining bolt and remove the unit from the mounting bracket.

Refitting

30 Refitting is a reversal of removal, but make sure that the wiring connector locking arrangement engages then insert the red tag. Ensure also that the earth lead retaining bolt is securely tightened.

WIRING DIAGRAM FOR FRONTERA
(AS OF MODEL YEAR 1992)

WIRING IDENTIFICATION

COLOUR CODING	COLOUR	CIRCUITS
B	BLACK	STARTER & GROUNDING CIRCUITS
W	WHITE	CHARGING CIRCUIT
R	RED	LIGHTING CIRCUIT
G	GREEN	SIGNAL CIRCUIT
Y	YELLOW	INSTRUMENT CIRCUIT
L	BLUE	WIPER CIRCUIT
O	ORANGE	
Br	BROWN	
Lg	LIGHT GREEN	
GY	GREY	
P	PINK	
Sb	SKY BLUE	
V	VIOLET	

EXAMPLE: ——— 0.5   G R ———

WIRE SIZE (0.5mm2)
GREEN
RED (STRIPE)

CAUTIONARY NOTE

PLEASE REFER TO THE WIRING COLOUR CODE CHART ABOVE BEFORE INVESTIGATING ELECTRICAL FAULTS TO ENSURE THAT VEHICLE CIRCUITS AND WIRES ARE CORRECTLY IDENTIFIED.

IT IS IMPORTANT TO BE AWARE OF THE DIFFERENCES BETWEEN THE USE OF COLOUR CODES ON FRONTERA VEHICLES AND THOSE NORMALLY ADOPTED BY VAUXHALL/OPEL

E.G.   BLACK   FRONTERA - GROUNDING CIRCUITS

             OPEL   - IGNITION

Information for wiring diagrams (early models)

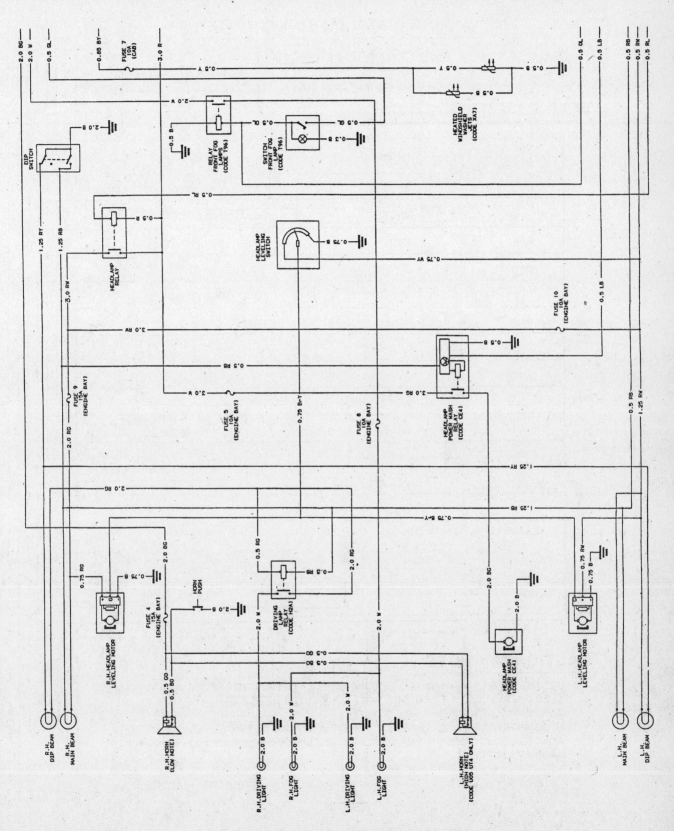

Typical wiring diagram (early models)

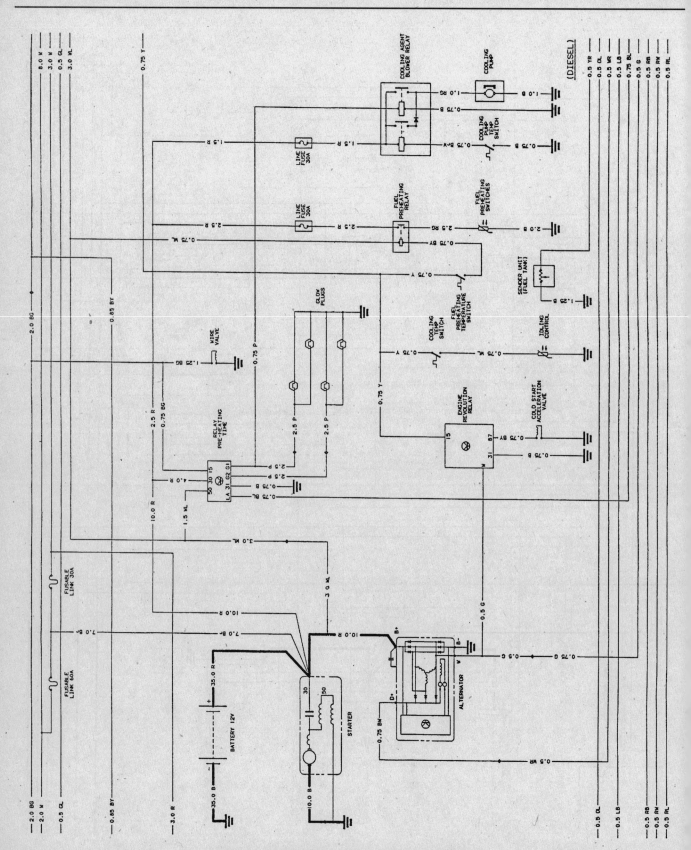

Typical wiring diagram (early models) - continued

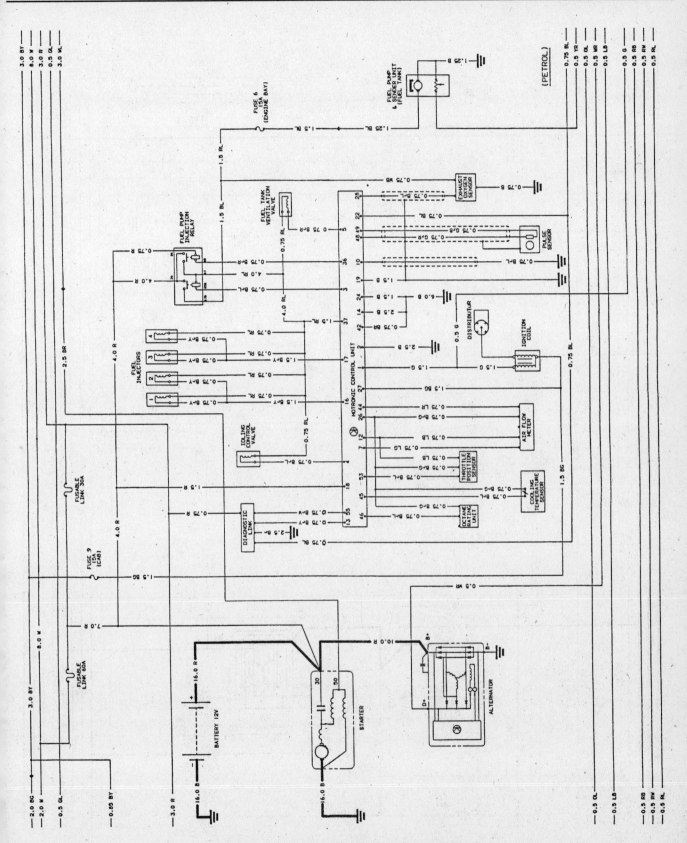

Typical wiring diagram (early models) - continued

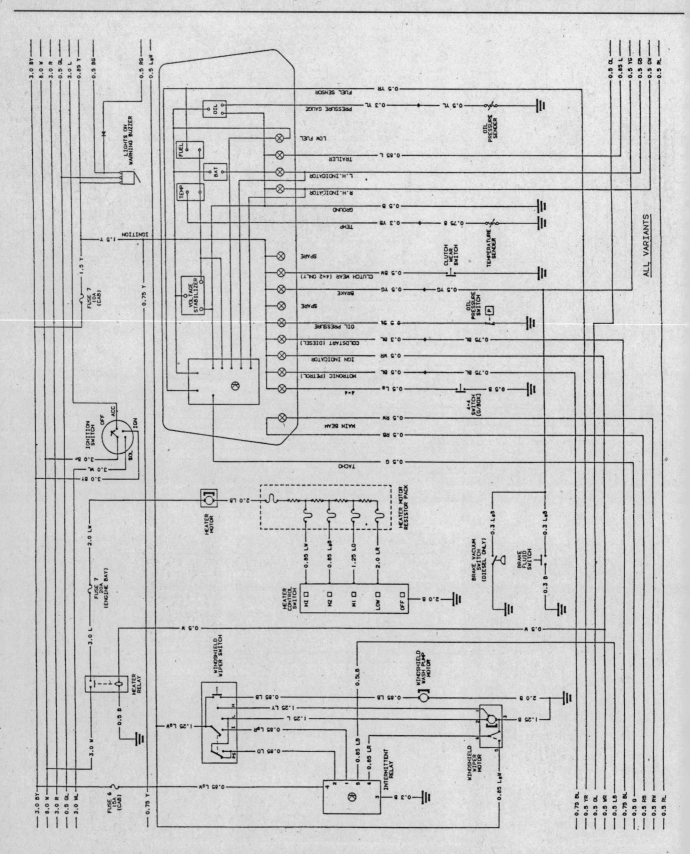

Typical wiring diagram (early models) - continued

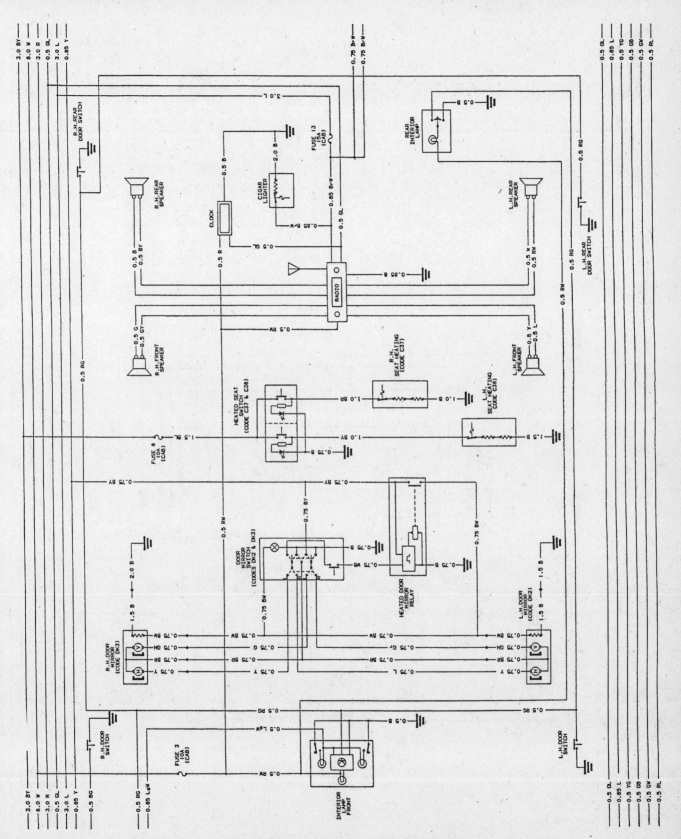

Typical wiring diagram (early models) - continued

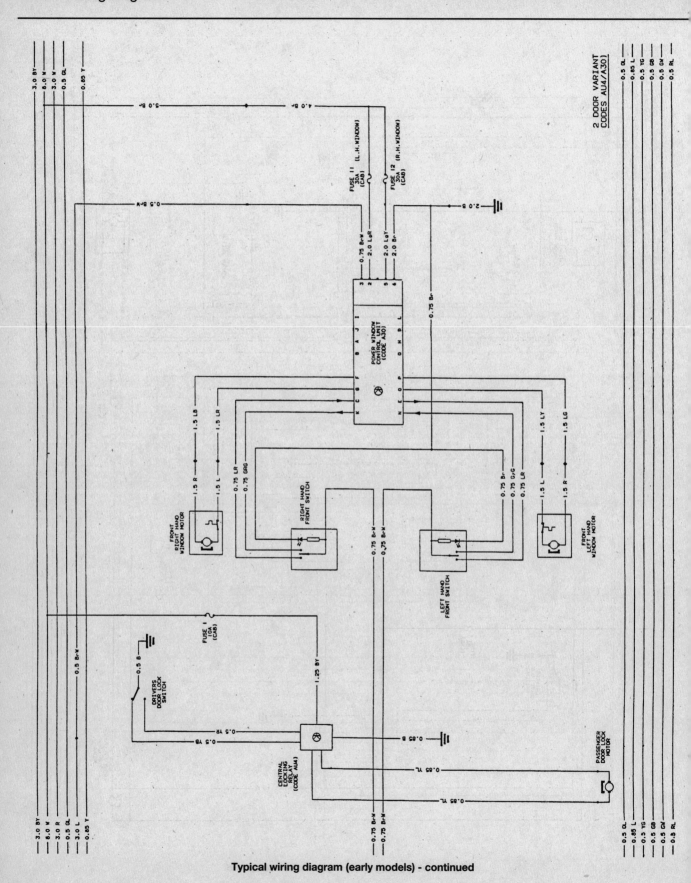

Typical wiring diagram (early models) - continued

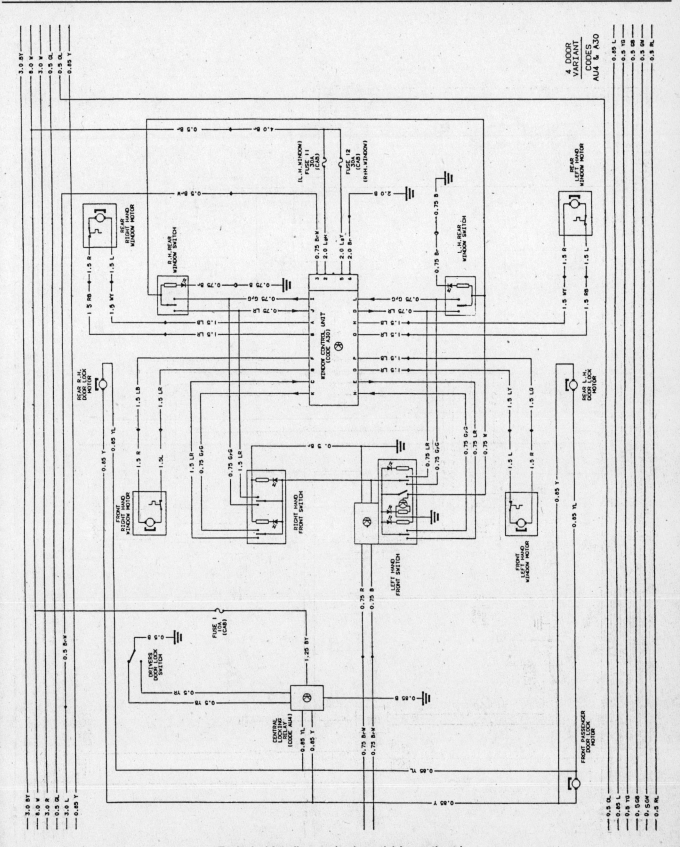

Typical wiring diagram (early models) - continued

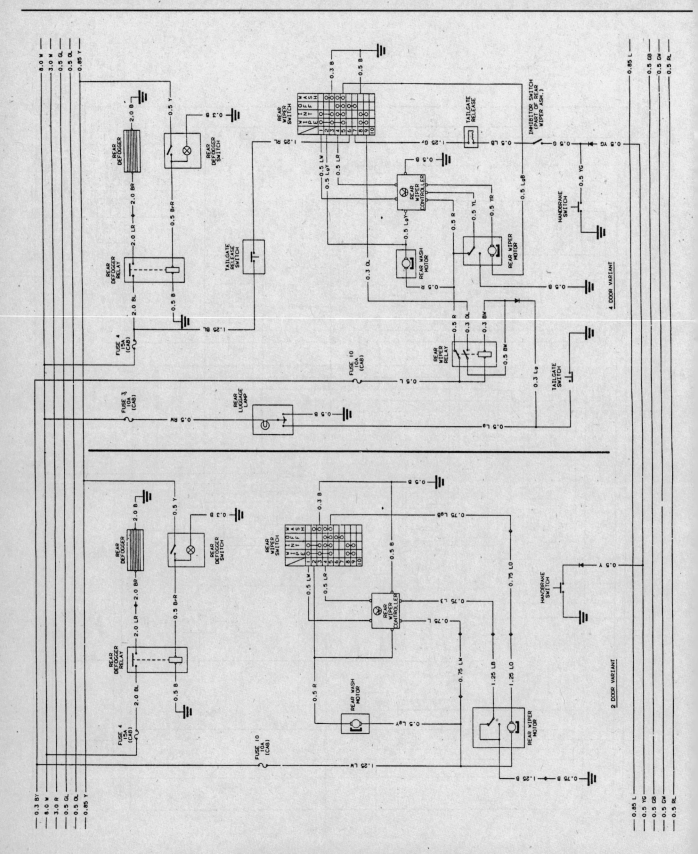

Typical wiring diagram (early models) - continued

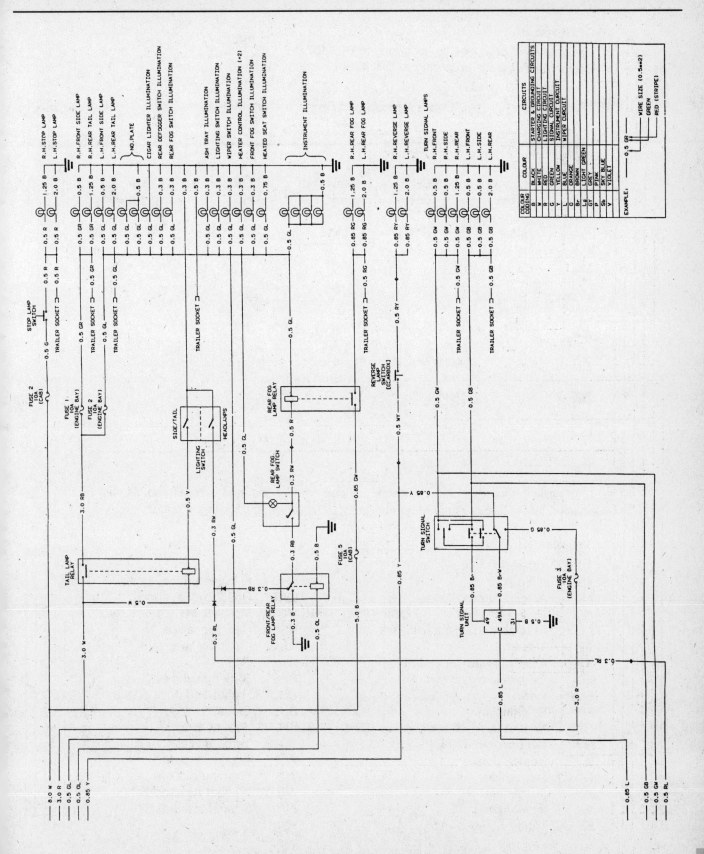

Typical wiring diagram (early models) - continued

GENERAL INFORMATION

Designation of components according to DIN 40719
Designation of leads according to DIN 47002

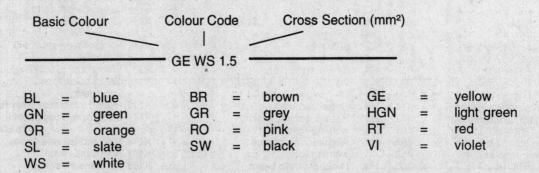

Basic Colour	Colour Code	Cross Section (mm²)

GE WS 1.5

BL	=	blue	BR	=	brown	GE	=	yellow
GN	=	green	GR	=	grey	HGN	=	light green
OR	=	orange	RO	=	pink	RT	=	red
SL	=	slate	SW	=	black	VI	=	violet
WS	=	white						

SYMBOLS

▲ = X 20 SE and X 22 XE only (Petrol)

△ = VM41B only (Diesel)

■ = 4 Door only

□ = 2 Door only

LEAD CONNECTIONS

A framed number, e.g. 322 indicates a circuit in which the lead is continued. At this position there is also a framed number, e.g. 107 referring back to the circuit.

ABBREVIATIONS

ABS	Anti-lock brake system	L	Left
AB	Airbag	LHD	Left-hand drive
AC	Air conditioning	LWR	Headlamp levelling
ACC	Accessory position - ignition switch	MOT	Motronic M1.5.4
ALDL	Assembly line diagnostic link	NSL	Rear fog lamps
AZV	Trailer hitch	NSW	Front fog lamps
DWA	Anti-theft warning system	R	Right
EDC	Electronic diesel control	RFS	Back up lamps
EMP	Radio	RHD	Right-hand drive
FH	Window lifter	SD	Sun roof
HS	Heated back window	SH	Seat heating
HW	Rear screen wiper	TD	Turbo diesel
HZG	Heater blower	WD	Washer nozzle
IMMO	Immobiliser	WS	Warning buzzer
INS	Instrument	WSW	Washer-headlamps
IRL	Interior lamp	ZV	Central locking
KBS	Wiring harness		

Information for wiring diagrams (later models)

Key to wiring diagrams - later models

Not all items fitted to all models

No	Description	Track
C/B1	Fuse	822, 843
E1	Sidelight, left	312
E2	Tail light, left	306
E4	Sidelight, right	317
E5	Tail light, right	314
E7	Headlight main beam, left	337
E8	Headlight main beam, right	345
E9	Headlight dipped beam, left	339
E10	Headlight dipped beam, right	343
E11	Instrument lighting	607, 608, 708
E14	Luggage compartment light	479
E16	Cigarette lighter illumination	442
E17	Reversing light, left	401
E18	Reversing light, right	404
E19	Heated rear window	453
E20	Foglight, front left	363
E21	Foglight, front right	366
E22	Headlight main beam, left	336
E23	Headlight main beam, right	346
E24	Foglight, rear left	352
E29	Luggage compartment light, rear	495, 496
E33	Ashtray lamp	409
E34	Heater control lamp	411
E39	Foglight, rear right	354
E41	Passenger compartment light delay	472 to 474
E61	Number plate light, left	302, 308
E62	Number plate light, right	304, 310
E71	Seat heating, left	979
E72	Seat heating, right	987
F1B	Fuse	200
F1D	Fuse	121, 225
F1E	Fuse	317
F2B	Fuse	202
F2D	Fuse	196
F2E	Fuse	312
F3B	Fuse	1034
F3D	Fuse	1046
F3E	Fuse	339
F4D	Fuse	136
F4E	Fuse	343
F5D	Fuse	450
F5E	Fuse	952, 965
F6D	Fuse	354
F6E	Fuse	113, 217
F7D	Fuse	660, 760
F7E	Fuse	902
F8D	Fuse	928, 954
F8E	Fuse	947
F9D	Fuse	281
F9E	Fuse	337
F10D	Fuse	684
F10E	Fuse	345
F11D	Fuse	511
F12D	Fuse	979
F13D	Fuse	373
F14D	Fuse	803
F15D	Fuse	461
F16D	Fuse	532
F17D	Fuse	453
F18D	Fuse	456
F19D	Fuse	188, 287
F20D	Fuse	440
F21D	Fuse	790
F22D	Fuse	787
F23D	Fuse	665, 765
F24D	Fuse	994

No	Description	Track
FL1	Fuse	111, 214
FL2	Fuse	108, 205
FL3	Fuse	105, 207
FL4	Fuse	124, 290
G1	Battery	100, 201
G2	Alternator	106, 107, 207 to 210
H1	Radio	417 to 434
H3	Direction indicator warning light	612, 614, 712, 714
H4	Oil pressure warning light	645, 745
H5	Brake fluid warning light	660, 760
H6	Hazard warning system warning light	617, 717
H7	Alternator/no-charge warning light	651, 751
H8	Headlight main beam warning light	605, 705
H9	Stop-light, left	376
H10	Stop-light, right	373
H11	Direction indicator light, front left	386
H12	Direction indicator light, rear left	384
H13	Direction indicator light, front right	394
H14	Direction indicator light, rear right	398
H15	Low fuel/fuel reserve warning light	619, 719
H16	Glow plug warning light	658
H17	Trailer direction indicator warning light	610, 710
H18	Horn (twin-tone)	460
H19	Headlamps 'on' warning light	490, 491
H23	Airbag warning light	790
H26	ABS warning light	648, 748
H30	Engine warning light	653, 753
H33	Direction indicator side repeater light left	388
H34	Direction indicator side repeater light right	392
H37	Loudspeaker, front left	426, 427
H38	Loudspeaker, front right	433, 434
H39	Loudspeaker, rear left	429, 430
H40	Loudspeaker, rear right	424, 425
H45	Four-wheel-drive warning light	656, 756
H47	Anti-theft alarm horn	1094
H48	Horn (twin-tone)	462
H52	Tweeter, front left	429, 430
H53	Tweeter, front right	436, 437
K1	Heated rear window relay	452, 453
K4	High beam relay	330, 331
K5	Front foglight relay	366, 367
K7	Fan relay	901, 902
K8	Intermittent wiper relay	502 to 506
K10	Indicator relay	378, 379
K18	Horn relay	460, 461
K31	Airbag control unit	779 to 792
K37	Central door locking control unit	801 to 807
K51	Radiator fan relay	941 to 943
K52	Radiator fan relay	946 to 948, 968 to 970
K60	AC compressor relay	960 to 962
K61	Motronic control unit	135 to 190
K68	Fuel injection relay	185 to 191
K70	Diesel control unit	243 to 285
K76	Glow time control unit	282 to 285
K80	Fuel filter heating relay (diesel)	233, 234
K89	Rear foglight relay	354, 355
K94	Anti-theft alarm control unit	1050 to 1094

No	Description	Track
K96	Radiator fan relay	124, 125
K97	Headlight washer delay relay	552 to 557
K111	Tailgate wiper control	519 to 523
K114	Engine main relay	284, 285
K115	Starter relay	119, 120, 223, 224
K117	Immobiliser control unit	1040 to 1048
K128	Electronic thermostat	927 to 929, 973 to 975
K140	Main beam/dipped beam relay	339 to 341
K145	Heated mirror time delay relay	894, 896
K147	Electric windows control unit	821 to 835, 846 to 872
K148	Side and tail lamps relay	318, 319
K157	Headlamp relay	326 to 328
K165	AC pressure switch override relay	924, 925, 954 to 956
K166	AC compressor control relay	935 to 937
K167	AC compressor control relay	920 to 922
L2	Ignition coil (DIS)	141 to 143
M1	Starter motor	111, 112, 212, 213
M2	Windscreen wiper motor	505 to 508
M3	Heater fan motor	124, 902, 905
M5	Windscreen washer pump	510
M8	Tailgate wiper motor	527, 529
M9	Tailgate washer pump	516, 546
M11	Radiator cooling fan motor	947, 968, 969
M12	Radiator fan motor	942
M13	Sunroof motor	
M13.1	Sunroof motor	993 to 997
M13.2	Microswitch timing box	993
M13.3	Microswitch timing box	995
M16	Electric window motor, rear left	849, 850
M17	Electric window motor, rear right	868, 869
M19	Central locking motor, rear left	812, 813
M20	Central locking motor, rear right	815, 816
M21	Fuel pump	196
M24	Headlight washer pump	557
M30	Electric mirror, driver's side	884 to 887
M31	Electric mirror, passenger side	891 to 894
M32	Central locking motor, front passenger door	806, 807
M33	Idle speed actuator	160, 161
M39	Headlight levelling motor, left	562 to 564
M40	Headlight levelling motor, right	570 to 572
M69	Tailgate wiper motor	538 to 540
M76	Central locking motor, tailgate	818, 819
M83	Electric window motor, front left	825, 827, 855, 857
M84	Electric window motor, front right	833, 835 to 865
P1	Fuel gauge	626, 726
P2	Coolant temperature gauge	629, 729
P3	Clock	413, 415
P4	Fuel level sensor	626, 726
P5	Coolant temperature sensor	629, 729
P7	Tachometer	636, 736
P8	Oil pressure gauge	642, 742
P9	Voltmeter	639, 739
P12	Coolant temperature indicator	167
P14	Distance sensor	633, 635, 734

13

Key to wiring diagrams - later models (continued)
Not all items fitted to all models

No	Description	Track
P17	Wheel sensor, front left	1017, 1019
P18	Wheel sensor, front right	1021, 1023
P19	Wheel sensor, rear left	1025, 1027
P20	Wheel sensor, rear right	1029, 1031
P29	Inlet manifold temperature sensor	173
P30	Coolant temperature sensor	261
P32	Exhaust gas oxygen sensor (heated)	190, 191
P34	Throttle valve potentiometer	161 to 163
P35	Crankshaft impulse sensor	151 to 153, 252 yo 254
P43	Speedometer	633, 733
P44	Air mass meter	179 to 182, 256 to 258
P46	Knock sensor	155 to 157
P53	Anti-theft sensor, driver's side	1066 to 1073
P54	Anti-theft sensor, passenger side	1076 to 1084
P57	Aerial	433, 434
P66	Needle movement sensor	248
P67	Pedal position sensor	242 to 247
P75	Immobiliser receiver	1042 to 1044
P76	Injection quality regulation	
P76.1	Fuel temperature sensor	266
P76.2	Control valve position sensor	26 8 to 270
P76.3	Injection quality actuator	272, 273
R3	Cigarette lighter	440
R5	Glow plugs	284 to 286
R13	Heated washer nozzle, left	577
R14	Heated washer nozzle, right	580
R30	Fan motor relay	910 to 914
S1	Ignition/starter switch	119 to 123, 223 to 227
S2	Light switch assembly	
S2.1	Light switch	322 to 327
S3	Heater fan switch	910 to 916
S4	Rear window & mirror switch	446 to 449
S5	Direction indicator switch assembly	383
S7	Reversing light switch	405
S8	Stop-light switch	373
S11	Brake fluid level switch	660, 760
S13	Handbrake 'on' switch	670, 770
S16	Courtesy light switch, driver's door	491
S17	Courtesy light switch, passenger's door	487
S19	Tailgate wash/wipe switch	518 to 523, 539 to 544

No	Description	Track
S20	Pressure switch	
S20.1	Compressor low pressure switch	937, 972
S20.2	Compressor high pressure switch	937, 972
S20.3	Compressor high pressure fan switch	935, 970
S21	Fog lamp switch	367 to 369
S22	Rear fog lamp switch	358, 360
S31	Courtesy light switch, left rear door	478
S32	Courtesy light switch, right rear door	484
S36	Courtesy light switch, tailgate	475, 496
S37	Electric window switch assembly (in driver's door)	
S37.1	Electric window switch, driver's window	853, 854
S37.2	Electric window switch, passenger window	871, 872
S37.3	Electric window switch, rear left	859, 862
S37.4	Electric window switch, rear right	874 to 876
S37.5	Electric window safety switch	856
S41	Anti-theft locking switch, driver's door	801, 802
S48	Wash/wipe switch assembly	
S48.1	Windscreen wiper switch	503 to 507
S48.2	Windscreen washer switch	508
S52	Hazard warning light (hazard flashers) switch	
S52.3	Indicator switch	384, 386
S57	Sunroof switch	992 to 997
S64	Horn switch	465, 468
S68	Electric mirror switch assembly	
S68.1	Electric mirror adjustment switch	882, 885
S68.2	Electric mirror heating switch	888, 889
S68.3	Electric mirror left/right switch	883 to 887
S77	Electric window switch, front left	825 to 827
S78	Electric window switch, front right	832 to 834
S79	Electric window switch, rear left	840 to 842

No	Description	Track
S80	Electric window switch, rear right	871 to 873
S88	Coolant temperature switch	125
S101	AC compressor switch	932, 935, 967, 970
S120	Anti-theft alarm bonnet switch	1058
S128	Coolant temperature switch	954, 955
S178	Indicator switch assembly	330 to 332
S143	Vacuum switch	664
S150	Four-wheel-drive switch	656, 756
S151	Anti-theft alarm tailgate override switch	1058
S208	Seat heating switch, left	979, 981
S209	Seat heating switch, right	985, 987
U4	ABS hydro aggregate system	
U4.4	ABS hydro aggregate pump	1018
U4.8	ABS control unit	1001 to 1036
U12	Heated fuel filter assembly	
U12.1	Temperature switch	234
U12.2	Heating resistor	233
U20	Airbag contact	783 to 785
U21	Airbag, driver's side	
U21.1	Airbag, driver's side squib	783, 785
U22	Airbag, passenger's side	
U22.1	Airbag, passenger's side squib	779, 781
U30	Oil pressure assembly	
U30.1	Oil pressure sensor	643, 743
U30.2	Oil pressure switch	645, 745
V23	Diode	489
V24	Diode	479
V25	Diode	668, 768
V26	Diode	539
V40	Diode	358, 359
X1 to 106	Wiring connectors	Various
Y1	AC compressor clutch	936, 961
Y5	Fuel solenoid valve	275
Y7	Fuel injectors	
Y7.1	Fuel injector	171, 172
Y7.2	Fuel injector	174, 175
Y7.3	Fuel injector	177, 178
Y7.4	Fuel injector	180, 181
Y18	EGR solenoid valve	166, 167, 279, 280
Y20	Injection regulation solenoid valve	277, 278
Y34	Fuel tank ventilation valve	163, 164

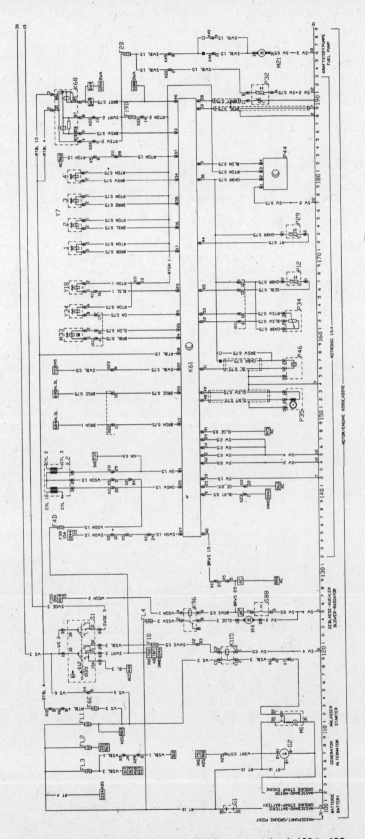

Typical wiring diagram (later models) - current track 100 to 199

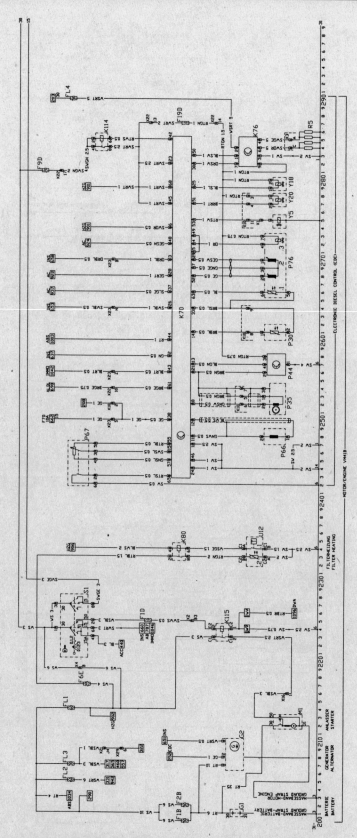

Typical wiring diagram (later models) - current track 200 to 299

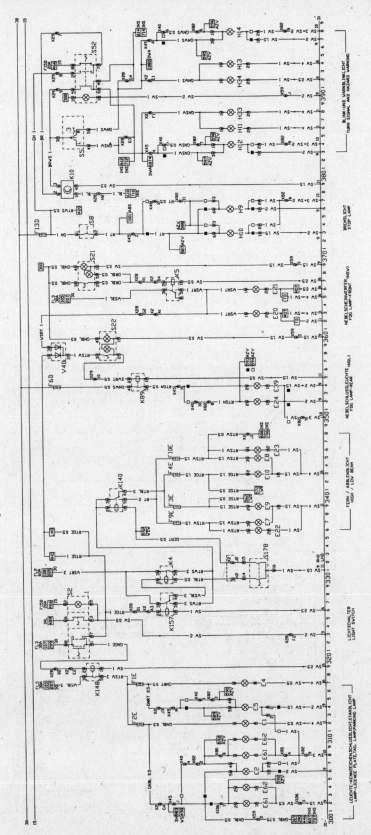

Typical wiring diagram (later models) - current track 300 to 399

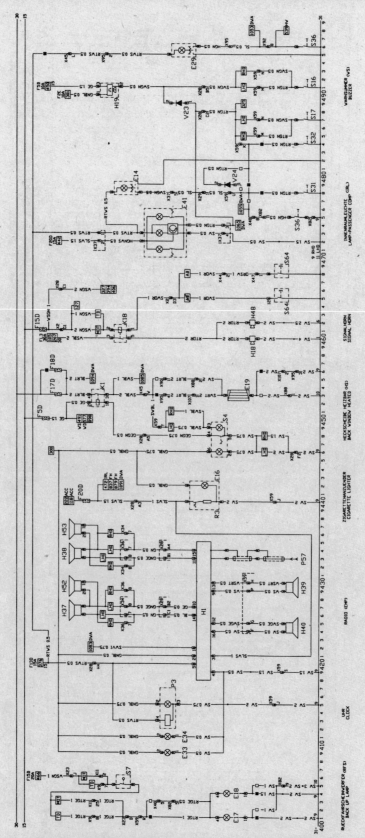

Typical wiring diagram (later models) - current track 400 to 499

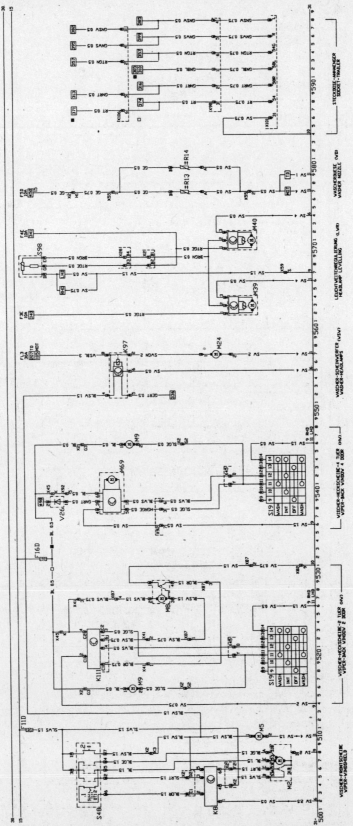

Typical wiring diagram (later models) - current track 500 to 599

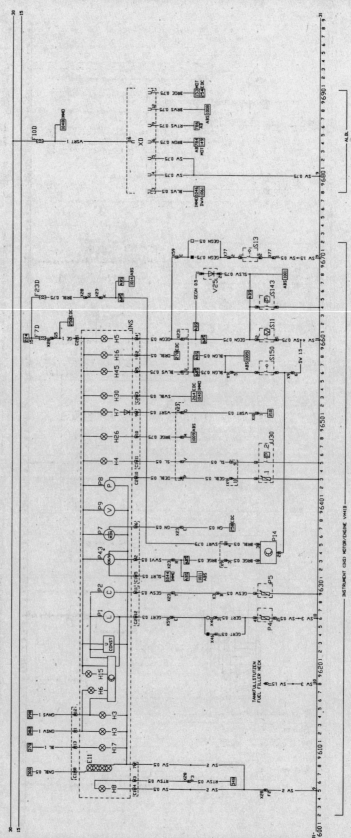

Typical wiring diagram (later models) - current track 600 to 699

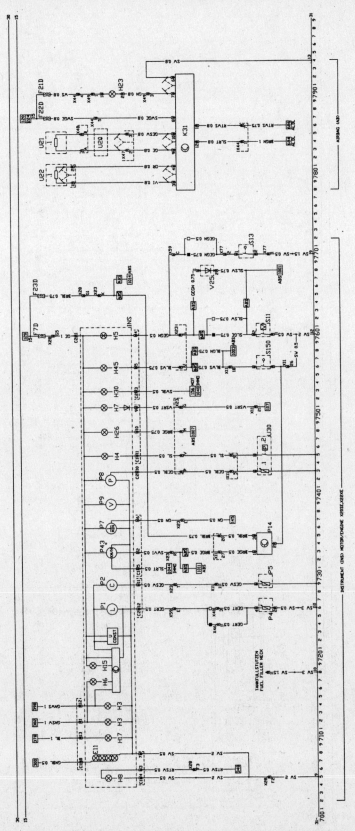

Typical wiring diagram (later models) - current track 700 to 799

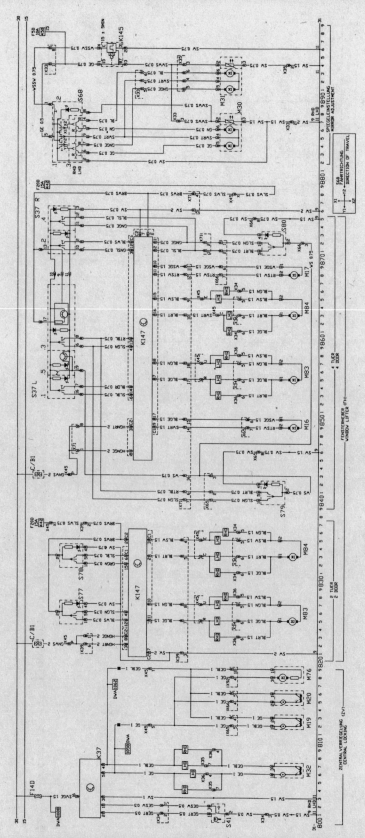

Typical wiring diagram (later models) - current track 800 to 899

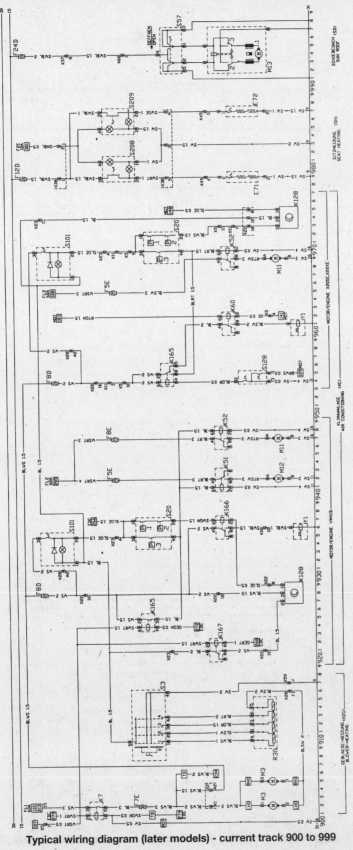

Typical wiring diagram (later models) - current track 900 to 999

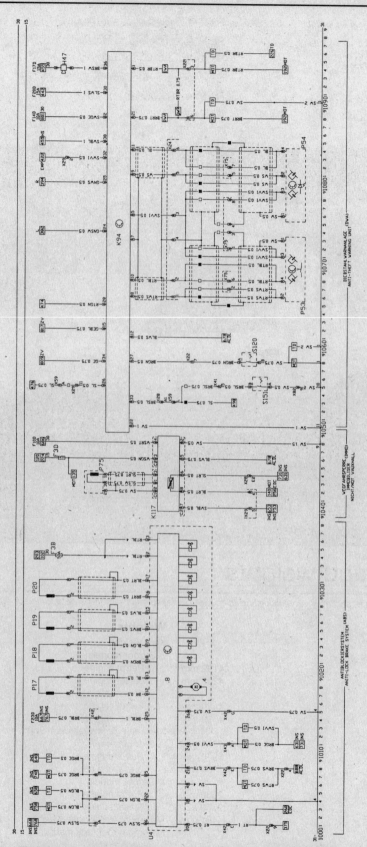

Typical wiring diagram (later models) - current track 1000 to 1099

Dimensions and Weights . . . . **REF•1**
Conversion Factors . . . . **REF•2**
Buying Spare Parts . . . . **REF•3**
Vehicle Identification . . . . **REF•3**
General Repair Procedures . . . . **REF•4**
Jacking and Vehicle Support . . . . **REF•5**
Radio/cassette unit Anti-theft System . . . . **REF•5**
Tools and Working Facilities . . . . **REF•6**
MOT Test Checks . . . . **REF•8**
Fault Finding . . . .**REF•12**
Glossary of Technical Terms . . . .**REF•20**
Index . . . .**REF•25**

Dimensions and weights

Note: *All figures are approximate, and may vary according to model. Refer to manufacturer's data for exact figures.*

Dimensions

Overall length:
  3-door:
    Hard-top model . . . . .4192 mm
    Soft-top model . . . . .4207 mm
  5-door:
    Pre 1995 model . . . . .4480 mm
    1995 on model . . . . .4692 mm
Overall width:
  Excluding mirrors . . . . .1780 mm
  Including mirrors . . . . .1950 mm
Overall height (unladen) . . . . .1753 mm
Wheelbase:
  3-door model . . . . .2330 mm
  5-door model . . . . .2760 mm
Ground clearance . . . . .191 mm

Weights

Kerb weight:
  3-door models:
    Petrol engine . . . . .1561 to 1700 kg
    diesel engine . . . . .1890 to 1825 kg
  5-door models:
    Petrol engine . . . . .1723 to 1800 kg
    diesel engine . . . . .1784 to 1920kg
Maximum gross vehicle weight:
  3-door models:
    Petrol engine . . . . .2100 to 2200 kg
    diesel engine . . . . .2510 kg
  5-door models:
    Petrol engine . . . . .2400 to 2510 kg
    diesel engine . . . . .2550 to 2600 kg
Maximum trailer nose weight .75 kg
Maximum roof rack load:
  3-door models . . . . .60 kg*
  5-door models . . . . .100 kg*
*Halve this figure if the vehicle is to be taken off-road and over rough terrain

Conversion factors

Length (distance)

Inches (in)	x 25.4	= Millimetres (mm)	x 0.0394	= Inches (in)
Feet (ft)	x 0.305	= Metres (m)	x 3.281	= Feet (ft)
Miles	x 1.609	= Kilometres (km)	x 0.621	= Miles

Volume (capacity)

Cubic inches (cu in; in^3)	x 16.387	= Cubic centimetres (cc; cm^3)	x 0.061	= Cubic inches (cu in; in^3)
Imperial pints (Imp pt)	x 0.568	= Litres (l)	x 1.76	= Imperial pints (Imp pt)
Imperial quarts (Imp qt)	x 1.137	= Litres (l)	x 0.88	= Imperial quarts (Imp qt)
Imperial quarts (Imp qt)	x 1.201	= US quarts (US qt)	x 0.833	= Imperial quarts (Imp qt)
US quarts (US qt)	x 0.946	= Litres (l)	x 1.057	= US quarts (US qt)
Imperial gallons (Imp gal)	x 4.546	= Litres (l)	x 0.22	= Imperial gallons (Imp gal)
Imperial gallons (Imp gal)	x 1.201	= US gallons (US gal)	x 0.833	= Imperial gallons (Imp gal)
US gallons (US gal)	x 3.785	= Litres (l)	x 0.264	= US gallons (US gal)

Mass (weight)

Ounces (oz)	x 28.35	= Grams (g)	x 0.035	= Ounces (oz)
Pounds (lb)	x 0.454	= Kilograms (kg)	x 2.205	= Pounds (lb)

Force

Ounces-force (ozf; oz)	x 0.278	= Newtons (N)	x 3.6	= Ounces-force (ozf; oz)
Pounds-force (lbf; lb)	x 4.448	= Newtons (N)	x 0.225	= Pounds-force (lbf; lb)
Newtons (N)	x 0.1	= Kilograms-force (kgf; kg)	x 9.81	= Newtons (N)

Pressure

Pounds-force per square inch (psi; lbf/in^2; lb/in^2)	x 0.070	= Kilograms-force per square centimetre (kgf/cm^2; kg/cm^2)	x 14.223	= Pounds-force per square inch (psi; lbf/in^2; lb/in^2)
Pounds-force per square inch (psi; lbf/in^2; lb/in^2)	x 0.068	= Atmospheres (atm)	x 14.696	= Pounds-force per square inch (psi; lbf/in^2; lb/in^2)
Pounds-force per square inch (psi; lbf/in^2; lb/in^2)	x 0.069	= Bars	x 14.5	= Pounds-force per square inch (psi; lbf/in^2; lb/in^2)
Pounds-force per square inch (psi; lbf/in^2; lb/in^2)	x 6.895	= Kilopascals (kPa)	x 0.145	= Pounds-force per square inch (psi; lbf/in^2; lb/in^2)
Kilopascals (kPa)	x 0.01	= Kilograms-force per square centimetre (kgf/cm^2; kg/cm^2)	x 98.1	= Kilopascals (kPa)
Millibar (mbar)	x 100	= Pascals (Pa)	x 0.01	= Millibar (mbar)
Millibar (mbar)	x 0.0145	= Pounds-force per square inch (psi; lbf/in^2; lb/in^2)	x 68.947	= Millibar (mbar)
Millibar (mbar)	x 0.75	= Millimetres of mercury (mmHg)	x 1.333	= Millibar (mbar)
Millibar (mbar)	x 0.401	= Inches of water (inH$_2$O)	x 2.491	= Millibar (mbar)
Millimetres of mercury (mmHg)	x 0.535	= Inches of water (inH$_2$O)	x 1.868	= Millimetres of mercury (mmHg)
Inches of water (inH$_2$O)	x 0.036	= Pounds-force per square inch (psi; lbf/in^2; lb/in^2)	x 27.68	= Inches of water (inH$_2$O)

Torque (moment of force)

Pounds-force inches (lbf in; lb in)	x 1.152	= Kilograms-force centimetre (kgf cm; kg cm)	x 0.868	= Pounds-force inches (lbf in; lb in)
Pounds-force inches (lbf in; lb in)	x 0.113	= Newton metres (Nm)	x 8.85	= Pounds-force inches (lbf in; lb in)
Pounds-force inches (lbf in; lb in)	x 0.083	= Pounds-force feet (lbf ft; lb ft)	x 12	= Pounds-force inches (lbf in; lb in)
Pounds-force feet (lbf ft; lb ft)	x 0.138	= Kilograms-force metres (kgf m; kg m)	x 7.233	= Pounds-force feet (lbf ft; lb ft)
Pounds-force feet (lbf ft; lb ft)	x 1.356	= Newton metres (Nm)	x 0.738	= Pounds-force feet (lbf ft; lb ft)
Newton metres (Nm)	x 0.102	= Kilograms-force metres (kgf m; kg m)	x 9.804	= Newton metres (Nm)

Power

Horsepower (hp)	x 745.7	= Watts (W)	x 0.0013	= Horsepower (hp)

Velocity (speed)

Miles per hour (miles/hr; mph)	x 1.609	= Kilometres per hour (km/hr; kph)	x 0.621	= Miles per hour (miles/hr; mph)

Fuel consumption*

Miles per gallon (mpg)	x 0.354	= Kilometres per litre (km/l)	x 2.825	= Miles per gallon (mpg)

Temperature

Degrees Fahrenheit = (°C x 1.8) + 32

Degrees Celsius (Degrees Centigrade; °C) = (°F - 32) x 0.56

* It is common practice to convert from miles per gallon (mpg) to litres/100 kilometres (l/100km), where mpg x l/100 km = 282

Spare parts are available from many sources, including maker's appointed garages, accessory shops, and motor factors. To be sure of obtaining the correct parts, it will sometimes be necessary to quote the vehicle identification number. If possible, it can also be useful to take the old parts along for positive identification. Items such as starter motors and alternators may be available under a service exchange scheme - any parts returned should be clean.

Our advice regarding spare parts is as follows.

Officially appointed garages

This is the best source of parts which are peculiar to your car, and which are not otherwise generally available (eg, badges, interior trim, certain body panels, etc). It is also the only place at which you should buy parts if the vehicle is still under warranty.

Accessory shops

These are very good places to buy materials and, components needed for the maintenance of your car (oil, air and fuel filters, light bulbs, drivebelts, greases, brake pads, touch-up paint, etc). Components of this nature sold by a reputable shop are usually of the same standard as those used by the car manufacturer.

Besides components, these shops also sell tools and general accessories, usually have convenient opening hours, charge lower prices, and can often be found close to home. Some accessory shops have parts counters where components needed for almost any repair job can be purchased or ordered.

Motor factors

Good factors will stock all the more important components which wear out comparatively quickly, and can sometimes supply individual components needed for the overhaul of a larger assembly (eg, brake seals and hydraulic parts, bearing shells, pistons, valves). They may also handle work such as cylinder block reboring, crankshaft regrinding, etc.

Tyre and exhaust specialists

These outlets may be independent, or members of a local or national chain. They frequently offer competitive prices when compared with a main dealer or local garage, but it will pay to obtain several quotes before making a decision. When researching prices, also ask what extras may be added - for instance fitting a new valve and balancing the wheel are both commonly charged on top of the price of a new tyre.

Other sources

Beware of parts or materials obtained from market stalls, car boot sales or similar outlets. Such items are not invariably sub-standard, but there is little chance of compensation if they do prove unsatisfactory. in the case of safety-critical components such as brake pads, there is the risk not only of financial loss, but also of an accident causing injury or death.

Second-hand components or assemblies obtained from a car breaker can be a good buy in some circumstances, but this sort of purchase is best made by the experienced DIY mechanic.

Vehicle identification

Modifications are a continuing and unpublicised process in vehicle manufacture, quite apart from major model changes. Spare parts manuals and lists are compiled upon a numerical basis, the individual vehicle identification numbers being essential to correct identification of the component concerned.

When ordering spare parts, always give as much information as possible. Quote the car model, year of manufacture and registration, chassis and engine numbers as appropriate.

The *Vehicle Identification Number (VIN)* plate is riveted to the bonnet lock crossmember, on the right-hand side of the lock, and is visible once the bonnet has been opened. The vehicle identification (chassis) number is also stamped onto the outside of the chassis member on the right-hand side; on 3-door models the number is located in the area underneath the rear wheel arch and on 5-door models it can be found in the area directly underneath the rear door **(see illustration)**. On certain models a *Service parts identification plate* is attached to the left-hand side of the engine compartment bulkhead; this plate carries details of the exact specification of all optional extras fitted at the factory.

The *engine number* can be found on the left-hand side of the cylinder block. The first five digits of the engine number form the engine identification code which is often referred to throughout this manual.

Chassis number location points

Whenever servicing, repair or overhaul work is carried out on the car or its components, it is necessary to observe the following procedures and instructions. This will assist in carrying out the operation efficiently and to a professional standard of workmanship.

Joint mating faces and gaskets

When separating components at their mating faces, never insert screwdrivers or similar implements into the joint between the faces in order to prise them apart. This can cause severe damage which results in oil leaks, coolant leaks, etc upon reassembly. Separation is usually achieved by tapping along the joint with a soft-faced hammer in order to break the seal. However, note that this method may not be suitable where dowels are used for component location.

Where a gasket is used between the mating faces of two components, ensure that it is renewed on reassembly, and fit it dry unless otherwise stated in the repair procedure. Make sure that the mating faces are clean and dry, with all traces of old gasket removed. When cleaning a joint face, use a tool which is not likely to score or damage the face, and remove any burrs or nicks with an oilstone or fine file.

Make sure that tapped holes are cleaned with a pipe cleaner, and keep them free of jointing compound, if this is being used, unless specifically instructed otherwise.

Ensure that all orifices, channels or pipes are clear, and blow through them, preferably using compressed air.

Oil seals

Oil seals can be removed by levering them out with a wide flat-bladed screwdriver or similar tool. Alternatively, a number of self-tapping screws may be screwed into the seal, and these used as a purchase for pliers or similar in order to pull the seal free.

Whenever an oil seal is removed from its working location, either individually or as part of an assembly, it should be renewed.

The very fine sealing lip of the seal is easily damaged, and will not seal if the surface it contacts is not completely clean and free from scratches, nicks or grooves. If the original sealing surface of the component cannot be restored, and the manufacturer has not made provision for slight relocation of the seal relative to the sealing surface, the component should be renewed.

Protect the lips of the seal from any surface which may damage them in the course of fitting. Use tape or a conical sleeve where possible. Lubricate the seal lips with oil before fitting and, on dual-lipped seals, fill the space between the lips with grease.

Unless otherwise stated, oil seals must be fitted with their sealing lips toward the lubricant to be sealed.

Use a tubular drift or block of wood of the appropriate size to install the seal and, if the seal housing is shouldered, drive the seal down to the shoulder. If the seal housing is unshouldered, the seal should be fitted with its face flush with the housing top face (unless otherwise instructed).

Screw threads and fastenings

Seized nuts, bolts and screws are quite a common occurrence where corrosion has set in, and the use of penetrating oil or releasing fluid will often overcome this problem if the offending item is soaked for a while before attempting to release it. The use of an impact driver may also provide a means of releasing such stubborn fastening devices, when used in conjunction with the appropriate screwdriver bit or socket. If none of these methods works, it may be necessary to resort to the careful application of heat, or the use of a hacksaw or nut splitter device.

Studs are usually removed by locking two nuts together on the threaded part, and then using a spanner on the lower nut to unscrew the stud. Studs or bolts which have broken off below the surface of the component in which they are mounted can sometimes be removed using a stud extractor. Always ensure that a blind tapped hole is completely free from oil, grease, water or other fluid before installing the bolt or stud. Failure to do this could cause the housing to crack due to the hydraulic action of the bolt or stud as it is screwed in.

When tightening a castellated nut to accept a split pin, tighten the nut to the specified torque, where applicable, and then tighten further to the next split pin hole. Never slacken the nut to align the split pin hole, unless stated in the repair procedure.

When checking or retightening a nut or bolt to a specified torque setting, slacken the nut or bolt by a quarter of a turn, and then retighten to the specified setting. However, this should not be attempted where angular tightening has been used.

For some screw fastenings, notably cylinder head bolts or nuts, torque wrench settings are no longer specified for the latter stages of tightening, "angle-tightening" being called up instead. Typically, a fairly low torque wrench setting will be applied to the bolts/nuts in the correct sequence, followed by one or more stages of tightening through specified angles.

Locknuts, locktabs and washers

Any fastening which will rotate against a component or housing during tightening should always have a washer between it and the relevant component or housing.

Spring or split washers should always be renewed when they are used to lock a critical component such as a big-end bearing retaining bolt or nut. Locktabs which are folded over to retain a nut or bolt should always be renewed.

Self-locking nuts can be re-used in non-critical areas, providing resistance can be felt when the locking portion passes over the bolt or stud thread. However, it should be noted that self-locking stiffnuts tend to lose their effectiveness after long periods of use, and should be renewed as a matter of course.

Split pins must always be replaced with new ones of the correct size for the hole.

When thread-locking compound is found on the threads of a fastener which is to be re-used, it should be cleaned off with a wire brush and solvent, and fresh compound applied on reassembly.

Special tools

Some repair procedures in this manual entail the use of special tools such as a press, two or three-legged pullers, spring compressors, etc. Wherever possible, suitable readily-available alternatives to the manufacturer's special tools are described, and are shown in use. In some instances, where no alternative is possible, it has been necessary to resort to the use of a manufacturer's tool, and this has been done for reasons of safety as well as the efficient completion of the repair operation. Unless you are highly-skilled and have a thorough understanding of the procedures described, never attempt to bypass the use of any special tool when the procedure described specifies its use. Not only is there a very great risk of personal injury, but expensive damage could be caused to the components involved.

Environmental considerations

When disposing of used engine oil, brake fluid, antifreeze, etc, give due consideration to any detrimental environmental effects. Do not, for instance, pour any of the above liquids down drains into the general sewage system, or onto the ground to soak away. Many local council refuse tips provide a facility for waste oil disposal, as do some garages. If none of these facilities are available, consult your local Environmental Health Department, or the National Rivers Authority, for further advice.

With the universal tightening-up of legislation regarding the emission of environmentally-harmful substances from motor vehicles, most current vehicles have tamperproof devices fitted to the main adjustment points of the fuel system. These devices are primarily designed to prevent unqualified persons from adjusting the fuel/air mixture, with the chance of a consequent increase in toxic emissions. If such devices are encountered during servicing or overhaul, they should, wherever possible, be renewed or refitted in accordance with the vehicle manufacturer's requirements or current legislation.

OIL CARE
FOLLOW THE CODE

OIL BANK LINE
0800 66 33 66

Note: It is antisocial and illegal to dump oil down the drain. To find the location of your local oil recycling bank, call this number free.

The jack supplied with the vehicle tool kit should only be used for changing the roadwheels - see *Wheel changing* at the front of this manual. When carrying out any other kind of work, raise the vehicle using a hydraulic (or trolley) jack, and always supplement the jack with axle stands positioned under the vehicle jacking points.

To raise the front of the vehicle, position the jack head underneath the front axle differential housing. Lift the vehicle to the required height and support it on axle stands positioned underneath the lifting points on the chassis, directly behind the engine rear mounting crossmember **(see illustration)**.

To raise the rear of the vehicle, position the jack head underneath the rear axle differential housing. Lift the vehicle to the required height and support it on axle stands. The stands can either be positioned underneath the rear axle, as near to the wheels as possible, or underneath the lifting points on the rear of the chassis. The lifting points are located just in front of the leaf spring front mountings on early models (leaf spring rear axle) or just behind the trailing link front mountings on later models (coil spring rear axle) **(see illustrations)**.

The jack supplied with the vehicle should be located underneath the lifting points on the front of the chassis or underneath the rear axle, as close to the wheel to be lifted as possible. Ensure that the jack head is correctly located before attempting to raise the vehicle.

Never work under, around, or near a raised vehicle, unless it is adequately supported in at least two places.

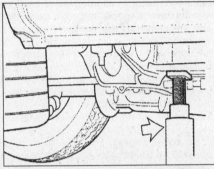

Position the axle stand or vehicle lifting jack under the front lifting point as shown

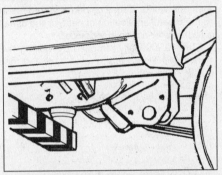

On early models with a leaf spring rear axle, the lifting points on the chassis are located in front of the leaf spring mountings

On later models with a coil spring rear axle, the lifting points on the chassis are located to the rear of the trailing link front mountings

Radio/cassette unit anti-theft system - precaution

The radio/cassette/CD player/autochanger unit fitted as standard equipment by Vauxhall is equipped with a built-in security code, to deter thieves. If the power source to the unit is cut, the anti-theft system will activate. Even if the power source is immediately reconnected, the radio/cassette unit will not function until the correct security code has been entered. Therefore if you do not know the correct security code for the unit, **do not** disconnect the battery negative lead, or remove the radio/cassette unit from the vehicle.

The procedure for reprogramming a unit that has been disconnected from its power supply varies from model to model - consult the handbook supplied with the unit for specific details or refer to your Vauxhall dealer.

Introduction

A selection of good tools is a fundamental requirement for anyone contemplating the maintenance and repair of a motor vehicle. For the owner who does not possess any, their purchase will prove a considerable expense, offsetting some of the savings made by doing-it-yourself. However, provided that the tools purchased meet the relevant national safety standards and are of good quality, they will last for many years and prove an extremely worthwhile investment.

To help the average owner to decide which tools are needed to carry out the various tasks detailed in this manual, we have compiled three lists of tools under the following headings: *Maintenance and minor repair, Repair and overhaul*, and *Special*. Newcomers to practical mechanics should start off with the *Maintenance and minor repair* tool kit, and confine themselves to the simpler jobs around the vehicle. Then, as confidence and experience grow, more difficult tasks can be undertaken, with extra tools being purchased as, and when, they are needed. In this way, a *Maintenance and minor repair* tool kit can be built up into a *Repair and overhaul* tool kit over a considerable period of time, without any major cash outlays. The experienced do-it-yourselfer will have a tool kit good enough for most repair and overhaul procedures, and will add tools from the *Special* category when it is felt that the expense is justified by the amount of use to which these tools will be put.

Maintenance and minor repair tool kit

The tools given in this list should be considered as a minimum requirement if routine maintenance, servicing and minor repair operations are to be undertaken. We recommend the purchase of combination spanners (ring one end, open-ended the other); although more expensive than open-ended ones, they do give the advantages of both types of spanner.

- ☐ *Combination spanners:*
  Metric - 8 to 19 mm inclusive
- ☐ *Adjustable spanner - 35 mm jaw (approx.)*
- ☐ *Spark plug spanner (with rubber insert) - petrol models*
- ☐ *Spark plug gap adjustment tool - petrol models*
- ☐ *Set of feeler gauges*
- ☐ *Brake bleed nipple spanner*
- ☐ *Screwdrivers:*
  Flat blade - 100 mm long x 6 mm dia
  Cross blade - 100 mm long x 6 mm dia
  Torx - various sizes (not all vehicles)
- ☐ *Combination pliers*
- ☐ *Hacksaw (junior)*
- ☐ *Tyre pump*
- ☐ *Tyre pressure gauge*
- ☐ *Oil can*
- ☐ *Oil filter removal tool*
- ☐ *Fine emery cloth*
- ☐ *Wire brush (small)*
- ☐ *Funnel (medium size)*
- ☐ *Sump drain plug key (not all vehicles)*

Repair and overhaul tool kit

These tools are virtually essential for anyone undertaking any major repairs to a motor vehicle, and are additional to those given in the *Maintenance and minor repair* list. Included in this list is a comprehensive set of sockets. Although these are expensive, they will be found invaluable as they are so versatile - particularly if various drives are included in the set. We recommend the half-inch square-drive type, as this can be used with most proprietary torque wrenches.

The tools in this list will sometimes need to be supplemented by tools from the *Special* list:

- ☐ *Sockets (or box spanners) to cover range in previous list (including Torx sockets)*
- ☐ *Reversible ratchet drive (for use with sockets)*
- ☐ *Extension piece, 250 mm (for use with sockets)*
- ☐ *Universal joint (for use with sockets)*
- ☐ *Flexible handle or sliding T "breaker bar" (for use with sockets)*
- ☐ *Torque wrench (for use with sockets)*
- ☐ *Self-locking grips*
- ☐ *Ball pein hammer*
- ☐ *Soft-faced mallet (plastic or rubber)*
- ☐ *Screwdrivers:*
  Flat blade - long & sturdy, short (chubby), and narrow (electrician's) types
  Cross blade - long & sturdy, and short (chubby) types
- ☐ *Pliers:*
  Long-nosed
  Side cutters (electrician's)
  Circlip (internal and external)
- ☐ *Cold chisel - 25 mm*
- ☐ *Scriber*
- ☐ *Scraper*
- ☐ *Centre-punch*
- ☐ *Pin punch*
- ☐ *Hacksaw*
- ☐ *Brake hose clamp*
- ☐ *Brake/clutch bleeding kit*
- ☐ *Selection of twist drills*
- ☐ *Steel rule/straight-edge*
- ☐ *Allen keys (inc. splined/Torx type)*
- ☐ *Selection of files*
- ☐ *Wire brush*
- ☐ *Axle stands*
- ☐ *Jack (strong trolley or hydraulic type)*
- ☐ *Light with extension lead*
- ☐ *Universal electrical multi-meter*

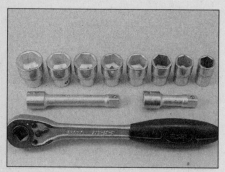

Sockets and reversible ratchet drive

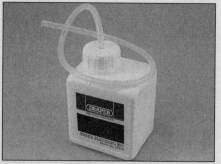

Brake bleeding kit

Torx key, socket and bit

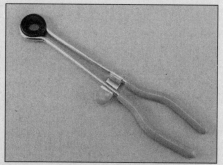

Hose clamp

Angular-tightening gauge

Special tools

The tools in this list are those which are not used regularly, are expensive to buy, or which need to be used in accordance with their manufacturers' instructions. Unless relatively difficult mechanical jobs are undertaken frequently, it will not be economic to buy many of these tools. Where this is the case, you could consider clubbing together with friends (or joining a motorists' club) to make a joint purchase, or borrowing the tools against a deposit from a local garage or tool hire specialist. It is worth noting that many of the larger DIY superstores now carry a large range of special tools for hire at modest rates.

The following list contains only those tools and instruments freely available to the public, and not those special tools produced by the vehicle manufacturer specifically for its dealer network. You will find occasional references to these manufacturers' special tools in the text of this manual. Generally, an alternative method of doing the job without the vehicle manufacturers' special tool is given. However, sometimes there is no alternative to using them. Where this is the case and the relevant tool cannot be bought or borrowed, you will have to entrust the work to a dealer.

- ☐ Angular-tightening gauge
- ☐ Valve spring compressor
- ☐ Valve grinding tool
- ☐ Piston ring compressor
- ☐ Piston ring removal/installation tool
- ☐ Cylinder bore hone
- ☐ Balljoint separator
- ☐ Coil spring compressors (where applicable)
- ☐ Two/three-legged hub and bearing puller
- ☐ Impact screwdriver
- ☐ Micrometer and/or vernier calipers
- ☐ Dial gauge
- ☐ Stroboscopic timing light
- ☐ Dwell angle meter/tachometer
- ☐ Fault code reader
- ☐ Cylinder compression gauge
- ☐ Hand-operated vacuum pump and gauge
- ☐ Clutch plate alignment set
- ☐ Brake shoe steady spring cup removal tool
- ☐ Bush and bearing removal/installation set
- ☐ Stud extractors
- ☐ Tap and die set
- ☐ Lifting tackle
- ☐ Trolley jack

Buying tools

Reputable motor accessory shops and superstores often offer excellent quality tools at discount prices, so it pays to shop around.

Remember, you don't have to buy the most expensive items on the shelf, but it is always advisable to steer clear of the very cheap tools. Beware of 'bargains' offered on market stalls or at car boot sales. There are plenty of good tools around at reasonable prices, but always aim to purchase items which meet the relevant national safety standards. If in doubt, ask the proprietor or manager of the shop for advice before making a purchase.

Care and maintenance of tools

Having purchased a reasonable tool kit, it is necessary to keep the tools in a clean and serviceable condition. After use, always wipe off any dirt, grease and metal particles using a clean, dry cloth, before putting the tools away. Never leave them lying around after they have been used. A simple tool rack on the garage or workshop wall for items such as screwdrivers and pliers is a good idea. Store all normal spanners and sockets in a metal box. Any measuring instruments, gauges, meters, etc, must be carefully stored where they cannot be damaged or become rusty.

Take a little care when tools are used. Hammer heads inevitably become marked, and screwdrivers lose the keen edge on their blades from time to time. A little timely attention with emery cloth or a file will soon restore items like this to a good finish.

Working facilities

Not to be forgotten when discussing tools is the workshop itself. If anything more than routine maintenance is to be carried out, a suitable working area becomes essential.

It is appreciated that many an owner-mechanic is forced by circumstances to remove an engine or similar item without the benefit of a garage or workshop. Having done this, any repairs should always be done under the cover of a roof.

Wherever possible, any dismantling should be done on a clean, flat workbench or table at a suitable working height.

Any workbench needs a vice; one with a jaw opening of 100 mm is suitable for most jobs. As mentioned previously, some clean dry storage space is also required for tools, as well as for any lubricants, cleaning fluids, touch-up paints etc, which become necessary.

Another item which may be required, and which has a much more general usage, is an electric drill with a chuck capacity of at least 8 mm. This, together with a good range of twist drills, is virtually essential for fitting accessories.

Last, but not least, always keep a supply of old newspapers and clean, lint-free rags available, and try to keep any working area as clean as possible.

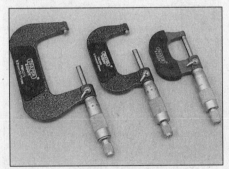
Micrometers

Dial test indicator ("dial gauge")

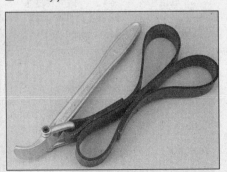
Strap wrench

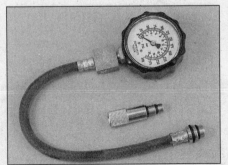
Compression tester

Fault code reader

This is a guide to getting your vehicle through the MOT test. Obviously it will not be possible to examine the vehicle to the same standard as the professional MOT tester. However, working through the following checks will enable you to identify any problem areas before submitting the vehicle for the test.

Where a testable component is in borderline condition, the tester has discretion in deciding whether to pass or fail it. The basis of such discretion is whether the tester would be happy for a close relative or friend to use the vehicle with the component in that condition. If the vehicle presented is clean and evidently well cared for, the tester may be more inclined to pass a borderline component than if the vehicle is scruffy and apparently neglected.

It has only been possible to summarise the test requirements here, based on the regulations in force at the time of printing. Test standards are becoming increasingly stringent, although there are some exemptions for older vehicles. For full details obtain a copy of the Haynes publication Pass the MOT! (available from stockists of Haynes manuals).

An assistant will be needed to help carry out some of these checks.

The checks have been sub-divided into four categories, as follows:

1 Checks carried out **FROM THE DRIVER'S SEAT**

2 Checks carried out **WITH THE VEHICLE ON THE GROUND**

3 Checks carried out **WITH THE VEHICLE RAISED AND THE WHEELS FREE TO TURN**

4 Checks carried out on **YOUR VEHICLE'S EXHAUST EMISSION SYSTEM**

1 Checks carried out **FROM THE DRIVER'S SEAT**

Handbrake

☐ Test the operation of the handbrake. Excessive travel (too many clicks) indicates incorrect brake or cable adjustment.

☐ Check that the handbrake cannot be released by tapping the lever sideways. Check the security of the lever mountings.

Footbrake

☐ Depress the brake pedal and check that it does not creep down to the floor, indicating a master cylinder fault. Release the pedal, wait a few seconds, then depress it again. If the pedal travels nearly to the floor before firm resistance is felt, brake adjustment or repair is necessary. If the pedal feels spongy, there is air in the hydraulic system which must be removed by bleeding.

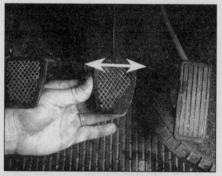

☐ Check that the brake pedal is secure and in good condition. Check also for signs of fluid leaks on the pedal, floor or carpets, which would indicate failed seals in the brake master cylinder.

☐ Check the servo unit (when applicable) by operating the brake pedal several times, then keeping the pedal depressed and starting the engine. As the engine starts, the pedal will move down slightly. If not, the vacuum hose or the servo itself may be faulty.

Steering wheel and column

☐ Examine the steering wheel for fractures or looseness of the hub, spokes or rim.

☐ Move the steering wheel from side to side and then up and down. Check that the steering wheel is not loose on the column, indicating wear or a loose retaining nut. Continue moving the steering wheel as before, but also turn it slightly from left to right.

☐ Check that the steering wheel is not loose on the column, and that there is no abnormal

movement of the steering wheel, indicating wear in the column support bearings or couplings.

Windscreen and mirrors

☐ The windscreen must be free of cracks or other significant damage within the driver's field of view. (Small stone chips are acceptable.) Rear view mirrors must be secure, intact, and capable of being adjusted.

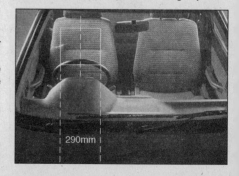

290mm

Seat belts and seats

Note: *The following checks are applicable to all seat belts, front and rear.*

☐ Examine the webbing of all the belts (including rear belts if fitted) for cuts, serious fraying or deterioration. Fasten and unfasten each belt to check the buckles. If applicable, check the retracting mechanism. Check the security of all seat belt mountings accessible from inside the vehicle.

☐ The front seats themselves must be securely attached and the backrests must lock in the upright position.

Doors

☐ Both front doors must be able to be opened and closed from outside and inside, and must latch securely when closed.

2 Checks carried out WITH THE VEHICLE ON THE GROUND

Vehicle identification

☐ Number plates must be in good condition, secure and legible, with letters and numbers correctly spaced – spacing at (A) should be twice that at (B).

☐ The VIN plate and/or homologation plate must be legible.

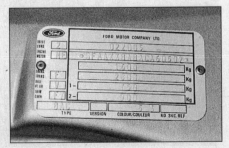

Electrical equipment

☐ Switch on the ignition and check the operation of the horn.

☐ Check the windscreen washers and wipers, examining the wiper blades; renew damaged or perished blades. Also check the operation of the stop-lights.

☐ Check the operation of the sidelights and number plate lights. The lenses and reflectors must be secure, clean and undamaged.

☐ Check the operation and alignment of the headlights. The headlight reflectors must not be tarnished and the lenses must be undamaged.

☐ Switch on the ignition and check the operation of the direction indicators (including the instrument panel tell-tale) and the hazard warning lights. Operation of the sidelights and stop-lights must not affect the indicators - if it does, the cause is usually a bad earth at the rear light cluster.

☐ Check the operation of the rear foglight(s), including the warning light on the instrument panel or in the switch.

Footbrake

☐ Examine the master cylinder, brake pipes and servo unit for leaks, loose mountings, corrosion or other damage.

☐ The fluid reservoir must be secure and the fluid level must be between the upper (**A**) and lower (**B**) markings.

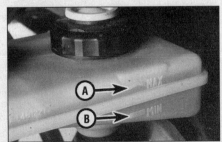

☐ Inspect both front brake flexible hoses for cracks or deterioration of the rubber. Turn the steering from lock to lock, and ensure that the hoses do not contact the wheel, tyre, or any part of the steering or suspension mechanism. With the brake pedal firmly depressed, check the hoses for bulges or leaks under pressure.

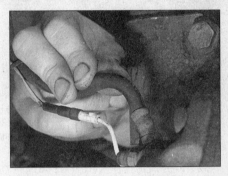

Steering and suspension

☐ Have your assistant turn the steering wheel from side to side slightly, up to the point where the steering gear just begins to transmit this movement to the roadwheels. Check for excessive free play between the steering wheel and the steering gear, indicating wear or insecurity of the steering column joints, the column-to-steering gear coupling, or the steering gear itself.

☐ Have your assistant turn the steering wheel more vigorously in each direction, so that the roadwheels just begin to turn. As this is done, examine all the steering joints, linkages, fittings and attachments. Renew any component that shows signs of wear or damage. On vehicles with power steering, check the security and condition of the steering pump, drivebelt and hoses.

☐ Check that the vehicle is standing level, and at approximately the correct ride height.

Shock absorbers

☐ Depress each corner of the vehicle in turn, then release it. The vehicle should rise and then settle in its normal position. If the vehicle continues to rise and fall, the shock absorber is defective. A shock absorber which has seized will also cause the vehicle to fail.

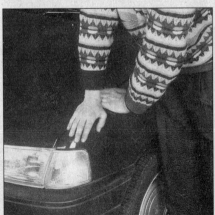

Exhaust system

☐ Start the engine. With your assistant holding a rag over the tailpipe, check the entire system for leaks. Repair or renew leaking sections.

3 Checks carried out WITH THE VEHICLE RAISED AND THE WHEELS FREE TO TURN

Jack up the front and rear of the vehicle, and securely support it on axle stands. Position the stands clear of the suspension assemblies. Ensure that the wheels are clear of the ground and that the steering can be turned from lock to lock.

Steering mechanism

☐ Have your assistant turn the steering from lock to lock. Check that the steering turns smoothly, and that no part of the steering mechanism, including a wheel or tyre, fouls any brake hose or pipe or any part of the body structure.

☐ Examine the steering rack rubber gaiters for damage or insecurity of the retaining clips. If power steering is fitted, check for signs of damage or leakage of the fluid hoses, pipes or connections. Also check for excessive stiffness or binding of the steering, a missing split pin or locking device, or severe corrosion of the body structure within 30 cm of any steering component attachment point.

Front and rear suspension and wheel bearings

☐ Starting at the front right-hand side, grasp the roadwheel at the 3 o'clock and 9 o'clock positions and shake it vigorously. Check for free play or insecurity at the wheel bearings, suspension balljoints, or suspension mountings, pivots and attachments.

☐ Now grasp the wheel at the 12 o'clock and 6 o'clock positions and repeat the previous inspection. Spin the wheel, and check for roughness or tightness of the front wheel bearing.

☐ If excess free play is suspected at a component pivot point, this can be confirmed by using a large screwdriver or similar tool and levering between the mounting and the component attachment. This will confirm whether the wear is in the pivot bush, its retaining bolt, or in the mounting itself (the bolt holes can often become elongated).

☐ Carry out all the above checks at the other front wheel, and then at both rear wheels.

Springs and shock absorbers

☐ Examine the suspension struts (when applicable) for serious fluid leakage, corrosion, or damage to the casing. Also check the security of the mounting points.

☐ If coil springs are fitted, check that the spring ends locate in their seats, and that the spring is not corroded, cracked or broken.

☐ If leaf springs are fitted, check that all leaves are intact, that the axle is securely attached to each spring, and that there is no deterioration of the spring eye mountings, bushes, and shackles.

☐ The same general checks apply to vehicles fitted with other suspension types, such as torsion bars, hydraulic displacer units, etc. Ensure that all mountings and attachments are secure, that there are no signs of excessive wear, corrosion or damage, and (on hydraulic types) that there are no fluid leaks or damaged pipes.

☐ Inspect the shock absorbers for signs of serious fluid leakage. Check for wear of the mounting bushes or attachments, or damage to the body of the unit.

Driveshafts (fwd vehicles only)

☐ Rotate each front wheel in turn and inspect the constant velocity joint gaiters for splits or damage. Also check that each driveshaft is straight and undamaged.

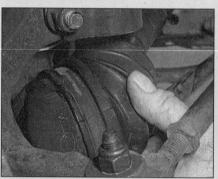

Braking system

☐ If possible without dismantling, check brake pad wear and disc condition. Ensure that the friction lining material has not worn excessively, (A) and that the discs are not fractured, pitted, scored or badly worn (B).

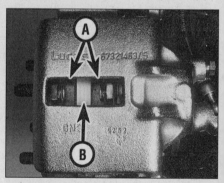

☐ Examine all the rigid brake pipes underneath the vehicle, and the flexible hose(s) at the rear. Look for corrosion, chafing or insecurity of the pipes, and for signs of bulging under pressure, chafing, splits or deterioration of the flexible hoses.

☐ Look for signs of fluid leaks at the brake calipers or on the brake backplates. Repair or renew leaking components.

☐ Slowly spin each wheel, while your assistant depresses and releases the footbrake. Ensure that each brake is operating and does not bind when the pedal is released.

☐ Examine the handbrake mechanism, checking for frayed or broken cables, excessive corrosion, or wear or insecurity of the linkage. Check that the mechanism works on each relevant wheel, and releases fully, without binding.

☐ It is not possible to test brake efficiency without special equipment, but a road test can be carried out later to check that the vehicle pulls up in a straight line.

Fuel and exhaust systems

☐ Inspect the fuel tank (including the filler cap), fuel pipes, hoses and unions. All components must be secure and free from leaks.

☐ Examine the exhaust system over its entire length, checking for any damaged, broken or missing mountings, security of the retaining clamps and rust or corrosion.

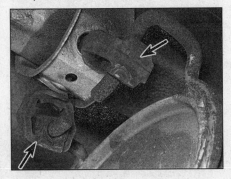

Wheels and tyres

☐ Examine the sidewalls and tread area of each tyre in turn. Check for cuts, tears, lumps, bulges, separation of the tread, and exposure of the ply or cord due to wear or damage. Check that the tyre bead is correctly seated on the wheel rim, that the valve is sound and

properly seated, and that the wheel is not distorted or damaged.

☐ Check that the tyres are of the correct size for the vehicle, that they are of the same size and type on each axle, and that the pressures are correct.

☐ Check the tyre tread depth. The legal minimum at the time of writing is 1.6 mm over at least three-quarters of the tread width. Abnormal tread wear may indicate incorrect front wheel alignment.

Body corrosion

☐ Check the condition of the entire vehicle structure for signs of corrosion in load-bearing areas. (These include chassis box sections, side sills, cross-members, pillars, and all suspension, steering, braking system and seat belt mountings and anchorages.) Any corrosion which has seriously reduced the thickness of a load-bearing area is likely to cause the vehicle to fail. In this case professional repairs are likely to be needed.

☐ Damage or corrosion which causes sharp or otherwise dangerous edges to be exposed will also cause the vehicle to fail.

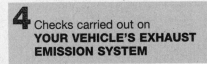

4 Checks carried out on YOUR VEHICLE'S EXHAUST EMISSION SYSTEM

Petrol models

☐ Have the engine at normal operating temperature, and make sure that it is in good tune (ignition system in good order, air filter element clean, etc).

☐ Before any measurements are carried out, raise the engine speed to around 2500 rpm, and hold it at this speed for 20 seconds. Allow

the engine speed to return to idle, and watch for smoke emissions from the exhaust tailpipe. If the idle speed is obviously much too high, or if dense blue or clearly-visible black smoke comes from the tailpipe for more than 5 seconds, the vehicle will fail. As a rule of thumb, blue smoke signifies oil being burnt (engine wear) while black smoke signifies unburnt fuel (dirty air cleaner element, or other carburettor or fuel system fault).

☐ An exhaust gas analyser capable of measuring carbon monoxide (CO) and hydrocarbons (HC) is now needed. If such an instrument cannot be hired or borrowed, a local garage may agree to perform the check for a small fee.

CO emissions (mixture)

☐ At the time of writing, the maximum CO level at idle is 3.5% for vehicles first used after August 1986 and 4.5% for older vehicles. From January 1996 a much tighter limit (around 0.5%) applies to catalyst-equipped vehicles first used from August 1992. If the CO level cannot be reduced far enough to pass the test (and the fuel and ignition systems are otherwise in good condition) then the carburettor is badly worn, or there is some problem in the fuel injection system or catalytic converter (as applicable).

HC emissions

☐ With the CO emissions within limits, HC emissions must be no more than 1200 ppm (parts per million). If the vehicle fails this test at idle, it can be re-tested at around 2000 rpm; if the HC level is then 1200 ppm or less, this counts as a pass.

☐ Excessive HC emissions can be caused by oil being burnt, but they are more likely to be due to unburnt fuel.

Diesel models

☐ The only emission test applicable to Diesel engines is the measuring of exhaust smoke density. The test involves accelerating the engine several times to its maximum unloaded speed.

Note: *It is of the utmost importance that the engine timing belt is in good condition before the test is carried out.*

☐ Excessive smoke can be caused by a dirty air cleaner element. Otherwise, professional advice may be needed to find the cause.

Engine

- ☐ Engine fails to rotate when attempting to start
- ☐ Engine rotates, but will not start
- ☐ Engine difficult to start when cold
- ☐ Engine difficult to start when hot
- ☐ Starter motor noisy or excessively-rough in engagement
- ☐ Engine starts, but stops immediately
- ☐ Engine idles erratically
- ☐ Engine misfires at idle speed
- ☐ Engine misfires throughout the driving speed range
- ☐ Engine hesitates on acceleration
- ☐ Engine stalls
- ☐ Engine lacks power
- ☐ Engine backfires
- ☐ Oil pressure warning light illuminated with engine running
- ☐ Engine runs-on after switching off
- ☐ Engine noises

Cooling system

- ☐ Overheating
- ☐ Overcooling
- ☐ External coolant leakage
- ☐ Internal coolant leakage
- ☐ Corrosion

Fuel and exhaust systems

- ☐ Excessive fuel consumption
- ☐ Fuel leakage and/or fuel odour
- ☐ Excessive noise or fumes from exhaust system

Clutch

- ☐ Pedal travels to floor - no pressure or very little resistance
- ☐ Clutch fails to disengage (unable to select gears).
- ☐ Clutch slips (engine speed increases, with no increase in vehicle speed).
- ☐ Judder as clutch is engaged
- ☐ Noise when depressing or releasing clutch pedal

Manual transmission

- ☐ Noisy in neutral with engine running
- ☐ Noisy in one particular gear
- ☐ Difficulty engaging gears
- ☐ Jumps out of gear
- ☐ Vibration
- ☐ Lubricant leaks

Driveshafts

- ☐ Vibration when accelerating or decelerating
- ☐ Clicking or knocking noise on turns (at slow speed on full-lock)

Differential and propellor shaft

- ☐ Vibration when accelerating or decelerating
- ☐ Low pitched whining; increasing with road speed

Braking system

- ☐ Vehicle pulls to one side under braking
- ☐ Noise (grinding or high-pitched squeal) when brakes applied
- ☐ Excessive brake pedal travel
- ☐ Brake pedal feels spongy when depressed
- ☐ Excessive brake pedal effort required to stop vehicle
- ☐ Judder felt through brake pedal or steering wheel when braking
- ☐ Brakes binding
- ☐ Rear wheels locking under normal braking

Suspension and steering

- ☐ Vehicle pulls to one side
- ☐ Wheel wobble and vibration
- ☐ Excessive pitching and/or rolling around corners, or during braking
- ☐ Wandering or general instability
- ☐ Excessively-stiff steering
- ☐ Excessive play in steering
- ☐ Lack of power assistance
- ☐ Tyre wear excessive

Electrical system

- ☐ Battery will not hold a charge for more than a few days
- ☐ Ignition/no-charge warning light remains illuminated with engine running
- ☐ Ignition/no-charge warning light fails to come on
- ☐ Lights inoperative
- ☐ Instrument readings inaccurate or erratic
- ☐ Horn inoperative, or unsatisfactory in operation
- ☐ Windscreen wipers inoperative, or unsatisfactory in operation
- ☐ Windscreen washers inoperative, or unsatisfactory in operation
- ☐ Electric windows inoperative, or unsatisfactory in operation
- ☐ Central locking system inoperative, or unsatisfactory in operation

Introduction

The vehicle owner who does his or her own maintenance according to the recommended service schedules should not have to use this section of the manual very often. Modern component reliability is such that, provided those items subject to wear or deterioration are inspected or renewed at the specified intervals, sudden failure is comparatively rare. Faults do not usually just happen as a result of sudden failure, but develop over a period of time. Major mechanical failures in particular are usually preceded by characteristic symptoms over hundreds or even thousands of miles. Those components which do occasionally fail without warning are often small and easily carried in the vehicle.

With any fault-finding, the first step is to decide where to begin investigations. Sometimes this is obvious, but on other occasions, a little detective work will be necessary. The owner who makes half a dozen haphazard adjustments or replacements may be successful in curing a fault (or its symptoms), but will be none the wiser if the fault recurs, and ultimately may have spent more time and money than was necessary. A calm and logical approach will be found to be more satisfactory in the long run. Always take into account any warning signs or abnormalities that may have been noticed in the period preceding the fault - power loss, high or low gauge readings, unusual smells, etc - and remember that failure of components such as fuses or spark plugs may only be pointers to some underlying fault.

The pages which follow provide an easy-reference guide to the more common problems which may occur during the operation of the vehicle. These problems and their possible causes are grouped under headings denoting various components or systems, such as Engine, Cooling system, etc. The Chapter and/or Section which deals with the problem is also shown in brackets. Whatever the fault, certain basic principles apply. These are as follows:

Verify the fault. This is simply a matter of being sure that you know what the symptoms are before starting work. This is particularly important if you are investigating a fault for someone else, who may not have described it very accurately.

Don't overlook the obvious. For example, if the vehicle won't start, is there fuel in the tank? (Don't take anyone else's word on this particular point, and don't trust the fuel gauge either!) If an electrical fault is indicated, look for loose or broken wires before digging out the test gear.

Cure the disease, not the symptom. Substituting a flat battery with a fully-charged one will get you off the hard shoulder, but if the underlying cause is not attended to, the new battery will go the same way. Similarly, changing oil-fouled spark plugs for a new set will get you moving again, but remember that the reason for the fouling (if it wasn't simply an incorrect grade of plug) will have to be established and corrected.

Don't take anything for granted. Particularly, don't forget that a new component may itself be defective (especially if its been rattling around in the boot for months), and don't leave components out of a fault diagnosis sequence just because they are new or recently-fitted. When you do finally diagnose a difficult fault, you'll probably realise that all the evidence was there from the start.

Engine

Engine fails to rotate when attempting to start

- ☐ Battery terminal connections loose or corroded (see *Weekly checks*)
- ☐ Battery discharged or faulty (Chapter 5)
- ☐ Broken, loose or disconnected wiring in the starting circuit (Chapter 5)
- ☐ Defective starter solenoid or switch (Chapter 5)
- ☐ Defective starter motor (Chapter 5)
- ☐ Starter pinion or flywheel ring gear teeth loose or broken (Chapters 2 and 5)
- ☐ Engine earth strap broken or disconnected (Chapter 5)

Engine rotates, but will not start

- ☐ Fuel tank empty
- ☐ Battery discharged (engine rotates slowly) (Chapter 5)
- ☐ Battery terminal connections loose or corroded (Chapter 1)
- ☐ Ignition components damp or damaged - petrol models (Chapters 1 and 5)
- ☐ Broken, loose or disconnected wiring in the ignition circuit - petrol models (Chapters 1 and 5)
- ☐ Worn, faulty or incorrectly-gapped spark plugs - petrol models (Chapter 1)
- ☐ Preheating system faulty - diesel models (Chapter 5)
- ☐ Fuel injection system fault - petrol models (Chapter 4)
- ☐ Stop solenoid faulty - diesel models (Chapter 4)
- ☐ Air in fuel system - diesel models (Chapter 4)
- ☐ Major mechanical failure (eg camshaft drive) (Chapter 2)

Engine difficult to start when cold

- ☐ Battery discharged (Chapter 5)
- ☐ Battery terminal connections loose or corroded (see *Weekly checks*)
- ☐ Worn, faulty or incorrectly-gapped spark plugs - petrol models (Chapter 1)
- ☐ Preheating system faulty - diesel models (Chapter 5)
- ☐ Fuel injection system fault - petrol models (Chapter 4)
- ☐ Other ignition system fault - petrol models (Chapters 1 and 5)
- ☐ Low cylinder compressions (Chapter 2)

Engine difficult to start when hot

- ☐ Air filter element dirty or clogged (Chapter 1)
- ☐ Fuel injection system fault - petrol models (Chapter 4)
- ☐ Low cylinder compressions (Chapter 2)

Starter motor noisy or excessively-rough in engagement

- ☐ Starter pinion or flywheel ring gear teeth loose or broken (Chapters 2 and 5)
- ☐ Starter motor mounting bolts loose or missing (Chapter 5)
- ☐ Starter motor internal components worn or damaged (Chapter 5)

Engine starts, but stops immediately

- ☐ Loose or faulty electrical connections in the ignition circuit - petrol models (Chapters 1 and 5)
- ☐ Vacuum leak at the throttle body or inlet manifold - petrol models (Chapter 4)
- ☐ Blocked injector/fuel injection system fault - petrol models (Chapter 4)

Engine idles erratically

- ☐ Air filter element clogged (Chapter 1)
- ☐ Vacuum leak at the throttle body, inlet manifold or associated hoses - petrol models (Chapter 4)
- ☐ Worn, faulty or incorrectly-gapped spark plugs - petrol models (Chapter 1)
- ☐ Uneven or low cylinder compressions (Chapter 2)
- ☐ Camshaft lobes worn (Chapter 2)
- ☐ Timing belt/chain incorrectly fitted (Chapter 2)
- ☐ Blocked injector/fuel injection system fault - petrol models (Chapter 4)
- ☐ Faulty injector(s) - diesel models (Chapter 4)

Engine misfires at idle speed

- ☐ Worn, faulty or incorrectly-gapped spark plugs - petrol models (Chapter 1)
- ☐ Faulty spark plug HT leads (where fitted) - petrol models (Chapter 1)
- ☐ Vacuum leak at the throttle body, inlet manifold or associated hoses - petrol models (Chapter 4)
- ☐ Blocked injector/fuel injection system fault - petrol models (Chapter 4)
- ☐ Faulty injector(s) - diesel models (Chapter 4)
- ☐ Distributor cap cracked or tracking internally - petrol models (where applicable) (Chapter 1).
- ☐ Uneven or low cylinder compressions (Chapter 2)
- ☐ Disconnected, leaking, or perished crankcase ventilation hoses (Chapter 4)

Engine misfires throughout the driving speed range

- ☐ Fuel filter choked (Chapter 1)
- ☐ Fuel pump faulty, or delivery pressure low (Chapter 4)
- ☐ Fuel tank vent blocked, or fuel pipes restricted (Chapter 4)
- ☐ Vacuum leak at the throttle body, inlet manifold or associated hoses - petrol models (Chapter 4)
- ☐ Worn, faulty or incorrectly-gapped spark plugs - petrol models (Chapter 1)
- ☐ Faulty spark plug HT leads (where fitted) - petrol models (Chapter 1)
- ☐ Faulty injector(s) - diesel models (Chapter 4)
- ☐ Distributor cap cracked or tracking internally - petrol models (where applicable) (Chapter 1)
- ☐ Faulty ignition coil - petrol models (Chapter 5)
- ☐ Uneven or low cylinder compressions (Chapter 2)
- ☐ Blocked injector/fuel injection system fault - petrol models (Chapter 4)

Engine (continued)

Engine hesitates on acceleration

- [ ] Worn, faulty or incorrectly-gapped spark plugs - petrol models (Chapter 1)
- [ ] Vacuum leak at the throttle body, inlet manifold or associated hoses (Chapter 4)
- [ ] Blocked injector/fuel injection system fault - petrol models (Chapter 4)
- [ ] Faulty injector(s) - diesel models (Chapter 4)

Engine stalls

- [ ] Vacuum leak at the throttle body, inlet manifold or associated hoses - petrol models (Chapter 4)
- [ ] Fuel filter choked (Chapter 1)
- [ ] Fuel pump faulty, or delivery pressure low - petrol models (Chapter 4)
- [ ] Fuel tank vent blocked, or fuel pipes restricted (Chapter 4)
- [ ] Blocked injector/fuel injection system fault - petrol models (Chapter 4)
- [ ] Faulty injector(s) - diesel models (Chapter 4)

Engine lacks power

- [ ] Timing belt/chain incorrectly fitted (Chapter 2)
- [ ] Fuel filter choked (Chapter 1)
- [ ] Fuel pump faulty, or delivery pressure low (Chapter 4)
- [ ] Uneven or low cylinder compressions (Chapter 2)
- [ ] Worn, faulty or incorrectly-gapped spark plugs - petrol models (Chapter 1)
- [ ] Vacuum leak at the throttle body, inlet manifold or associated hoses - petrol models (Chapter 4)
- [ ] Blocked injector/fuel injection system fault - petrol models (Chapter 4)
- [ ] Faulty injector(s) - diesel models (Chapter 4)
- [ ] Injection pump timing incorrect - diesel models (Chapter 4)
- [ ] Brakes binding (Chapters 1 and 10)
- [ ] Clutch slipping (Chapter 6)

Engine backfires

- [ ] Timing belt/chain incorrectly fitted (Chapter 2)
- [ ] Vacuum leak at the throttle body, inlet manifold or associated hoses - petrol models (Chapter 4)
- [ ] Blocked injector/fuel injection system fault - petrol models (Chapter 4)

Oil pressure warning light illuminated with engine running

- [ ] Low oil level, or incorrect oil grade (Chapter 1)
- [ ] Faulty oil pressure switch (Chapter 5)
- [ ] Worn engine bearings and/or oil pump (Chapter 2)
- [ ] High engine operating temperature (Chapter 3)
- [ ] Oil pressure relief valve defective (Chapter 2)
- [ ] Oil pick-up strainer clogged (Chapter 2)

Engine runs-on after switching off

- [ ] Excessive carbon build-up in engine (Chapter 2)
- [ ] High engine operating temperature (Chapter 3)
- [ ] Fuel injection system fault - petrol models (Chapter 4)
- [ ] Faulty stop solenoid - diesel models (Chapter 4)

Engine noises

Pre-ignition (pinking) or knocking during acceleration or under load

- [ ] Ignition timing incorrect/ignition system fault - petrol models (Chapters 1 and 5)
- [ ] Incorrect grade of spark plug - petrol models (Chapter 1)
- [ ] Incorrect grade of fuel (Chapter 1)
- [ ] Vacuum leak at the throttle body, inlet manifold or associated hoses - petrol models (Chapter 4)
- [ ] Excessive carbon build-up in engine (Chapter 2)
- [ ] Blocked injector/fuel injection system fault - petrol models (Chapter 4)

Whistling or wheezing noises

- [ ] Leaking inlet manifold or throttle body gasket - petrol models (Chapter 4)
- [ ] Leaking exhaust manifold gasket or pipe-to-manifold joint (Chapter 4)
- [ ] Leaking vacuum hose (Chapters 4, 5 and 10)
- [ ] Blowing cylinder head gasket (Chapter 2)

Tapping or rattling noises

- [ ] Worn valve gear or camshaft (Chapter 2)
- [ ] Ancillary component fault (coolant pump, alternator, etc) (Chapters 3, 5, etc)

Knocking or thumping noises

- [ ] Worn big-end bearings (regular heavy knocking, perhaps less under load) (Chapter 2)
- [ ] Worn main bearings (rumbling and knocking, perhaps worsening under load) (Chapter 2)
- [ ] Piston slap (most noticeable when cold) (Chapter 2)
- [ ] Ancillary component fault (coolant pump, alternator, etc) (Chapters 3, 5, etc)

Cooling system

Overheating

- [ ] Insufficient coolant in system (*Weekly Checks*)
- [ ] Thermostat faulty (Chapter 3)
- [ ] Radiator core blocked, or grille restricted (Chapter 3)
- [ ] Cooling fan faulty (Chapter 3)
- [ ] Inaccurate temperature gauge sender unit (Chapter 3)
- [ ] Airlock in cooling system (Chapter 3)
- [ ] Pressure cap faulty (Chapter 3)

Overcooling

- [ ] Thermostat faulty (Chapter 3)
- [ ] Inaccurate temperature gauge sender unit (Chapter 3)
- [ ] Cooling fan faulty (Chapter 3)

External coolant leakage

- [ ] Deteriorated or damaged hoses or hose clips (Chapter 1)
- [ ] Radiator core or heater matrix leaking (Chapter 3)
- [ ] Pressure cap faulty (Chapter 3)
- [ ] Coolant pump internal seal leaking (Chapter 3)
- [ ] Coolant pump-to-block seal leaking (Chapter 3)
- [ ] Boiling due to overheating (Chapter 3)
- [ ] Core plug leaking (Chapter 2)

Internal coolant leakage

- [ ] Leaking cylinder head gasket (Chapter 2)
- [ ] Cracked cylinder head or cylinder block (Chapter 2)

Corrosion

- [ ] Infrequent draining and flushing (Chapter 1)
- [ ] Incorrect coolant mixture or inappropriate coolant type (Chapter 1)

Fuel and exhaust systems

Excessive fuel consumption

- [ ] Air filter element dirty or clogged (Chapter 1)
- [ ] Fuel injection system fault - petrol models (Chapter 4)
- [ ] Faulty injector(s) - diesel models (Chapter 4)
- [ ] Ignition timing incorrect/ignition system fault - petrol models (Chapters 1 and 5)
- [ ] Tyres under-inflated (*Weekly checks*)

Fuel leakage and/or fuel odour

- [ ] Damaged or corroded fuel tank, pipes or connections (Chapter 4)

Excessive noise or fumes from exhaust system

- [ ] Leaking exhaust system or manifold joints (Chapters 1 and 4)
- [ ] Leaking, corroded or damaged silencers or pipe (Chapters 1 and 4)
- [ ] Broken mountings causing body or suspension contact (Chapter 1)

Clutch

Pedal travels to floor - no pressure or very little resistance

- [ ] Faulty hydraulic release system (Chapter 6)
- [ ] Broken clutch release bearing or fork (Chapter 6)
- [ ] Broken diaphragm spring in clutch pressure plate (Chapter 6)

Clutch fails to disengage (unable to select gears)

- [ ] Faulty hydraulic release system (Chapter 6)
- [ ] Clutch disc sticking on gearbox input shaft splines (Chapter 6)
- [ ] Clutch disc sticking to flywheel or pressure plate (Chapter 6)
- [ ] Faulty pressure plate assembly (Chapter 6)
- [ ] Clutch release mechanism worn or incorrectly assembled (Chapter 6)

Clutch slips (engine speed increases, with no increase in vehicle speed)

- [ ] Faulty hydraulic release system (Chapter 6)
- [ ] Clutch disc linings excessively worn (Chapter 6)
- [ ] Clutch disc linings contaminated with oil or grease (Chapter 6)
- [ ] Faulty pressure plate or weak diaphragm spring (Chapter 6)

Judder as clutch is engaged

- [ ] Clutch disc linings contaminated with oil or grease (Chapter 6)
- [ ] Clutch disc linings excessively worn (Chapter 6)
- [ ] Faulty or distorted pressure plate or diaphragm spring (Chapter 6).
- [ ] Worn or loose engine or gearbox mountings (Chapter 2)
- [ ] Clutch disc hub or gearbox input shaft splines worn (Chapter 6)

Noise when depressing or releasing clutch pedal

- [ ] Worn clutch release bearing (Chapter 6)
- [ ] Worn or dry clutch pedal bushes (Chapter 6)
- [ ] Faulty pressure plate assembly (Chapter 6)
- [ ] Pressure plate diaphragm spring broken (Chapter 6)
- [ ] Broken clutch disc cushioning springs (Chapter 6)

Transmission

Noisy in neutral with engine running

☐ Input shaft bearings worn (noise apparent with clutch pedal released, but not when depressed) (Chapter 7)*
☐ Clutch release bearing worn (noise apparent with clutch pedal depressed, possibly less when released) (Chapter 6)

Noisy in one particular gear

☐ Worn, damaged or chipped gear teeth (Chapter 7)*

Difficulty engaging gears

☐ Clutch fault (Chapter 6)
☐ Worn synchroniser units (Chapter 7)*

Jumps out of gear

☐ Worn synchroniser units (Chapter 7)*
☐ Worn selector forks (Chapter 7)*

Vibration

☐ Lack of oil (Chapter 1)
☐ Worn bearings (Chapter 7)*

Lubricant leaks

☐ Leaking output shaft oil seal (Chapter 7)
☐ Leaking housing joint (Chapter 7)*
☐ Leaking input shaft oil seal (Chapter 7)*

Although the corrective action necessary to remedy the symptoms described is beyond the scope of the home mechanic, the above information should be helpful in isolating the cause of the condition, so that the owner can communicate clearly with a professional mechanic.

Driveshafts

Vibration when accelerating or decelerating

☐ Worn inner constant velocity joint (Chapter 8)
☐ Bent or distorted driveshaft (Chapter 8)
☐ Worn intermediate bearing (Chapter 8)

Clicking or knocking noise on turns (at slow speed on full-lock)

☐ Worn outer constant velocity joint (Chapter 8)
☐ Lack of constant velocity joint lubricant, possibly due to damaged gaiter (Chapter 8)
☐ Worn intermediate bearing (Chapter 8)

Differential and propeller shaft

Vibration when accelerating or decelerating

☐ Worn universal joint (Chapter 8)
☐ Bent, distorted or unbalanced propeller shaft (Chapter 8)

Low pitched whining; increasing with road speed

☐ Worn differential (Chapter 8)

Braking system

Note: *Before assuming that a brake problem exists, make sure that the tyres are in good condition and correctly inflated, that the front wheel alignment is correct, and that the vehicle is not loaded with weight in an unequal manner. Apart from checking the condition of all pipe and hose connections, any faults occurring on the anti-lock braking system should be referred to a Vauxhall dealer for diagnosis.*

Vehicle pulls to one side under braking

☐ Worn, defective, damaged or contaminated brake pads/shoes on one side (Chapters 1 and 10)
☐ Seized or partially-seized brake caliper piston/wheel cylinder (Chapters 1 and 10)
☐ A mixture of brake pad/shoe lining materials fitted between sides (Chapters 1 and 10)
☐ Brake caliper/backplate mounting bolts loose (Chapter 10)
☐ Worn or damaged steering or suspension components (Chapters 1 and 11)

Noise (grinding or high-pitched squeal) when brakes applied

☐ Brake pad/shoe friction lining material worn down to metal backing (Chapters 1 and 10)
☐ Excessive corrosion of brake disc/drum (may be apparent after the vehicle has been standing for some time (Chapters 1 and 10)
☐ Foreign object (stone chipping, etc) trapped between brake disc and shield (Chapters 1 and 10)

Excessive brake pedal travel

☐ Faulty master cylinder (Chapter 10)
☐ Air in hydraulic system (Chapters 1 and 10)
☐ Faulty vacuum servo unit (Chapter 10)

Brake pedal feels spongy when depressed

☐ Air in hydraulic system (Chapters 1 and 10)
☐ Deteriorated flexible rubber brake hoses (Chapters 1 and 10)
☐ Master cylinder mounting nuts loose (Chapter 10)
☐ Faulty master cylinder (Chapter 10)

Excessive brake pedal effort required to stop vehicle

☐ Faulty vacuum servo unit (Chapter 10)
☐ Disconnected, damaged or insecure brake servo vacuum hose (Chapter 10)
☐ Primary or secondary hydraulic circuit failure (Chapter 10)
☐ Seized brake caliper/wheel cylinder piston (Chapter 10)
☐ Brake pads/shoes incorrectly fitted (Chapters 1 and 10)
☐ Incorrect grade of brake pads/shoes fitted (Chapters 1 and 10)
☐ Brake pad/shoe linings contaminated (Chapters 1 and 10)
☐ Faulty vacuum pump - diesel models (Chapter 10)

Judder felt through brake pedal or steering wheel when braking

☐ Excessive run-out or distortion of discs/drums (Chapters 1 and 10)
☐ Brake pad/shoe linings worn (Chapters 1 and 10)
☐ Brake caliper/backplate mounting bolts loose (Chapter 10)
☐ Wear in suspension or steering components or mountings (Chapters 1 and 11)

Brakes binding

☐ Seized brake caliper/wheel cylinder piston (Chapter 10)
☐ Incorrectly-adjusted handbrake mechanism (Chapter 10)
☐ Faulty master cylinder (Chapter 10)

Rear wheels locking under normal braking

☐ Rear brake pad/shoe linings contaminated (Chapters 1 and 10)
☐ Rear brake discs/drums warped (Chapters 1 and 10)

Suspension and steering

Note: *Before diagnosing suspension or steering faults, be sure that the trouble is not due to incorrect tyre pressures, mixtures of tyre types, or binding brakes.*

Vehicle pulls to one side

☐ Defective tyre (*Weekly checks*)
☐ Excessive wear in suspension or steering components (Chapters 1 and 11)
☐ Incorrect front wheel alignment (Chapter 11)
☐ Accident damage to steering or suspension components (Chapter 1)

Wheel wobble and vibration

☐ Front roadwheels out of balance (vibration felt mainly through the steering wheel) (Chapters 1 and 11)
☐ Rear roadwheels out of balance (vibration felt throughout the vehicle) (Chapters 1 and 11)
☐ Roadwheels damaged or distorted (Chapters 1 and 11)
☐ Faulty or damaged tyre (*Weekly checks*)
☐ Worn steering or suspension joints, bushes or components (Chapters 1 and 11)
☐ Wheel bolts loose (Chapters 1 and 11)

Excessive pitching and/or rolling around corners, or during braking

☐ Defective shock absorbers (Chapters 1 and 11)
☐ Broken or weak spring and/or suspension component (Chapters 1 and 11)
☐ Worn or damaged anti-roll bar or mountings (Chapter 11)

Wandering or general instability

☐ Incorrect front wheel alignment (Chapter 11)
☐ Worn steering or suspension joints, bushes or components (Chapters 1 and 11)
☐ Roadwheels out of balance (Chapters 1 and 11)
☐ Faulty or damaged tyre (*Weekly checks*)
☐ Wheel bolts loose (Chapters 1 and 11)
☐ Defective shock absorbers (Chapters 1 and 11)

Excessively-stiff steering

☐ Seized steering linkage balljoint or suspension balljoint (Chapters 1 and 11)
☐ Broken or incorrectly-adjusted auxiliary drivebelt (Chapter 1)
☐ Incorrect front wheel alignment (Chapter 11)
☐ Steering gear damaged (Chapter 11)

Suspension and steering (continued)

Excessive play in steering

- [ ] Worn steering column/intermediate shaft joints (Chapter 11)
- [ ] Worn track rod balljoints (Chapters 1 and 11)
- [ ] Worn steering gear (Chapter 11)
- [ ] Worn steering or suspension joints, bushes or components (Chapters 1 and 11)

Lack of power assistance

- [ ] Broken or incorrectly-adjusted auxiliary drivebelt (Chapter 1)
- [ ] Incorrect power steering fluid level (Weekly checks)
- [ ] Restriction in power steering fluid hoses (Chapter 1)
- [ ] Faulty power steering pump (Chapter 11)
- [ ] Faulty steering gear (Chapter 11)

Tyre wear excessive

Tyres worn on inside or outside edges

- [ ] Tyres under-inflated (wear on both edges) (Weekly checks)
- [ ] Incorrect camber or castor angles (wear on one edge only) (Chapter 11)

- [ ] Worn steering or suspension joints, bushes or components (Chapters 1 and 11)
- [ ] Excessively-hard cornering
- [ ] Accident damage

Tyre treads exhibit feathered edges

- [ ] Incorrect toe setting (Chapter 11)

Tyres worn in centre of tread

- [ ] Tyres over-inflated (Weekly checks)

Tyres worn on inside and outside edges

- [ ] Tyres under-inflated (Weekly checks)

Tyres worn unevenly

- [ ] Tyres/wheels out of balance (Chapter 1)
- [ ] Excessive wheel or tyre run-out (Chapter 1)
- [ ] Worn shock absorbers (Chapters 1 and 11)
- [ ] Faulty tyre (Weekly checks)

Electrical system

Note: For problems associated with the starting system, refer to the faults listed under Engine earlier in this Section.

Battery will not hold a charge for more than a few days

- [ ] Battery defective internally (Chapter 5)
- [ ] Battery terminal connections loose or corroded (Weekly checks)
- [ ] Auxiliary drivebelt worn or incorrectly adjusted (Chapter 1)
- [ ] Alternator not charging at correct output (Chapter 5)
- [ ] Alternator or voltage regulator faulty (Chapter 5)
- [ ] Short-circuit causing continual battery drain (Chapters 5 and 13)

Ignition/no-charge warning light remains illuminated with engine running

- [ ] Auxiliary drivebelt broken, worn, or incorrectly adjusted (Chapter 1)
- [ ] Alternator brushes worn, sticking, or dirty (Chapter 5)
- [ ] Alternator brush springs weak or broken (Chapter 5)
- [ ] Internal fault in alternator or voltage regulator (Chapter 5)
- [ ] Broken, disconnected, or loose wiring in charging circuit (Chapter 5)

Ignition/no-charge warning light fails to come on

- [ ] Warning light bulb blown (Chapter 13)
- [ ] Broken, disconnected, or loose wiring in warning light circuit (Chapter 13)
- [ ] Alternator faulty (Chapter 5)

Lights inoperative

- [ ] Bulb blown (Chapter 13)
- [ ] Corrosion of bulb or bulbholder contacts (Chapter 13)
- [ ] Blown fuse (Chapter 13)
- [ ] Faulty relay (Chapter 13)
- [ ] Broken, loose, or disconnected wiring (Chapter 13)
- [ ] Faulty switch (Chapter 13)

Instrument readings inaccurate or erratic

Instrument readings increase with engine speed

- [ ] Faulty voltage regulator (Chapter 13)

Fuel or temperature gauges give no reading

- [ ] Faulty gauge sender unit (Chapters 3 and 4)
- [ ] Wiring open-circuit (Chapter 13)
- [ ] Faulty gauge (Chapter 13)

Fuel or temperature gauges give continuous maximum reading

- [ ] Faulty gauge sender unit (Chapters 3 and 4)
- [ ] Wiring short-circuit (Chapter 13)
- [ ] Faulty gauge (Chapter 13)

Horn inoperative, or unsatisfactory in operation

Horn operates all the time

- [ ] Horn push either earthed or stuck down (Chapter 13)
- [ ] Horn cable-to-horn push earthed (Chapter 13)

Horn fails to operate

- [ ] Blown fuse (Chapter 13)
- [ ] Cable or cable connections loose, broken or disconnected (Chapter 13)
- [ ] Faulty horn (Chapter 13)

Horn emits intermittent or unsatisfactory sound

- [ ] Cable connections loose (Chapter 13)
- [ ] Horn mountings loose (Chapter 13)
- [ ] Faulty horn (Chapter 13)

Electrical system (continued)

Windscreen wipers inoperative, or unsatisfactory in operation

Wipers fail to operate, or operate very slowly

☐ Wiper blades stuck to screen, or linkage seized or binding (Chapters 1 and 13)
☐ Blown fuse (Chapter 13)
☐ Cable or cable connections loose, broken or disconnected (Chapter 13)
☐ Faulty relay (Chapter 13)
☐ Faulty wiper motor (Chapter 13)

Wiper blades sweep over too large or too small an area of the glass

☐ Wiper arms incorrectly positioned on spindles (Chapter 1)
☐ Excessive wear of wiper linkage (Chapter 13)
☐ Wiper motor or linkage mountings loose or insecure (Chapter 13)

Wiper blades fail to clean the glass effectively

☐ Wiper blade rubbers worn or perished (*Weekly checks*)
☐ Wiper arm tension springs broken, or arm pivots seized (Chapter 13)
☐ Insufficient windscreen washer additive to adequately remove road film (*Weekly checks*).

Windscreen washers inoperative, or unsatisfactory in operation

One or more washer jets inoperative

☐ Blocked washer jet (Chapter 1)
☐ Disconnected, kinked or restricted fluid hose (Chapter 13)
☐ Insufficient fluid in washer reservoir (*Weekly checks*)

Washer pump fails to operate

☐ Broken or disconnected wiring or connections (Chapter 13)
☐ Blown fuse (Chapter 13)
☐ Faulty washer switch (Chapter 13)
☐ Faulty washer pump (Chapter 13)

Washer pump runs for some time before fluid is emitted from jets

☐ Faulty one-way valve in fluid supply hose (Chapter 13)

Electric windows inoperative, or unsatisfactory in operation

Window glass will only move in one direction

☐ Faulty switch (Chapter 13)

Window glass slow to move

☐ Regulator seized or damaged, or in need of lubrication (Chapter 12)
☐ Door internal components or trim fouling regulator (Chapter 12)
☐ Faulty motor (Chapter 12)

Window glass fails to move

☐ Blown fuse (Chapter 13)
☐ Faulty relay (Chapter 13)
☐ Broken or disconnected wiring or connections (Chapter 13)
☐ Faulty motor (Chapter 12)

Central locking system inoperative, or unsatisfactory in operation

Complete system failure

☐ Blown fuse (Chapter 13)
☐ Faulty relay (Chapter 13)
☐ Broken or disconnected wiring or connections (Chapter 13)
☐ Faulty motor (Chapter 12)

Latch locks but will not unlock, or unlocks but will not lock

☐ Faulty master switch (Chapter 13)
☐ Broken or disconnected latch operating rods or levers (Chapter 12)
☐ Faulty relay (Chapter 13)
☐ Faulty motor (Chapter 12)

One solenoid/motor fails to operate

☐ Broken or disconnected wiring or connections (Chapter 13)
☐ Faulty operating assembly (Chapter 12)
☐ Broken, binding or disconnected latch operating rods or levers (Chapter 12)
☐ Fault in door latch (Chapter 12)

A

ABS (Anti-lock brake system) A system, usually electronically controlled, that senses incipient wheel lockup during braking and relieves hydraulic pressure at wheels that are about to skid.

Air bag An inflatable bag hidden in the steering wheel (driver's side) or the dash or glovebox (passenger side). In a head-on collision, the bags inflate, preventing the driver and front passenger from being thrown forward into the steering wheel or windscreen.

Air cleaner A metal or plastic housing, containing a filter element, which removes dust and dirt from the air being drawn into the engine.

Air filter element The actual filter in an air cleaner system, usually manufactured from pleated paper and requiring renewal at regular intervals.

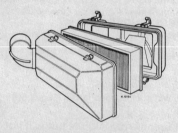

Air filter

Allen key A hexagonal wrench which fits into a recessed hexagonal hole.

Alligator clip A long-nosed spring-loaded metal clip with meshing teeth. Used to make temporary electrical connections.

Alternator A component in the electrical system which converts mechanical energy from a drivebelt into electrical energy to charge the battery and to operate the starting system, ignition system and electrical accessories.

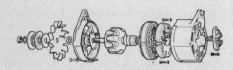

Alternator (exploded view)

Ampere (amp) A unit of measurement for the flow of electric current. One amp is the amount of current produced by one volt acting through a resistance of one ohm.

Anaerobic sealer A substance used to prevent bolts and screws from loosening. Anaerobic means that it does not require oxygen for activation. The Loctite brand is widely used.

Antifreeze A substance (usually ethylene glycol) mixed with water, and added to a vehicle's cooling system, to prevent freezing of the coolant in winter. Antifreeze also contains chemicals to inhibit corrosion and the formation of rust and other deposits that would tend to clog the radiator and coolant passages and reduce cooling efficiency.

Anti-seize compound A coating that reduces the risk of seizing on fasteners that are subjected to high temperatures, such as exhaust manifold bolts and nuts.

Anti-seize compound

Asbestos A natural fibrous mineral with great heat resistance, commonly used in the composition of brake friction materials. Asbestos is a health hazard and the dust created by brake systems should never be inhaled or ingested.

Axle A shaft on which a wheel revolves, or which revolves with a wheel. Also, a solid beam that connects the two wheels at one end of the vehicle. An axle which also transmits power to the wheels is known as a live axle.

Axle assembly

Axleshaft A single rotating shaft, on either side of the differential, which delivers power from the final drive assembly to the drive wheels. Also called a driveshaft or a halfshaft.

B

Ball bearing An anti-friction bearing consisting of a hardened inner and outer race with hardened steel balls between two races.

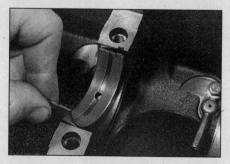

Bearing

Bearing The curved surface on a shaft or in a bore, or the part assembled into either, that permits relative motion between them with minimum wear and friction.

Big-end bearing The bearing in the end of the connecting rod that's attached to the crankshaft.

Bleed nipple A valve on a brake wheel cylinder, caliper or other hydraulic component that is opened to purge the hydraulic system of air. Also called a bleed screw.

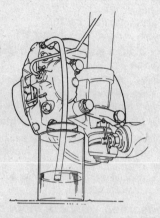

Brake bleeding

Brake bleeding Procedure for removing air from lines of a hydraulic brake system.

Brake disc The component of a disc brake that rotates with the wheels.

Brake drum The component of a drum brake that rotates with the wheels.

Brake linings The friction material which contacts the brake disc or drum to retard the vehicle's speed. The linings are bonded or riveted to the brake pads or shoes.

Brake pads The replaceable friction pads that pinch the brake disc when the brakes are applied. Brake pads consist of a friction material bonded or riveted to a rigid backing plate.

Brake shoe The crescent-shaped carrier to which the brake linings are mounted and which forces the lining against the rotating drum during braking.

Braking systems For more information on braking systems, consult the *Haynes Automotive Brake Manual*.

Breaker bar A long socket wrench handle providing greater leverage.

Bulkhead The insulated partition between the engine and the passenger compartment.

C

Caliper The non-rotating part of a disc-brake assembly that straddles the disc and carries the brake pads. The caliper also contains the hydraulic components that cause the pads to pinch the disc when the brakes are applied. A caliper is also a measuring tool that can be set to measure inside or outside dimensions of an object.

Camshaft A rotating shaft on which a series of cam lobes operate the valve mechanisms. The camshaft may be driven by gears, by sprockets and chain or by sprockets and a belt.

Canister A container in an evaporative emission control system; contains activated charcoal granules to trap vapours from the fuel system.

Canister

Carburettor A device which mixes fuel with air in the proper proportions to provide a desired power output from a spark ignition internal combustion engine.

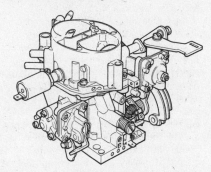

Carburettor

Castellated Resembling the parapets along the top of a castle wall. For example, a castellated balljoint stud nut.

Castellated nut

Castor In wheel alignment, the backward or forward tilt of the steering axis. Castor is positive when the steering axis is inclined rearward at the top.

Catalytic converter A silencer-like device in the exhaust system which converts certain pollutants in the exhaust gases into less harmful substances.

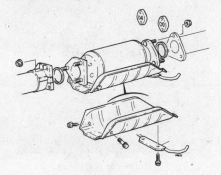

Catalytic converter

Circlip A ring-shaped clip used to prevent endwise movement of cylindrical parts and shafts. An internal circlip is installed in a groove in a housing; an external circlip fits into a groove on the outside of a cylindrical piece such as a shaft.

Clearance The amount of space between two parts. For example, between a piston and a cylinder, between a bearing and a journal, etc.

Coil spring A spiral of elastic steel found in various sizes throughout a vehicle, for example as a springing medium in the suspension and in the valve train.

Compression Reduction in volume, and increase in pressure and temperature, of a gas, caused by squeezing it into a smaller space.

Compression ratio The relationship between cylinder volume when the piston is at top dead centre and cylinder volume when the piston is at bottom dead centre.

Constant velocity (CV) joint A type of universal joint that cancels out vibrations caused by driving power being transmitted through an angle.

Core plug A disc or cup-shaped metal device inserted in a hole in a casting through which core was removed when the casting was formed. Also known as a freeze plug or expansion plug.

Crankcase The lower part of the engine block in which the crankshaft rotates.

Crankshaft The main rotating member, or shaft, running the length of the crankcase, with offset "throws" to which the connecting rods are attached.

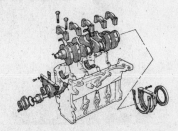

Crankshaft assembly

Crocodile clip See Alligator clip

D

Diagnostic code Code numbers obtained by accessing the diagnostic mode of an engine management computer. This code can be used to determine the area in the system where a malfunction may be located.

Disc brake A brake design incorporating a rotating disc onto which brake pads are squeezed. The resulting friction converts the energy of a moving vehicle into heat.

Double-overhead cam (DOHC) An engine that uses two overhead camshafts, usually one for the intake valves and one for the exhaust valves.

Drivebelt(s) The belt(s) used to drive accessories such as the alternator, water pump, power steering pump, air conditioning compressor, etc. off the crankshaft pulley.

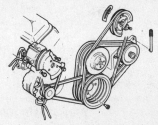

Accessory drivebelts

Driveshaft Any shaft used to transmit motion. Commonly used when referring to the axleshafts on a front wheel drive vehicle.

Driveshaft

Drum brake A type of brake using a drum-shaped metal cylinder attached to the inner surface of the wheel. When the brake pedal is pressed, curved brake shoes with friction linings press against the inside of the drum to slow or stop the vehicle.

Drum brake assembly

E

EGR valve A valve used to introduce exhaust gases into the intake air stream.

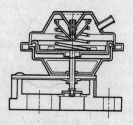

EGR valve

Electronic control unit (ECU) A computer which controls (for instance) ignition and fuel injection systems, or an anti-lock braking system. For more information refer to the *Haynes Automotive Electrical and Electronic Systems Manual*.

Electronic Fuel Injection (EFI) A computer controlled fuel system that distributes fuel through an injector located in each intake port of the engine.

Emergency brake A braking system, independent of the main hydraulic system, that can be used to slow or stop the vehicle if the primary brakes fail, or to hold the vehicle stationary even though the brake pedal isn't depressed. It usually consists of a hand lever that actuates either front or rear brakes mechanically through a series of cables and linkages. Also known as a handbrake or parking brake.

Endfloat The amount of lengthwise movement between two parts. As applied to a crankshaft, the distance that the crankshaft can move forward and back in the cylinder block.

Engine management system (EMS) A computer controlled system which manages the fuel injection and the ignition systems in an integrated fashion.

Exhaust manifold A part with several passages through which exhaust gases leave the engine combustion chambers and enter the exhaust pipe.

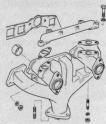

Exhaust manifold

F

Fan clutch A viscous (fluid) drive coupling device which permits variable engine fan speeds in relation to engine speeds.

Feeler blade A thin strip or blade of hardened steel, ground to an exact thickness, used to check or measure clearances between parts.

Feeler blade

Firing order The order in which the engine cylinders fire, or deliver their power strokes, beginning with the number one cylinder.

Flywheel A heavy spinning wheel in which energy is absorbed and stored by means of momentum. On cars, the flywheel is attached to the crankshaft to smooth out firing impulses.

Free play The amount of travel before any action takes place. The "looseness" in a linkage, or an assembly of parts, between the initial application of force and actual movement. For example, the distance the brake pedal moves before the pistons in the master cylinder are actuated.

Fuse An electrical device which protects a circuit against accidental overload. The typical fuse contains a soft piece of metal which is calibrated to melt at a predetermined current flow (expressed as amps) and break the circuit.

Fusible link A circuit protection device consisting of a conductor surrounded by heat-resistant insulation. The conductor is smaller than the wire it protects, so it acts as the weakest link in the circuit. Unlike a blown fuse, a failed fusible link must frequently be cut from the wire for replacement.

G

Gap The distance the spark must travel in jumping from the centre electrode to the side

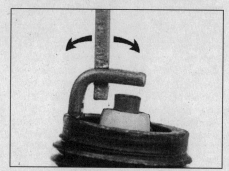

Adjusting spark plug gap

electrode in a spark plug. Also refers to the spacing between the points in a contact breaker assembly in a conventional points-type ignition, or to the distance between the reluctor or rotor and the pickup coil in an electronic ignition.

Gasket Any thin, soft material - usually cork, cardboard, asbestos or soft metal - installed between two metal surfaces to ensure a good seal. For instance, the cylinder head gasket seals the joint between the block and the cylinder head.

Gasket

Gauge An instrument panel display used to monitor engine conditions. A gauge with a movable pointer on a dial or a fixed scale is an analogue gauge. A gauge with a numerical readout is called a digital gauge.

H

Halfshaft A rotating shaft that transmits power from the final drive unit to a drive wheel, usually when referring to a live rear axle.

Harmonic balancer A device designed to reduce torsion or twisting vibration in the crankshaft. May be incorporated in the crankshaft pulley. Also known as a vibration damper.

Hone An abrasive tool for correcting small irregularities or differences in diameter in an engine cylinder, brake cylinder, etc.

Hydraulic tappet A tappet that utilises hydraulic pressure from the engine's lubrication system to maintain zero clearance (constant contact with both camshaft and valve stem). Automatically adjusts to variation in valve stem length. Hydraulic tappets also reduce valve noise.

I

Ignition timing The moment at which the spark plug fires, usually expressed in the number of crankshaft degrees before the piston reaches the top of its stroke.

Inlet manifold A tube or housing with passages through which flows the air-fuel mixture (carburettor vehicles and vehicles with throttle body injection) or air only (port fuel-injected vehicles) to the port openings in the cylinder head.

J

Jump start Starting the engine of a vehicle with a discharged or weak battery by attaching jump leads from the weak battery to a charged or helper battery.

L

Load Sensing Proportioning Valve (LSPV) A brake hydraulic system control valve that works like a proportioning valve, but also takes into consideration the amount of weight carried by the rear axle.

Locknut A nut used to lock an adjustment nut, or other threaded component, in place. For example, a locknut is employed to keep the adjusting nut on the rocker arm in position.

Lockwasher A form of washer designed to prevent an attaching nut from working loose.

M

MacPherson strut A type of front suspension system devised by Earle MacPherson at Ford of England. In its original form, a simple lateral link with the anti-roll bar creates the lower control arm. A long strut - an integral coil spring and shock absorber - is mounted between the body and the steering knuckle. Many modern so-called MacPherson strut systems use a conventional lower A-arm and don't rely on the anti-roll bar for location.

Multimeter An electrical test instrument with the capability to measure voltage, current and resistance.

N

NOx Oxides of Nitrogen. A common toxic pollutant emitted by petrol and diesel engines at higher temperatures.

O

Ohm The unit of electrical resistance. One volt applied to a resistance of one ohm will produce a current of one amp.

Ohmmeter An instrument for measuring electrical resistance.

O-ring A type of sealing ring made of a special rubber-like material; in use, the O-ring is compressed into a groove to provide the sealing action.

O-ring

Overhead cam (ohc) engine An engine with the camshaft(s) located on top of the cylinder head(s).

Overhead valve (ohv) engine An engine with the valves located in the cylinder head, but with the camshaft located in the engine block.

Oxygen sensor A device installed in the engine exhaust manifold, which senses the oxygen content in the exhaust and converts this information into an electric current. Also called a Lambda sensor.

P

Phillips screw A type of screw head having a cross instead of a slot for a corresponding type of screwdriver.

Plastigage A thin strip of plastic thread, available in different sizes, used for measuring clearances. For example, a strip of Plastigage is laid across a bearing journal. The parts are assembled and dismantled; the width of the crushed strip indicates the clearance between journal and bearing.

Plastigage

Propeller shaft The long hollow tube with universal joints at both ends that carries power from the transmission to the differential on front-engined rear wheel drive vehicles.

Proportioning valve A hydraulic control valve which limits the amount of pressure to the rear brakes during panic stops to prevent wheel lock-up.

R

Rack-and-pinion steering A steering system with a pinion gear on the end of the steering shaft that mates with a rack (think of a geared wheel opened up and laid flat). When the steering wheel is turned, the pinion turns, moving the rack to the left or right. This movement is transmitted through the track rods to the steering arms at the wheels.

Radiator A liquid-to-air heat transfer device designed to reduce the temperature of the coolant in an internal combustion engine cooling system.

Refrigerant Any substance used as a heat transfer agent in an air-conditioning system. R-12 has been the principle refrigerant for many years; recently, however, manufacturers have begun using R-134a, a non-CFC substance that is considered less harmful to

the ozone in the upper atmosphere.

Rocker arm A lever arm that rocks on a shaft or pivots on a stud. In an overhead valve engine, the rocker arm converts the upward movement of the pushrod into a downward movement to open a valve.

Rotor In a distributor, the rotating device inside the cap that connects the centre electrode and the outer terminals as it turns, distributing the high voltage from the coil secondary winding to the proper spark plug. Also, that part of an alternator which rotates inside the stator. Also, the rotating assembly of a turbocharger, including the compressor wheel, shaft and turbine wheel.

Runout The amount of wobble (in-and-out movement) of a gear or wheel as it's rotated. The amount a shaft rotates "out-of-true." The out-of-round condition of a rotating part.

S

Sealant A liquid or paste used to prevent leakage at a joint. Sometimes used in conjunction with a gasket.

Sealed beam lamp An older headlight design which integrates the reflector, lens and filaments into a hermetically-sealed one-piece unit. When a filament burns out or the lens cracks, the entire unit is simply replaced.

Serpentine drivebelt A single, long, wide accessory drivebelt that's used on some newer vehicles to drive all the accessories, instead of a series of smaller, shorter belts. Serpentine drivebelts are usually tensioned by an automatic tensioner.

Serpentine drivebelt

Shim Thin spacer, commonly used to adjust the clearance or relative positions between two parts. For example, shims inserted into or under bucket tappets control valve clearances. Clearance is adjusted by changing the thickness of the shim.

Slide hammer A special puller that screws into or hooks onto a component such as a shaft or bearing; a heavy sliding handle on the shaft bottoms against the end of the shaft to knock the component free.

Sprocket A tooth or projection on the periphery of a wheel, shaped to engage with a chain or drivebelt. Commonly used to refer to the sprocket wheel itself.

Starter inhibitor switch On vehicles with an

automatic transmission, a switch that prevents starting if the vehicle is not in Neutral or Park.

Strut See MacPherson strut.

T

Tappet A cylindrical component which transmits motion from the cam to the valve stem, either directly or via a pushrod and rocker arm. Also called a cam follower.

Thermostat A heat-controlled valve that regulates the flow of coolant between the cylinder block and the radiator, so maintaining optimum engine operating temperature. A thermostat is also used in some air cleaners in which the temperature is regulated.

Thrust bearing The bearing in the clutch assembly that is moved in to the release levers by clutch pedal action to disengage the clutch. Also referred to as a release bearing.

Timing belt A toothed belt which drives the camshaft. Serious engine damage may result if it breaks in service.

Timing chain A chain which drives the camshaft.

Toe-in The amount the front wheels are closer together at the front than at the rear. On rear wheel drive vehicles, a slight amount of toe-in is usually specified to keep the front wheels running parallel on the road by offsetting other forces that tend to spread the wheels apart.

Toe-out The amount the front wheels are closer together at the rear than at the front. On front wheel drive vehicles, a slight amount of toe-out is usually specified.

Tools For full information on choosing and using tools, refer to the *Haynes Automotive Tools Manual.*

Tracer A stripe of a second colour applied to a wire insulator to distinguish that wire from another one with the same colour insulator.

Tune-up A process of accurate and careful adjustments and parts replacement to obtain the best possible engine performance.

Turbocharger A centrifugal device, driven by exhaust gases, that pressurises the intake air. Normally used to increase the power output from a given engine displacement, but can also be used primarily to reduce exhaust emissions (as on VW's "Umwelt" Diesel engine).

U

Universal joint or U-joint A double-pivoted connection for transmitting power from a driving to a driven shaft through an angle. A U-joint consists of two Y-shaped yokes and a cross-shaped member called the spider.

V

Valve A device through which the flow of liquid, gas, vacuum, or loose material in bulk may be started, stopped, or regulated by a movable part that opens, shuts, or partially obstructs one or more ports or passageways. A valve is also the movable part of such a device.

Valve clearance The clearance between the valve tip (the end of the valve stem) and the rocker arm or tappet. The valve clearance is measured when the valve is closed.

Vernier caliper A precision measuring instrument that measures inside and outside dimensions. Not quite as accurate as a micrometer, but more convenient.

Viscosity The thickness of a liquid or its resistance to flow.

Volt A unit for expressing electrical "pressure" in a circuit. One volt that will produce a current of one ampere through a resistance of one ohm.

W

Welding Various processes used to join metal items by heating the areas to be joined to a molten state and fusing them together. For more information refer to the *Haynes Automotive Welding Manual.*

Wiring diagram A drawing portraying the components and wires in a vehicle's electrical system, using standardised symbols. For more information refer to the *Haynes Automotive Electrical and Electronic Systems Manual.*

Note: *References throughout this index are in the form - "Chapter number" • "page number"*

A

ABS - 10•17
Accelerator cable - 4A•2, 4B•5
Accelerator pedal - 4A•3, 4B•6, 4B•7
Accessory shops - REF•3
Acknowledgements - 0•4
Aerial - 13•17
Air bags - 0•5
Air conditioning - 1A•8, 1B•8, 1B•10, 3•12
Air dam - 12•5
Air filter - 1A•2, 1A•13, 1B•14, 4A•2, 4B•4
Air mass meter - 4B•7
Air nozzles - 3•12
Air temperature sensor - 4A•8, 4B•8
Airbag system - 13•18, 13•19
Airflow meter - 4A•7
Alternator - 1A•7, 1A•8, 1B•8, 1B•10, 5A•4, 5A•5
Anti-lock braking system (ABS) - 10•17
Anti-roll bar - 11•13, 11•15
Anti-theft alarm - 13•18, REF•5
Antifreeze - 0•14, 0•17, 1A•1, 1A•2, 1A•14, 1B•1, 1B•2, 1B•15
Asbestos - 0•5
Ashtray - 13•9
ATF - 0•17
Automatic transmission fluid - 0•17
Auxiliary drivebelt - 1A•7, 1A•8, 1B•8
Axle drive pinion oil seal - 9•3, 9•6
Axle oil - 1A•1, 1A•10, 1A•15, 1B•1, 1B•13, 1B•16

B

Badges - 12•18
Battery - 0•5, 0•14, 5A•2, 5A•3
Big-end bearings - 2G•14, 2G•18, 2H•18, 2H•22
Bleeding brakes - 10•2
Bleeding clutch - 6•4
Bleeding fuel system - 4B•6
Bleeding power steering - 11•19
Body electrical system - 13•1 et seq
Bodywork and fittings -
    12•1 et seq, REF•11
Bonnet - 12•6, 12•7
Brake fluid - 0•13, 0•17, 1A•11, 1B•14
Braking system - 1A•12, 1B•14,
    10•1 et seq, REF•8, REF•9, REF•10
Braking system fault finding - REF•17
Bulbs - 0•16, 13•7, 13•8
Bumpers - 12•5
Burning - 0•5
Bypass valve - 10•16

C

Cables - 4A•2, 4B•5, 10•16, 12•6
Calipers - 10•11, 10•12
Camshaft - 2A•4, 2A•7 to 2A•10, 2B•4, 2B•6, 2B•7, 2C•6, 2D•6, 2F•6, 2F•11, 2H•11, 2H•12
Camshaft sensor - 4A•8
Carpets - 12•2, 12•22

Cassette player - 13•16, REF•5
Catalytic converter - 4A•11, 4B•20, 4C•2, 4C•4, 4C•5
Central locking - 12•16
Centre console - 12•17, 12•24
Centre link - 11•15
Charcoal canister - 4C•2
Charging system - 5A•3
Cigarette lighter - 13•9
Clock - 13•13
Clutch - 6•1 et seq
Clutch fault finding - REF•15
Clutch fluid - 0•13
CO emissions (mixture) - REF•11
Coil - 5B•2
Coil spring - 11•15
Compression test - 2A•3, 2B•3, 2C•3, 2D•3, 2E•3, 2F•3
Connecting rods - 2G•11, 2G•12, 2G•18, 2H•12, 2H•16, 2H•21
Console - 12•17, 12•24
Contents - 0•2
Control arm - 11•11, 11•12
Conversion factors - REF•2
Coolant - 0•14, 0•17, 1A•1, 1A•2, 1A•14, 1B•1, 1B•2,, 1B•15
Coolant temperature
    sensor - 4A•7, 4B•7, 4B•8, 5C•3
*Cooling, heating and air
    conditioning systems* - 3•1 et seq
Cooling system fault finding - REF•15
Corrosion - 1A•9, 1B•12, REF•11
Courtesy light - 13•5, 13•6, 13•8
Crankcase - 2H•15
Crankcase emission
    control - 4C•1, 4C•2, 4C•4
Crankshaft - 2A•4, 2A•7, 2A•14, 2B•4, 2B•6, 2B•9, 2C•4, 2C•10, 2D•4, 2D•11, 2E•4, 2E•14, 2F•4, 2F•6, 2F•11, 2G•11, 2G•13, 2G•16, 2H•13, 2H•17, 2H•19
Crankshaft sensor - 4A•8, 4B•7
Crushing - 0•5
CV joint - 8•5, 8•6
Cylinder block - 2G•12, 2H•15
Cylinder head - 2A•10, 2B•8, 2C•4, 2C•7, 2D•4, 2D•7, 2E•4, 2E•6, 2F•4, 2F•7, 2G•9, 2G•10, 2H•7, 2H•9, 2H•10
Cylinder liners - 2H•12

D

Dents in bodywork - 12•3
Depressurisation - fuel injection
    system - 4A•4
*Diesel engine in-car repair
    procedures* - 2D•1 et seq, 2E•1 et seq, 2F•1 et seq
*Diesel engine removal and overhaul
    procedures* - 2H•1 et seq
Diesel injection equipment - 0•5
Differential fault finding - REF•16
Differential carrier - 9•4
Dimensions - REF•1
Direction indicator - 13•7, 13•8, 13•10
DIS module - 5B•2

Discs - 1A•8, 1A•9, 1B•11, 10•10, 10•9
Distributor - 5B•3
Doors - 12•7 to 12•10, 12•16, REF•9
Drivebelts - 1A•7, 1A•8, 1B•8, 1B•9, 1B•10
Driving light - 13•8, 13•10
Driveshafts - 1A•9, 1B•12, 8•4, 8•5, REF•10
Driveshafts -
    See *Propeller shafts and driveshafts*
Driveshafts fault finding - REF•16
Drivetrain - 1A•12, 1B•14
Driving light - 13•8, 13•10
Drop arms - 11•20
Drums - 1A•14, 1B•15, 10•10

E

Earth fault - 13•2
EGR system - 4C•2, 4C•3, 4C•4
Electric mirror - 12•17
Electric shock - 0•5
Electric window - 12•17, 13•4, 13•6
Electrical equipment - 1A•11, 1B•14, REF•9
Electrical system fault
    finding - 13•2, REF•18, REF•19
Electronic control unit (ABS) - 10•17
Electronic control unit (EDC) - 4B•8
Electronic control unit (fuel injection
    system) - 4A•8
Electronic Diesel Control (EDC)
    system - 4B•7
Emission control systems - 4C•1 et seq
Emissions - 1B•11, REF•11
Engine in-car repair procedures -
    2A•1 et seq, 2B•1 et seq, 2C•1 et seq,
    2D•1 et seq
Engine fault finding - REF•13, REF•14
Engine oil - 0•12, 1A•1, 1A•6, 1B•1, 1B•7
Environmental considerations - REF•4
Evaporative emission control - 4C•2
Exhaust emission - 1A•8, 1B•11, 4C•1, 4C•2, 4C•4, REF•11
Exhaust gas recirculation (EGR)
    system - 4C•2, 4C•3, 4C•4
Exhaust manifold - 4A•10, 4B•16
Exhaust specialists - REF•3
Exhaust system - 4A•11, 4B•20, REF•10

F

Facia - 12•25, 13•4, 13•6
Fan - 3•5, 3•6, 3•7
Fault finding - REF•12 et seq
Fault finding - braking system - REF•17
Fault finding - clutch - REF•15
Fault finding - cooling system - REF•15
Fault finding - differential and propeller
    shaft - REF•16
Fault finding - driveshafts - REF•16
Fault finding - electrical
    system - 13•2, REF•18, REF•19
Fault finding - engine - REF•13, REF•14
Fault finding - fuel and exhaust
    systems - REF•15
Fault finding -
    manual transmission - REF•16

Fault finding - suspension and
    steering - REF•17, REF•18
Filling - 12•3
Filter, air - 1A•2, 1A•13, 1B•14, 4A•2, 4B•4
Filter, fuel - 1A•13, 1B•8, 1B•14, 5C•2, 5C•3
Filter, oil - 1A•2, 1A•6, 1B•7, 2E•11, 2E•12
Fire - 0•5
Fixed window - 12•11, 12•18
Flat tyre - 0•8
Fluid leaks - 1A•9, 1B•11
Flywheel - 2A•14, 2B•9, 2C•10, 2D•11,
    2E•15, 2F•11
Fog light - 13•5, 13•8, 13•10
Free-wheeling hubs - 11•6
Front and rear axles - 9•1 et seq
*Fuel and exhaust systems - diesel engine
    models - 4B•1 et seq*
*Fuel and exhaust systems - petrol engine
    models - 4A•1 et seq*
Fuel and exhaust systems fault
    finding - REF•11, REF•15
Fuel filter - 1A•13, 1B•8, 1B•14, 5C•2, 5C•3
Fuel gauge - 4A•4, 4B•5
Fuel injection pump - 2F•6, 4B•10
Fuel injectors - 4A•5, 4B•14
Fuel lift pump - 4B•9
Fuel pump - 4A•4
Fuel tank - 1A•1, 1B•1, 4A•4, 4B•5
Fume or gas intoxication - 0•5
Fuses - 0•16, 5C•2, 5C•3, 13•3

G

Gaiters - 1A•9, 1B•12, 8•6
Gashes in bodywork - 12•3
Gaskets - REF•4
Gearbox - See *Transmission*
Gearbox oil - 0•17, 1A•1, 1A•10, 1A•15,
    1B•1, 1B•13, 1B•16
Gearchange lever - 7•2
Gearchange quadrant box - 7•3
Glossary of technical terms - REF•20 et seq
Glow plugs - 5C•2
Grille - 12•6

H

Halfshaft - 9•6
Handbrake 'on' warning light
    switch - 13•5, 13•6
Handbrake - 1A•14, 1B•15, 10•15,
    10•16, REF•8
Handles - 12•9, 12•10, 12•13, 12•14, 12•16
Hard top - 12•22
HC emissions - REF•11
Headlights - 1A•11, 1B•14, 13•5, 13•6,
    13•7, 13•9, 13•10, 13•16
Headlining - 12•22
Heat shield(s) - 4B•20
Heated seat - 13•6
Heater blower - 13•4, 13•6
Heating system - 3•9, 3•10, 3•11
Hinges - 1A•11, 1B•14
Horn - 13•5, 13•6, 13•14
Hoses - 1A•9, 1B•11, 3•2, 10•4
HT coil - 5B•2
Hub assembly - 11•8, 11•9

Hub bearing - 1A•10, 1A•14, 1B•13,
    1B•15, 11•9, REF•10
Hydraulic damper - 6•4
Hydraulic tappets - 2A•10
Hydraulic valve lifters - 2C•3, 2C•6
Hydrofluoric acid - 0•5

I

Idle speed - 1B•10, 4A•7
Idler pivot - 11•20
Idler pulleys - 2B•6, 2F•7
Ignition switch - 13•3, 13•5
Ignition system - petrol engine models -
    1A•13, 1A•16, 5B•1 *et seq*
Illumination bulbs - 13•9
Immobiliser - 13•18
Indicators - 13•7, 13•8, 13•10
Injection timing - 4B•12
Injectors - 4A•5, 4B•14
Inlet manifold - 4A•8, 4B•16
Input shaft - 7•4
Instruments - 1A•11, 1B•14, 13•4, 13•9,
    13•11, 13•13
Intake air temperature sensor - 4A•8
Intercooler - 4B•16
Interior light - 13•5, 13•6, 13•8
Introduction - 0•4

J

Jacking and vehicle support - REF•5
Joint mating faces - REF•4
Jump starting - 0•7

K

Knock sensor - 4A•8
Knuckle - 11•9

L

Leaf spring - 11•14
Leakdown test - 2D•3, 2E•3, 2F•3
Leaks - 0•9, 1A•9, 1B•11
Load proportioning valve - 1A•11, 1B•13
Load-sensing valve - 10•16
Locks - 1A•11, 1B•14, 12•7, 12•9, 12•10,
    12•14 to 12•16, 13•3, 13•5
Locknuts, locktabs and washers - REF•4
Long-range driving light - 13•8, 13•10
Loudspeakers - 13•16
Lubricants and fluids - 0•17

M

Main bearings - 2G•14, 2G•16, 2H•18, 2H•19
Maintenance schedule -
    petrol models - 1A•3
Maintenance schedule -
    diesel models - 1B•3
Manifolds - 4A•8, 4A•10, 4B•16
Manual gearbox - See *Transmission*
Manual gearbox oil - 0•17, 1A•1, 1A•10,
    1A•15, 1B•1, 1B•13, 1B•16
Master cylinder - 6•3, 10•13
Mirrors - 12•17, REF•8

Modulator (ABS) - 10•17
MOT test checks - REF•8 et seq
Motor factors - REF•3
Motronic M1.5 system - 5B•2
Motronic M1.5.4 system - 5B•2
Mountings - 2A•15, 2B•9, 2C•11, 2D•12,
    2E•15, 2F•11
Multi-function switch - 13•4, 13•5

N

Needle movement sensor - 4B•7
Nudge bar - 12•5
Number plate light - 13•8, 13•10

O

Oil cooler - 2A•13, 2B•9, 2D•10,
    2E•12, 2F•10
Oil filter - 1A•2, 1A•6, 1B•7, 2E•11, 2E•12
Oil pressure switch - 2E•12
Oil pump - 2A•12, 2B•9, 2C•10, 2D•10,
    2E•10, 2F•10
Oil seals - 2A•8, 2A•14, 2B•6, 2B•9, 2C•10,
    2D•11, 2E•14, 2F•11, 7•3, 9•3, 9•6,
    REF•4
Oil, axle - 1A•1, 1A•10, 1A•15, 1B•1,
    1B•13, 1B•16
Oil, engine - 0•12, 0•17, 1A•1, 1A•6,
    1B•1, 1B•7
Oil, transmission - 0•17, 1A•1, 1A•10,
    1A•15, 1B•1, 1B•13, 1B•16
Open circuit - 13•2
Output shaft oil seal - 7•3
Oxygen sensor - 4C•2

P

Pads - 1A•8, 1A•9, 1B•11, 10•4, 10•6
Panel illumination - 13•13
Panhard rod - 11•15
Pedals - 4B•6, 4B•7, 4A•3, 6•2, 6•3, 10•13
Petrol engine in-car repair procedures -
    2A•1 *et seq*, 2B•1 *et seq*, 2C•1 *et seq*,
    2G•1 *et seq*
Pipes - 10•4
Piston rings - 2G•15
Pistons - 2G•11, 2G•12, 2G•18, 2H•12,
    2H•16, 2H•21
Plastic components - 12•4, 12•18
Poisonous or irritant substances - 0•5
Power steering fluid - 0•13, 0•17
Power steering pump - 1A•8, 1B•8, 1B•10
Preheating system -
    diesel engine models - 5C•1 et seq
Pressure relief valve - 2E•11
Printed circuit - 13•13
Propeller shafts and
    driveshafts - 1A•10, 1B•12, 8•1 et seq
Propeller shaft fault finding - REF•16
Proportioning valve - 1A•11, 1B•13
Puncture - 0•8
Purge valve - 4C•2
Pushrods - 2F•7

Q

Quick Warm-up System - 4B•8

R

Radiator - 1A•14, 1B•15, 3•3
Radiator grille - 12•6
Radio - 13•16
Radio/cassette unit anti-theft system - REF•5
Rear light cluster - 13•8, 13•10
Regulator (window) - 12•11, 12•17
Relays - 5C•2, 5C•3, 13•3
Release bearing - 6•6
Repair procedures - REF•4
Reversing light switch - 7•4
Road test - 1A•11, 1B•14
Roadside Repairs - 0•6
Roadwheel nuts - 1A•11, 1B•13
Rocker arms - 2C•6, 2D•7, 2E•5, 2F•7
Roll over bar - 12•23
Routine maintenance and servicing - diesel engine models - 1B•1 *et seq*
Routine maintenance and servicing - petrol engine models - 1A•1 *et seq*
Routine maintenance - underframe - 12•2
Routine maintenance - upholstery and carpets - 12•2
Rust holes in bodywork - 12•3

S

Safety first - 0•5, 0•13
Scalding - 0•5
Scratches in bodywork - 12•3
Screw threads and fastenings - REF•4
Seat belts - 12•18, REF•9
Seats - 12•18, 13•6, REF•9
Secondary air injection system - 4C•2, 4C•3
Servo unit - 10•14
Shock absorber - 1A•10, 1B•12, 11•11, 11•14, REF•9, REF•10
Shoes - 1A•14, 1B•15, 10•5, 10•7
Short circuit - 13•2
Sidelight - 13•7
Slave cylinder - 6•4
Sliding window - 12•11
Solenoid valve - 4C•3
Spare parts - REF•3
Spark plugs - 1A•2, 1A•12, 1A•16
Speedometer - 7•4, 13•13
Spraying - 12•3
Springs - REF•10
Start up after overhaul - 2G•20, 2H•23
Starter motor - 5A•6

Starting and charging systems - 5A•1 *et seq*
Steering adjustment - 11•18
Steering angles - 11•21
Steering column - 11•17, REF•8
Steering column lock - 13•3, 13•5
Steering column multi-function switch - 13•4, 13•5
Steering gear - 11•18
Steering knuckle - 11•9
Steering mechanism - REF•10
Steering pump - 11•18
Steering wheel - 11•16, REF•8
Stop-light - 10•17, 13•4, 13•6
Sump - 2A•12, 2B•9, 2C•9, 2D•9, 2E•13, 2F•9
Sunroof - 12•18
Suspension and steering - 1A•9, 1A•12, 1B•12, 1B•14, 11•1 *et seq*, REF•9, REF•10
Suspension and steering fault finding - REF•17, REF•18
Switch illumination bulbs - 13•9
Switches - 3•7, 5C•2, 5C•3, 7•4, 13•3

T

Tachometer - 13•13
Tailgate - 12•11, 12•12, 12•13, 12•15, 12•16, 12•21, 13•16
Tailpipe - 4A•11, 4B•20
Tappets - 2A•10, 2H•11, 2H•12
Temperature control valve - 2D•11
Temperature gauge - 3•7
Thermostat - 3•4
Throttle housing - 4A•5
Throttle potentiometer - 4A•7
Throttle valve - 4B•9
Tie rod - 11•20, 11•21
Timing belt - 1A•16, 1B•16, 2A•4, 2A•5, 2A•7, 2A•8, 2B•4, 2B•6, 2F•5, 2F•6
Timing chain - 2C•4, 2C•5, 2D•5, 2D•6, 2E•10
Tools - REF•4
Tools and working facilities - REF•6 *et seq*
Top dead centre (TDC) for No 1 piston - locating - 2A•4, 2B•3, 2C•3, 2D•3, 2E•3, 2F•3
Torsion bar - 11•13
Towing - 0•9
Trailing link - 11•15
Transfer change lever - 7•2
Transmission - 2A•15, 2B•9, 2C•11, 2D•12, 2F•11, 7•1 *et seq*
Transmission fault finding - REF•16
Transmission oil - 0•17, 1A•1, 1A•10, 1A•15, 1B•1, 1B•13, 1B•16

Trim height - 11•6
Trim panels - 12•8, 12•18, 12•20, 12•21
Turbocharger - 4B•18, 4B•19
Tyre condition - 0•15
Tyre pressures - 0•15, 0•18
Tyre specialists - REF•3
Tyres - REF•11

U

Underbonnet check points - 0•10
Underframe - 12•2
Universal joints - 8•3
Unleaded petrol - 4A•3
Upholstery - 12•2
Upper control arm - 11•11, 11•12

V

Vacuum hose check valve - 10•15
Vacuum pump - 2E•13, 10•18
Vacuum reservoir - 10•18
Vacuum servo - 10•14
Vacuum valves - 4B•9
Valve clearances - 1B•15, 2D•4, 2F•4
Valve lifters - 2C•3, 2C•6
Valves - 2G•9, 2H•9
Vehicle identification - REF•3, REF•9
Vehicle support - REF•5
Ventilation system - 3•9, 3•12
Visco-clutch fan - 3•6
Voltage stabiliser - 13•13

W

Warning lights - 13•13
Washer system - 0•16, 13•16
Water pump - 3•7
Weekly Checks - 0•10 *et seq*
Weights - REF•1
Wheel alignment - 11•21
Wheel arch liners - 12•18
Wheel bearings - 1A•10, 1A•14, 1B•13, 1B•15, 11•9, REF•10
Wheel changing - 0•8
Wheel cylinder - 10•11
Wheel sensor - 10•18
Wheels - REF•11
Window regulator - 12•11, 12•17
Window release button - 12•15, 12•16
Windows - 12•10, 12•17
Windscreen - 12•18, REF•8
Wiper arm - 13•14
Wiper blades - 0•16
Wiper motor - 13•14
Wiring diagrams - 13•20 *et seq*
Working facilities - REF•7

Haynes Manuals – The Complete List

Title	Book No.
ALFA ROMEO	
Alfa Romeo Alfasud/Sprint (74 - 88) up to F	0292
Alfa Romeo Alfetta (73 - 87) up to E	0531
AUDI	
Audi 80 (72 - Feb 79) up to T	0207
Audi 80, 90 (79 - Oct 86) up to D & Coupe (81 - Nov 88) up to F	0605
Audi 80, 90 (Oct 86 - 90) D to H & Coupe (Nov 88 - 90) F to H	1491
Audi 100 (Oct 82 - 90) up to H & 200 (Feb 84 - Oct 89) A to G	0907
Audi 100 & A6 Petrol & Diesel (May 91 - May 97) H to P	3504
Audi A4 (95 - Feb 00) M to V	3575
AUSTIN	
Austin A35 & A40 (56 - 67) *	0118
Austin Allegro 1100, 1300, 1.0, 1.1 & 1.3 (73 - 82)*	0164
Austin Healey 100/6 & 3000 (56 - 68) *	0049
Austin/MG/Rover Maestro 1.3 & 1.6 (83 - May 95) up to M	0922
Austin/MG Metro (80 - May 90) up to G	0718
Austin/Rover Montego 1.3 & 1.6 (84 - 94) A to L	1066
Austin/MG/Rover Montego 2.0 (84 - 95) A to M	1067
Mini (59 - 69) up to H	0527
Mini (69 - Oct 96) up to P	0646
Austin/Rover 2.0 litre Diesel Engine (86 - 93) C to L	1857
BEDFORD	
Bedford CF (69 - 87) up to E	0163
Bedford/Vauxhall Rascal & Suzuki Supercarry (86 - Oct 94) C to M	3015
BMW	
BMW 1500, 1502, 1600, 1602, 2000 & 2002 (59 - 77)*	0240
BMW 316, 320 & 320i (4-cyl) (75 - Feb 83) up to Y	0276
BMW 320, 320i, 323i & 325i (6-cyl) (Oct 77 - Sept 87) up to E	0815
BMW 3-Series (Apr 91 - 96) H to N	3210
BMW 3- & 5-Series (sohc) (81 - 91) up to J	1948
BMW 520i & 525e (Oct 81 - June 88) up to E	1560
BMW 525, 528 & 528i (73 - Sept 81) up to X	0632
CITROËN	
Citroën 2CV, Ami & Dyane (67 - 90) up to H	0196
Citroën AX Petrol & Diesel (87 - 97) D to P	3014
Citroën BX (83 - 94) A to L	0908
Citroën C15 Van Petrol & Diesel (89 - Oct 98) F to S	3509
Citroën CX (75 - 88) up to F	0528
Citroën Saxo Petrol & Diesel (96 - 01) N to X	3506
Citroën Visa (79 - 88) up to F	0620
Citroën Xantia Petrol & Diesel (93 - 98) K to S	3082
Citroën XM Petrol & Diesel (89 - 00) G to X	3451
Citroën Xsara Petrol & Diesel (97 - Sept 00) R to W	3751
Citroën ZX Diesel (91 - 98) J to S	1922
Citroën ZX Petrol (91 - 98) H to S	1881
Citroën 1.7 & 1.9 litre Diesel Engine (84 - 96) A to N	1379
FIAT	
Fiat 126 (73 - 87) *	0305
Fiat 500 (57 - 73) up to M	0090
Fiat Bravo & Brava (95 - 00) N to W	3572
Fiat Cinquecento (93 - 98) K to R	3501
Fiat Panda (81 - 95) up to M	0793
Fiat Punto Petrol & Diesel (94 - Oct 99) L to V	3251
Fiat Regata (84 - 88) A to F	1167
Fiat Tipo (88 - 91) E to J	1625
Fiat Uno (83 - 95) up to M	0923
Fiat X1/9 (74 - 89) up to G	0273
FORD	
Ford Anglia (59 - 68) *	0001
Ford Capri II (& III) 1.6 & 2.0 (74 - 87) up to E	0283
Ford Capri II (& III) 2.8 & 3.0 (74 - 87) up to E	1309
Ford Cortina Mk III 1300 & 1600 (70 - 76) *	0070
Ford Cortina Mk IV (& V) 1.6 & 2.0 (76 - 83) *	0343
Ford Cortina Mk IV (& V) 2.3 V6 (77 - 83) *	0426
Ford Escort Mk I 1100 & 1300 (68 - 74) *	0171
Ford Escort Mk I Mexico, RS 1600 & RS 2000 (70 - 74)*	0139
Ford Escort Mk II Mexico, RS 1800 & RS 2000 (75 - 80)*	0735
Ford Escort (75 - Aug 80) *	0280
Ford Escort (Sept 80 - Sept 90) up to H	0686
Ford Escort & Orion (Sept 90 - 00) H to X	1737
Ford Fiesta (76 - Aug 83) up to Y	0334
Ford Fiesta (Aug 83 - Feb 89) A to F	1030
Ford Fiesta (Feb 89 - Oct 95) F to N	1595
Ford Fiesta (Oct 95 - 01) N-reg. onwards	3397
Ford Focus (98 - 01) S to Y	3759
Ford Granada (Sept 77 - Feb 85) up to B	0481
Ford Granada & Scorpio (Mar 85 - 94) B to M	1245
Ford Ka (96 - 02) P-reg. onwards	3570
Ford Mondeo Petrol (93 - 99) K to T	1923
Ford Mondeo Diesel (93 - 96) L to N	3465
Ford Orion (83 - Sept 90) up to H	1009
Ford Sierra 4 cyl. (82 - 93) up to K	0903
Ford Sierra V6 (82 - 91) up to J	0904
Ford Transit Petrol (Mk 2) (78 - Jan 86) up to C	0719
Ford Transit Petrol (Mk 3) (Feb 86 - 89) C to G	1468
Ford Transit Diesel (Feb 86 - 99) C to T	3019
Ford 1.6 & 1.8 litre Diesel Engine (84 - 96) A to N	1172
Ford 2.1, 2.3 & 2.5 litre Diesel Engine (77 - 90) up to H	1606
FREIGHT ROVER	
Freight Rover Sherpa (74 - 87) up to E	0463
HILLMAN	
Hillman Avenger (70 - 82) up to Y	0037
Hillman Imp (63 - 76) *	0022
HONDA	
Honda Accord (76 - Feb 84) up to A	0351
Honda Civic (Feb 84 - Oct 87) A to E	1226
Honda Civic (Nov 91 - 96) J to N	3199
HYUNDAI	
Hyundai Pony (85 - 94) C to M	3398
JAGUAR	
Jaguar E Type (61 - 72) up to L	0140
Jaguar MkI & II, 240 & 340 (55 - 69) *	0098
Jaguar XJ6, XJ & Sovereign; Daimler Sovereign (68 - Oct 86) up to D	0242
Jaguar XJ6 & Sovereign (Oct 86 - Sept 94) D to M	3261
Jaguar XJ12, XJS & Sovereign; Daimler Double Six (72 - 88) up to F	0478
JEEP	
Jeep Cherokee Petrol (93 - 96) K to N	1943
LADA	
Lada 1200, 1300, 1500 & 1600 (74 - 91) up to J	0413
Lada Samara (87 - 91) D to J	1610
LAND ROVER	
Land Rover 90, 110 & Defender Diesel (83 -95) up to N	3017
Land Rover Discovery Petrol & Diesel (89 - 98) G to S	3016
Land Rover Series IIA & III Diesel (58 - 85) up to C	0529
Land Rover Series II, IIA & III Petrol (58 - 85) up to C	0314
MAZDA	
Mazda 323 (Mar 81 - Oct 89) up to G	1608
Mazda 323 (Oct 89 - 98) G to R	3455
Mazda 626 (May 83 - Sept 87) up to E	0929
Mazda B-1600, B-1800 & B-2000 Pick-up (72 - 88) up to F	0267
Mazda RX-7 (79 - 85) *	0460
MERCEDES-BENZ	
Mercedes-Benz 190, 190E & 190D Petrol & Diesel (83 - 93) A to L	3450
Mercedes-Benz 200, 240, 300 Diesel (Oct 76 - 85) up to C	1114
Mercedes-Benz 250 & 280 (68 - 72) up to L	0346
Mercedes-Benz 250 & 280 (123 Series) (Oct 76 - 84) up to B	0677
Mercedes-Benz 124 Series (85 - Aug 93) C to K	3253
Mercedes-Benz C-Class Petrol & Diesel (93 - Aug 00) L to W	3511
MG	
MGA (55 - 62) *	0475
MGB (62 - 80) up to W	0111
MG Midget & AH Sprite (58 - 80) up to W	0265
MITSUBISHI	
Mitsubishi Shogun & L200 Pick-Ups (83 - 94) up to M	1944
MORRIS	
Morris Ital 1.3 (80 - 84) up to B	0705
Morris Minor 1000 (56 - 71) up to K	0024
NISSAN	
Nissan Bluebird (May 84 - Mar 86) A to C	1223
Nissan Bluebird (Mar 86 - 90) C to H	1473
Nissan Cherry (Sept 82 - 86) up to D	1031
Nissan Micra (83 - Jan 93) up to K	0931
Nissan Micra (93 - 99) K to T	3254
Nissan Primera (90 - Aug 99) H to T	1851
Nissan Stanza (82 - 86) up to D	0824
Nissan Sunny (May 82 - Oct 86) up to D	0895
Nissan Sunny (Oct 86 - Mar 91) D to H	1378
Nissan Sunny (Apr 91 - 95) H to N	3219
OPEL	
Opel Ascona & Manta (B Series) (Sept 75 - 88) up to F	0316
Opel Ascona (81 - 88) (Not available in UK see Vauxhall Cavalier 0812)	3215
Opel Astra (Oct 91 - Feb 98) (Not available in UK see Vauxhall Astra 1832)	3156
Opel Astra & Zafira Diesel (Feb 98 - Sept 00) (See Astra & Zafira Diesel Book No. 3797)	
Opel Astra & Zafira Petrol (Feb 98 - Sept 00) (See Vauxhall/Opel Astra & Zafira Petrol Book No. 3758)	
Opel Calibra (90 - 98) (See Vauxhall/Opel Calibra Book No. 3502)	
Opel Corsa (83 - Mar 93) (Not available in UK see Vauxhall Nova 0909)	3160
Opel Corsa (Mar 93 - 97) (Not available in UK see Vauxhall Corsa 1985)	3159
Opel Frontera Petrol & Diesel (91 - 98) (See Vauxhall/Opel Frontera Book No. 3454)	
Opel Kadett (Nov 79 - Oct 84) up to B	0634
Opel Kadett (Oct 84 - Oct 91) (Not available in UK see Vauxhall Astra & Belmont 1136)	3196
Opel Omega & Senator (86 - 94) (Not available in UK see Vauxhall Carlton & Senator 1469)	3157
Opel Omega (94 - 99) (See Vauxhall/Opel Omega Book No. 3510)	
Opel Rekord (Feb 78 - Oct 86) up to D	0543
Opel Vectra (Oct 88 - Oct 95) (Not available in UK see Vauxhall Cavalier 1570)	3158
Opel Vectra Petrol & Diesel (95 - 98) (Not available in UK see Vauxhall Vectra 3396)	3523
PEUGEOT	
Peugeot 106 Petrol & Diesel (91 - 01) J to X	1882
Peugeot 205 Petrol (83 - 97) A to P	0932
Peugeot 206 Petrol and Diesel (98 - 01) S to X	3757
Peugeot 305 (78 - 89) up to G	0538

* Classic reprint

Title	Book No.
Peugeot 306 Petrol & Diesel (93 - 99) K to T	3073
Peugeot 309 (86 - 93) C to K	1266
Peugeot 405 Petrol (88 - 97) E to P	1559
Peugeot 405 Diesel (88 - 97) E to P	3198
Peugeot 406 Petrol & Diesel (96 - 97) N to R	3394
Peugeot 505 (79 - 89) up to G	0762
Peugeot 1.7/1.8 & 1.9 litre Diesel Engine (82 - 96) up to N	0950
Peugeot 2.0, 2.1, 2.3 & 2.5 litre Diesel Engines (74 - 90) up to H	1607

PORSCHE
Title	Book No.
Porsche 911 (65 - 85) up to C	0264
Porsche 924 & 924 Turbo (76 - 85) up to C	0397

PROTON
Title	Book No.
Proton (89 - 97) F to P	3255

RANGE ROVER
Title	Book No.
Range Rover V8 (70 - Oct 92) up to K	0606

RELIANT
Title	Book No.
Reliant Robin & Kitten (73 - 83) up to A	0436

RENAULT
Title	Book No.
Renault 4 (61 - 86) *	0072
Renault 5 (Feb 85 - 96) B to N	1219
Renault 9 & 11 (82 - 89) up to F	0822
Renault 18 (79 - 86) up to D	0598
Renault 19 Petrol (89 - 94) F to M	1646
Renault 19 Diesel (89 - 96) F to N	1946
Renault 21 (86 - 94) C to M	1397
Renault 25 (84 - 92) B to K	1228
Renault Clio Petrol (91 - May 98) H to R	1853
Renault Clio Diesel (91 - June 96) H to N	3031
Renault Clio Petrol & Diesel (May 98 - May 01) R to Y	3906
Renault Espace Petrol & Diesel (85 - 96) C to N	3197
Renault Fuego (80 - 86) *	0764
Renault Laguna Petrol & Diesel (94 - 00) L to W	3252
Renault Mégane & Scénic Petrol & Diesel (96 - 98) N to R	3395
Renault Mégane & Scénic (Apr 99 - 02) T-reg onwards	3916

ROVER
Title	Book No.
Rover 213 & 216 (84 - 89) A to G	1116
Rover 214 & 414 (89 - 96) G to N	1689
Rover 216 & 416 (89 - 96) G to N	1830
Rover 211, 214, 216, 218 & 220 Petrol & Diesel (Dec 95 - 98) N to R	3399
Rover 414, 416 & 420 Petrol & Diesel (May 95 - 98) M to R	3453
Rover 618, 620 & 623 (93 - 97) K to P	3257
Rover 820, 825 & 827 (86 - 95) D to N	1380
Rover 3500 (76 - 87) up to E	0365
Rover Metro, 111 & 114 (May 90 - 98) G to S	1711

SAAB
Title	Book No.
Saab 90, 99 & 900 (79 - Oct 93) up to L	0765
Saab 95 & 96 (66 - 76) *	0198
Saab 99 (69 - 79) *	0247
Saab 900 (Oct 93 - 98) L to R	3512
Saab 9000 (4-cyl) (85 - 98) C to S	1686

SEAT
Title	Book No.
Seat Ibiza & Cordoba Petrol & Diesel (Oct 93 - Oct 99) L to V	3571
Seat Ibiza & Malaga (85 - 92) B to K	1609

SKODA
Title	Book No.
Skoda Estelle (77 - 89) up to G	0604
Skoda Favorit (89 - 96) F to N	1801
Skoda Felicia Petrol & Diesel (95 - 01) M to X	3505

SUBARU
Title	Book No.
Subaru 1600 & 1800 (Nov 79 - 90) up to H	0995

SUNBEAM
Title	Book No.
Sunbeam Alpine, Rapier & H120 (67 - 76) *	0051

SUZUKI
Title	Book No.
Suzuki SJ Series, Samurai & Vitara (4-cyl) (82 - 97) up to P	1942
Suzuki Supercarry & Bedford/Vauxhall Rascal (86 - Oct 94) C to M	3015

TALBOT
Title	Book No.
Talbot Alpine, Solara, Minx & Rapier (75 - 86) up to D	0337
Talbot Horizon (78 - 86) up to D	0473
Talbot Samba (82 - 86) up to D	0823

TOYOTA
Title	Book No.
Toyota Carina E (May 92 - 97) J to P	3256
Toyota Corolla (Sept 83 - Sept 87) A to E	1024
Toyota Corolla (80 - 85) up to C	0683
Toyota Corolla (Sept 87 - Aug 92) E to K	1683
Toyota Corolla (Aug 92 - 97) K to P	3259
Toyota Hi-Ace & Hi-Lux (69 - Oct 83) up to A	0304

TRIUMPH
Title	Book No.
Triumph Acclaim (81 - 84) *	0792
Triumph GT6 & Vitesse (62 - 74) *	0112
Triumph Herald (59 - 71) *	0010
Triumph Spitfire (62 - 81) up to X	0113
Triumph Stag (70 - 78) up to T	0441
Triumph TR2, TR3, TR3A, TR4 & TR4A (52 - 67)*	0028
Triumph TR5 & 6 (67 - 75) *	0031
Triumph TR7 (75 - 82) *	0322

VAUXHALL
Title	Book No.
Vauxhall Astra (80 - Oct 84) up to B	0635
Vauxhall Astra & Belmont (Oct 84 - Oct 91) B to J	1136
Vauxhall Astra (Oct 91 - Feb 98) J to R	1832
Vauxhall/Opel Astra & Zafira Diesel (Feb 98 - Sept 00) R to W	3797
Vauxhall/Opel Astra & Zafira Petrol (Feb 98 - Sept 00) R to W	3758
Vauxhall/Opel Calibra (90 - 98) G to S	3502
Vauxhall Carlton (Oct 78 - Oct 86) up to D	0480
Vauxhall Carlton & Senator (Nov 86 - 94) D to L	1469
Vauxhall Cavalier 1300 (77 - July 81) *	0461
Vauxhall Cavalier 1600, 1900 & 2000 (75 - July 81) up to W	0315
Vauxhall Cavalier (81 - Oct 88) up to F	0812
Vauxhall Cavalier (Oct 88 - 95) F to N	1570
Vauxhall Chevette (75 - 84) up to B	0285
Vauxhall Corsa (Mar 93 - 97) K to R	1985
Vauxhall/Opel Corsa (Apr 97 - Oct 00) P to X	3921
Vauxhall/Opel Frontera Petrol & Diesel (91 - Sept 98) J to S	3454
Vauxhall Nova (83 - 93) up to K	0909
Vauxhall/Opel Omega (94 - 99) L to T	3510
Vauxhall Vectra Petrol & Diesel (95 - 98) N to R	3396
Vauxhall/Opel 1.5, 1.6 & 1.7 litre Diesel Engine (82 - 96) up to N	1222

VOLKSWAGEN
Title	Book No.
Volkswagen 411 & 412 (68 - 75) *	0091
Volkswagen Beetle 1200 (54 - 77) up to S	0036
Volkswagen Beetle 1300 & 1500 (65 - 75) up to P	0039
Volkswagen Beetle 1302 & 1302S (70 - 72) up to L	0110
Volkswagen Beetle 1303, 1303S & GT (72 - 75) up to P	0159
Volkswagen Beetle Petrol & Diesel (Apr 99 - 01) T reg onwards	3798
Volkswagen Golf & Bora Petrol & Diesel (April 98 - 00) R to X	3727

Title	Book No.
Volkswagen Golf & Jetta Mk 1 1.1 & 1.3 (74 - 84) up to A	0716
Volkswagen Golf, Jetta & Scirocco Mk 1 1.5, 1.6 & 1.8 (74 - 84) up to A	0726
Volkswagen Golf & Jetta Mk 1 Diesel (78 - 84) up to A	0451
Volkswagen Golf & Jetta Mk 2 (Mar 84 - Feb 92) A to J	1081
Volkswagen Golf & Vento Petrol & Diesel (Feb 92 - 96) J to N	3097
Volkswagen LT vans & light trucks (76 - 87) up to E	0637
Volkswagen Passat & Santana (Sept 81 - May 88) up to E	0814
Volkswagen Passat Petrol & Diesel (May 88 - 96) E to P	3498
Volkswagen Passat 4-cyl Petrol & Diesel (Dec 96 - Nov 00) P to X	3917
Volkswagen Polo & Derby (76 - Jan 82) up to X	0335
Volkswagen Polo (82 - Oct 90) up to H	0813
Volkswagen Polo (Nov 90 - Aug 94) H to L	3245
Volkswagen Polo Hatchback Petrol & Diesel (94 - 99) M to S	3500
Volkswagen Scirocco (82 - 90) up to H	1224
Volkswagen Transporter 1600 (68 - 79) up to V	0082
Volkswagen Transporter 1700, 1800 & 2000 (72 - 79) up to V	0226
Volkswagen Transporter (air-cooled) (79 - 82) up to Y	0638
Volkswagen Transporter (water-cooled) (82 - 90) up to H	3452
Volkswagen Type 3 (63 - 73) *	0084

VOLVO
Title	Book No.
Volvo 120 & 130 Series (& P1800) (61 - 73) *	0203
Volvo 142, 144 & 145 (66 - 74) up to N	0129
Volvo 240 Series (74 - 93) up to K	0270
Volvo 262, 264 & 260/265 (75 - 85) *	0400
Volvo 340, 343, 345 & 360 (76 - 91) up to J	0715
Volvo 440, 460 & 480 (87 - 97) D to P	1691
Volvo 740 & 760 (82 - 91) up to J	1258
Volvo 850 (92 - 96) J to P	3260
Volvo 940 (90 - 96) H to N	3249
Volvo S40 & V40 (96 - 99) N to V	3569
Volvo S70, V70 & C70 (96 - 99) P to V	3573

AUTOMOTIVE TECHBOOKS
Title	Book No.
Automotive Air Conditioning Systems	3740
Automotive Brake Manual	3050
Automotive Carburettor Manual	3288
Automotive Diagnostic Fault Codes Manual	3472
Automotive Diesel Engine Service Guide	3286
Automotive Electrical and Electronic Systems Manual	3049
Automotive Engine Management and Fuel Injection Systems Manual	3344
Automotive Gearbox Overhaul Manual	3473
Automotive Service Summaries Manual	3475
Automotive Timing Belts Manual – Austin/Rover	3549
Automotive Timing Belts Manual – Ford	3474
Automotive Timing Belts Manual – Peugeot/Citroën	3568
Automotive Timing Belts Manual – Vauxhall/Opel	3577
Automotive Welding Manual	3053
In-Car Entertainment Manual (3rd Edition)	3363

* Classic reprint

CL13.4/02

All the products featured on this page are available through most motor accessory shops, cycle shops and book stores. Our policy of continuous updating and development means that titles are being constantly added to the range. For up-to-date information on our complete list of titles, please telephone: (UK) +44 1963 442030 • (USA) +1 805 498 6703 • (France) +33 1 47 78 50 50 • (Sweden) +46 18 124016 • (Australia) +61 3 9763 8100

Preserving Our Motoring Heritage

< The Model J Duesenberg Derham Tourster. Only eight of these magnificent cars were ever built – this is the only example to be found outside the United States of America

Almost every car you've ever loved, loathed or desired is gathered under one roof at the Haynes Motor Museum. Over 300 immaculately presented cars and motorbikes represent every aspect of our motoring heritage, from elegant reminders of bygone days, such as the superb Model J Duesenberg to curiosities like the bug-eyed BMW Isetta. There are also many old friends and flames. Perhaps you remember the 1959 Ford Popular that you did your courting in? The magnificent 'Red Collection' is a spectacle of classic sports cars including AC, Alfa Romeo, Austin Healey, Ferrari, Lamborghini, Maserati, MG, Riley, Porsche and Triumph.

A Perfect Day Out

Each and every vehicle at the Haynes Motor Museum has played its part in the history and culture of Motoring. Today, they make a wonderful spectacle and a great day out for all the family. Bring the kids, bring Mum and Dad, but above all bring your camera to capture those golden memories for ever. You will also find an impressive array of motoring memorabilia, a comfortable 70 seat video cinema and one of the most extensive transport book shops in Britain. The Pit Stop Cafe serves everything from a cup of tea to wholesome, home-made meals or, if you prefer, you can enjoy the large picnic area nestled in the beautiful rural surroundings of Somerset.

> John Haynes O.B.E., Founder and Chairman of the museum at the wheel of a Haynes Light 12.

< Graham Hill's Lola Cosworth Formula 1 car next to a 1934 Riley Sports.

The Museum is situated on the A359 Yeovil to Frome road at Sparkford, just off the A303 in Somerset. It is about 40 miles south of Bristol, and 25 minutes drive from the M5 intersection at Taunton.
Open 9.30am - 5.30pm (10.00am - 4.00pm Winter) 7 days a week, *except Christmas Day, Boxing Day and New Years Day*
Special rates available for schools, coach parties and outings Charitable Trust No. 292048